[FINANCE FOR NON-FINANCIAL MANAGERS]

SIXTH EDITION

D0634586

[FINANCE FOR NON-FINANCIAL MANAGERS]

SIXTH EDITION

PIERRE G. BERGERON
University of Ottawa

NELSON EDUCATION

NELSON EDUCATION

Finance for Non-Financial Managers, Sixth Edition
by Pierre G. Bergeron

Vice President, Editorial Director:
Evelyn Veitch

Editor-in-Chief, Higher Education:
Anne Williams

Senior Acquisitions Editor:
Craig Dyer

Senior Marketing Manager:
Dave Ward

Developmental Editor:
Toula Di Leo

Photo Researcher:
Melody Tolson

Permissions Coordinator:
Melody Tolson

Senior Content Production Manager:
Imoinda Romain

Production Service:
Integra Software Services Pvt. Ltd.

Copy Editor:
Michael Kelly

Proofreader:
Integra

Indexer:
Integra

Senior Production Coordinator:
Ferial Suleman

Design Director:
Ken Phipps

Managing Designer:
Franca Amore

Interior Design:
Jennifer Leung

Cover Design:
Courtney Hellam

Cover Image:
Robert Nicholas/gettyimages

Compositor:
Integra Software Services Pvt. Ltd.

Printer:
Edwards Brothers

COPYRIGHT © 2011, 2008 by Nelson Education Ltd.

Printed and bound in the United States
2 3 4 13 12 11

For more information contact Nelson Education Ltd., 1120 Birchmount Road, Toronto, Ontario, M1K 5G4. Or you can visit our Internet site at http://www.nelson.com

ALL RIGHTS RESERVED. No part of this work covered by the copyright herein may be reproduced, transcribed, or used in any form or by any means—graphic, electronic, or mechanical, including photocopying, recording, taping, Web distribution, or information storage and retrieval systems—without the written permission of the publisher.

For permission to use material from this text or product, submit all requests online at www.cengage.com/permissions. Further questions about permissions can be emailed to permissionrequest@cengage.com

Every effort has been made to trace ownership of all copyrighted material and to secure permission from copyright holders. In the event of any question arising as to the use of any material, we will be pleased to make the necessary corrections in future printings.

Library and Archives Canada Cataloguing in Publication Data

Bergeron, Pierre G.

Finance for non-financial managers / Pierre G. Bergeron. — 6th ed.

Includes index.
ISBN 978-0-17-650163-1

1. Business enterprises—Finance. I. Title.

HG4026.B46 2010 658.15
C2010-900675-5

ISBN 13: 978-0-17-650163-1
ISBN 10: 0-17-650163-0

To the memory of my beloved father

Paul E. Bergeron

■

a friend

■

a tutor

■

a motivator

who started me on the trail that

has led to this book, among others,

and introduced me to the measures

of excellence.

[BRIEF CONTENTS]

[CONTENTS]

Chapter 7

PLANNING, BUDGETING, AND CONTROLLING

Chapter 8

SOURCES AND FORMS OF FINANCING

Chapter 9

COST OF CAPITAL, CAPITAL STRUCTURE, AND FINANCIAL MARKETS

Chapter 10

TIME-VALUE-OF-MONEY CONCEPT

Chapter 11

CAPITAL BUDGETING

Chapter 12

BUSINESS VALUATION

[PREFACE]

Over the past 30 years, many managers and executives taking my seminars on *Finance for Non-Financial Managers* have expressed the need for a simple and basic financial management book, one that would easily clarify financial terms, concepts, and techniques, and help them apply the theory of finance to solve business problems. This book responds to that need.

This book is written for managers, executives, and business students (undergraduates, postgraduates, and graduates) who have little experience in the field of finance. It is aimed primarily at readers who wish to broaden their understanding of financial analysis, improve their decision-making skills, or upgrade old skills in the field of financial management and accounting.

I have written this book with the conviction that finance is a function that is far too important to be left only to financial specialists. Financial activities should be practised by non-financial managers who are responsible for resources and interested in improving the financial performance and destiny of their organizations.

This book will be particularly useful to (1) managers in all types of organizations who currently work in various non-financial functions such as marketing, production, human resources, engineering, or research and development; (2) financial analysts who want to adopt more rigid methodologies for solving financial problems; (3) accountants who want to learn how to analyze financial statements in a more comprehensive way and use them as decision-making instruments; (4) entrepreneurs of small and medium-sized businesses who feel the need to develop fundamental skills in financial control and financial planning; and (5) independent professionals, such as lawyers, engineers, and medical practitioners, who want to develop the financial side of their profession.

The various financial topics are presented in a format appropriate for both groups, for example, those who supply financial information (accountants) and those who use it (non-financial managers and financial analysts). One of the most important objectives of this book is to make the various topics presented in each chapter intelligible to all readers at different levels of education and experience.

In addition to managers and executives, business students will find this book instrumental in learning the essentials of financial statement analysis and capital budgeting techniques. It can be used for a one-semester course at colleges, for continuing education courses in finance at universities, in business courses for non-business majors, and in small business management and entrepreneurship courses.

Readers will find *Finance for Non-Financial Managers* informative and enjoyable. There is no need to present finance as an abstract or obtuse subject. Properly explained and presented, finance can be easily understood and, more importantly, applied to business situations so that non-financial managers and executives can be more effective. I have presented various financial management concepts and techniques in a simple way, using a common-sense approach, supported by many tables, figures, examples, and illustrations.

Finance for Non-Financial Managers is an attempt to repurpose my seminars, which are a source of joy and challenge, into another medium. I continue to be most gratified by the positive responses from the many users of the book, at all levels of businesses, who have found it very helpful. I wish every reader good luck and hope that you will be able to find those financial tools helpful for improving your decisions and, in the process, bring growth and financial affluence to your business.

Features of This Book

One major goal of this book is to offer better ways of navigating the textbook in order to learn and understand the dynamic and challenging financial management concepts, theories, and practices. To this end, this book includes several exclusive features, which are discussed below.

Chapter Outline and Learning Objectives

Each chapter begins with an outline of its contents and a clear statement of its learning objectives related to what will be covered in the chapter. This serves as a checklist to what will be learned. These objectives are directly keyed to end-of-chapter summaries.

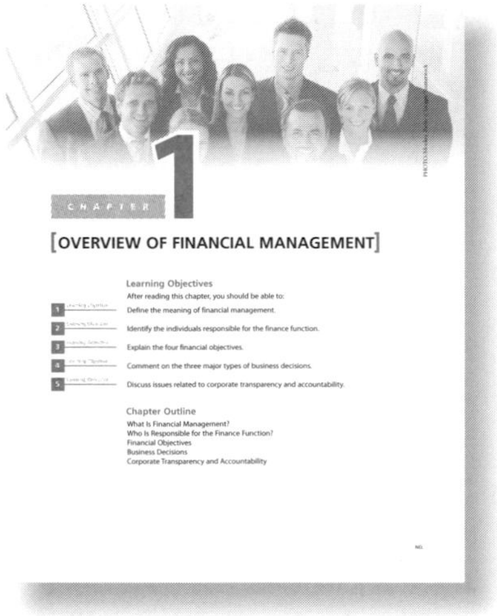
CHAPTER 1

[OVERVIEW OF FINANCIAL MANAGEMENT]

Learning Objectives

After reading this chapter, you should be able to:

1 Define the meaning of financial management.

2 Identify the individuals responsible for the finance function.

3 Explain the four financial objectives.

4 Comment on the three major types of business decisions.

5 Discuss issues related to corporate transparency and accountability.

Chapter Outline

What Is Financial Management?
Who Is Responsible for the Finance Function?
Financial Objectives
Business Decisions
Corporate Transparency and Accountability

NEL

Opening Case

Each chapter begins with an opening case (about a fictional business named CompuTech Inc.) with content that is linked to the subject of that particular chapter. The case contains the more important financial topics covered in the text. This feature will help students visualize how important financial concepts are logically tied to one another. These cases are also keyed to a series of self-test exercises located in appropriate chapter sections.

OPENING CASE

After spending ten years with different organizations, Len and Joan Miller decided to open their own retail business, CompuTech Sales and Service. While Len had worked for several computer retail stores, Joan was employed as a sales representative for a multinational computer organization. Both felt that their combined experience would prove to be a valuable asset for succeeding in their new venture.

However, before making their final decision, they decided to speak to a long-time friend and entrepreneur, Bill Murray, who had operated his own very successful retail business for the past 25 years. The intent of the meeting was to obtain some advice before launching their business. The following summarizes Bill's comments:

> The two most important factors for any business to be successful are products/services and management. There must be a demand for the products or services that you want to sell, and you must possess management skills (e.g., planning, organizing, leading, and controlling) and business skills (e.g., merchandising, pricing, sales, and promotion) if you are to realize your vision and objectives. You will also need operating and financial information to enable you to gauge the results of your ongoing business decisions. Although an accountant will help you set up your bookkeeping and accounting systems, you have to make sure that you have the ability to analyze your financial statements. Not being able to read financial statements is much like being a racing car driver who is unable to read the instruments on his dashboard. Like these instruments, financial statement analysis will help you see how well your business has done and, most importantly, what decisions you need to make to improve the financial performance of your retail operations.
>
> To succeed, your business will have to generate a healthy profit (efficiency) and be able to pay its bills on time (liquidity). In addition, your business must show signs of continuous growth in all segments, such as revenue and profit (prosperity). Be sure that you do not overburden your business with too much debt (stability).
>
> You will always be faced with three types of business decisions. The first are investing decisions, such as launching your business. This is not the only investing decision that you will make. If your business prospers, you will be faced with a series of investing decisions such as expanding your business, opening up new retail outlets, buying equipment for your business, and so on. Operating decisions are the second type of business decisions. They have to do with day-to-day operations. You will be continually faced with decisions such as pricing, advertising, hiring new employees, office expenses, and so on. Through your budgeting exercise, you will have to ensure that you keep your operating costs as low as possible in order to maximize your profit (efficiency). The third type is financing decisions. Once you know exactly how much it will cost you to start your business, you will have to approach investors such as lenders for financial support. These

NEL 3

Chapter Overview

Each chapter opens with an executive summary that gives a rich introductory outline of the major topics covered in the chapter. This opening summary highlights the key financial management themes covered in the text, thus giving an outline of what lies ahead.

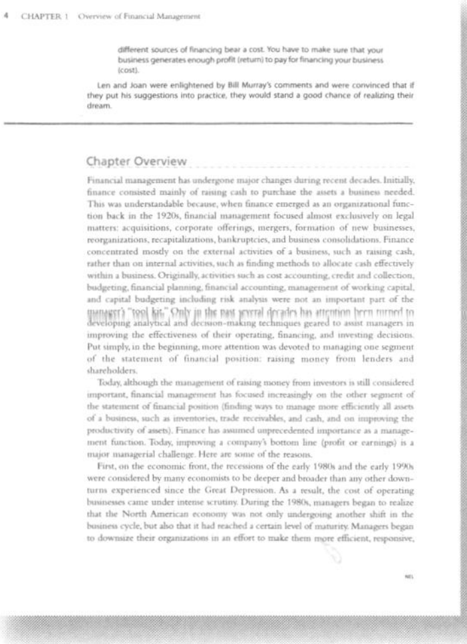

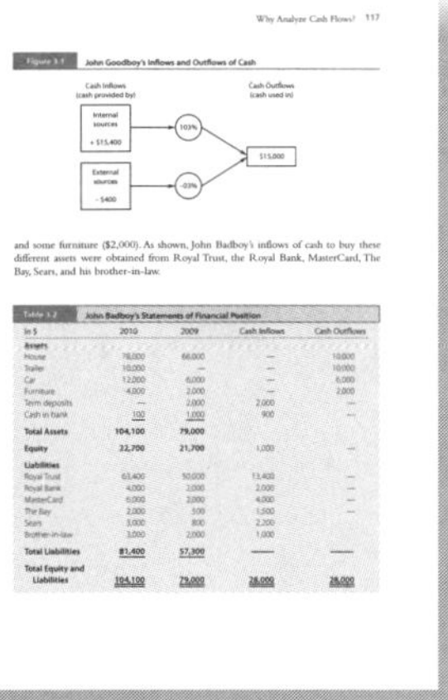

Figures and Tables

This book includes more than 175 figures and tables. These diagrams help to crystallize some of the more abstract financial concepts covered in the text, as well as to visualize how they are connected to one another.

In the News

Each chapter contains several illustrative examples drawn from the real world. These current real-life examples provide valuable insights about how Canadian financial management concepts and techniques are carried out by profit-driven and not-for-profit organizations.

Self-Test Exercises

The book is embedded with more than 80 self-test exercises. These exercises, which are directly connected to each chapter's opening case, can help the students apply *right away*, through personal reflection, many of the financial concepts and techniques explained in the text.

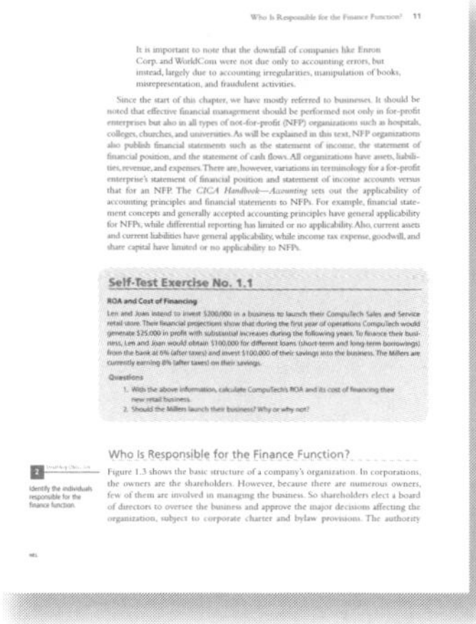

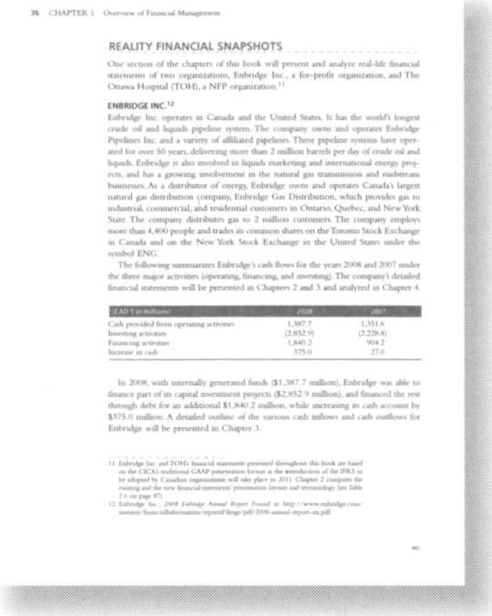

Reality Financial Snapshots

Two real-life financial statements are presented and analyzed in most chapters. This feature helps to connect the theory to the practice. Each section features a profit-driven organization (Enbridge Inc.) and a not-for-profit organization (The Ottawa Hospital).

Decision-Making in Action

This section, placed at the end of each chapter, shows how the theory covered in the text can be put into practical use within the framework of a specific situation. This allows students to comprehend how financial management concepts are applied within the decision-making process.

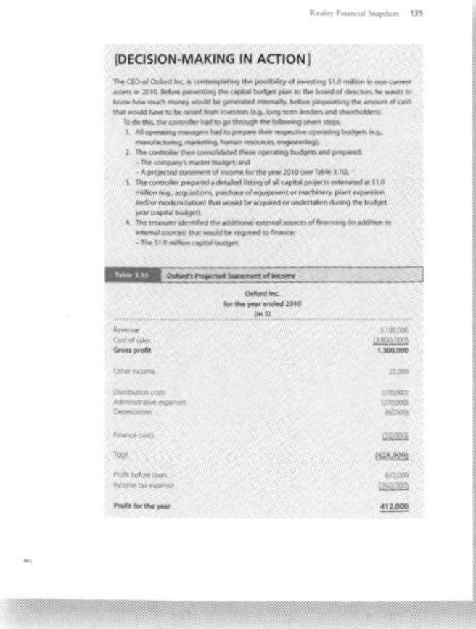

Financial Spreadsheets—Excel

A brief explanation about how Excel financial spreadsheets can be used to help students solve all types of computational problems. The objective of these spreadsheets is to allow students to devote more time on analysis and decision-making, and less on "number crunching."

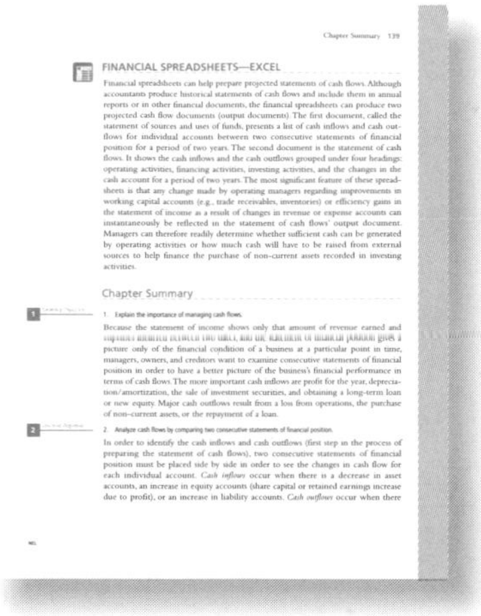
FINANCIAL SPREADSHEETS—EXCEL

Chapter Summary

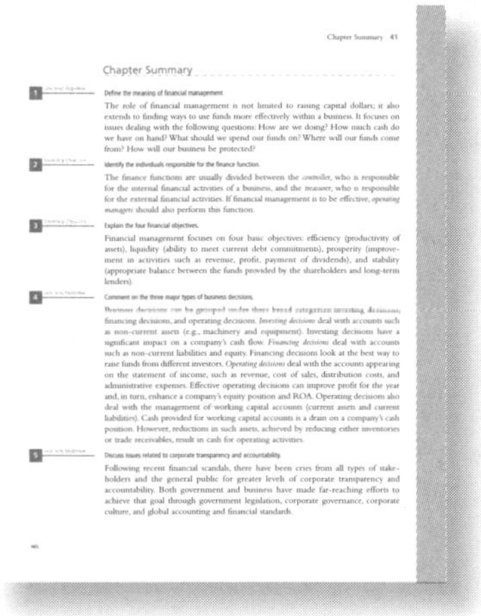
Chapter Summary

Chapter Summary

Each chapter closes with a summary of the major points presented in the text. The summary is directly linked to the learning objectives listed at the beginning of the chapter. These summaries provide a quick synopsis for review purposes.

Key Terms

A list of financial management terms is provided near the end of each chapter. Each key term, with a referenced page number, shows where the concept is explained in the text. Also, all key terms are collated in a glossary at the end of the book.

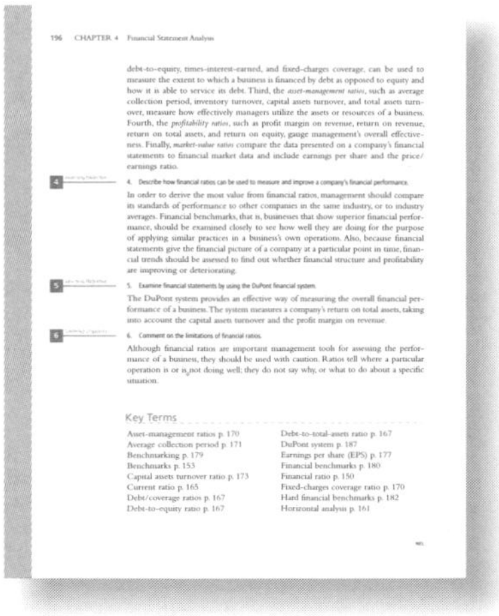
196 CHAPTER 4 Financial Statement Analysis

Key Terms

Review Questions

A set of end-of-chapter review questions is also provided. These questions are designed to help students test their understanding of the chapter's key themes.

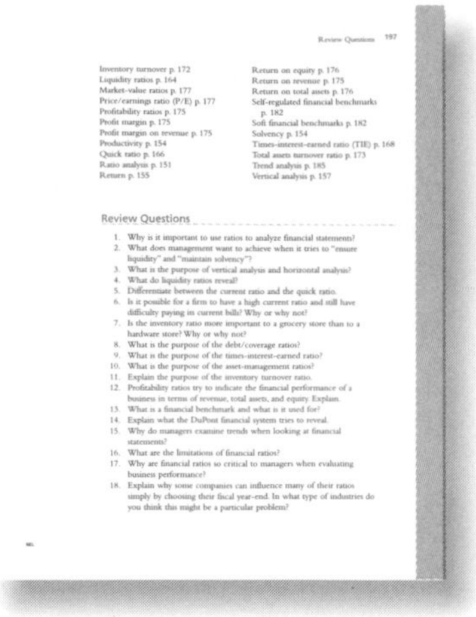

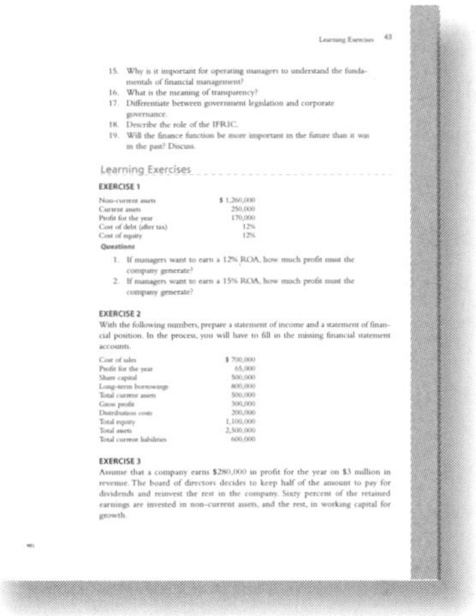

Learning Exercises

Several exercises are presented at the end of each chapter. These exercises give students the opportunity to gain a greater understanding of their own strengths and weaknesses in terms of their financial management competencies and skills. The exercises also provide a smoother transition into subsequent and more difficult problems contained in the cases.

Cases

Each chapter concludes with fictitious situations that allow students to apply the concepts and tools presented in the chapter. These cases will help students to sharpen their analytical skills and to validate the knowledge gained from the chapter.

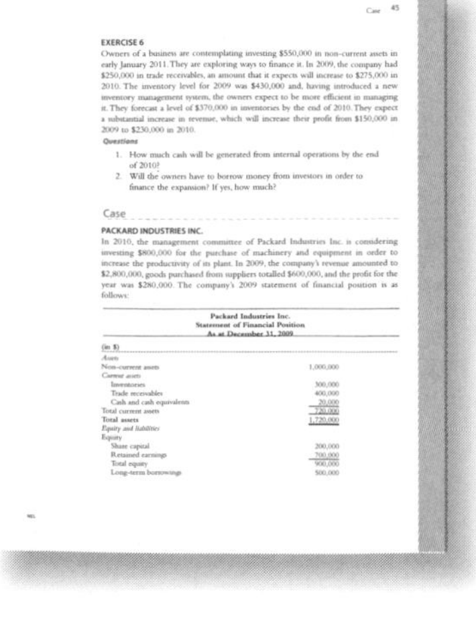

Glossary

All key terms are briefly defined at the end of the book. The glossary allows the students to review the more important terms associated with the material covered in the text.

[GLOSSARY]

A

Accounting: Process of recording and summarizing business transactions on a company's financial statements. p. 58

Accounting equation: Assets = Equity + Liabilities or Assets − Liabilities = Equity. p. 54

Accounting methods: Calculation of the book value rate of return by using data presented on financial statements. p. 524

Accrual method: Accounting method that considers sales when made and costs when incurred, regardless of when the transaction takes place. p. 62

Accrued liability: Represents what a company owes for services it has received and not yet paid or an expense that has been incurred but not recorded. p. 79

Adjustments in non-cash working capital accounts: The cash flow provided (or used) by working capital accounts such as trade receivables, inventories, and trade and other payables. p. 127

Administrative expenses: Expenses that are not directly related to producing and selling goods or services. p. 65

Aging of accounts receivable: A report showing how long trade receivables have been outstanding; it gives the percentage of receivables past due for one month, two months, or other periods. p. 270

Annual report: Report issued annually by corporations to their shareholders that contains their financial statements as well as management's opinion of the company's past year's operations and prospects for the future. p. 80

Annuity: A series of payments (or receipts) of fixed amount for a specified number of years. p. 486

Assessed value: Method used by municipal governments for determining the level of property taxes. p. 568

Asset-management ratios: Evaluate how efficiently managers use the assets of a business. p. 170

Assets: Resources that a business owns to produce goods and services (e.g., buildings, equipment, trade receivables, inventories). p. 71

Asset valuation: Methodology used to restate the numbers appearing on financial statements. p. 578

Auditor's report: Report prepared by an independent accounting firm that is presented to a company's shareholders. p. 82

Average collection period (ACP): Measures how many days it takes for customers to pay their bills. p. 171

B

Balanced scorecard (BSC): A process that can translate an organization's mission, vision, and strategies into a comprehensive set of quantifiable performance measures in addition to providing a framework for a strategic measurement and management system. p. 27

Benchmarking: Process of searching for the best practices by comparing oneself to a competitor's excellent performance. p. 179

Benchmarks: Excellent industry norms to which one's own financial ratios can be compared. p. 153

Bond: Long-term loan (10 to 30 years) that could be secured or unsecured. p. 387

Bookkeeping: Activity that involves collecting, classifying, and reporting accounting transactions. p. 53

Bookkeeping and accounting cycle: Steps involved in processing financial transactions for preparing financial statements. p. 54

Book value: The accounting value of an asset (the original cost minus total depreciation deductions made to date), shown on the financial statements as a firm's assets. p. 564

Break-even chart: Graphic that shows the effect of change in both revenue and costs on profitability. p. 220

Break-even point: Level of production where revenues equal total costs. p. 216

Break-even wedge: Method that helps managers to determine the most appropriate way of structuring operating costs (fixed versus variable). p. 231

Budgeting: Process by which management allocates corporate resources, evaluates financial outcomes, and

NEL G-1

New to This Edition

This new sixth edition has been modified to improve the clarity of many finance techniques and the relationship between the various concepts covered in the book. The explanation of the financial concepts and techniques, supported by numerous practical examples, continues to be a result of many questions and discussions that I have had with managers and executives during my seminars, including many suggestions made by reviewers of past editions. I have to point out, however, that while revising this text, I have not lost sight of its primary focus, which is to be an executive briefing instrument that will help students, managers, and executives grasp the more important financial relationships and issues.

The sixth edition maintains the unique and distinct features that were introduced in the previous editions such as the following:

- Well-defined learning objectives directly keyed to end-of-chapter summaries
- Opening cases (CompuTech Inc.) at the start of each chapter that are connected to each other with more than 80 insightful self-test exercises in appropriate chapter sections to help students apply *right away,* through personal reflection, many of the financial techniques presented in different sections of book
- Real-life financial statements of a profit-driven organization, *Enbridge Inc.*, and a not-for-profit organization, *The Ottawa General Hospital*, in all chapters that help to reinforce how financial concepts and theories are put to practical use in real-life organizations.

However, new distinctive and unique features have been introduced in this sixth edition. First, the text takes into account the recommendations made by the *International Accounting Standards Board (IASB)*, which has the objective of harmonizing and converging different generally accepted accounting principles (GAAP) developed in various countries over the past decades. To date, more than 100 countries have converged or are on a path to converge by using the *International Financial Reporting Standards (IFRS)*. In 2011, the Canadian *Handbook*, as it exists today, will be replaced by the IFRS. This book presents the revised structures and contents of the new financial statements, including some of the terms that will be used to list accounts presented in various sections of the statement of income, the statement of comprehensive income, the statement of changes in equity, the statement of financial position, and the statement of cash flows.

Second, a section dealing with "Corporate Transparency and Accountability" has been added in Chapter 1. This section deals with ways and means that (1) the government, through government legislation, attempts to prevent individuals and organizations from carrying out fraudulent activities; (2) profit-driven and not-for-profit organizations deal with these issues through corporate governance and corporate culture; and (3) the accounting profession, that is, the IASB through the IFRS, instructs all types of organizations on how to report information in their financial statements in order to make them more visible and open to inspection by stakeholders.

Third, a section focusing on "Financial Markets" has been added in Chapter 9. This section covers topics dealing with different types of markets (money markets, capital markets, primary and secondary markets, spot and future markets, mortgage and consumer credit markets, and physical asset markets). This new section also examines several concepts related to the stock market, such as the stock exchange, and differentiates between a privately held company and a publicly traded company, including the meaning of an initial public offering (IPO) and a listed company. It also examines various dividend theories, dividend policies, and dividend payment strategies.

Fourth, each chapter now includes several "In the News" inserts, which make a link between the theory presented in the chapter and real-life examples. This feature highlights how accounting and financial tools are used by profit-driven and not-for-profit organizations, and provides useful insights about what is going on the real world.

Fifth, the chapters have been reorganized under four broad categories to reflect the types of decisions made in organizations: (1) accounting, financial statements, and ratio analysis; (2) operating decisions; (3) financing decisions; and (4) investing decisions.

Sixth, more exercises, tables, and figures have been added to all chapters to add clarity to the many financial concepts and tools.

Supplementary Material

The supplement package to accompany the sixth edition of *Finance for Non-Financial Managers* has been modified from previous editions.

- The instructor's manual includes answers to the 250-plus review questions found at the end of each chapter in the text.
- There are more than 200 *Microsoft® PowerPoint® slides* that summarize the text's key concepts.

- A revised test bank contains over 2,000 multiple-choice, true/false, and fill-in-the-blank questions that are related to the chapter objectives.
- *Microsoft® Excel® Financial Spreadsheets* that accompany this revised edition were modified to reflect the presentation format of the financial statements as suggested by the International Financial Reporting Standards. The purpose of the spreadsheets is to help readers of *Finance for Non-Financial Managers* perform most financial calculations in the sixth edition of the book, allowing students to devote more time to the analytical and decision-making activities and less on "number crunching." The spreadsheets include two segments: the first helps to analyze financial statements; the second helps readers make business decisions related to the exercises and cases contained in the book. After taking just a few moments to input numbers drawn from financial statements into the spreadsheets, which contain more than 30 different financial analytical tools (e.g., 25 financial ratios, economic value added, Z-score, sustainable growth rate, DuPont financial calculation, and internal rate of return), readers can focus more on interpretation of financial statements and decisions and less on calculations.

The *Finance for Non-Financial Managers'* website (www.bergeron6e.nelson.com) contains a wealth of resources for both instructors and students. Students will find the following resources:

- Web links to major Canadian financial agencies and associations
- Comprehensive case studies that illustrate how to analyze and make decisions for each of three categories: operating decisions, investing decisions, and financing decisions
- Interactive quiz questions that test students' mastery of every learning objective in each chapter
- Lecture notes in PowerPoint format for each chapter
- Microsoft® Excel® Financial Spreadsheets

[ACKNOWLEDGMENTS]

Although I am the author of this book, the inspiration for the book's structure, content, and style emerged from the questions and discussions that I have had with many executives and managers who have attended my seminars during the past 30 years. They have helped me immensely in writing a pragmatic book in plain language that will surely help many readers understand more thoroughly the intricate discipline of financial management.

At Nelson Education, I am indebted to Herb Hilderley who, some 30 years ago, recognized the need for this type of book and provided me with the opportunity to make the first edition a reality. I also want to thank the world-class team at Nelson Education for the outstanding support they provided while I wrote this book: Craig Dyer, Senior Acquisitions Editor; Toula Di Leo, Developmental Editor; and Imoinda Romain, Content Production Manager, who were all calm, collected, and positive with me and kept things moving smoothly and promptly. I also want to thank Ross Meacher, the technical checker of this book. Special thanks on this team also goes to the copy editor, Michael Kelly, who diligently edited the manuscript and made many suggestions for improving accuracy, and to the proofreader at Integra, whose sharp eye found further corrections to make at time of proofreading. Simply put, everyone at Nelson Education has been great to work with throughout the entire project.

I want to extend my gratitude to the outstanding set of reviewers who provided me with constructive suggestions and whose diligent and thoughtful comments improved this sixth edition:

John Cavaliere, Sault College of Applied Arts & Technology
Pamela Blake, Nunavut Arctic College
Tammy Towill, Capilano University
Ken Hartford, St. Clair College
Andy Lin, Vancouver Island University

Finally, *un gros merci* to my wife Pierrette, for having put up with the demands and sacrifices of such an undertaking. As with previous books, Pierrette is always there giving me assistance, encouragement, empathy, and support.

Pierre G. Bergeron
Ottawa, Ontario

[ABOUT THE AUTHOR]

Pierre G. Bergeron is Adjunct Professor at the Telfer School of Management, University of Ottawa. He was formerly Secretary, Associate Dean (External Relations), and Assistant Dean (Undergraduate Programs) at the same university. He is President of Budgeting Concepts Inc., an Ottawa-based corporate financial planning consulting firm. He is a highly skilled educator with more than 30 years of experience.

Mr. Bergeron has occupied the position of Director in such federal government agencies as Industry Canada (Incentives Division) and Human Resources Canada (Financial Planning Division). In the private sector, he worked at Imperial Oil Limited in the Quebec Marketing Region and at the company's head office in Toronto in market analysis and capital project evaluation. He was also Director, Corporate Financial Planning, at Domtar Limited.

Mr. Bergeron is the author of seven books: *Modern Management in Canada; Introduction aux affaires; Gestion dynamique: concepts, méthodes et applications; Finance for Non-Financial Managers; Gestion Moderne: Théorie et Cas; Planification, Budgétisation et Gestion par Objectifs;* and *Capital Expenditure Planning for Growth and Profit*. The book *Finance for Non-Financial Managers* was so successful that it was adapted by an American publishing company under the new title *Survivor's Guide to Finance.* He has written extensively on finance, planning, budgeting, and capital budgeting for professional journals including *CAmagazine, CMA Magazine, CGA Magazine, Banker and ICB Review, Financial Post,* and *Optimum.* He is the recipient of the Walter J. MacDonald Award for his series of articles on capital budgeting decisions, which appeared in *CAmagazine.*

He also collaborated with Industry Canada in developing their Strategis website component called *Steps to Growth Capital* (strategis.ic.gc.ca/growth), a program designed to help entrepreneurs raise risk capital funds from venture capital markets. He also participated in producing *Tourism Is Your Business: A Financial Management Program for Canada's Lodging Industry*, and the *ABCs of Financial Performance Measures and Benchmarks for Canada's Tourism Sector*, seven finance-related guides and financial planning spreadsheets for the Canadian Tourism Commission for which he was awarded the J. Desmond Slattery Professional Marketing Award from Clemson University (South Carolina) for excellence. The two-segment financial planning spreadsheet was designed to help managers and financial analysts gauge the impact of business strategies, plans, and budgets on financial statements, and to make business decisions using the more sophisticated time-value-of-money investment yardsticks. A unique feature of this financial planning spreadsheet, available on Nelson's website (www.bergeron6e.nelson.com), is that it can perform just about any financial statement analysis and decision-making calculation included in the book *Finance for Non-Financial Managers.*

Mr. Bergeron is a graduate of the University of Ottawa and the University of Western Ontario.

PHOTO/Monkey Business Images/Shutterstock

CHAPTER 1

[OVERVIEW OF FINANCIAL MANAGEMENT]

Learning Objectives

After reading this chapter, you should be able to:

1 Learning Objective — Define the meaning of financial management.

2 Learning Objective — Identify the individuals responsible for the finance function.

3 Learning Objective — Explain the four financial objectives.

4 Learning Objective — Comment on the three major types of business decisions.

5 Learning Objective — Discuss issues related to corporate transparency and accountability.

Chapter Outline

What Is Financial Management?
Who Is Responsible for the Finance Function?
Financial Objectives
Business Decisions
Corporate Transparency and Accountability

OPENING CASE

After spending ten years with different organizations, Len and Joan Miller decided to open their own retail business, CompuTech Sales and Service. While Len had worked for several computer retail stores, Joan was employed as a sales representative for a multinational computer organization. Both felt that their combined experience would prove to be a valuable asset for succeeding in their new venture.

However, before making their final decision, they decided to speak to a long-time friend and entrepreneur, Bill Murray, who had operated his own very successful retail business for the past 25 years. The intent of the meeting was to obtain some advice before launching their business. The following summarizes Bill's comments:

> The two most important factors for any business to be successful are products/services and management. There must be a demand for the products or services that you want to sell, and you must possess management skills (e.g., planning, organizing, leading, and controlling) and business skills (e.g., merchandising, pricing, sales, and promotion) if you are to realize your vision and objectives. You will also need operating and financial information to enable you to gauge the results of your ongoing business decisions. Although an accountant will help you set up your bookkeeping and accounting systems, you have to make sure that you have the ability to analyze your financial statements. Not being able to read financial statements is much like being a racing car driver who is unable to read the instruments on his dashboard. Like these instruments, financial statement analysis will help you see how well your business has done and, most importantly, what decisions you need to make to improve the financial performance of your retail operations.
>
> To succeed, your business will have to generate a healthy profit (efficiency) and be able to pay its bills on time (liquidity). In addition, your business must show signs of continuous growth in all segments, such as revenue and profit (prosperity). Be sure that you do not overburden your business with too much debt (stability).
>
> You will always be faced with three types of business decisions. The first are investing decisions, such as launching your business. This is not the only investing decision that you will make. If your business prospers, you will be faced with a series of investing decisions such as expanding your business, opening up new retail outlets, buying equipment for your business, and so on. Operating decisions are the second type of business decisions. They have to do with day-to-day operations. You will be continually faced with decisions such as pricing, advertising, hiring new employees, office expenses, and so on. Through your budgeting exercise, you will have to ensure that you keep your operating costs as low as possible in order to maximize your profit (efficiency). The third type is financing decisions. Once you know exactly how much it will cost you to start your business, you will have to approach investors such as lenders for financial support. These

different sources of financing bear a cost. You have to make sure that your business generates enough profit (return) to pay for financing your business (cost).

Len and Joan were enlightened by Bill Murray's comments and were convinced that if they put his suggestions into practice, they would stand a good chance of realizing their dream.

Chapter Overview

Financial management has undergone major changes during recent decades. Initially, finance consisted mainly of raising cash to purchase the assets a business needed. This was understandable because, when finance emerged as an organizational function back in the 1920s, financial management focused almost exclusively on legal matters: acquisitions, corporate offerings, mergers, formation of new businesses, reorganizations, recapitalizations, bankruptcies, and business consolidations. Finance concentrated mostly on the external activities of a business, such as raising cash, rather than on internal activities, such as finding methods to allocate cash effectively within a business. Originally, activities such as cost accounting, credit and collection, budgeting, financial planning, financial accounting, management of working capital, and capital budgeting including risk analysis were not an important part of the manager's "tool kit." Only in the past several decades has attention been turned to developing analytical and decision-making techniques geared to assist managers in improving the effectiveness of their operating, financing, and investing decisions. Put simply, in the beginning, more attention was devoted to managing one segment of the statement of financial position: raising money from lenders and shareholders.

Today, although the management of raising money from investors is still considered important, financial management has focused increasingly on the other segment of the statement of financial position (finding ways to manage more efficiently all assets of a business, such as inventories, trade receivables, and cash, and on improving the productivity of assets). Finance has assumed unprecedented importance as a management function. Today, improving a company's bottom line (profit or earnings) is a major managerial challenge. Here are some of the reasons.

First, on the economic front, the recessions of the early 1980s and the early 1990s were considered by many economists to be deeper and broader than any other downturns experienced since the Great Depression. As a result, the cost of operating businesses came under intense scrutiny. During the 1980s, managers began to realize that the North American economy was not only undergoing another shift in the business cycle, but also that it had reached a certain level of maturity. Managers began to downsize their organizations in an effort to make them more efficient, responsive, and productive. Today, businesses are again facing extraordinary challenges in view of the slowdown in economic activity. As a result of the acute slump in world economies, many governments (e.g., Canada, the United States, the United Kingdom, Germany) are now helping (through "stimulus packages") financial institutions, car industries, housing industries, and other sectors of the economy in order to stimulate economic growth. In the meantime, many businesses are employing cost-cutting measures (e.g., closing plants, cutting back on production, laying off workers, reducing wages) in order to sustain their operating activities at a reasonable profit level.

Second, on the political side, governments began to open their national borders and push business strategies to fashion their companies and industries to be leaders in world markets. Both the *Free Trade Agreement*, which was implemented in 1989, and the *North American Free Trade Agreement*, which took effect in 1994, forced managers to rethink their cost structure, improve their manufacturing capabilities, and sharpen their international marketing strategies.

Third, with more global and open world economies, companies were forced to make structural changes to their organizations (removing organizational layers and introducing cross-functional teams and boundaryless, virtual, and network organizations) in order to make them more responsive to market demand.

Fourth, technological changes have compelled managers to alter their company's operations dramatically by producing new and/or better products or services, reducing their operating costs, modifying the size of their plants, and integrating operating activities. Technological change is taking place in all sectors of organizations, such as manufacturing (e.g., reengineering), administration (e.g., office automation), communication (e.g., information technology), and the increasing use of the Internet (e.g., websites to advertise and promote products and services).

Fifth, the product life cycle is now measured not in years, but in months. Whenever a company introduces a product or service into the market, "time risk," that is, the number of months or years it should take a company to recover its investment, has to be measured in order to determine a price structure that is acceptable.

Sixth, on the manufacturing side, managers have to not only find more innovative ways to produce their goods and provide services more efficiently, but also be concerned about quality objectives. Many Canadian firms have turned to total quality management (the Six Sigma, for example, which is a highly technical method used by engineers and statisticians to fine-tune products and processes) to gauge the quality of their products and services against world standards with a goal of near-perfection in meeting customer satisfaction. Today, many companies are getting certification from the International Organization for Standardization (ISO), which is an organization that develops and publishes standards that facilitate the international exchange of goods and services and assures constancy in quality management and quality assurance throughout the world. Companies are subscribing to the ISO certification because, increasingly, customers want them to do so. The ISO accreditation also makes it easier for companies to improve their chances of success on world markets by using the ISO certificate in their advertising programs and publications.

All these changes are putting a strain on the company's bottom line. And now, when organizational managers make operating, financing, and investing decisions, they have to gauge how these decisions affect their bottom line.

This chapter examines five key topics. The first topic focuses on the importance of financial management. We will learn that the fundamental role of financial management is to "manage" and "control" money and money-related matters within a business.

The second topic gives the profiles of individuals who are responsible for the finance function. We will learn that although the treasurer and the controller (both reporting to the chief financial officer, or CFO), play a key role in the management and control function of money, operating managers also play an important task in financial management as they are the ones who make critical business decisions. They are the ones who are responsible for the production, marketing, research and development, engineering, and administration functions, where key decisions affecting an organization's bottom line are made. Here are typical examples of such decisions:

- Should we increase our selling price?
- Should we spend more money on modernizing and/or buying new equipment?
- Should we hire more employees?
- Should we spend more money in research and development?
- Should we increase our advertising budget?

The third topic of this chapter pinpoints the four financial objectives. We will learn that all types of organizations (small and large, for-profit and not-for-profit, manufacturing and service) want to be efficient (generate a reasonable profit). They also want to be liquid in order to pay their bills on time. Also, all organizations want to prosper, that is, continue to grow in terms of revenue and profitability, and pay dividends to their shareholders. Finally, they want to be stable, that is, not bear a disproportionate amount of debt.

The fourth topic explores three basic types of business decisions. As shown on the right side of Figure 1.1, the first one has to do with *operating* decisions, that is, making sure that a company's bottom line is kept healthy. This is accomplished by ensuring that operating costs are maintained at a minimum level. Managers are also responsible for keeping their inventories and trade receivables at minimum levels. As shown in the figure, operating decisions will be examined in Chapter 5 (Profit Planning and Decision-Making); this chapter looks at how much revenue a business must earn when making decisions related to their operations (e.g., hiring more employees, changing the selling price, or spending more money in an advertising campaign) before making a profit. Chapter 6 (Working Capital Management) examines how current asset and current liability accounts shown on the statement of financial position should be managed in order to improve its cash conversion cycle. Chapter 7 (Planning, Budgeting, and Controlling) describes the importance of planning, budgeting, and controlling management functions and how plans, budgets, and projected financial statements are prepared. The second type of business decisions has to do with *financing*. All companies need money in order to function. Business managers can raise money from lenders and shareholders. As we will see in Chapter 8 (Sources and Forms of Financing), money can be obtained from different *sources* or institutions such as commercial banks, investment bankers, mortgage companies, and venture capitalists. Money also comes in different *forms* such as mortgages, bonds, common shares, and lease financing. Chapter 9 (Cost of Capital, Capital Structure, and Financial Markets) looks at the cost of raising money from these different institutions and explores how much debt a company should have compared to equity. The third type of business decision has to do with *investing*, that is, the acquisition of non-current assets such as the purchase of equipment or a business, the construction of a new plant, or the modernization of an existing one. As shown in Figure 1.1, investing decisions will be covered in three chapters. Chapter 10 (Time Value of Money Concepts) looks at the reasons managers should not count the cash earned in the future on a new project before it is discounted. Chapter 11 (Capital Budgeting) explores different time value of money yardsticks that can be used to gauge the viability or profitability of capital expenditure projects. Chapter 12 (Business Valuation) looks at different approaches for putting a price tag on an ongoing business.

The fifth and last topic examines "ways" and "means" that businesses and government organizations are putting in place to prevent individuals and organizations from carrying out fraudulent activities. We have all read and heard about corporate scandals

Figure 1.1 Business Decisions and Organization of This Text

Chapter 1	Overview of Financial Management	
Chapter 2	Accounting and Financial Statements	Accounting, Financial Statements, and Ratio Analysis
Chapter 3	Statement of Cash Flows	
Chapter 4	Financial Statement Analysis	
Chapter 5	Profit Planning and Decision-Making	Operating Decisions
Chapter 6	Working Capital Management	
Chapter 7	Planning, Budgeting, and Controlling	
Chapter 8	Sources and Forms of Financing	Financing Decisions
Chapter 9	Cost of Capital, Capital Structure, and Financial Markets	
Chapter 10	Time Value of Money Concepts	Investing Decisions
Chapter 11	Capital Budgeting	
Chapter 12	Business Valuation	

International Accounting Standards Board (IASB) Organization that develops, in the public interest, a single set of high-quality, understandable, and enforceable global standards that require transparent and comparable information in general-purpose financial statements.

International Financial Reporting Standards (IFRS) Accounting standards issued by the IASB.

dating back to the 1990s, from Bre-X Minerals to Enron Corp., WorldCom, Arthur Andersen, Hollinger International (Conrad Black), and the more recent Bernard L. Madoff of Investment Securities. Techniques and practices to make individuals and organizations more transparent and accountable that will be covered in this section include government legislation, corporate governance, corporate culture (business ethics), and global accounting and financial standards via the **International Accounting Standards Board (IASB)**'s[1] **International Financial Reporting Standards (IFRS)**. The objective of this organization is to harmonize and converge different generally accepted accounting principles (GAAP) developed in various countries over the past decades. Both the IASB and the International Organization of Securities Commissions (IOSCO) are working together to move toward global convergence where more than 100 countries have to date converged or are on a path to converge. In the News 1.1 gives an illustration of the difficulty that may arise from different accounting organizations regarding ways of presenting information in financial statements.

In The News [1.1]

Which Method Is More Accurate to Value Assets: Judgment or Market Prices?

Every time changes are announced, there are individuals or interest groups that are for the change, and others against. The changes regarding the global accounting standards announced by the IASB are no exception!

An important piece of this change has to do with the way that capital assets are presented on financial statements. Everyone now has an opinion, including politicians, bank lobbyists, Wall Street, bank regulators, economists, Securities Commissions, lawyers, the U.S. Congress, Bay Street, and Canadian accounting firms. Even some Canadian interest groups and U.S. interest groups do not see eye to eye with the new accounting regulations. Some say that some new accounting rules will weaken the banking system while others say that the "fair-value," or "mark-to-market" accounting system is the most correct and objective way to price assets. Who is right on these issues?

Source: Adapted from Duncan Mavin and Eoin Callan, "Warning on fair value; Accounting board calls U.S. changes 'crazy,'" *Financial Post*, April 21, 2009. Found at: http://www.nationalpost.com/story.html?id=1516597. For updates on the IFRS, visit www.iasb.org/IFRSs/IFRS.htm.

What Is Financial Management?

1 Learning Objective

Define the meaning of financial management.

Financial management ensures that a company uses its resources in the most efficient and effective way: maximizing the profit (or earnings) generated by a business, which ultimately increases the value of a business (its net worth or equity). What was called finance in the past is now referred to as financial management, reflecting the current emphasis on the importance of having all managers in a business participate in making

1. For recent updates on the work accomplished by the IASB, visit the website, www.iasb.org.

important decisions that affect the financial destiny of their respective organizational units and the company as a whole.

Financial management Activity involved in raising money and buying assets in order to obtain the highest possible return.

Financial management deals with two things: first, raising funds, and second, buying and utilizing assets in order to gain the highest possible return. An important objective of financial management is to ensure that the assets used in business produce a return that is higher than the cost of borrowed funds. For example, if an individual borrows money from a bank at 6% and lends it to a friend, he would certainly lend it for more than 6%. Using this example, we have two transactions. First, the individual *borrows* money from a bank, and second, lends it to a friend in the form of an *investment*. Businesses function in the same way. Managers borrow money from lenders and invest it in business assets for the purpose of earning a profit.

It would be pointless for a business to raise funds from investors at a cost of 10% and invest them in assets (i.e., a project) that generate only 7%. As shown in Figure 1.2, the objective of financial management is to ensure that the return on assets (ROA) generated by a business (here, 10%) is higher than the cost of money borrowed from investors—that is, lenders and shareholders (here, 7%). This figure shows that the statement of financial position has two sides. On the left, it lists assets such as non-current assets (e.g., cars, buildings, equipment), and current assets (e.g., inventories, trade receivables) that a business owns; on the right, the money raised from investors such as equity (shareholders), non-current liabilities (long-term borrowings), and current liabilities. Here is how the 10% and 7% figures were calculated. If the business invests $100,000 in assets (left side) and generates $10,000 in profit from its revenue, it will have earned 10% ($10,000 ÷ $100,000). If the business borrows the $100,000 from different sources such as commercial banks, term lenders, and mortgage companies and pays $7,000 in interest, the cost of financing would therefore be 7% ($7,000 ÷ 100,000).

In the main, financial management focuses on five important questions:

1. *How are we doing?* Everybody wants to know about a company's financial performance: managers, short- and long-term lenders, shareholders, suppliers, etc. They want answers to the following questions: Is the

Figure 1.2 **Relationship between ROA and Cost of Financing**

Statement of Financial Position

Assets • Non-current assets • Current assets	Equity and Liabilities • Equity • Non-current liabilities • Current liabilities
Return on assets 10%	Investors Cost of financing 7%

company profitable? How about the return on its assets? Is the company efficient and keeping its costs under control? Is the company adding value for its shareholders? As we will see in later chapters, a company's financial statements provide answers to these questions and help managers find ways to maximize profitability.

2. *How much cash do we have on hand?* Knowing how much cash a company has on hand is important to determine its liquidity and its ability to pay its bills on time. Here are typical questions related to liquidity issues: Can the business meet its payroll? Pay its suppliers on time? Service its line of credit or seasonal loan? How much cash can be generated internally, that is, from the business itself, within the next 12 months? Managers must know how much cash the company has on hand now and how much it will have in the future in order to determine how much it will need to borrow from external sources such as lenders and shareholders.
3. *What should we spend our money on?* Money can be spent on (a) operating activities such as salaries, advertising, freight, promotions, and insurance, including current assets such as inventories and trade receivables; and (b) investing activities, that is, non-current assets such as property, plant, machinery, and equipment. Managers must determine whether the money that will be spent on non-current assets for automation and expansion will generate a ROA that is higher than the cost of financing, and equally important, compensate for the risk. Because money can be invested in different projects bearing different risk levels, the return to be earned from various capital investments must therefore show different economic values. For example, managers may accept an 8% return on a project that bears a low risk and will not approve one even if it generates 15% because of higher risks.
4. *Where will our funds come from?* Once managers have identified how much money the business needs and how much cash it has on hand, they have to determine where cash can be obtained in the future. Suppliers? Bankers? Long-term investors such as shareholders, venture capitalists, or insurance companies?
5. *How will our business be protected?* One of the most important responsibilities of managers is to protect the investors' interests. It is important to recognize that managers are employed by shareholders and should therefore act on their behalf. However, managers have to reconcile the legitimate and sometimes conflicting objectives of various interest groups (e.g., unions, lenders, employees, customers, suppliers, communities, and government agencies). Because shareholders have a unique and legal status, managers must ensure that their interests are not compromised and that they are clearly protected.

> It is important to note that the downfall of companies like Enron Corp. and WorldCom were not due only to accounting errors, but instead, largely due to accounting irregularities, manipulation of books, misrepresentation, and fraudulent activities.

Since the start of this chapter, we have mostly referred to businesses. It should be noted that effective financial management should be performed not only in for-profit enterprises but also in all types of not-for-profit (NFP) organizations such as hospitals, colleges, churches, and universities. As will be explained in this text, NFP organizations also publish financial statements such as the statement of income, the statement of financial position, and the statement of cash flows. All organizations have assets, liabilities, revenue, and expenses. There are, however, variations in terminology for a for-profit enterprise's statement of financial position and statement of income accounts versus that for an NFP. The *CICA Handbook—Accounting* sets out the applicability of accounting principles and financial statements to NFPs. For example, financial statement concepts and generally accepted accounting principles have general applicability for NFPs, while differential reporting has limited or no applicability. Also, current assets and current liabilities have general applicability, while income tax expense, goodwill, and share capital have limited or no applicability to NFPs.

Self-Test Exercise No. 1.1

ROA and Cost of Financing

Len and Joan intend to invest $200,000 in a business to launch their CompuTech Sales and Service retail store. Their financial projections show that during the first year of operations CompuTech would generate $25,000 in profit with substantial increases during the following years. To finance their business, Len and Joan would obtain $100,000 for different loans (short-term and long-term borrowings) from the bank at 6% (after taxes) and invest $100,000 of their savings into the business. The Millers are currently earning 8% (after taxes) on their savings.

Questions

1. With the above information, calculate CompuTech's ROA and its cost of financing their new retail business.
2. Should the Millers launch their business? Why or why not?

Who Is Responsible for the Finance Function?

2 Learning Objective

Identify the individuals responsible for the finance function.

Figure 1.3 shows the basic structure of a company's organization. In corporations, the owners are the shareholders. However, because there are numerous owners, few of them are involved in managing the business. So shareholders elect a board of directors to oversee the business and approve the major decisions affecting the organization, subject to corporate charter and bylaw provisions. The authority

Figure 1.3 **Responsibility of Financial Management**

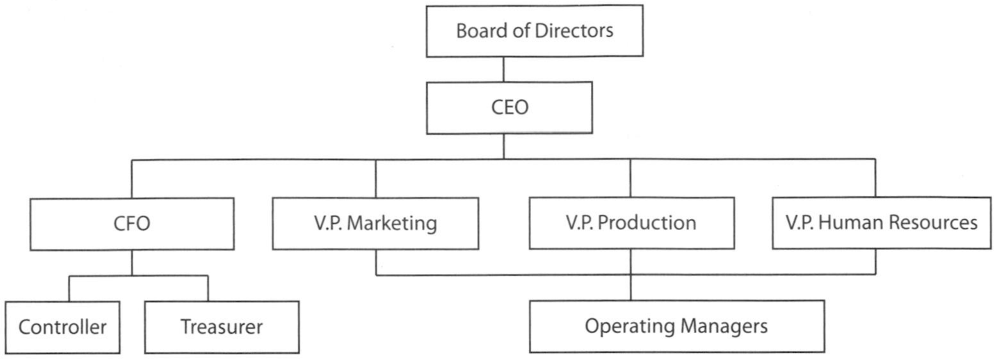

Chief executive officer (CEO)
Person who plays a major role in the complete management process and is responsible for the formulation of the strategic plans and seeing that they are effectively implemented.

Chief financial officer (CFO)
Person in charge of the finance function and responsible for all accounting functions and external activities.

Controller
Person responsible for establishing the accounting and financial reporting policies and procedures.

Treasurer
Person responsible for raising funds and regulating the flow of funds.

vested in the board of directors is assigned to a **chief executive officer (CEO)**. This person is personally accountable to the board and to the shareholders for the company's performance. The CEO is usually the president or the chair of the board of directors and is probably the single most important individual in any organization. The CEO plays a major role in the complete management process and is responsible for the formulation of the strategic plans and seeing that they are effectively implemented.

The **chief financial officer (CFO)** and the vice-presidents report to the CEO. The CFO is the executive in charge of the finance function and is responsible for all accounting functions and external activities. The title vice-president of finance is sometimes used instead.

The finance activities are carried out by the controller, the treasurer, and operating managers. As shown in Figure 1.3, both the controller and the treasurer report to the chief financial officer.

CONTROLLER

The **controller** establishes the accounting and financial reporting policies and procedures; maintains the accounting, auditing, and management control mechanisms; and analyzes financial results. Together with operating managers, the controller prepares annual budgets and financial plans and determines financial objectives and standards to ensure efficiency and adequate returns. This controllership function has to do with how funds are expensed and invested to satisfy consumer needs and shareholder interests.

TREASURER

The **treasurer**—that is, the person responsible for raising funds—looks after investors, plans investment strategies, analyzes tax implications, and gauges the impact of internal and external events on a firm's capital structure, or the relationship between liabilities and equity. The treasurer also regulates the flow of funds, determines dividend payments, recommends short- and long-term financing strategies, and cultivates relations with investors. In short, the treasurer is responsible for the liability and shareholder equity accounts shown on the statement of financial position.

Table 1.1 shows a list of typical activities of the finance function under the jurisdiction of the controller (controllership functions) and the treasurer (treasury functions).

OPERATING MANAGERS

Operating managers Person in charge of organizational units such as marketing, manufacturing, and human resources, and responsible for making operating and investing decisions.

Financial management is also a responsibility of **operating managers** (managers responsible for line and staff functions) in various organizational units such as marketing, manufacturing, human resources, research and development, and general administration. As shown in Figure 1.3, these managers report to various vice-presidents (marketing, production, human resources, etc.) and are responsible for analyzing operating and financial data, making decisions about asset acquisitions, and improving the operating performance of their respective organizational units and of the company as a whole.

People often think of finance as a function performed only by accountants, bookkeepers, treasurers, controllers, or financial analysts. Although these people play a key role in financial management and in the financial planning process, *all managers* are accountable for their decisions as they may impact, directly or indirectly, the financial performance of their business unit or organization.

A business is much like an aircraft—someone has to pilot it. In an aircraft, a pilot is responsible for analyzing various instruments on the dashboard to make sure that the flight will run smoothly, from takeoff to landing. For a business establishment, an operating manager is responsible for managing or piloting it, and the instruments

Table 1.1 The Functions of the Controller and the Treasurer

Functions of the Controller	Functions of the Treasurer
• General accounting	• Raising capital
• Cost accounting	• Investor relations
• Credit and collection	• Short-term borrowings
• Management information system	• Dividend and interest payments
• Trade and other payables	• Insurance
• Corporate accounting	• Analysis of investment securities
• Internal auditing	• Retirement funds
• Budgets and analysis	• Property taxes
• Payroll	• Investment portfolio
• Systems and procedures	• Cash flow requirements
• Planning	• Actuarial
• Controlling	• Underwriting policy and manuals
• Interpreting financial reports	• Tax administration

used to steer the business are financial statements. These financial statements reflect how well a business has done in the past and, based on goals and plans, how well it will perform in the future.

Business decisions of all types cut across all business functions such as marketing, manufacturing, administration, human resources, research and development, and after-sales services. Operators of businesses make many of these decisions on a daily basis. For example, some of these decisions may include the hiring of an employee, increasing the selling price of one or two product lines or services, cutting back some operating expenses, adding a bigger share of the budget to promotion and advertising, buying new equipment in order to make the business more efficient, and providing a better service to customers. These decisions have one thing in common: They impact on a business establishment's *financial performance* (statement of income) and *financial structure* (statement of financial position). These two financial documents inform operators of business establishments about the outcome of their decisions. Operating managers who have difficulty reading or interpreting financial statements are unable to effectively gauge how well their business has done, is currently doing, or will do in the future.

An aircraft pilot is in the best position to control his airplane (whether it is a small or large aircraft) for three reasons.

- He understands his operating environment.
- He knows exactly where he wants to go.
- He has an appreciation about what needs to be done in order to reach his destination.

An aircraft pilot does not delegate this most important activity. He may ask for advice or help, but in the end, he makes critical decisions based on his analysis and the input of others. The same should apply for businesses. It is the operating manager (CEO, vice-presidents, directors, managers) who is ultimately responsible for making important decisions and for determining the financial destiny of an organizational unit or business as a whole.

Operating managers are often tempted to hand over the analysis of financial statements to others, such as accountants or business consultants, because of their lack of understanding of accounting and finance. If accountants and business consultants don't have a crisp understanding or appreciation of an operator's business environment and operating functions, they risk making decisions that may be damaging to the financial health of the business.

Finance is a business function that is far too important to be left only to financial specialists or consultants. It is important that all managers (top, middle, or first-level) responsible for resources or budgets become familiar with the language of finance and with the different tools available for analyzing business performance and making vital business decisions. A manager who lacks these skills will not be in a position to contribute fully and effectively to improving the operational and financial performance of his business unit and that of the organization.

Financial Objectives

3 Learning Objective

Explain the four financial objectives.

As mentioned earlier, finance involves "handling money." There is no question that all organizations—small or large, public or private, manufacturing or service, government agencies or Crown corporations, for-profit or NFP—need money to function. All these organizations have this in common: They want to be *efficient*, they need to be *liquid* in order to pay their current bills on time, they do their best to *prosper*, and they want to secure a certain level of *stability*. These are the four most important financial objectives. Let's examine these four objectives.

EFFICIENCY

Efficiency
The relationship between profit (outputs) generated and assets employed (inputs).

Efficiency means the productivity of assets, which is the relationship between the profit generated and assets employed. In the language of finance, this is referred to as ROA, return on equity, and return on revenue (ROR). The objective of any organization is to ensure that a business's resources are used efficiently to produce an acceptable return. High profits satisfy investors and indicate that the assets of an organization are working hard. The more profit a business earns, the more cash it can invest in operations to finance its growth and to purchase non-current assets such as machinery and equipment. The notion of efficiency applies to not only for-profit enterprises but also NFP organizations; churches, hospitals, colleges, and universities want to ensure that they use their resources efficiently. If organizations can save money by using their resources wisely, more money will be available to invest in their organizations. When an organization deducts all costs from its revenue, businesses call this "profit" while a NFP organization may choose to call it a "surplus" or "excess of revenues over expenses."

Let's examine the meaning of efficiency. Figure 1.4 shows a business that generates $100,000 in revenue and earns $8,000 in profit. As shown, the company is earning $0.08 (or 8.0% of revenue) for every revenue dollar. If another business generates $10,000 in profit with the same amount in revenue, it may very well mean that it is more efficient; it will be earning $0.10 for every revenue dollar.

Figure 1.4 Return on Revenue

Statement of Income (in $)		%
Revenue	100,000	100.0
Cost of sales	(70,000)	(70.0)
Gross profit	30,000	30.0
Other costs	(15,000)	(15.0)
Profit before taxes	15,000	15.0
Income tax expense	(7,000)	(7.0)
Profit for the year	8,000	8.0

Return on Revenue

Let's now explore what this business can do with the $8,000 of profit or $0.08 for each revenue dollar. This is commonly referred to as *return on revenue.* As shown in Figure 1.5, this $8,000 could be reinvested in the business through retained earnings (say, $5,000 or $0.05). Retained earnings simply means the amount of money that will be kept by the business for reinvestment purposes. As shown in Figure 1.5, the company will invest $3,000 or $0.03 in non-current assets to purchase, for example, equipment and machinery, and $2,000 or $0.02 for every revenue dollar in current assets, or working capital accounts such as trade receivables and inventories (for day-to-day operating purposes). The balance of the cash ($3,000 or $0.03) will be used for external purposes. Here, the shareholders would receive $2,000 in dividends or $0.02 to compensate for the investment they have made in the business, and $1,000 or $0.01 will be used to repay the principal on the debt. The bottom line is this: If the $8,000 or $0.08 ROR begins to shrink to, say, $6,000 or even $3,000, the company will have less money to invest internally to help its growth, to invest in assets, and to satisfy its shareholders.

LIQUIDITY

Liquidity
Ability of a firm to meet its short-term financial commitments.

Liquidity is a company's ability to meet its short-term financial commitments. If a business increases its revenue, it will inevitably increase its working capital accounts such as inventories, trade receivables, and cash required for paying its employees, suppliers, and creditors on time. As shown in Figure 1.5, $2,000 or $0.02 for each revenue dollar is invested in such working capital accounts. If a business wants to grow but shows a reduction in its ROR performance (say, less than $0.08 per revenue dollar), it will have less cash from internal operations (retained earnings) to invest in working capital accounts, and may have to rely on short-term borrowings in order to keep growing. As a consequence, additional borrowings reduce a company's profit (because of increased finance costs) and further reduce its ROR.

Figure 1.5 Return on Revenue Objective

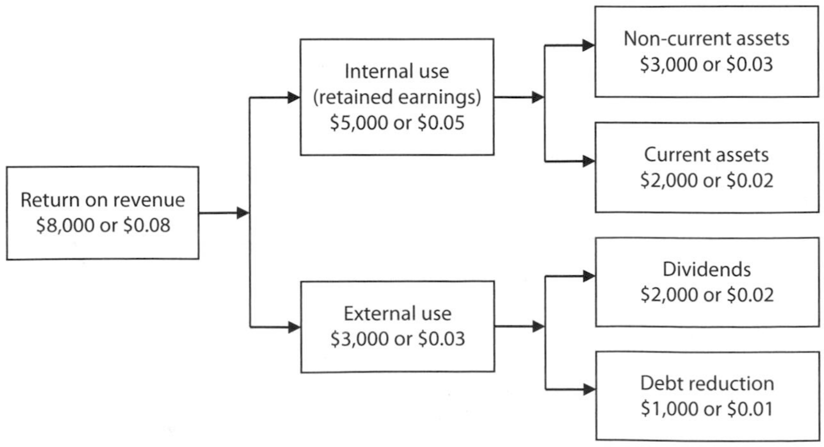

PROSPERITY

Prosperity
The ability of a firm to grow (i.e., revenue, profit, equity).

Prosperity means growth in all segments of a business: revenue, profit, dividend payments, non-current assets, equity, and working capital. If a company's ROR deteriorates, it may not be able to finance its growth through internally generated cash. Consequently, it would have difficulty investing in non-current assets such as equipment and machinery in order to expand its operations and improve its productivity (as shown in Figure 1.5, an amount of $3,000 or $0.03 for each revenue dollar is invested in non-current assets). Again, if the organization wants to invest in these types of assets, it may have to borrow (if internally generated cash is insufficient) from long-term lenders and shareholders to finance the purchase of non-current assets.

STABILITY

Stability
Relationship between debt and equity.

Stability refers to the financial structure of a business. Here, financial management ensures equilibrium between the cash provided by creditors and that provided by shareholders (relationship between debt and equity). If a business continues to borrow from lenders, it may have a high debt-to-equity ratio and as a result may not be able to meet its short- and long-term debt obligations, particularly if there is a slowdown in business activities caused by economic conditions. If the company's ROR is adequate, it will have enough cash (as shown in Figure 1.5, an amount of $3,000 or $0.03 for each revenue dollar is used for external activities) to pay dividends ($2,000 or $0.02 for each revenue dollar) and reduce the principal on its debt ($1,000 or $0.01 for each revenue dollar). If the company does not produce an adequate ROR, again it may have to borrow more from lenders and consequently produce a negative effect on its stability.

The bottom line is this: If a company wants to maintain or improve its stability, it must never lose sight of the first objective, to earn a suitable *return on revenue*. If successful, profit (or retained earnings) can be used to increase working capital and to purchase non-current assets (if required), to pay dividends, and to reduce debt without relying too extensively on debt financing.

Self-Test Exercise No. 1.2

Distribution of Profit

Len and Joan want to reinvest 70% of their $25,000 profit (see Self-Test Exercise No. 1.1 on page 11) in their business and use the rest to pay the principal on their loan. They expect to invest 50% of the reinvested earnings in working capital and 50% in non-current assets. CompuTech's 2009 revenue is estimated to be $350,000.

Question

On the basis of the above information, calculate, as a percentage of revenue, how much the Millers would keep in the business for growth purposes (i.e., working capital and the purchase of non-current assets), and how much would be used to pay off the principal on their loan.

Business Decisions

4 Learning Objective

Comment on the three major types of business decisions.

Figure 1.6 shows the three major types of business decisions made by managers: operating decisions, financing decisions, and investing decisions. For example, if managers want to invest $1.0 million in non-current assets (investing decisions), the cash required to purchase these assets would be provided by (1) internal activities (operating decisions) and (2) external activities (financing decisions). First, managers provide internal cash through operating decisions (profit for the year shown on the statement of income and improvement in the management of current asset and current liability accounts shown on the statement of financial position); second, shareholders and long-term lenders, through financing decisions, provide external funds. As shown in Figure 1.6, if the company provides $500,000 from internal operations and is able to obtain the rest from investors ($500,000), the $1.0 million in non-current assets (investing decisions) would be financed equitably.

The ideal situation is to finance, to the maximum, the purchase of non-current assets with internally generated cash. For example, if the company purchases the assets ($1.0 million) with $800,000 of internally generated cash, it would rely less on external financing and be able to enhance its financial stability.

Internal financing Cash provided from retained earnings, depreciation/amortization, and a reduction in working capital accounts.

Internal financing is provided from retained earnings—that is, the profit generated by the business—plus the depreciation/amortization that appears on the statement of income as a non-cash expense[2]—and by reducing current asset accounts such as trade receivables and inventories. In Figure 1.6, the box representing working capital (current assets and current liabilities) is shaded because managers can obtain cash only

Figure 1.6 Business Decisions

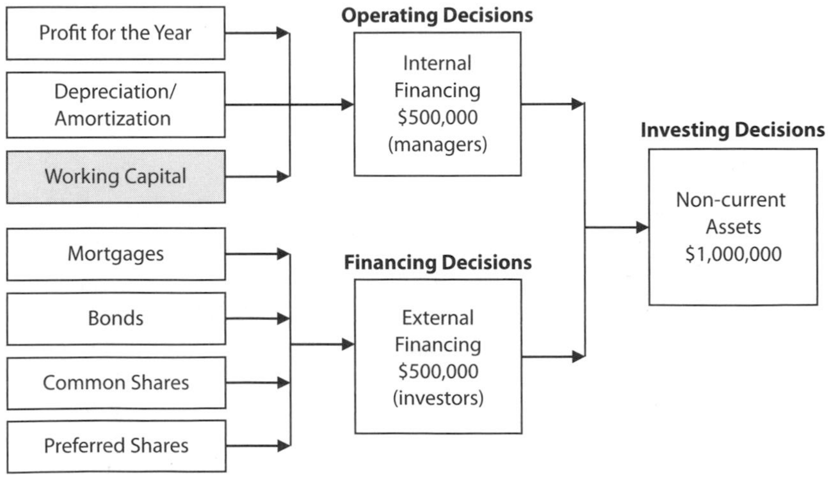

2. The notion of depreciation/amortization being considered a non-cash expense is explained in Chapter 2 on page 65.

if they are able to reduce accounts such as trade receivables and inventories. An increase in these accounts would be considered an outflow of cash. To illustrate, suppose that a plant manager wants to buy a $50,000 machine; it could be financed by a $50,000 reduction in inventories.

Figure 1.7 illustrates how the three types of business decisions appear on the statement of financial position. On the left are investments in non-current assets such as buildings, machinery, and equipment, and other assets or intangible assets such as research and development, goodwill, and patents. These two investing decisions or activities (I) appear in boxes with vertical lines.

External financing Cash obtained from investors (long-term lenders and shareholders).

The right side of the statement of financial position in Figure 1.7 shows the **external financing** decisions related to the provision of funds obtained from long-term lenders and shareholders. The two financing decisions or activities (F) appear in boxes with horizontal lines, one a portion of equity and the other, non-current liabilities. Obtaining funds from these two sources is the responsibility of the chief financial officer or the treasurer.

Managers can provide cash to a business through two sources: (1) profit for the year and (2) an improvement in working capital accounts. The centre of the statement of financial position shows to what extent operating decisions affect retained earnings

Figure 1.7 Business Decisions and The Financial Statements

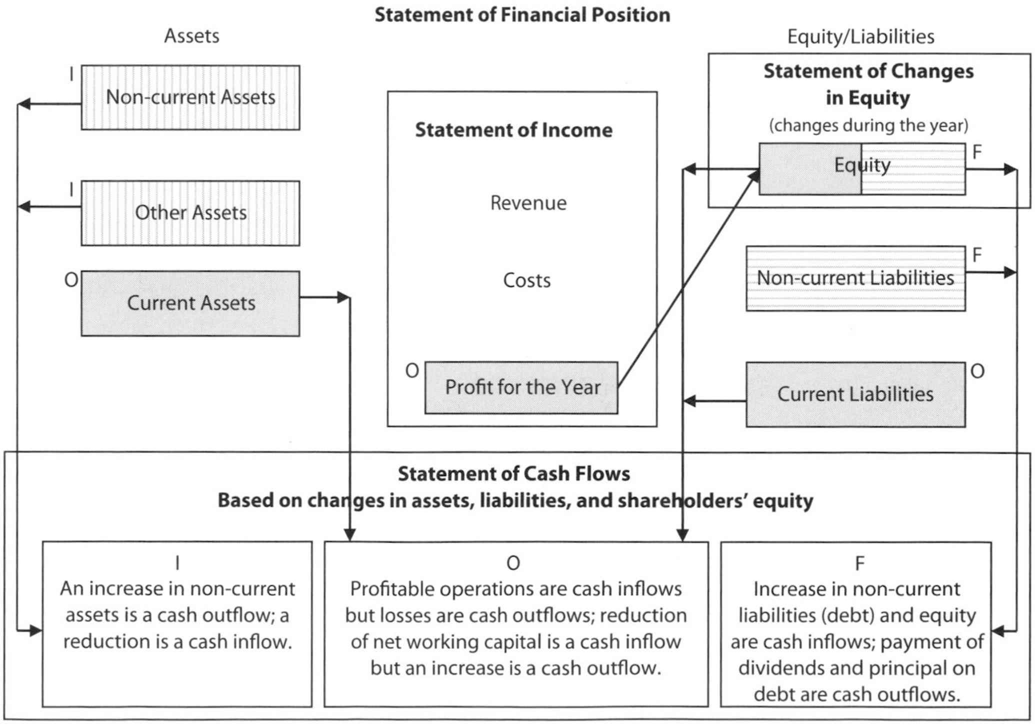

Source: Erich A. Helfert, *Techniques of Financial Analysis: A Guide to Value Creation*, 6th edition, 2000, Fig. 1.9, Page 18. Irwin/McGraw-Hill. Reprinted with permission.

(statement of financial position).[3] Operating decisions are the responsibility of all managers and include decisions that affect *every* account shown on the statement of income (e.g., revenue, costs). If managers make prudent operating decisions in marketing, manufacturing, production, administration, human resources, etc., they will help generate higher profit (O) and ultimately improve the ROR performance. As mentioned earlier, higher profit enables managers to pay dividends and to reinvest the rest in the business through retained earnings (shareholders' equity). As shown in Figure 1.7, profit for the year (shaded box) is reinvested in the business in the form of retained earnings and a portion of the equity comprises retained earnings (also shaded). The figure shows that managers are also responsible for the management of working capital accounts (current assets and current liabilities) that appear in the lower portion of the statement of financial position (also shaded box). The more efficient they are in managing these items (trade receivables, inventories, and trade and other payables), the more cash will be provided in the business (O).

The cash generated by the business (O) and obtained from investors (F) will be used to purchase non-current assets and other assets (I).

The lower portion of Figure 1.7 shows how these three types of business decisions affect a company's cash position. For instance, a decrease in the non-current asset accounts (e.g., through selling an asset such as a truck) would be considered an inflow of cash. An increase in liability and equity accounts (through borrowing from banks or the injection of additional funds from shareholders) would also be considered an inflow of cash, as is profit generated by a business.

This book explores in detail these three types of business decisions. After examining the structure of financial statements and how they can be analyzed in Chapters 2, 3, and 4, as mentioned earlier (see Figure 1.1, page 7), we will discuss operating decisions in Chapters 5, 6, and 7, financing decisions in Chapters 8 and 9, and investing decisions in Chapters 10, 11, and 12.

The rest of this chapter gives an overview of how these three types of business decisions can affect favourably the financial performance (statement of income) and financial structure (statement of financial position) of a business.

Investing decisions
Decisions related to the acquisition of non-current assets.

Non-current assets
Statement of financial position accounts such as land, buildings, equipment, and machinery.

INVESTING DECISIONS

As mentioned earlier, **investing decisions** deal with the acquisition of non-current assets (e.g., machinery, equipment). As shown in Figure 1.7, investing decisions have an impact on a company's cash flow. Acquiring non-current assets puts a drain on a company's cash position as it is considered an outflow of cash. However, a reduction in such assets, such as selling unproductive capital assets, is considered an inflow of cash.

Decisions dealing with **non-current** (also called **capital** or **fixed**) **assets** involve the purchase of equipment or machinery, and the more critical decisions such as plant

3. The statement of income is presented at the centre of the statement of financial position in Figure 1.7 strictly for presentation purposes. It shows how profit for the year increases the equity on the statement of financial position.

expansion, plant modernization to increase productivity, or investment in new facilities. These types of decisions are usually made during the capital budgeting process. Here, management examines the relationship between the cash invested in such assets and the anticipated cash that can be generated in the future by these assets. For example, if someone invests $100,000 in Canada Savings Bonds and earns $5,000 in interest, that person earns 5%. The same applies when managers invest in non-current assets. They want to measure two things: the expected ROA and how it compares to the cost of capital.

Here is an example of how investing decisions in non-current assets are calculated. Let's say that a company invests $1.0 million in the following assets:

Land	$ 100,000
Buildings	500,000
Machinery and equipment	400,000
Total investments	$1,000,000

Let's also assume that this investment produces $132,000 in profit each year. The following shows the calculation:

Revenue	$ 2,000,000
Cost of sales	(1,200,000)
Gross profit	800,000
Total costs	(560,000)
Profit before taxes	240,000
Income tax expense	(108,000)
Profit for the year	$ 132,000

Several capital budgeting techniques are used to gauge the economic desirability of such investments. For example, there is the ROA calculation that relates profit for the year to investment in non-current (or capital) assets. It is calculated as follows:

$$\frac{\textbf{Profit for the year}}{\textbf{Investment in non-current assets}} = \frac{\$132{,}000}{\$1{,}000{,}000} = 13.2\%$$

This means that the $1.0 million investment in non-current assets generates a 13.2% return. Managers must also consider whether the investment is worth the risk. Before making a decision, they would have to relate the return of that particular investment to both the cost of capital and the inherent risks associated with the project. For example, if the company borrows the entire amount from lenders at a before-tax cost of 10%, it means that the after-tax cost of capital would be 6% (assuming that the business is in a 40% tax bracket). In this particular instance, the company would earn 7.2% (13.2–6.0%) more than the cost of borrowing.

The project's risk would also be considered. Managers would have to gauge whether a 13.2% return on this particular investment is worth the risk. If this investment was in the high-risk category, such as an investment in an untried product, management may want to earn at least 25% to 30% to justify the investment. However, if the project is low risk, such as the expansion of an existing plant, it could require a much lower return on its investment (say, around 10%).

FINANCING DECISIONS

Financing decisions Decisions related to borrowing from long-term lenders and shareholders.

As shown in Figure 1.7(page 19), **financing decisions** deal with the accounts listed on the right side of the statement of financial position—that is, funds obtained from long-term lenders and shareholders. Financing decisions examine the best way cash can be raised from these investors. Financing decisions deal with five elements: matching principle, sources and forms of financing, cost of financing, weighted average cost of capital, and financing mix.

Matching principle Process of selecting the most appropriate financing source when buying an asset.

The Matching Principle. Essentially, the **matching principle** explores the selection of the most appropriate financing source of cash when buying assets. This means that short-term borrowings should be used to finance current assets while long-term borrowings should buy the more permanent assets such as non-current assets. For example, it would not make much sense to buy a house on a credit card such as MasterCard or Visa! Simply put, the matching principle calls for relating the maturity of the sources of cash and the maturity of the uses of cash.

Sources of financing Institutions that provide funds (e.g., commercial banks).

Forms of financing Financing instruments used to buy assets (e.g., term loans).

Sources and Forms of Financing. A business can obtain money from a wide range of sources and in different forms. **Sources of financing** are institutions that provide funds and include commercial banks, investment bankers, equipment vendors, government agencies, private venture capital companies, suppliers, trust companies, life insurance companies, mortgage companies, individuals, and shareholders. **Forms of financing** are the financing instruments used to purchase the assets. They include short-term loans (secured or unsecured), term or installment loans, revolving loans, lease financing, mortgages, bonds, preferred shares, and common shares.

Cost of financing Effective after-tax cost of raising funds from different sources (lenders and shareholders).

Cost of Financing. Another important element in financing decisions is determining the **cost of financing** when raising funds from different sources. This is critical because borrowed funds are used to purchase assets, and managers want to ensure that the return generated by the assets exceeds the cost of borrowed funds.

Weighted average cost of capital Composite weighted after-tax cost of raising funds from long-term investors (bonds, mortgages, common shares, preferred shares).

Weighted Average Cost of Capital. **Weighted average cost of capital** deals with the accounts shown on the right side of the statement of financial position. It involves the more permanent forms of financing such as mortgages, bonds, and preferred and common shares. These are referred to as *capital funds*, thus, their cost is known as *cost of capital*. In the earlier example of a $1.0 million investment in non-current assets, managers would have to determine the cost of each loan and the weighted cost of capital. For instance, if the business borrows $400,000 from a mortgage company at 12%, $300,000 from bondholders at 13%, and the rest ($300,000) from shareholders at, say, 15%,[4] the weighted average cost of capital would be 9.27%. Because finance costs on mortgage and bond financing are tax-deductible and the company is in a

4. This percentage is equivalent to what the shareholders could earn if they were to invest these funds elsewhere; it is sometimes referred to as the *opportunity cost*.

45% tax bracket, such financing options are more attractive than equity financing as dividends are paid with after-tax profit. The calculation is as follows:

Sources	Amount ($)	Proportion (%)	Before-tax Cost (%)		After-tax Cost (%)		Weighted Cost of Capital (%)
Mortgage	400,000	0.40	12.0	×	6.6	=	2.64
Bonds	300,000	0.30	13.0	×	7.1	=	2.13
Common shares	300,000	0.30	15.0	×	15.0	=	4.50
Weighted average Cost of capital	1,000,000	1.00					9.27

Financing mix
Proportion of funds raised from lenders and shareholders.

Financing Mix. Another component of financing decisions is determining the **financing mix**, proportion of funds that should be raised from lenders versus owners. As shown in the previous example, it would be advantageous to borrow as much as possible from lenders because that is the least expensive option (6.6% and 7.1% versus 15.0%). However, because lenders do not want to take all the risks related to the investment decisions, they will demand that an appropriate amount of funds be provided by shareholders. Equally important in financing decisions is a firm's ability to repay its debt obligation. If both the economy and the industry sectors are in a strong growth position, the company will generate healthy profits, be able to repay its loan without difficulty, and raise more funds from lenders rather than shareholders. However, if the economic indicators and the marketplace indicate slow growth, a low-leveraged position (meaning less money borrowed from lenders) would be more advantageous and less risky.

Self-Test Exercise No. 1.3

Cost of Financing and Weighted Average Cost of Capital

With the following information, calculate CompuTech's cost of financing and its weighted average cost of capital. Assume that the company's income tax rate is 33%.

Source	Amount (in $)
Share capital	100,000
Long-term borrowings (mortgage)	60,000
Trade and other payables	17,000
Short-term borrowings (term loan)	35,000

The bank charges 12.0% (before tax) for the term loan and 11.0% for the mortgage. The Millers expect to earn 8% on their savings.

Questions

1. Calculate the company's after-tax cost of financing.
2. Calculate the company's weighted average cost of capital.

OPERATING DECISIONS

Operating decisions Decisions related to accounts appearing on the statement of financial position (current assets and current liabilities) and the statement of income (e.g., revenue, cost of sales, distribution costs).

As shown in Figure 1.7(page 19), **operating decisions** deal with many accounts appearing on both the statement of financial position and the statement of income. These financial statements will be explained in detail in Chapter 2. As shown in the figure, operating decisions deal with accounts shown on the statement of financial position such as current assets and current liabilities (shaded boxes). In the statement of income, these accounts include revenue, cost of sales, distribution costs, and administrative expenses.

Operating Decisions Related to the Statement of Financial Position

Let's now examine how working capital decisions affect a company's cash flow performance.

Working capital accounts Statement of financial position accounts such as inventories, trade receivables, and cash (current assets), and trade and other payables and short-term borrowings (current liabilities).

Working Capital Accounts. **Working capital accounts** are statement of financial position accounts such as cash, trade receivables, and inventories (current assets), and trade and other payables and short-term borrowings (current liabilities).

Managing working capital means accelerating the movement of cash in a business. This movement of cash is referred to as the cash-conversion cycle. The faster inventories are turned over and trade receivables are collected, the more cash and profit a business earns.

Current assets are not productive assets, but they are necessary for a business to operate; it must sell on credit and carry a certain amount of inventories. However, it is necessary to determine the right amount of working capital that should be maintained. The faster working capital accounts are transformed into cash, the faster the cash can be invested into more productive assets such as equipment and machinery; this ultimately improves a company's profit performance.

Decisions related to managing *cash* determine the minimum level of cash that will satisfy business needs under normal operating conditions. Cash reserves (including marketable securities) should be sufficient to satisfy daily cash expenditures (salaries, suppliers, etc.).

Decisions related to *inventories* deal with lowering the amount of raw materials, unfinished goods, and finished goods. Turning over inventory rapidly can improve a company's cash position and, ultimately, its profitability and return on investment. Several techniques can be used to make such decisions, including the following:

- *Just-in-time inventory management process*, which is a supply system that attempts to reduce inventories.
- *Economic ordering quantity system*, which determines the optimal number of units that should be ordered each time goods are purchased from suppliers.

The intent here is to invest as little as possible in inventory because it is considered a non-productive asset. To illustrate, let's assume that managers can reduce inventory levels from, say, $400,000 down to $325,000 because of inventory management approaches such as just-in-time and economic ordering quantity. This means that the company will have an extra $75,000 in cash with which to work.

Decisions related to *trade receivables* deal with collecting receivables from customers as quickly as possible. For example, if a business has slow-paying customers (say, 90 days), management may decide to offer cash discounts off the original sale price to accelerate the cash flow and shorten the collection period (say, a 2% discount if the customer pays within 10 days). Before offering such discounts, however, management will want to analyze the cost of offering the discount versus the interest earned in the bank as a result of receiving payment from the customers more quickly. Management will want to get answers to the following questions:

- What is the status of our trade receivables (e.g., aging of the trade receivables)?
- What are our competitors' credit policies?
- How much will we lose in profit if we offer, say, a 2%, net 30-day discount?
- How much interest can be earned from the bank on the additional cash flow?

For example, if managers are able to reduce the level of trade receivables from, say, $300,000 down to $250,000, it means that the company will have an extra $50,000 in cash with which to operate.

Cash reserve decisions are usually based on planning assumptions such as the following:

- The practical minimum level of cash balance required to meet ongoing operating conditions.
- An amount necessary to absorb unforeseen expenditures.
- The level of cash required to exploit profitable business opportunities (e.g., special discounts on purchases or anticipation of an increase in the price of raw materials).

It is important to keep cash at a minimum because investment securities yield very little. It would therefore be more economically advantageous to invest excess cash into investment opportunities in order to earn a more attractive return.

Operating Decisions Related to the Statement of Income

Operating decisions can also increase a company's profitability in many ways. Some decisions cut across all organizational functions and activities affecting the statement of income, such as improving employee productivity, reducing waste, and eliminating useless activities. Here are a few budgeting approaches used by managers that can help improve profitability.

Demassing
Recession-driven technique to remove management layers from organizational charts to cut costs.

Demassing is a recession-driven technique that was used widely during the sharp economic downturn in the early 1980s. The purpose of this approach was to remove headquarters' staff and entire management layers and professional positions from organizational charts. Organizations were simply flattened. It has been reported that more than a third of U.S. middle-management positions were eliminated in 1981–1982 as a result of demassing exercises.

Planned downsizing
Systematic way of cutting costs.

Planned downsizing is similar to demassing except that it is a more systematic way of cutting costs. Guidelines used in planned downsizing include the following:[5]

5. For interesting reading on this subject, see Tomasso, Robert, M. *Downsizing: Reshaping the Corporation for the Future*, New York: AMACOM, 1987.

- Matching organizational structure with strategies.
- Pinpointing excess staff in the control and support of organizational units.
- Evaluating the effectiveness of organizational units.
- Performing a zero-based evaluation by questioning everything.
- Introducing norms and ratios such as allowing 1 staff position per 100 employees or maintaining computer-related expenses below 1%.
- Using strategic concepts such as product life cycles and value added to determine staff size.
- Enforcing sunset laws by closing down, decentralizing, or contracting out mature or aging activities before starting new ones.
- Flattening organizational pyramids by asking pertinent questions such as: How many management layers are really necessary? How many people can one manager manage? How can a manager's span of control be increased?

Productivity measures Ways of measuring organizational performance (i.e., ROA).

Productivity measures are essential for measuring the performance of organizational units. It is often said that organizational units without clearly defined goals are difficult to manage. Productivity indicators must first be identified for each organizational unit before the units can be made more productive. If organizational efficiencies and effectiveness for the most important activities performed by managers and employees are measured and used as goals, they can improve productivity and ultimately the bottom line because:

- Productivity is more likely to improve when expected results are measured;
- Productivity increases rapidly when expected benefits are shared with those who will produce them;
- The greater the alignment of employee expectations (needs) with organizational goals (targets), the greater the motivation to accomplish both; and
- When productivity measures are placed on a time scale, there is a greater likelihood of achieving the goals.

Rewarding simplification instead of needless complication can also produce positive financial effects. Jack Welch (former CEO at General Electric) was an advocate of keeping things simple at GE. As he pointed out, "The leader's unending responsibility must be to remove every detour, every barrier, to ensure that vision is first clear, and then real. The leader must create an atmosphere in the organization where people feel not only free to, but obliged to demand clarity and purpose from their leaders."[6] In the process, GE was able to improve its operating efficiencies and improve the bottom line by billions of dollars.

Cutting back useless activities and replacing them with productive work adds value to financial results.

6. Slater, Robert, *Jack Welch and the GE Way*, New York: McGraw Hill, 1999, p. 139.

Focusing on quality work instead of fast work can also increase operating margins and the bottom line. Doing work too quickly and too cheaply often inadvertently becomes costly because quality suffers. Several of the payoffs of improving quality include lower costs, increased productivity, worker pride, and customer loyalty. One tool that has produced positive benefits to the bottom line through cost reduction, productivity improvement, customer retention, cycle-time reduction, defect reduction, and product/service development is Six Sigma. It is a tool that has been adapted by companies such as GE, Motorola, Black & Decker, Bombardier, DuPont, Dow Chemical, and Federal Express. The Six Sigma four-step process includes measure, analyze, improve, and control. At GE, for example, Six Sigma was expected to generate $1.5 billion in 1999, while operating margins went from 14.8% in 1996 to 18.9% in 2000.[7]

Empowering workers through team building and communication can also produce synergistic effects on a company's operating performance. Empowerment is more than a trendy slogan; it has produced positive financial results. Working in teams creates a great sense of interdependence. Some plants have increased productivity substantially just by giving workers the option to decide how to perform their work. Workers learned to inspect their own work, management listened more actively to their suggestions, and employee dignity was greatly elevated.

Balanced scorecard (BSC)
A process that can translate an organization's mission, vision, and strategies into a comprehensive set of quantifiable performance measures in addition to providing a framework for a strategic measurement and management system.

The **balanced scorecard (BSC)** is a process that can help translate an organization's mission, vision, and strategies into a comprehensive set of quantifiable performance measures in addition to providing a framework for a strategic measurement and management system. The BSC measures organizational financial and non-financial performance from across four balanced *perspectives*: financial, customers, internal business processes, and learning and growth.[8]

Organizations that have embraced the balanced scorecard realized the following benefits:

- Provide everyone in an organization with a clear line of sight to the mission, vision, and strategy.
- Make strategies operational by translating them into performance measures and targets and achieve breakthrough performance.
- Provide an effective tool for communicating (1) the mission, vision, and strategy; and (2) the processes and systems required to implement the strategy.
- Perform as an integrating device, an umbrella, for a variety of diverse, often disconnected organizational programs such as quality, reengineering, process redesign, and customer service.

7. Welch, Jack, *Jack: Straight From the Gut*, New York: Warner Business Books, 2001, p. 336. For interesting readings on the subject of Six Sigma, refer to Pandre, Peter, Robert Neuman, and Roland Cavanagh, *The Six Sigma Way*, New York: McGraw Hill, 2000; and George, Michael L., *Lean Six Sigma*, New York: McGraw Hill, 2002.
8. For interesting reading on the subject of the BSC, refer to Kaplan, S. Robert and David P. Norton, *The Balanced Scorecard*, Cambridge, MA: Harvard Business School Press, 1996; and Niven, Paul R., *Balanced Scorecard*, New York: John Wiley & Sons, Inc., 2006.

- Provide a comprehensive view that overturns the traditional idea of an organization as a collection of isolated, independent functions and activities (the silo phenomenon).
- Help to break down corporate-level measures to lower levels in an organization so that team leaders and employees can see what they must do well in order to improve organizational efficiencies and effectiveness.
- Draw cause-and-effect roadmaps related to stakeholders, customers, internal processes, and employees.
- Demonstrate quantifiable and measurable results that can be monitored by everyone (from top to bottom) and, as a consequence, make them accountable for performance.

GROSS PROFIT

Gross profit Difference between revenue and cost of sales.

Decisions that affect the **gross profit** are revenue and cost of sales. Revenue comprises decisions affecting the number of units sold and the selling price. Decisions regarding the marketing variables (product, price, place, and promotion) determine, to a large extent, sales output and market share performance. Effective marketing decisions can improve a company's sales performance and, ultimately, its revenue. There are a number of ways management can determine the most appropriate selling price. These are markup percentages, cost-plus pricing, suggested retail price, psychological pricing, discounts, and geographic price policies.

For manufacturing businesses, cost of sales represents a substantial percentage (as much as 80%) of a company's total costs. For this reason, a great deal of attention is devoted to making a company's manufacturing operations more efficient by modernizing its plants (mechanization or automation), reducing waste, improving employee morale, and empowering workers.

Earnings before Interest and Taxes

Earnings before interest and taxes (EBIT) Profit before taxes and finance costs.

Decisions affecting **earnings before interest and taxes (EBIT)**, which is the profit before taxes and finance costs shown on the statement of income, are grouped under two categories of costs: distribution costs and administrative expenses. Many of the operating budgeting techniques explained earlier, such as planned downsizing, cutting useless activities, and empowering workers, are examples of how profit before taxes can be improved. In the past, incremental or traditional budgeting was used to prepare budgets for overhead units. To justify the amount of budget or funds to be allocated to such units, input-oriented budgeting techniques (emphasis on activities and functions or on objects of expenditures such as salaries, telephone, travel, and training) were frequently used. Today, more businesses are using results-oriented budgeting techniques where productivity measures (as in the case of the BSC) or some form of standards are applied to help justify and approve budget proposals. When preparing operating budgets for most overhead units, three broad operating decisions are often explored: economy, efficiency, and levels of service (quality of service). These concepts will be discussed in Chapter 7 (Planning, Budgeting, and Controlling), under the heading "Performance Indicators" on page 305.

Profit for the Year

Profit for the year Difference between profit before taxes and income tax expense.

The account that affects **profit for the year** is the income tax expense. It is the difference between profit before taxes and income tax expense.

Self-Test Exercise No. 1.4

Cash Flow Provided by Operating Activities

With the following information, calculate CompuTech's cash flow generated by the business. Between 2009 and 2010, inventories increased from $50,000 to $65,000, and during the same time period, trade receivables also increased from $35,000 to $45,000. The company also realized an increase in profit from $25,000 to $33,000.

Corporate Transparency and Accountability

5 Learning Objective

Discuss issues related to corporate transparency and accountability.

Transparency Extent to which business processes and related information resources, assets, and outcomes are visible and open to inspection by stakeholders.

Following the Bre-X, Enron, WorldCom, and now Madoff scandals, there have been cries from all types of stakeholders and the general public for greater levels of corporate transparency and accountability. **Transparency** can be defined as how business processes and related information resources, assets, and outcomes can be made more visible and open to inspection by stakeholders. What organizations now need more than ever are (1) corporate senior executives (public and private sector organizations) who have the ability to establish "social architectures" for openness, and (2) a new branch of management theory and practice to be called "transparency and accountability management."

Both governments and businesses have made far-reaching efforts to achieve that goal through government legislation, effective governance, more entrenched corporate culture, and global accounting and financial standards. Let's take a look at each one.

GOVERNMENT LEGISLATION

As a reaction to many financial scandals, including Enron and WorldCom, in 2002 the U.S. government enacted the *Sarbanes-Oxley Act*. The purpose of this legislation was to set new standards for all public company boards, management, and public accounting firms. The Act contained 11 titles, or sections, ranging from additional corporate board responsibilities to criminal penalties, and required the Securities and Exchange Commission to implement rulings on requirements to comply with the new law. The mandates and requirements for financial reporting include the following:

- Creation of a Public Company Accounting Oversight Board, to define processes and procedures for compliance audits.
- Auditor independence, to limit conflicts of interest.

- Corporate responsibility, to ensure that senior executives take individual responsibility for accuracy and completeness of corporate financial reports.
- Enhanced financial disclosures, to show reporting requirements for all transactions including off-statement of financial position's transactions, pro-forma figures, and stock transactions of corporate officers.
- Analysts' conflicts of interest, to specify measures designed to help restore investor confidence in the reporting of securities analysts.
- Commission resources authority, to define reporting processes of securities analysts.
- Studies and reports, to determine how the Securities and Exchange Commission should perform various studies and report their findings.
- Corporate and criminal fraud accountability, to describe specific criminal penalties for fraud by manipulation.
- White-collar crime penalty enhancement, to recommend stronger sentencing guidelines associated with white-collar crimes and conspiracies.
- Corporate tax returns, to state that the CEO should sign their company's tax return.
- Corporate fraud accountability, to identify corporate fraud and records tampering as criminal offenses.

This was not the first time that the U.S. government (the ultimate gatekeeper of public confidence in public markets) had introduced legislation to (1) build a stronger framework for effective governance, (2) establish high standards and healthy board dynamics, (3) set up guidance for effective corporate communications, and (4) show how red flags should be highlighted to signal the need for prompt investigation and action. There have been at least 10 powerful legislations enacted in the United States in the past 100 years. They include the *Sherman Antitrust Act* (1890) on monopolies; the *Clayton Antitrust Act* (1914) on unfair business practices; the *Securities Act* (on corporate transparency), and the *Banking Act* (on unfair banking practices), both enacted in 1933; the *Securities Exchange Act* (1934) on regulating the securities market; the *Investment Company Act* and the *Investment Advisers Act* (both 1940) on abusive investment company practices; the *Foreign Corrupt Practices Act* (1977) on bribery; the *Financial Institutions Reform, Recovery and Enforcement Act* (1989) on restoring confidence in savings-and-loan institutions; the *Comprehensive Thrift and Bank Fraud Prosecution and Taxpayer Recovery Act* (1990) on strengthening federal regulators' authority to combat financial fraud; and more recently, the *Sarbanes-Oxley Act* (2002) for greater agent and gatekeeper accountability for financial reporting.

Despite the enactment of all these laws with the primary intent of preventing accounting irregularities, investigations of corporate fraud continues to be alive and well (e.g., Conrad Black, Bernard Madoff, and the billions of dollars in bonuses paid to Merrill Lynch & Co. executives). It appears that government legislation to instill high ethical standards in the corporate arena is not enough. Corporate governance, corporate culture, and, now, global accounting and financial standards are financial and management practices that have been introduced in many for-profit and NFP organizations, and will continue to be reinforced in many others.

CORPORATE GOVERNANCE

Because boards of directors bear the ultimate authority and accountability for an organization's affairs, much attention has been focused on how board members should *govern* their organizations. Individuals involved in governance include the regulatory body (e.g., CEO, the board of directors, management, and shareholders) and other stakeholders (suppliers, employees, creditors, customers, and the community at large). **Governance** can be defined as the process of decision-making and the process by which decisions are implemented (or not implemented).

Governance
Process of decision-making and the process by which decisions are implemented (or not implemented).

The fundamental elements of effective corporate governance include honesty, trust and integrity, openness, performance orientation, responsibility and accountability, mutual respect, and commitment to the organization. A key responsibility of effective directors and top-level managers is to *develop* a model of governance that aligns and instills these values throughout their organization and to *evaluate* the model periodically for its effectiveness.

The more commonly publicized principles of effective corporate governance include the following:

- Right and equitable treatment of shareholders.
- Interests of other stakeholders.
- Role and responsibilities of the board.
- Integrity and ethical behaviour of all members of the organization.
- Full disclosure of corporate documents and transparency of information and conduct.

Corporate governance principles and codes of conduct have been developed in many countries and issued from different stock exchanges, corporations, institutional investors, or associations of directors and managers with the support of government and international organizations. For example, companies quoted on the Toronto Stock Exchange (TSX) need not follow, on a formal basis, the recommendations of their respective national codes but must *disclose* whether they follow the recommendations in those documents and, if not, provide explanations concerning divergent practices, which ultimately exert a considerable pressure on organizations for compliance.

CORPORATE CULTURE

Since the beginning of the 20th century, Canadian organizations have always tried to sustain their competitive stamina in order to compete effectively on world markets. During the past 100 years, top-level managers have tried to transform their ways of managing their organizations by changing their corporate culture, that is, "doing things the right way." There is no question that productivity, efficiency, and high-quality goods and services are essential elements that make businesses prosper in the global arena. Although financial statements are simply a reflection of how well organizations perform, the manner in which organizations are managed is the means for achieving higher levels of profitability. Each time that organizations have been plagued with productivity and motivational problems, new approaches to management were discovered to solve the problems of the time. Since the start of the 20th century, we have experienced five management waves, all aimed at improving productivity, efficiency, employee motivation, quality, and assurance.

The first management wave began at the beginning of the 20th century, and is considered the classical, mechanistic, or *scientific movement*, when a group of writers, consultants, and researchers found logic, order, and common sense to be the prerequisites to organizing work and increasing productivity. A set of management principles emerged from this first wave and, as a result, productivity and employee motivation were improved.

The second management wave began in the early 1930s when it was realized that organizations and people should not be viewed as "pawns," motivated only by financial incentives. The pendulum had swung toward a more people-oriented approach: This was the behavioural or *humanistic movement*. A new set of values emerged from this second wave, to the effect that people should be treated as human beings. Again, there was an upswing in productivity and employee motivation.

The third management wave came about during the mid-1940s. To some extent, it was the resurgence of the scientific movement, that is, the *quantitative approach*, which led to the application of mathematical and statistical solutions such as optimization models, information models, computer simulation, linear programming, work scheduling, and operations research. Although the quantitative movement contributed mainly to decision-making, particularly in the area of planning and controlling, it had, and still has, considerable influence on the practice of management (i.e., Edwards Deming's approach to Total Quality Management and the Six Sigma approach). Once more, there was a bounce in productivity, efficiency, and product quality.

The fourth management wave started in the early 1960s, when a more integrative and unifying approach to management was seen to be needed. Topical management subjects at the time were styles of leadership, the systems approach, and management processes. The search for the most appropriate style of leadership was in fashion. Should a manager be autocratic or democratic, an X or Y type, results-oriented or people-oriented? In the end, most researchers and writers concluded that an organization should be viewed as a system, that managers should use the style that best meets the needs of a particular situation, and that management should be regarded as a process. There was (and still is) a plethora of articles, books, and seminars on these various topics. Once more, a rise in productivity, employee motivation, and product quality surfaced.

It was in the early 1980s that the fifth management wave emerged. When North American managers began to realize that they were losing ground to other countries, including Japan, France, Germany, and even England, they wanted to know why and the study of comparative management was born. Today, not only are countries comparing their management approaches, even North American companies are searching to find the "magic of management" that makes one organization more successful than another. It all started with Ouchi's *Theory Z: How American Business Can Meet the Japanese Challenge*,[9] which compared the North American style of management to the Japanese style, which was followed by Peters and Waterman's book *In Search of Excellence*.[10] The lesson was clear. The excellent companies had one thing in common: a strong sense of shared values, norms, and beliefs about people, products, services, and innovation. It was clear that a strong **corporate culture**, that is a shared system of values and beliefs within an organization, was the foundation of a company's success. North American organizations are now caught up in clarifying the meaning and significance of organizational culture and how strong corporate values can be adapted within their own organizations. In the News 1.2 gives an example of RONA's values and rules. To many, the value factors appear to supercharge organizational performance. As mentioned in the preceding sections on government legislation and corporate governance, the focus of many top-level managers is on the reinforcement of ethical standards within their organizations.

Corporate culture
Shared system of values and beliefs within an organization.

In The News [1.2]

RONA's Values and Rules of Ethics That Guide Behaviour

If an organization wants to practise good behaviour, all it has to do is write a set of values and live by them!

RONA is a classic example about how a company goes through the process of adapting to exceptional working habits. As pointed out by Robert Dutton, president and CEO of RONA Inc., "It is desirable to draw up a set of written rules to which we can refer."

From the start, RONA's employees have drawn strength by adhering to their shared vision and living out deeply entrenched values. Here are some of the terms to which employees hold fast: service, honesty, integrity, professionalism, unity, respect, search for the common good, and sense of responsibility. To many employees, "living" these words that are part of the company's "Code of Conduct" represents a commitment at two levels: collective and individual. The bottom line is this: everybody wins—customers, investors, suppliers, and business partners. Above all, every stakeholder appears to trust RONA.

Source: Adapted from RONA, *Code of Conduct*. Found at: http://www.rona.ca/content/code-conduct_annual-reports-other-documents_investor relations. Accessed October 8, 2009. You can download RONA's complete document of the Code of Conduct in PDF version by visiting their site.

9. Ouchi, William G., *Theory Z: How American Business Can Meet the Japanese Challenge*, Don Mills, Ontario: Addison-Wesley Publishing Company, 1981, p. 4.
10. Peters, Thomas J., and Robert H. Waterman, *In Search of Excellence*, New York: Harper & Row Publishers, Inc., 1982.

GLOBAL ACCOUNTING AND FINANCIAL STANDARDS

One way to improve transparency and accountability is by introducing a common international accounting and financial language. This is precisely the role and purpose of the International Accounting Standards Committee (IASC), which was established in 1973. Until 2001, it had published only 41 International Accounting Standards (IASs). It was in the early 2000s that problems started to emerge when multinationals had to prepare financial statements with a set of different standards for different jurisdictions; it became more difficult to make cross-country comparisons. It was then that the International Organization of Securities Commissions (IOSCO) asked the IASC to review and reinforce global standards and to solve the financial instruments problem. The IASC's key objective was to put in place "global convergence."

In April 2001, a new structure of the IASB was set up and it had the exclusive responsibility for establishing IFRS.

In 2005, a new era in global conduct of business, for a worldwide adaptation of reporting rules and standards, emerged. As a consequence, most national GAAP standards were reduced in importance or were being phased out as countries all over the world began to adapt the IFRS. In Canada, Canadian GAAP will be eliminated and replaced by IFRS in 2011.

The push to converge existing different financial reporting standards was clear: to facilitate the free flow of capital so that, for instance, investors in Canada would be willing to finance businesses in other countries without having to go through the financial statement "interpretation process." The IFRS would therefore help investors to easily read financial statements from different countries written in a "common language."

Figure 1.8 shows the interaction between the various organizational units involved in the administration of global accounting and financial standards. The IASC Foundation includes 19 Trustees (six from North America, seven from Europe, four from Asia Pacific, and one each from Africa and South America).

Figure 1.8 **Organizational Structure of Global Accounting and Financial Standards**

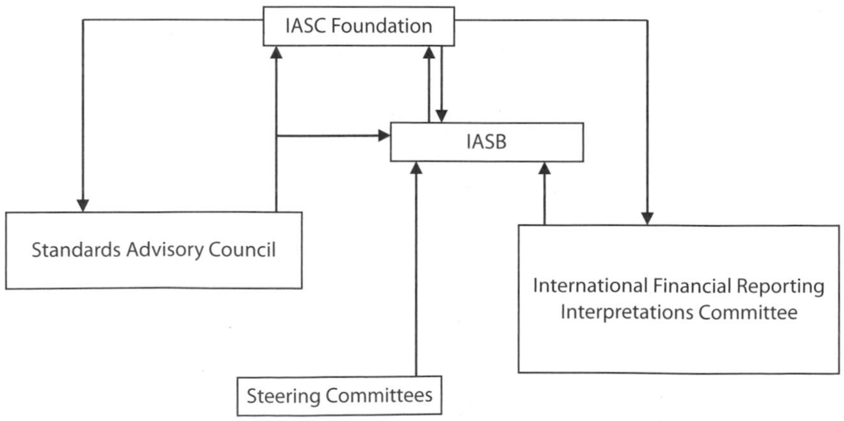

The IASB, which is the principal body within the new structure, has 12 full-time and 2 part-time members. The Board's key responsibilities are to (1) develop and issue IFRS and Exposure Drafts, and (2) approve interpretations developed by the International Financial Reporting Interpretations Committee (IFRIC).

The Standards Advisory Council (SAC), which consists of some 45 members, provides a forum for organizations and individuals interested in international financial reporting. The Council meets three times each year and has a responsibility to:

- Advise the Board on priorities;
- Inform the Board of the implications of suggested standards for potential users and those responsible for preparing financial statements; and
- Give advice to the Board or to the Trustees.

The IFRIC, which consists of 12 members appointed by the Trustees, has a responsibility to:

- Interpret the application of IFRS and provide timely guidance on financial reporting issues;
- Publish draft interpretations for public comment; and
- Report to the Board and obtain Board approval for final Interpretations.

The IOSCO also works with the *IASB* and its objective is to link together securities regulators, such as the Ontario Securities Commission (OSC), the Securities and Exchange Commission (SEC), and others, to promote cooperation and high standards of regulation on a global basis. In the News 1.3 gives some statistics about the number of countries that have adopted the IFRS.

In The News [1.3]

The World Is Going with the IFRS

The IFRS train is moving fast. One destination, Canada, and arrival date, January 1, 2011.

Although most countries in the world will be adopting the single IFRS, depending on where a country is located on the world map, the acceptance level on the "IFRS continuum" varies.

Recent surveys indicate that publicly traded companies located in most countries are adopting the IFRS. However, the degree of acceptance of the new standards ranges from "okay" to "not-so-okay"! The adopted standards happen to be the European model backed by the IASB and not the United States. GAAP system supported by the Financial Accounting Standards Board (FASB). Up until the early part of May 2009, 95% of 59 countries surveyed have adopted or intend to converge with the IFRS, and 72% (39 countries) that have the intention to move toward the convergence system have adopted a formal policy to go ahead with it. Included in the 39 are 25 EU members.

Source: Adapted from Stephen Taub, "World going IFRS," *CFO,* February 24, 2003. Found at: http://www.cfo.com/article.cfm/3008402?f=search. For IFRS adoption by country, visit http://www.pwc.com/us/en/issues/ifrs-reporting/country-adoption/index.jhtml.

REALITY FINANCIAL SNAPSHOTS

One section of the chapters of this book will present and analyze real-life financial statements of two organizations, Enbridge Inc., a for-profit organization, and The Ottawa Hospital (TOH), a NFP organization.[11]

ENBRIDGE INC.[12]

Enbridge Inc. operates in Canada and the United States. It has the world's longest crude oil and liquids pipeline system. The company owns and operates Enbridge Pipelines Inc. and a variety of affiliated pipelines. These pipeline systems have operated for over 50 years, delivering more than 2 million barrels per day of crude oil and liquids. Enbridge is also involved in liquids marketing and international energy projects, and has a growing involvement in the natural gas transmission and midstream businesses. As a distributor of energy, Enbridge owns and operates Canada's largest natural gas distribution company, Enbridge Gas Distribution, which provides gas to industrial, commercial, and residential customers in Ontario, Quebec, and New York State. The company distributes gas to 2 million customers. The company employs more than 4,400 people and trades its common shares on the Toronto Stock Exchange in Canada and on the New York Stock Exchange in the United States under the symbol ENG.

The following summarizes Enbridge's cash flows for the years 2008 and 2007 under the three major activities (operating, financing, and investing). The company's detailed financial statements will be presented in Chapters 2 and 3 and analyzed in Chapter 4.

(CAD $ in millions)	2008	2007
Cash provided from operating activities	1,387.7	1,351.6
Investing activities	(2,852.9)	(2,228.8)
Financing activities	1,840.2	904.2
Increase in cash	375.0	27.0

In 2008, with internally generated funds ($1,387.7 million), Enbridge was able to finance part of its capital investment projects ($2,852.9 million), and financed the rest through debt for an additional $1,840.2 million, while increasing its cash account by $375.0 million. A detailed outline of the various cash inflows and cash outflows for Enbridge will be presented in Chapter 3.

11. Enbridge Inc. and TOH's financial statements presented throughout this book are based on the CICA's traditional GAAP presentation format as the introduction of the IFRS to be adopted by Canadian organizations will take place in 2011. Chapter 2 compares the existing and the new financial statements' presentation layouts and terminology (see Table 2.6 on page 87).

12. Enbridge Inc., *2008 Enbridge Annual Report*. Found at: http://www.enbridge.com/investor/financialInformation/reportsFilings/pdf/2008-annual-report-en.pdf.

THE OTTAWA HOSPITAL[13]

TOH is a multi-campus, academic health sciences centre, servicing 1.5 million residents of Ottawa and eastern Ontario, both in English and French. It boasts specialty centres in cancer, heart, kidney, and vision care, as well as rehabilitation services. The following presents some statistics for the period of April 1, 2007 to March 31, 2008.

Staff members	11,566
Physicians	1,150
Volunteers	1,992
Admissions	46,089
Average length of stay (days)	8.6
Outpatient visits	908,010
Births	6,940
Number of beds	1,066
External funding for research	$79,000,000

The following summarizes TOH's flow of cash for the years 2008 and 2007. The hospital's detailed financial statements will be presented in Chapters 2 and 3 and analyzed in Chapter 4.

(CAD $ in thousands)	2008	2007
Operating activities	6,742	57,287
Financing and investing activities	(38,681)	(3,443)
Net decrease (increase) in bank indebtedness	(31,939)	53,844

As will be explained in Chapter 3 (see page 131), NFP organizations' cash flow statements combine financing and investing activities under one heading. A detailed outline of the various cash inflows and cash outflows for TOH will be presented in that chapter.

[DECISION-MAKING IN ACTION]

The management committee of Flint Ltd. is considering investing $1.0 million in non-current assets for expansion purposes, and an additional $200,000 for working capital (e.g., inventories and trade receivables). Currently, the profit generated by the company is $500,000, which represents a 5.0% ROR of $10.0 million. The investment proposal was presented to the board of directors for consideration and approval.

To finance the $1.2 million investment, Flint's CFO explained that a certain portion of the expansion would be financed by internally generated cash (operating activities). He indicated that (1) the revenue for the budget year would show a 10% increase over the current year, and

13. *2008 Ottawa Hospital Annual Report.* Found at http://www.ottawahospital.on.ca/about/reports/FS2008-e.pdf.

(2) the ROR (as a result of cost-cutting activities, particularly in manufacturing) would be increased to 7.0%.

The CFO explained that the profit was to be allocated as follows:

- Sixty percent for internal use; half of the funds would be allocated toward working capital (current assets) and the rest in non-current assets; and
- Forty percent would be used for external purposes, of which 60% would be used to pay dividends and the rest to reduce the principal on the debt.

Based on the feasibility study prepared by the controller's department, he explained that the capital expansion program would generate lucrative profits. However, in order to finance the purchase of these assets, he would have to raise capital funds from a lending institution at a cost estimated at 10% (before tax). The shareholders were prepared to invest $200,000 toward the capital projects, and an amount of $100,000 would be obtained from the bank for financing the working capital requirements. The shareholders are looking for at least a 12% return on their investment.

The board of directors indicated that if the project generated 15%, they would consider approving it. However, before approval, they wanted answers to the following questions:

Question 1: How much cash would be generated internally (operating activities)?

Question 2: How much cash would have to be raised from external sources (financing activities)?

Question 3: How does the ROA of the project (investing activities) compare to the weighted average cost of capital (financing activities)?

Question 4: Should the board of directors approve the capital project?

Question 5: On the basis of the above information, what is the breakdown of the financing package?

The CFO provided the following explanation to these questions:

Answer to Question 1

An amount of $462,000 would be generated internally based on the following assumptions:

- Revenue for the budget year will be $11,000,000 (a 10% increase over the current year);
- A 7% ROR would generate $770,000 in profit ($11,000,000 × 7%);
- An amount of 60% or $462,000 ($770,000 × 60%) would be reinvested in the business in the form of retained earnings and the remaining 40% (or $308,000) would be used for external use; $184,800 (or 60% of $308,000) for the payment of dividends, and $123,200 (or 40%) for the payment of principal on the debt.

Answer to Question 2

External financing would be as follows: $200,000 from shareholders and $438,000 from long-term lenders. Here is the calculation (in $).

a. Funds generated from operating activities:		
Profit for the year (retained earnings)		462,000
Working capital requirements	(200,000)	
Short-term borrowings	100,000	(100,000)
Funds provided by operating activities		362,000
b. Investing activities:		
Non-current assets		(1,000,000)
Shortfall		(638,000)

c. Financing activities:

Share capital	200,000	
Long-term borrowings	438,000	638,000
		$ 0

Answer to Question 3

ROA is 16.7%, and weighted average cost of capital is 7.86%. The calculations are as follows:

a. ROA is 16.7%

$$\frac{\textbf{Profit}}{\textbf{Total assets}} = \frac{\$200{,}000}{\$1{,}200{,}000} = 16.7\%$$

b. Weighted average cost of capital is 7.86%

Source	Amount (in $)	Proportion		After-Tax Cost (%)		Weighted Average Cost of Capital (%)
Share capital	200,000	0.31	×	12.0	=	3.72
Long-term borrowings	438,000	0.69	×	6.0	=	4.14
Total capital raised	638,000	1.00				7.86

Answer to Question 4

The board of directors would probably approve the project for the following reasons:

- The project's ROA compared to the weighted average cost of capital is favourable (16.7% compared to 7.86%).
- The project's ROA exceeds the board's expectations (16.7% ROA compared to the 12% objective).

Answer to Question 5

The project would be financed in the following way:

Based on the $1.0 million purchase of the capital assets:

- 36% ($362,000) by internally generated cash and 64% ($638,000) by external financing (share capital and long-term borrowings);

Based on the $1.2 million purchase of the capital assets and working capital:

- 44.8% or $538,000 ($100,000 from short-term borrowings and $438,000 from long-term borrowings) would be obtained from creditors while 55.2% or $662,000 would be funded by ownership interest ($462,000 provided from cash flow from operating activities and $200,000 from the shareholders).

FINANCIAL SPREADSHEETS—EXCEL

Financial spreadsheets can be downloaded from the Nelson Education Web site (http://www.bergeron6e.nelson.com). The objective of these spreadsheets is to perform most financial calculations (simple or complicated) contained in this text. In fact, most calculations done for this book and the Instructor's Manual were done with the help of these spreadsheets.

These spreadsheets allow more time for analyzing financial statements and less for "number crunching." The website includes Read Me Notes, which explain how to use the spreadsheets. As we go through the chapters of this book, some brief comments will be made regarding the application and the type of analysis that can be done with these spreadsheets.

The spreadsheets are divided into two parts: (A) Financial Statement Analysis and (B) Decision-Making Tools.

PART A: FINANCIAL STATEMENT ANALYSIS SPREADSHEETS (15 TEMPLATES)

Three templates are used to input data from financial statements onto the spreadsheets. They are referred to as input templates.

Template 1: Statement of Income
Template 2: Statement of Comprehensive Income and Statement of Changes in Equity
Template 3: Statement of Financial Position

Twelve output templates are used for analytical purposes.

Template 4: Statement of Sources and Uses of Funds
Template 5: Statement of Cash Flows
Template 6: Vertical Analysis of the Statement of Income
Template 7: Horizontal Analysis of the Statement of Income
Template 8: Vertical Analysis of the Statement of Financial Position
Template 9: Horizontal Analysis of the Statement of Financial Position
Template 10: Financial Ratios (26 ratios)
Template 11: DuPont System
Template 12: Cash Flow, EBIT, and earnings before interest, taxes, depreciation and amortization (EBITDA)
Template 13: Economic Value Added (EVA)
Template 14: Sustainable Growth Rate
Template 15: Financial Health Score

PART B: DECISION-MAKING TOOLS (12 TEMPLATES)

Template 1: Break-Even Analysis Using the Contribution Margin
Template 2: Break-Even Analysis Using the PV Ratio
Template 3: Operating Leverage
Template 4: Cost of Capital for Privately Owned Company
Template 5: Cost of Capital for Publicly Owned Company
Template 6: Capital Project Analysis (cash flow, NPV, internal rate of return (IRR), profitability index (PI))
Template 7: Monthly Cash Budget
Template 8: Lease–Buy Decision
Template 9: Revenue and Manufacturing Budgets
Template 10: Cash Discounts
Template 11: Credit Terms
Template 12: Economic Ordering Quantity

Chapter Summary

1 Learning Objective

Define the meaning of financial management.

The role of financial management is not limited to raising capital dollars; it also extends to finding ways to use funds more effectively within a business. It focuses on issues dealing with the following questions: How are we doing? How much cash do we have on hand? What should we spend our funds on? Where will our funds come from? How will our business be protected?

2 Learning Objective

Identify the individuals responsible for the finance function.

The finance functions are usually divided between the *controller*, who is responsible for the internal financial activities of a business, and the *treasurer*, who is responsible for the external financial activities. If financial management is to be effective, *operating managers* should also perform this function.

3 Learning Objective

Explain the four financial objectives.

Financial management focuses on four basic objectives: efficiency (productivity of assets), liquidity (ability to meet current debt commitments), prosperity (improvement in activities such as revenue, profit, payment of dividends), and stability (appropriate balance between the funds provided by the shareholders and long-term lenders).

4 Learning Objective

Comment on the three major types of business decisions.

Business decisions can be grouped under three broad categories: investing decisions, financing decisions, and operating decisions. *Investing decisions* deal with accounts such as non-current assets (e.g., machinery and equipment). Investing decisions have a significant impact on a company's cash flow. *Financing decisions* deal with accounts such as non-current liabilities and equity. Financing decisions look at the best way to raise funds from different investors. *Operating decisions* deal with the accounts appearing on the statement of income, such as revenue, cost of sales, distribution costs, and administrative expenses. Effective operating decisions can improve profit for the year and, in turn, enhance a company's equity position and ROA. Operating decisions also deal with the management of working capital accounts (current assets and current liabilities). Cash provided for working capital accounts is a drain on a company's cash position. However, reductions in such assets, achieved by reducing either inventories or trade receivables, result in cash for operating activities.

5 Learning Objective

Discuss issues related to corporate transparency and accountability.

Following recent financial scandals, there have been cries from all types of stakeholders and the general public for greater levels of corporate transparency and accountability. Both government and business have made far-reaching efforts to achieve that goal through government legislation, corporate governance, corporate culture, and global accounting and financial standards.

Key Terms

Balanced scorecard (BSC) p. 27
Chief executive officer (CEO) p. 12
Chief financial officer (CFO) p. 12
Controller p. 12
Corporate culture p. 33
Cost of financing p. 22
Demassing p. 25
Earnings before interest and taxes (EBIT) p. 28
Efficiency p. 15
External financing p. 19
Financial management p. 9
Financing decisions p. 22
Financing mix p. 23
Forms of financing p. 22
Governance p. 31
Gross profit p. 28
Internal financing p. 18
International Accounting Standards Board (IASB) p. 8
International Financial Reporting Standards (IFRS) p. 8
Investing decisions p. 20
Liquidity p. 16
Matching principle p. 22
Non-current assets p. 20
Operating decisions p. 24
Operating managers p. 13
Planned downsizing p. 25
Productivity measures p. 26
Profit for the year p. 29
Prosperity p. 17
Sources of financing p. 22
Stability p. 17
Transparency p. 29
Treasurer p. 12
Weighted average cost of capital p. 22
Working capital accounts p. 24

Review Questions

1. Define the meaning of financial management.
2. Why is it important for managers to ask questions such as "How are we doing?" and "How will our business be protected?"
3. Differentiate between the role of the treasurer and the role of the controller.
4. What are the four financial objectives? What do they mean?
5. Comment on the importance of the "return on revenue" financial objective.
6. Who is responsible for the business decisions in a business?
7. Differentiate between internal financing and external financing.
8. What are investing decisions and financing decisions?
9. What are non-current assets?
10. What are working capital accounts?
11. What do we mean by the "matching principle"?
12. What is the "weighted average cost of capital"?
13. What is an operating decision? Give some examples.
14. How can "productivity indicators" and "rewarding quality work" improve the bottom line?

15. Why is it important for operating managers to understand the fundamentals of financial management?
16. What is the meaning of transparency?
17. Differentiate between government legislation and corporate governance.
18. Describe the role of the IFRIC.
19. Will the finance function be more important in the future than it was in the past? Discuss.

Learning Exercises

EXERCISE 1

Non-current assets	$ 1,260,000
Current assets	250,000
Profit for the year	170,000
Cost of debt (after tax)	12%
Cost of equity	12%

Questions

1. If managers want to earn a 12% ROA, how much profit must the company generate?
2. If managers want to earn a 15% ROA, how much profit must the company generate?

EXERCISE 2

With the following numbers, prepare a statement of income and a statement of financial position. In the process, you will have to fill in the missing financial statement accounts.

Cost of sales	$ 700,000
Profit for the year	65,000
Share capital	500,000
Long-term borrowings	800,000
Total current assets	500,000
Gross profit	300,000
Distribution costs	200,000
Total equity	1,100,000
Total assets	2,500,000
Total current liabilities	600,000

EXERCISE 3

Assume that a company earns $280,000 in profit for the year on $3 million in revenue. The board of directors decides to keep half of the amount to pay for dividends and reinvest the rest in the company. Sixty percent of the retained earnings are invested in non-current assets, and the rest, in working capital for growth.

Questions

1. On the basis of the above information, calculate, as a percentage of revenue, how much would be kept in the company for growth purposes (i.e., working capital and non-current assets), and how much would be used to pay dividends.
2. Explain who is responsible for making the split between the amount of funds to be retained in the business and the amount to be paid in dividends.
3. What do you think the board of directors would do if the profit for the year increased to $350,000?

EXERCISE 4

Make a list of the following accounts under their respective business decisions:

Change in long-term borrowings
Profit for the year
Acquisition of a business
Depreciation/amortization
Share capital issue
Change in trade receivables
Net change in short-term borrowings
Sale of non-current assets
Change in trade and other payables
Additions to property, plant, and equipment

EXERCISE 5

Sources	Amounts
Trade and other payables	$200,000
Short-term borrowings	250,000
Mortgage	500,000
Long-term borrowings	250,000
Share capital	300,000
Retained earnings	800,000

The before-tax bank charges are 11.0% for the short-term borrowings, 10.0% for the long-term borrowings, and 10.5% on the mortgage. The shareholders expect to earn 16%. Assume that the company's income tax rate is 50%.

Questions

1. Calculate the company's after-tax cost of borrowing.
2. Calculate the company's weighted average cost of capital.

EXERCISE 6

Owners of a business are contemplating investing $550,000 in non-current assets in early January 2011. They are exploring ways to finance it. In 2009, the company had $250,000 in trade receivables, an amount that it expects will increase to $275,000 in 2010. The inventory level for 2009 was $430,000 and, having introduced a new inventory management system, the owners expect to be more efficient in managing it. They forecast a level of $370,000 in inventories by the end of 2010. They expect a substantial increase in revenue, which will increase their profit from $150,000 in 2009 to $230,000 in 2010.

Questions

1. How much cash will be generated from internal operations by the end of 2010?
2. Will the owners have to borrow money from investors in order to finance the expansion? If yes, how much?

Case

PACKARD INDUSTRIES INC.

In 2010, the management committee of Packard Industries Inc. is considering investing $800,000 for the purchase of machinery and equipment in order to increase the productivity of its plant. In 2009, the company's revenue amounted to $2,800,000, goods purchased from suppliers totalled $600,000, and the profit for the year was $280,000. The company's 2009 statement of financial position is as follows:

Packard Industries Inc.
Statement of Financial Position
As at December 31, 2009

(in $)	
Assets	
Non-current assets	1,000,000
Current assets	
Inventories	300,000
Trade receivables	400,000
Cash and cash equivalents	20,000
Total current assets	720,000
Total assets	1,720,000
Equity and liabilities	
Equity	
Share capital	200,000
Retained earnings	700,000
Total equity	900,000
Long-term borrowings	500,000

Current liabilities	
Trade and other payables	170,000
Short-term borrowings	150,000
Total current liabilities	320,000
Total liabilities	820,000
Total equity and liabilities	1,720,000

In 2010, management expects revenue to increase by 10%, and with cutbacks in different segments of their business activities, ROR is expected to improve to 12%. Cost of sales as a percentage of revenue is expected to show an improvement and decline to 20%.

Management also expects improvements in the working capital accounts. The company's objective is to lower trade receivables to $370,000, with inventory levels expected to reach $280,000.

Questions

1. Calculate the company's return on total assets for the year 2009.
2. How much cash will be provided by internal operations in 2010, in particular by the following:
   - Retained earnings
   - Inventories
   - Trade receivables
3. How much will management have to get from external activities (shareholders and lenders) to proceed with an $800,000 investment in non-current assets?

PHOTO/Wrangler/Shutterstock

CHAPTER 2

ACCOUNTING AND FINANCIAL STATEMENTS

Learning Objectives

After reading this chapter, you should be able to:

1 Learning Objective — Explain the activities related to bookkeeping.

2 Learning Objective — Describe the accounting function and give an outline of the four financial statements.

3 Learning Objective — Examine the contents and the structure of the statement of income and the statement of comprehensive income, the statement of changes in equity, and the statement of financial position.

4 Learning Objective — Explain the meaning of analysis in financial management.

5 Learning Objective — Discuss the importance of decision-making in financial management.

6 Learning Objective — Draw a comparison between the GAAP and IFRS financial statements' presentation profiles.

7 Learning Objective — Explain the contents and structure of the financial statements prepared for NFP organizations.

Chapter Outline

- Bookkeeping
- Accounting
- Financial Statements
- Analysis
- Decision-Making
- Financial Statements (GAAP versus IFRS)
- Not-For-Profit (NFP) Organizations

OPENING CASE

After their discussion with Bill Murray, Len and Joan did some additional homework in light of Bill's comments. They felt that Bill's advice about pinpointing operational and financial objectives was critical for formulating operational plans that would help them succeed.

Len and Joan also felt that it was important for them to learn how to set up a bookkeeping and accounting system. They knew that relevant and timely information was critical for analyzing all aspects of their retail operations and making key decisions. They asked Bill if he knew an accountant. He suggested May Ogaki, a chartered accountant with experience in counselling small businesses.

During their first meeting, Len and Joan indicated to May that they were looking for an integrated information system that would provide them with different types of operational and financial data. They would need a cash register that could generate reports about their sales, purchases, inventories, costs, etc. Len made the following comments:

> As far as I'm concerned, the cash register should be considered the most important information instrument in our business. It should provide us with daily, weekly, and monthly operational data. Anything that we buy and sell will go through the cash register. With a good software program integrated to our cash register, we should be able to know exactly what products are moving and when, the amount of inventories we have in stock at all times, when we should be ordering goods from suppliers, how much profit we make on each product line, how much sales each salesperson in the store makes, etc. In addition, we need an accounting software program that can provide us with financial statements such as the statement of financial position, the statement of income, and the statement of cash flows. This software should also help us prepare our monthly operating budget.

May understood the kind of information they sought. She recommended that accounting software programs such as Simply Accounting, for example, would provide the type of financial information they needed. May indicated that she would investigate further and meet with them to recommend specifically, on the basis of their requirements, the type of programs they should get.

However, before leaving, May asked Len and Joan to think about the type of accounts or ledgers that they would like to see on their financial statements. As May pointed out,

> This is the first step that you have to go through in the bookkeeping and accounting process. Once you know the information that you want to analyze to help you make your decisions, it will be easy for me to determine the type of operational and financial reports that should be produced by your customized software program.

May also recommended a basic course in accounting to understand some of the fundamentals of accounting and financial terms and concepts. Although it was important to have an accountant prepare the financial statements annually for income tax purposes, Len and Joan should be able to read and analyze their own financial statements. Just like a pilot who reads aircraft instruments, owners and managers should be able to understand and interpret their own financial statements. This point simply validated what Bill Murray told them during their first meeting.

Chapter Overview

Managers, owners, lenders, and investors want to know the financial health of the firms they deal with. They may want to analyze reports that summarize the financial performance and condition of the business. The financial performance is presented in a two-statement report called the statement of income and the statement of comprehensive income, also known as the "statement of operations," the "profit and loss statement," or the "statement of earnings." The financial structure of a business is presented in another report called the statement of financial position (SFP), also referred to as the "balance sheet" or the "statement of financial condition."

Financial statements Financial reports, which include the two-statement report called the statement of income and the statement of comprehensive income, the statement of changes in equity, the statement of financial condition, and the statement of cash flows.

The term **financial statements** is generally used to reflect the fact that several financial reports, such as those mentioned above, are included in annual reports. This chapter examines the contents and the structure of these financial statements. Chapter 3 profiles the fourth financial statement called the statement of cash flows.

Accounting is considered the language of business; it is used to present financial information about business activities. It shows the results of managerial decisions dealing with all segments of a business such as marketing, manufacturing, administration, engineering, human resources, and distribution. Accounting is the methodology that gives data about the financial performance and financial structure of a business.

Every day, hundreds or even thousands of activities take place in a business: Goods are sold on a cash or credit basis; materials are purchased; salaries, rent, and hydro bills are paid; customers pay their accounts; and goods that were purchased on credit are paid for. If managers want to know, on a daily, monthly, or yearly basis, the financial results of all these transactions, they must have them collected and recorded in a logical and methodical manner. For example, if managers want to know:

- The profit performance of their business, they will refer to the statement of income.
- How much the business owns or owes, they will refer to the SFP.

- How much profit the business has accumulated that has not been distributed to shareholders and the amount of dividends that was paid to their shareholders this year and the additional financial contributions that the shareholders have invested in the business, they will look at the SCE.
- How much cash was generated or used by the business, they will look at the statement of cash flows.

Managers who want to know how their business performed in the past, how it is doing now, and what decisions they should make to improve its financial position must refer to a variety of reports. For example, they will refer to the *operational reports*, produced by a management information system, and the *financial reports*, produced by bookkeeping and accounting systems. This chapter gives an overview of the methodology used by accountants for preparing these financial statements. The ultimate objective of financial management is to help managers analyze financial statements and to make sound financial decisions.

Bookkeeping and accounting are the touchstones of business information. Managers need information to plan and control their operations. Once managers have formulated their operational and financial objectives, and prepared their strategic and operational plans, the next logical step in the management process is to implement the plans and compare performance with projections.

Operating and financial data that are presented clearly and logically make it easy for managers to review and analyze performance and make decisions to solve problems or exploit opportunities. The planning and controlling management functions cannot be performed effectively if managers are deprived of such basic operational and financial information. Therefore, the purpose of bookkeeping and accounting activities is to ensure that managers are provided with the right kind of information at the right time.

Financial management embraces four broad activities: bookkeeping, accounting, analysis, and decision-making. This chapter explores these four activities covered under seven key topics. The first topic looks at bookkeeping. As shown in Figure 2.1, bookkeeping is the activity aimed at systematically recording, electronically or manually, financial transactions incurred by a business, on a day-by-day basis, in different sets of journals and ledgers. It involves collecting, classifying, and recording information that arises from the multitude of transactions taking place in a business. As shown in the figure, these transactions are first recorded in books of original entry known as *journals* and are subsequently recorded in books of final entry known as *ledgers*.

The second topic explains the accounting function, which involves the preparation of the four financial statements, that is, the (1) two-statement report, which includes the income statement and the statement of comprehensive income; (2) the statement of changes in equity; (3) the statement of financial position; and (4) the statement of cash flows (see Figure 2.1). This section gives a general profile of these four financial statements.

Figure 2.1 **The Bookkeeping and Accounting Process**

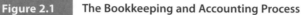

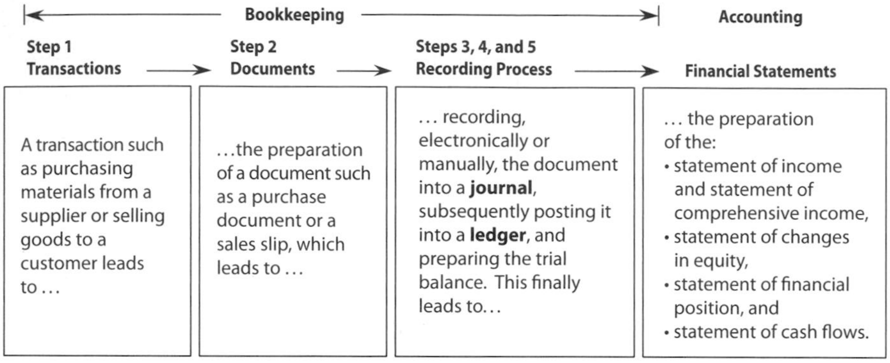

Bookkeeping
Accounting
Step 1
Transactions
Step 2
Documents
Steps 3, 4, and 5
Recording Process
Financial Statements
A transaction such as purchasing materials from a supplier or selling goods to a customer leads to . . .
. . .the preparation of a document such as a purchase document or a sales slip, which leads to . . .
. . . recording, electronically or manually, the document into a **journal**, subsequently posting it into a **ledger**, and preparing the trial balance. This finally leads to. . .
. . . the preparation of the:
• statement of income and statement of comprehensive income,
• statement of changes in equity,
• statement of financial position, and
• statement of cash flows.

The third topic explains in detail the structure and contents of the statement of income and the statement of comprehensive income, the SCE, and the SFP. As mentioned earlier, the statement of cash flows will be explained in Chapter 3. Accounting is a more specialized, creative, and comprehensive activity because accountants must present data in financial statements to inform managers, creditors, shareholders, and government agencies about the financial performance of a business. Because these financial statements are structured in a standardized format, they can be easily read, understood, and analyzed. For instance, if you want to know what a business owns, you look at the asset component of the SFP; if you want to know how much a business owes and the nature of its liabilities, you look at the equity and liabilities components of the statement. The financial statements presented in this text are based, in large measure, on the set of rules established by the International Accounting Standards Board (IASB)'s International Financial Reporting Standards (IFRS). Accounting is a profession with certain requirements and standards of education, accreditation, and conduct. In order to measure the financial affairs of a business, accountants must follow established rules, procedures, and standards established by the IASB. These rules govern how accountants measure, process, and communicate financial information.

The fourth topic looks at analysis, which consists of interpreting financial statements. The information presented on financial statements should be considered not merely as statistics, but as information that should be examined carefully to see how well (or badly) a business is doing. For example, the reader may want to know about the following:

- The company's profit performance: How much profit is the company generating? What is the return on assets (ROA)?
- The company's inventories and trade receivables: Are they at reasonable levels?
- The relationship between the company's current assets and current liabilities: Is it acceptable?
- The company's long-term borrowings: Is it in line with the amount of money the owners have put into the business?

The fifth topic explains the importance of decision-making. It is not enough to record, arrange, and analyze data. To make decisions to improve the financial performance and financial structure of their businesses, managers must use financial information. For example, the information will help to:

- Set the right price for their products and services;
- Establish the most appropriate credit policy;
- Maintain optimal inventory levels;
- Assess the financial viability of capital investments for new plants or the expansion or modernization of existing ones; and
- Determine the most appropriate source of cash needed to finance operations.

The sixth topic compares the general profiles of the financial statements using the *CICA Handbook*'s generally accepted accounting principles (GAAP) to those prepared under the IASB's IFRS. The three financial statements that will be compared are the statement of income, the SCE, and the SFP.

The seventh topic looks at the contents and structure of financial statements prepared by not-for-profit (NFP) organizations. It shows some of the unique financial features as they apply to preparing financial statements for these types of organizations. The NFP organizations' financial statements include the SFP the statement of operations, the statement of changes in net assets, and the statement of cash flows. The statement of cash flows will be explained in Chapter 3.

Bookkeeping

1 Learning Objective

Explain the activities related to bookkeeping.

Bookkeeping
Activity that involves collecting, classifying, and reporting accounting transactions.

Bookkeeping involves collecting, classifying, and reporting transactions taking place each day in different departments of a business. Some transactions take place in the sales department, others in the trade receivables department or manufacturing plant. All business transactions are recorded under five broad categories or headings of accounts:

- *Assets*, or what a business owns
- *Equity*, or what it owes to shareholders
- *Liabilities*, or what it owes to creditors
- *Revenue*, or how much it earned as a result of selling its goods or services
- *Costs (or expenses)*, or how much it costs to produce and sell its goods or services

Chart of accounts
A set of categories by which accounting transactions are recorded.

Bookkeeping begins with the preparation of a **chart of accounts**, which establishes the categories by which transactions of the business are recorded. These are much like the accounts that an individual has at home, such as bankbook, car, house, cottage, credit card, clothing, food, insurance, salary, holidays, etc. The number of accounts that a business sets up depends largely on the needs and desires of management.

The bookkeeping process will be examined under three headings: the accounting equation, the accounting cycle, and the trial balance.

THE ACCOUNTING EQUATION

Double-entry bookkeeping System for posting financial transactions so that the accounting equation remains in balance.

Each time a business transaction takes place, at least two accounts are affected. This is referred to as **double-entry bookkeeping**, meaning that every business transaction results in two account entries. For example, when a business buys a truck with borrowed funds from a banker, both the asset and liability accounts are affected. If a business pays its mortgage with cash, both its asset and liability accounts are also affected. If shareholders invest money in a business, and the funds are used to buy a truck, two accounts are also affected, assets and equity.

Accounting equation Assets = Equity + Liabilities or Assets − Liabilities = Equity

Once all the double-entry transactions have been completed, the financial position of a business can be expressed by the following equation, referred to as the **accounting equation**:

Assets = Equity + Liabilities

It can also be expressed in the following way:

Assets − Liabilities = Equity

The basic structure of the SFP is based on this accounting equation. One side of the SFP shows a listing of all asset accounts (e.g., trade receivables, equipment), and the other side a listing of all equity and liability accounts (e.g., share capital, trade, and other payables). Both sides must be equal, that is, they must balance. This is probably the reason the SFP is also called the *balance sheet*.

THE ACCOUNTING CYCLE

Bookkeeping and accounting cycle Steps involved in processing financial transactions for preparing financial statements.

There are several steps involved from the time that a transaction is processed in a business to the time that the transaction is reported in one of the financial statements. This **bookkeeping and accounting cycle** includes five steps. As shown in Figure 2.1, step 1 has to do with transactions, step 2 with the preparation of documents, and steps 3 to 5 with electronic or manual recording and posting in addition to the preparation of the trial balance.

Step 1. The first step is a business transaction (e.g., investing money in a business, buying a truck, selling goods or services, paying salaries).

Step 2. Each transaction is accompanied by a document (e.g., a deposit slip from the bank, a sales slip, a purchase document, a cheque stub).

Step 3. Through the bookkeeping system, each transaction is recorded in different sets of books: journals and ledgers. As indicated earlier, each business transaction affects at least two accounts. By recording the business transactions using the double-entry system, accountants can be assured that the total of all accounts are in balance, and an arithmetic error is automatically brought into the open by a lack of balance. Because some transactions are recorded on the left side of the financial documents

Debit
Accounting entries recorded on the left side of an account.

Credit
Accounting entries recorded on the right side of an account.

and others on the right, each side is given a name. The word **debit** refers to entries recorded on the left side of an account; the word **credit** to entries recorded on the right. As shown in Figure 2.2, when all accounts are closed at the end of an accounting period, the asset and cost accounts have debit balances and the equity, liability, and revenue accounts have credit balances.

There are some basic rules that determine whether a transaction should be a debit or a credit. These rules are summarized below:

	Assets	Equity	Liabilities
Debit	Increases	Decreases	Decreases
Credit	Decreases	Increases	Increases

As shown in Figure 2.2, debits and credits can also be registered in revenue and cost accounts. For this reason, the credit and debit rules can be expanded to apply to these two accounts and can be read as follows:

	Revenue	Costs
Debit	Decreases	Increases
Credit	Increases	Decreases

As shown in Figure 2.2, when the revenue and cost accounts are tabulated, there is usually a surplus called *profit*. The arrow shows that this profit (costs deducted from revenue) is transferred into the equity account in the SFP in the form of retained earnings. As shown in the figure, a credit in equity or revenue accounts increases the wealth of a business. Conversely, a debit in the cost or equity accounts reduces the wealth of a business. This explains why this profit (or earnings) is automatically added to the equity account.

Figure 2.2 Debits and Credits

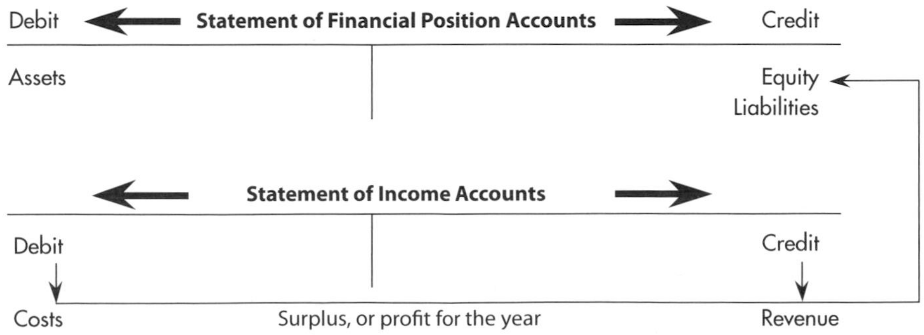

Journals
Also referred to as books of original entry, used to record accounting transactions in chronological order.

Journalizing
Process of recording, electronically or manually, transactions in a journal (e.g., sales journal, salaries journal).

Ledgers
Also referred to as books of final entry, show all amounts debited and credited in individual accounts (e.g., trade receivables, revenue, inventories and salaries) including a running balance.

Posting
Process of transferring recorded transactions from the journals to the appropriate ledger accounts (e.g., revenue, trade receivables).

Trial balance
Statement that ensures that the general ledger is in balance (debit transactions equal credit transactions).

As mentioned earlier, the books used to record accounting transactions are journals and ledgers. **Journals**, sometimes referred to as the books of original entry, are used to record transactions in a chronological order—that is, as they happen. There could be several types of journals, such as the sales journal, the purchase journal, and the salaries journal. The process of recording transactions, electronically or manually, in the journals is called **journalizing**.

Step 4. The fourth step in the process is to transfer the amounts recorded in the journals into ledgers. Journals do not show the outstanding balance of each account after each transaction has been recorded. For this purpose, a second set of books called ledgers is created. A **ledger** is very much like a chequebook. It shows all amounts debited and credited in each account, including its running balance. As mentioned earlier, ledgers for a home would include hydro, credit card, mortgage, salary, and food accounts. If a person wants to know how much he owns or owes, the outstanding balance for each of these accounts would give the answer. If a person wants to know how much salary he earned, or the expenses incurred for telephone, groceries, or entertainment during a given year, separate accounts would provide the answers.

A business operates with similar accounts, which are called ledgers or the books of final entry. All transactions recorded in journals are subsequently transferred to the appropriate ledger accounts; this process is called **posting**. Ledgers provide a running balance for each account. Ledger accounts are usually given a number to facilitate the process of recording the transactions, whether the recording is done manually or electronically.

THE TRIAL BALANCE

Step 5. The fifth and final step in the bookkeeping and accounting cycle is called *closing the books.* It is done at the end of an accounting period (i.e., the end of a month or the end of a fiscal year). To ensure that all transactions recorded during the period are error-free—that is, the sum of all debits equals the sum of all credits—the outstanding account balances are listed under their appropriate column in the **trial balance**.

As shown in Table 2.1, Eastman Technologies Inc.'s trial balance for the year 2009 is done by listing, in parallel columns, the total of all debit and credit balances for each account or ledger. Once this has been done, the debit and credit columns of the trial balance are added. If the debit column equals the credit column, it means that there should be no arithmetical error; all accounts are in balance. Because the ledger accounts are used to prepare the financial statements, it is preferable, before commencing this exercise, to do a trial balance. The accounts shown in this trial balance will be used to prepare Eastman Technologies Inc.'s statement of income and the statement of comprehensive income (Table 2.2 on page 63), the SCE (Table 2.3 on page 70), and the SFP (Table 2.4 on page 72). The trial balance shown in Table 2.1 identifies the financial statement (SFP, SI, or SCE) in which each account will appear.

Table 2.1 Trial Balance

Eastman Technologies Inc.
Trial Balance as at December 31, 2009
(in $)

	Debit		Credit	
Cash	22,000	SFP		
Revenue			2,500,000	SI
Prepaid expenses	60,000	SFP		
Finance costs	35,000	SI		
Cost of sales	1,900,000	SI		
Retained earnings (beginning of year)			205,000	SCE
Trade receivables	300,000	SFP		
Accrued expenses			20,000	SFP
Sales salaries	140,000	SI		
Income tax expense	97,500	SI		
Taxes payable			80,000	SFP
Advertising expenses	20,000	SI		
Long-term borrowings			800,000	SFP
Inventories	218,000	SFP		
Trade and other payables			195,000	SFP
Notes payable			150,000	SFP
Non-current assets (at cost)	1,340,000	SFP		
Depreciation	40,000	SI		
Accumulated depreciation			140,000	SFP
Share capital			300,000	SFP
Office salaries	170,000	SI		
Dividends	47,500	SCE		
Lease	20,000	SI		
Other income (from investments)			20,000	SI
Total	4,410,000		4,410,000	

SCE = Statement of Changes in Equity
SFP = Statement of Financial Position
SI = Statement of Income

Some of the most common errors that will cause inequality in trial balance totals include the following:

- One of the columns of the trial balance was added incorrectly.
- One amount of an account balance was improperly reported on the trial balance.
- A debit balance that should have been recorded on the trial balance as a credit (or vice versa) was omitted entirely.
- One side of an account was computed incorrectly.

- An erroneous amount was reported as a debit or as a credit in an account.
- A debit entry was recorded as a credit, or vice versa.
- A debit or a credit entry was omitted.

With some other errors, the debit column will still be equal to the credit column in the trial balance. These errors include the following:

- Failure to record an entire transaction.
- Recording the same erroneous amount for both the debit and the credit.
- Recording the same transaction more than once.
- Recording one part of a transaction in the wrong account.

Self-Test Exercise No. 2.1

The Trial Balance

After opening their computer sales and service store, the Millers went through the following four transactions:

1. They invested $100,000 in cash in the business.
2. They purchased on credit $10,000 worth of goods from several suppliers.
3. They sold on a cash basis $13,000 worth of products and services.
4. They paid $3,000 for salaries.

With the above information, prepare the following:

1. Journal entries
2. Ledgers
3. Trial balance

Accounting

2 Learning Objective

Describe the accounting function and give an outline of the four financial statements.

Accounting
Process of recording and summarizing business transactions on a company's financial statements.

Statement of income
Financial statement that shows a summary of revenue and costs for a specified period of time.

The function of **accounting** governs the way the financial statements shown in Figure 2.3 are presented. The IASB, via the IFRS, specifies the structure in which the accounts should be presented on the statement of income and the statement of comprehensive income, the SCE, the SFP, and the statement of cash flows. Here is an overview of these financial statements.

The upper left side of Figure 2.3 shows a two-statement format, (1) the statement of income and (2) the statement of comprehensive income. Table 2.2 on page 63 gives a profile of these two financial statements. The **statement of income** is much like a "movie" of the business. It shows the flow of revenue and costs incurred by a business during a given period (e.g., one month, say, June 1 to June 30, or one year, say, January 1 to December 31). The statement of income shows profitability performance at three levels (boxes 1 to 3): gross profit, profit before taxes, and profit for the year. The **statement of comprehensive income** includes other comprehensive income/(loss), net of tax in a single statement, and

Figure 2.3 Financial Statements

Statement of Income and Statement of Comprehensive Income

1. Revenue
   – Cost of sales
   = Gross profit
2. – Distribution costs, administrative expenses, and finance costs, plus other income
   = Profit before taxes
3. – Income tax expense
   = Profit for the year
4. Other comprehensive income/(loss) for the year, net of tax
   = Total comprehensive income/(loss) for the year

Statement of Changes in Equity

1. Beginning of year
   - Share capital
   - Contributed surplus
   - Retained earnings
   - Accumulated other comprehensive income/(loss)
2. Transactions made during the year
   - Share capital (e.g., shares issued)
   - Contributed surplus (e.g., options exercised)
   - Retained earnings (profit less dividends)
   - Accumulated other comprehensive income/(loss) for the year (e.g., currency translation)
3. End of year
   - Share capital
   - Contributed surplus
   - Retained earnings
   - Accumulated other comprehensive income/(loss)

Statement of Financial Position

1. Non-current assets	3. Equity
	4. Non-current liabilities
2. Current assets	5. Current liabilities

Statement of Cash Flows

1. Operating Activities
   - Profit for the year
   - Adjustments
2. Financing Activities
3. Investing Activities
4. Cash Balance

Statement of comprehensive income
Financial statement that shows items of income and expense that are not recognized in the statement of income.

Total comprehensive income/(loss) for the year
Transactions and other events (e.g., asset revaluation) that will have an impact in the equity account.

highlights items of income and expense that are not recognized in the statement of income such as exchange differences on translating foreign operations, available-for-sale financial assets, and changes in the revaluation of property, plant, and equipment and intangible assets. The statement subsequently reports all these changes in the appropriate equity section of the SCE. As shown in the figure, the statement of comprehensive income shows the fourth level of profitability (box 4), that is, **total comprehensive income/(loss) for the year**, which is the change in equity during a period resulting from transactions and other events (e.g., asset revaluation).

As shown in Figure 2.3, the **statement of changes in equity** represents the interest of the shareholders of a business. It shows the cumulative net results in equity with respect to share capital, contributed surplus, retained earnings, and accumulated other comprehensive income/(loss) for the year. The statement specifies the carrying amount of these four components of equity at the beginning and end of the year.

Statement of changes in equity
Represents the interest of the shareholders of a business, showing the cumulative net results in equity with respect to share capital, contributed surplus, retained earnings, and accumulated other comprehensive income/(loss) for the year.

Statement of financial position
Financial statement that shows a "snapshot" of a company's financial condition (assets, equity, and liabilities).

Statement of cash flows
Financial statement that shows where funds come from (cash inflows) and where they went (cash outflows).

In the case of retained earnings, for example, the statement shows (1) the amount of profit[1] in a business that was "not distributed" to shareholders since the business was started, (2) the profit earned and dividends paid during a current operating year, and (3) the amount of earnings remaining in the business at the end of the period.

The **statement of financial position** is a "snapshot" of a company's financial condition. As shown in Figure 2.3, this statement is divided into five sections. The left side shows what the business owns, or its assets. Asset accounts are grouped under two headings: non-current assets and current assets.

The right side shows what a business owes to its shareholders (owners) and creditors (lenders). The right side of the SFP shows the equity account, which is money provided by the shareholders to a business. Debts are also grouped under two headings: non-current liabilities and current liabilities.

The **statement of cash flows** shows where cash came from (cash inflows) and where it went (cash outflows) between two accounting periods. The figure shows that this statement is divided into four sections: (1) operating activities (principal revenue-generating activities and changes or adjustments in the balances of working capital accounts such as trade receivables and inventories), (2) financing activities (changes in the size of the equity and long-term borrowings), (3) investing activities (acquisition or disposition of long-term assets or non-current assets such as buildings and equipment), and (4) cash balance (changes in the balance of cash on hand and cash equivalents).

Figure 2.4 gives a visual comparison of the relationship between the SFP and the statement of income. As indicated earlier, the SFP shows a "snapshot" of the financial condition of a business at a given point in time (say, December 31). For this reason, the SFP reads "as at December 31." On the other hand, the statement of income is much like a "movie" of what went on during an operating period of a business (say, from January 1 to December 31). This is the reason the statement of income reads "for the period ended December 31."

There is a parallel between an individual and a business in terms of growth (in the first case, the weight; in the second, the wealth). Suppose that both John Pound and ABC Inc. were born and started, respectively, in 1970. At the end of the first year, John weighed 20 pounds and ABC Inc. had accumulated $100,000 in profit for the year or earnings. Each year, during the next 40 years, John's daily activities included eating (intake of food and drinks) and exercising (burning of calories). On the other hand, ABC Inc. earned revenue and incurred costs. For both John and ABC, 40 12-month movies were produced—one for each year. This information would be recorded in the statement of income. Also, at the end of each year, John could have weighed himself to find out how many pounds he had gained (or lost) and would record the results in his diary. In the case of ABC Inc., the accumulated

1. The words *profit* and *earnings* mean the same thing will be used interchangeably throughout this text.

Figure 2.4 **Relationship Between the Statement of Financial Position and the Statement of Income**

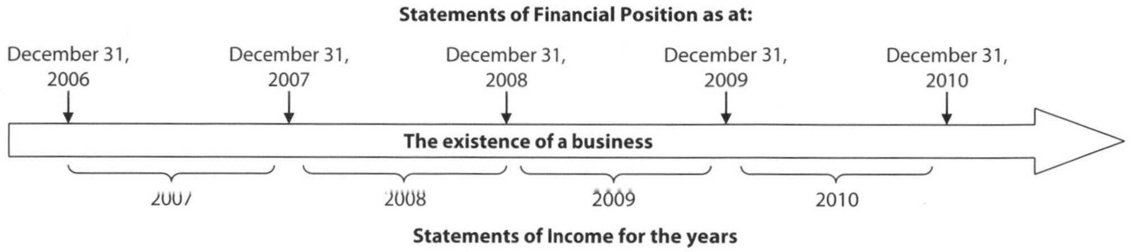

gains would be recorded in the SFP under the heading "Retained earnings." The number of pounds that John gained (or lost) each year would be added (or subtracted) to the previous year's accumulated weight. In the case of ABC Inc., each time it generated a profit (or loss), that number would also be added or subtracted from the previous year's SFP in the section called "Retained earnings" (under "Equity").

Now, assuming that on January 1, 2010, John's weight was 170 pounds (beginning of the year) and increased to 180 pounds (end of the year), his weight would have increased by 10 pounds. However, during the 12-month period, suppose he actually gained 15 pounds, but 5 pounds was removed through liposuction a few days before he stepped on the scale. The removal of excess pounds would be equivalent to what is paid in dividends and recorded in the SCE under the heading "Retained earnings." Similar to the evolution of John's weight pattern, ABC Inc.'s earnings and dividends would also be recorded in the same fashion on the financial statements. This information would be recorded as follows:

	John Pound	ABC Inc.
Beginning of year (January 1, 2010)		
On the scale	170 pounds	
Last year's statement of financial position		$1,000,000
Change during the year		
Changes in weight	+15 pounds	
Statement of income (profit for the year)		+ $ 200,000
Adjustment during the year		
Removal of excess fat	–5 pounds	
Net change	+10 pounds	
SCE under the heading "Retained earnings" (dividends)		– $ 100,000
SCE (net change)		+ $ 100,000
End of year (December 31, 2010)		
On the scale	180 pounds	
This year's statement of financial position		$ 1,100,000

There are two ways of reporting financial statements: the cash method and the accrual method.

Cash method
Accounting method of recording business transactions when cash is received or disbursed.

The **cash method** keeps a record of cash receipts from sales and from disbursements of expenses. In this case, the business recognizes revenue when cash or its equivalent is received, irrespective of when the goods or services are delivered. Costs are treated in a similar way. At the end of an accounting period, the costs are deducted from revenues, and the excess gives the profit or loss for the period. This accounting method is limited to small businesses (such as variety stores) where most transactions are on a cash basis. For this reason, all financial reports or statements discussed in this book, unless otherwise stated, use the accrual method.

Accrual method
Accounting method that considers sales when made and costs when incurred, regardless of when the transaction takes place.

The **accrual method** records revenue when goods are sold or services rendered. For example, if a business makes a sale, whether on a cash or credit basis, or buys goods, also on either a cash or credit basis, it assumes that the revenues and the costs have been incurred. Although a sale is made on credit (and cash has not been received) or goods are purchased from suppliers on credit (and payment has not been made), the statement of income shows the respective revenue and cost transactions in the appropriate accounts. The most important accounts that differentiate cash basis from accrual basis are the trade receivables and trade and other payables.

The main purpose of the accrual method is to obtain a measure of the results of business operations by allocating, to each fiscal period, the appropriate revenue and cost items. In accounting, this process is called *matching expenses with revenues.* This concept is important in order to reflect, in a realistic way, the "true" profit generated by a business during a particular operating period.

Financial Statements

3 Learning Objective

Examine the contents and the structure of the statement of income and the statement of comprehensive income, the statement of changes in equity, and the statement of financial position.

Let's now examine the contents and structure of these financial statements in more detail. Eastman Technologies Inc.'s statement of income and the statement of comprehensive income are shown in Table 2.2, the SCE in Table 2.3, and the SFP in Table 2.4. The information contained in these financial statements is drawn from the trial balance (see Table 2.1 on page 57). Eastman's statement of cash flows will be explained in Chapter 3.

STATEMENT OF INCOME AND STATEMENT OF COMPREHENSIVE INCOME

Table 2.2 shows the Eastman Technologies' statement of income and statement of comprehensive income. These two statements are so closely connected that they are often presented in a single statement.

STATEMENT OF INCOME

Everyone associated with a business wants to know if it is making a profit and, if so, how much. This is what the statement of income does. This financial statement summarizes the revenue and costs for a period of time (one month, six months, or a year). As shown in the statement (Table 2.2), all cost and expense figures are bracketed and

Table 2.2 The Statement of Income and the Statement of Comprehensive Income

Eastman Technologies Inc.
Statement of Income
for the year ended December 31, 2009
(in $)

Revenue		2,500,000	
Cost of sales		(1,900,000)	
Gross profit		600,000	Level 1
Other income		20,000	
Distribution costs:			
Sales salaries	(140,000)		
Advertising expenses	(20,000)		
Total distribution costs		(160,000)	
Administrative expenses:			
Office salaries	(170,000)		
Lease	(20,000)		
Depreciation	(40,000)		
Total administrative expenses		(230,000)	
Finance costs		(35,000)	
Total other income and costs		(405,000)	
Profit before taxes		195,000	Level 2
Income tax expense		(97,500)	
Profit for the year		97,500	Level 3

Eastman Technologies Inc.
Statement of Comprehensive Income
for the year ended December 31, 2009
(in $)

Profit for the year	97,500	
Other comprehensive income/(loss)	—	
Exchange differences on translating foreign operations	—	
Gain or loss on property revaluation	—	
Actuarial gains (losses) on defined benefit pension plans	—	
Total other comprehensive income/(loss) for the year	—	
Total comprehensive income	97,500	Level 4

all revenue or income figures are without brackets. The statement of income for Eastman Technologies Inc. for the year ended December 31, 2009 is to be read in a step-down fashion. As shown in the table, the statement of income shows three levels of profitability: (1) gross profit, (2) profit before taxes, and (3) profit for the year. Also, the accounts shown on the statement of income can be grouped in two distinct sections:

1. The *operating section*, which shows the gross profit and the profit before taxes.
2. The *owners' section*, which shows the profit for the year or the amount left for the shareholders.

A company has two main sources of income. The major origin of income is the revenue generated from the sale of its main products and services. The second source includes other income such as interest received from investments. The more important costs associated with a business are cost of sales, distribution costs, and administrative expenses. These costs are directly linked to the ongoing operating activities of a business. Finance costs, on the other hand, are less significant and are also included in the statement of income.

Operating Section

Operating section
Section of the statement of income that shows a company's gross profit and profit before taxes.

The **operating section** of the statement of income includes two levels of profitability: the gross profit and the profit before taxes.

Gross profit (also referred to as gross margin) is the difference between revenue and cost of sales. It is the profit a business makes after paying for the cost of producing the goods.

Revenue	$2,500,000
Cost of sales	(1,900,000)
Gross profit	$600,000

It is called gross profit because no other costs have been deducted, and it represents the amount of money left over to pay for other general expenses such as distribution costs and administrative expenses. Gross profit is the starting point for earning a satisfactory level of profitability.

Revenue
What a business earns for the sale of its products and services.

Revenue (also referred to as net sales) is what a business earns for the sale of its products and services. It represents items actually delivered or shipped to customers during the fiscal period. Revenue is the amount a company has received or expects to receive after allowing for discounts off list prices, sales returns, prompt payment discounts, and other deductions from the original sale price. Sales taxes (GST/HST) are not included in the revenue amount. Essentially, revenue is the amount that a business receives in order to cover all operating costs or expenses and to generate a profit. Revenue is an important figure because it is used to calculate the fundamental financial soundness of a business. For example, this figure is used to determine a company's level of productivity (relationship between revenue and total assets) and efficiency (relationship between revenue and profit for the year). Although annual reports show only one level of revenue, internal company documents would show two levels of revenue, gross revenue and net revenue, which are presented below:

Gross revenue	$2,700,000
Less: discounts, returns, and allowances	(200,000)
Net revenue	$2,500,000

Cost of sales
Cost incurred in making or producing goods that are sold.

Cost of sales (also known as cost of goods sold) is the cost incurred in making or producing the goods that were sold. It is by far the largest expense in the statement of income for a manufacturing enterprise (in many cases, it may represent as much as 80% of a company's total costs). It includes three major items: materials purchased from suppliers, transportation cost or freight-in for goods shipped from suppliers to the company's plants, and all costs associated with the manufacturing process to make the goods, such as wages and depreciation on the plant's equipment and machinery In the case of a retailer, the goods purchased from suppliers and the freight-in for goods shipped from suppliers are considered cost of sales. Service-based industries such as motels, bowling alleys, advertising agencies, and recreational services do not incur manufacturing costs, but may show instead as cost of sales, all costs or expenses associated with the delivery of the services that the business offers. As shown in Table 2.2, gross profit is the difference between revenue and cost of sales.

Other income
Revenue that is not directly related to the central operations of a business.

Other income is revenue that is not directly related to the central operations of a business. It can include interest earned on investments (e.g., short-term deposits) and rental income for renting parts of premises not needed for business operations.

Distribution costs
Costs incurred by a marketing organization to promote, sell, and distribute its goods and services.

Distribution costs are incurred by a marketing organization to promote, sell, and distribute its goods and services. These costs include advertising, sales salaries, sales commissions, trade shows, sales supplies, delivery expenses, and sales promotions.

Administrative expenses
Expenses that are not directly related to producing and selling goods or services.

Administrative expenses are all other expenses not directly related to producing, distributing, or selling goods. They include expenses incurred by organizational units such as human resources, accounting, legal, finance, computers, consultants, insurance, and depreciation (a non-cash expense) on machinery and equipment. In the case of equipment, when it was first purchased, office equipment was considered a capital expenditure. For such purchases, a useful life is usually estimated before it would wear out or be replaced by new technology. It would then be depreciated over its useful life, and the cost would therefore be amortized, or spread, over that same time period (e.g., five or ten years). Typical assets that are capitalized include factory equipment, computers, tools, machinery, and buildings.

Depreciation
An accounting entry allocating the cost of a non-current asset against revenue over an asset's life and an estimated decrease in the value of non-current assets due to wear and tear and/or obsolescence.

Depreciation is defined as an accounting entry allocating the cost of a non-current asset (e.g., plant, equipment, machinery) against revenue over an asset's life and an estimated decrease in the value of non-current assets due to wear and tear and/or obsolescence. It is a function of matching costs with revenue. Depreciation expenses could be shown in various sections of the statement of income where non-current assets are employed, including cost of sales, distribution costs, and administrative expenses. For example, a truck (distribution costs) may last seven years; a building (manufacturing costs), 40 years; and furniture (administrative expenses), 15 years. Although a non-current asset may be purchased on a cash basis during a particular year, because it will be used for say, seven years, the business will apportion the cost over the useful life of that asset.

There are different ways of calculating depreciation. The two most widely used methods are straight-line depreciation and accelerated depreciation. Let's examine how these two depreciation methods work.

Straight-line depreciation. This method is the most widely used and the simplest to calculate. It allocates an equal portion of the non-current asset to be amortized each year over its estimated useful life. It is calculated as follows:

$$\textbf{Depreciation} = \frac{\textbf{Purchase cost} - \textbf{scrap/salvage value}}{\textbf{Estimated useful life in years}}$$

For example, if a non-current asset such as a semi-trailer truck costs $100,000 and has a useful life of five years and no salvage value, the yearly depreciation amount would be $20,000.

$$\textbf{Depreciation} = \frac{\$100{,}000}{5} = \$20{,}000$$

Accelerated depreciation. The accelerated depreciation method can use, for example, the sum-of-the-years'-digits method of calculation. This method shifts depreciation forward in an asset's life. It increases early charges and reduces those that come in a later period during the life of the non-current assets. The sum-of-the-years'-digits calculation uses the estimated life of an asset as the common denominator. The numerators of the fractions are the years in the asset's life. Using the same $100,000 cost to illustrate this method of calculation, the arithmetic works this way:

1. If the life of the asset is five years, each individual year would be listed as follows: 1, 2, 3, 4, and 5; if it is ten years, it would go from 1 to 10.
2. The sum of the digits for each year would be added as follows:

$$1 + 2 + 3 + 4 + 5 = 15.$$

3. A fraction is identified for each year as follows: 1/15, 2/15, 3/15, 4/15, and 5/15.

Each fraction, starting with the last year, is multiplied by the original $100,000 investment. The calculation to find the depreciation is therefore done in the following way:

$$\textbf{Cost} \times \frac{\textbf{Number of years of depreciation remaining}}{\textbf{Sum of total digits of the asset's useful life}}$$

Year	Fraction		Cost of the Assets		Depreciation	Net Book Value	Depreciated (%)
1	5/15	×	$100,000	=	$ 33,333	$ 66,667	33.3
2	4/15	×	100,000	=	26,667	40,000	60.0
3	3/15	×	100,000	=	20,000	20,000	80.0
4	2/15	×	100,000	=	13,333	6,667	93.3
5	1/15	×	100,000	=	6,667	—	100.0
Total					$100,000		

Profit before taxes Difference between gross profit and expenses (distribution costs and administrative expenses), the addition of other income, and the subtraction of finance costs.

Profit before taxes is the difference between gross profit and all costs (distribution costs, administrative expenses, and finance costs) plus other income. There are sometimes hundreds of expenses included in these categories, ranging from salaries (a large amount) to legal fees (usually a small amount). This level of profitability is almost entirely affected by decisions made by managers (e.g., cost of sales, distribution costs, and administrative expenses); therefore, managers are directly accountable for the "profit before taxes" performance. Here is the calculation:

Gross profit	$600,000
Plus other income	20,000
Sub-total	620,000
Less: distribution costs	(160,000)
administrative expenses	(230,000)
finance costs	(35,000)
Total	(425,000)
Profit before taxes	$ 195,000

Managers are continually obsessed about their bottom-line results. They always try to find ways to maintain or improve profitability in order to satisfy their shareholders. In the News 2.1 gives an example about how cost-cutting activities improved profitability despite a slump in sales activities.

In The News [2.1]

How Cost-Cutting Can Help Profitability Despite a Decrease in Sales Volume

There are three ways of improving the bottom line: increase sales volume, increase selling prices, or cut costs. When times are tough and there is an economic downturn, the third option often appears to be the most realistic one!

This is what Dell Inc., the world's second-largest producer of personal computers, did when their sales estimates fell flat. When customers decided to defer buying new PCs, Dell's sales went south by 23%, or $12.3 billion (U.S.). However, analysts painted a rosier picture by predicting revenue to reach $12.7 billion. Nevertheless, there was a positive side to the story. By excluding some costs, profits reached 24 cents a share, a slight rise over the 23-cent prediction made by analysts. The solution was not overly complicated—costs were simply trimmed! As pointed out by Michael Dell, the company's CEO, jobs were abolished and offloaded to a select group of manufacturing business associates. The cure appears to have worked; by 2011, it is expected that Dell will have reduced its costs by $4 billion, and in the process, will have boosted profitability.

Source: Adapted from Bloomberg, "Dell's sales miss estimates on slumping PC demand," *Globe and Mail*, May 29, 2009, p. B8. For Dell's financial updates, visit www.dell.ca and click on "Investor Relations."

Owners' section Section of the statement of income that shows the amount of money left to the shareholders (i.e., profit for the year).

Owners' Section

The **owners' section** deals with the amount of money left to the shareholders, that is, "the bottom line." A company's shareholders are its owners, and they are entitled to receive a share of the company's earnings.

Therefore, profit for the year belongs to the shareholders. In our example shown in Table 2.2, Eastman Technologies Inc. earned $97,500 in profit. It is the responsibility of the board of directors to decide how much of this amount will be paid to the shareholders in dividends and how much will be left in the business in the form of retained earnings. The portions of the profit paid to shareholders and retained in the business appear in the SCE under the section, "Retained earnings."

Income Tax Expense Calculation

Income tax expense The total amount of taxes due to federal and provincial governments on the taxable income earned by the business during the current fiscal accounting period.

Income tax expense is the total amount of taxes due to federal and provincial governments on the taxable income earned by the business during the current fiscal accounting period. The amount is calculated by multiplying the taxable income for the period by the appropriate tax rate (a 50% income tax rate is used in this case for illustration purposes only). Income tax expense does not include other types of taxes, such as payroll and property taxes that are included in cost of sales and other costs and expenses.

Profit before taxes	$195,000
Income tax expense	(97,500)
Profit for the year	$ 97,500

Corporate income tax expense calculations take into account an appropriate tax rate for a particular corporation, costs and expenses, and business losses (if any). Here is a brief description of these three elements.

Income tax A percentage of taxable income paid to the provincial or federal governments based on taxable income less certain tax deductions.

Corporate and other income tax rates. **Income tax** is a percentage of taxable income paid to the provincial or federal governments. The tax is levied on a base of taxable income less certain tax deductions. When calculating the combined federal and provincial taxes, several variations must be noted. Any general figure applied arbitrarily can prove to be misleading. Provincial tax rates vary from province to province, and a number of abatements or special deductions exist. For instance, the deductions are particularly significant in the taxation of small-business income, income derived from manufacturing and processing operations in Canada, and income from production of minerals, oil, and gas.

All *costs and expenses* incurred by a business such as salaries, purchases, and advertising can be claimed against revenue, thereby reducing a business's taxable income. Also, finance costs are considered a business expense and hence are generally deductible in calculating taxable business income. Rent and lease payments are also considered deductible business expenses. However, repayment of principal on a loan, and dividends on both common and preferred shares, are not deductible and are paid with the profit or earnings for the year.

Business losses that took place during prior years are also tax deductible. For example, a company that incurs a loss may carry it back over the three previous years or it may carry forward that loss and deduct it from the taxable income of the next seven years. The *Income Tax Act* provides detailed explanation of such tax-deductible losses.

In arriving at taxable income, businesses may deduct *capital cost allowance (CCA)* on non-current assets (e.g., trucks, buildings). This topic will be discussed on page 73. Through CCA, provision is made for businesses to recover, over some time frame, the original amount invested in non-current assets without having to pay tax on the portion of the investments.

Self-Test Exercise No. 2.2

The Statement of Income

With the following accounts, prepare CompuTech's statement of income for the year ended December 31, 2009.

Purchases	$ 175,000
Sales salaries	80,000
Advertising	3,000
Travel	2,000
Revenue	350,000
Finance costs	10,000
Freight-in	2,000
Income tax expense	13,000
Sales commissions	2,000
Depreciation/amortization	38,000

STATEMENT OF COMPREHENSIVE INCOME

A business has the option of presenting the statement of comprehensive income for a given period as part of the statement of income or as a separate statement.

Comprehensive income comprises all components of *profit or loss* and of *other comprehensive income/(loss)*. The components of other comprehensive income/(loss) comprise the following:

- Changes in revaluation (property, plant, and equipment).
- Actuarial gains and losses on recognized defined benefit plans.
- Gains and losses arising from translating the financial statements of foreign operations.
- Gains and losses on remeasuring available-for-sale assets.

As shown in the lower portion of Table 2.2, Eastman Technologies Inc.'s statement of comprehensive income shows the profit for the year amount of $97,500, which is drawn from the statement of income, and other accounts (in this example, no transactions). As shown in the table, the total comprehensive income for the year amounts to $97,500 (profit level 4).

STATEMENT OF CHANGES IN EQUITY

The owners' (shareholders') equity represents the interest of the owners with regards to changes in various components such as share capital, contributed surplus, retained earnings, and other comprehensive income/(loss) for the year. This statement shows the increases and decreases in equity accounts during an accounting period.

This statement shows for each component the following:

1. The amounts at the start of the fiscal or accounting period; these amounts should agree with the equity figures appearing in the previous year's SFP.

2. The changes in the current operating year.
3. The amounts left in equity at the end of the fiscal year; this amount determines the equity figure that will appear in the company's current year's SFP.

Table 2.3 shows Eastman's SCE for the years 2009 and 2008. As shown, there was a change in the share capital account in the amount of $15,000 between 2008 and 2009. Under the retained earnings section, it shows the profit for the year figure in the amount of $97,500, which was drawn from the statement of income, in Table 2.2. An amount of $47,500 was paid out in dividends. The $255,000 amount in retained earnings as at December 31, 2009, is the same as the amount shown on the SFP (see Table 2.4). Also, the total equity amounts for the year 2009 ($555,000) and year 2008 ($490,000) are also the same as the amounts shown on the SFP.

Table 2.3 The Statement of Changes in Equity

Eastman Technologies Inc.
Statements of Changes in Equity
for the years ended December 31
(in $)

	2009	2008
Share capital		
Balance at beginning of year	285,000	285,000
Common shares issued	15,000	—
Dividend reinvestment and share purchase plan	—	—
Shares issued on exercise of stock options	—	—
Balance at end of year	300,000	285,000
Contributed surplus		
Balance at beginning of year	—	—
Stock-based compensation	—	—
Options exercised	—	—
Balance at end of year	—	—
Retained earnings		
Balance at beginning of year	205,000	205,000
Profit applicable to common shareholders	97,500	—
Dividends paid to shareholders	(47,500)	—
Balance at end of year	255,000	205,000
Total other comprehensive income/(loss) for the year		
Balance at beginning of year	—	—
Change in currency translation	—	—
Change in property revaluation	—	—
Balance at end of year	—	—
Total equity	555,000	490,000

STATEMENT OF FINANCIAL POSITION

Table 2.4 shows Eastman's SFP (also called the "balance sheet"); it gives a "position statement" of the company as at December 31, 2009 and 2008. The SFP is like a photograph in that it gives a picture of the size of each major account of a business at a particular moment; it does not show changes in each account from the previous year's financial statement. And, like an X-ray, the SFP gives a report about the health of a business at the close of an accounting period. Each separate item reported on this statement is called an account. Every account has a name and a dollar amount, which is the balance reported at the end of the accounting period. We will begin by discussing the meaning and significance of the major SFP classification of accounts.

The SFP is made up of assets, equity (also known as net worth), and liabilities. As shown on Eastman's SFP (Table 2.4), the total of all assets for both years equals the equity and liability side of the statement. Usually, the SFP's assets, equity, and liability accounts are grouped under several sub-accounts, namely non-current assets, investments, intangible assets, share capital, retained earnings, non-current liabilities, and current liabilities.

Assets

Assets
Resources that a business owns to produce goods and services (e.g., buildings, equipment, trade receivables, inventories).

Property, plant, and equipment
Types of assets that are considered permanent and are to be used over an extended period of time, that is, many years (previously called *capital assets* or *fixed assets*).

Assets are the physical items (tangible) or rights (intangible) owned by a business. Assets have a monetary value attached to them and usually appear under two headings: non-current assets and current assets. Some businesses with other assets, such as investments and intangible assets, will show them separately.

Non-current assets include two types of assets. First, we have the **property, plant, and equipment** (previously called *capital assets*[2] or *fixed assets*). These types of assets are considered permanent and are to be used over an extended period of time (many years). The word "used" is important because it characterizes the major difference between non-current assets and current assets. Non-current assets have either a limited life span (buildings, equipment, machinery) or an unlimited one (land). They are usually listed on the SFP at the price they were purchased for, at "book value" (historical cost less accumulated depreciation, which is the sum of all annual depreciation since the purchase of the non-current assets). However, a company may experience significant changes in the value of some assets and will consequently "write up," or increase, their value. In other instances, the company will "write down" an asset (decrease its value). These adjustments are shown in the statement of comprehensive income. For example, a write-up would take place when the value of a piece of land appreciates significantly, while a write-down would be done when a non-current asset suddenly becomes obsolete, that is, not useful to the company.

2. The term *capital assets* will be used interchangeably with the term *property, plant, and equipment* throughout this text.

Table 2.4 The Statement of Financial Position

Eastman Technologies Inc.
Statements of Financial Position
for the years ended December 31
(in $)

	2009	2008
Assets		
Non-current assets		
Property, plant, and equipment	1,340,000	1,050,000
Accumulated depreciation	(140,000)	(100,000)
Total non-current assets	1,200,000	950,000
Current assets		
Inventories	218,000	185,000
Trade receivables	300,000	280,000
Prepaid expenses	60,000	55,000
Cash and cash equivalents	22,000	18,000
Total current assets	600,000	538,000
Total assets	1,800,000	1,488,000
Equity and liabilities		
Equity		
Share capital	300,000	285,000
Contributed surplus	—	—
Retained earnings	255,000	205,000
Total other comprehensive income/(loss)	—	—
Total equity	555,000	490,000
Non-current liabilities		
Long-term borrowings	800,000	600,000
Current liabilities		
Trade and other payables	195,000	175,000
Short-term borrowings	150,000	135,000
Accrued expenses	20,000	18,000
Taxes payable	80,000	70,000
Total current liabilities	445,000	398,000
Total liabilities	1,245,000	998,000
Total equity and liabilities	1,800,000	1,488,000

Non-current assets (other than land) have a finite life span and wear out over a number of years. Because of this, a company will allocate a certain amount of the total value of the non-current asset over many years; this allocated amount is called depreciation. For example, if a building with an original cost of $2,000,000 has a 20-year physical life span, $100,000 will be allocated as an expense each year. Although this $100,000 is not a cash outlay, it is considered an expense and registered as such (as was indicated earlier) in the statement of income. If the building has been used for four years, the SFP will show an accumulated depreciation of $400,000 deducted from the original or purchase price of the building. The difference between non-current assets (at cost) and the accumulated depreciation is called *net non-current assets*, or *book value*.

Intangible assets
Assets that cannot be seen, touched, or physically measured and are included in the non-current asset section of the SFP.

The second category of non-current assets includes **intangible assets**, that is, those assets that cannot be seen, touched, or physically measured. There are two primary forms of intangible assets. First, there are the legal intangibles, also known as intellectual property, such as trade secrets, customer lists, copyrights, patents, trademarks, and goodwill. These types of assets generate legal property rights defensible in a court of law. Second, there are the competitive intangibles such as knowledge activities. Human capital is the primary source of competitive intangibles for modern-day organizations.

Capital Cost Allowance

Capital cost allowance (CCA)
A tax deduction that Canadian tax laws allow a business to claim for the loss in value of non-current assets due to wear and tear and/or obsolescence.

Whereas depreciation is a usage rate established by each individual business operator for the purpose of calculating profit, **capital cost allowance (CCA)** is a rate established by Canada Revenue Agency that is used by all businesses for different categories of assets for the purpose of calculating income tax expense. The income tax regulations stipulate that all businesses must use these rates to calculate their income tax expense, even though the same asset may become obsolete after five years in one business, but last ten years in another business.

In arriving at taxable income, businesses may deduct CCA on non-current assets. Through CCA, provision is made for businesses to recover, over some time frame, the original amount invested without having to pay tax on the depreciated portion of the investments. As a general rule, depreciated assets fall into one of over 30 asset classes that are defined for tax purposes. Maximum CCA rates, ranging from 4% to 100% per year, are prescribed for each class. For example, the CCA rate for general machinery, which falls in class 8, has a maximum rate of 20%, while buildings that fall in class 1 show a maximum CCA rate of 4%. As will be shown in the next paragraphs, these rates are applied against declining asset balances in each class.

Irrespective of the rate of depreciation and method of depreciating non-current assets used to calculate the profit for the year of a business, Canada Revenue Agency establishes a set of percentages for different categories or groups of capital assets. For example, automotive equipment falls under class 10, with a current rate of 30%. The calculation of the CCA is done on a declining basis similar to the sum-of-the-years'-digits method. (CCA never brings down the value of the asset to zero.) The CCA for each year is obtained by multiplying the maximum rate allowed (e.g., 50%) by the beginning of the year balance. Using the $100,000 example from above, CCA is calculated as follows:

Year	Value at Beginning of Year	CCA Rate	CCA	Value at End of Year
1	$100,000	50% ÷ 2*	$25,000	$75,000
2	75,000	50%	37,500	37,500
3	37,500	50%	18,750	18,750
4	18,750	50%	9,375	9,375
5	9,375	50%	4,687	—

* Income tax regulations allow only half of the CCA rate for the first year.

Self-Test Exercise No. 2.3

Depreciation and Capital Cost Allowance

On its SFP, CompuTech shows equipment purchased for $125,000 and a vehicle purchased for $35,000. The rate of depreciation (straight-line) and CCA for these non-current assets are as follows:

	Straight-line depreciation	Capital cost allowance
1. Equipment	25%	40%
2. Vehicle	20%	30%

Question

For the first five years of operation, calculate the amount of depreciation and CCA for the above-mentioned non-current assets.

Miscellaneous Assets

Miscellaneous assets Assets such as bonds and shares purchased from other businesses.

Miscellaneous assets are similar to marketable securities, except that they are invested for a longer period. They include items such as cash surrender value of life insurance; amounts due from directors, officers, and employees of the company; bonds and shares purchased from other companies; and investments or advances made to subsidiary and affiliated companies.

Intangible assets. As mentioned earlier, intangible assets are assets that cannot be touched, weighed, or measured. They represent values of trademarks, goodwill, franchises, and patents. These items are not tangible but represent some value to the owners of a business. Goodwill, for example, arises when a firm purchases another firm for a price that is higher than the value of the tangible assets. This difference represents the potential earning power resulting from its name or reputation. Also, company trademarks such as Coca-Cola, McDonald's arch, Apple, and Microsoft, are worth millions of dollars. Usually, intangible assets have little value if a business goes bankrupt.

Current assets Assets such as inventories and trade receivables expected to be turned into cash, usually in one year or less.

Current assets are defined as cash or other assets expected to be turned into cash, usually in one year or less, that is, during the operating cycle. Current assets include inventories, trade receivables, prepaid expenses, notes receivables, and cash and cash equivalents.

Inventories
Monetary value a company places on the material it has purchased or goods it has manufactured.

The **inventory** account describes the monetary value a company places on the material it has purchased or goods it has manufactured. Usually, a manufacturer has three types of accounts under inventories:

- *Raw materials*, which represent the goods purchased from various suppliers to be used for manufacturing purposes.
- *Work-in-process*, which includes the goods or materials tied up in various stages of the production process, somewhere between raw materials and finished goods.
- *Finished goods*, which are the products ready for sale.

Because inventories are not a source of profit, management makes an effort to keep them at low levels or to move them as fast as possible. Inventories are recorded at cost, not the price at which the firm hopes to sell them.

Trade receivables
Money owed to the company by its regular business customers for the purchase of goods or services.

Trade receivables represent money owed to the company by its regular business customers for the purchase of goods or services, which can be collected within a reasonable time period (usually between 30 and 90 days). To reduce the size of the cash tied up in this account, some businesses formulate credit policies and collection procedures to minimize the time it takes to turn receivables into cash. In view of the fact that some customers don't pay their bills, an account called *allowance for doubtful accounts* is created, which is an amount estimated by management regarding how much is not expected to be collected. Because this account is a negative asset account, it will be deducted from the regular trade receivables to reflect the true value of that particular account. Usually, allowance for doubtful accounts is not shown separately on the SFP as it is assumed that a reasonable amount has been made. This is how the calculation is done:

Trade receivables before allowance for doubtful accounts	$ 330,000
Allowance for doubtful accounts	(30,000)
Trade receivables	$ 300,000

Prepaid expenses
Payments made for services that have not yet been received.

Prepaid expenses are payments made for services that have not yet been received. A prepaid expense is an expense that is recorded before services were received. Rent, insurance, office supplies, or property taxes are typical examples of such items. For example, Eastman may pay $8,000 for its insurance premium on June 30. If this is a one-year insurance policy and Eastman's accounting cycle closes on December 31, half of the premium, $4,000, will be registered as a prepaid expense. This amount will be charged to the next year's accounting period. If Eastman decides to cancel its policy on December 31, the insurance company will owe Eastman $4,000. This is why such items are considered assets. Another example is office and computer supplies bought in bulk and then gradually used up over several months. Annual property taxes may be paid at the start of the taxation year, and these amounts should be allocated over all the months covered by the property taxes.

Notes receivable are written promises that have a specific maturity date. A note receivable may be the result of the settlement of an account by a customer that does not have the cash to pay the account according to the company's credit terms.

Cash and cash equivalents include all funds such as bills, coins, and cheques that are on hand or readily available from the bank account. A certain reservoir of cash is usually kept on hand in order to pay current bills and to take advantage of specific opportunities, such as cash discounts. Cash equivalents may include *marketable securities*, items such as term deposits or shares that can be readily converted into cash (in less than one year), and are regarded as an added reservoir of cash. Because the company will obtain a greater return on these types of assets than on its bank account, the company will buy securities.

EQUITY

Equity
Funds provided in a business by its shareholders, that is, share capital, contributed surplus, retained earnings, and total other comprehensive income/(loss).

Equity is an important source of funds for financing a business. This money comes from the owners or shareholders of a business in the form of a capital account (if it is a sole proprietorship), partners' account (if it is a partnership), or share capital (if it is a corporation). The money that has been paid by shareholders is referred to as *share capital*. It also includes contributed surplus, retained earnings (that portion of the net earnings that have been earned by the business over a period of years and not paid out as dividends to the shareholders), and total other comprehensive income/(loss).

Share capital
Amount of money that is put into the business by the shareholders.

Share capital represents the amount of money that is put into the business by the shareholders. These could be common shares (certificates of ownership in a company) or preferred shares (shares that rank ahead of common shares in their claims on dividends and in their claim on assets in the event of liquidation).

Contributed surplus, also called *paid-in capital (PIC)*, represents the difference between a share's par value and what shareholders paid when they bought newly issued shares.

Retained earnings
The profit generated by the business for which the owners have not claimed the amount in the form of dividends.

Retained earnings represent the profit generated by the business for which the owners have not claimed the amount in the form of dividends. This represents the profit for each year that has been accumulated and reinvested into the business to finance the purchase of non-current or current assets or to pay off the principal on the debt. If a company makes a profit during a given year, the amount in the retained earnings account shown on the current year's SFP is greater than the amount shown on the previous year's SFP. Conversely, if the company incurs a loss, the retained earnings account drops accordingly.

Total other comprehensive income/(loss) comprises items such as changes in revaluation of property, plant, and equipment, and the gains and losses on remeasuring available-for-sale assets.

Liabilities

Liabilities
The debts of a business.

Liabilities represent the debts of a business. They are the credit that persons or other businesses (other than the shareholders) have extended to a business in order to provide some financial assistance for purchasing the assets. Liabilities are also divided into two distinct groups: non-current liabilities and current liabilities.

Non-current liabilities Debts that are not due for a least one year.

Non-current liabilities include accounts that are not due for at least one year. They include items such as mortgages, contracts, or long-term notes and loans, such as bonds. These items are often used to finance the purchase of non-current assets. A mortgage is a long-term borrowing for which a company has pledged certain non-current assets (land and buildings) to serve as collateral. This assures lenders that the value of some assets will be made available to them if the company ceases to operate or if it is sold or liquidated. A long-term note is similar to notes payable (current liabilities) except that this item is to be repaid beyond a one-year period.

Future Income Taxes Payable

Future income taxes payable Future tax liability resulting from the difference between depreciation and CCA.

Because companies use depreciation rates that are different from the CCA rate allowed by governments to calculate income tax expense, in many instances businesses pay less taxes than they should, particularly during the first several years of the asset utilization. This future tax liability is a result of a temporary difference between book (accounting) value of assets and liabilities and their tax value. These are referred to as **future income taxes payable**, previously called deferred taxes.

Using the $100,000 example, the five-year straight-line depreciation rate (equivalent to 20%), and the 50% CCA rate, the future income taxes payable would be calculated as follows:

Years	CCA @ 50%	Internal depreciation @ 20%	Difference between CCA and depreciation	Difference in annual future taxes payable (tax rate @ 50%)	Difference cumulative future taxes payable
1	$25,000	$20,000	$ 5,000	$2,500	– $ 2,500
2	$37,500	$20,000	$17,500	$8,750	– $11,250
3	$18,750	$20,000	– $ 1,250	– $ 625	– $10,625
4	$ 9,375	$20,000	– $10,625	– $5,312	– $ 5,313
5	$ 4,687	$20,000	– $15,313	– $7,656	$ 2,343

With the above depreciation and CCA rates, let's now produce the first year's statement of income. As shown in Table 2.5, depreciation is used as an expense while CCA is used to calculate the company's income tax expense. The first column is used to calculate the company's income tax expense using CCA. Column 3 shows the company's internal document called the "profit and loss statement" for the year when using the company's five-year depreciation rate (or 20%), while column 2 shows the company's "statement of income," that is, the statement that is included in the annual report. The depreciation expense, the income tax expense paid in that year, and the amount of future income taxes payable that the company owes to the government all appear in the statement. The profit for the year in columns 2 and 3 are the same ($40,000); the only difference between the two columns is the timing of payment of the taxes. The company paid $2,500 less in taxes due to a higher CCA rate. Therefore, the company owes this amount to the government in the form of future income taxes payable. It is like an interest-free loan.

Table 2.5 The Statement of Income and the Profit and Loss Statement (In $)

	1 Accountant's Worksheet	2 Statement of Income	3 P & L Statement
Revenue	300,000	300,000	300,000
Cost of sales	(150,000)	(150,000)	(150,000)
Gross profit	150,000	150,000	150,000
Operating costs	(50,000)	(50,000)	(50,000)
CCA/depreciation	(25,000)	(20,000) ←	(20,000)
Total costs	(75,000)	(70,000)	(70,000)
Profit before taxes	75,000	80,000	80,000
Income tax expense			
- Current (50%)	(37,500) →	(37,500)	(40,000)
- Future income tax payable	(2,500) →	(2,500)	——
	(40,000)	(40,000)	(40,000)
Profit for the year	35,000	40,000	40,000

Self-Test Exercise No. 2.4

Future Income Taxes Payable

By using the information contained in Self-Test Exercise Nos. 2.2 and 2.3, calculate CompuTech's:

1. Future income taxes payable during the first five years; and
2. Statement of income using year 2 of the CCA and depreciation rates.

Current liabilities
Debts that a business must pay within one year (i.e., trade and other payables).

Trade and other payables
Money owed to suppliers of goods or services that were purchased on credit.

Current liabilities are what a business has to pay its creditors, monies that are owed within a short time (less than one year). Normally, such debts are used to finance the current assets. Current liabilities include trade and other payables, short-term borrowings, current portion of long-term debt, accrued expenses, and current income taxes payable.

Trade and other payables usually represent the most current debts of a business. This is the money owed to suppliers of goods or services that were purchased on credit.

Notes payable are written promises to repay a specified sum of money within a short period (usually less than one year). However, it should be noted that notes payable can also be recorded as a non-current liability, depending on their term.

Current income taxes payable are taxes to be paid to the government within the current operating year.

Current portion of long-term debt is the amount of long-term borrowings that the company will have to pay within the current operating year (e.g., mortgage).

Accrued liability
Represents what a company owes for services it has received and not yet paid or an expense that has been incurred but not recorded.

Accrued liability accounts represent what a company owes for services it has received and not yet paid or an expense that has been incurred but not recorded. These liabilities are the opposite of prepaid expenses. Normally, a business records expenses as soon as the invoice is received for operating costs, even though it doesn't pay the invoice until several weeks later. However, certain unrecorded expenses must be identified when a business closes its books. For instance, if employees are paid every second week, and the company closes its books on December 31, it may have to record that it owes (as a liability) its employees salaries for the unpaid period prior to December 31. The following are typical examples of accrued liabilities:

- Accumulated vacation and sick leave pay.
- Interest on debt that hasn't come due by year-end.
- Property taxes that should be charged for the year but have not been paid yet.
- Warranty and guarantee work that will be done during the following year on products already sold.

Self-Test Exercise No. 2.5

Statement of Financial Position

With the following accounts, prepare CompuTech's SFP as at December 31, 2009.

Trade receivables	$35,000
Cash and cash equivalents	15,000
Short-term borrowings	30,000
Share capital	100,000
Non-current liabilities	60,000
Property, plant, and equipment	170,000
Prepaid expenses	5,000
Current portion of long-term borrowings	5,000
Retained earnings	25,000
Accumulated depreciation/amortization	38,000
Trade and other payables	17,000
Inventories	50,000

Annual Reports

The main source of financial data about publicly traded companies is included in the annual report. The annual report is the primary direct communication from

Annual report
Report issued annually by corporations to their shareholders that contains their financial statements as well as management's opinion of the company's past year's operations and prospects for the future.

management to a company's shareholders. Essentially, an **annual report** contains two statements. First is a letter from the president that expresses management's opinion of its company's operating results during the past year and prospects (development and strategies) for the future. Although corporations prepare and disseminate quarterly reports to shareholders and regulatory bodies, these reports are very brief. Second, the annual report includes the four financial statements, that is, the statement of income and the statement of comprehensive income, the SCE, the SFP, and the statement of cash flows. Both the letter and the statements provide an overview of the company's operating activities and financial performance. Annual reports are issued to the shareholders, and most companies publish them on their websites. Each year, the CEO of publicly owned corporations presents their annual report to the shareholders, which gives them the opportunity to ask questions to senior managers. In the News 2.2 gives an example about how shareholders can challenge a CEO at such meetings.

In The News [2.2]

How Shareholders Can Challenge a CEO at the Annual General Meeting

Reprimanding someone for good reason happens all the time, and to all types of individuals occupying important positions: federal and provincial politicians, religious leaders, city officials, hospital and school administrators, and government bureaucrats. Even CEOs are not immune from being called to order!

At one of Exxon Mobil Corp.'s annual shareholders' meeting, CEO Rex W. Tillerson was rebuked by one of the company's shareholders for two reasons: first, for not doing enough for the environment, and second, for his compensation package. The CEO quickly defended the company's position on climate change and indicated that oil and gas would continue to be the world's dominant fuels for another 20 years and meet up to two-thirds of the world's demand. On the issue of compensation, most shareholders appeared to be on the same page as that of the CEO when they were informed that the company had made the most significant profit ever for a U.S.-based company: $45.2 billion in 2008, at the time when oil prices reached unprecedented levels of $150 a barrel.

Source: Adapted from Associated Press, "Exxon shareholders grill CEO on environment, pay," *Globe and Mail*, May 28, 2009, p. B8. For more information on Exxon's strategies related to energy and the environment, visit www.exxonmobil.com/corporate and click on "energy & environment."

The following is a *management statement* written to the shareholders that appears in Enbridge's annual report, which is in two sections: financial reporting and internal control over financial reporting.

> To the Shareholders of Enbridge Inc.
>
> **Financial Reporting**
>
> Management is responsible for the accompanying consolidated financial statements and all other information in this Annual Report. The consolidated financial statements have been prepared in

accordance with Canadian generally accepted accounting principles and necessarily include amounts that reflect management's judgment and best estimates. Financial information contained elsewhere in this Annual Report is consistent with the consolidated financial statements.

The Board of Directors and its committees are responsible for all aspects related to governance of the Company. The Audit, Finance & Risk Committee of the Board, composed of directors who are unrelated and independent, has a specific responsibility to oversee management's efforts to fulfill its responsibilities for financial reporting and internal controls related thereto. The Committee meets with management, internal auditors and independent auditors to review the consolidated financial statements and the internal controls as they relate to financial reporting. The Audit, Finance & Risk Committee reports its findings to the Board for its consideration in approving the consolidated financial statements for issuance to the shareholders.

Internal Control over Financial Reporting

Management is also responsible for establishing and maintaining adequate internal control over financial reporting. The Company's internal control over financial reporting includes policies and procedures to facilitate the preparation of relevant, reliable and timely information, to prepare consolidated financial statements for external reporting purposes in accordance with generally accepted accounting principles and provide reasonable assurance that assets are safeguarded.

Management assessed the effectiveness of the Company's internal control over financial reporting as of December 31, 2008, based on the framework established in Internal Control—Integrated Framework issued by the Committee of Sponsoring Organizations of the Treadway Commission (COSO).[3] Based on this assessment, management concluded that the Company maintained effective internal control over financial reporting as of December 31, 2008.

PricewaterhouseCoopers LLP, independent auditors appointed by the shareholders of the Company, conducts an examination of the consolidated financial statements in accordance with Canadian generally accepted auditing standards.

3. COSO is a voluntary private-sector organization, established in the United States to give guidance to executive management and governance entities on critical aspects of organizational governance, business ethics, internal controls, enterprise risk management, fraud, and financial reporting.

Patrick D. Daniel	J. Richard Bird
President & Chief Executive Officer	Executive Vice President &
February 12, 2009	Chief Financial Officer

Auditor's report Report prepared by an independent accounting firm that is presented to a company's shareholders.

Canadian federal corporate law requires that every federally incorporated limited company appoint an auditor to represent shareholders and report to them annually on the company's financial statements. In Canada, the **auditor's report** includes the following:

1. The auditor's opinion on the financial statements.
2. A statement that the financial statements are prepared in accordance with generally accepted accounting principles applied on a basis consistent with that of the preceding year.
3. A description of the scope of the examination (the audit itself). The auditor's report usually comments on the auditing procedures and any tests made to support the accounting records and presents evidence to show that they were made in accordance with generally accepted auditing standards.

The following is Enbridge's auditor's statement addressed to the shareholders included in the annual report. The auditor's statement is also covered under two sections: consolidated financial statements and internal control over financial reporting.

Consolidated Financial Statements

We have audited the accompanying consolidated statements of financial position of Enbridge Inc. as at December 31, 2008 and December 31, 2007, and the related consolidated statements of earnings, comprehensive income, shareholders' equity and cash flows for each of the years in the three year period ended December 31, 2008. These financial statements are the responsibility of the Company's management. Our responsibility is to express an opinion on these financial statements based on our audits.

We conducted our audits of the Company's financial statements as at December 31, 2008 and December 31, 2007 and for each of the years in the three year period ended December 31, 2008 in accordance with Canadian generally accepted auditing standards and the standards of the Public Company Accounting Oversight Board (United States). Those standards require that we plan and perform an audit to obtain reasonable assurance about whether the financial statements are free of material misstatement. An audit of financial statements includes examining, on a test basis, evidence supporting the amounts and disclosures in the financial statements. A financial statement audit also includes assessing the accounting principles used and significant estimates made by management, and evaluating the overall financial statement presentation. We believe that our audits provide a reasonable basis for our opinion.

In our opinion, these consolidated financial statements referred to above present fairly, in all material respects, the financial position of the Company as at December 31, 2008 and December 31, 2007, and the results of its operations and its cash flows for each of the years in the three year period ended December 31, 2008 in accordance with Canadian generally accepted accounting principles.

Internal Control over Financial Reporting

We have also audited Enbridge Inc.'s internal control over financial reporting as at December 31, 2008, based on the criteria established in Internal Control—Integrated Framework issued by the Committee of Sponsoring Organizations of the Treadway Commission (COSO). The Company's management is responsible for maintaining effective internal control over financial reporting and for its assessment of the effectiveness of internal control over financial reporting, included in the accompanying Management's Report on Internal Control Over Financial Reporting. Our responsibility is to express an opinion on the effectiveness of the Company's internal control over financial reporting based on our audit.

We conducted our audit of internal control over financial reporting in accordance with the standards of the Public Company Accounting Oversight Board (United States). Those standards require that we plan and perform the audit to obtain reasonable assurance about whether effective internal control over financial reporting was maintained in all material respects. An audit of internal control over financial reporting includes obtaining an understanding of internal control over financial reporting, assessing the risk that a material weakness exists, testing and evaluating the design and operating effectiveness of internal control based on the assessed risk, and performing such other procedures as we consider necessary in the circumstances. We believe that our audit provides a reasonable basis for our opinion.

A company's internal control over financial reporting is a process designed to provide reasonable assurance regarding the reliability of financial reporting and the preparation of financial statements for external purposes in accordance with generally accepted accounting principles. A company's internal control over financial reporting includes those policies and procedures that (i) pertain to the maintenance of records that, in reasonable detail, accurately and fairly reflect the transactions and dispositions of the assets of the company; (ii) provide reasonable assurance that transactions are recorded as necessary to permit preparation of financial statements in accordance with generally accepted accounting principles, and that receipts and expenditures of the company are being made only in accordance with authorizations of management and directors of the company; and (iii) provide reasonable assurance regarding prevention or timely detection of unauthorized acquisition, use, or disposition of the company's assets that could have a material effect on the financial statements.

Because of its inherent limitations, internal control over financial reporting may not prevent or detect misstatements. Also, projections of any evaluation of effectiveness to future periods are subject to the risk that controls may become inadequate because of changes in conditions, or that the degree of compliance with the policies or procedures may deteriorate.

In our opinion, the Company maintained, in all material respects, effective internal control over financial reporting as at December 31, 2008 based on criteria established in Internal Control—Integrated Framework issued by the COSO.

Calgary, Alberta, Canada PricewaterhouseCoopers LLP
February 12, 2009 Chartered Accountants

A typical annual report contains the following sections: financial highlights, letters to the shareholders (one from the CEO and the other from the external auditors), review of operations, financial statements, management's discussion and analysis, footnotes and supplementary information, summary of significant accounting policies, five-year summary of financial and statistical data, and names of the board of directors and corporate officers.

Footnotes are essential to financial statements; in fact, they are an integral, inseparable part of an annual report. Writing the footnotes is a necessary but difficult task as the management has to explain sometimes complex issues in a relatively small space. Without footnotes, financial statements would be incomplete since they provide adequate disclosure about relevant information so that the shareholders can make informed decisions and at the same time protect their interests. The two types of footnotes disclose:

- The main accounting methods used by the business; and
- Information that cannot be incorporated in the main body of the financial statements (e.g., details regarding share ownership, long-term operating leases, maturity dates, interest rates, collateral, or other security provisions, lawsuits, employees' retirement and pension plans).

Analysis

4 Learning Objective

Explain the meaning of analysis in financial management

Once the financial statements have been prepared, the information can be analyzed and interpreted. Many techniques exist for analyzing financial statements. What is important, however, is ensuring that the right type of information has been gathered and presented in a way that will assist managers, lenders, and shareholders to analyze the data in a meaningful way.

Here are typical analytical techniques that will be examined in Chapters 3 and 4.

- *Statement of cash flows*, which gives a picture of the changes taking place between two consecutive statements of financial position, that is, where the funds came from (inflows of cash) and where they went (outflows of cash).
- *Horizontal analysis*, which gives a picture of the company's historical growth pattern regarding its financial structure and profitability.
- *Vertical analysis*, which helps financial analysts compare different numbers on a SFP and statement of income (through ratios) in a more meaningful way.
- *Ratio analysis*, which expresses different sets of numbers contained in financial statements as ratios: liquidity ratios, debt-coverage ratios, asset-management ratios, and profitability ratios.
- *Break-even analysis*, which shows the relationship between revenues, expenses (fixed and variable), and profits.
- *Operational analysis*, which uses information contained in financial statements and management information reports to evaluate the efficiency, effectiveness, and productivity of a business.

Decision-Making

5 Learning Objective

Discuss the importance of decision-making in financial management.

This last activity of financial management gets to the heart of the management process—decision-making. Bookkeeping, accounting, and analysis are the key steps in financial management because they provide important information to management, which will assist in making prudent decisions. Decision-making techniques will also be reviewed in subsequent chapters. The information contained in financial statements and the analysis of this data provide answers to the following questions:

- How much money should we borrow?
- Should we borrow on a short-term or a long-term basis?
- How much inventory should be kept on hand?
- Should we buy or lease an asset?
- Should we invest in this project? Expand this operation? Modernize our plant?
- How much credit should we extend?
- How quickly should our company grow?

- What size of capital commitments should our company tackle this year? Next year?
- What level of risk does this project present?
- How should we administer our current assets and current liabilities?
- What is the optimal level of capital structure?
- What price should we set for our products?
- How can we compare the financial viability of different projects coming from various divisions, and how can we rate them?

Important business decisions can have consequential effects on a company's financial statements. A company that decides to invest in a major undertaking such as building a new manufacturing facility, launching a new product line, or buying another business would alter just about every account on its financial statements (e.g., revenue, cost of sales, finance costs, non-current assets, current assets, equity, non-current liabilities, and current liabilities). In the News 2.3 gives an example of such a critical decision.

In The News [2.3]

How a Strategic Decision Impacts a Company's Financial Statements

It sometimes takes hundreds of tactical and operational decisions to improve a company's financial performance; however, it only takes one bold strategic decision to make it happen.

Oracle does not intend to only be in the database, middleware, applications businesses, streamlining business processes for many industries such as banking, communications, health sciences, and insurance. Larry Ellison, Oracle's CEO, announced in May 2009 his intention to get into the selling of low-cost laptop computers, a sector considered to be one of the fastest-growing segments in the technology business. This strategic move will take place once he has completed the proposed $7 billion acquisition of computer maker Sun Microsystems Inc., a company that controls the Java computer language. This daring strategic decision would put Oracle in direct competition with companies like Dell Inc., Acer Inc., Hewlett-Packard Co., and Google. There is no question that Oracle would like to get a slice of the 20 to 30 million netbooks in this market, which happens to show the fastest sales growth in the technology industry, and in the process, enhance its financial profile.

Source: Adapted from Reuters, Clare Baldwin and Jim Finkle, "Oracle's Ellison considers foray into netbooks," *The Ottawa Citizen*, June 3, 2009, p. D2. For more information about Oracle's extraordinary and diverse operations, visit www.oracle.com.

Financial Statements (GAAP versus IFRS)

6 Learning Objective

Draw a comparison between the GAAP and IFRS financial statements' presentation profiles.

Table 2.6 draws a comparison of the financial statements prepared under the CICA's principles and conventions, namely, GAAP and the convergence toward the new format suggested by the IASB's IFRS. As shown in the table, the structure of the statement of income, the SFP, and the SCE are somewhat different from the traditional way of presenting them, and even some of the terms used to describe financial accounts shown on these various statements are also different.

Table 2.6 Financial Statements—GAAP versus IFRS

	GAAP		IFRS
	Income Statement		**Statement of Income and Statement of Comprehensive Income**
	Sales revenue		Revenue
	Cost of sales		Cost of sales
1	Gross profit	1	Gross profit
	Operating expenses		Other income
	Selling expenses		Distribution costs
	Administrative expenses		Administrative expenses
	Total operating expenses		
2	Operating income		Finance costs
	Other income		Total
	Other expenses		
	Extraordinary expenses	2	Profit before taxes
3	Income before taxes	3	Profit for the year
			Profit for the year
			Total other comprehensive income/(loss) for the year
4	Net income	4	Total comprehensive income
	Balance Sheet		**Statement of Financial Position**
	Assets		Assets
	Current assets		Non-current assets
	Capital assets		Current assets
	Intangible assets		Total assets
	Total assets		
			Equity
	Liabilities		
	Current liabilities		Liabilities
	Long-term debts		Non-current liabilities
	Total liabilities		Current liabilities
			Total liabilities
	Shareholders' equity		
	Total liabilities and equity		Total equity and liabilities
	Statement of changes in equity		**Statement of changes in equity**
	Share capital		Share capital
	Preferred shares		Preferred shares
	Common shares		Common shares
	Contributed surplus		Contributed surplus
	Retained earnings		Retained earnings
	Total shareholders' equity		Total other comprehensive income/(loss) for the year
			Total equity

As shown in the table, the *income statement* prepared under the GAAP conventions presented four levels of profitability: gross profit, operating income, income before taxes, and net income. As shown, the other income and other expenses (finance costs) were excluded from the operating section of the income statement. Other expenses such as "extraordinary expenses" were part of the non-operating section of the income statement. The statement of income based on the IFRS conventions shows three levels of profitability: gross profit, profit before taxes, and profit for the year. As shown, other income and finance costs are included in the operating section of the statement. The statement of comprehensive income (shaded) can be part of the income statement or can be shown as a separate statement. This statement shows a fourth level of profitability, that is, total comprehensive income. This statement is made up of the (1) profit for the year, which is drawn from the statement of income; and (2) other comprehensive income/(loss) items for the year, net of tax, such as the following:

- Changes in revaluation surplus for property, plant, and equipment and intangible assets.
- Certain actuarial gains/losses on defined benefit plans.
- Gains/losses arising on translation of financial statement of foreign operations.
- Gains/losses arising from remeasuring securities available for sale.
- Gains/losses on cash flow hedges.[4]

The sum of the profit for the year and total other comprehensive income/(loss) for the year produces the total comprehensive income.

The middle section of Table 2.6 compares the statements of financial position. As shown, both the sequence in presenting the assets and liabilities, and some of the terms used to describe various accounts are different. Under the GAAP convention, current assets and current liabilities are shown first instead of the more permanent assets and liabilities. Under the IFRS convention, non-current assets (capital assets) are shown ahead of current assets. Equity is shown ahead of liabilities, and non-current liabilities (long-term debt) appear before current liabilities.

The SCE shown in the lower part of the table contains similar sections (e.g., share capital, retained earnings) with one exception: IFRS's format shows the total other comprehensive income/(loss) for the year as a component of the statement. Total other comprehensive income/(loss) for the year is drawn from the statement of comprehensive income.

4. Hedge accounting is regarded as one of the most complex aspects of IAS39. The aim of hedge accounting is to provide an offset to the mark-to-market of the derivatives (assets or liabilities) in the profit and loss account. It is a topic that focuses on reducing earnings' volatility (interest rate risk, foreign exchange risk, commodity risk, etc.) and too intricate to be effectively covered in an introductory financial management book.

Not-For-Profit (NFP) Organizations

7 Learning Objective

Explain the contents and structure of the financial statements prepared for NFP organizations.

The NFP industry in Canada is huge. Universities, religious institutions, research centres, museums, hospitals, and social service agencies such as public charities help communities and less-privileged people. These types of organizations administer a variety of programs ranging from infant day-care programs to antipoverty programs. Most NFP organizations manage programs just like a business with a system that is reinforced by NFP accounting rules. Individuals responsible for managing these programs are accountable for realizing the mission and objectives of the program.

Corporations are formed to operate these programs. Just like in the private sector, NFP organizations are legally approved entities distinct from the individuals who have created them. These corporations have their own continuing existence and, like individuals, have their own set of responsibilities, powers, and liabilities.

Not-for-profit organizations Organizations that operate exclusively for social, educational, professional, religious, health, charitable, or any other NFP purpose.

The *CICA Handbook* dedicates section 4400 to the manner in which accounting should be practised by NFP organizations. The CICA defines **not-for-profit organizations** as "entities, normally without transferable ownership interests, organized and operated exclusively for social, educational, professional, religious, health, charitable or any other not-for-profit purpose. A not-for-profit organization's members, contributors and other resource providers do not, in such capacity, receive any financial return directly from the organization."[5]

Just like the for-profit organizations, NFP organizations have to prepare financial statements that normally include the following:

- Statement of financial position
- Statement of operations
- Statement of changes in net assets
- Statement of cash flows

The following paragraphs give a brief description, structure, and contents of the first three financial statements for a fictitious NFP organization called Ontario Foundation for Community Care. The statement of cash flows for NFP organizations will be explained in Chapter 3.

STATEMENT OF FINANCIAL POSITION

The statement of financial position (also known as the balance sheet) shows on one side the resources required by an organization to function properly, called *assets*, and on the other side the claims of outsiders against those resources, known as *liabilities* and *net assets*. The main purpose of this statement is to show the NFP organization's economic resources (assets), its financial obligations (liabilities), and net assets as of a specific date. The accounting equation for the NFP organization

5. The Canadian Institute of Chartered Accountants, Accounting Recommendations, *CICA Handbook*, July 2003, p. 4012.

and the Ontario Foundation for Community Care for the year 2010 are as follows:

Assets	=	Net assets	+	Liabilities
$410,000	=	$200,000	+	$210,000

In the case of for-profit organizations, the total amount of assets equals equity plus liabilities. As shown above, for NFP organizations, equity is called *net assets*, fund balances, or accumulated surplus or deficit. The SFP for the Ontario Foundation for Community Care is as follows:

Ontario Foundation for Community Care
Statement of Financial Position
as at December 31
(in $)

	2010	2009
Assets		
Non-current assets		
Buildings and equipment (net)	300,000	222,000
Investments	40,000	13,000
Total non-current assets	340,000	235,000
Current assets		
Trade receivables	30,000	15,000
Grants receivable	10,000	5,000
Cash and term deposits	30,000	25,000
Total current assets	70,000	45,000
Total assets	410,000	280,000
Net assets and liabilities		
Net assets		
Net assets invested in capital assets	140,000	100,000
Net assets restricted for endowment	60,000	20,000
Total net assets	200,000	120,000
Liabilities		
Long-term borrowings	150,000	115,000
Current liabilities		
Trade and other payables	40,000	30,000
Accrued liabilities	10,000	8,000
Current mortgage payable	10,000	7,000
Total current liabilities	60,000	45,000
Total liabilities	210,000	160,000
Total net assets and liabilities	410,000	280,000

The first section of the asset component of the SFP is called non-current assets and includes two sections: buildings and equipment, and investments. *Non-current assets* are investments held in land, buildings, and equipment, and these items are normally shown at the cost of acquiring them less the appropriate depreciation.

These *investments* are recorded in the books at the lower of cost and market value. Non-current asset purchases could be made for either investment purposes or for operational purposes. The second section is called current assets, which include trade receivables, grants receivable, and cash and term deposits. Just like the for-profit business's SFP, *trade receivables* represent money due to the NFP organization for goods and services rendered to its users; *grants receivable* are pledges made by individuals, foundations, corporations, and government agencies that will be received during the current operating year; and *cash* and *term deposits* is money that is readily available to the organization. As shown, the total assets for the year 2010 amount to $410,000.

The first section of the net assets and liabilities side of the statement is called net assets. *Net assets* represent the organization's residual amount in its assets after deducting all debts used to purchase these assets. It shows the net resources the organization has in order to function properly and provide its services in an efficient and effective manner. The $200,000 amount in net assets includes the following:

1. The net book value invested in capital assets in the amount of $140,000, which is made up of non-current assets ($300,000) less $160,000, which is the sum of the mortgage payable—current in the amount of $10,000 and long-term borrowings in the amount of $150,000; and
2. Net book assets attributable to endowments for $60,000. An *endowment contribution* is a restricted contribution and constitutes resources that are maintained permanently with external constraints. These endowment funds are usually held in securities that are under the control of a professional money manager who operates under specific instructions from the board of directors of the NFP organization.

On the liability section of the statement, we have long-term borrowings, which is the money that was loaned to the NFP organization for buying or renovating its building or equipment. This section may also include *deferred contributions* in the form of restricted contributions and unrestricted contributions related to expenses of future periods. A *contribution* is a gift made to an NFP organization. Such gifts could be in the form of cash, other assets, or a cancellation of a debt. Government funding is considered a contribution. A *restricted contribution* is a gift that is subject to stipulations imposed by the donor and specifies the purpose of the gift (e.g., purchase of a specific asset or the development of a specific program). An *unrestricted contribution* is open and has no specific constraints regarding the purpose of the gift. Looking at the lower portion of the SFP, the three current liabilities include *trade and other payables*, *accrued liabilities*, and *current mortgage payable*, which are obligations that the NFP organization has to pay within the current operating year. These are the most immediate claims against assets. These three accounts amount to $60,000. As shown, the total amount of liabilities for the Ontario Foundation for Community Care is $210,000 and net asset and liability sections for the year 2010 amounts to $410,000.

STATEMENT OF OPERATIONS

The statement of operations shows the revenues and expenses incurred by the NFP organization. The purpose of this statement is to show how much surplus (or deficit) was generated by an organization during an operating year. It also shows the level of efficiencies of the organization. As shown below, the statement of operations lists the various sources of revenues (grants, contributions, investment income, and other income generated by services provided by the organization) for the Ontario Foundation for Community Care. After deducting the total amount of expenses from revenue, the organization made a $40,000 surplus, also called "excess of revenues over expenses."

Ontario Foundation for Community Care
Statement of Operations
for the year ended December 31, 2010
(in $)

Revenues		
Contributions, gifts, grants	25,000	
Direct public support	115,000	
Investment income	10,000	
Program service revenue (e.g., seminars)	200,000	
Government grants (federal)	50,000	
Government grants (provincial)	40,000	
Total		440,000
Expenses		
Services (salaries, benefits, materials)	(320,000)	
Depreciation of non-current assets	(20,000)	
Interest on mortgage	(10,000)	
Fund raising activities	(50,000)	
Total		(400,000)
Excess of revenues over expenses		40,000

STATEMENT OF CHANGES IN NET ASSETS

The statement of changes in net assets shows the changes in fund balances and presents information regarding the net resources the NFP has available to provide its services (for-profit businesses use the statement of retained earnings). As shown below, this statement shows the accumulation of the organization's net assets with regard to endowments and capital assets.

Ontario Foundation for Community Care Statement of Changes in Net Assets for the year ended December 31, 2010 (in $)	
Net assets	
Balance, beginning of year	120,000
Excess of revenues over expenses	40,000
Endowment contributions	40,000
Balance, end of year	200,000

REALITY FINANCIAL SNAPSHOTS

The following pages present the financial statement of the for-profit organization, Enbridge, and NFP organization, The Ottawa Hospital (TOH).

ENBRIDGE[6]

Enbridge's annual report contains five financial statements, the Consolidated Statements of Earnings and the Consolidated Statements of Comprehensive Income for the years 2006 to 2008, the Consolidated Statements of Shareholders' Equity for the years 2006 to 2008, the Consolidated Statements of Financial Position for the years 2007 and 2008, and the Consolidated Statements of Cash Flows for the years 2007 to 2008. This last statement will be explained in Chapter 3 (see page 133). The financial statements contain numerous footnotes that are included in the annual report and can be viewed on their website (www.enbridge.com).

Enbridge's statement of earnings shows the two main sources of revenues emanating from commodity sales plus transportation and other services. Between 2006 and 2008, revenues increased by 51.5%. Expenses are broken down under three major categories, commodity costs, operating and administrative, and depreciation and amortization. During the three-year period, expenses increased by 55.4%. All other non-operating revenues and expenses are listed separately (e.g., income from equity investments, etc.). In 2008, return on revenues (earnings) was 8.2%, compared to 5.8% in 2006. Enbridge's financial performance will be analyzed in detail in Chapter 4 (see page 190).

Consolidated Statements of Earnings

(in millions of Canadian dollars, except per share amounts)

Year Ended December 31	2008	2007	2006
Revenues			
Commodity sales	13,431.9	9,536.4	8,264.5
Transportation and other services	2,699.4	2,383.0	2,380.0
	16,131.3	11,919.4	10,644.5

6. Enbridge Inc., *2008 Enbridge Annual Report*. Found at: http://www.enbridge.com/investor/financialInformation/reportsFilings/pdf/2008-annual-report-en.pdf.

Expenses			
Commodity costs	12,792.0	9,009.5	7,824.6
Operating and administrative	1,312.2	1,163.7	1,084.2
Depreciation and amortization	658.4	596.9	587.4
	14,762.6	10,770.1	9,496.2
	1,368.7	1,149.3	1,148.3
Income from Equity Investments	177.1	167.8	180.3
Other Investment Income	202.7	195.1	107.8
Interest Expense	(550.8)	(550.0)	(567.1)
Gain on Sale of Investment in CLH	694.6	—	—
	1,892.3	962.2	869.3
Non-controlling Interests	(55.7)	(45.9)	(54.7)
	1,836.6	916.3	814.6
Income Taxes	(508.9)	(209.2)	(192.3)
Earnings	1,327.7	707.1	622.3
Preferred Share Dividends	(6.9)	(6.9)	(6.9)
Earnings Applicable to Common Shareholders	1,320.8	700.2	615.4
Earnings per Common Share	3.67	1.97	1.81
Diluted Earnings per Common Share	3.64	1.95	1.79

Enbridge's earnings shown in the statement below are drawn from the consolidated statements of earnings. Other comprehensive income/(loss) increased from \$36.0 million to \$317.8 million between 2006 and 2008 and comprehensive income increased by 150.0% over the same time period.

Consolidated Statements of Comprehensive Income

(in millions of Canadian dollars, except per share amounts)

Year Ended December 31	2008	2007	2006
Earnings	1,327.7	707.1	622.3
Other Comprehensive Income (Loss)			
Change in unrealized gains/(losses) on cash flow hedges, net of tax	(127.4)	96.4	—
Reclassification to earnings of realized cash flow hedges, net of tax	(1.3)	(6.7)	—
Other comprehensive gain/(loss) from equity investees	49.2	(19.8)	—
Non-controlling interest in other comprehensive income	(19.6)	4.9	—
Change in foreign currency translation adjustment	576.8	(447.1)	87.6
Change in unrealized gains/(losses) on net investment hedges, net of tax	(159.9)	174.9	(51.6)
Other Comprehensive Income/(Loss)	317.8	(197.4)	36.0
Comprehensive Income	1,645.5	509.7	658.3

The following statement shows Enbridge's consolidated statement of shareholders' equity. This statement has six sections: preferred shares, common shares, contributed surplus, retained earnings, accumulated other comprehensive income/(loss), and reciprocal shareholding.

Consolidated Statements of Shareholders' Equity

(in millions of Canadian dollars)

Year ended December 31	2008	2007	2006
Preferred Shares	125.0	125.0	125.0
Common Shares			
Balance at beginning of year	3,026.5	2,416.1	2,343.8
Common shares issued	—	566.4	—
Dividend reinvestment and share purchase plan	131.3	17.7	18.4
Shares issued on exercise of stock options	36.2	26.3	53.9
Balance at End of Year	3,194.0	3,026.5	2,416.1
Contributed Surplus			
Balance at beginning of year	25.7	18.3	10.0
Stock-based compensation	14.5	8.9	10.5
Options exercised	(2.3)	(1.5)	(2.2)
Balance at End of Year	37.9	25.7	18.3
Retained Earnings			
Balance at beginning of year	2,537.3	2,322.7	2,098.2
Earnings applicable to common shareholders	1,320.8	700.2	615.4
Common share dividends	(489.3)	(452.3)	(403.1)
Dividends paid to reciprocal shareholder	14.6	13.7	12.2
Cumulative impact of change in accounting policy	—	(47.0)	—
Balance at End of Year	3,383.4	2,537.3	2,322.7
Accumulated Other Comprehensive Income/(Loss)			
Balance at beginning of year	(285.0)	(135.8)	(171.8)
Other comprehensive income/(loss)	317.8	(197.4)	36.0
Cumulative impact of change in accounting policy	—	48.2	—
Balance at End of Year	32.8	(285.0)	(135.8)
Reciprocal Shareholding			
Balance at beginning of year	(154.3)	(135.7)	(135.7)
Participation in common shares issued	—	(18.6)	—
Balance at End of Year	(154.3)	(154.3)	(135.7)
Total Shareholders' Equity	6,618.8	5,275.2	4,610.6
Dividends Paid per Common Share	1.32	1.23	1.15

Enbridge's statements of financial position show a 24.1% increase in total assets. This increase was financed by a 23.6% increase in debt and a 25.5% increase in shareholders' equity. The proportion of debt to total assets decreased from 73.5% in 2007 to 73.2% in 2008.

Consolidated Statements of Financial Position

(in millions of Canadian dollars)

December 31	2008	2007
Assets		
Current Assets		
Cash and cash equivalents	541.7	166.7
Accounts receivable and other	2,322.5	2,388.7
Inventory	844.7	709.4
	3,708.9	3,264.8
Property, Plant and Equipment, net	16,389.6	12,597.6
Long-Term Investments	2,491.8	2,076.3
Deferred Amounts and Other Assets	1,318.4	1,182.0
Intangibles Assets	225.3	212.0
Goodwill	389.2	388.0
Future Income Taxes	178.2	186.7
	24,701.4	19,907.4
Liabilities and Shareholders' Equity		
Current Liabilities		
Short-term borrowings	874.6	545.6
Accounts payable and other	2,411.5	2,213.8
Interest payable	101.9	89.1
Current maturities of long-term debt	533.8	605.2
Current portion of non-recourse long-term debt	184.7	61.1
	4,106.5	3,514.8
Long-Term Debt	10,154.9	7,729.0
Non-Recourse Long-Term Debt	1,474.0	1,508.4
Other Long-Term Liabilities	259.0	253.9
Future Income Taxes	1,290.8	975.6
Non-Controlling Interests	797.4	650.5
	18,082.6	14,632.2
Shareholders' Equity		
Share capital		
Preferred shares	125.0	125.0
Common shares	3,194.0	3,026.5
Contributed surplus	37.9	25.7
Retained earnings	3,383.4	2,537.3
Accumulated other comprehensive income/(loss)	32.8	(285.0)
Reciprocal shareholding	(154.3)	(154.3)
	6,618.8	5,275.2
Commitments and Contingencies	24,701.4	19,907.4

THE OTTAWA HOSPITAL[7]

The following pages show TOH's three financial statements, namely the Statement of Operations, the Statement of Changes in Net Assets, and the SFP for the years 2007

7. *2008 Ottawa Hospital Annual Report*. Found at http://www.ottawahospital.on.ca/about/reports/FS2008-e.pdf.

and 2008. The Statement of Cash Flows will be presented in Chapter 3 (see page 134). The financial statements contain numerous footnotes that are included in the annual report and can be viewed on their Web site (www.ottawahospital.on.ca). As shown, the structure and contents of TOH's financial statements are somewhat different from Enbridge.

TOH's statement of operations is divided into three parts: revenue, expenses, and other revenues or expenses generated from non-operating activities. As shown, in 2008, 80.7% of the revenue was obtained from the Ministry of Health and Long-Term Care and the bulk of expenses were incurred in salaries, wages, employee benefits, and medical staff remuneration for a total of 72.5% of the hospital's total expenses. For both years, TOH recorded revenues that exceeded the expenses.

Statement of Operations

(in thousands of dollars)

Year ended March 31	2008	2007
Revenue		
Patient care:		
Ministry of Health and Long-Term Care	702,015	641,219
Other	97,351	94,162
Other funding	15,350	15,147
Marketed services	8,398	7,688
Amortization of deferred contributions related to equipment	7,830	7,770
Recoveries and other	38,340	37,803
Investment	859	1,288
	870,143	805,077
Expenses		
Salaries and wages	444,305	409,967
Employee benefits	118,364	108,316
Medical staff remuneration	65,690	58,956
Medical and surgical	47,816	47,250
Drugs	50,610	52,307
Supplies and other	118,458	104,415
Amortization of equipment	20,358	19,927
Interest on bank indebtedness	880	567
	866,481	801,705
Excess of Revenue over Expenses before Undernoted Items	3,662	3,372
Parking Operations	10,005	9,343
Amortization of Deferred Contributions Related to Buildings	8,803	6,081
Amortization of Buildings and Land Improvements	(15,169)	(13,119)
Excess of Revenue over Expenses	7,301	5,677

The statement of changes in net assets shows the value of capital assets in TOH's books as at March of each year. In 2008, the hospital had $182.4 million in net capital assets, up from $163.0 million over 2007 for an 11.9% increase.

Statement of Changes in Net Assets

(in thousands of dollars)

Year ended March 31	Investment in Capital Assets	Unrestricted	Total 2008	Total 2007
Balance, Beginning of Year	163,035	(142,087)	20,948	15,271
Excess of Revenue over Expenses	7,301	7,301	5,677	
Net Change in Investment in Capital Assets	19,334	(19,334)	—	—
Balance, End of Year	182,369	(154,120)	28,249	20,948

Between 2007 and 2008, TOH's total assets increased by 7.5%. Current assets show an increase of 10.4% and an increase of 6.9% in capital assets.

Statement of Financial Position

(in thousands of dollars)

March 31	2008	2007
Assets		
Current Assets:		
Cash held in trust	20,228	18,741
Accounts receivable	41,249	36,724
Inventories	9,674	9,205
Prepaid expenses	4,309	3,664
	75,460	68,334
Capital Grants Receivable	13,499	5,392
Investments	43,459	47,417
Capital Assets	434,802	406,655
Receivable from Royal Ottawa Health Care Group–Vested Benefits	493	493
	567,713	528,291
Liabilities, Deferred Contributions, and Net Assets		
Current Liabilities:		
Bank indebtedness	51,294	19,355
Accounts payable and accrued liabilities	179,768	194,123
Payable to TOH Residence Corporation	2,389	1,729
Deferred contributions related to trust funds	20,228	18,741
	253,679	233,948
Long-term Liabilities		
Employee future benefits	15,959	13,945
Deferred Contributions Related to Capital Assets	269,826	259,450
Net Assets:		
Investment in capital assets	182,369	163,035
Unrestricted deficiency	(154,120)	(142,087)
	28,249	20,948
Commitments, Contingencies, and Guarantees		
	567,713	528,291

[DECISION-MAKING IN ACTION]

The CEO of Oxford Inc. was reviewing the December 31, 2010, financial statements prepared by his controller. The controller confirmed that these financial statements were prepared in accordance with generally accepted accounting principles in order to make it easy for managers, lenders, owners, etc. to analyze and interpret their content and make enlightened decisions.

The CEO noticed that the statement of income contained three levels of profitability: gross profit, profit before taxes, and profit for the year. The first level of profit indicates how much profit was earned by Oxford after paying the cost of manufacturing, that is, purchases, freight-in, and all other expenses related to producing goods. The second level, profit before taxes, shows the amount of profit that Oxford made after deducting, from gross profit, all expenses (distribution costs and administrative expenses and other costs) and the addition of other income. This is the level of profit that managers are accountable for as they are directly responsible for making decisions related to revenue and expenses. These two profit levels deal with the operating section of the statement of income.

The third level of profit (profit for the year) shows how much income tax expense is deducted from profit before taxes. The shareholders then decide what to do with this third level of profit: pay dividends or reinvest it in the business in the form of retained earnings.

The CEO noticed that although Oxford earned $260,000 in profit for the year, it generated $315,000 in cash ($260,000 + $55,000 for depreciation, which is a non-cash expense).

Oxford Inc.
Statement of Income
for the year ended December 31, 2010
(in $)

Revenue		4,500,000	
Cost of sales		(3,500,000)	
Gross profit		1,000,000	Level 1
Other income		20,000	
Distribution costs	(300,000)		
Administrative expenses	(200,000)		
Depreciation	(55,000)		
Other expenses	(35,000)	(590,000)	
Total		(570,000)	
Profit before taxes		430,000	Level 2
Income tax expense		(170,000)	
Profit for the year		260,000	Level 3

He also noticed that the second financial statement, the SCE (which includes the statement of retained earnings), had little value to his managers but showed important information about the amount of profit or earnings that had been invested back into Oxford since it was started. He noticed that as of January 1, 2010, a total of $1,100,000 had been reinvested in Oxford. During the current operating year, $50,000 was paid out in dividends and deducted from the $260,000 profit for the year (or earnings), and the balance of $210,000 was reinvested in Oxford. At the end of the year, Oxford had accumulated $1,310,000 in retained earnings. This amount also appears in the current year's SFP under the heading "Equity."

Oxford Inc.
Statement of Retained Earnings
for the year ended December 31, 2010
(in $)

Retained earnings (beginning of year)		1,100,000
Earnings for the year	260,000	
Dividends	(50,000)	210,000
Retained earnings (end of year)		1,310,000

The third financial statement is the SFP. The CEO noticed that this financial statement was divided into two sections: what Oxford owns (assets) and what it owes to its shareholders (equity) and creditors (liabilities).

The asset section was further divided into two sections. The first grouping of accounts includes non-current assets or those that are tangible, such as land, buildings, machinery, and equipment. Because these assets are used over an extended period of years, the original cost of the assets can be depreciated (accumulated depreciation) over their respective useful lives. The worth of these tangible assets in the company books is recorded as net property, plant, and equipment (also known as capital assets and non-current assets). This grouping of accounts also includes intangible assets such as goodwill, patents, etc. The second grouping of accounts includes current assets or those assets that can be converted into cash within the operating year.

Two groups of individuals finance the assets listed on the company's books: shareholders and creditors. This is the reason the shareholder and liabilities' side of the SFP is divided into two sections: equity and liabilities. The equity section also contains two subgroups: share capital and retained earnings. Share capital is the amount of money that has been invested in the business by the shareholders themselves. On the other hand, retained earnings is the amount of money that has been reinvested in the business since its inception. This money belongs to the shareholders, but they have decided to leave it in the business in order to finance assets.

The liability section also includes two subgroups. The first group lists the long-term borrowings. These liabilities are usually used to help finance the purchase of the non-current assets. These debts are due only after the current operating year (2 to approximately 15 years). The second group, current liabilities, usually finance current assets. These liabilities must be paid within the next operating year (12 months).

Oxford Inc.
Statement of Financial Position
as at December 31, 2010
(in $)

Assets		
Non-current assets		
Property, plant, and equipment	2,450,000	
Accumulated depreciation	(650,000)	
Total property, plant, and equipment	1,800,000	
Intangible assets	65,000	
Total non-current assets		1,865,000
Current assets		
Inventories	750,000	
Trade receivables	450,000	
Prepaid expenses	30,000	
Marketable securities	50,000	
Cash and cash equivalents	35,000	
Total current assets		1,315,000
Total assets		3,180,000
Equity and liabilities		
Equity		
Share capital	400,000	
Retained earnings	1,310,000	
Total equity		1,710,000
Long-term borrowings		900,000
Current liabilities		
Trade and other payables	130,000	
Accrued expenses	50,000	
Current portion of long-term borrowings	40,000	
Short-term borrowings	350,000	
Total current liabilities		570,000
Total liabilities		1,470,000
Total equity and liabilities		3,180,000

FINANCIAL SPREADSHEETS—EXCEL

The financial spreadsheets available from Nelson's website include three input templates: the statement of income, the statement of comprehensive income and the SCE, and the SFP. These templates comprise two types of cells, protected cells (non-shaded) and unprotected cells (shaded). Most cells on these three templates are unprotected because the analyst will want to input financial data from an organization's financial statements for three consecutive years. These templates are linked to one another as some data is automatically transcribed onto another. For example, the profit for the year shown on the statement of income is copied in the appropriate line on the SCE and the total retained earnings (end of year) is transcribed onto the SFP under equity. Most cells on templates 4 to 15 are protected because they are output documents (analytical documents) useful to analyze a company's financial performance from different angles (ratios, vertical analysis, horizontal analysis, DuPont system, cash flow, the economic value added, sustainable growth, and the Z-score). Most financial ratios contained in this book are calculated by these spreadsheets; they can save many hours of tedious calculations that can be committed instead to more important work such as analysis and decision-making.

Chapter Summary

1 Learning Objective

Explain the activities related to bookkeeping.

Bookkeeping involves collecting, classifying, and reporting transactions taking place each day in different departments of a business. Bookkeeping begins with the preparation of a chart of accounts. Each time a business transaction takes place, at least two accounts are affected (debit and credit); this is referred to as double-entry bookkeeping. The bookkeeping and accounting process includes five steps: (1) a business transaction, (2) preparation of documents and recording and posting transactions in (3) journals, (4) ledgers, and (5) the preparation of the trial balance. In its simplest form, the financial picture of a business can be expressed by the following formula:

Assets = Equity + Liabilities

2 Learning Objective

Describe the accounting function and give an outline of the four financial statements.

The main purpose of accounting is to prepare the financial statements, namely, the statement income and the statement of comprehensive income, the SCE, the SFP, and the statement of cash flows.

3 Learning Objective

Examine the contents and the structure of the statement of income and the statement of comprehensive income, the statement of changes in equity, and the statement of financial position.

Four key financial statements were reviewed. The *statement of income* presents the operating results, that is, revenues and expenses and profit for a given period of time. The *statement of comprehensive income* shows items of income and expense that are not recognized in the statement of income. The *statement of changes in equity* represents the interest of the shareholders of a business and shows the cumulative net results in equity with respect to share capital, contributed surplus, retained earnings, and accumulated other comprehensive income/(loss). The *statement of financial position*, which describes a company's financial position at a given moment in time, contains a list of the assets (what a company owns), equity (owners who have a claim on the assets), and liabilities (creditors who have a claim on the assets). Canadian federal corporate law requires that every federally incorporated limited company appoint an auditor to represent shareholders and report to them annually on the company's financial statements. The more important areas examined include corporate income tax rates, small business deductions, business expenses and deductions, business losses, and CCA. *Depreciation* is an accounting entry allocating the cost of a non-current asset against revenue over an estimated asset's life. There are several ways of calculating depreciation, and two were presented in this chapter: the straight-line method and the accelerated method. *Capital cost allowance* is the rate of depreciation established by Canada Revenue Agency and is used by all businesses for calculating their income taxes. Because companies use depreciation rates that are different from the CCA rate allowed by governments to calculate income taxes, in many instances businesses pay less tax than they should, particularly during the first several years of the asset utilization. This means that the company owes taxes (liability) to the government. These are referred to as future income taxes payable.

4 Learning Objective

Explain the meaning of analysis in financial management.

Once the financial statements have been drawn up, the information can be analyzed and interpreted. Some of the more popular analytical tools include the statement of cash flows, horizontal and vertical analysis, ratio analysis, and break-even analysis.

5 Learning Objective

Discuss the importance of decision-making in financial management.

Decision-making is the process of using information for the purpose of improving the financial performance of a business. Some of the more important decisions made by managers include the following: How much money should we borrow? Should we buy or lease? Should we invest in this project? What level of risk does this project present?

6 Learning Objective

Draw a comparison between the GAAP and IFRS financial statements' presentation profiles.

The presentation format of the statement of income, the SFP, and the SCE and some of the terms used to describe the accounts contained in these statements under the IFRS conventions are different from the traditional way of presenting them under the GAAP convention.

7 Learning Objective

Explain the contents and structure of the financial statements prepared for NFP organizations.

NFP organizations operate exclusively for social, educational, professional, religious, health, charitable, or any other NFP purpose. In their annual reports, these organizations must also prepare financial statements: the SFP, the statement of operations, the statement of changes in net assets, and the statement of cash flows.

Key Terms

Accounting p. 58
Accounting equation p. 54
Accrual method p. 62
Accrued liability p. 79
Administrative expenses p. 65
Annual report p. 80
Assets p. 71
Auditor's report p. 82
Bookkeeping p. 53
Bookkeeping and accounting cycle p. 54
Capital cost allowance (CCA) p. 73
Cash method p. 62
Chart of accounts p. 53
Cost of sales p. 65
Credit p. 55
Current assets p. 74
Current liabilities p. 78
Debit p. 55
Depreciation p. 65
Distribution costs p. 65
Double-entry bookkeeping p. 54
Equity p. 76
Financial statements p. 50
Future income taxes payable p. 77
Income tax p. 68
Income tax expense p. 68
Intangible assets p. 73
Inventories p. 75
Journalizing p. 56
Journals p. 56
Ledgers p. 56
Liabilities p. 76
Miscellaneous assets p. 74
Non-current liabilities p. 77
Not-for-profit organizations p. 89
Operating section p. 64
Other income p. 65
Owners' section p. 67
Posting p. 56
Prepaid expenses p. 75
Profit before taxes p. 67
Property, plant, and equipment p. 71
Retained earnings p. 76
Revenue p. 64
Share capital p. 76
Statement of cash flows p. 60
Statement of changes in equity p. 60
Statement of comprehensive income p. 59
Statement of financial position p. 60
Statement of income p. 58
Total comprehensive income/(loss) for the year p. 59
Trade and other payables p. 78
Trade receivables p. 75
Trial balance p. 56

Review Questions

1. What are financial statements and what do they include?
2. What activities are involved in bookkeeping?
3. Explain the accounting equation.
4. What are journals and ledgers?
5. What is the purpose of a trial balance?

6. Explain the different sections of the statement of income.
7. What does the statement of changes in equity show?
8. What is the connection between the retained earnings amount shown in the statement of changes in equity and the statement of financial position?
9. Is there a difference between the book value of accounts shown on the statement of financial position and market value? Explain.
10. What is the basic structure of the statement of financial position?
11. Differentiate between non-current assets and current assets.
12. What are the four sections included in the statement of cash flows?
13. What is the purpose of the auditor's report?
14. Explain why you think auditors write in a company's annual report the following statement: "These consolidated financial statements are the responsibility of the company's management. Our responsibility is to express an opinion on these consolidated financial statements based on our audits."
15. Differentiate between cash accounting and accrual accounting.
16. What are future income taxes payable?
17. What is the difference between depreciation and capital cost allowance?
18. What is a not-for-profit organization?
19. Name the financial statements prepared by not-for-profit organizations?

Learning Exercises

EXERCISE 1

Jim Benson opens a retail store called The Bead Shop. During the first month of operation, Jim goes through the following accounting transactions:

1. Invests $100,000 in cash in the business.
2. Buys $50,000 worth of equipment on credit he obtained from the bank.
3. Buys $60,000 worth of goods from different suppliers, pays $30,000 in cash, and puts the rest on credit.
4. Spends $5,000 in cash for advertising.
5. Sells $20,000 worth of goods on credit.
6. Pays $15,000 in cash for salaries.
7. Pays $10,000 to the bank toward the loan.
8. Pays $5,000 to a supplier.
9. Pays $13,000 for some merchandise that he had purchased on credit.
10. Pays a salary of $3,000.

Questions

Using the previous transactions, prepare the following:

a) The journal entries
b) The ledgers
c) The trial balance

EXERCISE 2

At the end of December 31, 2010, Cougar Inc.'s accounts are as follows:

Office salaries	$30,000
Finance costs	3,000
Depreciation (administration)	2,000
Cost of sales	300,000
Income tax expense	35,000
Sales salaries	40,000
Interest income	6,000
Gross revenue	520,000
Advertising	10,000
Lease (administration)	3,000
Promotional expenses	2,000
Sales discounts	20,000
Travel expenses	3,000
Rental charges	5,000

Question

With the above accounts, prepare Cougar's statement of income for the year ended December 31, 2010.

EXERCISE 3

On its statement of financial position, a company shows buildings purchased for $700,000, equipment purchased for $350,000, and machinery purchased for $170,000. The depreciation and capital cost allowance rates for these non-current assets are as follows:

	Capital Cost Allowance	Straight Line Depreciation
1. Buildings	5%	7%
2. Equipment	20%	25%
3. Machinery	15%	30%

Question

For the first five years of operation, calculate the amount of depreciation and capital cost allowance for the above-mentioned non-current assets.

EXERCISE 4

ABC Inc.'s revenue and costs for the year 2010 amounted to the following:

Revenue	$500,000
Cost of sales	300,000
Gross profit	200,000
Operating expenses	100,000

The company's statement of financial position shows the gross value of non-current assets worth $100,000. The company's straight line depreciation rate for the asset is 15%, and Canada Revenue Agency's CCA is 30%. The company's income tax rate is 50%.

Questions

On the basis of the above information:

1. Calculate the company's future income taxes payable during the first five years.
2. Prepare the statement of income using year 2 of the CCA and depreciation rates.

EXERCISE 5

At the end of December 31, 2010, Cougar Inc.'s accounts are as follows:

Accumulated depreciation	$100,000
Current income taxes payable	5,000
Long-term borrowings	25,000
Inventories	90,000
Trade receivables	60,000
Non-current assets (at cost)	300,000
Trade and other payables	40,000
Mortgage payable	130,000
Accrued expenses	10,000
Future income taxes payable	5,000
Share capital	100,000
Prepaid expenses	10,000
Intangible assets	20,000
Cash and cash equivalents	25,000
Retained earnings	80,000
Short-term borrowings	10,000

Question

With the above accounts, prepare Cougar Inc.'s statement of financial position as at December 31, 2010.

EXERCISE 6

An accountant employed by Zimmerman Electronics Inc. was reviewing the following balances shown in the company's ledgers for the year 2010:

Mortgage payable	$80,000
Prepaid insurance	2,000
Marketable securities	5,000
Sales returns	50,000
Cash and cash equivalents	5,000
Advertising	50,000
Trade receivables	15,000
Gross revenue	650,000
Trade and other payables	12,000
Buildings (net)	100,000

Cost of sales	300,000
Short-term notes payable	10,000
Retained earnings (December 31, 2009)	40,000
Finance costs	10,000
Land	25,000
Office salaries	70,000
Share capital	15,000
Lease	20,000
Insurance	10,000
Depreciation (administration)	20,000
Income tax expense	10,000
Dividends	10,000
Interest income	15,000
Inventories	20,000
Sales salaries	100,000

Questions

1. With the above account balances, prepare the following financial statements:
   a) Statement of income
   b) Retained earnings (section of the statement of changes in equity)
   c) Statement of financial position
2. Calculate the company's cash flow for the year.

EXERCISE 7

On the basis of the information provided below, prepare the following four financial statements for Linden International Inc. for the year 2010.

1. Statement of income
2. Statement of comprehensive income
3. Statement of changes in equity
4. Statement of financial position

Income tax expense	$600,000
Change in property revaluation (loss)	35,000
Current assets	6,500,000
Cost of sales	7,500,000
Distribution costs	900,000
Common shares issued	895,000
Accumulated other comprehensive income/(loss) beginning of year	0
Finance costs	90,000
Stock-option compensation	40,000
Profit before taxes	1,750,000
Retained earnings (end of year)	5,000,000
Dividends paid	150,000
Other income	40,000
Gross profit	3,500,000
Share capital (end of year)	3,395,000
Contributed surplus (beginning of year)	60,000

Non-current liabilities	5,000,000
Change in currency translation (income)	40,000
Retained earnings (beginning of year)	4,000,000
Administrative expenses	800,000
Total liabilities	8,000,000
Total assets	16,500,000

PHOTO/Yuri Arcurs/Shutterstock

CHAPTER 3

[STATEMENT OF CASH FLOWS]

Learning Objectives

After reading this chapter, you should be able to:

1 Learning Objective — Explain the importance of managing cash flows.

2 Learning Objective — Analyze cash flows by comparing two consecutive statements of financial position.

3 Learning Objective — Explain the basic structure of the statement of cash flows.

4 Learning Objective — Describe the structure of the statement of cash flows for not-for-profit organizations.

Chapter Outline

OPENING CASE

In February 2009, Len and Joan Miller started their computer retail business. During the first several months of operations, sales objectives were realized, and expenses were in line with their budget. As part of their original plans, the Millers were thinking about opening a new retail outlet. In fact, they were thinking of opening several retail outlets in different cities over the next 10 years. They understood, however, that in any start-up venture, business survival was a primary focus. They realized that any cash invested in CompuTech Sales and Service had to "return a suitable level of profit." They also recognized that some of the cash required to open new retail stores would have to come from their existing business. They remembered Bill Murray's comments that in order to maintain stability, they should not rely on cash from lenders as the only source of growth funds, but should also rely on cash generated from internal operations (profit for the year). As far as the Millers were concerned, the key was to minimize operating expenses during the first few years of operations and put a reasonable amount of cash into products and services in order to generate profitable revenue.

The Millers' goal for 2009 and 2010 was to develop a good understanding of the computer retail business in terms of customer needs, supplier arrangements, and day-to-day operating activities. They understood the importance of cash flows. They had often heard from course instructors and long-time business entrepreneurs that "cash is king." They remembered vividly the discussion they had with one of their instructors when he said that having the money when you need it is as important as being able to predict when you'll get it.

In line with their cash flow philosophy, the Millers did not want to open up a new retail outlet until 2011. They realized after speaking with various lenders that financing choices to expand their business quickly, particularly for a successful business venture, were extensive, and the terms and conditions could be varied. Their intention (and cash flow strategy) was to generate as much cash as possible from CompuTech during 2009 and 2010, invest a minimal amount of cash for the purchase of some equipment during these two years, and reduce their debt in order to prepare themselves for future growth.

The Millers' longer-term plan was to open a new retail outlet during the latter part of 2011 estimated to cost around $350,000. In light of their investment plan, they had to implement a cash flow strategy that could lead them successfully toward their expansion program. They wanted to ensure that they had a balanced financing package. They were aiming for a 20% increase in revenue in 2010 and a 90% increase in 2011. The following summarizes CompuTech's key financial figures. As shown, the investment in property, plant, and equipment is expected to be minimal in 2010 (only $40,000) with a substantial increase ($350,000) in 2011. To pay for these investments, the Millers would have to obtain cash from their business operations. Part of the cash would come from profit and depreciation in the amount of $73,000 ($33,000 + $20,000 + $20,000) for the year 2010 and $157,000 ($77,000 + $40,000 + $40,000) for the year 2011, and long-term borrowings would provide $150,000 in 2011. Appendix A at the end of this book presents CompuTech's financial statements: the statements of income, the statements of comprehensive income, the statements of changes in equity, and the statements of financial position for the years 2009 to 2011.

(in $000s)	2009	2010	2011
Revenue	$ 350	$ 420	$ 800
Profit for the year	25	33	77
Depreciation/amortization	38	40	80
Purchase of property, plant, and equipment	170	40	350
Long-term borrowings	60	(10)	150

Chapter Overview

The previous chapter examined the contents and structure of the statement of income and the statement of comprehensive income, the statement of changes in equity, and the statement of financial position. As indicated:

- The *statement of income* and *the statement of comprehensive income* are like a movie in that they show the amount of revenue earned and expenses incurred between two dates or during a given time period.
- The *statement of changes in equity* tells how much profit (earnings) has been accumulated by a business since it began its operations, the profit for the year that the business earned (drawn from the statement of income) during the current operating year, the amount of dividends paid to its shareholders during the current operating year, and the amount of profit retained in the business. It also shows the amount of cash that was invested in the business by shareholders.
- The *statement of financial position*, like a snapshot, gives a picture of what a business owns, and what it owes to creditors, and to the shareholders at a given point in time.

These financial statements have a specific purpose, giving important information about the financial performance and financial condition of a business. However, they do not show the cash flow that takes place between two consecutive accounting periods; this is what the *statement of cash flows* (also called the statement of changes in financial position) does.

To illustrate the meaning of change, let's examine six accounts drawn from, say, Judy's statements of financial position for the years 2009 and 2010. As shown on the following page, the two columns (2010 and 2009) give a picture of what Judy owns and what she owes at the end of these two accounting periods. You cannot tell what changes took place if you look at only one column or one year. But if you list the accounts of two consecutive statements of financial position side by side, you can readily observe the changes. As shown, each change produces either a cash inflow or a cash outflow.

In $	2010	2009	Cash Inflows	Cash Outflows
1. Bank loan	20,000	5,000	15,000	—
2. Mortgage payable	140,000	100,000	40,000	—
3. Visa loan	2,000	1,000	1,000	—
4. Watch	1,000	—	—	1,000
5. Car	30,000	5,000	—	25,000
6. House	180,000	150,000	—	30,000
Total			56,000	56,000

Let's examine the meaning and significance of these changes. As shown, in 2009 Judy owed $5,000 to the bank; in 2010, she owed $20,000. This change means that Judy borrowed an additional $15,000 from the bank in 2010. Because she borrowed (or received) money from the bank, this change is called a *cash inflow*. To find out what she did with the money, we have to look at other statement of financial position accounts; these will be identified later. Also, the mortgage account shows a $40,000 increase between the two accounting periods (from $100,000 to $140,000). This means that Judy borrowed an additional amount from a mortgage company. This loan is also considered a cash inflow. Again, we're not sure yet what Judy did with the cash. Furthermore, Judy's Visa loan account shows a $1,000 change. Again, Judy borrowed $1,000 on her credit card. The changes in these three accounts show that Judy pocketed or took in $56,000 in cash. Now, let's see what she did with this cash.

By examining the other accounts in the statement of financial position, we see that Judy purchased a $1,000 watch because the 2009 watch account on the statement of financial position had a nil balance, and a $1,000 amount is shown in 2010. This acquisition is considered a purchase and therefore a *cash outflow*. We can assume that Judy took the $1,000 amount borrowed from Visa to make that purchase. Also in 2010, Judy's car account increased by $25,000. In 2009 this account showed $5,000, which increased to $30,000 in 2010. This means that Judy purchased a car. We can assume that she used the bank loan ($15,000) and some of the mortgage money ($40,000) to buy the car. Also in 2010, Judy had a $30,000 solarium installed in her house. As shown, in 2009, Judy's house account was $150,000; it increased to $180,000 in 2010. In order to make this addition to her house, she must have taken what was left over from the mortgage after the car purchase.

We can see from these simple examples the changes in various accounts that took place between Judy's two accounting periods, that is, where she got the money from (cash inflows) and where it went (cash outflows). Judy obtained $56,000 from three different sources (bank loan, mortgage, and Visa), purchased a watch and a car, and made some renovations to her house. As will be shown in many examples in this chapter, the totals of all cash inflows and cash outflows must *always be equal.* In other words, when adding all the changes between two statements of financial position from either the asset, equity, or liability accounts, the sources always equal the uses. This makes sense, because each time a transaction takes place, it affects two accounts, a cash outflow (e.g., purchase of a car) and a cash inflow (e.g., bank loan).

This chapter examines the concepts related to the management of cash flows. In particular, it focuses on four key topics. The first one looks at why it is important to examine the flow of cash between two accounting periods and what is meant by "cash is king." The second topic explores the meaning of cash flows and the basic rules that can be applied to determine whether a change between two accounting periods for a particular account is considered a *cash inflow* or a *cash outflow.* It shows that by looking at two consecutive statements of financial position, one can readily determine whether a change between accounts (e.g., inventories, trade, and other payables, or mortgage) is considered a cash inflow (cash provided by) or a cash outflow (cash used in). The third and fourth topics give the outline of the basic structure and contents of the statement of cash flows for organizations with different ambitions, the for-profit businesses and the not-for-profit (NFP) organizations. It also presents the various accounts of the statement of financial position that are included in the statement of cash flows called *adjustments in non-cash working capital accounts.*

Why Analyze Cash Flows?

1 Learning Objective

Explain the importance of managing cash flows.

Financial analysts, lenders, investors, and managers are all interested in the flow of cash within a business and, more importantly, the changes taking place in cash-related activities from year to year. They often say that "cash is king" because businesses need cash to function. For example, they need cash to pay their bills on time and to invest in non-current assets such as machinery and equipment for modernization or expansion purposes. They want to know where cash came from (provided by cash inflows) and what it was spent on (used in or cash outflows). More importantly, they want to know how much the company will spend in future years and how it will be provided. For instance, if a company wants to invest $1.0 million in capital assets (property, plant, and equipment) during the next budget year (cash outflows), management will surely want to know where the cash needed to finance these assets will be coming from (cash inflows).

This type of analysis and decision-making process brings management to the heart of financial management: the procurement and the allocation of cash. This process is referred to as **cash flows**. Changes in various accounts of the statement of financial position indicate the flows of cash resulting from management decisions. The statement of cash flows shows the amount of cash invested in (used in) non-current asset accounts and where these funds are obtained (from lenders or shareholders) or provided by (cash inflows).

Cash flows
Has to do with the procurement (cash provided by) or allocation (cash used in) of cash.

Figure 1.6 in Chapter 1 on page 18 illustrates this point. It shows that a business purchased $1.0 million worth of assets (investing decisions). One-half of the funds used to finance these investments was provided by internal sources (operating decisions), that is, the business itself; the other half was provided by external sources (financing decisions), that is, investors (shareholders and long-term lenders).

To help explain how this works, let's examine two consecutive statements of financial position (as at December 31) of two individuals, John Goodboy (Table 3.1) and John Badboy (Table 3.2). Table 3.1 shows that John Goodboy obtained $21,000 from different sources (cash inflows) and used $21,000 (cash outflows) to purchase different assets and to pay several loans. As shown in the table and as mentioned earlier, the inflows of cash equals the outflows of cash.

In the "Cash Inflows" column, it shows that John cashed in a term deposit and borrowed a little from the Royal Bank, The Bay, and Sears. However, the major portion of the cash inflow was provided by equity ($16,400). This is the surplus (like profit) that John had left over from his salary after paying off the living expenses he incurred during the year. For example, he could have earned $60,000 in salary and spent $43,600 for living expenses (e.g., rent, food, entertainment, hydro).

As shown in the "Cash Outflows" column, John made some renovations to his house, and bought a trailer, a car, and some furniture. In addition, he paid off part of his debts to Royal Trust, MasterCard, and his brother-in-law. As shown in

Table 3.1 John Goodboy's Statements of Financial Position

In $	2010	2009	Cash Inflows	Cash Outflows
Assets				
House	70,000	68,000	—	2,000
Trailer	8,000	—	—	8,000
Car	9,000	6,000	—	3,000
Furniture	4,000	2,000	—	2,000
Term deposits	1,000	2,000	1,000	—
Cash in bank	3,000	1,000		2,000
Total Assets	**95,000**	**79,000**		
Equity	38,100	21,700	16,400	—
Liabilities				
Royal Trust	48,000	50,000	—	2,000
Royal Bank	5,000	2,000	3,000	—
MasterCard	1,000	2,000	—	1,000
The Bay	1,000	500	500	—
Sears	900	800	100	—
Brother-in-law	1,000	2,000	—	1,000
Total Liabilities	**56,900**	**57,300**		
Total Equity and Liabilities	**95,000**	**79,000**	**21,000**	**21,000**

Table 3.1, John actually disbursed $15,000 in cash to buy different assets: renovations to his house ($2,000), a trailer ($8,000), a car ($3,000), and some furniture ($2,000).

The following shows what John Goodboy had to do to finance the purchase of these four assets for $15,000. An amount of $15,400 came from his personal funding, called internal sources, such as the surplus he had left over from his salary after paying off his living expenses and term deposits. Even though John was able to purchase $15,000 worth of assets, he had enough to reduce his overall outstanding debt by $400. Here is the breakdown.

Internal Cash Flows (personal funding)	**Provided by**	**Used in**	**Difference**
Term deposits	$1,000	—	
Cash in the bank	—	$2,000	
Equity (salary less expenses)	16,400	—	
Total	$17,400	$2,000	$15,400
External Cash Flows (from debt)			
Royal Trust	—	2,000	
Royal Bank	3,000	—	
MasterCard	—	1,000	
The Bay	500	—	
Sears	100	—	
Brother-in-law	—	1,000	
Total	$3,600	$4,000	$ (400)
Cash Inflows Grand Total			$15,000

As shown in Figure 3.1, John obtained $15,400 in cash from internal sources in order to buy these assets. As indicated earlier, John did not require any financing from external sources like a bank or a mortgage company; in fact, he reduced his overall debts by $400.

John Badboy's financial position, shown in Table 3.2, gives a different picture. The asset accounts show a net increase of $25,100 between 2009 and 2010, to $104,100, with a corresponding total increase in the equity and liability accounts. This is $9,100 more than John Goodboy's $95,000 amount in total assets for the year 2010. The main difference, however, lies in the way that John Badboy financed the purchase of the additional $25,100 assets. In total, he required $28,000 to buy the following: installation of new windows in his house ($10,000), a trailer ($10,000), a car ($6,000),

Figure 3.1 John Goodboy's Inflows and Outflows of Cash

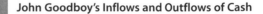

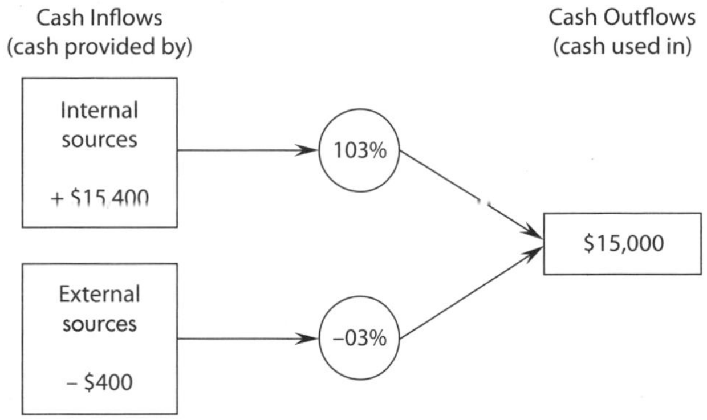

and some furniture ($2,000). As shown, John Badboy's inflows of cash to buy these different assets were obtained from Royal Trust, the Royal Bank, MasterCard, The Bay, Sears, and his brother-in-law.

Table 3.2 John Badboy's Statements of Financial Position

In $	2010	2009	Cash Inflows	Cash Outflows
Assets				
House	78,000	68,000	—	10,000
Trailer	10,000	—	—	10,000
Car	12,000	6,000	—	6,000
Furniture	4,000	2,000	—	2,000
Term deposits	—	2,000	2,000	—
Cash in bank	100	1,000	900	—
Total Assets	**104,100**	**79,000**		
Equity	**22,700**	**21,700**	1,000	—
Liabilities				
Royal Trust	63,400	50,000	13,400	—
Royal Bank	4,000	2,000	2,000	—
MasterCard	6,000	2,000	4,000	—
The Bay	2,000	500	1,500	—
Sears	3,000	800	2,200	
Brother-in-law	3,000	2,000	1,000	
Total Liabilities	**81,400**	**57,300**		
Total Equity and Liabilities	**104,100**	**79,000**	**28,000**	**28,000**

The following shows what John Badboy had to do to finance the purchase of these four assets valued at $28,000. As shown, $3,900 came from his own personal funding while $24,100 came from external sources or lenders.

Internal Cash Flows (personal funding)	**Provided by**	**Used in**	**Difference**
Term deposits	$2,000	—	—
Cash in the bank	$900	—	—
Equity (salary less expenses)	1,000	—	—
Total	$3,900	—	$3,900
External Cash Flow (from debt)			
Royal Trust	$13,400	—	
Royal Bank	2,000	—	
MasterCard	4,000	—	
The Bay	1,500	—	
Sears	2,200	—	
Brother-in-law	1,000	—	
Total	$24,100		$24,100
Cash Inflow Grand Total			$28,000

As shown in Figure 3.2, in order to buy these assets John Badboy obtained the cash almost entirely from external sources—to be exact, $24,100, or 86.1% of the total. Only $3,900 was generated internally, by withdrawing money from his bank and term deposits, and a small amount of equity, that is, the surplus between his salary and living expenses. John Badboy is spending almost every dollar that he earns! If he continues this practice year after year, it will not be long before he finds himself in a severe financial crunch.

Figure 3.2 **John Badboy's Inflows and Outflows of Cash**

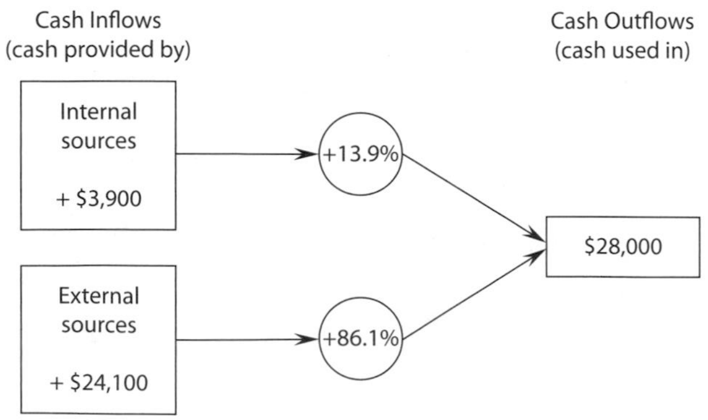

Self-Test Exercise No. 3.1

Identifying the Inflows and the Outflows of Cash

By using CompuTech's financial statements, identify whether the following changes are considered cash inflows or cash outflows.

	2010	2009	Cash Inflows	Cash Outflows
Property, plant, and equipment	$210,000	$170,000		40,000
Trade receivables	45,000	35,000		10,000
Cash and cash equivalents	21,000	15,000		6,000
Long-term borrowings	50,000	60,000	10,000	
Short-term borrowings	35,000	30,000		5,000

Cash Flow Analysis

2 Learning Objective

Analyze cash flows by comparing two consecutive statements of financial position.

Before presenting the structure of the statement of cash flows, let's examine the key drivers related to the cash inflows and the cash outflows and some of the basic rules that can help determine what constitutes a cash inflow and a cash outflow

KEY CASH FLOW DRIVERS

Cash inflows
These include profit for the year, proceeds from sale of non-current assets, proceeds from sale of investment securities, and obtaining loans or new equity.

Cash outflows
These include a loss from operation, the purchase of non-current assets, and the purchase of investment securities.

As shown in Table 3.3, some of the more important **cash inflows** include profit for the year, sale of non-current assets, sale of investment securities, increase in long-term borrowings, increase in share capital, and decrease in working capital accounts (e.g., trade receivables and inventories). **Cash outflows** take place when a company experiences a loss, purchases non-current assets, buys investment securities, reduces its long-term borrowings, increases its working capital accounts, or pays dividends.

In the News 3.1 gives an example of how a reduction in profit, a key cash inflow driver, can hamper a company's projects.

Table 3.3 Key Cash Flow Drivers

Cash Inflows (cash provided by)	Cash Outflows (cash used for)
• Profit for the year	• Loss for the year
• Proceeds from sale of non-current assets	• Purchase of non-current assets
• Proceeds from sale of investments	• Purchase of investment securities
• Proceeds from long-term borrowings	• Payment of long-term borrowings
• Proceeds from issue of share capital	• Purchase of share capital
• Decrease in working capital accounts	• Increase in working capital accounts

In The News [3.1]

How a Reduction in Profit Can Hamper a Company's Cash Flow, and Ultimately, Stall Its Capital Projects

Cash flow is much like a reservoir: There are inflows and outflows of cash, and the tap is the device that regulates the speed. At times, management has to open or close the cash flow apparatus, depending on how fast business activities can generate funds that are often needed to start or complete capital projects.

This is what happened at Nexen Inc. Its multi-million dollar capital project came to a halt during the middle of 2009 as a result of dramatic reductions in sales and profitability. The impact of a slowdown in general economic activities caused Nexen, Canada's fourth-leading independent oil explorer, to put the brakes on its $6.1-billion Long Lake project. As a result, the company's profit performance during the second quarter of 2009 dropped by as much as 95%. To be specific, Nexen's Long Lake project earned only $20 million (or four cents a share), dropping from $380 million (or 72 cents a share) from the previous year. The suspension of this capital project caused a series of negative impacts on the company's activities, including its drive for generating more cash flows, which resulted in putting a "freezing effect" on the funds that were needed to continue drilling. In fact, cash inflows dropped to $443 million (or 85 cents a share) from a projected $946 million (or $1.78 a share). All of this was due in large measure to a reduction in oil prices by as much as 52% from the previous year. When Nexen's revenue drops to $1.2 billion, down from $2.07 billion in the previous year, it does not require an "exceptional intellect" to realize the effect that this would have on cash flow performance.

Source: Adapted from Reuters, "Nexen profit, cash flow plummet," *Ottawa Citizen*, July 17, 2009, p. F3. For updates on Nexen's capital project activities, see www.Nexeninc.com.

COMPARATIVE STATEMENTS OF FINANCIAL POSITION

Consecutive statements of financial position Consecutive statements of financial position help to determine whether a change in each account is a cash inflow or a cash outflow.

Table 3.4 presents Eastman Technologies Inc.'s **consecutive statements of financial position** for the years 2009 and 2008 (as at December 31). By placing these two consecutive statements of financial position side by side, we can analyze Eastman's cash inflows and cash outflows, or the cash flow changes that took place between these two accounting periods.

Table 3.4 presents a list of all cash inflows and cash outflows in Eastman's major accounts listed under assets, equity, and liabilities. The table shows how the cash flows emerged in Eastman's consecutive statements of financial position. Eastman obtained $352,000 from different accounts and used the same amount to purchase assets and increase some of the working capital accounts. These working capital accounts (current assets and current liabilities) are shaded and will be explained later (page 127) as to: (1) the accounts included in the *adjustments in non-cash working capital accounts*, and (2) why they are part of *operating activities.* We will analyze, in the next section, the significance and meaning of each change in cash flows shown in Eastman's financial statements. But first, let's examine some simple guidelines that can help determine

Table 3.4 **Comparative Statements of Financial Position**

Eastman Technologies Inc.
Cash Inflows and Cash Outflows
(in $)

Assets	2009	2008	Cash Inflows	Cash Outflows
Non-current assets (at cost)	1,340,000	1,050,000		290,000
Accumulated depreciation	(140,000)	(100,000)	40,000	—
Non-current assets (net)	1,200,000	950,000		
Current assets				
Inventories	218,000	185,000	—	33,000
Trade receivables	300,000	280,000	—	20,000
Prepaid expenses	60,000	55,000	—	5,000
Cash and cash equivalents	22,000	18,000	—	4,000
Total current assets	600,000	538,000	—	—
Total assets	1,800,000	1,488,000	—	—
Equity				
Share capital	300,000	285,000	15,000	—
Retained earnings	255,000	205,000	50,000	—
Total equity	555,000	490,000		
Liabilities				
Long-term borrowings	800,000	600,000	200,000	—
Current liabilities				
Trade and other payables	195,000	175,000	20,000	—
Notes payable	150,000	135,000	15,000	—
Accrued expenses	20,000	18,000	2,000	—
Taxes payable	80,000	70,000	10,000	—
Total current liabilities	445,000	398,000	—	—
Total equity and liabilities	1,800,000	1,488,000	352,000	352,000

Note: Here is the reason why the inflows equals the outflows: If you buy something, you need to get the same amount of cash from somewhere!

whether a change in a statement of financial position account is sometimes considered a cash inflow while in other cases, a cash outflow.

GUIDELINES FOR IDENTIFYING CASH INFLOWS AND CASH OUTFLOWS

Cash inflows and cash outflows are associated with specific types of changes in a statement of financial position. Figure 3.3 shows some basic guidelines to follow in

Figure 3.3 **Guidelines for Identifying Whether an Account Is a Cash Inflow or a Cash Outflow**

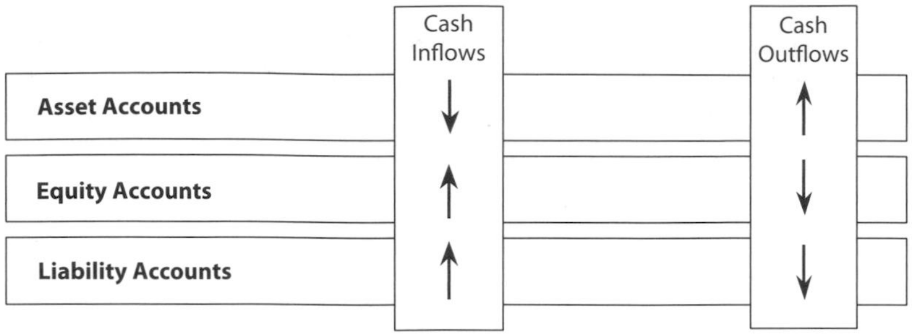

order to determine whether an asset, an equity, or a liability account is a cash inflow or cash outflow.

Cash inflow guidelines
A cash inflow takes place when there is a decrease in an asset account or an increase in an equity or liability account.

Cash inflows (or **cash provided by**) take place when there is:

- A decrease in asset accounts;
- An increase in the equity accounts (share capital or retained earnings increase due to profit from operations); or
- An increase in liability accounts.

Cash outflow guidelines
A cash outflow takes place when there is an increase in an asset account or a decrease in an equity or liability account.

Cash outflows (or **cash used for**) take place when there is:

- An increase in asset accounts;
- A decrease in equity (dividends paid or retained earnings decrease due to loss from operations); or
- A decrease in liability accounts.

By applying these guidelines to Eastman Technologies Inc.'s financial statements for the years 2009 and 2008, we can easily determine the company's cash inflows and cash outflows (see Table 3.4). The inflows and outflows of cash for these accounts are listed in Table 3.5. As shown, the cash inflow and cash outflow guidelines identified earlier have been applied. The table shows that Eastman obtained $352,000 worth of cash from eight different accounts (e.g., increase in share capital, long-term borrowings, trade, and other payables) and used the cash for five different accounts (e.g., increase in non-current assets, inventories, trade receivables).

Now that we have a basic understanding of the meaning of cash inflows and cash outflows, and how they can be identified, let's turn to the structure of the statement of cash flows and see how it is prepared.

Table 3.5 **Cash Inflows and Cash Outflows**

Eastman Technologies Inc.
for the year ended 2009
(in $)

Cash Inflows	
Increase in accumulated depreciation	40,000
Increase in share capital	15,000
Increase in retained earnings	50,000
Increase in long-term borrowings	200,000
Increase in trade and other payables	20,000
Increase in notes payable	15,000
Increase in accrued expenses	2,000
Increase in taxes payable	10,000
Total cash inflows	352,000
Cash Outflows	
Increase in non-current assets	290,000
Increase in inventories	33,000
Increase in trade receivables	20,000
Increase in prepaid expenses	5,000
Increase in cash and cash equivalents	4,000
Total cash outflows	352,000

Self-Test Exercise No. 3.2

Pinpointing the Cash Inflows and Cash Outflows

On the basis of Len and Joan Miller's personal statements of financial position shown below, identify whether each account is a cash inflow or a cash outflow.

	2010	**2009**	**Cash Inflows**	**Cash Outflows**
Assets				
House	$205,000	$136,000	______	______
Car	22,000	6,000	______	______
Furniture	8,500	7,000	______	______
RRSPs	30,000	20,000	______	______
Savings bonds	5,000	4,000	______	______
Short-term deposits	2,000	2,000	______	______
Total assets	$272,500	$175,000		
Equity	$111,000	$80,000	______	______
Liabilities				
Mortgage	112,000	79,000	______	______
Car loan	24,000	3,000	______	______
Toronto Dominion Bank	21,000	11,000	______	______
Amex	4,500	2,000	______	______
Total liabilities	161,500	95,000	______	______
Total equity and liabilities	$272,500	$175,000	$______	______

The Statement of Cash Flows

3 Learning Objective

Explain the basic structure of the statement of cash flows.

Cash budget
A treasury function that determines the cash flow of business at the micro level to determine the level of liquidity.

Let's begin by saying that cash flows can be examined at two levels: micro and macro. At the *micro level*, cash flows looks at short-term operating statements such as the monthly cash receipts and disbursements incurred by a business. The financial tool used to determine cash flows at this level is called the **cash budget**. This is one aspect of the treasury function. The objective is to ensure that the company has enough cash on hand to pay the company's ongoing bills (e.g., salaries, purchases, advertising, etc.) and current borrowings as they come due. On the other hand, if the company has enough reserves in cash, the treasurer would invest the surplus in short-term securities. This type of analysis and decision-making has to do with liquidity.

At the *macro level*, cash flow deals with solvency and the ability of a business to do the following:

1. Generate cash from its operations (profit for the year plus depreciation/amortization and the adjustments in non-cash working capital accounts).
2. Pay its long-term borrowings and dividends.
3. Purchase property, plant, and equipment (capital assets included in the capital budget).

While the operating cash receipts and disbursements show the liquidity performance of a business, the information dealing with solvency and liquidity appears in the statement of cash flows. It helps to assess a company's ability to generate cash internally, to repay debts, to reinvest in capital assets, and to pay dividends. The information is relevant to operating activities, financing activities, and investing activities.

Preparing the statement of cash flows is a relatively complex task, but interpreting it is somewhat easy and of great importance to stakeholders. To prepare this statement, the financial information has to be drawn from: (1) the statement of financial position, (2) the statement of income, and (3) the statement of changes in equity (e.g., retained earnings).

Three key steps involved in the preparation of Eastman Technologies Inc.'s statement of cash flows are as follows:

1. The cash inflows and the cash outflows must be identified. This was already done and presented in Table 3.4 on page 121.
2. The list of accounts affecting the adjustments of the non-cash working capital accounts must also be prepared. These are the current asset and current liability accounts shaded in Table 3.4 on page 121 and listed in Table 3.7 on page 127.
3. By using the information obtained in steps 1 and 2, the statement of cash flows can be prepared (see Table 3.9 on page 129). The table identifies from which statement (statement of income, statement of changes in equity, and statement of financial position) the accounts producing cash inflows and cash outflows are drawn.

The cash flow statement presented in Table 3.9 lists these cash inflows and cash outflows under three main headings:

- Operating activities (including adjustments in non-cash working capital accounts)
- Financing activities
- Investing activities

Let's now continue the several steps involved in the process of preparing the statement of cash flows presented in Table 3.9.

OPERATING ACTIVITIES

Operating activities The portion of the statement of cash flows that shows how much cash was provided by the business itself (e.g., profit for the year, depreciation/amortization, and adjustments in non-cash working capital accounts).

Operating activities deal with the principal revenue-producing activities generated by a business itself (internally generated cash). There are three important cash-generated items in this section: profit for the year, depreciation/amortization, and adjustments in non-cash working capital accounts.

Profit for the Year and Depreciation/Amortization

Eastman Technologies Inc. earned $97,500 in profit in 2009 (see Table 3.6). By adding back $40,000 in depreciation to this figure, the company generated $137,500 in cash. Depreciation is added back to profit for the year as this account is only a book entry and does not represent a "real" cash outflow like paying expenses such as salaries and leases.

In the News 3.2 gives an example about how a recession-driven economy can affect an organization's operating performance (bottom line) and, ultimately, cash flow generated from operating activities.

Table 3.6 Statement of Income

Eastman Technologies Inc.
for the year ended 2009
(in $)

Revenue	2,500,000
Cost of sales	(1,900,000)
Gross profit	600,000
Other income/expenses (net)	(15,000)
Expenses	(350,000)
Depreciation	(40,000)
Total	(405,000)
Profit before taxes	195,000
Income tax expense	(97,500)
Profit for the year	97,500

In The News [3.2]

How a Recession-Driven Economy Can Affect Cash Flows

Recession is a word that describes "a period of temporary economic decline during which trade and industrial activities are reduced." It is a word that causes great fear or nervousness amongst leaders of profit-driven and even NFP organizations. In fact, this type of gloomy economic movement often constrains individuals or businesses to grow.

One of Ottawa's finest cultural institutions, the National Arts Centre (NAC), was one of hundreds of organizations in Canada that faced serious drops in sales performance due to the 2008 recession-driven economy. Expected lowered sales and a projected $3.8-million budget shortfall forced the NAC to cut back on its operating budget and in the process eliminate 40 jobs over a two-year period. Also, the economic slowdown compelled the NAC to cut back on its programming activities and some core administrative services. As pointed out by Jayne Watson, the NAC's director of communications, "The impact of the recession has affected our business lines," from parking to restaurant sales. It also had serious repercussions on catering, box office sales, and even fundraising.

Source: Adapted from Cassadra Drudi, "Recession forces NAC to cut up to 40 jobs," *Ottawa Citizen*, June 10, 2009, p. C1. To learn more about the National Arts Centre, visit www.nac-can.ca.

Adjustments in Non-Cash Working Capital Accounts

The statement of cash flows does not usually give a detailed listing of the cash flows generated by a company's individual working capital accounts (current assets and current liabilities). However, because working capital accounts are an important element

Self-Test Exercise No. 3.3

Making the Adjustments in Non-Cash Working Capital Accounts Statement

With the following accounts, drawn from CompuTech's statement of financial position, (1) identify those that are considered *working capital accounts* and (2) prepare the adjustments in non-cash working capital accounts statement.

Accounts	2010	2009
Trade and other payables	$20,000	$17,000
Retained earnings	58,000	25,000
Long-term borrowings	50,000	60,000
Trade receivables	45,000	35,000
Property, plant, and equipment	210,000	170,000
Inventories	65,000	50,000
Cash and cash equivalents	21,000	15,000
Accumulated depreciation/amortization	78,000	38,000
Short-term borrowings	40,000	35,000
Prepaid expenses	5,000	5,000

Table 3.7 Adjustments in Non-Cash Working Capital Accounts

Eastman Technologies Inc.
for the year ended 2009
(in $)

Cash Inflows			
Increase in trade and other payables	20,000		Drawn from working capital accounts in the statement of financial position, that is, current assets and current liabilities
Increase in notes payable	15,000		
Increase in accrued expenses	2,000		
Increase in taxes payable	10,000	47,000	
Cash Outflows			
Increase in inventories	33,000		
Increase in trade receivables	20,000		
Increase in prepaid expenses	5,000	58,000	
Adjustments in non-cash working capital accounts		11,000	

Adjustments in non-cash working capital accounts
The cash flow provided (or used) by working capital accounts such as trade receivables, inventories, and trade and other payables.

in the management of a company's cash flow, the company will produce a detailed statement called the **adjustments in non-cash working capital accounts** (see Table 3.7). This statement shows whether individual working capital accounts are generating cash (cash inflows) or using cash (cash outflows). Although a company's net increase in working capital may not change dramatically, this does not mean that all accounts are under control. Non-cash working capital accounts include all current assets (excluding cash), and all current liability accounts. These accounts are all drawn from the statement of financial position.

The seven working capital accounts shown in Table 3.7 are drawn from the statement of financial position (see the shaded portion of the statement of financial position in Table 3.4 on page 121) and show a net cash outflow of $11,000. This means that the business used $11,000 over the past 12-month period to carry on its day-to-day business operations. In this particular case, by adding back depreciation ($40,000) to the profit for the year ($97,500), the statement of income generated $137,500 in cash, and the working capital accounts shown on the statement of financial position produced an $11,000 cash outflow (see Table 3.9 on page 129). As shown in the upper portion of the statement of cash flows under the heading "Operating Activities" in Table 3.9, the total cash generated from the business's operations amounts to $126,500.

Financing activities
Portion of the statement of cash flows that shows how much cash was provided (or used) from external sources (e.g., proceeds from the issue of shares or borrowings, repaying long-term debt, or payment of dividends).

FINANCING ACTIVITIES

Financing activities deal with the proceeds received from the sale of shares, the repayment of long-term borrowings, the borrowing of long-term debt, and the

Table 3.8 Statement of Retained Earnings

Eastman Technologies Inc.
for the year ended 2009
(in $)

Retained earnings (beginning of year)		205,000
Profit for the year	97,500	
Dividends	(47,500)	(50,000)
Retained earnings (end of year)		255,000

payment of dividends. With the exception of the payment of dividends, which is obtained from the statement of changes in equity (retained earnings), this information is drawn from the SFP. Cash inflows and cash outflows under financing activities deal with the *long-term financing transactions*, that is, those appearing on the middle section of the statement of financial position under the heading "Equity and non-current liabilities." As shown in Table 3.9 under the heading "Financing Activities," Eastman Technologies Inc. obtained a total of $167,500. First, the company paid $47,500 in dividends (see Table 3.8); second, it borrowed $200,000 from its long-term lenders; and finally, the shareholders invested $15,000 in the business.

All accounts appearing under operating and financing activities generated $294,000 in cash. Now, what did Eastman do with this money? The next section answers this question.

In the News 3.3 gives an example about how a company could pay off its debts by simply raising cash from a common share issue.

In The News [3.3]

One Way to Pay Off a Debt Is by Selling More Shares

As the expression goes, "There's more than one way to skin a cat." The same applies in business when a company wants to raise cash. It can obtain additional funds by increasing its earnings, by reducing its working capital requirements, by increasing its debt, or even by selling more shares.

Imax Corporation, producer of the world's largest cinema screen, the IMAX screen (covering an area as much as eight stories high and the most widely used system for large-format, special-venue film presentations), decided to pay down its debt by as much at $70.1 million. It did so by going through a public offering and selling more than 9.8 million common shares at a price of $7.15 a share. The Canadian-based company intends to use the net proceeds to reduce its debt, as well as for some general corporate purposes.

Source: Adapted from "Imax expects $70.1 M from share offering," *Ottawa Citizen*, June 3, 2009, p. D3. To learn more about Imax, go to www.Imax.com and click on "Company Info."

Table 3.9 Statement of Cash Flows

Eastman Technologies Inc.
for the year ended 2009
(in $)

		Source Document
Operating Activities		
Profit for the year	97,500.00	Statement of Income
Depreciation	40,000.00	Statement of income
Adjustments in non-cash working capital	(11,000.00)*	Statement of financial position
Net cash from operating activities	126,500.00	
Financing activities		
Payment of dividends	(47,500.00)	Statement of changes in equity
Long-term borrowings	200,000.00	Statement of financial position
Share capital	15,000.00	Statement of financial position
Net cash from financing activities	167,500.00	
Investing activities		
Purchase of non-current assets	(290,000.00)	Statement of financial position
Increase in cash	(4,000.00)	Statement of financial position
Cash at beginning of year	18,000.00	
Cash at end of year	22,000.00	

* Numbers with brackets signify an outflow of cash.

INVESTING ACTIVITIES

Investing activities That portion of the statement of cash flows that shows how much cash was provided (or used) to buy or sell non-current assets (e.g., purchase or proceeds from the sale of a building).

Investing activities deal with the acquisition and disposal of assets shown in the upper portion of the statement of financial position (non-current assets). This section shows the cash flow provided by or used for buying or selling non-current assets. As shown in Table 3.9, Eastman invested $290,000 for the purchase of non-current assets.

Self-Test Exercise No. 3.4

Identifying the Cash Flow Statement Activities

Indicate under which activity (operating, financing, or investing) the following accounts belong in the statement of cash flows:

	Activity
Notes receivable (short-term)	____________
RRSP	____________
Computers	____________
Long-term borrowings	____________
Profit for the year	____________
Notes payable (short-term)	____________
Depreciation	____________
Inventories	____________
Car	____________

Self-Test Exercise No. 3.5

The Statement of Cash Flows

From the following financial statements, prepare CompuTech Sales and Service's statement of cash flows for the year 2010.

CompuTech Sales and Services
Statement of Income
for the year ended 2010
(in $)

Revenue	420,000
Cost of sales	(209,000)
Gross profit	211,000
Other income	5,000
Costs/expenses	(156,000)
Finance costs	(14,000)
Total	(165,000)
Profit before taxes	46,000
Income tax expense	(13,000)
Profit for the year	33,000

CompuTech Sales and Services
Statements of Financial Position
as at December 31
(in $)

	2010	**2009**
Non-current assets		
Property, plant, and equipment	210,000	170,000
Accumulated depreciation/amortization	(78,000)	(38,000)
Total non-current assets	132,000	132,000
Current assets		
Inventories	65,000	50,000
Trade receivables	45,000	35,000
Prepaid expenses	5,000	5,000
Cash and cash equivalents	21,000	15,000
Total current assets	136,000	105,000
Total assets	268,000	237,000
Equity		
Share capital	100,000	100,000
Retained earnings	58,000	25,000
Total equity	158,000	125,000
Long-term borrowings	50,000	60,000
Current liabilities		
Trade and other payables	20,000	17,000
Short-term borrowings	35,000	30,000
Current portion of long-term borrowings	5,000	5,000
Total current liabilities	60,000	52,000
Total equity and liabilities	268,000	237,000

As indicated before, both operating and financing activities generated $294,000, and the company used $290,000 for buying the non-current assets shown in the investing activities section. In total, the net amount from these three activities gives a surplus of $4,000 for a net increase in the company's bank account. As shown in the company's 2010 and 2009 statements of financial position (Table 3.4), the cash and cash equivalents account increased from $18,000 to $22,000.

Statement of Cash Flows for Not-For-Profit Organizations

4 Learning Objective

Describe the structure of the statement of cash flows for not-for-profit organizations.

In Chapter 2, the structure and contents of NFP organizations' statement of financial position, statement of operations, and statement of changes in net assets were explained for the fictitious NFP organization called the Ontario Foundation for Community Care. The following paragraphs describe the fourth financial statement, the statement of cash flows.

The NFP organization's statement of cash flows reports the total of the cash generated from operations by the NFP organization and the elements of cash flows that took place in financing and investing activities. This statement complements the other financial statements. As shown in the Ontario Foundation for Community Care's statement of cash flows below, the first segment shows the inflows and the outflows of cash generated by operations. As shown, the Ontario Foundation for Community Care generated a net inflow of cash in the amount of $52,000. This amount includes the $40,000 surplus and $20,000 in depreciation; both amounts are drawn from the statement of operations (see page 92). The net cash inflows also include an amount of $8,000 for adjustments in non-cash working capital accounts. This amount is the product of the following accounts shown on the statement of financial position (see page 90):

Cash Outflows		
Increase in trade receivables	$(15,000)	
Increase in grants receivable	(5,000)	$(20,000)
Cash Inflows		
Increase in trade and other payables	$10,000	
Increase in accrued liabilities	2,000	12,000
Net cash outflows		$(8,000)

This statement illustrates the organization's ability to generate cash internally in order to sustain its operations, that is, providing its services and meeting its contractual obligations. The segment dealing with cash flows from financing and investing activities ($47,000) shows the cash flow that was received from external sources ($38,000 and $40,000) that was used to finance the acquisition of buildings and equipment ($98,000) and investments ($27,000).

Ontario Foundation for Community Care Statement of Cash Flows for the year ended December 31, 2010 (in $)	
Cash flows from operating activities	
Excess of revenues over expenses	40,000
Depreciation of buildings and equipment	20,000
Adjustments in non-cash working capital accounts	(8,000)
Net cash generated through operating activities	**52,000**
Cash flows from financing and investing activities	
Purchase of buildings and equipment	(98,000)
Purchase of investments	(27,000)
Long-term borrowings	38,000
Contributions from cash endowments	40,000
Net cash used in financing and investing activities	**(47,000)**
Net decrease (increase) in cash and term deposits	**(5,000)**
Cash and term deposits, beginning of year	25,000
Cash and term deposits, end of year	30,000

REALITY FINANCIAL SNAPSHOTS

The following pages present the statement of cash flows of the for-profit organization, Enbridge, and the NFP organization, The Ottawa Hospital (TOH).

ENBRIDGE[1]

Enbridge's annual report includes the statements of cash flows for the years 2006 to 2008. The following outlines the company's cash flows for these three operating years. As shown, Enbridge's operating activities generated a total of $4,054.6 million. This amount was used to finance the purchase of $6,679.3 million in long-term investments and additions to property, plant, and equipment. To finance the rest of the purchase of investments, Enbridge borrowed from different sources an amount of $3,012.5 million, and its cash balance increased by $387.8 million. Enbridge's Statements of Cash Flows contains numerous footnotes that are included in the annual report and can be viewed on its website (www.enbridge.com).

(in $mil)	2008	2007	2006	Total
Operating activities	1,387.7	1,351.6	1,315.3	4,054.6
Investing activities	(2,852.9)	(2,228.8)	(1,597.6)	(6,679.3)
Financing activities	1,840.2	904.2	268.1	3,012.5
(Increase) decrease in cash	(375.0)	(27.0)	14.2	(387.8)

The following gives the details of Enbridge's Consolidated Statements of Cash Flows for the three activities.

1. Enbridge Inc., *2008 Enbridge Annual Report*. Found at: http://www.enbridge.com/investor/financialInformation/reportsFilings/pdf/2008-annual-report-en.pdf.

(in $mil) Year ended December 31	2008	2007	2006
Cash provided by operating activities			
Earnings	1,327.7	707.1	622.3
Depreciation and amortization	658.5	596.9	587.4
Unrealized (gains)/losses on derivative instruments	(120.3)	32.3	—
Equity earnings in excess of cash distributions	(81.6)	(35.2)	(54.2)
Gain on reduction of ownership interest	(12.3)	(33.9)	—
Gain on sale of investment in CLH	(694.6)	—	—
Gain on sale of investment in Inuvik Gas	(5.7)	—	—
Future income taxes	258.1	40.8	(21.0)
Goodwill and asset impairment losses	22.7	—	—
Allowance for equity funds used during construction	(58.9)	(15.1)	(1.5)
Non-controlling interests	55.7	45.9	54.7
Other	48.7	19.2	3.9
Changes in operating assets and liabilities	(10.3)	(6.4)	123.7
	1,387.7	1,351.6	1,315.3
Investing activities			
Acquisitions	—	—	(101.4)
Long-term investments	(659.3)	(20.3)	(362.3)
Sale of investment in CLH	1,369.0	—	—
Settlement of investment in Inuvik Gas	13.5		—
Settlement of CLH hedges	(47.0)	—	—
Additions to property, plant, and equipment	(3,635.7)	(2,299.2)	(1,205.9)
Affiliate loans, net	—	15.6	28.0
Change in construction payable	106.6	75.1	44.0
	(2,852.9)	(2,228.8)	(1,597.6)
Financing activities			
Net change in short-term borrowings	329.0	(262.3)	(266.9)
Net change in commercial paper and credit facility draws	750.8	336.8	188.2
Net change in non-recourse short-term debt	31.6	43.1	57.7
Debenture and term note issues	497.8	1,342.2	1,125.0
Debenture and term note repayments	(602.0)	(634.5)	(400.0)
Net change in Southern Lights project financing	1,238.3	—	—
Non-recourse long-term debt issues	6.4	14.4	2.8
Non-recourse long-term debt repayments	(65.1)	(58.8)	(60.5)
Distributions to non-controlling interests	(9.9)	(18.2)	(31.3)
Common shares issued	29.4	583.8	63.1
Preferred share dividends	(6.9)	(6.9)	(6.9)
Common share dividends	(359.2)	(435.4)	(403.1)
	1,840.2	904.2	268.1

Increase (decrease) in cash and cash equivalents	375.0	27.0	(14.2)
Cash and cash equivalents at beginning of year	166.7	139.7	153.9
Cash and cash equivalents at end of year	541.7	166.7	139.7

THE OTTAWA HOSPITAL[2]

TOH's Statements of Cash Flows is structured differently from those prepared by for-profit organizations. The NFP organizations' statement of cash flows contains two main activities: (1) operating activities and (2) financing and investing activities. As shown below, cash provided by operating activities over the two-year period amounted to $64,029 thousand and the net amount in financing and investing activities totalled $42,124 thousand over the two-year period; the remaining amount of $21,905 thousand was used to decrease the bank indebtedness. TOH's Statements of Cash Flows contains numerous footnotes that are included in the annual report and can be viewed on its website (www.ottawahospital.on.ca).

The following presents the hospital's Statements of Cash Flows for the years 2008 and 2007.

Year ended March 31 (in $000s)	**2008**	**2007**
Cash provided by (used for)		
Operating activities:		
Excess of revenue over expenses	7,301	5,677
Items not involving cash:		
Amortization of capital assets	35,527	33,046
Amortization of deferred contributions related to capital assets	(16,633)	(13,851)
Loss on disposal of assets	14	—
Net increase in employee future benefits	2,014	2,762
Net change in non-cash working capital	(21,481)	29,653
	6,742	57,287
Financing and investment activities:		
Purchase of capital assets	(63,688)	(64,502)
Net increase in capital grants receivable	(8,107)	(1,966)
Deferred contributions related to capital assets received	27,009	49,485
Increase in deferred contributions related to trust funds	1,487	5,710
Increase in payable to TOH Residence Corporation	660	715
Net decrease in investments	3,958	7,115
	(38,681)	(3,443)
Net decrease (increase) in bank indebtedness	(31,939)	53,844
Bank indebtedness, beginning of year	(19,355)	(73,199)
Bank indebtedness, end of year	(51,294)	(19,355)

2. *2008 Ottawa Hospital Annual Report.* Found at: http://www.ottawahospital.on.ca/about/reports/FS2008-e.pdf.

[DECISION-MAKING IN ACTION]

The CEO of Oxford Inc. is contemplating the possibility of investing $1.0 million in non-current assets in 2010. Before presenting the capital budget plan to the board of directors, he wants to know how much money would be generated internally, before pinpointing the amount of cash that would have to be raised from investors (e.g., long-term lenders and shareholders).

To do this, the controller had to go through the following seven steps:

1. All operating managers had to prepare their respective operating budgets (e.g., manufacturing, marketing, human resources, engineering);
2. The controller then consolidated these operating budgets and prepare:
   - The company's master budget; and
   - A projected statement of income for the year 2010 (see Table 3.10).
3. The controller prepared a detailed listing of all capital projects estimated at $1.0 million (e.g., acquisitions, purchase of equipment or machinery, plant expansion and/or modernization) that would be acquired or undertaken during the budget year (capital budget).
4. The treasurer identified the additional external sources of financing (in addition to internal sources) that would be required to finance:
   - The $1.0 million capital budget;

Table 3.10 **Oxford's Projected Statement of Income**

Oxford Inc.
for the year ended 2010
(in $)

Revenue	5,100,000
Cost of sales	(3,800,000)
Gross profit	**1,300,000**
Other income	22,000
Distribution costs	(270,000)
Administrative expenses	(270,000)
Depreciation	(60,000)
Finance costs	(50,000)
Total	**(628,000)**
Profit before taxes	672,000
Income tax expense	(260,000)
Profit for the year	**412,000**

- The working capital accounts (e.g., trade receivables, inventories); and
- The amount of money that will be paid in dividends (an amount of $155,674 shown in Table 3.11) during 2010.

5. The controller then prepared the company's monthly cash budget and the projected statement of financial position for the year 2010.
6. The controller compared individual accounts shown on the company's projected statement of financial position for 2010 to the 2009 accounts. This information identified the cash inflows and cash outflows for each account. (This information is shown on the right side of Table 3.12.)
7. The final step was the preparation of the projected statement of cash flows (Table 3.13). The cash flow changes between the two accounting periods generated from each activity are as follows:

– Operating activities:	$367,000
– Financing activities:	$644,326
– Investing activities:	($1,000,000)
– Change in the cash account:	($11,326)

As shown, about 37% of the investing activities would be financed by operating activities, the rest by financing activities.

By using the information contained in Table 3.13, the CEO will be able to inform the board of directors how much inflow of cash will be generated from the business itself (from operating activities) versus investors (financing activities) to finance the $1.0 million purchase of the property, plant, and equipment.

To many stakeholders, all businesses pivot around cash, and all decisions depend on the cash on hand. The statement of cash flows shows a company's cash flow performance. It shows how well Oxford performed in the past in terms of cash flows and how much cash the company should generate in the future to buy the non-current assets listed in the capital budget.

By looking at Table 3.13, the board of directors will have enough information to determine whether the business should proceed with the purchase of the $1.0 million worth of capital assets. The CEO should therefore be prepared to answer the following questions:

- Should operating managers redo their operating budgets in order to squeeze more cash from the business (more than the $412,000 profit)?

Table 3.11 Oxford's Projected Statement of Changes in Equity

Oxford Inc.
for the year ended 2010
(in $)

Retained earnings (beginning of year)		1,310,000
Profit for the year	412,000	
Dividends	(155,674)	256,326
Retained earnings (end of year)		1,566,326

Table 3.12 **Oxford's Comparative Statements of Financial Position**

Oxford Inc.
Statement of Sources and Uses of Funds
(in $)

Assets	Projected 2010	Year-end 2009	Cash Inflows	Cash Outflows
Non-current assets				
Property, plant, and equipment (at cost)	3,450,000	2,450,000	—	1,000,000
Accumulated depreciation	(710,000)	(650,000)	60,000	—
Property, plant, and equipment (net)	2,740,000	1,800,000		
Intangible assets	65,000	65,000	—	—
Total non-current assets	2,805,000	1,865,000		
Current assets				
Inventories	850,000	750,000	—	100,000
Trade receivables	550,000	450,000	—	100,000
Prepaid expenses	25,000	30,000	5,000	—
Marketable securities	50,000	50,000	—	—
Cash and cash equivalents	46,326	35,000	—	11,326
Total current assets	1,521,326	1,315,000		
Total assets	4,326,326	3,180,000		
Equity				
Share capital	500,000	400,000	100,000	—
Retained earnings	1,566,326	1,310,000	256,326	—
Total equity	2,066,326	1,710,000		
Liabilities				
Long-term borrowings	1, 600,000	900,000	700,000	—
Current liabilities				
Trade and other payables	170,000	130,000	40,000	—
Accrued expenses	50,000	50,000	—	—
Current portion of long-term debt	40,000	40,000	—	—
Short-term borrowings	400,000	350,000	50,000	—
Total current liabilities	660,000	570,000		
Total liabilities	2,260,000	1,470,000		
Total equity and liabilities	4,326,326	3,180,000	1,211,326	1,211,326

Table 3.13 **Oxford's Projected Statement of Cash Flows**

Oxford Inc.
for the year ended 2010
(in $)

Operating activities		
Profit for the year	412,000	
Adjustments		
Depreciation	60,000	
Adjustments in non-cash working capital accounts	(105,000)	
Net cash from operating activities		367,000
Financing activities		
Payment of dividends	(155,674)	
Long-term borrowings	700,000	
Share capital	100,000	
Cash flow from financing activities		644,326
Investing activities		
Purchase of property, plant, and equipment	(1,000,000)	
Cash flow from investing activities		(1,000,000)
Increase in cash		(11,326)
Cash at beginning of year	35,000	
Cash at end of year	46,000	
Adjustments in non-cash working capital accounts		
Cash inflows		
Trade and other payables	40,000	
Prepaid expenses	5,000	
Short-term borrowings	50,000	95,000
Cash outflows		
Inventories	(100,000)	
Trade receivables	(100,000)	(200,000)
Adjustments in non-cash working capital accounts		(105,000)

- Should operating managers examine whether more cash could be squeezed from working capital (e.g., trade receivables and inventories), where there is a net cash outflow in the amount of $105,000?
- Should Oxford pay less than the $155,674 amount in dividends? What impact would this have on the shareholders' views about Oxford?
- Will Oxford be able to raise the $700,000 from the long-term lenders? What's the cost of capital?
- Will Oxford be able to raise the $100,000 from the shareholders? Should the company ask for more or less?
- If Oxford is unable to obtain more cash from internal or external sources, should the company then cut back the $1.0 million amount in the capital budget? Where should the cuts take place? What impact will these cuts have on the business?

FINANCIAL SPREADSHEETS—EXCEL

Financial spreadsheets can help prepare projected statements of cash flows. Although accountants produce historical statements of cash flows and include them in annual reports or in other financial documents, the financial spreadsheets can produce two projected cash flow documents (output documents). The first document, called the statement of sources and uses of funds, presents a list of cash inflows and cash outflows for individual accounts between two consecutive statements of financial position for a period of two years. The second document is the statement of cash flows. It shows the cash inflows and the cash outflows grouped under four headings: operating activities, financing activities, investing activities, and the changes in the cash account for a period of two years. The most significant feature of these spreadsheets is that any change made by operating managers regarding improvements in working capital accounts (e.g., trade receivables, inventories) or efficiency gains in the statement of income as a result of changes in revenue or expense accounts can instantaneously be reflected in the statement of cash flows' output document. Managers can therefore readily determine whether sufficient cash can be generated by operating activities or how much cash will have to be raised from external sources to help finance the purchase of non-current assets recorded in investing activities.

Chapter Summary

1 Learning Objective

Explain the importance of managing cash flows.

Because the statement of income shows only that amount of revenue earned and expenses incurred between two dates, and the statement of financial position gives a picture only of the financial condition of a business at a particular point in time, managers, owners, and creditors want to examine consecutive statements of financial position in order to have a better picture of the business's financial performance in terms of cash flows. The more important cash inflows are profit for the year, depreciation/amortization, the sale of investment securities, and obtaining a long-term loan or new equity. Major cash outflows result from a loss from operations, the purchase of non-current assets, or the repayment of a loan.

2 Learning Objective

Analyze cash flows by comparing two consecutive statements of financial position.

In order to identify the cash inflows and cash outflows (first step in the process of preparing the statement of cash flows), two consecutive statements of financial position must be placed side by side in order to see the changes in cash flow for each individual account. *Cash inflows* occur when there is a decrease in asset accounts, an increase in equity accounts (share capital or retained earnings increase due to profit), or an increase in liability accounts. *Cash outflows* occur when there is an increase in asset accounts, a decrease in owners' equity (dividends paid or retained earnings decrease due to loss from operations), or a decrease in liability accounts.

3 Learning Objective

Explain the basic structure of the statement of cash flows.

The statement of cash flows gives a complete picture of the cash inflows and cash outflows of a business under three distinct headings: operating activities, financing activities, and investing activities. It also shows the changes in the cash and cash equivalent account between two accounting periods.

4 Learning Objective

Describe the structure of the statement of cash flows for not-for-profit organizations.

NFP organizations also produce a statement of cash flows. Unlike the for-profit organizations, the NFP organization's statement of cash flows contains two headings: (1) operating activities and (2) financing and investment activities.

Key Terms

Adjustments in non-cash working capital accounts p. 127
Cash budget p. 124
Cash flows p. 114
Cash inflows p. 119
Cash inflow guidelines p. 122
Cash outflows p. 119
Cash outflow guidelines p. 122
Consecutive statements of financial position p. 120
Financing activities p. 127
Investing activities p. 129
Operating activities p. 125

Review Questions

1. Why is it important for managers to analyze changes in the flow of cash between two consecutive accounting periods?
2. Differentiate between cash inflows and cash outflows.
3. What do we mean by internal sources of financing?
4. What do we mean by external sources of financing?
5. Identify some of the key cash inflows and cash outflows.
6. Why is depreciation/amortization considered a cash inflow?
7. Why are working capital accounts part of the operating activities shown on the statement of cash flows?
8. Comment on the key guidelines that can be used to identify whether a change in the accounts shown on a statement of financial position

between two consecutive accounting periods is considered a cash inflow or a cash outflow.

9. Identify the basic structure of the statement of cash flows.
10. What is the purpose of the statement of adjustments in non-cash working capital accounts?
11. Comment on the more important items that are usually shown under the operating activities section in the statement of cash flows.
12. What financial statements are used to prepare the statement of cash flows?
13. Comment on the more important items that are usually shown under the financing activities section in the statement of cash flows.
14. Comment on the more important items that are usually shown under the investing activities section in the statement of cash flows.
15. How does the statement of cash flows complement the other financial statements, that is, the statement of income and the statement of financial position?
16. How can managers use the statement of cash flows to make important business decisions?

Learning Exercises

EXERCISE 1

Identify, under the appropriate heading, whether the following changes are considered an inflow of cash or an outflow of cash.

In $	This Year	Last Year	Cash Inflows	Cash Outflows
House	134,600	130,000	________	________
Trailer	12,000	—	________	________
Furniture	5,600	4,000	________	________
Mortgage payable	75,000	60,000	________	________
RRSP	23,000	20,000	________	________
Loan made to a friend	—	5,000	________	________
Car loan	12,000	8,000	________	________
Visa	1,250	600	________	________
The Bay	—	450	________	________
Cash in the bank	3,000	2,000	________	________
Marketable securities	12,000	10,000	________	________
Total			$________	$________

EXERCISE 2

On the basis of Vicky Subbarao's statements of financial position shown on the following page, identify whether each account is an outflow of cash or an inflow of cash.

In $	This Year	Last Year	Cash Inflows	Cash Outflows
Asset				
House	145,000	136,000	______	______
Cottage	65,000	—	______	______
Land	—	40,000	______	______
Car	12,000	6,000	______	______
Computers	7,500	3,000	______	______
Savings bonds	5,000	4,000	______	______
RRSP	20,000	16,000	______	______
Cash	2,000	4,000	______	______
Total assets	256,500	209,000		
Equity	105,000	92,000	______	______
Liabilities				
Mortgage	112,000	99,000	______	______
Bank of Montreal loan	21,000	11,000	______	______
Bank loan	14,000	3,000	______	______
Visa	1,500	2,000	______	______
Sears	3,000	2,000	______	______
Total liabilities	151,500	117,000	______	______
Total equity and liabilities	256,500	209,000	$______	$______

EXERCISE 3

Indicate under which activity (operating, financing, or investing) the following accounts belong in the statement of cash flows:

	Activity
Trade receivables	______
Land	______
Mortgage payable	______
Profit for the year	______
Trade and other payables	______
Depreciation	______
Inventories	______
Prepaid expenses	______
Share capital (common)	______
Buildings	______
Accrued expenses	______
Current taxes payable	______
Equipment	______
Long-term borrowings	______
Purchase of a company	______
Dividends	______
Share capital (preferred)	______

EXERCISE 4

With the following accounts, identify those that are considered working capital accounts and prepare the adjustments in non-cash working capital account statement.

Accounts	This Year	Last Year
Trade receivables	$ 230,000	$ 210,000
Non-current assets	550,000	450,000
Inventories	350,000	290,000
Prepaid expenses	50,000	40,000
Accumulated depreciation	210,000	180,000
Dividends	40,000	32,000
Trade and other payables	240,000	190,000
Revolving loan	90,000	100,000
Mortgage payable	120,000	110,000
Accrued expenses	20,000	30,000
Share capital	50,000	40,000
Short-term borrowings	82,000	34,000
Profit for the year	48,000	39,000

EXERCISE 5

With the following financial statements, prepare the following:

- The adjustments in non-cash working capital accounts statement
- The statement of cash flows

Statement of Income
for the year ended December 31, 2009
(in $)

Revenue	550,000
Cost of sales	(200,000)
Gross profit	350,000
Other income	10,000
Costs/expenses	(210,000)
Total	200,000
Profit before taxes	150,000
Income tax expense	(60,000)
Profit for the year	90,000

Statement of Changes in Equity
for the year ended December 31, 2009
(in $)

Retained earnings	2009	2008
Balance at beginning of year	210,000	210,000
Profit for the year	90,000	—
Dividends	(70,000)	—
Balance at end of year	230,000	210,000
Share capital		
Balance at beginning of year	71,000	71,000
Shares issued	—	—
Balance at end of year	71,000	71,000

Statements of Financial Position
as at December 31
(in $)

	2009	2008
Non-current assets		
Property, plant, and equipment	400,000	350,000
Accumulated depreciation	(100,000)	(65,000)
Property, plant, and equipment (net)	300,000	285,000
Current assets		
Inventories	300,000	230,000
Trade receivables	250,000	200,000
Cash and cash equivalents	3,000	4,000
Total current assets	553,000	434,000
Total assets	853,000	719,000
Equity		
Share capital	71,000	71,000
Retained earnings	230,000	210,000
Total equity	301,000	281,000
Liabilities		
Non-current liabilities		
Long-term borrowings	200,000	122,000
Current liabilities		
Trade and other payables	200,000	178,000
Accrued expenses	32,000	38,000
Short-term borrowings	120,000	100,000
Total current liabilities	352,000	316,000
Total liabilities	552,000	438,000
Total equity and liabilities	853,000	719,000

Cases

CASE 1
AUSTIN INDUSTRIES INC.

In 2010, the management committee of Austin Industries Inc. would like to invest $75,000 in property, plant, and equipment. The board of directors would like to approve the decision, but first they must find out how much cash will be generated by the operations in 2010. The members of the board also have the options of raising more funds from the shareholders and increasing their long-term borrowings.

On the basis of the information shown on Austin Industries Inc.'s 2010 projected statement of financial position, identify the cash inflows and the cash outflows for the year 2010.

Austin Industries Inc. Projected Statements of Financial Position as at December 31 (in $000s)		
	2010	2009
Non-current assets		
Property, plant, and equipment	150	75
Accumulated depreciation	(41)	(26)
Total non-current assets	109	49
Current assets		
Inventories	75	53
Trade receivables	30	22
Term deposits	—	11
Cash	7	15
Total current assets	112	101
Total assets	221	150
Equity		
Share capital	64	38
Retained earnings	95	67
Total equity	159	105
Liabilities		
Non-current liabilities		
Long-term borrowings	26	8
Current liabilities		
Trade and other payables	18	15
Notes payable	3	15
Other current liabilities	15	7
Total current liabilities	36	37
Total liabilities	62	43
Total equity and liabilities	221	150

In 2010, management of Austin Industries Inc. expects to generate $38,000 in profit. The board of directors will pay $10,000 in dividends to the shareholders.

Questions

On the basis of this information, prepare the following statements:

1. The adjustments in non-cash working capital accounts statement projected for the year 2010.
2. The projected statement of cash flows for the year 2010.

CASE 2
GRANT ELECTRONICS INC.

The management committee of Grant Electronics Inc. was studying a feasibility report prepared by its economics department regarding the expansion of a plant to increase their production capacity. The CEO, Jim Smart, indicated that the expansion program would cost approximately $5.6 million in non-current assets (property, plant, and equipment) and that he was hoping that at least half of the funds to finance this expansion program would be financed through internally generated cash. The investment would take place during the early part of 2011.

He therefore asked his management team (vice-president of marketing, vice-president of production, executive vice-president, treasurer, manager responsible for trade receivables, and several managers in the production department) to prepare a summary report about how much cash they expect to generate within their respective operations during the remaining six months of 2010. He indicated that he would like to review their respective plans in 30 days.

At the meeting, Jim Smart asked each team member to make a brief statement indicating how much cash they would be able to generate before the end of 2010. The vice-president of marketing indicated that despite the slowdown in economic conditions, the company would be able to increase its overall revenue by 3.2% over 2009. He also indicated that the introduction of two new product lines and the increased effectiveness in its after-sales service would help the company marginally increase its market share. He stated that the industry would grow by only 1.5%. He was convinced that based on his organization's forecasts the company would reach $10.2 million in revenue.

The executive vice-president, on the other hand, mentioned that a new planning and budgeting management process, which Grant Electronics introduced some 24 months ago, was starting to show positive results. He had asked all managers in different organizational units to re-think their operating budgets for the next six months and said that the introduction of the Balanced Scorecard management technique helped various units to streamline their priorities, objectives, and strategies with those of the corporation. As a result, the company would improve its return on revenue (ROR) from 3.4% to 4.1%.

The vice-president for production gave a breakdown of the plant and equipment that would be included in the capital budget proposal. He further emphasized that the modernization program would generate manufacturing economies and efficiencies that were included in the 4.1% ROR. He added that 80% of the $5.6 million capital investment in non-current assets was included in the manufacturing department's capital expenditure budget program.

The chief financial officer indicated that the projected financial statements included an amount of $1.3 million for depreciation and amortization and that he had asked the manager responsible for the trade receivables department to give him an update about the amount of receivables that would be shown on the statement of financial position by the end of the year. He also mentioned that although there was a three-day improvement in the average collection period, the total amount of receivables outstanding would show a $700,000 increase.

The vice-president responsible for production indicated that all managers responsible for the production and manufacturing sectors of the company looked at every possibility to improve the inventory turnover by using the just-in-time and the economic ordering quantity methods. These techniques were used to introduce ways for improving the management of inventories and providing the lowest costs possible in order to sustain their operations. Despite the improved efficiencies and effectiveness in inventory management, the levels of inventories for raw materials, work-in-process, and finished goods would increase by $800,000.

The treasurer was asked to give an account about how much cash could be raised from various sources. He mentioned that an amount of $400,000 could be raised from the bank to finance the increased levels of trade receivables and inventories and that he had approached several long-term lenders who showed a willingness to finance part of the capital expenditure project for the amount of $1.2 million. He also pointed out that Grant Electronics would continue to pay its common shareholders their annual dividends in the amount of $600,000 but that he would be able to raise $500,000 from them by issuing new common shares. The treasurer also pointed out that the cash in the bank would increase from $600,000 to $782,000 by the end of 2010. He also pointed out that because of some changes in the accounting procedures, the current taxes payable would increase by $100,000.

The manager responsible for the trade and other payables department indicated that he had approached several suppliers for the purpose of extending the time delay for paying their bills. This effort produced positive results in view of the fact that despite the increased amount of purchases that the company would make before the end of the year, he was able to extend its trade and other payables by $200,000.

Questions

1. On the basis of the above information, prepare the following:
   a. The adjustments in non-cash working capital accounts for the year 2010.
   b. The statement of cash flows for the year 2010.
2. Is the company able to raise more than half of the cash from internally generated funds (as mentioned by the CEO) to finance the capital budget proposal?

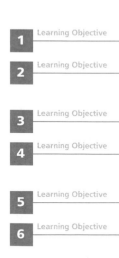

PHOTO/Thorsten Rust/Shutterstock

CHAPTER 4

[FINANCIAL STATEMENT ANALYSIS]

Learning Objectives

After reading this chapter, you should be able to:

1 Learning Objective — Explain why financial statements need to be analyzed.

2 Learning Objective — Evaluate a company's statement of financial position and statement of income by using vertical and horizontal analysis.

3 Learning Objective — Analyze financial statements by using meaningful ratios.

4 Learning Objective — Describe how financial ratios can be used to measure and improve a company's financial performance.

5 Learning Objective — Examine financial statements by using the DuPont financial system.

6 Learning Objective — Comment on the limitations of financial ratios.

Chapter Outline

Why Analyze Financial Statements?
Two-Dimensional Views of Financial Statements
Financial Ratios
External Comparisons
The DuPont Financial System
Limitations of Financial Ratios

OPENING CASE

Since CompuTech Sales and Service started, the Millers have been obtaining their company's financial statements from accountant May Ogaki each month. The data presented on the financial statements allows the Millers to analyze their financial performance on a continual basis.

As May pointed out, the information presented on the financial statements is critical to gauge the results of past decisions and to determine what has to be done in the future. The Millers remembered vividly the points made by Bill Murray regarding the requirements needed to keep a business liquid, stable, productive, and profitable. This is exactly what the Millers considered when analyzing their financial statements. CompuTech Sales and Service's financial statements for 2010 presented in Appendix A at the end of this book will be used for working on the Self-Test Exercises of this chapter.

The first requirement was for the Millers to pay their current bills on time or to be *liquid*. In 2010, CompuTech bought $209,000 worth of goods from different suppliers. The Millers always paid their invoices on time (usually within 30 days). They felt that this was important if CompuTech was to maintain a healthy working relationship with its suppliers. Also, being in a favourable liquid position, the business could take advantage of cash and trade discounts. The business had $90,000 in bank loans (short- and long-term borrowings). In order to maintain a certain level of "trustworthiness" with their banker, the Millers made sure that all debt commitments were honoured each month.

The second requirement was *stability*, maintaining a level of debt that CompuTech could afford. The Millers did not want to overextend themselves into too much debt for two reasons. First, the more debt that the business had to carry the more costly it was. They realized that a heavy debt load would have an adverse effect on profit performance, particularly if finance costs increased, even by 1% or 2%. Also, the Millers' strategy in 2010 was to keep their level of debt as low as possible (even reducing it) to allow them more leverage to finance the opening of a new store by 2011.

The third requirement was *productivity*. To the Millers, productivity meant getting the "biggest bang for each invested dollar." Productivity meant generating the highest level of revenue with the least amount of resources (assets). For example, they realized that dollars invested in inventories ($65,000) and trade receivables ($45,000), although necessary, did not generate any profit. For this reason, they wanted the investment level in working capital accounts as low as possible. In total, CompuTech had $268,000 invested in assets, and each dollar generated $1.57 in revenue ($420,000 ÷ $268,000). To find out whether CompuTech was productive, the Millers had to obtain information from different sources (e.g., banks, industry associations, Dun & Bradstreet) to compare their firm's performance against the industry and other competing firms. This information was used as benchmarks for making decisions.

The last requirement for long-term growth and success was *profitability*. This had to do with the level of profit CompuTech would generate compared to revenue, assets, and equity. The Millers realized the importance of making effective investment and operating decisions in order to maximize profitability. High profit level is a sign of efficiency. In 2010, for example, the Millers expect to earn 7.9 cents for every revenue dollar ($33,000 ÷ $420,000). As far as they were concerned, return on revenue was one of the most important financial objectives.

Improving profitability would be achieved if revenue could be increased while being vigilant in spending their budget dollars (e.g., cost of sales and expenses). They knew that the more profit the business earned, the more expansion could be funded by internally generated cash and less from external sources (e.g., lenders).

Chapter Overview

Financial ratio Comparison or relationship between numbers shown on financial statements.

Financial statement analysis is not limited to assessing cash inflows and cash outflows. Another important tool used to gauge the financial health of a business is ratio analysis. A **financial ratio** is the comparison or relationship between different numbers appearing on a statement of financial position and/or a statement of income. This relationship is usually expressed in terms of a ratio or a percentage.

Business managers, suppliers, investors, and market analysts do not look only at the makeup of financial statements, that is, the "cosmetics." Just because a statement of financial position balances, or is prepared by professional accountants and audited by renowned accounting firms, does not mean that a business is in a healthy financial position. A person who knows how to read financial statements can readily detect whether a business is financially sound or suffers from financial anemia.

As discussed in Chapter 2, the purpose of the initial two steps in financial management (bookkeeping and accounting) is to prepare financial statements. The next two steps involve the analysis of business performance for the purpose of assessing financial strengths and weaknesses, and making operating, financing, and investing decisions.

When looking at a statement of financial position or a statement of income, it is relatively easy to gauge how much profit a business has made, how much debt it owes to its creditors, or the amount of funds owners have invested in it. However, in order to evaluate business performance in more depth and with more precision, managers and investors use financial ratios to gauge liquidity, debt, coverage, asset management, profitability, and market value.

Hundreds of ratios can be used to gauge financial performance and management competence. Using a proliferation of ratios for evaluating financial performance of a business can, however, confuse more than enlighten. Some ratios are deficient because they (1) can mislead, (2) do not give a complete picture of a financial situation, (3) do not have a practical application, and (4) show in a roundabout manner what other ratios show more clearly. For example, what would be the point of comparing current liabilities to equity, or distribution expenses to non-current assets? The real objective of ratio analysis is to reduce the large number of accounts (or items) contained in financial statements to a relatively small number of meaningful relationships. Important relationships (ratios) depend to a large measure on the purpose of the ratios selected and should relate components in which a logical decision-making relationship exists between the two elements.

Ratios can be regarded as diagnostic tools. Just as a doctor measures various characteristics of the blood, someone evaluating a company measures the various relationships of numbers shown on financial statements. Just as a blood test can show symptoms of a disease, the study of numbers on financial statements reveals symptoms of problems or of management errors that require correction.

As indicated earlier, a ratio is simply a comparison of one account to another to express the size of an item in relation to the other. For instance, if you wanted to express how sunny a month was, you could calculate the ratio of sunny days to rainy days. Dividing the number of sunny days (say, 15) by the number of rainy days (say 15) gives a ratio of 1. Alternatively, you could work out the ratio of sunny days to total days. In this case, you divide the number of sunny days in the month (15) by the total number of days in the month (30) to give 0.50 or 50%.

After reading this chapter, you will be able to analyze financial statements, and gauge the financial soundness and profitability of any business. This chapter shows how to meaningfully compare numbers appearing on statements of financial position and statements of income. Here are a few examples of how numbers shown on financial statements can be compared and for what reasons:

Compare ...	**to see whether the ...**
• current assets to current liabilities	• company is able to meet its payroll and pay its suppliers on time.
• trade receivables to revenue	• company is collecting its receivables quickly enough.
• inventories to cost of sales	• company's inventory is turning over quickly enough.
• finance costs to profit	• business can service its debt.
• total debts to total assets	• company has too much debt.
• total assets to revenue	• company's assets are productive.
• profit to revenue	• company as a whole is efficient.

Ratio analysis Helps readers of financial statements to assess the financial structure and performance of a business.

Ratio analysis helps readers of financial statements assess the financial structure and profitability performance of businesses by exploring answers to the following questions:

- Is this company able to meet its current debt obligations?
- Are the company's assets being managed efficiently (doing things right) and effectively (doing the right things)?
- Are the business's trade receivables and inventories at suitable levels?
- Will the company be able to meet its long-term borrowing commitments?
- Can the company service its debt comfortably?
- Is the company profitable?

- How does the company's financial structure and profitability compare with those of others in the same industry?
- Is the shareholders' return on investment satisfactory?
- Do investors have a high regard for the company?

This chapter covers six major themes. The first theme examines the reasons financial statements should be analyzed. Those are ensuring that a business (1) preserves a certain level of liquidity; (2) maintains its solvency, that is, keeping a reasonable level of debt compared to equity; (3) uses its assets in the most productive way; (4) maximizes its return on its investments; and (5) secures long-term prosperity.

The second theme looks at two broad approaches of analyzing financial statements: (1) vertical analysis of financial statements, a technique that converts all the elements on the financial statements to percentages, and (2) horizontal analysis of financial statements, an approach that helps to compare the financial results of a particular period to previous or future years.

The third theme explains the more important financial ratios used by businesses to measure a company's financial performance. They can be grouped under five categories: (1) liquidity ratios, (2) debt/coverage ratios, (3) asset-management ratios, (4) profitability ratios, and (5) market-value ratios.

The fourth theme explains how a company's financial statements can be compared to external financial results. This theme focuses on financial benchmarks, comparing a company's financial performance to specific highly successful competitors and to its industry as a whole.

The fifth theme illustrates how the DuPont financial system can be used as an effective way of measuring the overall financial performance of a business. This system measures a company's return on total assets, taking into account the non-current asset turnover and the profit before taxes.

The last theme explains the limitations of financial ratios and that while they are important management tools for assessing the performance of a business, they should be used with caution.

Why Analyze Financial Statements?

1 Learning Objective

Explain why financial statements need to be analyzed.

Managers analyze financial statements for two main reasons. First, to examine the past in order to gauge how well a business performed in terms of meeting its financial objectives related to efficiency, liquidity, prosperity, and stability. Second, to formulate goals and strategies that will help improve the company's future financial performance. One important characteristic of good business goals is the element of precision and meaningfulness. Financial ratios are considered vital instruments that can make financial analysis and decision-making useful and unambiguous.

Analyzing financial statements through ratios helps managers, market analysts, or investors find out what is good or bad about a business. While ratios give only signals about what is wrong or right, they can easily trigger a process that can help managers dig a little deeper in order to find answers to questions, solve problems, or improve performance.

Financial statements become valuable instruments when managers or analysts are able to make the connection between different accounts or groups of accounts shown on the statement of income and the statement of financial position. Furthermore, this information can be quite revealing when compared to competitors and industry norms that can be used as **benchmarks** (considered excellent industry norms to which one's own financial performance can be compared). Only once the analysis is completed can corrective measures be taken to improve the financial performance.

Benchmarks
Excellent industry norms to which one's own financial ratios can be compared.

The real value of financial statement analysis lies in the fact that it can be used to help predict a company's future financial performance. If the analysis is done effectively, managers can anticipate future conditions and, more importantly, make decisions that will improve the future financial performance for their business.

It is important to analyze financial statements for five reasons: (1) to ensure liquidity, (2) to maintain solvency, (3) to improve the productivity of assets, (4) to maximize return, and (5) to secure long-term prosperity. Let's examine the relevance of these five objectives.

ENSURE LIQUIDITY

In business, being liquid is just as important as generating an adequate return. No business activity is more important than being able to transact daily with customers so that the business can pay employees, bills, and debt on time. To operate with some degree of comfort, a business must have enough cash (liquidity) to pay its day-to-day expenses and retire other liabilities on schedule. An important ratio that can test a company's liquidity position is the relationship between all current asset accounts, such as trade receivables and inventories, to all current liability accounts that must be paid within a reasonable time period (e.g., a year), such as trade and other payables and short-term borrowings.

Stakeholders that are interested in measuring liquidity are short-term lenders, suppliers, employees, and owners.

Businesses that want to improve their profit performance (maximize return) must implement effective cash management strategies such as the following:

- Accelerating cash receipts by speeding billing and collection processes.
- Delaying disbursements to maximize the use of cash.
- Reducing working capital requirements (e.g., inventories and trade receivables).
- Monitoring the operating cycle, which can help gauge cash goals (i.e., number of days it takes from the purchase of inventories to collecting receivables from customers).

Some of the financial ratios that can provide answers to these concerns include the cash ratio, the current ratio, the quick ratio, the working capital ratio, and the cash conversion cycle.

MAINTAIN SOLVENCY

Solvency
Ability to service or pay all debts (short- and long-term).

Solvency can be defined as a company's ability to pay its debts. Solvency ratios attempt to determine whether a business is overextended in debt. This analysis helps to pinpoint whether a firm has (or will have) the ability to pay its principal on debt, finance costs, lease payments, and any other fixed obligations as they become due. Cash flow performance and capital structure (proportion of debt to equity) can help determine the solvency prospects of a company in order to avoid getting into financial trouble. There is no question that maintaining solvency is essential for any business. If a business defaults on its debt obligations, it can lead to legal proceedings that could easily put a strain on its day-to-day activities and even derail its operations.

Both managers and investors are always on the alert for the threat of insolvency that applies to both current and longer-term operating conditions. When a business is insolvent, its liabilities exceed assets and it is operating with a negative equity. Nevertheless, if a company operates with a positive equity structure, it can still be insolvent if it has difficulty in servicing its debt payments. For this reason, financial measures are used to test whether a business is financially solvent. This can be examined from two angles:

- *Financial structure*, which examines whether a company has too much debt compared to what owners have invested in the business (equity).
- *Debt-paying ability*, which examines whether a business has the ability to service its debt with relative ease. Here, solvency is analyzed from two angles:
  a. *Short-term solvency* tests (i.e., quick ratio, current ratio)
  b. *Long-term solvency* tests (i.e., debt-service coverage ratio, fixed-charges coverage)

Testing the solvency of a business is of prime interest to market analysts, investment portfolio managers, private investors, investment bankers, and other stakeholders. They will usually test a firm's solvency performance before deciding whether to make or renew a loan. These financial ratios can determine the financial profile of a firm in terms of its creditworthiness and judge whether it will have enough cash to repay its loans (interest and principal) and pay dividends on time.

Productivity
A measure of performance that gauges how resources are used.

IMPROVE THE PRODUCTIVITY OF ASSETS

Productivity is a key financial objective for any business. **Productivity** is a measure of performance that gauges how resources are used. This measure relates goods or services sold (outputs) and resources used to make them (inputs). At the micro level, a productivity measure for a manufacturing department could be the relationship between the number of units produced (say, 100,000 widgets) and the resources required (people, equipment, materials) to produce them (say, $100,000). In this particular case, it would cost the company $1.00 for each widget. If it costs $1.00 for company A and $1.10 for company B, company A would be considered more productive.

Financial statements can also be used to gauge the overall productivity of a business, that is, at the macro level. Comparing revenue (outputs) to total assets (inputs) gauges productivity. For instance, if company A sells $5 million worth of goods and services and utilizes $2.5 million worth of assets, it means that for every dollar's worth of assets, the company generates $2.00 worth of goods and services. If company B sells $5 million worth of goods and services and utilizes $5 million dollars worth of assets, it utilizes $1.00 worth of assets to produce $1.00 worth of goods and services and would therefore be considered less productive than company A.

The total assets figure is an important number that is used to measure the financial health of a business. As shown in Table 7.13 on page 338, the financial health score, or the *Z-score*, that is used to measure corporate health uses total assets as a denominator for four ratios out of five. The bottom line is that management wants to utilize the least amount of resources to produce the maximum amount of goods or services (revenue); in short, management wants to manage a "speedboat," one that moves quickly and is agile, rather than a large "barge" that moves slowly and awkwardly. As will be discussed in the section on "Asset-Management Ratios," beginning on page 170, managers can use four ratios to measure productivity: average collection period, inventory turnover, capital assets turnover (property, plant, and equipment), and total assets turnover. Both current assets (inventories and trade receivables) and capital assets are used to measure productivity.

MAXIMIZE RETURN

Return
Adequate cash and profit to finance a company's growth.

In business, the word *return* is synonymous with survival. To survive, a business must earn adequate profit and cash flow that will in turn earn a suitable **return** to investors and provide adequate cash to finance its working capital requirements and to buy non-current assets. Ratios such as return on revenue (ROR), return on assets (ROA), and return on invested capital can readily show whether a business is generating enough profit to satisfy its day-to-day operating needs and longer-term financial aspirations.

Profitability can be improved by a combination of the following:

- Increasing sales volume and/or unit selling price.
- Reducing expenses (e.g., cost of sales, distribution cost, or administrative expenses).

- Reducing the use of borrowed funds (finance costs).
- Cutting back non-productive assets (e.g., working capital and non-current assets).

As will be covered later in this chapter, the use of financial ratios through the vertical analysis technique of the statement of income can help set the stage for improved profitability and return performance. The first step is to convert all numbers in the statement of income from dollar figures to percentages (or ratios). Each line on the statement of income is compared to revenue. Once the percentages or ratios have been calculated, they can be used to analyze past performance and can be compared to specific competitors and to industry-wide statistics. As shown below, this analysis can readily help managers pinpoint operating efficiencies (or inefficiencies) and profitability.

Sales Revenue (%)	**2008**	**2009**	**2010**
Revenue	100.0%	100.0%	100.0%
Cost of sales	80.0	81.0	79.0
Gross profit	20.0	19.0	21.0
Costs/expenses	15.0	16.0	15.0
Profit before taxes	5.0%	3.0%	6.0%

As shown above, ROR (or for every dollar's worth of revenue) was reduced from 5 cents to 3 cents between 2008 and 2009. Managers have to find out the reasons for this deterioration in operating efficiencies. More importantly, they will have to formulate financial goals for each operating line on the statement of income (e.g., 79 cents in cost of sales and 15 cents in costs/expenses for 2010). Also, they will have to determine strategies and plans that will help realize the 2010 goals in order to improve their gross profit and profit before tax performance. To illustrate the importance of this simple analysis, if the revenue objective for 2010 is $10 million, a 6% ROR would generate $600,000 in profit before taxes. If the ROR performance is maintained at the 2009 operating efficiency level (3.0% level), the level of profit before taxes would be reduced to $300,000. Vertical analysis helps to pinpoint what should be done for each account on the statement of income in order to improve profitability (here, by an extra $300,000) and return. Tables 4.1 and 4.2 show Eastman Technologies' vertical analysis for its statements of financial position and statements of income, respectively, for the years 2008 and 2009.

ROA also measures the level of profitability. For example, if profit before taxes increases from $300,000 to $600,000 between 2009 and 2010 with a corresponding growth in total assets from $3 million and $4 million, this means that the company's return performance would be increased from 10% ($300,000 ÷ $3,000,000) to 15% ($600,000 ÷ $4,000,000).

Table 4.1 Vertical Analysis of the Statement of Financial Position

Eastman Technologies Inc.
Statements of Financial Position
as at December 31
(in $)

Assets	2009	%	2008	%
Non-current assets				
Property, plant, and equipment	1,340,000	74.44	1,050,000	70.56
Accumulated depreciation	(140,000)	(7.77)	(100,000)	(6.72)
Total non-currents assets	1,200,000	66.67	950,000	63.84
Current assets				
Inventories	218,000	12.11	185,000	12.43
Trade receivables	300,000	16.67	280,000	18.82
Prepaid expenses	60,000	3.33	55,000	3.70
Cash and cash equivalents	22,000	1.22	18,000	1.21
Total current assets	600,000	33.33	538,000	36.16
Total assets	1,800,000	100.00	1,488,000	100.00
Equity				
Share capital	300,000	16.67	285,000	19.15
Contributed surplus	—	—	—	—
Retained earnings	255,000	14.16	205,000	13.78
Total other comprehensive income/(loss)	—	—	—	—
Total equity	555,000	30.83	490,000	32.93
Liabilities				
Non-current liabilities				
Long-term borrowings	800,000	44.45	600,000	40.32
Current liabilities				
Trade and other payables	195,000	10.83	175,000	11.76
Short-term borrowings	150,000	8.33	135,000	9.07
Accrued expenses	20,000	1.11	18,000	1.21
Taxes payable	80,000	4.45	70,000	4.71
Total current liabilities	445,000	24.72	398,000	26.75
Total liabilities	1,245,000	69.17	998,000	67.07
Total equity and liabilities	1,800,000	100.00	1,488,000	100.00

SECURE LONG-TERM PROSPERITY

If a company is able to achieve the above four fundamental financial objectives, it could very well realize its most important and all-inclusive long-term objective: prosperity, that is, the ability of a business to grow smoothly, a concern for

Table 4.2 Vertical Analysis of the Statement of Income

Eastman Technologies Inc.
Statements of Income
for the period ended December 31
(in $)

	2009	sales (%)	2008	sales (%)
Revenue	2,500,000	100.0	2,250,000	100.0
Cost of sales	(1,900,000)	(76.0)	(1,743,000)	(77.5)
Gross profit	600,000	24.0	507,000	22.5
Other income	20,000	0.8	18,000	0.8
Distribution costs:				
Sales salaries	(140,000)	(5.6)	(128,000)	(5.7)
Advertising expenses	(20,000)	(0.8)	(19,000)	(0.9)
Total distribution costs	(160,000)	(6.4)	(147,000)	(6.6)
Administrative expenses:				
Office salaries	(170,000)	(6.8)	(155,000)	(6.9)
Lease	(20,000)	(0.8)	(20,000)	(0.9)
Depreciation	(40,000)	(1.6)	(30,000)	(1.3)
Total administrative expenses	(230,000)	(9.2)	(205,000)	(9.1)
Finance costs	(35,000)	(1.4)	(23,000)	(1.0)
Total other income and expenses	(405,000)	(16.2)	(357,000)	(15.9)
Profit before taxes	195,000	7.8	150,000	6.6
Income tax expense	(97,500)	(3.9)	(75,000)	(3.3)
Profit for the year	97,500	3.9	75,000	3.3

all stakeholders. Growth funds (a topic that will be discussed in the section, "Sustainable Growth Rate," in Chapter 7, beginning on page 335) come from several sources:

- Internally generated cash flows (cash flows from operating activities)
- Externally generated cash flows (lenders and shareholders)
- Reduced dividends
- Reduced amount of cash invested in capital assets such as property, plant, and equipment

Typical questions that stakeholders usually ask are:

- Do we have sufficient resources to grow (physical, financial, human)?
- Where will growth funds come from? Internal sources? External sources? How much?
- Do we have enough borrowing power to finance our growth?
- Will we have enough cash to service the new debt and equity (finance costs and dividends)?
- Will the incremental ROR and earnings (or profit) before interest and taxes (EBIT) be positive? If yes, to what extent?

Horizontal analysis gives a clear indication of the growth patterns (past and future) for various accounts appearing on financial statements. Tables 4.3 and 4.4 show Eastman Technologies' horizontal analysis of the company's statements of financial position and statements of income, respectively, for the years 2008 and 2009. These financial statements reveal, for example, that an 11.1% increase in revenue for the forecast period (2009) will generate a 30% increase in profit. It will also require a 21% increase in total assets whereby the growth funds will come from equity for an increase of 13.3% (new capital from shareholders and/or an increase in retained earnings), and a 33.3% increase in long-term borrowings and an 11.8% increase in current liabilities. These numbers provide managers and investors the opportunity to query whether the growth rate for each element on the financial statements is feasible.

Now that we understand why ratios are important to analyze financial statements and to help make important operating, financing, and investing decisions, let's now examine how financial statements can be analyzed. First, we will look at the analysis of financial statements from two angles, vertical analysis and horizontal analysis, and then examine the more commonly used financial ratios, what they measure, and how they are calculated.

2 Learning Objective

Evaluate a company's statement of financial position and statement of income by using vertical and horizontal analysis.

Two-Dimensional Views of Financial Statements

As explained in the previous section, financial statements can be examined globally from two angles, from a vertical or horizontal perspective.

VERTICAL ANALYSIS

Vertical analysis Method of listing (1) all numbers on the statement of financial position to a percentage of total assets, and (2) all numbers on the statement of income to a percentage of revenue.

One of the most frequently used approaches in probing statements of financial position and statements of income is to list the individual items on the financial statements in percentages. This is called **vertical analysis**, *common-size ratios*, or *common-size statement analysis*.

As shown in Table 4.1, each component of Eastman's statements of financial position related to assets is expressed as a percentage of total assets, and each component related to equity and liabilities is expressed as a percentage of total equity and liabilities. Vertical analysis is useful for comparing the performance of one business to another or one division to another, because it ignores the difference in the size of the individual accounts. All elements are converted on comparable terms—a percentage.

Vertical analysis also reveals the change in mix between several elements of a statement of financial position and between consecutive statements of financial position. For example, Table 4.1 shows that, in 2008, current assets represented 36.16% out of every asset dollar of the company. In 2009, this ratio was reduced to 33.33%. This is evidenced by the fact that trade receivables, inventories, and prepaid expenses all decreased in percentage terms. The same analysis can be performed for each component in the equity and liability accounts.

Vertical analysis of the statement of income provides the same type of information. As shown in Table 4.2, each component of Eastman's statement of income is converted to a percentage of revenue. Eastman's profit performance improved over the accounting period; in 2009, for every dollar of revenue, it made 3.9% (or cents) compared to 3.3% (or cents) in 2008. Although the overall profitability performance of the company improved, it is evident that some accounts improved and others deteriorated. For example, cost of sales went from 77.5% to 76.0%, which improved the company's gross profit from 22.5% to 24.0%. Salary and lease accounts improved, while depreciation showed an increase.

Vertical analysis not only enables management to compare financial statements from one year to the next between companies or operating divisions, but also can reveal sufficient information for management to answer the following types of questions:

- Is our company's financial structure in line with that of the industry?
- Is the ratio of the company's current assets to total assets favourable?
- Is the investment in property, plant, and equipment (capital assets) in the right proportion?
- Are the manufacturing costs too high?
- Are the costs or expenses too high?
- Is the ratio of profit to revenue adequate?

In the News 4.1 gives an example about how a company's financial statements can be profiled from different angles, that is, from year-to-year (horizontal analysis) and by comparing figures of the same year (vertical analysis).

HORIZONTAL ANALYSIS

Horizontal analysis
Shows percentage change of accounts shown on two consecutive financial statements.

Horizontal analysis is done by reviewing two consecutive financial statements and then comparing the differences between the two periods. The comparison shows the growth or decline in each component of a financial statement, both in absolute dollars and as a percentage. For example, if two consecutive statements of income show figures of $900,000 in 2010 and $990,000 in 2011, horizontal analysis will show the $90,000 increase and a 10% growth.

In The News [4.1]

A Company's Financial Performance Can Be Profiled from Different Angles, from Year-to-Year, and by Comparing Figures of the Same Year

Profiling a company's financial statements is more than just looking at numbers or understanding what they mean. It has to do with *who* is analyzing the numbers and *what* information should be looked at. For example, a 1.7 times liquidity ratio is of little or no interest to investors. However, this number is critical to a banker who has to decide whether a line of credit should be extended to a business.

Different types of numbers were presented in newspapers to profile the financial performance of Adobe Systems Corporation, the creator and manufacturer of successful products such as Acrobat, Adobe Air, Photoshop Elements, and Cold Fusion. Adobe had to navigate the negative waves of the recession during the spring of 2008. As mentioned in a newspaper article, Adobe showed signs that it was capable of outpacing the performance of other California software giants by demonstrating it through horizontal and vertical ratios. Undoubtedly, these ratios were of moderate interest to some readers, but of vital concern to others. On the *horizontal analysis* side, when looking at the statement of income, the article indicated that Adobe's sales declined by 21% and that during the second quarter, LiveCycle sales would drop by as much as 16%. On the *vertical analysis* side, the article stated that profits, as a percent of sales, would be 33%. Looking at another number from a different angle, net income dropped to 24 cents a share ($126.1 million) from 40 cents a share a year earlier (or $219.1 million).

Source: Adapted from Bert Hill, "Adobe expects summer recovery for Ottawa-developed products," *Ottawa Citizen,* June 18, 2009, p. D2. For additional information about Adobe's financial performance, visit www.adobe.com and click on "Investor Relations."

Tables 4.3 and 4.4 show horizontal analyses for Eastman's statements of financial position and statements of income, respectively. In Table 4.3, Eastman's statements of financial position show significant changes in certain accounts. For example, total non-current assets show a 26.3% growth while total current assets increased by 11.5%. The lower part of the statements of financial position shows an increase of 13.3% in Eastman's equity, an increase of 33.3% in its long-term borrowings, and an 11.8% increase in current liabilities.

Self-Test Exercise No. 4.1

Vertical Analysis of Financial Statements

By using CompuTech's financial statements in Appendix A at the end of the book, prepare a vertical analysis of the company's (a) statements of financial position and (b) statements of income for the years 2009 to 2011. For the statements of financial position, do the calculations only for total non-current assets, total current assets, total equity, total long-term borrowings, total current liabilities, and total liabilities. For the statements of income, do the calculations only for gross profit, profit before taxes, and profit for the year.

Table 4.3 Horizontal Analysis of the Statement of Financial Position

Eastman Technologies Inc.
Statements of Financial Position
as at December 31
(in $)

Assets	2009	2008	Amount of Change	Change (%)
Non-current assets				
Property, plant, and equipment	1,340,000	1,050,000	290,000	27.6
Accumulated depreciation	(140,000)	(100,000)	(40,000)	40.0
Total non-currents assets	1,200,000	950,000	250,000	26.3
Current assets				
Inventories	218,000	185,000	33,000	17.8
Trade receivables	300,000	280,000	20,000	7.1
Prepaid expenses	60,000	55,000	5,000	9.1
Cash and cash equivalents	22,000	18,000	4,000	22.2
Total current assets	600,000	538,000	62,000	11.5
Total assets	1,800,000	1,488,000	312,000	21.0
Equity				
Share capital	300,000	285,000	15,000	5.2
Contributed surplus	—	—	—	—
Retained earnings	255,000	205,000	50,000	24.4
Total other comprehensive income/(loss)	—	—	—	—
Total equity	555,000	490,000	65,000	13.3
Liabilities				
Non-current liabilities				
Long-term borrowings	800,000	600,000	200,000	33.3
Current liabilities				
Trade and other payables	195,000	175,000	20,000	11.4
Short-term borrowings	150,000	135,000	15,000	11.1
Accrued expenses	20,000	18,000	2,000	11.1
Taxes payable	80,000	70,000	10,000	14.3
Total current liabilities	445,000	398,000	47,000	11.8
Total liabilities	1,245,000	998,000	247,000	24.7
Total equity and liabilities	1,800,000	1,488,000	312,000	21.0

Table 4.4 **Horizontal Analysis of the Statement of Income**

Eastman Technologies Inc.
Statements of Income
for the period ended December 31
(in $)

	2009	2008	Amount of Change	Change (%)
Revenue	2,500,000	2,250,000	250,000	11.1
Cost of sales	(1,900,000)	(1,743,000)	(157,000)	9.0
Gross profit	600,000	507,000	93,000	18.3
Other income	20,000	18,000	2,000	11.1
Distribution costs:				
Sales salaries	(140,000)	(128,000)	(12,000)	9.4
Advertising expenses	(20,000)	(19,000)	(1,000)	5.3
Total distribution costs	(160,000)	(147,000)	13,000	8.8
Administrative expenses:				
Office salaries	(170,000)	(155,000)	(15,000)	9.7
Lease	(20,000)	(20,000)	—	—
Depreciation	(40,000)	(30,000)	(10,000)	33.3
Total administrative expenses	(230,000)	(205,000)	(25,000)	12.2
Finance costs	(35,000)	(23,000)	(12,000)	52.2
Total other income and expenses	(405,000)	(357,000)	(48,000)	13.4
Profit before taxes	195,000	150,000	45,000	30.0
Income tax expense	(97,500)	(75,000)	(22,500)	30.0
Profit for the year	97,500	75,000	22,500	30.0

Table 4.4 shows a 30% increase in profit. Individual components that have contributed to this significant increase include revenue, which shows a larger increase than the cost of sales (11.1% versus 9.0%). Although sales salaries increased by only 9.4%, there was a hefty 52.2% increase in finance costs.

Self-Test Exercise No. 4.2

Horizontal Analysis of Financial Statements

By using CompuTech's financial statements in Appendix A at the end of the book, prepare a horizontal analysis of the company's (a) statements of financial position and (b) statements of income for the years 2010 and 2011. For the statements of financial position, do the calculations only for total non-current assets, total current assets, total equity, total long-term borrowings, and total liabilities. For the statements of income, do the calculations only for revenue, gross profit, profit before taxes, and profit for the year.

Financial Ratios

3 Learning Objective

Analyze financial statements by using meaningful ratios.

This section examines 16 ratios that can be grouped under three categories:

- *Statement of financial position ratios*, which relate two accounts shown on the statement of financial position
- *Statement of income ratios*, which show the relationship between two accounts on the statement of income
- *Combined ratios*, which relate numbers on the statement of financial position to the numbers on the statement of income

Statement of financial position, statement of income, and combined ratios can also be regrouped under five other categories in order to measure a company's financial performance.

a. *Liquidity ratios* measure the ability of a firm to turn assets into cash to meet its short-term cash obligations.
b. *Debt/coverage ratios* are used to evaluate the capital structure, that is, the proportion of funds a business borrows from creditors and owners to finance the purchase of assets, and the firm's ability to service its debt.
c. *Asset-management ratios* evaluate how efficiently managers use the assets of a business.
d. *Profitability ratios* measure the overall operating effectiveness of a business by comparing profit level to revenue, assets, and equity.
e. *Market-value ratios* are used to assess the way investors and stock markets react to a company's performance.

This section examines these five groups of financial ratios. The 16 ratios identified in Table 4.5 will be defined and examined within the context of Eastman Technologies Inc.'s statements of income and statements of financial position shown in Tables 2.2 on page 63 and 2.4 on page 72, respectively in Chapter 2.

Table 4.5 Commonly Used Financial Ratios

A. Liquidity Ratios
   1. Current ratio (times)
   2. Quick ratio (times)

B. Debt/Coverage Ratios
   3. Debt-to-total assets (%)
   4. Debt-to-equity (times)
   5. Times-interest-earned (times)
   6. Fixed-charges coverage (times)

C. Asset-Management Ratios
   7. Average collection period (days)
   8. Inventory turnover (times)
   9. Capital assets turnover (times)
   10. Total assets turnover (times)

D. Profitability Ratios
   11. Profit margin on revenue (%)
   12. Return on revenue (%)
   13. Return on total assets (%)
   14. Return on equity (%)

E. Market-Value Ratios
   15. Earnings per share ($)
   16. Price/earnings ratio (times)

LIQUIDITY RATIOS

Liquidity ratios
Measure the ability of a firm to meet its cash obligations.

Liquidity ratios examine the current accounts shown on the statement of financial position, that is, the relationship between current assets and current liabilities. These two groupings of accounts are referred to as working capital. By referring to Table 2.4, we can calculate Eastman's net working capital in 2009 as follows:

Current assets	$600,000
Current liabilities	445,000
Net working capital	$155,000

Liquidity ratios measure the short-term solvency and help judge the adequacy of liquid assets or meeting short-term obligations as they come due. The $155,000 in net working capital is the level of funds Eastman has to operate with on a day-to-day basis—that is, to pay on time its trade and other payables, short-term bank borrowings, and weekly operating expenses such as wages and salaries. Some businesses may experience financial difficulty because they cannot pay obligations as they come due and not always because they are not profitable.

The most commonly used liquidity ratios are the current ratio and the quick ratio.

Current Ratio

Current ratio
Gauges general business liquidity.

The **current ratio**, also referred to as the working capital ratio, is calculated by dividing current assets by current liabilities. It is an excellent way to gauge business liquidity because it measures to what extent current assets exceed current liabilities.

Eastman's current ratio is computed as follows:

$$\frac{\textbf{Current assets}}{\textbf{Current liabilities}} = \frac{\$600,000}{\$445,000} = \textbf{1.35 times}$$

This means that Eastman has $1.35 of current assets for every dollar of current liabilities. The current ratio has a general weakness in that it ignores the *composition* of the current asset accounts, which may be as important as their relationship to current liabilities. Therefore, before judging the liquidity position of a business, it is always prudent to examine other factors, such as the ratio of the industry in which it operates, the composition of the company's current assets, and the season of the year. For example, a business that has a 2 to 1 current ratio with, say, 80% of its current assets in inventories would not be as liquid as a company in the same industry that has a 1.5 to 1 ratio with only 30% of its current assets comprising inventories. Therefore, current ratio analysis must be supplemented by other working capital ratios such as the quick ratio.

Rule of thumb. A common rule of thumb suggests that an acceptable current ratio should be around 2 to 1, that is, every dollar's worth of current liabilities should be backed up by at least two dollars' worth of current assets. This makes sense because if the firm could realize only one-half of the values stated in the statement of financial position, if liquidating current assets, it would still have adequate funds to pay all current liabilities. Nevertheless, a general standard for this ratio is not useful because it fails to recognize that an appropriate current ratio is a function of the nature of a company's business and would vary with different operating cycles of different businesses. It is more pertinent to use industry averages than overall standards. For example, for distilleries, it may take several years before raw materials are converted into finished products. Consequently, these businesses require a considerable amount of working capital to finance operations. In other industries such as meat packers, the production process is shorter and businesses are able to receive cash from sales much more quickly and have money available to pay their current bills. Consequently, companies operating under such conditions can operate with less working capital.

Quick Ratio

Quick ratio
Shows the relationship between the more liquid current assets and all current liabilities.

The **quick ratio**, also called the acid-test ratio, measures the relationship between the more liquid current asset accounts such as cash, marketable securities, and trade receivables, and the current liability accounts. This ratio complements the current ratio because the problem in meeting current liabilities may rest on delays or even in the inability to convert inventories into cash to meet current obligations, particularly in periods of economic disturbance. This is a more rigorous measure of the short-term liability-paying ability of a business as the least-liquid current asset, inventories, is not included in the calculation because this account takes more time to be converted into cash. The quick ratio does assume that trade receivables are of good quality and will be converted into cash over the next 12 months.

Eastman's quick ratio, which includes trade receivables ($300,000), prepaid expenses ($60,000), and cash and cash equivalents ($22,000), is calculated as follows:

$$\frac{\textbf{Quick assets}}{\textbf{Current liabilities}} = \frac{\$382{,}000}{\$445{,}000} = 0.86 \text{ times}$$

Rule of thumb. An acceptable quick ratio is about 1 to 1; this means that Eastman's second liquidity position also does not appear to be acceptable. However, before passing final judgment on Eastman's liquidity position, it would be preferable to evaluate the company's historical working capital performance and compare it to industry standards or norms.

Self-Test Exercise No. 4.3

Liquidity Ratios

By using CompuTech's financial statements in Appendix A at the end of the book, calculate the company's current ratio and quick ratio for the year 2010.

DEBT/COVERAGE RATIOS

Debt/coverage ratios Measures the capital structure of a business and its debt-paying ability.

Debt/coverage ratios deal with debt, the funds borrowed by a business to finance the purchase of its assets. Two questions are usually asked when gauging indebtedness. First, what should be the best mix of funds provided by lenders and the owner to buy assets (debt ratios)? Second, will the business be able to service its contractual loan agreement, that is, pay the finance costs and principal each month (coverage ratios)? The most commonly used debt/coverage ratios are debt-to-total-assets ratio, debt-to-equity ratio, times-interest-earned ratio, and fixed-charges coverage ratio.

Debt-to-Total-Assets Ratio

Debt-to-total-assets ratio Measures how much debt a business uses to finance all assets.

The **debt-to-total-assets ratio** (also called debt ratio) measures the proportion of all debts (current and long-term) injected into a business by lenders to finance all assets shown on the statement of financial position. The more debt employed by a firm, the more highly leveraged it is. This ratio is calculated by dividing total debt by total assets.

This ratio is important to lenders because they want to ensure that shareholders invest a sufficient amount of funds in the business in order to spread the risk more equitably. For Eastman, the 2009 ratio is computed as follows:

$$\frac{\textbf{Total liabilities}}{\textbf{Total assets}} = \frac{\$1,245,000}{\$1,800,000} = 69\%$$

This means that 69% of Eastman's assets are financed by debt, and thus lenders bear the greatest portion of risk. This suggests that creditors may have difficulty in collecting their loan from the business in the event of bankruptcy or liquidation.

Rule of thumb. Usually when this ratio exceeds 50%, creditors may be reluctant to provide more debt financing. However, as with all other ratios, it is important to assess the type or nature of the assets owned by the business, as that may very well influence how far lenders will go in funding the operations. The book value of assets, for example, may be much less than their market value. Also, a business may obtain more funds from lenders to construct a plant in an industrial park located in a large metropolitan area than for one located in an economically depressed region. Furthermore, non-current assets, such as property, plant, and equipment, may have little value except to an ongoing business and for this reason some find this ratio to be only of academic interest.

Debt-to-Equity Ratio

Debt-to-equity ratio Measures the proportion of debt used compared to equity to finance all assets.

The **debt-to-equity ratio** is actually redundant if the debt-to-total-assets ratio is used because the two ratios convey the same information. The debt-to-equity ratio is explained here because financial publications that provide industry average ratios for comparison purposes often cite the debt-to-equity ratio instead of the debt-to-total-assets ratio. Therefore, it is important to be familiar with this measure. This ratio also shows whether a company is using debt prudently or has gone too far and is overburdened with debt that may cause problems. It is important to show the relative proportion of lenders' claims compared to ownership claims because this proportion (or percentage) is used as a measure of debt exposure. Companies with debt-to-equity ratios above 1 are probably relying too much on debt.

In the case of Eastman, the 2009 ratio works out to:

$$\frac{\textbf{Total debt}}{\textbf{Total equity}} = \frac{\$1,245,000}{\$555,000} = 2.24 \textbf{ times}$$

Eastman uses over two dollars in borrowed funds compared to each dollar provided by shareholders. The debt-to-equity ratio shows that a considerable amount of assets is being financed by debt rather than by equity and that the company would find it difficult to borrow additional funds without first raising more equity capital. Management would probably be subjecting the firm to the risk of bankruptcy if it sought to increase the debt-to-equity ratio any further by borrowing additional funds. For this reason, it would be advantageous for Eastman to start thinking about trying to lower its total debt and/or increase owners' equity over the next year in an effort to improve its financial structure.

Times-Interest-Earned Ratio

Times-interest-earned ratio (TIE)
Measures to what extent a business can service its interest charges on debt.

The **times-interest-earned ratio (TIE)** measures to what extent a business can service its debt, or the business's ability to pay back the interest charges (or finance costs as named on the statement of income) as per agreement. Take the example of a potential homeowner who is seeking a loan to buy a $200,000 house. Here, the bank would be interested not only in the value of the house in relation to how much the home buyer is prepared to put into the house, but also the buyer's ability to repay the loan on a month-to-month basis. An acceptable ratio is around 30%, that is, for every dollar's worth of gross salary, the loan repayment should not exceed 30 cents. For example, if a home buyer earns $5,000 a month and is in the 40% tax bracket, $1,500 (or 30%) would go against the loan, $2,000 would be used to pay income taxes, and the remaining $1,500 would be left for monthly living expenses. The higher the loan repayment in proportion to the buyer's gross salary, the less the buyer would have left to pay for ongoing living expenses.

This is what the TIE ratio reveals. It is determined by dividing earnings (or profit, as named on the statement of income) before interest charges and taxes (EBIT) by interest charges. The ratio measures the extent to which profit before taxes can decline before the business is unable to meet its annual interest charges.

This ratio shows the number of dollars of EBIT that is available to pay each dollar of interest. Adding the earnings before taxes ($195,000) and interest charges ($35,000) and dividing the sum by interest charges makes the calculation. This $230,000 would be equivalent to the homebuyer's $5,000 gross salary. A higher ratio adds more certainty to the estimate of the business's ability to pay all interest charges as agreed.

The calculation is always done on a before-tax basis, because interest charges are a tax-deductible expense. Referring to Table 2.2, Eastman's ratio is computed as follows:

$$\frac{\textbf{Earnings before taxes + Interest charges}}{\textbf{Interest charges}} = \frac{\$195{,}000 + \$35{,}000}{\$35{,}000} = \textbf{6.57 times}$$

This means that the company has $6.57 of EBIT available per dollar of interest charges to pay the interest charges and taxes. Because interest charges and taxes amount to only $3.78 ($1.00 + $2.78), the rest is profit. Here is another way of describing this ratio.

EBIT	$6.57
Interest charges	1.00
EBT	5.57
Income tax expense	2.78
EAIT	$2.79

With each $6.57 EBIT, Eastman pays $1.00 toward the interest charges and is left with $5.57 in earnings before taxes. Because the company is in the 50% tax bracket, Eastman pays $2.78 in income taxes and is therefore left with $2.79 to:

- Pay dividends;
- Pay the principal on the debt; and
- Reinvest the rest in the business as retained earnings.

The lower the ratio, the riskier it is. To illustrate, if the TIE ratio is reduced to 3.0, it means that the company would be left with only $2.00 (after paying the interest charges) to pay income taxes, the principal on the loan, and dividends, and to reinvest profit (retained earnings) in the business.

This ratio complements the debt ratios in providing additional information about the company's ability to meet debt obligations. However, it still does not present a complete picture. The ultimate question is one of whether the company can meet its commitments to "all" creditors. Thus, a ratio based on all fixed charges, which is explained in the next segment, is helpful.

Rule of thumb. A comfortable TIE ratio is in the 4.0 to 5.0 range. An acceptable ratio in each of the past five fiscal years should be covered at least 3.0 to 4.0 times for industrial businesses and 2.0 times for utilities. Utilities operate with little or no competition, and rate boards establish rates that allow them to generate an acceptable return on their investment while an industrial company's profit for the year is more volatile and unpredictable and thus requires a higher safety margin.

Fixed-Charges Coverage Ratio

This ratio is similar to the TIE ratio. However, it is more inclusive in that it recognizes that many firms incur long-term obligations under scheduled rental or lease payments. The cumulative total of those obligations, lease payments plus interest charges,

Fixed-charges coverage ratio
Measures to what extent a business can service all its fixed charges (e.g., interest charges, leases).

comprise a firm's total annual fixed charges. The **fixed-charges coverage ratio** is calculated by dividing the sum of the earnings before taxes and all fixed charges, by fixed charges. Fixed charges can include items such as lease payments, interest charges, principal repayment, and sinking funds or the annual payment required to amortize a bond. These types of outlays are regarded as unavoidable. The Eastman 2009 ratio is computed as follows:

$$\frac{\textbf{Earnings before taxes + Interest charges + Lease}}{\textbf{Interest charges + Lease}} = \frac{\$195,000 + \$35,000 + \$20,000}{\$35,000 + \$20,000}$$

$$= \textbf{4.54 times}$$

Other fixed charges, such as lease payments, reduce the margin of error held in Eastman's operating results. This ratio is being used more often because of the increasing popularity of long-term lease agreements. It shows how much earnings before taxes is left to pay for all fixed charges.

In the News 4.2 gives an example about how a successful business can be driven to the edge of closing its doors due to a heavy debt load.

In The News [4.2]

Too Much Debt Can Drive a Successful Business to the Edge of Closing Its Doors

It does not matter how many years a company has been in business, how successful it has been, the quality of products or services it has offered to its clients, what it offers in term of guarantees, or what its creed says, bankruptcy can always unexpectedly appear at its doorstep. When it happens, something has to be done, and quickly!

It was in June of 2009 that Eddie Bauer, one of America's most recognized icons, filed for Chapter 11 bankruptcy protection. At the time of the announcement, the company had 400 stores in the United States and Canada. This was the second time in the company's history that it filed for bankruptcy. Eddie Bauer, which started in Seattle in 1920, accumulated so much debt that management had difficulty complying with the conditions stipulated in a $225-million senior term loan. Like many businesses during the recession period, the company had been showing losses resulting from declining sales volume. In the first quarter alone, sales dropped by as much as 16%. As a result, the company hired investment bankers to come up with a plan to show how to cut costs and conserve cash. The company now operates 370 stores with 10,000 employees worldwide.

Source: Adapted from Reuters, "Eddie Bauer files for protection," *Ottawa Citizen,* June 18, 2009, p. C1. For more information on Eddie Bauer's financial performance, go to www.eddiebauer.com, and click on "Company Info."

ASSET-MANAGEMENT RATIOS

Asset-management ratios
Evaluate how efficiently managers use the assets of a business.

Asset-management ratios, sometimes referred to as *activity ratios*, *operating ratios*, or *management ratios*, measure the efficiency with which a business uses its corporate assets or resources (i.e., inventories, trade receivables, non-current assets) to earn a profit. The intent of these ratios is to answer one basic question: Does the amount of each category of asset shown on the statement of financial position seem too high or too low in view of what the firm has accomplished or wants to realize in the future? The more commonly used asset-management ratios are the average collection period, the inventory turnover, the capital assets (or property, plant, and equipment, as named in the statement of financial position) turnover, and the total assets turnover.

Self-Test Exercise No. 4.4

Debt/Coverage Ratios

By using CompuTech's financial statements in Appendix A at the end of the book, calculate the company's debt-to-total-assets ratio, debt-to-equity ratio, TIE ratio, and fixed-charges coverage ratio for the year 2010.

Average Collection Period

Average collection period (ACP) Measures how many days it takes for customers to pay their bills.

The **average collection period (ACP)** measures how long a firm's average sales dollar (revenue) remains in the hands of its customers. A longer collection period automatically creates a larger investment in assets and may even indicate that the firm is extending credit terms that are too generous. However, management must be aware of competitive credit practices in order to offer similar credit terms so as not to lose sales as a result of too-stringent credit policies. The main point is that investment in trade receivables has a cost, and excess trade receivables means that too much debt or equity is being used by the business. If so, the business would not be as capital-efficient as it could be.

The average collection period is calculated in two steps. The first step is calculating the average daily sales, which is done by dividing the total annual revenue by 365 days. Eastman's average daily sales are \$6,849 (\$2,500,000 ÷ 365). The second step is dividing the average daily sales into trade receivables. Eastman's average collection period is 44 days and is calculated as follows:

$$\frac{\textbf{Trade receivables}}{\textbf{Average daily sales}} = \frac{\$300,000}{\$6,849} = \textbf{44 days}$$

If Eastman were able to collect its receivables within 30 days, the company would reduce its trade receivables by \$95,886 (\$6,849 × 14 days) and thus add this amount to the company's treasury to be invested in more productive assets. The question for Eastman is: How long should sales credit be? The manager responsible has to decide whether the average collection period is getting out of hand. If so, actions would have to be taken to shorten credit terms, shut off credit to slow payers, or step up collection efforts.

Inventory turnover Measures the number of times a year a company turns over its inventories.

Inventory Turnover

Inventory turnover (also called inventory utilization ratio) measures the number of times a company's investment in inventories is turned over during a given year. An inventory item "turns" each time a firm buys or repurchases another similar item for stock. The number of times that the cycle recurs during the year represents that product's annual turnover rate. To be sure, a company's statement of financial position does not show individual items. For this reason and for practical purposes, this ratio looks at the total average annual turnover rate. The higher the turnover ratio, the better, because a company with a high turnover requires a smaller investment in inventories than one producing the same level of revenue with a low turnover rate. Company management has to be sure, however, to keep inventories at a level that is just right in order not to miss sales.

While both revenue and cost of sales could be used in the calculation, they give different results because revenue exceeds cost of sales by the amount of the gross profit. Cost of sales (not revenue) should be used as the numerator for calculating the inventory turnover ratio as the denominator (inventories) is valued at cost, and the purpose is to assess the adequacy of the physical turnover of that inventory.

Another point to remember is that since a company's revenue takes place over a 12-month period (moving-picture concept) while inventory is computed at a specific point in time (still-photography concept), it would be more appropriate to use the average inventory for the year. Usually, we can calculate that by taking the beginning plus ending inventory and dividing it by two. Quarterly and even monthly inventories can also be used.

This ratio indicates the efficiency in turning over inventory and can be compared with the experience of other companies in the same industry. It also provides some indication as to the adequacy of a company's inventories for the volume of business being handled. If a company has an inventory turnover rate that is above the industry average, it means that a better balance is being maintained between inventories and cost of sales. As a result, there will be less risk for the business of being caught with top-heavy inventories in the event of a decline in the price of raw materials or finished products. Here is how Eastman's 2009 inventory ratio is calculated.

$$\frac{\textbf{Cost of sales}}{\textbf{Inventories}} = \frac{\$1,900,000}{\$218,000} = 8.7 \text{ times}$$

Eastman turns the average item carried in its inventory 8.7 times during the year. Of course, not every item in the company's stock turns at the same rate. Nevertheless, the overall average provides a logical starting point for positive inventory management. If Eastman were able to turn over its inventory faster, say, up to 10 times a year, it would reduce its inventories from \$218,000 down to \$190,000 (\$1,900,000 ÷ 10) and thus add an extra \$28,000 to the company's treasury.

In the News 4.3 gives an example about how fresh liquidity can facilitate a company's credit and supplier agreements.

In The News [4.3]

Fresh Liquidity Can Help a Company Facilitate Its Credit and Supplier Agreements

Everyone knows what happens when an individual is short of cash. After paying its fix commitments such as mortgage and other debts, the individual hopes to have enough to provide for basic necessities such as food, medication, and clothing. For a quick solution, and to go over the hurdle quickly, the individual usually meets his or her creditors for one purpose: to consolidate debts.

This is what Air Canada did during the summer of 2009. The company raised $1.02 billion from different stakeholders, an amount needed to avoid a second brush with bankruptcy in six years. Included in this deal was a renegotiated $700-million package with GE Canada Finance Holding Co., Export Development Corporation Canada, Aeroplan Canada Inc., and ACE Aviation Holdings. This financial package helped Air Canada refinance some of its debt obligations and made available an additional $600 million in working capital, an amount critically needed to meet its short-term obligations. Stakeholders that came to the rescue of Air Canada included suppliers, main credit card processors, a creditor involved in a sale and leaseback amendments for three aircraft, and Boeing, which conveniently modified the arrangements for the purchase of future aircraft.

Source: Adapted from Reuters, Wojtek Dabrowski, "Air Canada raises $1B in fresh liquidity," *Ottawa Citizen*, June 30, 2009, p. D2. For more up-to-date news about Air Canada, visit www.aircanada.ca, and click on "About Air Canada."

Capital Assets Turnover

Capital assets turnover ratio Measures how intensively a firm's capital assets are used to generate revenue.

The **capital** (or property, plant, and equipment, as named in the statement of financial position) **assets turnover ratio** (also called *fixed assets utilization ratio*) measures how intensively a firm's capital assets, such as property, plant, and equipment, are used to generate revenue. A low capital assets turnover implies that a firm has too much investment in non-current assets relative to revenue; it is basically a measure of productivity.

The following shows how Eastman's 2009 capital assets turnover ratio is calculated.

$$\frac{\textbf{Revenue}}{\textbf{Capital assets}} = \frac{\$2,500,000}{\$1,200,000} = 2.1 \text{ times}$$

This means that the company generates $2.10 worth of revenue for every dollar invested in capital assets. If a competing firm has a $3.00 ratio, it implies that it is more productive as every dollar invested in capital assets produces an extra $0.90 in revenue. If a business shows a weakness in this ratio, its plant may be operating below capacity, and managers should be looking at the possibility of selling the less-productive assets.

There is one problem with the use of capital assets turnover for comparison purposes. If the capital assets turnover ratio of a firm with assets that were acquired many years ago is compared to a company that has recently automated its operations to make them more efficient or productive, the more modern firm may have a lower capital assets turnover ratio than the older and less-productive company simply because of the increased amount of capital assets.

Total Assets Turnover

Total assets turnover ratio Measures how intensively a firm's total assets are used to generate revenue.

The **total assets turnover ratio** measures the turnover or utilization of all of a firm's assets, both capital assets and current assets. It also gives an indication of the efficiency with which assets are used; a low ratio means that excessive assets are employed to generate revenue and/or that some assets (capital or current assets) should be liquidated or reduced. This ratio is very useful as an initial indicator of a problem with revenue or an excessive accumulation of assets. When managers see that this ratio is too low, they may have to modify their sales objectives and plans, examine the growth in the marketplace and competitors, or determine if their asset base is too large. Eastman's 2009 total assets turnover is as follows:

$$\frac{\textbf{Revenue}}{\textbf{Total assets}} = \frac{\$2,500,000}{\$1,800,000} = 1.4 \text{ times}$$

In this case, the company produces \$1.40 worth of revenue for every dollar invested in total assets. If Eastman is able to reduce its investment in trade receivables and inventories and/or sell a division or capital assets that are a burden on the company's operating performance, it would increase the total assets turnover ratio and thus would be more productive.

Self-Test Exercise No. 4.5

Asset-Management Ratios

By using CompuTech's financial statements in Appendix A at the end of the book, calculate the company's average collection period, inventory turnover, capital assets turnover, and total assets turnover for 2010.

Self-Test Exercise No. 4.6

Using Financial Ratios as a Management Tool to Improve Cash Flow

The Millers are trying to find ways to improve their cash flow situation during 2010. After looking closely at their working capital accounts, they feel that additional cash could be generated internally if the trade receivables and inventories were managed more efficiently. Calculate how much cash CompuTech could generate within the next six months if the Millers were able to improve (a) the average collection period to 30 days, and (b) the inventory turnover to 4.5 times.

Self-Test Exercise No. 4.7

Cash Flow Forecast

By using the company's statement of income shown in Appendix A at the end of the book and the information contained in Self-Test Exercise No. 4.6, calculate the amount of cash that CompuTech could generate before the end of December 31, 2010.

PROFITABILITY RATIOS

Profitability ratios
Measure the overall efficiency and effectiveness of a business.

Profitability ratios deal with bottom-line performance and measure the extent to which a business is successful in generating profit relative to revenue, assets, and equity. These ratios show the level of business efficiency and effectiveness, and reflect the results of a large number of policies and decisions. Therefore, profitability ratios show the combined effects or operating results of liquidity, asset management, and debt management. The most commonly used profitability ratios are profit margin on revenue, ROR, return on total assets, and return on equity.

Profit Margin on Revenue

Profit margin
Represents the profit before tax, after adjusting for non-operating accounts such as other income and finance costs.

Profit margin can be defined as the sum of the profit before taxes, adjusting for non-operating accounts such as other income and finance costs. In the case of Eastman, here is how profit margin is calculated for the year 2009:

Profit before taxes		$195,000
Other income	– 20,000	
Finance costs	+35,000	+15,000
Profit margin		$210,000

Profit margin on revenue
Measures the operating efficiency of a business.

Profit margin on revenue, or *net operating margin* (operating income), is computed by dividing profit margin by revenue. This ratio is an excellent measure of a firm's ability to make any financial gains because the calculation excludes non-operating items, such as finance costs and other income, which are not part of the mainstream operating activities of a business. The main purpose of this ratio is to assess the effectiveness of management in generating operating income.

Eastman's profit margin on revenue is as follows:

$$\frac{\textbf{Profit margin}}{\textbf{Revenue}} = \frac{\$210,000}{\$2,500,000} = 8.4\%$$

In the case of Eastman, the company generates 8.4 cents in operating margin for every dollar's worth of revenue.

Return on Revenue

Return on revenue
Measures a company's overall ability to generate profit from each revenue dollar.

Return on revenue represents an important measure of a company's financial performance after recognizing its finance costs and income tax obligation. This ratio gauges the firm's overall ability to squeeze profit from each revenue dollar. This ratio measures the overall profitability of a business and is calculated by dividing profit for the year by revenue. Profit-seeking businesses are keenly interested in maximizing their ROR, as this bottom-line figure represents funds either distributed to shareholders in the form of dividends or retained and reinvested in the business (see Figure 1.5 on page 16).

Eastman's 2009 ROR is calculated as follows:

$$\frac{\textbf{Profit for the year}}{\textbf{Revenue}} = \frac{\$97,500}{\$2,500,000} = 3.9\%$$

For every dollar's worth of revenue, Eastman earns 3.9 cents in profit. The higher the ratio, the more beneficial it is to the wealth of the business and to its shareholders. For effective analysis, this ratio should also be compared to historical company performance, used as a platform for planning purposes, and compared to the industry average or specific firms competing in the industry.

The ROR ratio has a limitation in that it is based on profit after deducting finance costs. If the company has increased its debt substantially, the result may be a decrease in profit because of the finance costs deduction, even if the return on the shareholders' investment has actually increased. The profit margin on revenue overcomes this problem and provides another view of profitability.

Return on Total Assets

Return on total assets
Gauges the performance of assets employed in a business.

The **return on total assets** ratio measures profit performance in relation to all assets committed. This ratio might be viewed as a measure of the efficiency or productivity of total asset usage. It is calculated by dividing profit for the year by total assets. Eastman's 2009 return on total assets is computed as follows:

$$\frac{\textbf{Profit for the year}}{\textbf{Total assets}} = \frac{\$97{,}500}{\$1{,}800{,}000} = 5.4\%$$

To have any meaning, this ratio should also be compared to the industry average or to competing firms. Another way of measuring the effectiveness of this ratio is by comparing it to the company's weighted average cost of capital. See Figure 1.2 on page 9. The difference between these two numbers would identify, to a certain extent, the economic value added (EVA). This will be discussed in Chapter 9 (see Table 9.3 on page 431).

Return on Equity

Return on equity
Measures the yield shareholders earn on their investment.

The **return on equity** ratio relates the profit to equity. This ratio is critical to shareholders because it shows the yield they earn on their investments. It also allows shareholders to judge whether the return made on their investment is worth the risk. Eastman's 2009 return on equity ratio is calculated as follows:

$$\frac{\textbf{Profit for the year}}{\textbf{Equity}} = \frac{\$97{,}500}{\$555{,}000} = 17.6\%$$

This means that for every dollar invested in the business by the shareholders, 17.6 cents is earned. By most standards, this profit for the year performance would be judged relatively good.

Self-Test Exercise No. 4.8

Profitability Ratios

By using CompuTech's financial statements in Appendix A at the end of the book, calculate the company's profit margin on revenue, ROR, return on total assets, and return on equity for 2010.

MARKET-VALUE RATIOS

Up to this point, we have examined *financial statement ratios*, which are calculated by using information drawn from financial statements. The next two ratios are market-value ratios, which are used to analyze the way investors and stock markets are reacting to a company's performance.

Market-value ratios Measurement tools to gauge the way investors react to a company's market performance.

Market-value ratios relate the data presented in a company's financial statements to financial market data and provide some insight into how investors perceive a business as a whole, including its strength on the securities markets.

These ratios would be impossible to calculate for Eastman or any company whose stock is not actively traded on the stock market (e.g., Toronto or New York stock exchanges). Only public companies have to report market-value ratios at the bottom of their financial statements. If a company's liquidity, asset-management, debt/coverage, and profitability ratios are all good, the chances for its market ratios would be excellent, and its share price would also be on the high side. The more commonly used market-value ratios are earnings per share and the price/earnings ratio.

Earnings per Share

Earnings per share (EPS) Measures how much profit is available to each outstanding share.

Earnings per share (EPS) is calculated by dividing the profit for the year after preferred dividends—that is, profit for the year available to common shareholders—by the number of common shares outstanding. Assuming that Eastman has 40,000 outstanding shares in 2009, the calculation would be as follows:

$$\textbf{Earnings per share} = \frac{\textbf{Profit for the year}}{\textbf{Number of shares outstanding}} = \frac{\$97,500}{40,000} = \$2.44$$

EPS is a measure that both management and shareholders pay attention to because it is widely used in the valuation of common shares, and is often the basis for setting specific strategic goals and plans. Normally, market analysts do not have to calculate the results as they are readily available in the financial pages of daily newspapers.

Price/Earnings Ratio

Price/earnings ratio (P/E) Indicates how much investors are willing to pay per dollar of reported profits.

The **price/earnings ratio (P/E)** is one of the most widely used and understood ratios in share value and securities analysis. The P/E ratio shows how much investors are willing to pay per dollar of reported profits. The P/E ratio is the market price of common shares divided by the earnings (profit) per common share. In the case of Eastman, we assume here that in 2009, the company's common share market price was $30.00. Daily newspaper stock market pages include EPS and P/E ratio, which are considered primary stock valuation criteria. This ratio is probably the most useful and widely used financial ratio because it takes into account all other ratios combined into one figure.

The price/earnings ratio is calculated as follows:

$$\textbf{Price/earnings ratio} = \frac{\textbf{Price per common share}}{\textbf{Earnings per common share}} = \frac{\$30.00}{\$2.44} = \textbf{12.3 times}$$

Eastman's 12.3 P/E ratio is more meaningful when compared to the P/E ratios of other companies. If a competitor is generating a P/E ratio of 10, Eastman's P/E ratio is above the competitor, suggesting that it could be regarded as somewhat less risky, or having better growth prospects, or both.

Table 4.6 summarizes Eastman's 16 important financial ratios that were calculated in this chapter.

Table 4.6 Eastman Technologies Inc.'s 2009 Financial Ratios

Liquidity Ratios

1. Current Ratio

$$\frac{\text{Current assets}}{\text{Current liabilities}} = \frac{\$600{,}000}{\$445{,}000} = 1.35 \text{ times}$$

2. Quick Ratio

$$\frac{\text{Quick assets}}{\text{Current liabilities}} = \frac{\$382{,}000}{\$445{,}000} = 0.86 \text{ times}$$

Debt/Coverage Ratios

3. Debt-to-Total-Assets Ratio

$$\frac{\text{Total liabilities}}{\text{Total assets}} = \frac{\$1{,}245{,}000}{\$1{,}800{,}000} = 69\%$$

4. Debt-to-Equity Ratio

$$\frac{\text{Total debt}}{\text{Total equity}} = \frac{\$1{,}245{,}000}{\$555{,}000} = 2.24 \text{ times}$$

5. Times-Interest-Earned Ratio

$$\frac{\text{Earnings before taxes} + \text{Interest charges}}{\text{Interest charges}} = \frac{\$195{,}000 + \$35{,}000}{\$35{,}000} = 6.57 \text{ times}$$

6. Fixed-Charges Coverage Ratio

$$\frac{\text{Earnings before taxes} + \text{Interest charges} + \text{Lease}}{\text{Interest charges} + \text{Lease}} = \frac{\$195{,}000 + \$35{,}000 + \$20{,}000}{\$35{,}000 + \$20{,}000} = 4.54 \text{ times}$$

Asset-Management Ratios

7. Average Collection Period

$$\frac{\text{Trade receivables}}{\text{Average daily sales}} = \frac{\$300{,}000}{\$6{,}849} = 44 \text{ days}$$

8. Inventory Turnover

$$\frac{\text{Cost of sales}}{\text{Inventories}} = \frac{\$1{,}900{,}000}{\$218{,}000} = 8.7 \text{ times}$$

9. Capital Assets Turnover

$$\frac{\text{Revenue}}{\text{Capital assets}} = \frac{\$2{,}500{,}000}{\$1{,}200{,}000} = 2.1 \text{ times}$$

10. Total Assets Turnover

$$\frac{\text{Revenue}}{\text{Total assets}} = \frac{\$2{,}500{,}000}{\$1{,}800{,}000} = 1.4 \text{ times}$$

Profitability Ratios

11. Profit Margin on Revenue

$$\frac{\text{Profit margin}}{\text{Revenue}} = \frac{\$210{,}000}{\$2{,}500{,}000} = 8.4\%$$

12. Return on Revenue

$$\frac{\text{Profit for the year}}{\text{Revenue}} = \frac{\$97{,}500}{\$2{,}500{,}000} = 3.9\%$$

13. Return on Total Assets

$$\frac{\text{Profit for the year}}{\text{Total assets}} = \frac{\$97{,}500}{\$1{,}800{,}000} = 5.4\%$$

14. Return on Equity

$$\frac{\text{Profit for the year}}{\text{Equity}} = \frac{\$97{,}500}{\$555{,}000} = 17.6\%$$

Market-Value Ratios

15. Earnings per Share

$$\text{Earnings per share} = \frac{\text{Profit for the year}}{\text{Number of shares outstanding}} = \frac{\$97{,}500}{40{,}000} = \$2.44$$

16. Price/Earnings Ratio (P/E)

$$\text{Price/earnings ratio} = \frac{\text{Price per common share}}{\text{Earnings per common share}} = \frac{\$30.00}{\$2.44} = 12.3 \text{ times}$$

External Comparisons

4 Learning Objective

Describe how financial ratios can be used to measure and improve a company's financial performance.

As indicated earlier, financial ratios are useful for comparing financial performance for companies that operate in the same industry. It is important, however, when using external comparisons to not only compare businesses performing similar operations but also ensure that the financial ratios are calculated in the same way. For example, it would be meaningless to compare the inventory turnover of a company that calculates this ratio by using cost of sales to another business that uses revenue. External comparisons will be covered under four headings: financial benchmarks, comparing company to specific competitors, comparing company to industry, and trend analysis.

FINANCIAL BENCHMARKS

Benchmarking
Process of searching for the best practices by comparing oneself to a competitor's excellent performance.

An effective way to learn from others is benchmarking. **Benchmarking** is the process of searching for the best practices among competitors or non-competitors that have led to their superior performance. It is looking for companies that are doing "something excellent" and learning about their best practices, and then adapting them for your own company. By aspiring to be as good as the best in the industry, managers can set their own ambitions and use this tool as a way to at least catch up if not to become better than the benchmarked company.

Benchmarking is a management technique that was pioneered by Xerox Corporation during the late 1970s as part of an effort to respond to international competition in the photocopier industry. Benchmarking is an effective tool that can help business operators identify and solve problems, formulate strategic plans to achieve specific targets, and implement processes geared to improving their operations. It can help operators better understand their industry in terms of innovative practices and creative solutions that have been applied in different businesses. As mentioned at the beginning of this chapter, a benchmark is an industry norm that a business operator can use to compare his own operating and financial performance and is recognized as the standard of excellence.

Benchmarks can be grouped under four categories. *Process benchmarks* focus on discrete work processes and operating systems. These benchmarks focus, for example, on the effectiveness of a customer's operating service, customer billing, the way orders are filled and goods received, employee recruitment programs, or even management's planning process. They can help managers to focus on improving efficiencies, lowering costs, or increasing revenues, which can all lead to improving the bottom line.

Performance benchmarks focus on product and service comparisons to help pinpoint the effectiveness of a business establishment's strategies related to prices, technical quality, product or services features, speed, and reliability.

Strategic benchmarks (also called outside-of-industry benchmarks) give notice to operators on how effective their business establishment is able to compete within their industry by using excellent norms achieved by businesses that are operating outside their own industry (e.g., hotel versus restaurant). These benchmarks help to influence the long-term competitive patterns of a business and the benefits can accrue within the long term.

Internal benchmarks look at excellent operating systems within a company's own establishments for the purpose of applying processes and systems uniformly throughout its operations. For example, a business that has five restaurants located in different locations will make comparisons amongst all of them to determine the one that shows the best operating results so that others can learn from these organizational units. These excellent business units are referred to as "champions." This method can also be used for comparing similar operating systems employed in different operating functions such as in the marketing department versus the human resources department.

The following are the steps involved when introducing a benchmarking process:[1]

Step 1: Pinpoint what needs to be benchmarked (e.g., a service, a process).
Step 2: Pinpoint the organization or organizations that will be used as leaders or the "best-in-class" in the activity or field that will be benchmarked.
Step 3: Research and examine the data that needs to be collected. The data must provide meaningful comparison.
Step 4: Identify your own current operating performance and gauge the gaps (if any) that exist with the benchmarking organization or business establishment.
Step 5: Formulate the performance levels that you want to achieve within the planning period (short, medium, and long term).
Step 6: Obtain agreement from senior management and communicate to all levels of management and employees what needs to be done to implement the process.
Step 7: Pinpoint realistic objectives to be achieved and the strategies needed to reach them.
Step 8: Put in place an action plan that will help achieve each objective.
Step 9: Implement the action plans and monitor the process to determine achievement levels and find solutions if goals are not realized.
Step 10: Re-evaluate and update the benchmarks based on more recent performance data.

Financial benchmarks Financial performance ratios that can be calculated by using dollar figures shown on financial statements (statement of income and statement of financial position) for the purpose of pinpointing excellent financial performance.

Financial benchmarks are financial performance ratios that can be calculated by using dollar figures shown on financial statements (statement of income and statement of financial position) for the purpose of pinpointing excellent financial performance. These points of reference are recognized as the standard of excellence against which an operator can compare his performance measures.

Financial benchmarks can also be grouped under four categories: liquidity, debt/coverage, asset management, and profitability. However, certain financial benchmarks should be interpreted with some degree of caution. For example, what is an excellent

1. For interesting reading on this subject, refer to Robert Camp, *Benchmarking: The Search for Industry Best Practices That Lead to Superior Performance*, New York: Quality Press, 1989.

ROR or debt-to-total-assets performance for a particular business operating in a specific industry could be marginal to others operating in a different industry. Because of this, financial benchmarks will be categorized under three groups: hard financial benchmarks, soft financial benchmarks, and self-regulated financial benchmarks. Table 4.7 shows under which of these three categories the 14 financial statement ratios described in this chapter fall under and why.

Table 4.7 Financial Benchmarks

Financial Ratios	Category	Benchmark	Reasons
A. Liquidity Ratios			
1. Current ratio (times)	S SR	1.5 times	S • Aging of trade receivables and nature of inventories (i.e., perishable) • Composition of working capital accounts (e.g., inventories versus trade receivables) SR Depends on cash needs, credit policies, and agreement with suppliers
2. Quick ratio (times)	S SR	1.0 times	S Aging of trade receivables SR Depends on cash needs and credit policies
B. Debt/Coverage Ratios			
3. Debt to total assets (%)	S	50%	Type of assets and location of business
4. Debt to equity (times)	S	1 to 1	Type of assets and location of business
5. Times-interest-earned (times)	H	4–5 times	
6. Fixed charges coverage (times)	H	4–5 times	
C. Asset-Management Ratios			
7. Average collection period (days)	SR	N/A	Depends on credit policies
8. Inventory turnover (times)	S	N/A	Level of profit margin and type of inventories (i.e., perishable)
9. Capital assets turnover (times)	S SR	N/A	S Nature of industry, age of capital assets SR Automated versus labour intensive plant
10. Total assets turnover (times)	S SR	N/A	S Nature of industry, age of capital assets SR Depends on cash needs, credit policies agreement with suppliers, and automated versus labour-intensive plant
D. Profitability Ratios			
11. Profit margin on revenue (%)	S	N/A	Nature of business
12. Return on revenue (%)	S	N/A	Nature of business
13. Return on total assets (%)	SR	N/A	Depends on cost of capital
14. Return on equity (%)	S	N/A	Level of risk

S = Soft H= Hard SR = Self-regulated

Hard financial benchmarks
Financial targets that can be applied to any business or industry to gauge financial performance.

Hard financial benchmarks are financial targets that can be applied to just about any business and industry to gauge financial performance. For example, the ability to service debt can be applied as a measurement tool in any sector or business establishment. To illustrate, a person who is looking for a mortgage to finance his house must demonstrate that he is able to pay (or service) the monthly payments. Banks calculate this ratio for anyone applying for a mortgage, whether the person works for a small or large business establishment, a government organization, or a retail store.

Soft financial benchmarks
Most financial benchmarks fall in this category and should be used with some degree of interpretation.

Soft financial benchmarks are financial targets (most financial benchmarks fall in this category) that should be used with some degree of interpretation for two reasons. First, these financial benchmarks vary from industry to industry (depending on the nature of the operation). For example, liquidity ratios for manufacturers would be different from service establishments where inventories are not an important component of working capital. Second, soft financial benchmarks can vary from business to business depending on the nature or composition of certain accounts shown on a business's financial statements. Here are two examples.

- A business that sells perishable goods to food stores or restaurants will want to collect its bills more quickly than one selling durable goods such as computers and DVDs to wholesalers or retailers. The average collection period would be different.
- A business that operates with depreciated assets will show a higher level of productivity (related to revenue) than a business that is a manufacturing plant that is highly automated and only two or three years old.

Self-regulated financial benchmark
Financial targets that are determined by a business's own policies and practices and other financial measures.

Self-regulated financial benchmarks are financial ratios that are contingent on (1) a company's own policies and practices and/or (2) other financial performance measures. For example, a business that offers a 2%/10-day net 30 will probably show a better average collection than a business that has a different credit policy.

Reading industry and trade journals, and attending trade shows and public symposia help to keep managers and employees aware of what others are doing and gives them ideas for how to improve their own company's practices.

COMPARING COMPANY TO SPECIFIC COMPETITORS

As indicated earlier, the first step in benchmarking is to select, from trade journals or periodicals, the companies that are showing the best financial results in their respective industries for managing their resources (e.g., current assets, trade receivables, capital assets turnover). For example, teams in various sectors of a company could embark on benchmarking journeys and try to find solutions to improve various aspects of the company's financial results.

For example, Standard & Poor's Compustat Services, Inc. produces all types of historical and current financial ratios about individual firms and industries. If a company wants to improve its working capital accounts, debt structure, or profit performance, it should refer to the Report Library and look for companies that excel in these specific areas. The next logical step would be to analyze and ask questions about why that company's performance is superior.

Table 4.8 shows a partial list of the type of financial information that can be drawn from the *Compustat Report Library* on a company basis and industry-wide basis.

Table 4.8 Benchmarking the Corporation

Partial List of Financial Information That Can Be Drawn from Standard & Poor's Compustat Services, Inc. Library Report

Statement of Income Reports

- Annual Statement of Income—11 Years
- Comparative Statement of Income
- Comparative Composite Statement of Income
- Trend Statement of Income
- Common Size Statement of Income
- Quarterly Common Size Statement of Income
- 12-Month Moving Statement of Income

Statement of Financial Position Reports

- Annual Statement of Financial Position—11 Years
- Annual Statement of Financial Position—With Footnotes
- Composite Historical Annual Statement of Financial Position
- Trend Statement of Financial Position
- Common Size Statement of Financial Position
- Quarterly Trend Statement of Financial Position

Statement of Cash Flows

- Statement of Cash Flows (Annual and Quarterly)
- Cash Statement by Source and Use (Annual and Quarterly)
- 12-Month Moving Statement of Cash Flows
- Working Capital Statement (Annual and Quarterly)

Ratio Reports

- Annual Ratio
- Quarterly Ratio
- Comparative Annual Ratio

Market Reports

- Daily Market Date—Seven Days
- Daily Adjusted Prices

Summary Reports

- Profitability
- Trend—Five Years

Graphics Library

- Fundamental Financial Data
- Six-Month and One-Year Daily Price
- Company Segment Pie Chart
- Geographic Segment Pie Chart
- Ten-Year Monthly Price/Earnings

As shown in the table, there is certainly no lack of information that can be drawn from annual financial reports for comparative purposes. If a business is in the food industry, information can be drawn for all public corporations in that industry, while focusing on the ratios of those companies that are considered excellent.

COMPARING COMPANY TO INDUSTRY

To be of any value, the ratio of a particular operation or business should be compared to the sector or industry in which the business operates. To illustrate how ratios can be used as measurement tools, let's examine Table 4.9 and compare Eastman's 16 ratios to those of the industry.

By looking at Table 4.9, it is possible to see whether Eastman's management should be satisfied or concerned about the financial structure and profitability position of the business. The arrows opposite the ratios indicate better financial performance.

On *liquidity*, Eastman appears to be in a difficult position compared to the industry. Maybe there is no reason for concern if the company is able to meet its current commitments on time. If the current ratio were too high, say 3.5 or 4.0, it could mean that the company had money tied up in assets that had low earning power, because cash or marketable securities are low profit generators. A high liquidity ratio could

Table 4.9 Comparative Ratio Analysis of Eastman Technologies Inc. with Industry

Eastman Technologies Inc. with Industry

Ratios	Eastman Technologies		Industry	
A. Liquidity Ratios				
1. Current ratio (times)	1.35		2.00	←
2. Quick ratio (times)	0.86		1.25	←
B. Debt/Coverage Ratios				
3. Debt-to-total-assets (%)	69		55	←
4. Debt-to-equity (times)	2.24		1.52	←
5. Times-interest-earned (times)	6.6	←	6.0	
6. Fixed-charges coverage (times)	4.5	←	4.12	
C. Asset-Management Ratios				
7. Average collection period (days)	44	←	53	
8. Inventory turnover (times)	8.7	←	6.3	
9. Capital assets turnover (times)	2.1		4.3	←
10. Total assets turnover (times)	1.4		2.1	←
D. Profitability Ratios				
11. Profit margin on sales (%)	8.4	←	6.2	
12. Return on sales (%)	3.9	←	2.4	
13. Return on total assets (%)	5.4	←	4.4	
14. Return on equity (%)	17.6	←	14.3	
E. Market-Value Ratios				
15. Earnings per share ($)	2.44	←	2.11	
16. Price/earnings ratio (times)	12.3	←	10.0	

also mean that management should reduce inventories and trade receivables and put the proceeds into more productive uses.

On *debt/coverage*, the company appears to be in a more precarious position than the industry. This means that the creditors are more exposed, that is, they bear a greater amount of risk. Although Eastman has a higher debt ratio, its fixed debt commitments are slightly better than the industry (6.6 compared to 6.0). Nevertheless, the high debt-to-total-assets ratio and debt-to-equity ratio suggest that Eastman has reached, if not exceeded, its borrowing capacity.

On *asset management*, Eastman is doing a good job with the management of its current assets, but shows signs of weakness in the administration of capital and total assets. Both the average collection period and the inventory turnover indicate that management is keeping the trade receivables and inventories at minimum levels. These ratios are also in line with the liquidity ratios that deal with the current portion of the assets shown on the statement of financial position. The capital assets turnover and total assets turnover indicate that, overall, the business has too many assets (mainly capital assets) for the level of revenue. It also means that the capital assets are not working hard enough. The only way to correct this situation is by increasing revenue or by liquidating (if possible) some of its capital assets.

On *profitability*, Eastman is doing well on all counts. Profit margin and profit in relation to revenue, assets, or equity are healthy. The profit level is particularly encouraging, despite the fact that capital assets and debt burden are higher than the industry.

On *market value*, Eastman is also doing well. Both the EPS and price/earnings ratio exceed those of the industry. Although Eastman is not a publicly owned company, these ratios are shown here for illustration purposes.

TREND ANALYSIS

Comparing one set of figures for a given year to those of the industry gives a good picture of the financial structure and profitability level of a particular business. However, this analysis does not give a full picture of the situation, because it does not take into account the element of time. Comparative analysis gives a snapshot view of the financial statements at a given point in time; it is like still photography. For a more complete picture, ratios of one company should be compared to those of the industry over a period of several years, like a motion picture; this would show whether the financial statements are improving or deteriorating.

Trend analysis
Analyzing a company's performance over a number of years.

Trend analysis is illustrated in Figure 4.1. Four of Eastman's ratios are compared with the industry over a four-year period (from 2007 to 2010); they are the current ratio, debt to total assets, capital assets turnover, and return on total assets.

Eastman's *current ratio* has always been inferior to that of the industry. The gap widened between 2007 and 2008, and reached a 0.65 spread in 2010 (1.35 versus 2.00). This means that the company decreased the level of receivables and inventories, or increased its current liabilities. Although the current ratio is a good indicator of current

Figure 4.1 Trend Analysis

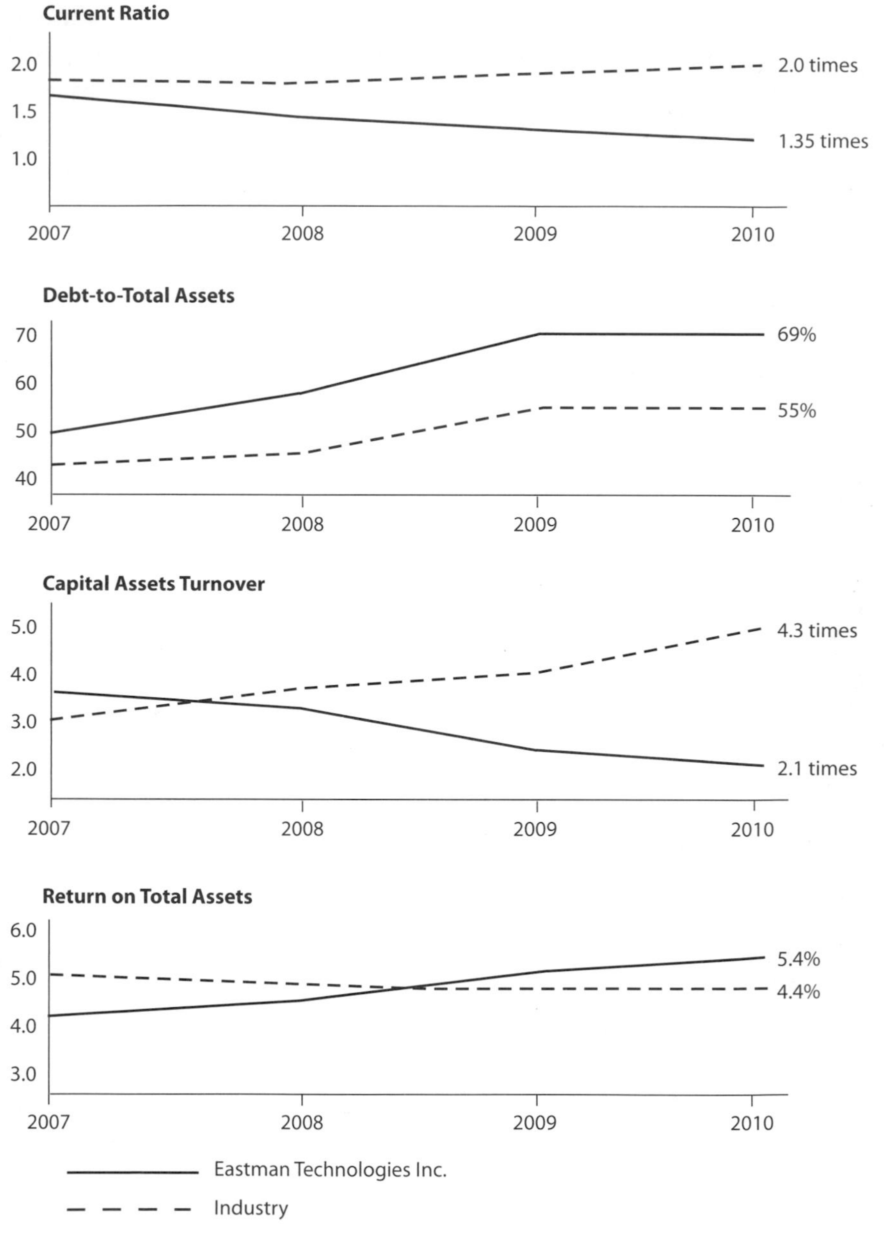

asset management, management and creditors may want to learn more about individual current asset accounts by looking at average collection period and inventory turnover.

The *debt-to-total-assets* ratio has deteriorated over the years. While Eastman finances 69 cents of each asset by debt, the industry is at only 55 cents. The debt-ratio position was weak in 2007 and continued to deteriorate. The company probably invested large sums of money in capital assets that, as can be seen in the capital assets turnover, are not being very productive in relation to the industry.

Eastman's *capital assets* turnover dropped from 4.0 to 2.1 between 2007 and 2010, meaning that Eastman's capital assets are less productive. Not only has the management of current assets been marginal over the past four years, but also the acquisition of capital assets during the 2007–2010 period seems to indicate that Eastman has a surplus of non-productive capital assets. This means that Eastman management should examine closely all capital asset accounts to see what can be done to improve the ratio. If management sees a growth trend in sales, it might not want to change anything; however, if sales are projected to improve only marginally, it may have to sell some of the capital assets in order to make all assets work at full capacity.

Return on total assets shows a strong position for Eastman. It is operating at a level one point higher than the industry (5.4 versus 4.4). The profitability position of Eastman surpassed that of the industry in 2008; the industry's trend declined over the four-year period, while Eastman's profit performance during the same period improved considerably. In short, Eastman's profitability position is healthy despite the fact that the debt ratio and the capital assets turnover are weaker than the industry.

The DuPont Financial System

5 Learning Objective

Examine financial statements by using the DuPont financial system.

DuPont System
Presentation of financial ratios in a logical way to measure ROA.

The **DuPont system** is a financial analysis system that has achieved international recognition. DuPont brought together the key financial ratios in a logical presentation to assist management in measuring ROA. The system shows the various components affecting ROA, such as profit, non-current and current assets, and the most important figures appearing on the statement of income and the statement of financial position. Figure 4.2 shows a modified and simplified version of the DuPont financial system.

The numbers in the upper portion of the diagram deal with the statement of financial position, and show how current assets (inventories, trade receivables) and capital assets are employed. To calculate the total assets turnover, you divide revenue by total assets.

The numbers in the lower portion of the diagram deal with statement of income accounts. They give the profit performance in relation to revenue. By multiplying the total assets turnover by the profit margin on revenue, we obtain the ROA figure of 11.7%. Refer to page 175 for an explanation about how the profit margin is calculated. For Eastman, the calculation is as follows: before-tax profit ($195,000) + finance costs ($35,000) – other income ($20,000) = profit margin ($210,000).

Eastman's 2009 ROA was calculated by multiplying the 1.39 total assets turnover ratio by the 8.4 profit margin on revenue. This gives an 11.67% ROA performance. If the company wants to increase this ratio, it will have to improve the capital assets turnover ratio and/or the profit margin on revenue.

Figure 4.2 The DuPont Financial System

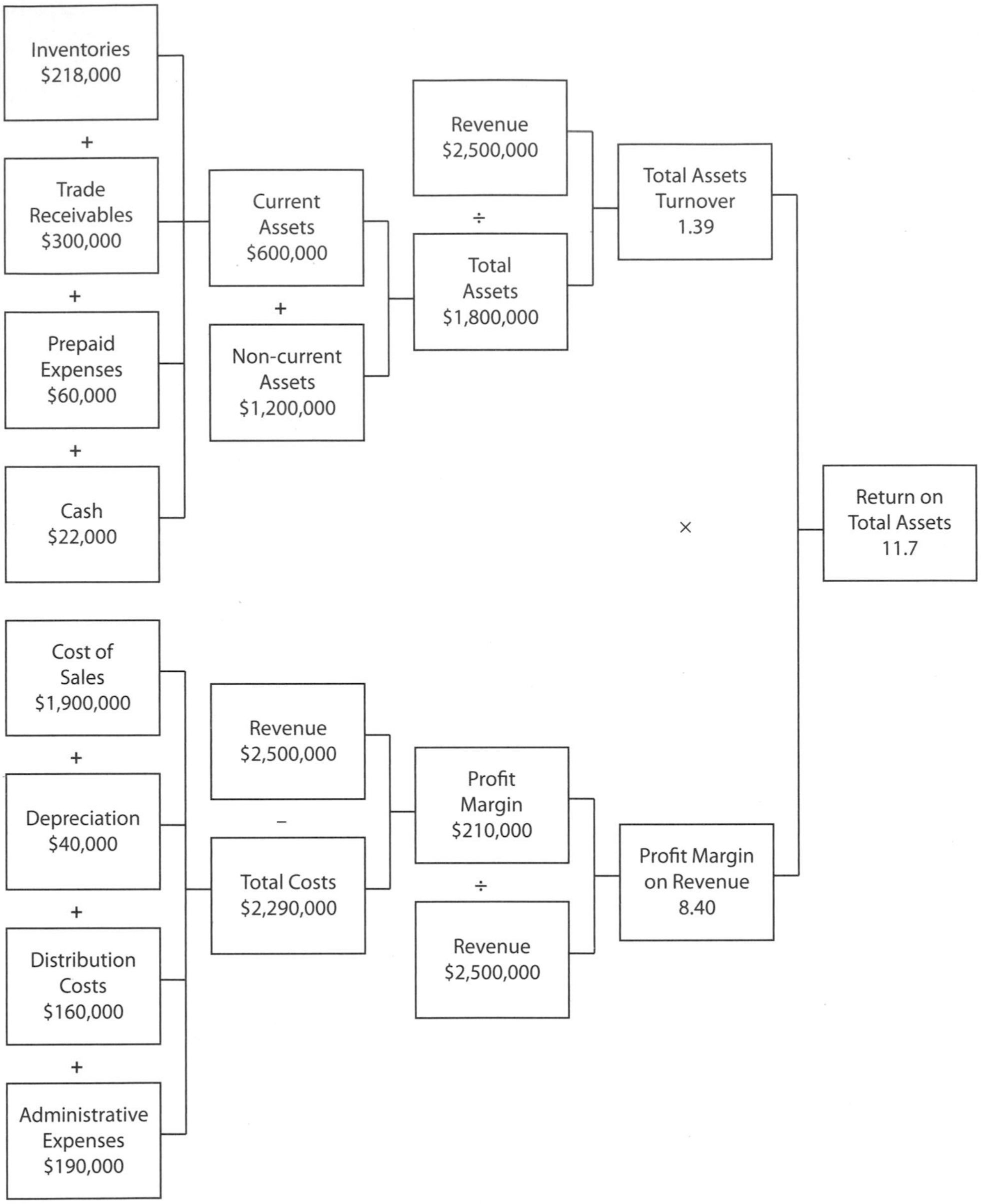

Limitations of Financial Ratios

6 Learning Objective

Comment on the limitations of financial ratios.

Although financial ratios can be effective tools for gauging financial performance and managerial effectiveness, they should not be used blindly. First, they should be used as only one instrument in the management tool kit. Essentially, a financial ratio gives an indication of the weak and strong points in a business. Ratios will not say why something is going wrong and what to do about a particular situation; they only

Self-Test Exercise No. 4.9

Calculating the ROA Using the DuPont Financial System

By using CompuTech's financial statements in Appendix A at the end of the book, calculate the following:

A. The company's 2010 ROA by using the DuPont financial system.
B. The company's 2011 ROA by using the DuPont financial system.

Is there an improvement? Why or why not?

pinpoint where a problem exists. For example, the inventory turnover may have gone from 10 to 7 over a period of three years, and the industry average may be at 9; this means that management will have to investigate further to find out what is going wrong and what to do about it.

A second limitation of financial ratios emerges when a particular set of ratios in a business is compared to other businesses or industry averages. Although there are accepted accounting principles and conventions for constructing financial statements, several different numbers can be used to calculate a ratio. As explained earlier, for calculating the inventory turnover, one business may use the cost of sales as the numerator, while another may use its revenue. Even though both companies are part of the same industry, and are equally efficient in the management of inventory, they will show different ratios. In another situation, a business may use the profit margin to calculate its total assets turnover, while another may use the profit for the year. It is important to remember that before comparing ratios, some of the numbers on the financial statements may have to be adjusted for comparison purposes.

Third, the fact that different operating methodologies can be used to run a business may render the comparison of financial ratios irrelevant. For instance, one business may lease most of its assets while another may own them. In this situation, some of the ratios, such as debt-to-total-assets ratio, TIE ratio, total assets turnover ratio, and return on total assets, would be unrelated.

A fourth limitation is the inflation factor. Inflation can make the ratio of a particular business look good or bad over time, when trends are examined. For example, inventory turnover may have deteriorated over a three-year period; the problem here may not be due to the increase in physical inventory, but rather to a substantial increase in the cost of sales. Also, an increase in return on total assets may not mean that the company is more efficient; it may reflect the fact that sales prices (and not volume) have increased rapidly and that the capital assets, which are shown on the financial statements at cost, have remained unchanged.

Finally, because statements of financial position reflect the financial situation of a business at a particular point in time, usually at the end of a fiscal period (e.g., as at December 31), this may result in a weak ratio, which might not be the case if the same calculation were done using the June figures.

Although financial ratios have limitations, a business operator should not shy away from using them. As long as a manager knows how to use them, understands their limitations, and accepts the fact that they are used as indicators and as one of many management tools, he will be in a better position to use them wisely, effectively, and with some degree of caution.

REALITY FINANCIAL SNAPSHOTS

The following paragraphs present the financial performance of the for-profit organization, Enbridge, and the not-for-profit organization, The Ottawa Hospital (TOH). The financial data used to calculate these ratios are drawn from the two organizations' financial statements presented on pages 93 to 98.

ENBRIDGE[2]

The following show Enbridge's financial ratios for the years 2007 and 2008 under the four categories:

Years	2007	2008
Liquidity ratios:		
Net working capital (millions of $)	–250	–398
Current ratio (times)	0.93	0.90
Quick ratio (times)	0.73	0.70
Debt/coverage ratios:		
Debt-to-total-assets (percent)	73.50	73.20
Times-interest-earned ratio (times)	2.67	4.34
Asset-management ratios:		
Average collection period (days)	73.15	52.55
Inventory turnover (times)	12.70	15.14
Capital assets turnover (times)	0.95	0.98
Total assets turnover (times)	0.60	0.65
Profitability ratios:		
Gross profit to revenue (percent)	24.41	20.70
Profit margin to revenue (percent)	9.64	8.48
Profit for the year to revenue (percent)	5.93	8.23
Return on total assets (percent)	3.55	5.37
Return on equity (percent)	13.40	20.06

Liquidity ratios. The company's net working capital is negative for both years as Enbridge has more current liabilities than current assets. In 2008, Enbridge had $3,709 million in current assets and $4,106 million in current liabilities. For this reason, Enbridge appears to be in a delicate liquidity situation.

Debt/coverage ratios. The company's debt-to-total-assets ratio showed a moderate increase between 2007 and 2008. While total assets increased by 24.1% (capital assets

2. Enbridge Inc., *2008 Enbridge Annual Report.* Found at http://www.enbridge.com/investor/financialInformation/reportsFilings/pdf/2008-annual-report-en.pdf.

alone showed a 30.1% increase), total debt and total equity showed a 23.6% and 25.5% increase, respectively. A large part of Enbridge's assets are still being financed by debt. TIE showed a significant increase (2.67 versus 4.34) between the two accounting periods. This is due to a very small increase in interest charges (0.15%) with a corresponding significant increase in income before taxes (100.44%).

Asset-management ratios. The management of assets showed an increase in the productivity of assets. The four ratios, average collection period (73.1 versus 52.5), inventory turnover (12.7 versus 15.1), capital assets turnover (0.95 versus 0.98), and total assets turnover (0.60 versus 0.65) all showed an improvement between the two accounting periods.

Profitability ratios. Because of the substantial increase (87.8%) in earnings performance and the continued increase (but not as hefty) in Enbridge's revenue (35.3%), total assets (24.1%), capital assets (30.1%), and owners' equity (25.5%), the profitability performance showed an increase in (1) profit for the year (from 5.9% to 8.2%), (2) return on total assets (from 3.6% to 5.4%), and (3) return on equity (from 13.4% to 20.1%).

THE OTTAWA HOSPITAL[3]

Unlike for-profit organizations, not-for-profit (NFP) organizations like TOH do not focus on profitability objectives. They have a *social responsibility.* A key objective for managers responsible for NFP organizations is to make use of resources in the most "efficient" and "effective" way. As shown in Figure 7.3 on page 307, managers responsible for NFP and for-profit organizations must ensure that they pursue the rights goals and not waste resources. The mission statement of TOH includes the following:

- Be a compassionate provider of patient-centred health services.
- Provide a wide variety of educational opportunities across all health care disciplines.
- Develop, share, and apply new knowledge and technology in the delivery of patient care.
- Play an active role in promoting and improving health.

Although TOH increased its surplus (bottom line) by less than 1.0%, from $3,372 thousand in 2007 to $3,662 thousand in 2008, as noted in the hospital's mission statement, financial results were not one of the hospital's most important priorities. This can be confirmed by the hospital's key success factors and core values, which are as follows:

Key success factors

- Set new standards in patient care, education, and research.
- Inspire innovation, learning, and growth.
- Build financial strength.
- Create enabling environments.
- Drive change through advocacy and partnerships.

3. *2008 Ottawa Hospital Annual Report.* Found at: http://www.ottawahospital.on.ca/about/reports/FS2008-e.pdf.

Core values

- Compassion
- A commitment to quality
- Working together
- Respect for the individual

The key financial success factors related to "build financial strength" will be achieved through the following:

- Operating the hospital within a balanced operating budget and proving that it can deliver comprehensive cost-effective health care services while being fiscally responsible (TOH has operated within its budget for the past three years).
- Injecting external funding (TOH received millions of dollars in grants from different organizations, such as the Ministry of Health, the Government of Ontario, the Ontario Regional Cancer Network, Honeywell Limited, and the general public) for financing different projects and programs.
- Developing strong links with partner organizations to better address their patients' needs (e.g., TOH has developed strong links with the University of Ottawa, Montfort Hospital, and other organizations to develop programs such as: a Regional Electronic Health Record, a Regional Cancer Plan, Regional Mental Health Services, a Regional Geriatric Assessment Program, Regional Satellite Dialysis Services, and a Regional Infection Control Network).
- Pursuing its volunteer program (TOH has about 2,000 volunteers—women and men, young and old—to enhance the quality of care offered at the hospital).
- Continuing the Ottawa Hospital Foundation (TOH put into motion a three-year, $100-million campaign and received gifts from individuals and organizations).

[DECISION-MAKING IN ACTION]

So far, in the first several chapters we have covered quite a few financial concepts and techniques, such as ratio analysis, vertical and horizontal analysis, internal and external financing, cash inflows and cash outflows, and depreciation as a source of cash. Let's now see how these financial concepts and techniques can be used to analyze financial information and, most importantly, to make decisions that will improve a company's bottom line and cash flow performance.

Referring to Eastman Technologies' financial statements, let's assume that management is formulating its financial objectives for 2010 and making the following projections:

Statement of income objectives

- Revenue is expected to show a 15% growth.
- Cost of sales as a percent of revenue is expected to improve to 75%.
- Operating expenses as a percent of revenue (ex-cluding depreciation) will also improve, to 13.2%.
- Depreciation will be $56,000.
- Other income/expenses will be maintained at $15,000.
- Income tax rate will be maintained at 50%.

Statement of financial position objectives

- Trade receivables will be reduced to 37 days.
- Inventory turnover will be improved to 10 times.
- Shareholders will invest $100,000 in common shares in the company.
- Capital budget is estimated at $400,000.

Retained earnings statement objectives

- The board of directors wants to pay $50,000 in dividends.

If management wants to invest $400,000 in capital assets such as equipment and machinery, how much money will the company have to borrow from lenders? As shown in Table 4.10, the company will have to borrow $148,949. The following shows how this number was calculated.

- A 15% increase over the $2,500,000 revenue in 2010 will produce $2,875,000.
- A 75% efficiency performance (as a percent of revenue) at the production level (versus 76% in 2009) will produce $2,156,250 in cost of sales.
- Expenses, as a percent of revenue, will decrease to 13.2% (versus 14.0% in 2009), or an estimated $379,500.
- Depreciation expense will reach $56,000 in 2010. Total expenses are therefore estimated at $450,500, representing 15.7% of revenue (versus 16.2% in 2009).
- The average collection period target of 37 days (compared to 44 days in 2009) will produce $8,551 in cash inflow despite the 15% revenue increase. The calculation is as follows:

2009	trade receivables	$300,000
2010	target of 37 days (average daily revenue of $7,877 × 37)	291,449
Net additional cash inflow		$8,551

The projected statement of financial position also shows inventories generating an extra $2,375 in cash inflow (turnover will improve to 10 times compared to 8.7 times). The calculation is as follows:

2009 inventories	$218,000
2010 target of 10 times (cost of sales $2,156,250 ÷ 10)	215,625
Net additional cash inflow	$2,375

As shown in the lower portion of Table 4.10, a total of $201,051 will be generated internally from operating activities. Under "Investing activities," the company will invest $400,000 in its capital budget (non-current assets). Because the operating activities will generate $201,051, the company will have to borrow $148,949 from long-term lenders; shareholders will invest $100,000 in the business and be paid $50,000 in dividends. This means that to finance its capital budget, Eastman will generate approximately 50% of the funds internally and the rest from external sources.

Table 4.10 Decision-Making in Action

In $	2009	Projected 2010	Revenue (%)	Objective
Statement of Income Assumptions				
Revenue	2,500,000	2,875,000	100.0	15% growth
Cost of sales	(1,900,000)	(2,156,250)	(75.0)	
Gross profit	600,000	718,750	25.0	
Other income/expenses	(15,000)	(15,000)	(0.5)	
Distribution and administrative expenses	(350,000)	(379,500)	(13.2)	
Depreciation	(40,000)	(56,000)	(2.0)	
Total	(405,000)	(450,500)	(15.7)	
Profit before taxes	195,000	268,250	9.3	
Income tax expense	(97,500)	(134,125)	(4.6)	
Profit for the year	97,500	134,125	4.7	
Statement of Financial Position Assumptions Related to Working Capital Accounts				
Trade receivables	44 days	$291,449		37 days
Inventory turnover	8.7 times	$215,625		10 times
Operating activities (in $)				
Profit for the year	134,125			
Adjustments				
Depreciation	56,000			
Trade receivables	8,551			
Inventories	2,375			
Cash flow from operating activities		201,051		
Financing activities				
Share capital	100,000			
Dividends	(50,000)			
Long-term borrowings	148,949			
Total financing activities		198,949		
Investing activities		(400,000)		

FINANCIAL SPREADSHEETS—EXCEL

The financial spreadsheets that complement this book calculate most financial ratios covered in this chapter. Once the financial data is inputted into the three input documents (statement of income, statement of changes in equity, and the statement of financial position), the spreadsheet calculates financial ratios on output documents that are presented on six templates focusing exclusively on financial ratios. They include the following:

- Vertical analysis of the statement of income
- Horizontal analysis of the statement of income
- Vertical analysis of the statement of financial position
- Horizontal analysis of the statement of financial position
- Financial ratios (26 ratios covered under four categories: liquidity, debt-coverage, asset-management, profitability)
- DuPont system

These financial spreadsheets can calculate ratios for a period of three years. The two key benefits of these spreadsheets are the following:

1. An analyst can spend more time analyzing a company's historical financial performance.
2. A manager can spend more time making decisions and finding solutions about how to improve the financial performance of a business's operations from different angles (liquidity, debt-coverage, asset-management and profitability) and less time on number crunching.

Chapter Summary

1 Learning Objective

Explain why financial statements need to be analyzed.

Financial statements should be analyzed in order to ensure liquidity, maintain solvency, improve the productivity of assets, generate a maximum return, and secure long-term prosperity.

2 Learning Objective

Evaluate a company's statement of financial position and statement of income by using vertical and horizontal analysis.

Analysts who constantly examine financial statements will look at them from different angles. *Vertical analysis* converts all the elements on the financial statements to percentages. *Horizontal analysis* compares the financial results of a particular period to those of previous periods in terms of absolute dollars and percentages.

3 Learning Objective

Analyze financial statements by using meaningful ratios.

Financial ratios can be grouped under five main categories. *Liquidity ratios*, such as current ratio and quick ratio or acid test, measure a company's ability to meet its short-term debts. Second, the *debt/coverage ratios*, such as debt-to-total-assets, debt-to-equity, TIE, and fixed-charges coverage, can be used to measure the extent to which a business is financed by debt as opposed to equity and how it is able to service its debt. Third, the *asset-management ratios*, such as average collection period, inventory turnover, capital assets turnover, and total assets turnover, measure how effectively managers utilize the assets or resources of a business. Fourth, the *profitability ratios*, such as profit margin on revenue, ROR, return on total assets, and return on equity, gauge management's overall effectiveness. Finally, *market-value ratios* compare the data presented on a company's financial statements to financial market data and include earnings per share and the price/earnings ratio.

4 Learning Objective

Describe how financial ratios can be used to measure and improve a company's financial performance.

In order to derive the most value from financial ratios, management should compare its standards of performance to other companies in the same industry, or to industry averages. Financial benchmarks, that is, businesses that show superior financial performance, should be examined closely to see how well they are doing for the purpose of applying similar practices in a business's own operations. Also, because financial statements give the financial picture of a company at a particular point in time, financial trends should be assessed to find out whether financial structure and profitability are improving or deteriorating.

5 Learning Objective

Examine financial statements by using the DuPont financial system.

The DuPont system provides an effective way of measuring the overall financial performance of a business. The system measures a company's return on total assets, taking into account the capital assets turnover and the profit margin on revenue.

6 Learning Objective

Comment on the limitations of financial ratios.

Although financial ratios are important management tools for assessing the performance of a business, they should be used with caution. Ratios tell where a particular operation is or is not doing well; they do not say why, or what to do about a specific situation.

Key Terms

Asset-management ratios p. 170
Average collection period (ACP) p. 171
Benchmarking p. 179
Benchmarks p. 153
Capital assets turnover ratio p. 173
Current ratio p. 165
Debt/coverage ratios p. 167
Debt-to-equity ratio p. 167
Debt-to-total-assets ratio p. 167
DuPont system p. 187
Earnings per share (EPS) p. 177
Financial benchmarks p. 180
Financial ratio p. 150
Fixed-charges coverage ratio p. 170
Hard financial benchmarks p. 182
Horizontal analysis p. 160

Review Questions

1. Why is it important to use ratios to analyze financial statements?
2. What does management want to achieve when it tries to "ensure liquidity" and "maintain solvency"?
3. What is the purpose of vertical analysis and horizontal analysis?
4. What do liquidity ratios reveal?
5. Differentiate between the current ratio and the quick ratio.
6. Is it possible for a firm to have a high current ratio and still have difficulty paying its current bills? Why or why not?
7. Is the inventory ratio more important to a grocery store than to a hardware store? Why or why not?
8. What is the purpose of the debt/coverage ratios?
9. What is the purpose of the TIE ratio?
10. What is the purpose of the asset-management ratios?
11. Explain the purpose of the inventory turnover ratio.
12. Profitability ratios try to indicate the financial performance of a business in terms of revenue, total assets, and equity. Explain.
13. What is a financial benchmark and what is it used for?
14. Explain what the DuPont financial system tries to reveal.
15. Why do managers examine trends when looking at financial statements?
16. What are the limitations of financial ratios?
17. Why are financial ratios so critical to managers when evaluating business performance?
18. Explain why some companies can influence many of their ratios simply by choosing their fiscal year-end. In what type of industries do you think this might be a particular problem?

19. Financial ratios are analyzed by four groups of individuals: managers, short-term lenders, long-term lenders, and equity investors. What is the primary emphasis of each group in evaluating ratios?

Learning Exercises

EXERCISE 1

Mary Pascal is having some problems with her cash flow. She asks her accountant to find a solution that would generate more cash from her working capital. The accountant indicates that if Mary were to manage her trade receivables and inventories more efficiently, she would be able to improve her cash flow performance. With the following information, calculate how much cash Mary could generate within the next four months if she were able to improve her average collection period to 35 days and the inventory turnover to 6 times.

Revenue	$ 2,500,000
Cost of sales	1,700,000
Trade receivables	300,000
Inventories	400,000

EXERCISE 2

Helen Wiseman, owner of a convenience store, is going to meet her banker hoping for an increase in her working capital loan. She figures that an additional loan would increase her finance costs by an extra $10,000. Before seeing her banker, she asks her accountant to determine whether she would have difficulty in servicing her debt with the additional finance costs.

With the following information, calculate the company's TIE ratio and fixed-charges coverage ratio. If you were the banker, would you consider approving the loan? Why or why not?

	Statement of Income (in $)
Revenue	600,000
Cost of sales	(200,000)
Gross profit	400,000
Expenses	
Sales salaries	(150,000)
Rent	(20,000)
Office salaries	(90,000)
Advertising	(23,000)
Finance costs	(30,000)
Total expenses	(313,000)
Profit before taxes	87,000
Income tax expense	(25,000)
Profit for the year	62,000

EXERCISE 3

After being in business for six years, Graham Mason, owner of a small retail store, is considering buying a new information system that would provide him with better operating and financial information. Graham feels that the new system would help him have much better control over his inventories so that he would be able to manage his purchases more wisely. He is also interested in making major renovations to his store.

After going through some detailed calculations, he determines that he would have to invest around $250,000 to have his plans completed by December 31, 2010. Graham is considering borrowing some money from the bank. However, before meeting his banker, he asks his accountant to figure out how much cash he would be able to squeeze from his operations (internally) to help him finance his two projects.

Graham feels that he would be able to improve his average collection period to 40 days and turn his inventory three times a year by December 31 of 2010. With the following information, calculate how much cash Graham could raise internally by December 2010.

Statement of Financial Position
as at December 31, 2010
(in $)

Inventories	200,000	Trade and other payables	150,000
Trade receivables	100,000	Notes payable	50,000
Cash	25,000	Future income taxes payable	50,000
Total	325,000	Total	250,000

Statement of Income
for the year ended December 31, 2010
(in $)

Revenue	500,000
Cost of sales	(300,000)
Gross profit	200,000
Other expenses	(135,000)
Depreciation	(15,000)
	(150,000)
Profit before taxes	50,000
Income tax expense	(25,000)
Profit for the year	25,000

EXERCISE 4

Fauquier Resources Inc.'s current revenue is $20.0 million and the sales and marketing department expects that it will reach $30.0 million by next year. At the moment, trade receivables are $3.5 million; inventories, $4.5 million; and non-current assets, $6.0 million. The company expects these assets to increase at the same percentage rate as that of revenue.

Based on his calculations, the treasurer anticipates a $2.5 million increase in the company's cash balance, and that trade and other payables will increase from $5.0 to $7.0 million. According to the company's operational plans, the profit for the year is expected to reach $4.0 million and the board of directors has approved a $1.5 million dividend payout. The company's income tax rate is at 40%.

Question

Will the company require any external financial cash flows next year? If yes, how much?

Cases

CASE 1: PICKWICK RESTAURANTS

Jaclyn Hargrove is the owner of six Pickwick Restaurants. For the past 10 years, she has always relied on her accountant to provide the analysis of her financial statements. Jaclyn feels that if she were able to read her financial statements, she would be able to improve the analysis of her financial performance. More importantly, she would be able to improve the decisions that touch on all aspects of her business, from the management of working capital to making investments.

Jaclyn has just purchased accounting software that would provide her with monthly, quarterly, and yearly financial statements and, more importantly, all types of ratios that would help her improve her analysis and decisions.

To help her understand the meaning of her financial statements, Jaclyn asks you for some advice. She shows you her December 31, 2010, statement of financial position and statement of income and asks you to calculate and explain the meaning of the more important financial ratios.

To help Jaclyn understand financial ratios, calculate the 2010 financial ratios by using the 2010 statement of financial position and statement of income, and explain to her the meaning and significance of each ratio.

a) current ratio
b) quick ratio
c) debt-to-total-assets ratio
d) debt-to-equity ratio
e) times-interest-earned ratio
f) fixed-charges coverage ratio
g) average collection period
h) inventory turnover ratio
i) capital assets turnover ratio
j) total assets turnover ratio
k) profit margin on revenue ratio
l) return on revenue ratio
m) return on total assets ratio
n) return on equity ratio

Statement of Financial Position
as at December 31, 2010
(in $)

Non-current assets		Equity	
Property, plant, and equipment	2,600,000	Preferred shares	100,000
Accumulated depreciation	(700,000)	Common shares	500,000
Total non-current assets	1,900,000	Retained earnings	560,000
		Total equity	1,160,000
		Long-term borrowings	1,640,000
Current assets		**Current liabilities**	
Inventories	1,100,000	Trade and other payables	710,000
Trade receivables	900,000	Notes payable	250,000
Term deposits	120,000	Accruals	260,000
Cash	90,000	Current income taxes payable	90,000
Total current assets	2,210,000	Total current liabilities	1,310,000
Total assets	4,110,000	Total equity and liabilities	4,110,000

Statement of Income
for the year ended December 31, 2010
(in $)

Revenue		4,500,000
Cost of sales		(3,300,000)
Gross profit		1,200,000
Other income		20,000
Expenses		
Distribution costs	(350,000)	
Rent	(100,000)	
Administrative expenses	(345,000)	(795,000)
Finance costs		(120,000)
Depreciation		(50,000)
Total other income/costs		(945,000)
Profit before taxes		255,000
Income tax expense		(127,500)
Profit for the year		127,500

CASE 2: IMPERIAL ELECTRONICS LTD.

Imperial Electronics Ltd. is a publicly owned company with 100,000 common shares outstanding. At the last executive committee meeting, Sandra Redgrave, CEO of the company, informed the board members of the economic slowdown that she anticipated during the next several years. She also told them that several U.S. firms were considering becoming more aggressive in the industry, particularly in the Canadian market.

Because of these external threats, management of Imperial Electronics Ltd. anticipates more difficult times ahead. For this reason, company management is now trying to watch its financial ratios more closely in order to keep the firm under control.

On the basis of the information contained in the company's financial statements, calculate and comment on Imperial Electronics Ltd.'s December 31, 2009, financial ratios by comparing them to the industry average. The common shares are valued on the stock market at $120.00.

a) current ratio
b) quick ratio
c) debt-to-total-assets ratio
d) debt-to-equity ratio
e) times-interest-earned ratio
f) fixed-charges coverage ratio
g) average collection period
h) inventory turnover ratio
i) capital assets turnover ratio
j) total assets turnover ratio
k) profit margin on revenue ratio
l) return on revenue ratio
m) return on total assets ratio
n) return on equity ratio
o) earnings per share ratio
p) price/earnings ratio

In July 2010, management of Imperial Electronics Ltd. is planning to invest substantial sums of money ($3,000,000) in capital assets for modernization and expansion purposes. The management committee is considering the possibility of borrowing funds from external sources. However, before meeting the investors, members of the management committee want to examine the amount that could be generated internally before June 30, 2010.

Industry financial ratios are as follows:

a) current ratio	1.95 times
b) quick ratio	1.03 times
c) debt-to-total-assets ratio	55%
d) debt-to-equity ratio	1.21 times
e) times-interest-earned ratio	6.43 times
f) fixed-charges coverage ratio	4.51 times
g) average collection period	35.00 days
h) inventory turnover ratio	7.00 times
i) capital assets turnover ratio	5.10 times
j) total assets turnover ratio	2.90 times
k) profit margin on revenue ratio	9.10%
l) return on revenue ratio	2.10%
m) return on total assets ratio	6.00%
n) return on equity ratio	21.00%
o) earnings per share	$8.50
p) price/earnings ratio	10.30 times

Assuming that the company is just as efficient as the industry in managing its inventories and trade receivables, calculate the amount of cash it could generate by June 30, 2010. Also, assume that in 2010 revenue will increase by 9%, ROR will be 5%, depreciation will increase to $400,000, and cost of sales in relation to revenue will improve to 72%.

Imperial Electronics Ltd.
Statement of Income
for the year ended December 31, 2009
(in $)

Revenue		30,000,000
Cost of sales		(23,000,000)
Gross profit		7,000,000
Expenses:		
Distribution costs	(2,500,000)	
Lease	(125,000)	
Depreciation	(300,000)	
Administrative expenses	(1,700,000)	
Total expenses		(4,625,000)
Finance costs		(400,000)
Total		(5,025,000)
Profit before taxes		1,975,000
Income tax expense		(900,000)
Profit for the year		1,075,000

Imperial Electronics Ltd.
Statement of Financial Position
as at December 31, 2009
(in $)

Non-current assets		Equity	
Property, plant, and equipment	8,200,000	Common shares	2,500,000
Depreciation	(2,000,000)	Retained earnings	3,300,000
Property, plant, and equipment	6,200,000	Total equity	5,800,000
		Long-term borrowings	4,200,000
Current assets		**Current liabilities**	
Inventories	4,100,000	Trade and other payables	2,500,000
Trade receivables	3,500,000	Notes payable	1,600,000
Prepaid expenses	250,000	Accruals	220,000
Term deposits	200,000	Current income tax payable	80,000
Cash	150,000	Total current liabilities	4,400,000
Total current assets	8,200,000	Total liabilities	8,600,000
Total assets	14,400,000	Total equity and liabilities	14,400,000

CASE 3: ADC PLUMBING AND HEATING LTD.

Albert Ellis owns a small plumbing and heating business. His main activities consist of installing and repairing piping systems, plumbing fixtures, and equipment such as water heaters, particularly for the residential market. His accountant and advisor prepared his financial statements for the current year. The statement of financial position and the statement of income for the year 2009 are presented below.

ADC Plumbing and Heating Ltd.
Statement of Financial Position
as at December 31, 2009
(in $)

Non-current assets		Equity	
Property, plant, and equipment	300,000	Shares held by Albert	130,000
Depreciation	(50,000)	Retained earnings	150,000
Property, plant, and equipment	250,000	Total equity	280,000
		Long-term borrowings	150,000
Current assets		**Current liabilities**	
Inventories	10,000	Trade and other payables	200,000
Trade receivables	330,000	Short-term borrowings	50,000
Cash	90,000	Total current liabilities	250,000
Total current assets	430,000	Total liabilities	400,000
Total assets	680,000	Total equity and liabilities	680,000

ADC Plumbing and Heating Ltd.
Statement of Income
for the period ended December 31, 2009
(in $)

Revenue		1,500,000
Cost of sales		(750,000)
Gross profit		750,000
Expenses:		
Distribution costs	(350,000)	
Lease	(25,000)	
Depreciation	(30,000)	
Administrative expenses	(200,000)	
Total expenses		(605,000)
Finance costs		(30,000)
Total		(635,000)
Profit before taxes		115,000
Income tax expense		(40,000)
Profit for the year		75,000

Albert and his accountant are considering making a few decisions that will impact the financial statements.

1. If Albert was to use $80,000 of his cash from the business to pay off some of his trade and other payables, how will this transaction alter his current ratio, quick ratio, and debt-to-total-assets ratio.
2. Albert is trying to keep his inventories at a minimum with an amount of only $10,000. However, another plumbing and heating contractor is going out of business in a different town and is selling his inventories, valued at $100,000, for only $60,000.

(a) Albert's son, who is not presently an owner of the business, is considering buying the inventory for cash and, in return, would gain a part ownership in the business. How would this transaction modify the company's current ratio, quick ratio, and debt-to-total-assets ratio?

(b) Instead of having his son become a shareholder of the business, Albert borrows a working capital loan from the bank for $60,000 at 10% interest. How would that decision affect the ratios identified in (a), as well as the times-interest-earned ratio?

(c) If Albert was to borrow the $60,000 on a long-term basis, how would this decision alter the ratios identified in (a), as well as the times-interest-earned ratio?

PHOTO/Dean Mitchell/Shutterstock

CHAPTER 5

[PROFIT PLANNING AND DECISION-MAKING]

Learning Objectives

After reading this chapter, you should be able to:

1 Learning Objective

Explain various cost concepts related to break-even analysis such as fixed and variable costs, the relationship between revenue and costs, the contribution margin, the relevant range, and relevant costs.

2 Learning Objective

Draw the break-even chart and calculate the break-even point, the cash break-even point, and the profit break-even point, and explain how they can be applied in different organizations.

3 Learning Objective

Differentiate between different types of cost concepts such as committed and discretionary costs, controllable and non-controllable costs, and direct and indirect costs.

Chapter Outline

OPENING CASE

Now that the Millers have been in business for close to two years, they are continuously faced with operating and investing decisions such as the following:

- Should we increase our advertising budget? By how much?
- Should we hire more part-time or full-time sales associates? Should we let some go? How many?
- Should we introduce a new product line?
- Should we open a new retail outlet?
- Should we reduce our selling price for a product line? Increase it? By how much?
- Should we introduce a new service?

The Millers realize that the key element that will determine whether they should proceed with some of these decisions is whether the increase in revenue will be adequate to generate sufficient profit. For example, if an additional $2,000 in advertising is spent, how much more revenue should be generated in order to pay for this cost and to generate a profit? Although the Millers had been making some of these decisions by using their instinct and good judgment, they were looking for a decision-making tool that could help validate their feelings. Len had heard that break-even analysis (also called operating leverage) is an effective tool that could be used for that purpose. He therefore decided to meet with May Ogaki, the Millers' accountant, to learn more about how this tool could be used to improve the effectiveness of his decisions. During the meeting, May made the following comments:

> Break-even analysis is an excellent and effective decision-making tool and is very easy to apply. Before using this tool, however, what you need to do is to carefully differentiate your store's costs in terms of what is fixed and what is variable. You will have to draw on your cost accounting knowledge and skills if you want to use the break-even technique as a reliable decision-making instrument. As you are fully aware, some of your costs are relatively easy to classify between fixed and variable. For example, costs such as the goods you buy from suppliers and sales commissions vary directly with revenue and, for this reason, they are considered "variable." The more you sell, the more you buy goods from suppliers. However, costs such as leasing and office salaries do not vary with the level of sales activities (revenue). For that reason, they are considered "fixed."
>
> Other costs, however, are more difficult to differentiate; for example, you may want to classify some of your sales associates' salaries as fixed and some as variable. Advertising could also be considered fixed or variable. It all depends on how you look at these costs. For instance, should you set a "fixed budget" for advertising a product line, or should you increase your advertising budget if you sell more of a certain product line? Once you have determined exactly how each item (e.g., advertising, sales salaries) shown on your operating budget should be considered (fixed or variable), the break-even calculation can be done rather quickly and easily.
>
> The allocation of your store's overhead costs to each department is also an important element to consider when calculating the break-even point

for different product lines. For example, how will you want to distribute your finance costs, your depreciation expense, and office salaries against each product line? You will have to go through this cost accounting allocation process if you want to get the full benefit of the break-even technique.

Len felt that the break-even calculation would be an excellent tool and considered investing some time and effort in understanding cost accounting in order to improve the effectiveness of his decisions.

Chapter Overview

If a business operated without fixed costs (e.g., rent, salaries), its managers would not have to be concerned about incurring a loss. In fact, managers of this unusual type of business would not have to go through detailed calculations to set prices for different products nor evaluate the level of risk associated with the business. If variable costs (e.g., purchases, sales commissions) were the only element to be deducted from revenue to arrive at a profit, profit planning would be relatively simple. In this instance, all that would be required would be to deduct, say, a $5.00 variable cost from a $7.00 price per unit to obtain a $2.00 profit. Irrespective of whether a business sold 20 or 100,000 widgets, it would make a $2.00 profit on each unit. The absence of fixed costs would not only facilitate the preparation of profit plans and detailed operating budgets but also allow the business to operate at minimal or no risk. Under these operating conditions, chances for incurring a loss would be virtually nonexistent.

However, businesses do not operate under such favourable conditions. The fact that businesses have to pay ongoing fixed costs creates an element of the unknown. Recognizing that fixed costs must be paid, managers need a complete knowledge of the number of widgets that should be sold. In addition, they need to know at what price each product should be sold, the exact costs that will be incurred in producing each widget, and the total costs that will be generated by the business if *x* or *y* widgets are sold.

If managers are to plan their profit in a proficient manner, and measure precisely the risk they are prepared to take, they should be able to calculate, analyze, and compare the projected sales volume, the unit selling price for each product, and all costs associated with running the business. If, on the other hand, managers are unable to forecast their costs and revenue with reasonable accuracy, the chances of achieving a favourable profit level are minimized.

As shown in Figure 1.1 on page 7, this is the first chapter related to operating decisions. In large measure, break-even analysis has to do with day-to-day managerial decisions that can have an impact (favourable or unfavourable) on a company's bottom line. However, this tool can also be useful for managers to make capital investment decisions (investing decisions) such as modernizing a plant or investing in a new facility.

Break-even analysis is a straightforward yet very powerful managerial tool that can help managers make a wide range of important decisions that touch on all types of business activities. Here are a few examples.

For *pricing decisions*, break-even analysis helps to analyze the effect of changing prices and volume relationships on levels of profit. For example, if a software company decides to increase or decrease its selling price per unit by 5% with no change in variable costs and fixed costs, break-even analysis would make it easy for managers to determine whether the change will have a positive or negative impact on profitability. Nevertheless, the most difficult variable element to pin down in this particular analysis is the reaction of competitors.

New product, new plant, new sales representative, new sales office, or new advertising campaign decisions are typical decisions that break-even analysis can help with. For example, break-even analysis can help determine the incremental sales volume level that is required in order to justify an investment, given the projected unit selling price and operating costs.

Modernization or *automation decisions* can be made more clearly with break-even analysis as it can disclose profit implications. All that is required within the break-even analysis framework is to determine to what extent variable costs (e.g., direct labour) can be substituted for by fixed costs (e.g., finance costs or depreciation). For example, if management wants to invest $1.0 million to automate a plant, additional costs (presumably most of them fixed) associated with the automation program would replace the use of workers and the reduction of wages (variable costs). Break-even analysis helps to study the interplay between the various types of costs affecting a business and the impact they have on profit performance.

Expansion decisions involve the study of the impact that incremental volume has on profitability. When a business reaches full operating capacity at one of its plants, management must decide whether to use its resources to expand the existing plant or to build a new one. The key question is this: Will the incremental volume and cost levels have a positive (or negative) effect on profitability? Because expansion programs impact variable costs, fixed costs, economies of scale, and profitability, break-even analysis helps to analyze the interplay between each of these variables.

Profit decisions deal with what a company needs to do in order to achieve a certain level of profitability. For example, if a company is operating at a loss or sub-par performance and wants to achieve a profit objective, say, 10% return on assets, the break-even analysis tool will help company management decide on the following in order to achieve the objective:

- How many units should we sell?
- At what price should we sell our product or service?
- What should our fixed costs be?
- What should each unit cost be?
- Which product or service should we push?

This chapter examines how break-even analysis can be used as a decision-making instrument. In particular, it focuses on three key topics. The first topic deals with various cost concepts related to break-even analysis—in particular, fixed costs, variable costs, and semi-variable costs—and how these various costs affect a company's bottom line. It also explains the contribution margin concept and its importance, the relevant range, and relevant costs.

The second topic explains the break-even analysis in terms of how the break-even chart can be drawn and how the break-even point is calculated. This segment also explains the cash break-even point, the profit break-even point, and the relevance of sensitivity analysis. It looks at how break-even analysis can be applied to different areas of an organization such as company-wide, district or sales territory, service centre, and retail store. This segment also clarifies the relevance of break-even wedges.

The third topic explains other cost concepts such as committed versus discretionary costs, controllable versus non-controllable costs, and direct versus indirect costs.

Cost Concepts Related to Break-Even Analysis

1 Learning Objective

Explain various cost concepts related to break-even analysis such as fixed and variable costs, the relationship between revenue and costs, the contribution margin, the relevant range, and relevant costs.

Cost-volume-profit analysis
Tool used for analyzing how volume, price, product mix, and product costs relate to one another.

Calculating the profit generated by a business, a product, or a service at different levels of production requires a total awareness of how volume, price, product mix, and product costs relate to one another. The tool used for analyzing the behaviour of these different variables, how they relate to one another, and how they affect profit levels, is called **cost–volume–profit analysis**. The major advantage of understanding the cost–volume–profit concept is that it helps managers determine the interrelationships among all costs affecting profits. The next three sections related to cost concepts examine (1) cost behaviour, that is, the meaning of fixed and variable costs; (2) the anatomy of profit, that is, the relationship of costs to changes in the level of production; and (3) some basic break-even concept terminology, that is, the meaning of the break-even point, the contribution margin, the PV ratio, the relevant range, and relevant costs.

COST BEHAVIOUR

All costs included in statements of income and budgets can be classified under two distinct groups: fixed costs and variable costs.

Fixed costs
Costs that remain constant at varying levels of production.

Fixed costs. Costs that remain constant at varying levels of production are called **fixed costs**, also known as *period costs*, *time costs*, *constant costs*, or *standby costs*. Although there might be subtle variations between each of these terms, they all have an element of "fixedness" and all must be paid with the passage of time. Such costs do not change as a result of variations in levels of production. Some of these costs are inescapable because they are essential for operating purposes. The following are typical examples of fixed costs:

- Rent or lease
- Finance costs

- Property insurance
- Property taxes
- Office salaries
- Depreciation
- Protection services
- Telephone
- Professional fees

Figure 5.1 shows the relationship between fixed costs and volume.

Variable costs
Costs that fluctuate directly with changes in volume of production.

Variable costs. Costs that vary directly with fluctuations in production levels are referred to as **variable costs**, also known as *direct costs*, *out-of-pocket costs*, or *volume costs*. As the volume of a business increases, so do these costs. For example, if a business produces 100 widgets at a per-unit cost of $0.10 for material A and $0.20 for material B, the firm would therefore incur a total variable cost of $30. If the firm sells 1,000 units, the costs would increase to $300.

Such costs are called variable because they vary "almost" automatically with volume. The following are typical examples of variable costs:

- Sales commissions
- Direct labour
- Packing materials
- Freight-in or freight-out
- Overtime premiums
- Equipment rentals
- Materials
- Fuel

Figure 5.2 shows the relationship between variable costs and volume.

In the News 5.1 gives an example regarding the way variable costs (in this case, labour) can change as a result of variations of ongoing operating activities.

Figure 5.1 Relationship of Fixed Costs to Volume

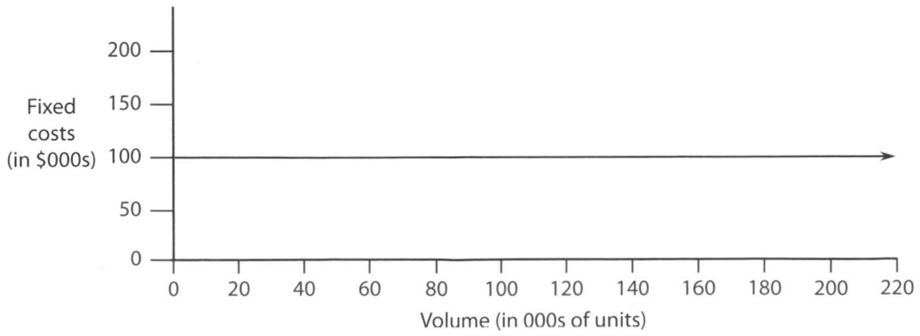

Figure 5.2 Relationship of Variable Costs to Volume

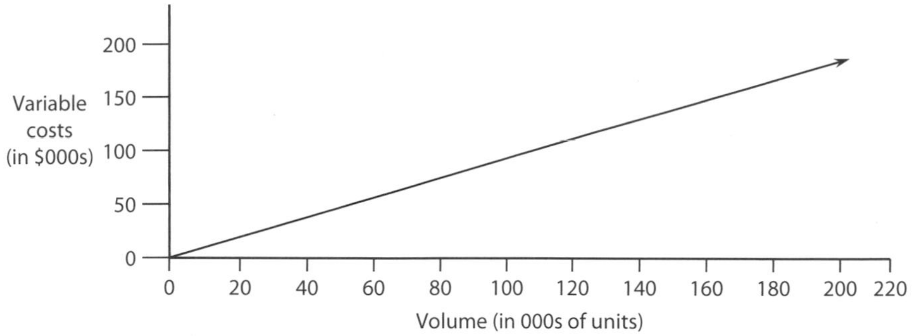

In The News [5.1]

An Organization's Variable Costs Usually Move Upward When it Has to Respond to an Influx of Incremental Activities

Variable costs can behave like magic. They are conveniently placed on the statement of income: These costs increase when more work or additional activities take place, and can easily decrease when there is less work or a reduction in activities.

Let's examine what is happening in the federal bureaucracy. In 2009, the number of public service employees is growing as Canada's deficit is on an upward move. In its annual report, the Public Service Commission indicated that the public service continued to show an increase over the past 10 years and that another 9,072 jobs were added in 2008, a 4.5% increase over the previous year. That growth included all types of jobs, from full-time permanent jobs to student jobs. As mentioned in the report, the factors that contributed the most to this growth included (1) the government's spending spree, injecting billions of dollars into several federal departments (stimulus packages), and (2) the public service renewal plan to bring more new blood into the government's workforce with an annual target of 4,000 students (23,000 students were hired as part of a $20 million stimulus package). In 2009, with a possible majority government around the corner, the public service will come under scrutiny and the possibility of slashing programs is real, which would cause the number of workers to plummet. So, more programs equal more jobs and spending; a reduced level of program activities means fewer workers and, consequently, less spending.

Source: Adapted from Kathryn May, "As deficit grows, so does bureaucracy," *Ottawa Citizen*, October 14, 2009, p. A1. To learn more about the application of the break-even point, go to http://entrepreneurs.about.com/od/businessplan/a/breakeven.htm.

Semi-variable costs Costs that change disproportionately with changes in output levels.

Semi-variable costs. While some costs vary directly and proportionately with volume, others have some characteristics of both fixed and variable costs; in other words, these costs, called **semi-variable costs**, possess different degrees of variability, or they change in a disproportionate way with changes in output levels. For this reason, these types of costs are considered semi-variable (or semi-fixed).

Let's consider four examples. First, there is electricity in a house. House owners have to pay a basic fixed cost each month (say $100.00) even if they don't use any electricity; in fact, the owner could be away on holidays for several months and still receive a $100.00 bill from the hydro company. However, the owners would have to pay additional costs if they were at home using electrical equipment (e.g., stove, toasters, heaters, dryers). This cost would vary according to the number of people living in the house and the extent to which electrical appliances are used.

Second, a business owner may pay a fixed rent to operate a business up to a certain volume level. When that level is reached, the owner may have no choice but to increase the space in order to meet increased production. If this is the case, these costs would be considered fixed for a specific period or up to a certain capacity or range of production.

Third, a business owner may pay *x* dollars for raw materials at *y* level of production, but when that level of operation is exceeded, less may be paid because of increased purchase discounts.

Fourth, if a business owner wants to produce an extra volume of units with the same production crew, after regular hours, time-and-a-half or double time may have to be paid. These direct or variable costs would not vary proportionately with volume increments, and would surely not fit the linear cost pattern.

As shown in Figure 5.3, it is important to separate fixed and variable costs for different levels of volume. This helps to prepare operating budgets in a more proficient manner. Once the costs are identified under their respective categories, they can be related to specific levels of volume. One way of separating costs is by percentage of capacity. As shown in Figure 5.4, a business may incur a total cost of $10.00 per unit (fixed and variable costs between periods A and B) up to 40% of capacity. At that point (B to C), costs will be increased by $2.00 per unit in order to exceed the 40% level of production capacity; this would bring total unit cost to $12.00. Between points C and D (up to 60% of capacity), costs remain the same (fixed costs will not change, while variable costs per unit can still vary proportionately with volume). Again, in order to go beyond the 60% capacity level, the business may increase costs from $12.00 to $14.00. As shown on the figure, costs move from $14.00 to $16.00 (F to G) at the 80% capacity level and remain at that point (G to H) up to 100% capacity.

Figure 5.3 **Relationship of Semi-Variable and Semi-Fixed Costs to Volume**

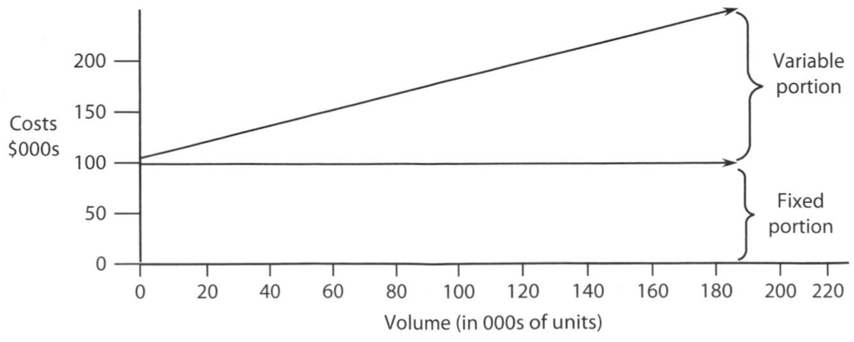

Figure 5.4 **Relationship of Costs to Changes in Level of Production**

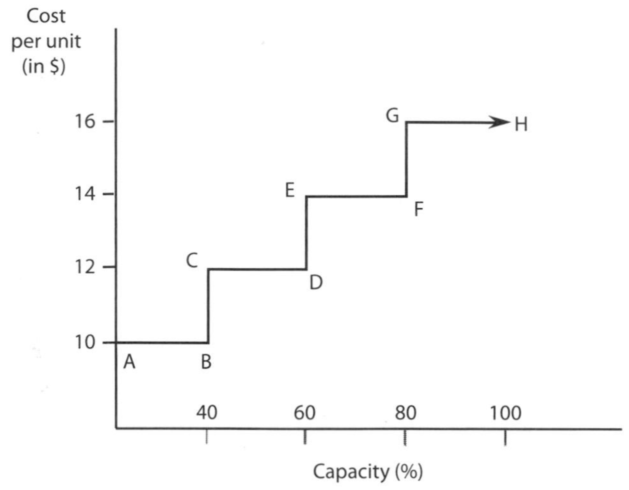

Self-Test Exercise No. 5.1

Fixed and Variable Costs

CompuTech's Statement of Income shows the following cost items:

- Purchases (included in cost of sales)
- Commissions
- Salaries (distribution)
- Advertising
- Travel
- Salaries (administration)
- Leasing
- Finance costs
- Depreciation/amortization
- Freight in (included in cost of sales)

Which of the above costs are considered fixed and which are considered variable?

ANATOMY OF PROFIT

If operating costs changed in the same proportion as that of revenue, or if profits had a linear relationship with costs or revenue, this chapter would be irrelevant. However, as indicated earlier, costs behave in a variety of ways with respect to revenue. If budgets and profit plans are to be prepared in a meaningful way, it is important for management to be completely familiar with the way costs change within specific time periods, at different levels of production, and even with changes in methods of operation.

Knowing the structure of costs, and how costs affect profits when volume changes, enables management to make well-informed decisions. The cost-volume-profit analysis helps managers establish prices in a more prudent way. Establishing accurate prices for a business is the key to achieving profit goals and, ultimately, to determining the success of a business.

The factors that affect profit levels are the following:

- Volume of production
- Prices
- Costs (fixed and variable)
- Changes in product mix

Managers who understand the interrelationships among the above factors and how they each affect profit can more readily realign their operations to changing market conditions. They can identify the relative profitability levels of different product lines, establish prices more effectively, have a better product mix, and, most importantly, be in a better position to make operating changes that will best optimize the use of financial, physical, material, and human resources.

Specifically, analyzing the relationships among costs, volume, and profit enables a manager to answer fundamental questions, such as the following:

- How much volume do we need to sell before hiring another employee?
- At what sales volume should we change our method of operation; for example, should we maintain the existing warehouse or should we move to a larger one?
- Which products require streamlining, from a cost point of view, if we are to improve our profit performance?
- Should we change our product mix?
- When should we purchase another piece of equipment?
- Should we reduce the level of output of product A and increase that of product B?

One of the most effective techniques used in profit planning, solving problems, and making rational decisions is called break-even analysis.

In the News 5.2 gives an example about how a business can improve its financial condition by removing fixed costs (in this case, finance costs) from its statement of income during difficult times.

In The News [5.2]

Reducing Fixed Costs Can Help a Business's Financial Condition in Difficult Times

There is a positive side to incurring fixed costs: They can always be replaced by variable costs without damaging operating activities, and at the same time, they make it possible for a company to obtain a better return on its investments.

On June 30, 2009, Quebecor World Inc., which employs more than 20,000 people worldwide, was given permission by creditors in the United States and Canada to go through a financial restructuring

In The News [5.2] (continued)

process that would allow the company to escape from bankruptcy protection. The approved change included a debt-for-equity exchange. In other words, new shares (variable costs), to be traded on the Toronto Stock Exchange, would replace debts (fixed costs). Quebecor, which is a company that prints books, magazines, directories, and advertising materials increased its debt load at a time when industry trends were in an overcapacity mode, when there were cutthroat price wars, and when the demand for printed materials was spiraling downwards.

Source: Adapted from Barbara Shecter, "Quebecor World creditors approve restructuring," *Ottawa Citizen*, June 24, 2009, p. D3. For more information about Quebecor's financial position, see www.quebecor.com/Home.aspx?Culture=en, and click on "Investor Center."

BREAK-EVEN CONCEPT

Cost behaviour can be understood more easily in a cost–volume–profit relationship when break-even analysis is used. The importance of break-even analysis is that it projects the impact of management decisions made today on future profit levels. This technique helps management to see, well in advance, profit performance resulting from changes in methods of operations. The break-even method gives a picture of the effect that changes in price, costs, and volume have on profit.

Break-even point Level of production where revenues equal total costs.

The break-even analysis deals with the **break-even point**, which can be defined as that point where, at a specific level of revenues, a business ceases to incur losses and begins to make a profit. In other words, it is at that level of operation where profit levels stand at zero, or where total revenues equal total costs. Before examining the break-even chart, let's examine several important concepts, namely, the contribution margin, relevant range, and relevant costs. These concepts will help us to further understand the technicalities of break-even analysis.

Contribution margin The difference between revenues and variable costs.

Contribution margin analysis. So far, fixed, variable, and semi-variable costs have been explained. These different cost concepts suggest that every time a business produces a unit, it increases its revenue and reduces the loss up to a point where total revenues equal total costs. If revenue continues to climb past the break-even point, profits are realized. There is another way of looking at this. Each time a business produces a unit, the revenue generated on each unit "contributes" to paying for fixed costs. Simply put, when variable costs are deducted from revenues, we are left with an amount that, when cumulated, will be used to pay off fixed costs and then realize a desired profit level. The difference between the revenues generated and the variable costs is called the **contribution margin**. The contribution margin is the level of profit that contributes to paying for fixed costs and, eventually, realizing a profit. For example, assume that John's monthly fixed expenses for his house are $2,000 (i.e., mortgage, hydro, insurance, etc.). Let's also assume that John works on a commission basis (say, a job in direct marketing) and earns, on average, $25 an hour. It would take 80 hours for John to pay all his fixed expenses ($2,000 ÷ 25 hours). In other words, every hour of work (or $25) contributes toward the fixed expenses. If John works 81 hours, the money

Table 5.1 The Statement of Income and the Contribution Margin

Revenue		$1,000,000
Less variable costs:		
Direct material	$(500,000)	
Direct labour	(250,000)	
Total variable costs		(750,000)
Contribution margin		250,000
Less fixed costs:		
Manufacturing	(150,000)	
Administration	(50,000)	
Total fixed costs		(200,000)
Profit before taxes		$50,000

that he would earn during the last hour would contribute toward a surplus (profit). If John works 40 hours a week (or 160 hours a month), he would make a $2,000 surplus [(160 hours × $25 = $4,000) – $2,000]. Contribution margin is also known as *marginal contribution*, *profit pick-up*, *cash margin*, or *margin income*.

Rearranging information shown on a statement of income can help identify (or calculate) the contribution margin. Table 5.1 shows how contribution margin relates to revenue, fixed and variable costs, and profit before taxes.

The contribution margin can also be expressed on a per-unit basis, as the difference between unit selling price and unit variable cost. This information becomes extremely valuable for decision-making purposes. If the contribution margin is positive, management knows how much money is earned on each unit sold, which will contribute to meeting fixed costs and realizing a profit. The contribution can also be expressed by a ratio called the *marginal contribution ratio*, *contribution ratio*, or *marginal income ratio*. The term that will be used in this chapter is **profit-volume (PV)** ratio.

Profit-volume (PV) ratio
The contribution margin expressed on a per-unit basis.

Table 5.2 shows how to calculate the contribution by using the PV ratio for varying volume levels. As shown in the table, the difference between revenue and variable costs gives a contribution of $250,000 or a PV ratio of 0.25 ($250,000 ÷ $1,000,000). If revenue increases by 25%, to $1,250,000, the contribution becomes

Table 5.2 Calculating the Contribution Using the PV Ratio

	Base Case	Ratio	Increased Revenues	Decreased Revenues
Revenue	$1,000,000		$1,250,000	$600,000
Variable costs	(750,000)	0.75	(937,500)	(450,000)
Contribution margin	250,000	0.25 (PV)	312,500	150,000
Fixed costs	(200,000)		(200,000)	(200,000)
Profit/(loss) before taxes	$50,000		$112,500	$(50,000)

$312,500 and the PV ratio still remains at 0.25 ($312,500 ÷ $1,250,000). If revenue drops to $600,000 and produces a contribution of $150,000, as shown, the PV ratio is still 0.25 ($150,000 ÷ $600,000).

The contribution margin approach offers significant benefits for examining pricing alternatives. Management can readily determine the impact each increase or decrease in price has on volume, revenue, and profit; this analysis helps streamline production operations in order to reach optimum cost levels.

Self-Test Exercise No. 5.2

The Contribution Margin and the PV Ratio

With the following information, calculate CompuTech's (a) income before taxes, (b) contribution margin, and (c) PV ratio.

Purchases (cost of sales)	$205,000	Salaries (administration)	$38,000
Freight in (cost of sales)	4,000	Revenue	420,000
Salaries (distribution)	60,000	Depreciation/amortization	40,000
Commissions	3,000	Leasing	7,000
Travel	3,000	Finance costs	14,000
Advertising	5,000		

Relevant range
Costs (fixed and variable) that apply to a certain level of production.

Relevant range. Changes in the operating variable costs alter the PV ratio, which in turn affects the profit level. As was indicated earlier, fixed costs can change from period to period, or from one level of output to another. These kinds of costs (fixed and variable), which apply to a certain level of production, are referred to as **relevant range**, and must be budgeted as accurately as possible, because they have a direct impact on the profitability level of a firm in both the short term and the long term. Cost analysis for costs incurred within a specific period must be considered within a designated range of volume levels. If the management of a business decides to increase its manufacturing capacity, more additional costs (fixed costs) will be incurred, or overtime (variable costs) at time-and-a-half or double time will have to be taken into account. Figure 5.5 shows graphically an example of relevant range. In this particular case, the cost information used to budget for a particular year would be relevant for volume of production within the 0 to 1,000 range ($5,000), the 1,000 to 2,000 range ($10,000), and the 2,000 to 3,000 range ($15,000).

Relevant costs
Cost alternatives that managers can choose from to operate a business.

Relevant costs. **Relevant costs** arise when management has the option of choosing among several cost alternatives to operate a business. Cost variations among the options are called *differential costs.* For example, if management is currently spending $20,000 in operating costs for distributing $50,000 worth of goods, two cost options may be analyzed for making a plant more cost efficient and increasing profitability. As

Figure 5.5 **Example of Relevant Range**

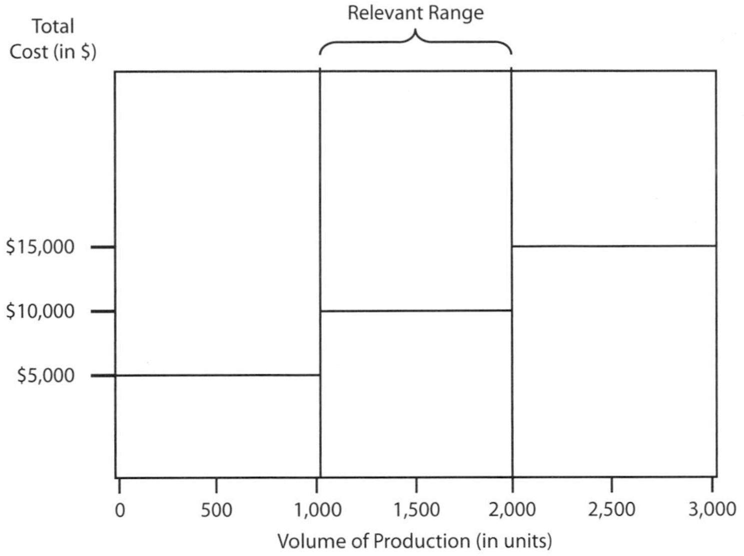

shown in Table 5.3, option A shows that an additional $10,000 in variable costs and $15,000 in fixed costs would have to be incurred. Option B shows an additional $14,000 in variable costs (less efficient than option A) and $13,000 in fixed costs (more efficient than option A). The table shows the differential between the two options. The $20,000 that is already spent for distributing the $50,000 worth of goods is not taken into account in this analysis because it has already been spent. These costs are sometimes referred to as "sunk costs." The only costs that are relevant for the purpose of this analysis are the uncommitted or unspent costs, which are $25,000 for option A and $27,000 for option B. These options should be analyzed because of the $2,000 cost differential. As shown in the table, option A gives a $5,000 profit compared to $3,000 for option B.

Table 5.3 **Differential Costs Between Two Cost Options**

	Option A	Option B	Differential
Revenue	$50,000	$50,000	—
Current costs	(20,000)	(20,000)	—
Variable costs	(10,000)	(14,000)	$4,000
Fixed costs	(15,000)	(13,000)	(2,000)
Total relevant costs	(25,000)	(27,000)	2,000
Total costs	(45,000)	(47,000)	2,000
Profit	$5,000	$3,000	$2,000

The net cost or profit advantage of choosing option A is $2,000.

Break-Even Analysis

2 Learning Objective

Draw the break-even chart and calculate the break-even point, the cash break-even point, and the profit break-even point, and explain how they can be applied in different organizations.

The next four sections look at break-even analysis, in particular (1) the break-even chart, (2) how various break-even points (regular break-even, cash break-even, and profit break-even) are calculated, (3) where break-even analysis can be applied, and (4) the break-even wedges.

THE BREAK-EVEN CHART

Break-even chart
Graphic that shows the effect of change in both revenue and costs on profitability.

The **break-even chart** is a relatively simple way of picturing the effect of change in both revenue and costs on profitability. Figure 5.6 shows the break-even chart for a firm that sells widgets. As shown, there are different parts in a break-even chart, listed below:

- Revenue — line OD
- Revenue zone — area OED
- Fixed-cost line — line AB
- Fixed-cost zone — area AOEB
- Total-cost line — line AC
- Total-cost zone — area AOEC
- Profit zone — area ZCD
- Loss zone — area AOZ

Figure 5.6 The Break-Even Chart

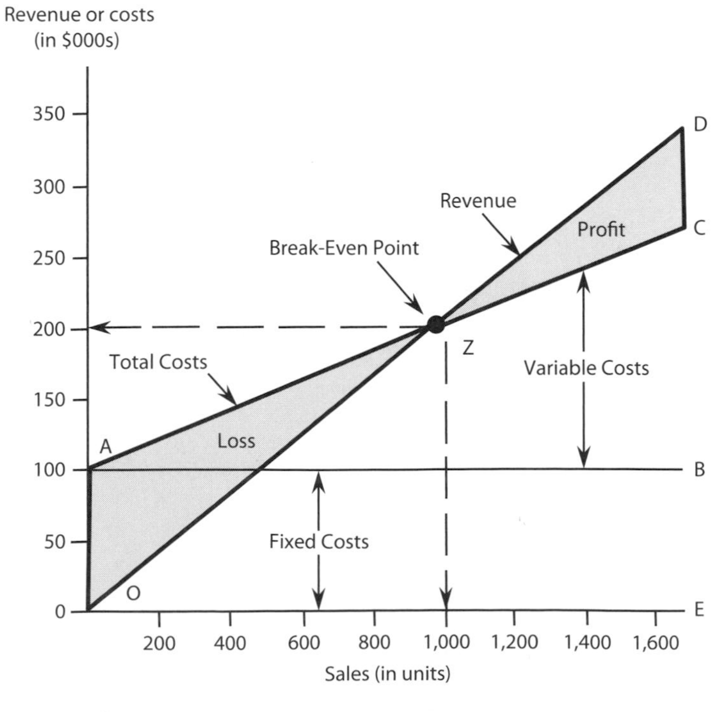

As shown in Figure 5.6, the horizontal axis represents the number of units sold, while the vertical axis represents total revenue and total costs.

Fixed costs (line AB) are shown parallel to the volume-in-units line. Fixed costs are $100,000 and remain unchanged, whether at 0, 600, or 1,600 units.

Revenue (line OD) slopes upward at an angle. As the company sells more units, revenue increases proportionately.

Total costs (line AC) portrays a gradual slope that intersects the revenue line at the 1,000-unit mark. The line begins at $100,000 (fixed costs), and slopes at an angle that is less steep than the revenue line.

The *loss zone* (area AOZ) represents losses if the company sells less than 1,000 units. If the company's unit selling price is maintained at $200 and fixed costs and variable costs are kept at the stated levels, losses range from $100,000, at zero unit sales, to $100 at 999 units.

The *profit zone* (area ZCD) represents the profits made by the company. Any volume of sales made over the 1,000-unit mark (horizontal axis) or $200,000-revenue mark (vertical axis) represents a profit to the company.

The profit and cost schedule shown in Table 5.4 was used to construct the break-even chart shown in Figure 5.6. The table shows numerically the change in profit at varying levels of sales units—from 200 to 1,600. For example, at 200 widgets with an average selling price per unit of $200, the company's revenue amounts to $40,000. At any level of sales volume, the company's fixed costs remain unchanged at $100,000. If the unit variable costs are $100, the total variable cost is $20,000 at the 200-unit volume level. At that level, total costs (fixed and variable) amount to $120,000 and the company realizes a loss in the amount of $80,000.

At 400 units, the loss is reduced to $60,000; at 1,000 units, revenue is at $200,000, fixed costs remain at $100,000, and variable costs reach a level of $100,000, for a total cost of $200,000. At that point, the company is showing neither a loss nor a profit, as costs equal revenue. It is at this particular sales-volume level that break-even takes

Table 5.4 The Profit and Cost Schedule

Sales Units	Unit Price	Revenue	Fixed Costs	Variable Costs	Total Costs	Profit (Loss)
0	$200	0	($100,000)	0	$(100,000)	$(100,000)
200	200	$ 40,000	(100,000)	$ (20,000)	(120,000)	(80,000)
400	200	80,000	(100,000)	(40,000)	(140,000)	(60,000)
600	200	120,000	(100,000)	(60,000)	(160,000)	(40,000)
800	200	160,000	(100,000)	(80,000)	(180,000)	(20,000)
1,000	200	200,000	(100,000)	(100,000)	(200,000)	—
1,200	200	240,000	(100,000)	(120,000)	(220,000)	20,000
1,400	200	280,000	(100,000)	(140,000)	(240,000)	40,000
1,600	200	320,000	(100,000)	(160,000)	(260,000)	60,000

place. Additional volume will improve the company's profit position. With sales units reaching levels of 1,400 and 1,600, the company generates profits of $40,000 and $60,000, respectively.

CALCULATING THE BREAK-EVEN POINTS

The break-even chart gives a visual presentation of the different variables affecting profitability. However, if the intent is to establish the quantity and revenue break-even points, and the variables, such as sales units, fixed costs, and unit variable costs are known, the graph can be formulated algebraically. The following information is needed for an algebraic solution:

SP = selling price per unit
VC = variable cost per unit
FC = fixed costs
N = quantity of units sold at break-even

By definition, we know that, at break-even, total revenue equals total cost. If:

$$\textbf{total revenue} = SP \times N$$

and

$$\textbf{total costs} = (VC \times N) + FC$$

therefore break-even is:

$$(SP \times N) = (VC \times N) + FC$$

The above formula can also be presented in the following way:

$$N\ (SP - VC) = FC$$

or

$$N = FC/(SP - VC)$$

By using the information from Table 5.4, we get:

$$FC = \$100{,}000$$
$$SP = \$200$$
$$VC = \$100$$

The contribution margin ($SP - VC$) is $100 (i.e., $200 minus $100).

By applying the above information to the break-even algebraic formula, we get the following break-even results for quantity and for revenue.

Unit break-even point
Number of units that must be sold in order to cover total costs.

Unit break-even point is:

$$\text{BEP} = \frac{\textbf{Fixed costs}}{\textbf{Price per unit} - \textbf{Variable costs per unit (or Unit contribution)}}$$

$$\text{BEP} = \frac{\$100{,}000}{\$200 - \$100} = \frac{\$100{,}000}{\$100} = 1{,}000 \text{ units}$$

Revenue break-even point
Revenue that must be reached in order to cover total costs.

Revenue break-even point is calculated in two steps:
Step 1: Find the PV ratio or unit contribution.

$$\text{PV} = \frac{\textbf{Unit contribution}}{\textbf{Unit selling price}} = \frac{\$100}{\$200} = 0.50$$

Step 2: Find the revenue break-even point.

$$\text{BEP} = \frac{\textbf{Fixed costs}}{\textbf{PV}} = \frac{\$100{,}000}{0.50} = \$200{,}000$$

If the break-even volume is multiplied by the unit selling price, the same answer is obtained: 1,000 units × $200 = $200,000.

Self-Test Exercise No. 5.3

The Break-Even Point

The Millers are thinking of introducing a new product line in their store. For this exercise, assume the following:

- Total fixed costs allocated to the department are estimated at $15,000.
- Total number of units expected to be sold are 10,000 based on a market study.
- Total variable costs are $20,000.
- Unit selling price is $4.50.

Based on the information above:

1. What is the break-even point in units?
2. What is the break-even point in revenue?
3. Should they go ahead with their plan?

Cash break-even point. The break-even model can also be applied to solve cash-management problems. Most costs, such as rent, salaries, hydro, insurance, raw materials, or telephone, are cash outlays. There are, however, other costs that are non-cash items, such as depreciation/amortization; even though they are treated as expenses, they do not entail an actual outflow of cash.

If we refer to the revenue and cost information in Table 5.4, and assume that the $100,000 fixed cost includes an amount of $25,000 for depreciation, the fixed cash disbursements would therefore be $75,000.

Cash break-even point Number of units or revenue that must be reached in order to cover total cash fixed costs (total fixed costs less depreciation/amortization).

In this case, the **cash break-even point** can be defined as the number of units or revenue that must reached in order to cover total cash fixed costs. The cash break-even point for both quantity and revenue would be calculated as follows:

Quantity (or unit) break-even point is:

$$\text{Cash BEP} = \frac{\text{Fixed costs} - \text{Depreciation}}{\text{Price per unit} - \text{Variable costs per unit}}$$

$$= \frac{\$100{,}000 - \$25{,}000}{\$200 - \$100} = \frac{\$75{,}000}{\$100} = 750 \text{ units}$$

Revenue break-even point is:

$$\text{Revenue cash BEP} = \frac{\text{Fixed costs} - \text{Depreciation}}{\text{PV}}$$

$$= \frac{\$75{,}000}{0.50} = \$150{,}000$$

Profit break-even point. Companies are interested in more than just breaking even. Some establish profit objectives to determine the sales units that should be sold in order to reach the stated objective. If this is the case, all that is needed is to modify the break-even formula. The **profit break-even point** can be defined as the number of units or revenue that must be reached in order to cover total costs plus a profit objective. Referring to our base data shown in Table 5.4, and assuming that $10,000 is the objective, we can calculate the profit break-even points for both quantity and revenue as follows:

Profit break-even point Number of units or revenue that must be reached in order to cover total costs plus a profit objective.

Quantity (or units) break-even point is:

$$\text{Profit BEP} = \frac{\text{Fixed costs} + \text{Profit objective}}{\text{Price per unit} - \text{Variable costs}}$$

$$= \frac{\$100{,}000 + \$10{,}000}{\$200 - \$100} = 1{,}100 \text{ units}$$

Revenue break-even point is:

$$\text{Profit BEP} = \frac{\text{Fixed costs} + \text{Profit}}{\text{PV}}$$

$$= \frac{\$110{,}000}{0.50} = \$220{,}000$$

The various quantity and revenue break-even points are summarized below:

	Quantity (in units)	Revenue
Regular break-even	1,000	$200,000
Cash break-even	750	$150,000
Profit break-even	1,100	$220,000

Sensitivity analysis. Any change in revenue, whether it comes from increased unit selling price, change in product mix, or a reduction in fixed or variable costs, will have favourable or unfavourable effects on a company's profitability. For example, referring to the base data in Table 5.4, a reduction of $20,000 in fixed costs (to $80,000) would reduce the break-even point to 800 units or $160,000 in revenue. Similarly, reducing variable costs to $80 (assuming that fixed costs are at the original level of $100,000) would reduce the break-even point to 833 units [($100,000 ÷ ($200 – $80)]. A simultaneous decline of both costs would improve the company's profitability substantially and reduce the break-even point to 667 units [($80,000 ÷ ($200 – $80)]. The opposite takes place if fixed and variable costs are increased. A change in unit selling price would also have an effect on profitability. If, for instance, the company faces a $20 per unit variable cost increase, and it wishes to maintain its break-even point at the 1,000 mark, the company would have to increase the unit selling price by $20 to $220. Obviously, this assumes that the increase in unit selling price would have no adverse effect on units sold.

Before deciding to make changes in the methods of operation, or to purchase new equipment, it is important to make a **sensitivity analysis** of different break-even points representing changes in unit sales, selling price, unit variable costs, and fixed costs.

Sensitivity analysis
Technique that shows to what extent a change in one variable (e.g., selling price, fixed costs) impacts the break-even point.

Self-Test Exercise No. 5.4

The Cash and Profit Break-Even Points

The Millers have been approached by a supplier to sell a new product line. Based on the supplier's estimates, CompuTech could sell as many as 1,500 units. The suggested retail price for each unit is $14.50. The purchase price for each unit is $7.00. The amount of fixed costs allocated to that particular department is $6,000, which includes a $1,000 amount for depreciation. On the basis of this information calculate the following:

1. Contribution margin
2. PV ratio
3. Revenue break-even by using the PV ratio
4. Cash break-even point in units and in revenue
5. Profit generated
6. Profit break-even point in units and in revenue

Self-Test Exercise No. 5.5

Sensitivity Analysis

Using the information contained in the Self-Test Exercise No. 5.3 on page 223 (The Break-Even Point), if fixed costs were increased by $5,000 and variable costs and unit selling price remained unchanged, what would be the new PV ratio and break-even point in units and in revenue?

WHERE THE BREAK-EVEN POINT CAN BE APPLIED

The break-even system can be used in just about any type of business or any area of a company's operations where variable and fixed costs exist and where products or services are offered. For example, a break-even chart can be applied in any of the following areas: company-wide, district or sales territory, service centre, retail store, plant, production centre, department, product division, or machine operation.

Let us examine how the break-even points can be presented for four of the above areas: company-wide, district or sales territory, service centre, and retail store.

Company-wide. Figure 5.7 shows a company-wide break-even chart. It indicates the various components of all elements entering into the total cost line. For example,

Figure 5.7 Company-Wide Break-Even Chart

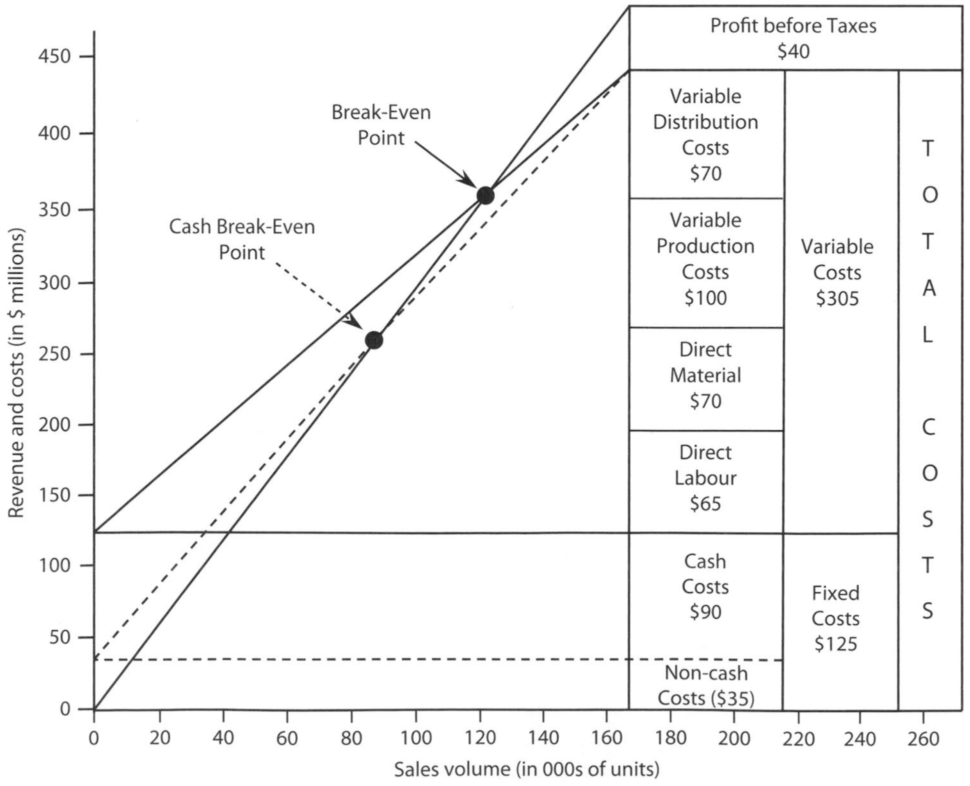

the chart shows the company's revenue is $470 million. Total variable costs are $305 million and include variable distribution costs ($70 million), variable production costs ($100 million), direct material ($70 million), and direct labour ($65 million). Total fixed costs amount to $125 million made up of cash fixed costs in the amount of $90 million and $35 million for non-cash costs (depreciation). The company's profit before taxes is $40 million. On the basis of this information, the company's break-even point is $356 million and cash break-even point is $256 million. The calculation is as follows:

	(in $000s)
Revenue	470,000
Total variable costs	(305,000)
Contribution margin	165,000
Total fixed costs	(125,000)
Profit before taxes	40,000

PV ratio is 0.351 ($165,000,000 ÷ $470,000,000).
The company's break-even point is $356 million ($125,000,000 ÷ 0.351)
The company's cash break-even point is $256 million ($90,000,000 ÷ 0.351).

Self-Test Exercise No. 5.6

Company-wide Break-Even Point

Given the information about CompuTech below, calculate the following:

1. Contribution margin and profit before taxes
2. Revenue break-even point
3. Cash break-even point

Purchases (cost of sales)	$205,000	Salaries (administration)	$38,000
Freight in (cost of sales)	4,000	Revenue	420,000
Salaries (distribution)	60,000	Depreciation/amortization	40,000
Commissions	3,000	Leasing	7,000
Travel	3,000	Finance costs	14,000
Advertising	5,000		

District or sales territory. The break-even point is also useful for analyzing whether it is economically attractive to open a sales office in a particular area. In this case, the fixed costs are rental charges, clerical staff, hydro, depreciation of office equipment, etc. Fixed costs would also include a portion of head-office fixed expenses. The variable costs would include sales commissions, travel, and living allowances. The break-even chart for a district or sales territory is shown in Figure 5.8.

The break-even analysis may become useful for determining whether a sales office should be located in the centre core of the business district, where high fixed costs

Figure 5.8 **District or Sales Territory Break-Even Chart**

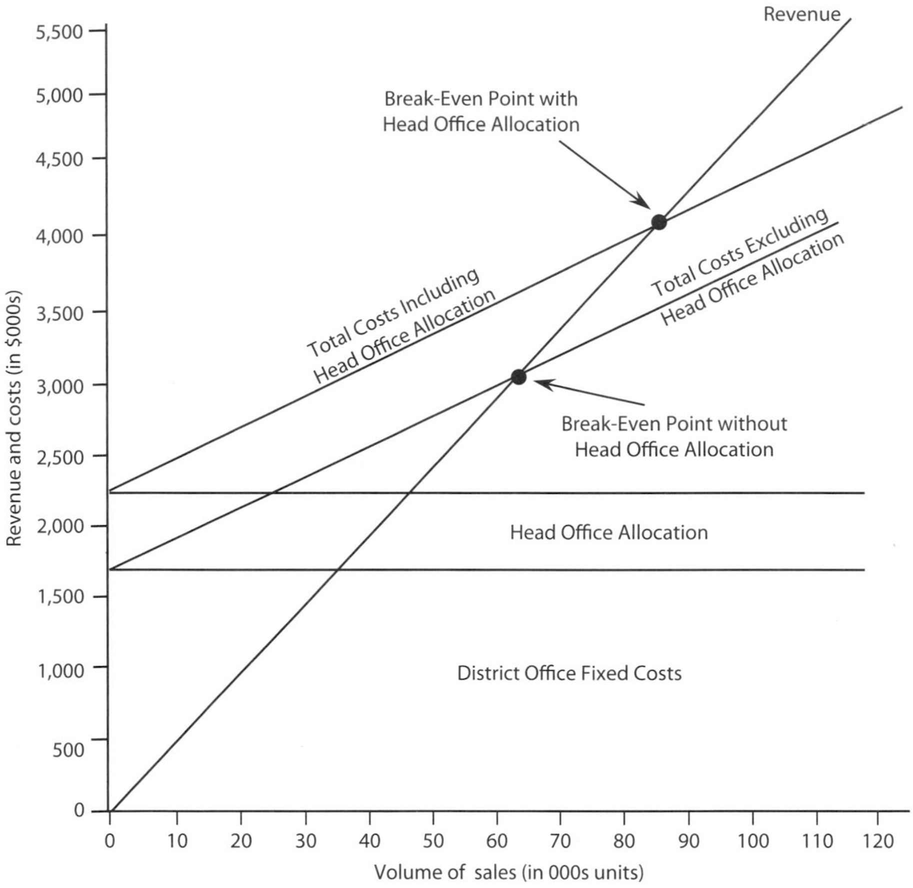

would be incurred and variable costs would be minimized, or in an area remote from the city core, where fixed costs are lower and variable costs higher. In weighing the two possibilities, the marketing manager would have to consider the market potential, the market share objectives, and the revenue for the short and medium term. Let's take the example of a company that is contemplating opening a sales office with a small staff. The initial market study indicates that the company could obtain a reasonable share of the market if the company had a sales staff present in the community. The sales department estimates $5.0 million in revenue during the first year and expects variable costs to be around 45.5% of revenue. As shown in Figure 5.8, the district office fixed cost is estimated at $1.6 million. However, because some headquarters staff would provide services (administration, computers, etc.) to the district office, an amount of $625,000 in overhead costs would be allocated to the sales office. Management's first-year objective is to realize a $500,000 profit before taxes. Based on this information, the sales manager is quite enthusiastic about the new sales office and is prepared to go ahead with the decision. The following information supports his decision:

(in $000s)			
Revenue		5,000	
Office variable costs		(2,275)	
Contribution margin		2,725	PV 0.545
District office overhead costs	(1,600)		
Head office fixed costs	(625)		
Total fixed costs		(2,225)	
Profit before taxes		500	

Break-even point with head office allocation is $4,082,569 ($2,225,000 ÷ 0.545) or 82% ($4,082,569 ÷ $5,000,000) of the revenue target, and the break-even point without head office allocation would be $2,935,780 ($1,600,000 ÷ 0.545) or 59% ($2,935,780 ÷ $5,000,000) of the revenue target.

Self-Test Exercise No. 5.7

Product Line Analysis Using the Break-Even Point

With the following information, calculate the break-even point for CompuTech's product lines A, B, and C.

- Revenue

Product line A	$ 45,000
Product line B	$ 21,750
Product line C	$ 35,000

- Cost of sales for the three product lines is 45%, 50%, and 52% of revenue respectively.
- Fixed costs are estimated at $32,000.

Service centre. Break-even analysis works exceptionally well for activities that produce specific units of output. Here, fixed costs and direct costs can be related to specific levels of operation. Like a retail store, a service unit does not produce specific production units; while fixed costs can be readily identified, variable costs cannot be related to a specific level of operation. The break-even concept can be applied to service operations but with subtle differences. The break-even chart for a service centre is shown in Figure 5.9. The vertical axis represents revenue and costs; the horizontal axis represents revenue. The dollar scale of the horizontal and vertical lines is identical because the break-even chart deals with dollar measurements in both instances. The fixed-costs line is parallel to the horizontal line, while the revenue line has a 45-degree slant. Variable costs vary not with the quantity of units sold, but with the dollar amount, with the slope of the line determined by the PV ratio. For example, if the variable costs represented 50% of revenue, variable costs would increase by a factor of 0.50 every time a dollar sale is made. As shown in Figure 5.9, the service department breaks even at $62,000 ($31,000 ÷ 0.50). This is based on $100,000 revenue generated by the service, a 50% cost directly related to providing the service

Figure 5.9 **Service Centre Break-Even Chart**

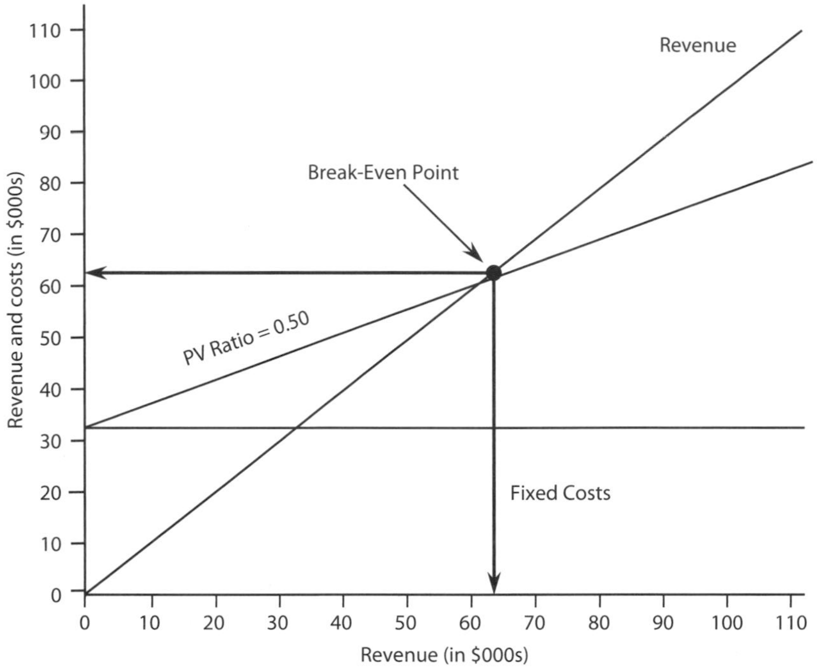

($50,000), and a $31,000 amount of fixed costs. As shown below, the service department's profit before taxes is $19,000.

Revenue	$ 100,000	
Variable costs	(50,000)	
Contribution margin	50,000	PV 0.50
Fixed costs	(31,000)	
Profit before taxes	$ 19,000	

Retail store. As shown in Table 5.5, the break-even point can also be calculated for a retail store. First, we must determine the number of products that would be sold and the unit-selling price for each. As shown in the table, the total revenue amounts to $500,000. Based on that forecast, variable costs, which include purchases and commissions, amount to $275,000 and $25,000, respectively. By deducting total variable costs from total revenue, we find that the store's contribution margin is $200,000. This margin contributes to pay for the $100,000 in fixed costs; the remaining $100,000 is profit before taxes. As indicated in the table, the store breaks even at $250,000, or 50% of its revenue forecast.

BREAK-EVEN WEDGES

Managers have different ways of structuring the cost profile of their businesses. They make their decisions based on two major factors: the level of risk they are prepared to take, and the level of expected sales volume. Some managers may favour a high

Table 5.5 Retail Store Break-Even Point

	Suits	Jackets	Shirts	Ties	Socks	Overcoats	Total
Number of units	800	200	700	900	2,400	500	
Unit price	$300.00	$150.00	$50.00	$30.00	$7.50	$300.00	
Revenue subtotal	$240,000	$30,000	$35,000	$27,000	$18,000	$150,000	
Revenue							$500,000
Variable costs							
Purchases							$(275,000)
Commissions							(25,000)
Total variable costs							(300,000)
Contribution margin							200,000
Fixed costs							(100,000)
Profit before taxes							$100,000

$$\frac{\text{Contribution margin}}{\text{Sales revenue}} = \frac{\$200{,}000}{\$500{,}000} = 0.40, \text{ or } \$0.40$$

$$\frac{\text{Fixed costs}}{\text{PV ratio}} = \frac{\$100{,}000}{0.40} = \$250{,}000$$

Break-even wedge Method that helps managers to determine the most appropriate way of structuring operating costs (fixed versus variable).

volume and a low PV ratio; others, a low volume and a high PV ratio. Some may prefer high fixed costs and low variable costs while others prefer low fixed costs and high variable costs. Figure 5.10 shows different possibilities. The **break-even wedge** is the method that helps managers to determine the most appropriate way of structuring these operating costs (fixed versus variable).

For example, with an extremely high and stable level of sales, it would be preferable for Company A to build a highly automated plant with high fixed costs and low unit variable costs. Management of Company B is not as optimistic about sales levels; it would therefore go for a plant that is not as highly automated (lower fixed costs), but it would have to pay higher unit variable costs (direct labour). Company A would therefore have a competitive advantage over B if the economy is strong and there is a large demand for the product. Profits are amplified when the company has reached its break-even point. If, however, the economy is weak and production levels are low, Company B would have a distinct competitive advantage over Company A because its fixed costs would be lower.

Figure 5.10 shows four companies with different cost structures and PV ratios. Each company shows a different profit wedge. As indicated earlier, Companies A and B have the same break-even points, but Company A has higher fixed costs and a higher PV ratio than Company B. Although Company A's profits are amplified after the break-even point, it is more vulnerable if sales volume falls short of the break-even point. As shown, the loss zone is more pronounced for Company A than for Company B.

Figure 5.10 **Break-Even Wedges**

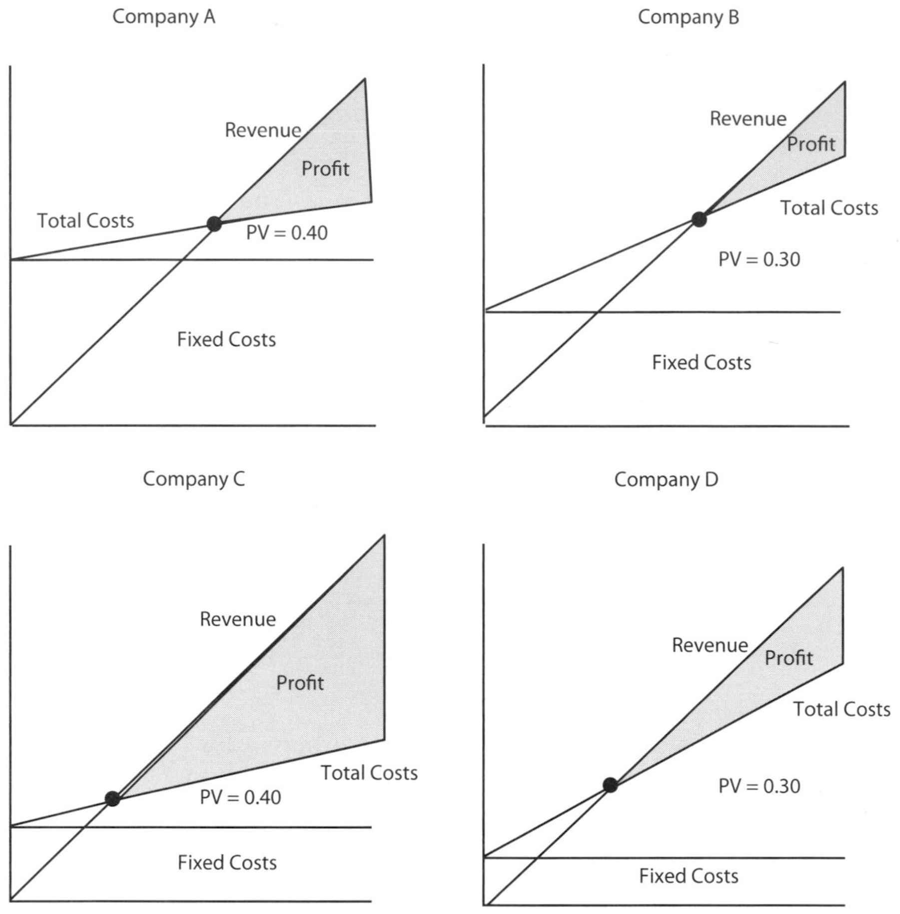

Companies C and D have lower fixed costs. The revenue line is the same as those of Companies A and B, but the profit levels are reached earlier. For example, Company C's profit structure (PV ratio) is similar to that of Company A, but Company C generates a profit on each sales dollar at a lower level of production. Profits generated by Companies B and D follow a similar pattern.

The major advantage of Companies A and C is that profits amplify faster once they have reached the break-even point (producing a wider wedge or bigger PV ratio). These companies are, however, more vulnerable to losses in a slow economy. Companies B and D have similar revenue and variable-cost patterns (the slope of the lines are identical), which produce a similar wedge in the profit zone.

In the News 5.3 gives an example about how a company can increase its PV ratio (or the break-even wedge) by changing its cost structure (more fixed costs and less variable costs), and subsequently, generate more profits over the long term.

In The News [5.3]

Trading Variable Costs for Upfront Costs Can Have Positive Long-Term Financial Benefits

You can trade fixed costs for variable costs, or vice versa, to improve your bottom line. The factor that will determine the type of trade has to do with how much variable costs can replace fixed costs (or upfront costs) and, at the same time, what you want to accomplish.

Atlantic Packaging Ltd. is a company with three paper mills and a vertically integrated producer of packaging finished products. The company started its operations in the late 1940s and it was in 1960 that it began using recycled contents. In 2008, Todd Kostal, director of purchasing and logistics at Atlantic Packaging Ltd., made an analysis of the company's energy costs (electricity, gas, and water) and contacted Enersource Hydro Mississauga to participate in their Electricity Retrofit Incentive Program (ERIP). By installing a more energy-efficient lighting system at its 140,000-square-foot Mississauga plant, the company was able to reduce its energy use for lighting by 60%. According to company officials, they not only wanted to cut back on energy savings but also wanted the plant to be brighter and offer a much nicer environment. As pointed out by Colin Anderson, CEO of Ontario Power Authority, "Companies that are turning these initiatives down at the boardroom are being shortsighted since they are looking at the upfront costs at the expense of long-term benefits."

Source: Adapted from Mary Teresa Bitti, "Seeing the new light," *Financial Post*, June 23, 2009, p. FP12. For more information about Enersource Hydro, visit www.enersource.com.

Other Cost Concepts

3 Learning Objective

Differentiate between different types of cost concepts such as committed and discretionary costs, controllable and non-controllable costs, and direct and indirect costs.

Managers classify costs in different categories. So far, we have made the distinction between fixed and variable costs and have shown that there are also costs that can be classified as semi-fixed or semi-variable. Costs must be classified in separate and distinct categories when preparing a cost–volume–profit analysis. Let us examine other cost concepts and see how they can be used for purposes of analysis and control.

COMMITTED VERSUS DISCRETIONARY COSTS

Fixed costs can be grouped in two distinct categories: committed and discretionary.

Committed fixed costs
Costs that must be incurred in order to operate a business.

Committed fixed costs are those that cannot be controlled and that must be incurred in order to operate a business. They include depreciation on buildings and equipment and salaries paid to managers.

Discretionary fixed costs
Costs that can be controlled by managers.

Discretionary fixed costs are those that can be controlled by managers from one period to another if necessary. For example, expenditures on research and development, training programs, advertising, and promotional activities can be increased or decreased from one period to the next.

It is important to recognize the difference between committed and discretionary fixed costs for cost–volume–profit analysis purposes. As shown in Figure 5.11, for a challenging anticipated planning period, management may decide to cut back some discretionary fixed costs in order to bring the break-even point from B to A.

Figure 5.11 Committed versus Discretionary Fixed Costs

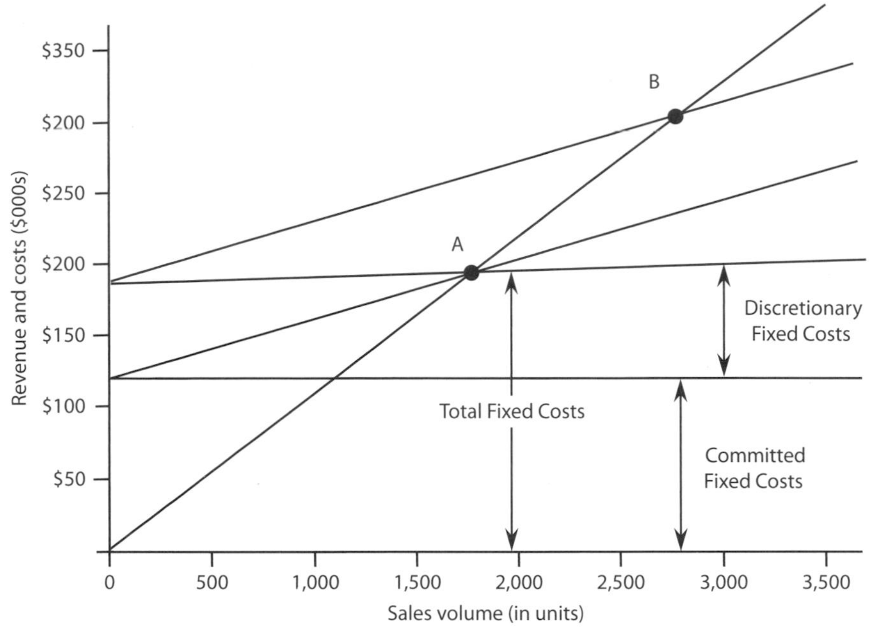

CONTROLLABLE VERSUS NON-CONTROLLABLE COSTS

Accountability is important in the management process. For this reason, it is vital to separate all costs that are within the jurisdiction of a manager from those that are not.

Budgets are allocated to individual managers, and they have to give an account whether they operate within budget ceilings. If certain costs over which managers have control exceed the budget, the managers must explain why. Typical **controllable costs** for plant managers are maintenance, production supplies, overtime, waste, and equipment. Certain other costs are incurred over which they have no control, such as the example given earlier about the opening of a district or sales office (see Figure 5.8 on page 228). In that particular instance, the district manager would not have to account for the head office cost allocations. Typical **non-controllable costs** are depreciation, insurance, supervisor's salary, and other overhead costs (e.g., allocated costs).

Controllable costs Costs that operating managers are accountable for.

Non-controllable costs Costs that are not under the direct control of operating managers.

It is important to distinguish between these two types of costs for reporting purposes. On the manager's budget reports, costs should be grouped under these two categories, and managers should be expected to account only for variances over which they have control.

DIRECT VERSUS INDIRECT COSTS

Costs may be direct or indirect. **Direct costs** are directly related to a specific activity, product, program, project, or objective. These costs would be avoided if an activity was eliminated or incurred if the activity was performed.

Direct costs Materials and labour expenses that are directly incurred when making a product.

Table 5.6(a) Direct and Indirect Costs

	Product A	Product B	Product C	Total
Revenue	$100,000	$90,000	$75,000	$265,000
Direct costs	(25,000)	(55,000)	(50,000)	(130,000)
Indirect costs	(30,000)	(30,000)	(30,000)	(90,000)
Total costs	(55,000)	(85,000)	(80,000)	(220,000)
Profit	$45,000	$5,000	$(5,000)	$45,000

Table 5.6(b) Direct and Indirect Costs

	Product A	Product B	Total
Revenue	$100,000	$90,000	$190,000
Direct costs	(25,000)	(55,000)	(80,000)
Indirect costs	(45,000)	(45,000)	(90,000)
Total costs	(70,000)	(100,000)	(170,000)
Profit	$30,000	$(10,000)	$20,000

Indirect costs
Costs that are necessary in the production cycle but that cannot be clearly allocated to specific products or services.

Indirect costs are not associated with a specific activity, product, program, project, or objective. Typical indirect costs include overhead (e.g., head office allocation), which is usually apportioned among different operating or production units. For example, Table 5.6(a) shows a company that produces three different products, each generating identifiable direct costs. A total of $90,000 in indirect costs or overhead costs is allocated equally ($30,000) to the products. As shown, products A and B are producing positive net results while product C is showing a $5,000 loss. Under these circumstances, management may contemplate the possibility of abandoning product C. If this is the case, the absorption of the $90,000 overhead (if these costs cannot be reduced with the abandonment of product C) would therefore have to be split between products A and B. As shown in Table 5.6(b), this would reduce the profit position of these two products, and even produce a negative result for product B. In addition to apparently losing money on product B, the company would reduce its overall profitability from $45,000 to $20,000. The company would, therefore, be in a better position if it continued to manufacture product C.

[DECISION-MAKING IN ACTION]

Let's now examine how the break-even concept can be applied within the context of decision-making. The left side of Table 5.7 shows the statement of income of Widget Inc. As indicated, the company has a $100,000 profit before tax objective. Management is considering the following decisions:

1. Should we increase our selling price by 5%?
2. Should we increase our advertising budget by $30,000?

3. Should we hire a new sales representative? Cost is estimated at $60,000.
4. What would our break-even revenue be if we were to reduce our variable costs by 3%?
5. How much revenue must we achieve to earn an extra $20,000 in profit before taxes?

To make these decisions, the Widget Inc. managers must first rearrange the statement of income by putting all variable costs and all fixed costs under two distinct groupings. As shown under the rearranged statement of income in the middle section of Table 5.7, it is assumed that the company's variable costs amount to $1,700,000 and generate $800,000 in contribution margin. Total fixed costs amount to $700,000. By regrouping the variable and fixed costs, it is possible to calculate the PV ratio. As shown, the PV ratio is 0.32, calculated by dividing the $800,000 contribution margin by the $2,500,000 revenue amount. This means that for every dollar's worth of revenue, the company is generating $0.32 in contribution margin. The PV ratio is required for the managers to make the decisions. For example, dividing fixed costs by the PV ratio shows that the company would have to sell $2,187,500 or 87.5% of its revenue objective in order to break-even.

The right side of Table 5.7 presents the number of units sold and, for each unit, the selling price, variable costs, and contribution margin. The contribution is maintained at 0.32, or $3.20 per unit.

Let's now look at the five managerial decisions.

Decision 1: Should we increase our selling price by 5%?

If the selling price is increased by 5%, the unit selling price would therefore be $10.50, increasing the contribution margin to $3.70, or 0.37. Dividing the fixed costs ($700,000) by the new contribution margin shows that the company's new break-even point would be $1,891,892. Because its revenue would be increased to $2,625,000 ($2,500,000 × 105%), the company would now break even at 72.7% ($1,891,892 ÷ $2,625,000) of its revised revenue forecast. This looks like a good

Table 5.7 Decision-Making in Action

Widget Inc. Statement of Income		Rearranged Statement of Income			
Revenue	$2,500,000	Revenue	$2,500,000	250,000	(no. of units)
Cost of sales	(1,900,000)	Variable costs		$10.00	(unit selling price)
Gross profit	600,000	Cost of sales	(1,600,000)		
		Distribution costs	(50,000)		
Distribution costs	(300,000)	Administrative expenses	(50,000)		
Administrative expenses	(200,000)	Total variable costs	(1,700,000)	(6.80)	(cost per unit)
Subtotal	(500,000)	Contribution margin	800,000	$3.20	(unit contribution)
		Fixed costs			
Profit before taxes	$100,000	Cost of sales	(300,000)		
		Distribution costs	(250,000)		
		Administrative expenses	(150,000)		
		Total fixed costs	(700,000)		
		Profit before taxes	$100,000		
		PV ratio	0.32	0.32	

decision because the break-even point for achieving the revenue targets would be reduced from 87.5% to 72.7%. However, before increasing its selling price, the managers would have to consider the effect of a change in the selling price on sales volume or revenue; that is, how many customers would be lost as a result of this change. The same calculations (sensitivity analysis) could be done for a 3% increase, a 2% decrease, etc.

Decision 2: Should we increase our advertising budget by $30,000?

If the advertising budget is increased by $30,000, total fixed costs would be increased to $730,000. Dividing these fixed costs by the PV ratio (0.32) shows that the break-even point would be increased to $2,281,250 (instead of $2,187,500), a difference of $93,750. Before increasing the advertising budget, management would have to determine whether the extra $30,000 cost would be able to generate an additional $93,750 in revenue. If it is estimated that the $30,000 would generate, say, an extra $175,000 in revenue, then the higher advertising budget would be justified.

Decision 3: Should we hire a new sales representative? Cost is estimated at $60,000.

The arithmetic here is similar to that of decision 2. Fixed costs would increase to $760,000 and the new break-even point would rise to $2,375,000 ($760,000 ÷ 0.32). Because the existing break-even point is $2,187,500, it means that the company would have to generate an extra $187,500 ($2,375,000 – $2,187,500) in revenue. Could the new sales representative generate this much revenue within the first year? If not, how about the second or third year?

Decision 4: What would our break-even revenue be if we were to reduce our variable costs by 3%?

A 3% reduction would bring the total variable costs to $1,649,000 and increase the PV ratio to 0.34. The arithmetic is done as follows:

Revenue	$2,500,000
Variable costs	(1,649,000)
Contribution margin	$851,000
PV ratio	0.34

Here, the break-even point would be reduced to $2,058,823 (from $2,187,500) or 82.3% of the revenue objective (instead of 87.5%).

Decision 5: How much revenue must we achieve to earn an extra $20,000 in profit before tax?

If management wants to realize a $120,000 profit objective, revenue would have to be $2,562,500 ([$700,000 + $120,000] ÷ 0.32). This means that the company's revenue would have to be increased by 2.5% ($2,562,500 – $2,500,000) ÷ $2,500,000.

FINANCIAL SPREADSHEETS—EXCEL

Templates 1 and 2 of the decision-making tools components of the financial spreadsheets accompanying this manual can calculate the break-even points using the contribution margin and the PV ratio. The objective of Template 1 (Break-Even Analysis Using the Contribution Margin) calculates the break-even point in units and in revenue of a business decision by using the contribution margin. The objective of Template 2 (Break-Even Analysis Using the PV Ratio) calculates the revenue break-even point using the PV ratio. The break-even point for these two templates can be done for three consecutive years.

Chapter Summary

1 Learning Objective

Explain various cost concepts related to break-even analysis such as fixed and variable costs, the relationship between revenue and costs, the contribution margin, the relevant range, and relevant costs.

Break-even analysis can be used in business to make different types of decisions, such as pricing decisions, new product decisions, modernization decisions, and expansion decisions. However, in order to make the right decision, management must have a complete knowledge of its business's operating-cost structure. Cost–volume–profit analysis consists of analyzing the interrelationships among volume of production, fixed costs, and variable costs. Fixed costs remain constant and do not vary with different levels of production. Variable costs vary in direct proportion to changes in level of output. There are also semi-fixed or semi-variable costs that vary at different levels of production. Break-even analysis is the method that helps management determine at what point profit or loss takes place. The break-even point is the level of output where a business stops incurring a loss and begins to make a profit. The contribution margin is the difference between the selling price of a product and the variable costs. This difference is used to pay for fixed costs, and to earn a profit. Relevant range has to do with costs (fixed and variable) that apply to a certain level of production. Relevant costs have to do with alternative ways that managers can choose from to operate a business

2 Learning Objective

Draw the break-even chart and calculate the break-even point, the cash break-even point, and the profit break-even point, and explain how they can be applied in different organizations.

The break-even chart gives a visual presentation of the interrelationships between revenues, variable costs, fixed costs, and total costs. The break-even point can be calculated by using this formula:

$$N = FC \div (SP - VC)$$

The cash break-even point determines how many units a business must sell in order to pay for its cash costs. The profit break-even point determines the number of units a business must sell in order to achieve a targeted profit objective. Sensitivity analysis is used to gauge the various break-even points when there are changes in any one of the variables, such as unit selling price, volume of production, fixed costs, or variable costs. Break-even analysis can be applied in many areas, including sales territories, retail stores, plants, departments, product divisions, production centres, service centres, and machine operation. The break-even wedge is a method that helps managers determine the most appropriate way to structure operating costs (fixed versus variable).

3 Learning Objective

Differentiate between different types of cost concepts such as committed and discretionary costs, controllable and non-controllable costs, and direct and indirect costs.

Costs can also be broken down into committed fixed costs versus discretionary fixed costs, controllable versus non-controllable costs, and direct versus indirect costs.

Key Terms

Break-even chart p. 220
Break-even point p. 216
Break-even wedge p. 231
Cash break-even point p. 224
Committed fixed costs p. 233
Contribution margin p. 216
Controllable costs p. 234
Cost–volume–profit analysis p. 210
Direct costs p. 234
Discretionary fixed costs p. 233
Fixed costs p. 210
Indirect costs p. 235
Non-controllable costs p. 234
Profit break-even point p. 224
Profit-volume (PV) ratio p. 217
Relevant costs p. 218
Relevant range p. 218
Revenue break-even point p. 223
Semi-variable costs p. 212
Sensitivity analysis p. 225
Unit break-even point p. 223
Variable costs p. 211

Review Questions

1. What is the relevance of break-even analysis?
2. Differentiate between fixed and variable costs.
3. Why are some costs called "semi-fixed"?
4. Explain the meaning and the significance of the contribution margin.
5. Comment on the more important elements that affect profit levels.
6. What do we mean by relevant range?
7. What do we mean by relevant costs?
8. Draw a hypothetical break-even chart.
9. What is a PV ratio?
10. Why would someone use the PV ratio instead of the unit contribution margin?
11. Why should managers be interested in calculating the profit break-even point?
12. How can the contribution margin be calculated?
13. Differentiate between the break-even point and the cash break-even point.
14. What is the significance of calculating the cash break-even point?
15. What is the usefulness of sensitivity analysis?
16. Differentiate between committed fixed costs and discretionary fixed costs.
17. What is the difference between direct costs and indirect costs? Give an example for each.
18. What is the significance of using the break-even wedge analysis when analyzing the break-even point?

19. How can the break-even analysis help managers make pricing decisions? Give an example.
20. "The major factor that will underlie the cost structure of a business is the level of risk that managers are prepared to take, and the level of expected sales volume." Explain.

Learning Exercises

EXERCISE 1

For this exercise, consider the following information:

- Total fixed costs are estimated at $100,000.
- Total units expected to be sold are 50,000.
- Total variable costs are $300,000.
- Unit selling price is $8.00.

Now calculate the following:

1. Break-even point in units
2. Break-even point in revenue

EXERCISE 2

A company expects to sell 75,000 widgets at a price of $10.00. The unit variable costs are estimated at $8.00 and the fixed costs are estimated at $125,000. On the basis of this information calculate the following:

1. Contribution margin
2. PV ratio
3. Revenue break-even by using the PV ratio
4. Profit generated

EXERCISE 3

Using the information contained in exercise 1 (above), if rent were increased by $25,000 and variable costs and unit selling price remained unchanged, what would be the new PV ratio and break-even point in units and in revenue?

EXERCISE 4

With the following information, calculate the break-even point for a retail store.

- Revenue

Product line A	$ 100,000
Product line B	$ 200,000
Product line C	$ 600,000

- Cost of sales for the three product lines is 50%, 45%, and 55% of revenue respectively.
- Fixed costs are estimated at $350,000.

EXERCISE 5

With the information outlined below, calculate the following:

1. Profit
2. Break-even point in revenue
3. Cash break-even point

Depreciation	$ 30,000	Office supplies	$ 3,000
Plant direct wages	100,000	Revenue	550,000
Plant supervision	60,000	Overtime	30,000
Advertising	30,000	Rent	35,000
Plant insurance	20,000	Property taxes	10,000
Sales commissions	100,000	Raw materials	100,000

EXERCISE 6

The owner/manager of a beverage and food retail outlet intends to invest $400,000 in another retail store. His objective is to make at least $75,000 in profit before taxes, or 18.75% return on his investment. Based on his market study, he estimates selling 200,000 coffees, 100,000 donuts, 75,000 sandwiches, and 75,000 soups.

The unit selling prices for these different products are $1.75 for coffee, $1.00 for donuts, $2.25 for sandwiches, and $1.75 for soups. Based on his current purchasing costs from existing suppliers, his cost of sales are estimated at 15%, 20%, 40%, and 25% of revenue for coffee, donuts, sandwiches, and soups, respectively. His other annual costs include rent ($100,000), salaries ($235,000), heating and hydro ($45,000), municipal taxes ($35,000), and a variety of other costs ($40,000).

a. With the above information, (1) construct the statement of income and (2) calculate the owner/manager's break-even point in dollars.
b. Based on his forecast, should he go ahead with the project?
c. If his cost of sales was to be reduced by 10%, how would that affect his break-even point?
d. If his rent and salaries increase by $25,000 and $50,000, respectively, how would these changes affect his break-even point (assume that the variable costs remain at the original estimate)?
e. If changes take place simultaneously in both c and d, how would these changes affect his break-even point?
f. If the owner/manager wants to make a $150,000 profit before taxes based on his original cost estimates, how much revenue must his retail outlet generate?

EXERCISE 7

Company A and Company B are both selling $2.5 million worth of goods. Company A's PV ratio is 0.40 while B shows 0.60. Company B's fixed costs are $1.0 million, which puts the business at a competitive disadvantage versus A, which has $500,000 in fixed costs.

1. On the basis of the above information, if revenues were to increase by 20% for both businesses next year, how much profit before taxes would each generate?
2. On the basis of the above information, if revenues were to decrease by 20% for both businesses next year, how much profit before taxes would each generate?
3. Because of the varying cost structures, discuss the implications it has on both companies' profit performance.

Cases

CASE 1: QUICK PHOTO LTD.

Tony Kasabian was just about ready to put the finishing touches on a business plan that he was to present to a local banker for financing his new venture, Quick Photo Ltd. The investment proposal contained a marketing plan designed to capture a good share of the southern Ontario digital print market. Tony was interested in buying several new high-technology digital film printers manufactured in Japan capable of providing online photo finishing and processing of top-quality prints from digital camera cards and CDs. His retailing plan consisted of operating digital print processors in kiosks in several Ontario high-traffic malls, including locations in Don Mills, Ottawa, Windsor, London, and Kingston. He felt that his business concept was in line with the trend of developing high-quality photo finishing services.

However, he realized that his banker would be asking him many questions about the market size, his competitors, his revenue targets for the next several years, and, most important, his marketing assumptions backing up his sales forecast. Therefore, before finalizing his business plan, Tony asked his friend, a recent commerce graduate, to help him calculate the number of prints that he would have to process each year in order to cover his fixed costs and earn a reasonable profit.

On average, Tony figured out that he would charge $0.32 per print, a price consistent with competitors' charges for work of similar quality: most prints would be 4×6; some would be 5×7 and 8×10. Quick Photo's statement of income for the first year of operations is as follows:

Number of prints developed		5,000,000
Revenue		$1,600,000
Cost of sales		
Direct materials	$(250,000)	
Direct labour	(265,000)	
Depreciation	(78,000)	
Supervision	(80,000)	
Total cost of sales		(673,000)
Gross profit		$927,000
Operating expenses		

Distribution costs		
Salaries	$(230,000)	
Sales commission	(110,000)	
Advertising	(25,000)	
Subtotal		$(365,000)
Administration expenses		
Salaries	(185,000)	
Insurance	(20,000)	
Rent	(60,000)	
Depreciation	(33,000)	
Subtotal		(298,000)
Finance costs		(35,000)
Total		(698,000)
Profit before taxes		229,000
Income tax expense		(101,000)
Profit for the year		$128,000

1. Calculate Tony's break-even point in revenue and the cash break-even point in revenue.
2. How many prints a year and what level of revenue must Tony reach if he wants to realize an objective of $275,000 in profit before taxes?
3. Calculate Tony's annual revenue break-even point by using the PV ratio if he is to realize the $275,000 profit before tax objective.
4. If he increases his advertising budget by $20,000, what would be Tony's new yearly break-even point in prints and in revenue? How many additional prints must Tony develop in order to increase his revenue to cover the incremental advertising budget?
5. If Tony reduces his direct material costs for processing the prints by $25,000, what would be his new break-even point in units and in revenue?

CASE 2: V & A CARPET CLEANING SERVICES

In March 2000, Vincent and Anne-Marie Finney started their carpet-cleaning services business in Toronto. The business was geared primarily at married couples, a market that they felt was growing rapidly. Vincent and Anne-Marie had worked during the previous 10 years as salaried employees for different types of organizations and were frustrated with the fact that their future was in the hands of employers. They decided to start V & A Carpet Cleaning Services, a residential carpet-cleaning service located in the Toronto area. After 10 years of tremendous success in the business, the couple decided to launch a franchise operation.

They placed advertisements in different daily newspapers across Canada promoting the franchise business. Bill and Jill Robinson of Ottawa saw the advertisement and called V & A Carpet Cleaning Services to obtain information about the economics and advantages of managing a carpet-cleaning franchise operation. The Finneys provided the following information:

- Average revenue for cleaning carpets in each household is $120.
- A 20% sales commission per contract is secured by a sales representative.
- Machine operators receive $30 for cleaning the carpets in each household.
- Average costs for gas and maintenance for trucks for each household is $5.50.
- Maintenance charges are $400 per machine for each 100 houses cleaned.
- Monthly rental charges for office and small warehouse for inventories is $1,200.
- Annual depreciation for the equipment is $500.
- Monthly salary paid to Bill and Jill totals $3,500.
- A $1,400 monthly salary for office employees.
- A $500 yearly expense for various insurance policies.
- A $125 monthly expense for utilities and telephone.
- A yearly $10,000 fee for the franchise.
- A $5.00 franchise fee for each household cleaned.

On the basis of the above information, calculate the following:

1. How many households would Bill and Jill have to clean each year in order to start making a profit?
2. How much revenue would they have to earn each year in order to break-even?
3. How many households would they have to clean each year if they want to earn a yearly profit of $45,000 before tax?
4. Prepare a statement of income on the basis of earning $45,000 in profit before taxes.

PHOTO/Pakhnyushcha/Shutterstock

CHAPTER 6

[WORKING CAPITAL MANAGEMENT]

Learning Objectives

After reading this chapter, you should be able to:

1 Learning Objective — Define the meaning and importance of the cash conversion cycle.

2 Learning Objective — Explain different strategies related to managing inventories.

3 Learning Objective — Discuss various techniques related to trade receivables management.

4 Learning Objective — Comment on managing cash and cash equivalents.

5 Learning Objective — Show how current liability accounts can be managed to improve the cash flow cycle.

Chapter Outline

Cash Conversion Cycle
Managing Inventories
Managing Trade Receivables
Managing Cash and Cash Equivalents
Managing Current Liabilities

OPENING CASE

During the third year of operation, the Millers were spending more time on the management of their working capital accounts such as inventories and trade receivables. This is quite understandable because during the early years of any business, a considerable amount of funds are invested in working capital. The following shows the evolution of CompuTech's current assets, net working capital, total assets, and revenue between the years 2009 and 2011.

In 000s of $	2009	2010	2011	Increase (%)
Current assets	105	136	235	124%
Current liabilities	52	60	132	154%
Net working capital	53	76	103	94%
Total assets	237	268	637	169%
Revenue	350	420	800	129%

As shown, the Millers' current assets increased by 124% between 2009 and 2011 while current liabilities show a 154% growth. Revenue increased by 129%. In order to improve their financial performance, the Millers recognize that they have to be very cautious as to how they manage their working capital accounts.

Len and Joan are beginning to realize that managing working capital accounts is more complex and time consuming than managing non-current assets (e.g., capital assets). In the case of capital assets (e.g., investing in a new store), they have to go through a detailed capital budgeting process using time value of money yardstick analysis in order to make their decision. This will be discussed in Chapters 10 and 11. However, once that decision is made, nothing much can be done. They have to live with the consequences, good or bad. On the other hand, managing working capital accounts is a daily activity and has to be done in a meticulous and knowledgeable way.

The Millers know that they have to maintain a certain amount of inventories in their store and sell goods and services on credit. These working capital accounts represent essential investments and must be made in order to generate revenue. However, the Millers realize that they have to be wise in the way that they spend their cash in these unproductive but necessary accounts. As Len pointed out:

> Too much investment in inventories and trade receivables is considered a drain on CompuTech's cash flow position and can even blemish the return on our assets. The more that we have to invest in these accounts, the more we will have to borrow from short-term lenders. And of course, the larger the loan, the more finance costs CompuTech has to pay, which ultimately reduces profitability.

The Millers must therefore ensure that just enough cash is invested in working capital accounts to meet their day-to-day operating needs and maximize profitability but not so much that such unproductive assets represent a cash drain on CompuTech. For this reason, the Millers have to manage on a continual basis each current asset and current liability account to ensure that they know exactly how much cash is needed (current assets) and how much cash is required (current liabilities).

Chapter Overview

In Chapter 1, *working capital* referred to all accounts appearing in the current accounts of the statement of financial position, that is, current assets and current liabilities. In the early years of financial management, working capital included only current asset accounts such as inventories, trade receivables, and cash and cash equivalents. These assets are essential for operating a business. Maintaining inventories and trade receivables, having money in the bank to pay ongoing bills, and holding money in marketable securities such as short-term investments are surely not productive assets. However, if a company is to produce goods and sell its products, a certain amount of cash must be tied up in these types of accounts. What is important for a business, however, is to ensure that a minimum amount of funds is tied up in these current asset accounts; as stated above, just enough to ensure that it can meet its day-to-day operations and maximize profitability but not so much that such unproductive assets represent a cash drain on the business. Managing current assets is a critical factor as it represents a major portion (in many cases, about half) of a manufacturing company's total assets.

Today, working capital is defined more broadly. It includes current liabilities, such as trade and other payables, notes payable, other accruals, or all loans that are due within a 12-month period (see Table 6.1 for a typical list of working capital accounts). A current liability, such as trade and other payables, is interest-free. Therefore, it is worthwhile for a business to take advantage of this type of short-term liability to finance its business activities. However, a business should be careful not to jeopardize its position by not being able to meet its short-term obligations.

Net working capital
The difference between current assets and current liabilities.

Net working capital is defined as the difference between current assets and current liabilities. As shown in Table 6.1, for instance, if a company's current assets total $1,420,000 and its current liabilities are $720,000, the net working capital is $700,000 (current ratio of 1.97 times).

Working capital management
Managing individual current asset and current liability accounts to ensure proper interrelationships among them.

Working capital management refers to all aspects of the management of individual current asset and current liability accounts, ensuring proper interrelationships among all current asset accounts, all current liability accounts, and other statement of financial position accounts such as non-current assets and long-term borrowings.

Table 6.1 Working Capital Accounts

Current assets		Current liabilities	
Inventories	$ 755,000	Trade and other payables	$400,000
Trade receivables	500,000	Accrued wages	50,000
Prepaid expenses	40,000	Taxes payable	20,000
Cash and cash equivalents	125,000	Notes payable	50,000
		Bank loan	200,000
Total current assets	$1,420,000	Total current liabilities	$720,000

Net working capital is the difference between current assets and current liabilities.

Working capital accounts require more time than non-current assets such as land, buildings, machinery, and equipment. The level of investment in each of the working capital accounts usually changes on a day-to-day basis, and in order to effectively manage the business, managers must always know how much cash is required in each of these accounts. Mismanagement of current accounts can be costly; excess current assets mean a drain on profits and can be a source of undue risk. Not enough current assets, on the other hand, may entail revenue loss as a shortage of inventories, for example, may mean that goods wanted by customers are not readily available.

This chapter deals with how current asset and current liability accounts should be managed in order to maximize an organization's profitability. The accounts that will be examined in this chapter are inventories, trade receivables, accruals (prepaid expenses), cash, and marketable securities under current assets; and trade and other payables, accruals (wages and taxes), and working capital loans under current liabilities.

Goal of working capital management To accelerate the cash flow cycle in a business after sales have been made.

The **goal of working capital management** is to accelerate the cash flow cycle in a business after sales have been made. The faster the cash circulates, the more profitable it is to the business, because it means that a company has less cash tied up in unproductive (but necessary) assets. Let's use Table 6.1 as an example. If inventories and trade receivables were reduced by $100,000 and $75,000 respectively, the company would be able to acquire $175,000 in investment securities, say at 4% (before tax), and earn $7,000 in interest annually. Instead, company management would probably want to invest this excess cash in more productive assets such as plant modernization or new equipment, which would generate a 20% return on the assets each year, as long as the inventories and trade receivables are kept at the new level.

In the News 6.1 illustrates how the reduction in shipments of goods or supply cuts are tools used to manage inventories and accelerate the cash flow cycle.

In The News [6.1]

Time, Uncertainty and Economies of Scale Are Three Key Reasons for Keeping Stock, However, It Takes a "Whiz Team" to Figure Out How Much Exactly Is Needed

Inventory levels can be used as a barometer to predict changes in the general economic conditions. When inventories start to pile up, it is a signal that economic activities are slowing down, but when inventories begin to shrink, businesses can start up the manufacturing engines to increase production.

Articles in financial newspapers often talk about inventory levels, and dozens of websites put out numbers relating to inventory activities. These statistics include data related to all types of sectors such as manufacturing, wholesaling, retailing, and the selling of durable goods, non-durable goods, crude oil, etc. Here are a few extracts from Bloomberg's website that show what economists have to draw meaning from in order to make their economic predictions:

- Inventories at U.S. wholesalers dropped in August for a 12th consecutive month, clearing the way for a pickup in orders as sales improve.
- Distributors will likely increase bookings after companies drew down inventories at a record pace in the first half of the year.

In The News [6.1] (continued)

- Value of goods on hand at distributors stood at $381.2 billion in August, the lowest level since July 2006.
- Today's report showed auto inventories dropped 2.3% as sales jumped 7.7%, the biggest gain since 1999. That pushed the industry's inventory-to-sales ratio for August down to 1.57 months, the lowest level since May 2008.
- Factory inventories, which account for about a third of the total, fell 0.8% in August, the smallest drop in three months.

Source: Adapted from Bloomberg, Courtney Schlisserman, "Inventories at U.S. wholesalers fall for 12th month," www.bloomberg.com, accessed October 16, 2009. For more information on a variety of topics related to inventories, see www.investopedia.com/terms/i/inventory.asp.

Days of working capital
The number of DWC a business holds to meet average daily sales requirements.

There are two broad approaches for measuring the productivity of cash within a business: days of working capital (DWC) and cash conversion efficiency (CCE). The objective of the **days of working capital** measurement is to calculate the number of DWC a business holds in order to meet its average daily sales requirements. The lower the number of days, the more efficient a business is in managing its working capital. Consider, for example, Eastman Technologies Inc., which was introduced in Chapters 2 and 3. In this case, the company shows 47.2 DWC for 2009. This ratio is calculated as follows:

$$\frac{\text{(Inventories + Trade receivables) − Trade and other payables}}{\text{Revenue} \div 365}$$

The information used to calculate Eastman's DWC is drawn from the statement of income (Table 2.2 on page 63) and the statement of financial position (Table 2.4 on page 72).

$$\frac{(\$218{,}000 + \$300{,}000) - \$195{,}000}{\$2{,}500{,}000 \div 365} = \frac{\$323{,}000}{\$6{,}849} = 47.2 \text{ days}$$

Cash conversion efficiency
Measures how quickly a business converts revenue to cash flow from its operations or operating activities.

The **cash conversion efficiency** calculation measures the efficiency with which a business converts revenue to cash flows within its operations. The financial data used for calculating Eastman's CCE ratio is drawn from Table 3.9 on page 129, the statement of cash flows, and Table 2.2 on page 63, the statement of income.

$$\frac{\text{Operating activities}}{\text{Revenue}} = \frac{\$126{,}500}{\$2{,}500{,}000} = 5.1\%$$

By themselves, Eastman Technologies' cash performance ratios do not mean much unless they are compared to previous years' financial performance and to industry standards. The higher the ratio, the more efficient a company is in generating cash. Using the Eastman example, for every sales dollar, the company produces 5.1 cents in operating cash flows. If the company were to increase its cash flows to $200,000 with the same level in revenue, the ratio would be 8.0%, or 8 cents.

Managing working capital accounts means reducing costs related to working capital accounts, keeping inventories and trade receivables as low as possible, investing short-term excess cash, while increasing trade and other payables. All this allows a business to do more business. Increasing revenue is not the only answer to improving profitability; all accounts that are affected as a result of incremental revenue must be managed efficiently and effectively.

An important criterion for measuring financial performance is return on assets (ROA). The accounts appearing under current assets are in the denominator of the ROA equation; consequently, if working capital accounts are minimized, ROA is improved.

As shown in Figure 1.1 on page 7, this is the second chapter dealing with the topic related to operating decisions. This is logical because the management of working capital accounts deals with decisions associated with operating activities and must be scrutinized on a day-to-day basis.

This chapter explores the importance of managing working capital accounts. In particular, it focuses on five key topics. The first topic explains the importance of the cash conversion cycle, how it is used, and the flow of cash within the operating cycle of a business. The second topic examines different decision models that businesses use to manage inventories in a more efficient and effective way. The third topic explores different strategies used for managing trade receivables, in particular, setting credit terms, granting credit to customers, billing customers, monitoring payments made by customers, collecting trade receivables, and ensuring adequate credit insurance. The fourth topic looks at how cash and cash equivalents can be made productive, different ways to improve the collection of cash, and several strategies that can be used to manage near-cash accounts such as marketable securities. The last topic explains how current liabilities such as trade and other payables, accruals, and working capital loans can improve profitability if managed appropriately.

Self-Test Exercise No. 6.1

Measuring Working Capital Efficiencies

Using CompuTech Inc.'s financial statements in Appendix A on page A-1, calculate the following:

a) For 2009 and 2010, the company's days of working capital
b) For 2010, the company's cash conversion efficiency ratio

To calculate the CCE ratio for 2010, refer to Self-Test Exercise No. 3.5 (The Statement of Cash Flows) on page 130.

Cash Conversion Cycle

1 Learning Objective

Define the meaning and importance of the cash conversion cycle.

Cash conversion cycle Periodic transformation of cash through working capital accounts such as inventories, trade receivables, and trade and other payables.

An important concept related to the management of working capital accounts is the **cash conversion cycle**, presented in Figure 6.1. It can be defined as the periodic transformation of cash through working capital accounts such as inventories, trade receivables, and trade and other payables. As shown, working capital accounts can be displayed on a wheel, and the faster the wheel turns, the faster and more effectively management can use the cash generated from revenue. The goal is to identify the number of days it takes to perform each activity shown on the wheel. For example, if it takes 12 days for customers to make their purchase decisions, 6 days for the credit manager to approve a new customer, 19 days to process goods in the plant, and 9 days to bill customers, the objective would be to reduce the number of days for each of these activities. If, overall, it takes 95 days for cash to circulate in a business, the objective would be to reduce this to, say, 80 days. In Chapter 4, under the heading "Decision-Making in Action" on page 193, we examined how the use of financial ratios such as inventory turnover and average collection period to gauge the management of working capital accounts can help improve cash flows.

Figure 6.2 looks at the flow of cash in terms of a *boomerang*. As shown, business activities start with cash and eventually end with cash. The business buys inventories, and pays wages to employees in its plant to transform raw materials into finished

Figure 6.1 The Cash Conversion Cycle

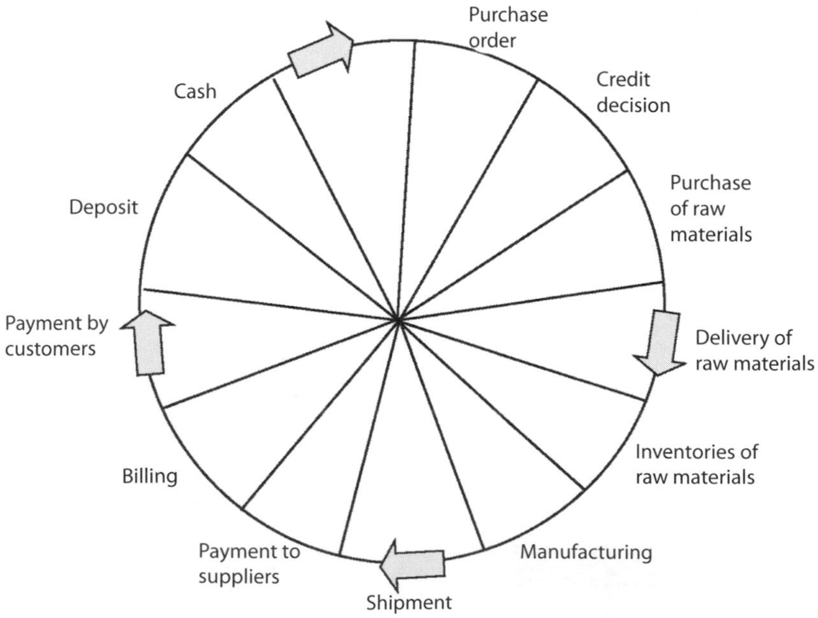

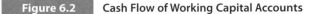

Figure 6.2 Cash Flow of Working Capital Accounts

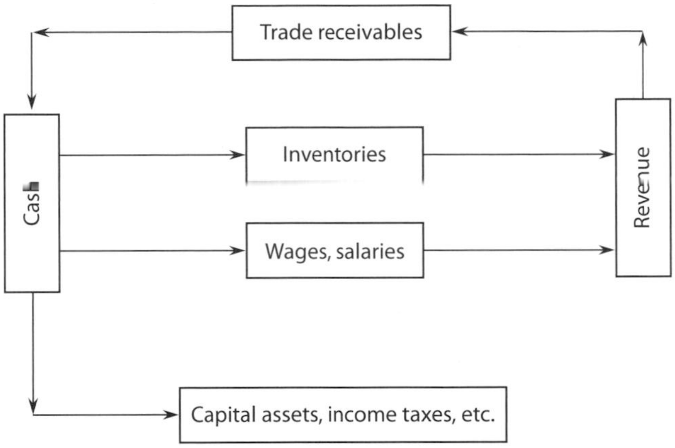

goods for shipment to customers (revenue). Usually, customers buy goods on credit (trade receivables) and when it is collected, the business once again has cash, which is used to buy more inventories, produce more goods, and the transformation process goes on and on. Some of the cash collected from customers is used to buy other things such as non-current assets (capital assets), or to pay the principal on a debt, income taxes, and even dividends.

Table 6.2 shows how Eastman Technologies' cash conversion cycle for the years 2008 and 2009 were calculated. As shown, both inventories and trade receivables are used to calculate the company's operating cycle. Essentially, the **operating cycle** represents the length of time (in days) that both inventories and trade receivables take to be converted into cash. Here is how the conversion periods for both accounts are calculated.

Operating cycle The number of days inventories and trade receivables take (in days) to be converted into cash.

$$\textbf{Inventory conversion period} = \frac{\textbf{Inventories}}{\textbf{Cost of sales} \div \textbf{365}}$$

$$\textbf{Trade receivables conversion period} = \frac{\textbf{Trade receivables}}{\textbf{Revenue} \div \textbf{365}}$$

While the operating cycle shown in Table 6.2 for 2009 is 85.7 days, it is partly offset by the trade and other payables deferral period of 37.5 days. The trade and other payables deferral period calculation is as follows:

$$\textbf{Trade and other payables deferral period} = \frac{\textbf{Trade and other payables}}{\textbf{Cost of sales} \div \textbf{365}}$$

Table 6.2 Eastman Technologies' Cash Conversion Cycle

	2009	2008
Liquidity ratios		
Current ratio	1.35	1.35
Quick ratio	0.86	0.89
Cash conversion cycle		
Inventory conversion period	41.9 days	38.7 days
Receivables conversion period	43.8 days	45.4 days
Operating cycle	85.7 days	84.1 days
Less: Trade and other payables deferral period	37.5 days	36.6 days
Cash conversion cycle	48.2 days	47.5 days

As shown, Eastman Technologies' cash conversion cycle for 2008 was 47.5 days and increased to 48.2 days in 2009. While the company increased its operating cycle by 1.6 days, it also increased its payable deferral period by 0.9 days, which indicates that the company was able to defer slightly its payments for purchases, thereby producing a net increase in the cash conversion period of 0.7 days.

Cash management is usually assigned to a high-level manager in a business—usually the chief financial officer (CFO) or the treasurer. As mentioned earlier, the goal is to ensure that cash flows into a business as quickly as possible and is used wisely. Figure 6.3 gives a visual presentation of how cash flows in and out of a business, in this case, Eastman Technologies Inc. The numbers shown in the figure were drawn from Table 3.9 on page 129, Eastman's statement of cash flows. At the centre of the system lies the cash pool (or cash reservoir). As shown on the right side of Figure 6.3, cash flows in and out of operating activities. Customers pay for goods or services and Eastman pays suppliers for goods purchased, wages to employees, and income taxes to the government. As shown on the left side of Figure 6.3, there is also cash flowing in and out of the financing activities. Lenders and shareholders provide money to Eastman (cash inflows), shareholders receive dividends, and lenders obtain repayment of the principal (cash outflows). As shown, cash from shareholders and lenders flows into the cash pool. Cash also flows in and out of investing activities. For example, if Eastman were to sell some non-current assets, that would be considered a cash inflow. However, in most cases, cash flows out of investment activities (also on the left side of Figure 6.3) because businesses continually buy non-current assets such as equipment and machinery. Overall, Eastman's operations generated $126,500 in cash (operating activities), received $167,500

Figure 6.3 **The Flow of Cash at Eastman Technologies Inc.**

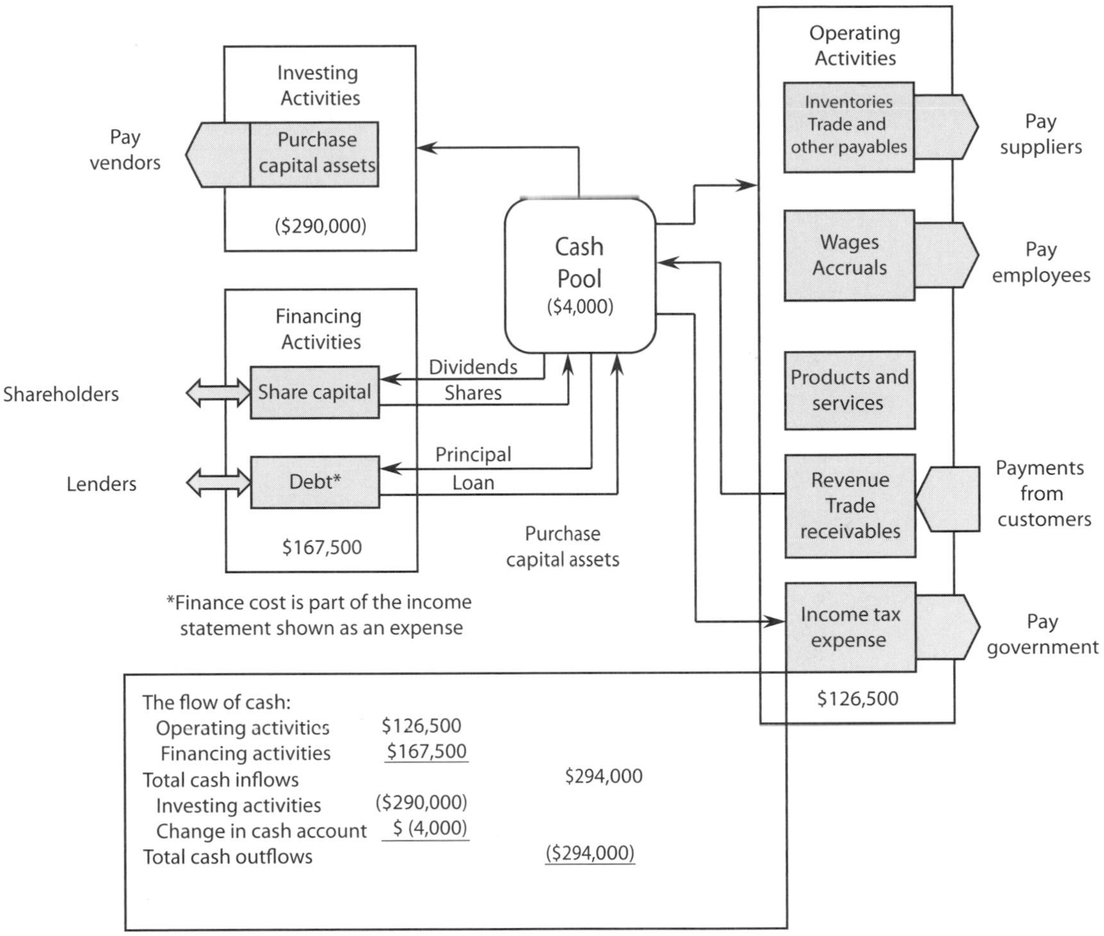

from external sources (financing activities), and invested $290,000 in capital assets (investing activities).

Table 6.3 shows how the acceleration of the cash flow improves a company's cash position. The shaded portion of the table shows the difference between profit and cash flow and how the improvement in working capital accounts can accelerate the flow of cash. The upper portion of the table shows the amount of profit generated each month. The middle section (current performance) shows the amount of cash generated by the business by collecting 10% of revenue within the first month, 50% in the second month, and 40% in the third month. An amount of 50% for purchases is paid during the same month that goods are purchased and the remaining 50% during the following month. The lower portion of the table (targeted performance) shows how cash flow is improved by collecting the trade receivables more quickly and by paying the suppliers more slowly.

Table 6.3 Acceleration of the Cash Flow Cycle

Profit Forecast	January	February	March	April
Revenue	$300,000	$400,000	$440,000	$480,000
Purchases (50% of revenue)	(150,000)	(200,000)	(220,000)	(240,000)
Operating expenses	(120,000)	(150,000)	(160,000)	(170,000)
Total expenses	(270,000)	(350,000)	(380,000)	(410,000)
Profit	$ 30,000	$ 50,000	$ 60,000	$ 70,000 ←
Cash Flow Forecast (current performances)				
Beginning cash balance	$100,000	$220,000	$370,000	$589,000
Collections*				
10% cash payment	30,000	40,000	44,000	48,000
50% in 30 days	100,000	150,000	200,000	220,000
40% in 60 days	80,000	80,000	120,000	160,000
Total cash available	210,000	270,000	364,000	428,000
Cash flow from operations** (profit + depreciation)	35,000	55,000	65,000	75,000
Purchases***				
50% cash payment	(75,000)	(100,000)	(110,000)	(120,000)
50% in 30 days	(50,000)	(75,000)	(100,000)	(110,000)
Total disbursements	(125,000)	(175,000)	(210,000)	(230,000)
Ending cash balance	$220,000	$370,000	$589,000	$862,000 ←
Cash Flow Forecast (targeted performance)				
Beginning cash balance	$100,000	$235,000	$430,000	$685,000
Collections*				
50% cash payment	150,000	200,000	220,000	240,000
40% in 30 days	80,000	120,000	160,000	176,000
10% in 60 days	20,000	20,000	30,000	40,000
Total cash available	250,000	340,000	410,000	456,000
Cash flow from operations** (profit + depreciation)	35,000	55,000	65,000	75,000
Purchases***				
20% cash payment	(30,000)	(40,000)	(44,000)	(48,000)
80% in 30 days	(120,000)	(160,000)	(176,000)	(192,000)
Total disbursements	(150,000)	(200,000)	(220,000)	(240,000)
Ending cash balance	$235,000	$430,000	$685,000	$976,000 ←

* Assumes sales of $200,000 per month for November and December.
** Assumes $5,000 depreciation expense.
*** Assumes purchases of $100,000 in December.

The following summarizes the cash balance at the end of each month as a result of managing these two working capital accounts more efficiently and the cumulative cash improvement for the four-month period.

	January	February	March	April
Current performance*	$120,000	$150,000	$219,000	$273,000
Targeted performance	$135,000	$195,000	$255,000	$291,000
Monthly cash flow improvement	$15,000	$45,000	$36,000	$18,000
Cumulative cash flow improvement	$15,000	$60,000	$96,000	$114,000

*These numbers are calculated by subtracting the beginning cash balance from the ending cash balance for individual months. For example, in January the amount is $120,000, the difference between $220,000 and $100,000.

By improving the management of only two working capital accounts (trade receivables and trade and other payables), the business was able to improve its cash position by $15,000 in January, $45,000 in February, $36,000 in March, and $18,000 in April for a cumulative improvement of $114,000.

The rest of the chapter explains how individual working capital accounts can be managed.

Self-Test Exercise No. 6.2

The Cash Conversion Cycle

Using CompuTech Inc.'s 2009 and 2010 financial statements in Appendix A on page A-1, calculate the following for the company:

a) Inventory conversion period
b) Trade receivables conversion period
c) Operating cycle
d) Trade and other payables deferral period
e) Cash conversion cycle

Managing Inventories

2 Learning Objective

Explain different strategies related to managing inventories.

The objective of inventory management is to replenish inventories or stocks in such a way that associated order and holding costs are kept to a minimum in order to enhance profitability.

Turning inventories more rapidly improves cash flows, profit, and ROA. One more way for a firm to analyze its management effort is by calculating the annual inventory turnover rate, or the number of times a business sells, or turns, its investment in inventories in the course of a year. It is an activity indicator that relates an investment in inventory directly to sales volume (for a retail or wholesale business) or cost of sales (for a manufacturer).

The turnover rate calculation is significant because of its direct relationship to cash flows and profit. Thus, the faster the inventories turn over, the lower the investment in inventories. Most managers understand that moving merchandise more rapidly is the key to profitability.

To calculate the inventory turnover rate, the annual cost of sales or revenue must be divided by the average investment in inventories.

Maintaining the right level of inventories can be compared to maintaining an appropriate level of water in a bathtub. If water flows out of the tub more rapidly than into it, the tub will soon be empty. However, if more water is let in than out, the tub will overflow. The same principle applies in inventory management. On one side, inventories are used continuously to produce manufactured goods and, on the other, raw materials keep flowing into the storage area. The idea is to determine two things: (1) the proper level of investment that should be kept in inventories, and (2) how much inventories should be purchased, and at what interval, to maintain an appropriate level of stock.

A delay in shipment lengthens the cash conversion period and hinders cash flows. To avoid delays in shipment, a firm should have a well-organized shipping process.

In the News 6.2 gives an example about the importance of inventory management within the context of an industry, and the impact that demand has on inventory levels and how it can influence selling prices and, ultimately, profitability.

In The News [6.2]

Cutting Back on Inventories Is a Balancing Act between Inventory Levels and Meeting Customer Needs

Sometimes, a prolonged level of severe economic movement can be boosted up by one annual predetermined activity or even an unplanned event. It only takes one such incident for a business or an industry to start selling *en masse* and for inventory levels to shrink, generating revenue, profit, and, most importantly, cash.

As a rule, this is what happens in the fall when students go back to school. In August of 2009, U.S. retailers took advantage of the "back-to-school" bounce as students began to stock up on classroom supplies and children's clothing for the upcoming academic year. Retail Metrics, a market research company, indicated that despite the retail sales decline of 2.3% in August, and a prolonged 12-month drop, it was, however, the smallest drop in revenue since September 2008. Even if the back-to-school event helped retailers to sell more, they are still going through difficult times. Because of the previous 12-month economic downturn, retailers had to keep inventories low. This meant offering fewer choices for parents and students, that is, fewer designs, colours, and sizes. Maintaining inventories at low levels and, at the same time, enticing buyers to buy more, requires the analysis of a foggy statistics.

Source: Adapted from Alexandra Frean, "U.S. retailers benefit from back-to-school bounce," *The Times*, London. © Times Newspapers Ltd. 2009. To read more about Retail Metrics, see www.retailmetrics.net/corp.asp.

An inventory control system should answer two essential needs:

- It should maintain a current record of the amount of each inventory item held in stock.
- It should be able to locate that stock.

Neither element should be left to chance or memory. Accountants refer to this system as *perpetual inventory*. The sale and purchase of each item in inventory is logged on a computerized stock sheet. Then, at any time, the computer program specifies the total inventory of each item held in stock. The computer system should also identify the exact location of the items, which prevents shipping delays, as employees do not have to search for stock in the warehouse. The perpetual inventory system also helps to determine the reorder points for each item on the stock ledger sheets or computerized inventory software program when the economic ordering quantity system (to be discussed later) is applied.

A periodic count of every item in stock is the first fundamental principle of sound inventory management. The physical count serves two primary objectives:

- It enables a business to verify the accuracy of its accounting procedures that keep track of the investment in inventories. As the exact amount of each item in stock is verified, it confirms the value of the investment.
- The physical count provides the basic data necessary to perform an item analysis of the inventory.

Item analysis enables a firm to control its investment in inventories. This analysis measures the amount of investment in each item in stock against the amount actually required, based on the firm's recent sales experience. It identifies the specific source of any overinvestment in inventories.

TYPES OF INVENTORIES

Before examining the techniques used to make inventory decisions, let us look at the different things that are inventoried. These include office supplies such as pencils, paper, and pens, and spare parts, which are used by manufacturing operations in the event of breakdowns. However, the three most important **types of inventories** for most manufacturing operations are raw materials, work-in-process, and finished goods.

Types of inventories
Raw materials, work-in-process, and finished goods.

Raw material inventories consist of goods purchased for the purpose of manufacturing goods. This type of inventory is influenced by the level of production, the reliability of sources of supply, and the efficiency of scheduling purchases and production operations.

Work-in-process inventories consist of partially assembled or incomplete goods in the production cycle. Such inventories are not ready for sale.

Finished inventories consist of products that are ready to be sold and shipped to customers.

INVENTORY DECISION MODELS

Inventory management means determining the optimal level of inventory that should be kept in stock at all times. Three models will be discussed here: material requirements planning, just-in-time inventory management, and economic ordering quantity.

Material requirements planning (MRP)
Method for developing a schedule to help coordinate and utilize resources in production.

Material requirements planning (MRP) is excellent for developing a production schedule to help coordinate and utilize resources (materials, people, and equipment) more effectively. The greater breadth and variety of product lines, together with increasingly expensive inventories, spurred management to adopt computers and use them to manage the huge amounts of production-related information in an entirely new way. By using MRP, it is possible to link individual departments in the production flow from a planning and scheduling point of view.

The MRP system that is based on anticipated shipments of finished goods uses that finished unit schedule to derive subassembly schedules and component schedules. To develop these schedules for individual departments requires a thorough understanding of how components feed into subassemblies, and how subassemblies in turn feed into the finished products. This information is referred to as a bill of materials for a finished end item.

When planning material requirements, it is also necessary to know the timing relationships between various departments and the production cycle times within each department. Knowing the bill of materials for that final assembled item and those timing relationships can help managers use the schedule for final assembly. They can also derive the schedules by which subassemblies would have to be produced in preceding time periods, and by which components would have to be produced in even earlier time periods. In addition, it helps to ensure that the components and subassemblies will come together according to the final assembly schedule.

Just-in-time inventory management
An inventory management technique that obtains supplier materials just when they are needed.

Using the **just-in-time inventory management** process helps to reduce inventories, speed the cash conversion cycle, and increase profitability (see Figure 6.1). In the past two decades, the Japanese supply system called just-in-time (JIT), or *kanban*, has received a great deal of attention. It includes frequent (even daily) deliveries of parts or supplies, which help to reduce working inventories. This system places responsibility on the supplier for "no defects," as well as responsibility for scheduled delivery of exactly the right quantity with "no excuses." Thus, safety stock and production-line float can be eliminated.

To make near-perfect coordination feasible, suppliers are encouraged or even required to locate plants very close to their customer's production line. These and other coordination activities in planning and production dramatically reduce in-process inventories, improve product quality, reduce the need for inspection, and increase saleable output per day.

Economic ordering quantity (EOQ)
Method that determines the optimum quantity of goods that should be ordered at any single time.

Another commonly used approach for determining optimal levels of inventories is the **economic ordering quantity (EOQ)** model. The main purpose of this technique is to minimize total inventory costs, consisting of ordering costs and carrying costs. Inventory decisions are influenced by the reorder point, which is the level of inventories that is held at the time a new order is placed, and the reorder quantity, which is the quantity ordered each time. Before examining the EOQ model, let's look at the different types of costs associated with inventory management. Inventory costs fall into two groups: ordering costs and holding costs.

Ordering costs Category of costs associated with the acquisition of goods (e.g., receiving, inspecting, accounting).

Ordering costs include the following:

- The actual cost of the merchandise acquired
- The administrative costs of scheduling, entering, and receiving an order
- The labour costs of receiving, inspecting, and shelving each order
- The cost of accounting and paying for the order

Because inventory acquisition costs rise as a business places more orders, the frequency of acquisitions should be kept to a minimum. Everyone recognizes the direct costs of acquiring inventories: the purchase price of the merchandise. However, many overlook other acquisition costs, which increase the actual cost of any particular order, and the inverse relationship they have to the size of the average investment in inventories.

Two facts concerning these costs are relevant here. First, the administrative, accounting, and labour costs associated with any order are far more significant than many people realize. Indeed, the cumulative acquisition costs from numerous orders can exert a significant downward effect on earnings. Second, the cumulative acquisition costs remain relatively constant regardless of the size of the order involved.

Holding costs Category of costs associated with the storing of goods in inventories (e.g., insurance, rent).

Holding costs are the category of costs associated with holding or storing goods in inventory. It is this cost that most people associate with inventories. Included in this category would be the following:

- The costs of maintaining and managing warehouses or other storage facilities
- The costs of safety systems for guarding inventories
- The costs of inventory shrinkage that might occur from spoilage, theft, or obsolescence
- The costs of company funds tied up in inventory (opportunity costs or finance costs)

Holding costs rise as the size of inventory increases. Because annual inventory carrying costs rise as the average size of an investment increases, each component of these costs should be examined with a view to keeping them at a minimum.

In contrast to acquisition costs, holding costs may be viewed as variable costs in the sense that more units held in inventory result in an increase in these costs. The financial or opportunity costs increase in exact proportion to the size of the investment. However, other carrying costs also increase, although the proportions are less precise. Therefore, as investment is increased, warehouse costs also increase because the firm needs more space to store more inventories. As the investment grows, the firm will also experience rising insurance and maintenance costs, as well as an increase in expenses from deterioration or obsolescence. Estimates of holding costs ranging from 20% to 30% of the value of inventories are not uncommon. The basic economic ordering quantity equation states that the ideal reorder quantity is as follows:

$$\mathbf{EOQ} = \sqrt{\frac{\mathbf{2 \times (order\ cost) \times (yearly\ demand)}}{\mathbf{(annual\ carrying\ cost\ for\ one\ unit)}}}$$

If a business sells 5,000 units of product per year, the ordering costs are $50.00 per order, and the carrying costs are $0.80 per unit per year, we find that the company should reorder 790 units each time it places an order. The calculation is as follows:

$$\mathbf{EOQ} = \sqrt{\frac{\mathbf{2 \times \$50.00 \times 5,000}}{\mathbf{\$0.80}}} = \mathbf{790\ units}$$

Table 6.4 shows the total ordering and holding costs for ordering different quantities during the year. Column 1 shows the number of orders the company can place during the year; it ranges from one to ten orders. Column 2 presents the number of units it would have to order each time an order is made. For example, by placing five orders, the company would order 1,000 units each time. Column 3 indicates the annual cost for placing the orders. For instance, ordering five times during the year would cost the company $250.00 ($50.00 × 5). Column 4 shows the average number of units that the company would have in its warehouse, depending on the number of orders it places. If only one order or 5,000 units is placed during the year, the average number of units the company would have in stock would be 2,500 (5,000 ÷ 2). Column 5 presents the average dollar investment. If the holding cost per unit, which includes maintenance, spoilage, finance costs, etc., is $5.35, the average dollar

Table 6.4 The Economic Ordering Quantity

Number of Orders	Order Quantity (units)	Annual Order Cost ($50.00 per order)	Average Unit Inventories (column 2 ÷ 2)	Average Dollar Investment (column 4 × $5.35)	Annual Holding Costs (column 5 × 15%)	Ordering Cost + Holding Cost (column 3 + column 6)
1	2	3	4	5	6	7
1	5,000	$50	2,500	$13,375	$2,006	$2,056
2	2,500	100	1,250	6,687	1,003	1,103
5	1,000	250	500	2,675	401	651
6	833	300	416	2,226	334	634
8	625	400	312	1,669	250	650
10	500	500	250	1,337	200	700

investment if the company places one order per year is \$13,375 (2,500 × \$5.35). Column 6 shows the annual holding costs, which can be calculated in two ways. The first is to multiply 15%, which represents the annual holding costs, by the average dollar investment and obtain \$2,006 (\$13,375 × 15%). The second is to multiply the annual holding costs per unit of \$0.80 by the average unit inventory and obtain the same answer, \$2,006 (2,500 × \$0.80). Column 7 shows the sum of column 3 (ordering costs) and column 6 (annual holding costs). As shown, 833 units (closest to 790) is the combination that costs the least (\$634.00).

Self-Test Exercise No. 6.3

The Economic Ordering Quantity

The Millers are thinking of marketing one of their products more aggressively. Current sales are 2,000 units per year and are expected to increase by 25%. Current carrying costs are estimated at \$0.23 per unit, and order costs are estimated at \$1.50. The Millers want to minimize their inventory costs. Calculate CompuTech's economic ordering quantity for the expected increased sales volume.

INVENTORY REPLENISHMENT

Inventory replenishment Decision related to when to order goods from supplier.

Another extension of the EOQ is the decision related to **inventory replenishment**. Supposing that the company decides to order 790 units each time it places an order. The next decision is to decide the frequency of the orders. Figure 6.4 shows graphically the factors that are taken into account for replenishing inventories. The key factors to take into account for determining inventory replenishment are the following:

- The minimum and maximum levels of inventories the business will want to have in stock prior to the point of placing a new order
- The total time it takes from the purchase to the receipt of the goods (LT)
- When the order should be placed (RP)

Self-Test Exercise No. 6.4

Monthly Inventory Replenishment

The Millers have decided to increase their advertising to push one of their product lines. Increased sales are estimated at 2,500 units per year, and they are expected to increase by a further 60% next year. Current carrying costs are estimated at \$0.10 per unit, and the order costs are estimated at \$3.50. The Millers want to minimize their inventory costs.

a) What is the new economic ordering quantity?
b) How many orders should be placed each month once the new sales level is reached?

Figure 6.4 Inventory Replenishment

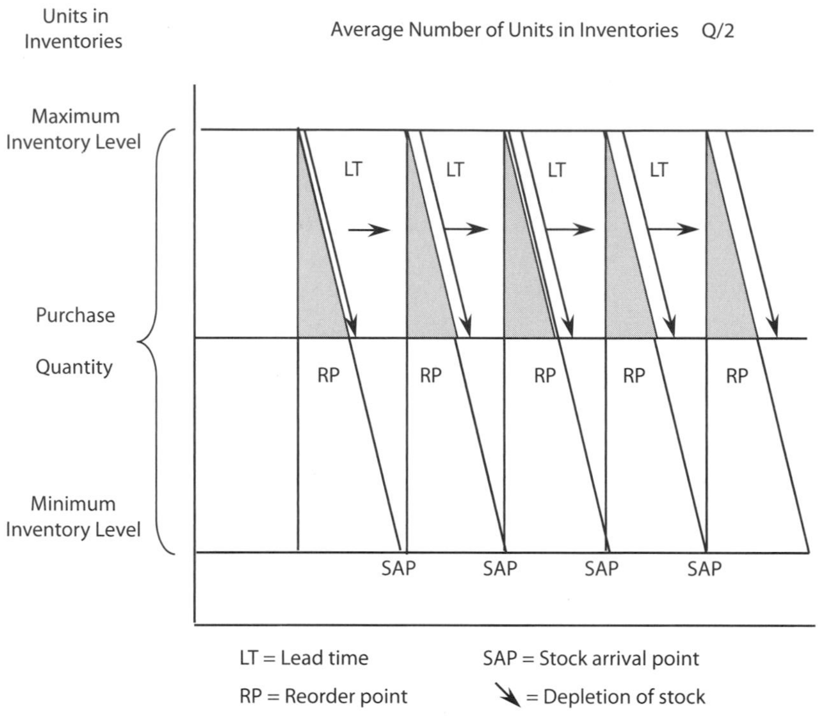

Managing Trade Receivables

3 Learning Objective

Discuss various techniques related to trade receivables management.

Because most firms sell on credit, and for most of them credit accounts for the bulk of their revenue, it is important to manage the trade receivables effectively. The level of trade receivables is determined in two ways: first, by the volume of sales made on credit; and second, by the time it takes for customers to pay off their accounts.

The mission of the credit manager is to set credit terms, grant credit to customers, bill the customers, monitor payments made by customers, collect trade receivables, and ensure adequate credit insurance. Let's review each of these activities.

SET CREDIT TERMS

Credit terms Conditions under which credit is extended, especially how quickly the customer is expected to pay the account.

It is the responsibility of the credit manager to decide what **credit terms** a firm should adopt. These terms are greatly influenced by the industry of which the firm is part. A basic element of credit terms to businesses is the length of time given to customers to pay their accounts.

Trade discounts can help a company's cash flow at the expense of earnings and may very well be a good trade-off. For example, a business may allow a 2% discount off the original sale price of goods if a customer pays an invoice within 10 days of shipment and charge the full amount for payment within 30 days (i.e., 2/10, N/30). However, before deciding to offer trade discounts, the credit manager estimates the costs and benefits that will result. Should a firm offer its customers a policy of 2/10, N/30? Or 1/10, N/30? Or 2/10, N/45? To answer this question, the credit manager must explore the following points.

First, the manager measures the benefits. When a customer pays in accordance with the discount terms, it shortens a company's average collection period and accelerates cash flows. At the same time, the investment in trade receivables is reduced, as are the costs associated with carrying that investment. Cash discounts presumably benefit both parties in the transaction: The customers reduce their purchase costs when taking the discount, and the firm enjoys a better cash flow and a lower investment in trade receivables.

Second, the credit manager calculates the effective price when offering a purchase discount. The bottom line is this: Before introducing discounts into credit terms, the credit manager recognizes how such allowances affect a company's profit performance.

Before changing the policy, the credit manager must go through a detailed calculation. To illustrate, let's assume that a company sells products with an average unit-selling price of $400.00. The cost of manufacturing or buying materials from suppliers is $250.00. Furthermore, in that particular industry, customers have the habit of paying 60 days after purchase. As shown below, if the cost of money is 10%, it would be more advantageous for the firm to offer the 2/10, N/30, because the profit generated when customers pay in 10 days is $146.69, compared to $145.89 if they continue to pay in 60 days. Here is the arithmetic. If the customer benefits from the 2% discount, line 1 shows that the company would receive $392.00 ($400.00 × 98%) instead of $400.00. Whether the company offers a 2% discount or not, line 2 indicates that the company would have to pay $250.00 to manufacture the product or to buy it from a supplier. Line 3 shows the finance costs for both options. The company would have to pay a $0.68 [$250.00 × 10% × (10/365)] finance cost to finance the $250.00 purchase if payment is received in 10 days, and $4.11 [$250.00 × 10% × (60/365)] if payment is received in 60 days. Line 4 shows that the company would make $5.37 [$392.00 × 10% × (50/365)] if the $392.00 is deposited in the bank for the 50-day period and earns 10%. Based on this calculation, line 5 shows that there is an economic advantage to offering the 2% discount.

Line		10-Day Payment	60-Day Payment
1.	Effective selling price	$392.00	$400.00
2.	Purchase (or manufacturing) costs	(250.00)	(250.00)
3.	Finance cost (10 and 60 days)	(0.68)	(4.11)
4.	Interest on investment (50 days)	5.37	—
5.	Profit	$146.69	$145.89

Self-Test Exercise No. 6.5

Trade Discount Policies

CompuTech sells goods with an average retail sales price of $250.00 to industrial accounts. These customers usually pay 65 days after the date of purchase. Cost of sales for each unit is $110.00. If CompuTech's cost of borrowing is 11%, should the Millers offer 1/10, N/30 to these accounts?

GRANT CREDIT TO CUSTOMERS

The second activity of the credit manager is the granting of credit. Two questions must be asked in the context of credit analysis: Should credit be granted to a customer? If yes, how much? The criteria used by firms to rate borrowers can be summarized as the six "C's" that will be discussed in Chapter 8 on page 376: character, collateral, capacity, capital, circumstances, and coverage.

In order to shorten the cash conversion cycle, the credit decision should be made as soon as a purchase order is received. Therefore, it is important to approve in advance lines of credit for major customers. In other words, the credit manager should anticipate customers' needs before they exceed their credit limits (see Figure 6.1).

Little is lost if a customer does not use the full credit line. However, customers who do increase their purchases will find their orders delivered more promptly if credit is pre-approved. Indeed, pre-approved credit facilitates the completion of a sale and improves a firm's service capability. A faster response inevitably offers a competitive advantage.

The same approach can be used for new customers. It is preferable to check the credit worthiness of a new account in advance, before receiving a larger order. Obtaining the information for a credit check—bank checks, supplier checks—can take several days and thus lengthen the cash conversion cycle. Moreover, if the delay is too long, the business may risk losing the sale to a competitor with a more efficient credit-decision process.

However, reliable credit analysis should not be sacrificed for the sake of speedy approval. Even a modest increase in bad-debt losses (if some customers do not pay their bills) can offset the benefits from a lower cash conversion cycle. At the same time, any element in the administrative process that delays the completion of a sale hampers the smooth flow of cash into a business.

Let's review the types of credit analysis that businesses go through when granting credit to consumers and businesses.

Credit-scoring system System used to analyze the creditworthiness of potential customers.

Consumer credit. Credit-scoring systems are often used to analyze the creditworthiness of potential customers. Under a **credit-scoring system**, the credit clerks are given specific guidelines for rating a potential customer as a good or bad risk. This system is used by businesses offering credit cards to thousands of consumers (e.g., retail stores and banks). Table 6.5 shows a typical credit-scoring system. As shown, several variables are examined, and each is given a weight. This weight has been determined by taking a sample of existing customers and finding the factors that distinguish those who pay their accounts promptly from those who are slow payers. In this case, the variables

Table 6.5 Credit Scoring System

Variable	Measurement	Value	Weight	Weighted Value
Age	In years as reported	36	0.4	14.4
Marital status	Coded 1 (yes) or 0 (no)	1	20.0	20.0
Occupation	Coded 1 to 5 for different professions	4	4.3	17.2
Time on last job	In years as reported	6	0.9	5.4
Annual income	In thousands of dollars as reported	45.0	0.6	27.0
Residence	Coded 1 to 5 for different postal zones	3	4.6	13.8
Home ownership	Number of years owned as reported	4	1.2	4.8
Telephone	Coded 1 (yes) or 0 (no)	1	15.0	15.0
Total credit score				117.6

include age, marital status, occupation, time on last job, annual income, residence, home ownership, and telephone; the credit score totals 117.6. The credit clerk will then decide, using the predetermined guidelines, what steps should be taken with each consumer. For example, the guidelines may stipulate that if the score is less than 60 points, credit will be denied; if it is between 60 and 80, the customer will be investigated further; and if it is greater than 80, credit will be granted. Under these guidelines, the consumer in our example would be granted credit.

Business credit. Granting credit to commercial enterprises involves a different type of analysis. Here, the firm may want to go through an analysis of the potential customer and obtain information regarding its credit standing. In certain cases, the firm will ask for a credit report, such as the one provided by Dun & Bradstreet or Standard & Poor's. Typical information provided by credit institutions is summarized in Table 6.6.

On the basis of the information obtained, the firm will specify the type of account that should be granted (open account or other arrangement), the credit period (when payment is due), the size of the discount, and the discount period.

Table 6.6 Information Shown on Business Credit Reports

Summary	Classification code for line business, year business started, rating, principal executives (owners).
Report information	Payments, sales worth, number of employees, trends.
Payments	How business pays its bill (i.e., amounts owing, amounts past-due, terms of sales, manner of payments, and supplier comments).
Finance	Financial conditions and trend of business (statement of financial position and statement of income).
History	Names, birthdates, and past business experience of the principals or owners; affiliations; ownership; outside interests of the principal owners.
Operations	Nature of the premises, neighbourhood, size of floor space, production facilities.

Credit policy
Decision about the extent of credit that should be extended to customers.

Decisions about the extent of credit to be provided to customers are determined by a firm's **credit policy**. If a business has a restrictive credit policy, it will most likely sell less, have less invested in inventories and trade receivables, and have fewer bad debts. Conversely, as a firm relaxes its credit terms, it sells more goods to a wider range of customers, including poorer credit risks; this in turn increases bad debts.

An integrated management analysis should precede any change in a firm's credit terms or policies. There is a close connection between selling and credit. Because most firms do not really have a choice of selling on credit or for cash, the most important decision for a business is when to change the credit policy of the firm over time. An ROI framework is appropriate for comparing credit alternatives because it focuses on the investment a firm makes in trade receivables. It also allows a business to systematically consider potential revenue and operating profit, alternative credit terms including cash discount, and bad debt expenses. Changing credit terms, therefore, requires the analysis of certain links or relationships that should not be ignored when evaluating alternative credit terms and policies. The decision to extend credit consideration and carry the resulting investment in trade receivables focuses on a trade-off between (1) the cost of carrying the investment in trade receivables, and (2) the benefits of a larger sales volume.

The most important links are among the following:

- Credit terms and policy and the firm's total marketing effort
- Credit policy and the inventory level
- Credit policy and production capacity
- Credit policy and the efficiency of the firm's operations

To establish an appropriate credit policy, the credit manager must examine the changes in the level of operating income generated as a result of a relaxed credit policy and the extra investment in trade receivables and inventories. Table 6.7 shows

Table 6.7 Establishing a Credit Policy

	Existing Terms	Proposed Terms
Expected volume (units)	500,000	550,000
Expected revenue ($10.00 per unit)	$5,000,000	$5,500,000
Expected operating profit before bad debts (10% of revenue)	$500,000	$550,000
Expected bad debt expense*	$25,000	$55,000
Expected operating profit (after bad debts)	$475,000	$495,000
Incremental operating profit	—	$20,000
Expected collection period (days)	31	38
Average trade receivables	$425,000	$575,000
Inventories	$850,000	$900,000
Incremental investment	—	$200,000

* A 0.5% factor is used for calculating bad debts for existing credit terms and a 1.0% factor for the proposed terms.

$$\text{Return on investment} = \frac{\$20{,}000}{\$200{,}000} = 10\%$$

how to calculate changes in operating profit and investment resulting from a change in credit terms. In this case, if the firm's cost of capital is 12%, it will not go ahead with the proposed credit policy.

As shown in the table, the levels of inventories and trade receivables are affected by the proposed change in the credit policy. It is important to calculate the effect each change in credit policy has on working capital accounts.

Self-Test Exercise No. 6.6

Establishing a Credit Policy

In 2009, CompuTech sells on terms of net 30 days and is considering a change to net 45 days. The Millers want to invest the extra funds in their new retail store, hoping that this will generate a return on investment greater than 20%. The expected effect of the change in credit is summarized below. Should the Millers make the change?

(in $000s)	Net 30 Today	Proposed	Net 45 Change
Revenue	420	450	30
Profit for the year	33	36	3
Trade receivables	45	65	20

BILL THE CUSTOMERS

The invoice identifies the merchandise sold, the shipment date, and the amount due from the purchaser. Prompt completion and transmission of an invoice are important elements of the cash cycle for two reasons. First, few purchasers will pay for merchandise prior to the receipt of the invoice. Indeed, in most businesses, the invoice typically serves as the trigger for the payment process in the accounting system. Second, the invoice date usually initiates the payment period defined by a firm's selling terms.

Prompt completion and transmission of the invoice increases cash availability and earnings. A firm should not render a monthly statement of account to trigger customer payment. Rendering statements is a costly, time-consuming, and self-defeating administrative process. Also, allowing customers to pay in response to monthly statements, rather than to purchase invoices, adds from one to 30 days to the cash conversion cycle, as customers ignore the invoices and wait for the monthly statement. Issuing the invoice that completes a sale is the final step in the administrative process.

MONITOR PAYMENTS MADE BY CUSTOMERS

Irrespective of how a credit policy is determined, once it is adopted, collection must be monitored continually to gauge the effectiveness of the policy and how well it is applied. Several approaches can be used to gauge the effectiveness of a credit policy, to monitor the payment behaviour of customers over a period of time, and to take corrective action on delinquent accounts. The most common are (1) average collection period (in days), and (2) the aging of accounts receivable.

First, there is the *average collection period*, which is the average time it takes for customers to pay their accounts after credit sales have been made. This topic was discussed on page 171 in Chapter 4 (Financial Statement Analysis). Let us examine how average collection period works within the framework of monitoring payments made by customers. Assume that a business sold \$3.0 million last year and the same amount this year. However, the trade receivables increased from last year's \$450,000 to this year's \$500,000. This is an indication that customers paid their accounts more slowly over the past 12 months. The calculation is done as follows:

$$\textbf{Last year's average collection period} = \frac{\$450{,}000}{\$3{,}000{,}000} \times 365 = 54.8 \text{ days}$$

$$\textbf{This year's average collection period} = \frac{\$500{,}000}{\$3{,}000{,}000} \times 365 = 60.8 \text{ days}$$

The company shows a six-day deterioration in the average collection period.

Second, there is the *aging of accounts receivable*. While six days may seem like a small increase, the credit manager may want to examine in more detail the aging of its trade receivables. The credit manager may want to spot changes in customer-paying behaviour by preparing an aging schedule showing the percentage of each month's sales still outstanding at the end of successive months. The schedule gives a picture of any recent change in the makeup of the receivables. This type of information is presented in Table 6.8. As shown, the **aging of accounts receivable** is grouped by age category and by what percentage of receivables outstanding fall in each age category.

Aging of accounts receivable
A report showing how long trade receivables have been outstanding; it gives the percentage of receivables past due for one month, two months, or other periods.

Examining the aging process is an essential element of the trade receivables analysis; it identifies specific groupings of accounts within the total component that make up

Table 6.8 Aging of Accounts Receivable

	As a percentage of total receivables	
Receivables (%)	Last Year	This Year
Under 31 days old	60.4	54.2
Between 31 and 60 days	24.4	23.8
Between 61 and 90 days	7.2	10.4
Between 91 and 120 days	6.5	8.3
Over 120 days	1.5	3.3

an overinvestment. The aging schedule also shows how long trade receivables have been outstanding at a given point in time.

Self-Test Exercise No. 6.7

Impact of Revised Credit Policy on ROI

CompuTech is planning to change its credit policy. The product is characterized as follows.

Current selling price	\$10.00 per unit
Average cost	\$ 7.50 per unit
Current annual sales	4,000 units
Current terms of sale	net 30 days

The Millers wish to extend its credit period to terms of net 60 days. Allowing for the reaction of competitors, it is anticipated that such a move would produce the following results:

1. Sales are expected to increase to 5,000 units.
2. Bad debt losses are expected to increase by \$2,000 per year.

The marginal cost per unit for the increased number of units to be produced would be \$6.50. The company's income tax rate is 35%, and its required minimum rate of return on such investments is 16% after tax. Would you recommend that the Millers change the company's credit policy?

COLLECT TRADE RECEIVABLES

Effective credit collection begins by mailing invoices promptly. Once the invoice is mailed, the credit manager must examine, on a regular basis, the average collection period and take remedial action if targets are not realized. Several steps can be adopted to accelerate the collection of accounts from delinquent customers. First, there is the "dunning" approach, mailing a duplicate copy of the original invoice. Second, the credit manager can make a personal telephone call, which can serve as a routine, but stronger, reminder. Third, the credit manager can call on customers and initiate constructive counselling. Fourth, registered letters can be sent to delinquent accounts as notices that if payment is not received by a certain date, the firm will involve a third party (e.g., a collection agency) in the collection process. Finally, the most expensive way is to resort to formal legal charges.

CREDIT INSURANCE

Credit insurance provides protection against the cash drain caused by uncollectible trade receivables. Just as a vehicle theft or a warehouse fire can disrupt a business, the inability to collect a large receivable can cut off its cash flow. Not only can credit insurance prevent a cash flow crisis, it can also lead to higher earnings. Insurance protection on trade receivables can be secured in two ways:

Indemnification policy Insurance that a business takes against a catastrophic loss in cash.

The **indemnification policy** is insurance that a business takes against the catastrophic loss in cash that might occur when a large receivable becomes uncollectible because of debtor bankruptcy, debtor composition (reorganization of debt by creditors), or any other proceedings that reflect a debtor's insolvency.

Credit insurance policy
Insurance to cover losses suffered from a firm's trade receivables that become uncollectible.

A **credit insurance policy** provides coverage for losses suffered from any of a firm's trade receivables that become uncollectible. The coverage is subject to two practical limits. First, the insurance company can apply a deductible amount to each loss. Second, the insurance company can limit the maximum coverage for each debtor. Typically, those limits are tied to ratings established by national credit agencies such as Dun & Bradstreet. While premiums vary, the coverage may cost 0.25% to 0.5% of annual sales, which could be a small price to pay for survival. With this type of insurance, a company can be more liberal in granting credit to high-risk customers. If they don't pay, the insurance company would compensate the company.

Managing Cash and Cash Equivalents

4 Learning Objective

Comment on managing cash and cash equivalents.

Cash
Cash holdings and short-term deposits.

Cash consists of cash holdings and short-term deposits. Paying for ongoing obligations, such as the purchase of raw materials and the payment of salaries and current bills, is a constant drain on a company's cash pool. However, this cash pool is constantly being replenished by cash sales of inventories and the collection of trade receivables. The first part of this section examines the management of cash; the second part, the management of cash equivalents (e.g., marketable securities).

MANAGING CASH

This section examines why an adequate amount of cash should be maintained in reserve, how to make cash a productive asset, and strategies related to the collection of cash.

Why Maintain an Optimal Liquid Asset Balance?

The cash pool must be maintained at an appropriate level, and specific amounts must be designated for specific purposes (e.g., inventories, marketable securities, trade receivables). Maintaining a balanced cash pool is important for four reasons. First, it enables a business to conduct its ordinary operating transactions, such as paying current bills (e.g., utilities, salaries, supplies, and materials), and to partially finance its inventories and trade receivables. Second, an emergency fund is needed because of the difficulty in forecasting accurately the matching of cash receipts and cash disbursements. Third, it can be used for taking advantage of opportunities, such as cash discounts if bills are paid within a specified number of days. Finally, it can be used as an instrument for maintaining a credit standing with short-term lenders and suppliers.

Making Cash a Productive Asset

The main objective of cash management is to maintain a reasonable amount of cash so that profitability is not affected and payment of short-term commitments is possible. One way to increase profitability is to reduce the time lag between the date a payment is mailed by customers and the date it is deposited in the company's bank account to produce a return. For example, if a business can make 12% on short-term securities, and an amount of \$30,000 tied up in the mail arrives 20 days late, the company misses the opportunity of making \$197.26. The calculation is as follows:

$$\$30{,}000 \times 12\% \times \frac{\text{20-day delay}}{\text{365 days}} = \$197.26$$

If a company has hundreds or thousands of such cheques arriving late, it can easily miss the opportunity to make thousands of dollars each year in interest alone. The electronic payment communication system is an excellent way to reduce the time lag to a minimum.

Self-Test Exercise No. 6.8

Earning Interest on Investments

CompuTech can make 12% by investing its money in a long-term investment. If the Millers receive an amount of \$10,000, 20 days sooner than expected, how much would the company make?

Establishing a Minimum Cash Balance

One of the activities of cash management is to determine exactly how much cash is needed on hand to conduct the ongoing operations of a business. In order to manage cash effectively, a firm must synchronize its cash inflows with its cash outflows on a monthly basis. Cash planning is done through the cash budget (see Table 7.6 on page 323 in Chapter 7 for an example of a monthly cash budget). The cash budget allows a firm to ascertain the following:

- Flow of monthly cash receipts
- Flow of monthly cash disbursements
- Surplus or shortages of cash at the end of each month
- Amount of cash that should be invested in short-term securities (surplus) or that will be required from the bank in terms of a loan (shortage)

The objective of cash management is to set a minimum level of cash to satisfy business needs under normal operating conditions in order to increase organizational profitability, but without lessening business activities or exposing a firm to undue risk in meeting its financial obligations. Cash reserves (including marketable securities) should be sufficient to satisfy daily cash expenditures. What a business needs is the following:

- A practical minimum cash balance to operate with
- An amount necessary to absorb any unforeseen expenditures
- Some money to take advantage of profitable business opportunities (e.g., cash or special discounts on purchases, anticipation of an increase in the price of raw materials, acquiring a specialized piece of equipment at an attractive price)

Cash needs can be estimated using the following two steps:

Step 1: Determine the average daily cash expenditures over recent months.
Step 2: After recognizing the special characteristics of the business, estimate the appropriate cash reserves as a specific number of days' average cash outflow.

For example, if a business spends \$300,000 in cash each month, the average daily cash outflow is \$10,000 (\$300,000 ÷ 30). Here, the treasurer might determine that six days of cash are required to meet the average expenditures under normal business operations. If this is the case, management would need a \$60,000 cash balance (\$10,000 × 6 days).

Self-Test Exercise No. 6.9

Establishing the Minimum Cash Reserve

Len and Joan are examining the optimal level of liquid funds that they should keep on hold to pay their ongoing commitments. Over the past several months, the average monthly expenditures have been in the order of \$28,000 and they want to keep just enough cash on hand for a 10-day period. What should be CompuTech's minimum cash reserve?

Ways to Improve the Collection of Cash

There are different ways a firm can speed up cash receipts in order to make that asset productive.

There is the *customer's decision to purchase*. A customer's decision to purchase goods or services initiates the cash conversion cycle. Introducing the most rapid communication process to encourage a customer to place an order as quickly as possible is the first step in the cash conversion cycle (see Figure 6.1). A purchase order serves as the medium of communication. Customers should be able to transmit their orders to the company as quickly as possible.

Float
The amount of funds tied up in cheques that have been written but are still in process and have not yet been collected.

Also, there is the possibility of *reducing the negative float*. **Float** is defined as the time lag between the day that a cheque is mailed to the firm and the time the funds are received by the firm. There are three ways to improve a negative float, that is, eliminate idle cash.

Electronic funds transfer (EFT)
Means for transferring funds between customer and supplier by using the Internet or any other electronic medium.

The first is electronic communications. The **electronic funds transfer (EFT)** is an effective means of collecting payments from customers. Because EFT eliminates delays caused by the postal system, the administrative structure of a business, or the cheque-clearing process, it allows a business to use the collected funds more rapidly. This process transfers money from the sender or customer's bank account into the receiver or firm's bank account in a matter of hours.

Under the EFT, money is wired directly from a customer's bank account to a business's bank account. This system allows accounts to be debited and credited daily. At the end of each day, excess cash is invested in short-term deposits in order to generate additional earnings. Unfortunately, many businesses look only at personnel and equipment costs involved in these alternatives and overlook the one- to seven-day reduction in their cash conversion period that results from eliminating mail delays.

The EFT is generally suitable when a business has an ongoing relationship with a customer. Repeat customers usually make up the bulk of all sales, so using electronic funds transfer for them helps a business improve its service and accelerate cash flow. Today, many consumers use teller cards that give them access to cash 24 hours a day, 7 days a week. They use automatic tellers to transfer funds between accounts. Debit cards make it possible to transfer funds from a customer's bank account electronically to the account of the retailer. There is no need to send an invoice, wait for a cheque to arrive, and verify the cheque before making the deposit. Both EFT and the electronic data interchange (EDI) systems are changing the way of managing cash.

Regional banks Locations where customers pay their accounts (local bank), which are subsequently transferred to the seller's bank account.

The second process involves **regional banks**. Under this process, customers pay their accounts to banks, and the payment can be transferred to the company's account more quickly than by mail delivery. Collection accounts are established at a series of commercial banks strategically located around the country, and customers are encouraged to pay their bills in their region rather than sending the payments to a central location.

Post office box Location where customers pay their accounts (local post office box), which are subsequently transferred to the seller's bank account.

The third strategy is to establish a **post office box** in an area where the firm has many customers. The lockbox system is a procedure whereby a firm rents post office boxes in different cities and entrusts their management to banks, which monitor the lockboxes periodically. The firm instructs customers in a particular region to mail their cheques to regional post office box numbers rather than directly to the firm. As soon as cheques from customers arrive, they are verified, checked for completeness, and deposited in the firm's account. Although this system can be an effective means of improving the collection of cash, a business must weigh the bank's fees against the benefits that accrue from a shorter cash conversion period. Often, the profit potential of a more rapid cash flow can make the cost of the lockbox service insignificant.

The following compares the traditional payment system and the lockbox system.

Traditional Payment System	Lockbox System
1. Invoice is sent to the customer.	1. Invoice is sent to the customer.
2. Invoice and payment are sent to the company.	2. Invoice and cheque are sent to the company's post office lockbox.
3. Company processes payment and credits customers' account.	3. Bank processes payment and credits the customer's bank account.
4. Company deposits the cheque at the bank.	4. Bank advises the company of payment information.
5. Bank processes the cheque and forwards it to the customer's bank.	5. Bank forwards cheque to the customer's bank.
6. Customer's bank credits customer's account and returns cheque with the next bank statement.	6. Customer's bank credits customer's account and returns cheque with the next bank statement.

It is estimated that such a system can help reduce the time lag by three to four days.

MANAGING MARKETABLE SECURITIES

One of the responsibilities of the CFO (or the treasurer) is to adjust the company's cash balance on an ongoing basis, either by investing excess cash in temporary short-term securities or by securing extra cash through short-term bank borrowings.

It is more profitable for a business to invest cash in marketable securities, even if it is only for several days, than it is to leave it dormant in a bank account that does not generate interest. The main objective of managing marketable securities is to invest the temporary excess cash in order to increase profitability.

Funds are held in short-term marketable securities or temporary investments for three reasons:

1. To finance seasonal or cyclical operations (temporary working capital)
2. To finance known financial requirements, such as purchase of equipment or machinery
3. To invest funds received from the sale of long-term securities (shares or bonds)

Different types of marketable securities can be held by businesses, and the attributes of each one should be examined carefully before investing. Four main attributes should be considered. First, there is *maturity*, the length of time by which the principal amount of a marketable security must be paid back to the investor. Second, there is the *denomination*, the unit of transaction for buying or selling a short-term security. Third, there is *marketability*, or the ability of an investor to sell a marketable security. Finally, there is the *yield determination*, which is the method of earning a return on the investment.

Investment securities
Funds invested in short-term deposits such as treasury bills, bank deposits, etc.

There are different types of **investment securities**, such as Canada Treasury bills, bank deposits, commercial paper, finance company paper, Eurodollar deposits, Canadian government bonds, and corporate bonds with different maturity dates and yields. Depending on the length of time a treasurer wants to place funds, he or she will have to find the most suitable type of security, that is, the one that responds most favourably to the business's needs.

Strategies for Managing Marketable Securities

Managing marketable securities for a small business is relatively easy. The only requirement is the need to match the short-term investments with the excess cash shown in the monthly cash budget. A large business, on the other hand, must determine investment strategies that will optimize the return on investment. In many cases, businesses have millions of dollars tied up in cash or near-cash accounts. It is therefore important for such businesses to determine effective investment strategies in short-term marketable securities. There are six approaches.

First, there is the *do-nothing* option. In this case, the company simply lets the excess funds accumulate in its bank account. Here, funds are not invested in short-term securities, therefore profitability is sacrificed.

Second, there is the investment of funds on an *ad hoc basis*. This approach is accomplished when investment securities are synchronized with projected cash disbursements. This method is used by firms that, because of a shortage of resources or a lack of expertise within the company, do not want to devote much time and energy to this activity.

Third, there is the *riding-the-yield approach*. Here, the treasurer examines the investment portfolio and invests in the securities that will offer the highest interest rate. For example, he may sell off a long-term security before maturity and purchase a short-term security simply to obtain a higher yield.

Fourth, *guidelines* can be developed. This is particularly useful if many people are involved in investing in short-term securities (e.g., in insurance companies and trust companies). Such guidelines give the securities analysts procedures to be followed systematically in order to reflect senior management's viewpoint and take into consideration both return and risk.

Fifth, *control limits* are established, and the system allows the analysts to take action only when the cash balance reaches an upper or lower control limit. This approach does not specify which marketable securities should be bought or sold but states only when action should be taken.

The sixth option is the *portfolio approach*. Here, individual marketable securities are not examined as isolated investment opportunities but as part of a group of investments. In this case, both risks and returns are taken into consideration from a broader viewpoint—the portfolio perspective. There may be hundreds of different investment options, and each option is evaluated on the basis of a total investment strategy that is consistent with the financial objectives of the firm. Some securities may offer low return and low risk; others, high risk and high return.

Managing Current Liabilities

5 Learning Objective

Show how current liability accounts can be managed to improve the cash flow cycle.

The management of current liabilities is also part of working capital management. Current liabilities are the credit obligations that fall due within a 12-month period. For a business, it is important to determine which assets should be financed by short-term borrowings and which ones by long-term sources. A business should always maximize the use of its trade and other payables and accruals as sources of financing, because they are spontaneous and self-adjusting. This means that these accounts can expand and contract with changes in the levels of sales. When more sales are made, trade and other payables increase in roughly the same proportion. Similarly, when more people are on the payroll, wages and salaries payable increase.

The main objective of managing payables and accruals is to provide the business with a spontaneous source of financing at no cost. Some of the more popular sources and forms of short-term borrowings will be discussed in Chapter 8.

This section deals with sources of working capital financing. Leverage is the extent to which a firm's assets are supported by debt. We will deal here with short-term leverage, the funds that can be derived from suppliers (trade and other payables), various accruals, and working capital loans obtained from commercial banks. The intent of this section is to examine the benefits of leverage and how this type of financing can help realize higher earnings.

TRADE AND OTHER PAYABLES

Several guidelines must be respected if credit is to be used effectively. First, the sales budget should be prepared in order to find out when the raw materials financing will be required. Second, the manufacturing budget should also be established in order to ascertain salary and wage payments. Third, suppliers that offer the best products and services are selected, considering the credit terms that best meet the company's needs. Finally, the decision is made regarding when and how invoices should be paid.

Managing trade and other payables require a good relationship between the company and its suppliers. This means that when bills arrive, they should be paid according to the agreement, on the appropriate date. This allows a firm to maintain a good credit standing with its suppliers and ensures that they will continue to sell goods and provide services to it.

However, nothing prevents a firm from taking advantage of cost-free funds, such as trade and other payables. It is a matter of slowing disbursements, and ensuring, at the same time, that the suppliers maintain confidence in the firm as a "slow, but sure, payer."

A supplier contributes financing to a firm any time account credit consideration is extended. This trade credit allows a business to defer cash payment for a purchase in accordance with the supplier's selling terms. Conceptually, trade credit provides the same benefits to a business as any other form of leverage: It increases a company's cash capability and enables it to satisfy objectives that might remain out of reach in the absence of external financing. However, it is more closely connected with the cash flow cycle than any other form of financing; therefore, its use calls for deliberate cash planning that focuses on the following four points:

- The link between trade credit and cash capability
- Benefits the firm can derive from an alternative supplier's selling terms
- The relationship between trade credit and the cash flow process with the help of the average payment period calculation and the period that contributes positively to cash flows
- Good working relations with suppliers

Link between trade credit and cash capability. Trade credit is a significant source of financing for most businesses and, if it is properly administered within the planning and purchasing functions, can help a business increase its cash capability and obtain interest-free, permanently revolving loans in the form of an infinite series of single-payment loans.

The goal of trade and other payables management is to provide as much spontaneous financing as possible at zero cost to a business. A major advantage of trade credit is the flexibility it gives a business. It is at management's discretion to determine whether a cash discount should be taken, or whether it should stretch its trade and other payables beyond the credit period. "Leaning on credit" involves postponement of payment beyond the credit period. The opportunity cost of leaning on credit is a possible deterioration of a company's credit rating.

Credit is directly related to purchasing and is not an isolated activity; it is part of a comprehensive process that touches on the effective scheduling of products and services for sale to customers. In order to determine the amount of trade credit a business requires, management must know how many units it needs to buy and when to buy them. The key activities related to purchasing are as follows:

- Preparing a sales budget
- Preparing a production budget
- Determining what and when to purchase
- Determining which suppliers to use
- Determining what credit terms to accept
- Receiving purchases and ensuring quality
- Determining when and how to pay invoices

Benefits derived from alternative supplier's selling terms. Delaying disbursements generates more cash capability in a firm and increases profitability. The maximum cash disbursement period comes from two complementary management practices:

- Liability management
- Float management

In either instance, the objective remains the same—the retention of all cash in a business as long as possible. A business should not pay its bills before they become due. This is the guiding principle of liability management. Of course, a business should never abuse a creditor's consideration, nor should it exceed the requirements set by a supplier's required payment terms. But if management experiences a tight cash flow, it can delay cash disbursements beyond the credit terms.

In some industries, such as electronics and printing, the practice of stretching payables is common. In other industries, such as steel and food commodities, failure to observe supplier terms can eliminate any future credit consideration. Certainly, management should know where it stands before deferring any payment beyond its due date.

As indicated earlier, extending the average payable period, which is the relationship between trade credit and the cash flow process, increases cash capability and earnings. Average payable period measures the average length of time each dollar of trade credit is used. A common characteristic of trade credit is that it is spontaneous (i.e., self-adjusting). As revenue expands, a business necessarily buys more materials and parts, hence payables increases. Trade credit involves the acquisition of materials, parts, and supplies needed, and a delay between the date of their acquisition and the date of payment to the creditors increases the company's cash capability and earnings.

To calculate the average payable period and to find how it contributes to positive cash flow, trade and other payables is divided by the average daily purchases. For example, if the trade and other payables shown on a statement of financial position are $300,000, and the average daily purchases are $10,000, the average payment period is 30 days. Thus, each dollar of trade credit consideration contributed to a business remains in the bank account for 30 days before being returned to the supplier in the form of a cash payment. If the average payment period is extended to 45 days, trade and other payables increase to $450,000 ($10,000 × 45 days), which provides an extra $150,000 in cash.

Two important factors should be considered here:

- Payments to suppliers should not be extended to a point where relationships and goodwill are damaged.
- Cash discounts should be considered before making payments.

Self-Test Exercise No. 6.10

Slowing the Disbursements to Suppliers

CompuTech bought $209,000 worth of goods and services in 2009. The Millers think that it would be possible to delay paying their bills up to 50 days without jeopardizing their relationship with suppliers. At the moment, the company's trade and other payables are $20,000. If the company defers paying its bills to 50 days, how much financing would the company be able to obtain from that source?

Relationship between trade credit and cash flows. A trade discount can help increase profitability at the expense of cash flows; therefore, it is a matter of calculating the trade-off. Many businesses offer various types of trade discounts if a supplier wants to increase its cash flow position. A business can reinvest its accelerated cash flow rapidly and thus increase profitability. The earnings that the supplier loses from today's discounts could benefit it more in the future.

When a company decides to offer a trade discount, it may mean that its average collection period is long (45, 60, or even as high as 90 days). If this is the case, a company may offer trade discounts to get its customers to pay faster. This has two benefits:

- Accelerated cash flow
- Increase in profitability

If a supplier offers a trade discount, the business should take advantage of it, as long as the cost of borrowing from the bank is less than the supplier discount. Here is the effective cost of various early-payment discounts when annualized:

Discounts allowed for payment in 10 days	Annualized cost to the supplier
0.5%	9%
1%	18%
2%	37%

Figure 6.5 Annualized Finance Costs

$$\text{Annualized finance costs} = \left[\frac{\text{Discount percent}}{100 - \text{Discount percent}}\right] \times \left[\frac{365}{\text{Credit limit} - \text{discount period}}\right] =$$

$$\left[\frac{2\%}{100\% - 2\%}\right] \times \left[\frac{365}{30 - 10}\right] =$$

$$\left[\frac{2\%}{98\%}\right] \times \left[\frac{365}{20}\right] = 37.2\%$$

This means that if a supplier offers a 2% discount if paid within a 10 days, net 30-day payment option, the 2% discount translates into a 37% annual borrowing cost. Figure 6.5 shows how this percentage was calculated.

Working relationship with suppliers. A favourable working relationship with suppliers has a direct influence on a firm's cash capability. A good working relationship affects both the amount and the terms of the credit consideration a business receives. One may argue that making a major purchase from any supplier involves considerations that are beyond any potential credit consideration. To be sure, price structures, product lines, delivery schedules, and service capabilities remain relevant.

However, most businesses eventually establish ongoing relationships with their major suppliers; once such relationships are established, a business should seek to develop and maintain the maximum potential cash capability from each supplier's credit consideration.

Two management practices contribute to good supplier relations. First, a consistent payment pattern is a good practice. Erratic payments upset even the most patient suppliers. So long as they know when to expect payment for purchases, even if persistently late, they can feel comfortable with the relationship. Second, lines of communication should always be kept open. The more a supplier knows about a business, the more it can respond to the company's needs. After all, the business's purchases presumably are profitable sales for the supplier. The better the supplier responds to a business's needs, the more it can improve its own bottom line.

Opening lines of communication can help a business in two ways. First, by informing the suppliers of projected requirements for credit considerations, management may obtain an increased line of credit. In this way, a business can lay the groundwork for approval by giving suppliers the information that will facilitate the credit decision process. Second, it can help a business slip unscathed through a cash flow problem.

ACCRUALS

Accruals such as salaries and taxes payable are similar to trade credit in that they are spontaneous sources of financing. They differ from trade credit in that they are much less a decision variable; that is, a business is relatively constrained in what it can do to influence accruals as a source of financing. However, some techniques can be used to improve cash flow and profitability.

Salaries and wages payable. Some managers may not realize that they, together with their fellow employees, are a source of financing to their firm. Indeed, all employees help finance their firm because they are not paid for their services on a day-by-day basis. Instead, they are paid at the end of the week, every two weeks, or perhaps at the end of the month.

For firms operating seasonal businesses, wages and salaries payable represent a spontaneous and flexible source of financing. During the busiest part of the year, when more employees are hired in the production process, the amount of financing available from wages and salaries payable increases. From a management perspective, there is not much flexibility with this source of financing. However, some leeway exists when a firm may choose to pay its employees (including management) less frequently—for example, monthly rather than semi-monthly. But because there are laws that dictate how frequently employees must be paid, there is a limit to the amount of additional financing that can be obtained this way.

Taxes payable. Taxes payable are also a potential free source of financing. Taxes that are owed to various governments constitute another accrual that becomes part of short-term financing. Property taxes and income tax expense (provincial and federal) do not become due at the moment they are incurred; rather, their payment is delayed until a later date.

Taxes payable are a free source of financing because governments often do not charge finance costs on outstanding balances. However, if management must accumulate funds in a special chequing account in anticipation of a future tax payment, there is an opportunity cost as those funds cannot be used for anything else.

Because the timing of tax payment is specified by government agencies, including the Canada Revenue Agency, there is little that a business can do to manipulate this free source of short-term financing. An exception would occur if management deliberately decided to delay tax payments beyond the due date, even though a known penalty would result. There have been reported cases in foreign countries where firms have deliberately avoided paying taxes to their government, recognizing that the penalties for late tax payments were less than the interest rates charged by banks and other lenders on comparable amounts of financing.

Working capital loans Short-term loans made for the purpose of financing working capital accounts (e.g., inventories, trade receivables).

WORKING CAPITAL LOANS

Most companies will need some sort of **working capital loan**. In order not to waste its time and that of lenders, management should always make sure to match the sources of financing to the appropriate assets. (This topic will be covered in Chapter 8 beginning on page 374 under the heading, "The Matching Principle.")

As mentioned earlier, leverage is another term used for money borrowed from bankers. Because bank credit is a significant element in cash flow management, it is important to choose the type of loan that will maximize the firm's profitability and cash capability.

Basically, management should use short-term credit (that with a maturity of one year or less) to finance seasonal current assets, and long-term credit to finance non-current assets. It is important to match the maturities of sources and the maturities of uses of funds. Also, because there are so many different forms and sources of financing, management must ensure that they approach a lender that will meet their specific need, such as a short-term loan, term or installment loan, or revolving loan.

In the News 6.3 gives an example of the type of strategy that management can bring into play to accelerate the movement of cash in a business by speeding up sales, reducing inventories, and sweetening leasing and loan rates.

In The News [6.3]

Injecting Cash in a Business Can Accelerate the Cash Conversion Cycle

It takes cash to generate cash! Usually, what a company does to increase sales, profit, and cash is spend money on promotions, advertisement, discounts, and offers of all types of incentives.

This is what Toyota did in September 2009. It planned a $1-billion marketing campaign in North America to sell more cars, particularly the hybrid models (e.g., Prius). This outflow of cash was directed toward the media, buyers, and auto dealers. The marketing and advertising plan represented a 40% increase above what Toyota usually spends during that particular quarter. Toyota decided to embark on this ambitious marketing and advertising campaign in view of the fact that it had just experienced one of its worst periods of sales performance since it was founded in 1937. The company was expecting to show a loss for the second straight year. The first time in its history! Despite the fact that Toyota sold three models among the top ten sold in the U.S. government's sponsored "cash for clunkers" incentive program, it was not enough for the Toyota to show a profit!

Source: Adapted from Reuter, "Toyota plans $1B campaign to bump fourth-quarter sales," *Ottawa Citizen*, September 18, 2009, p. E2. For more information about Toyota Canada, go to www.toyota.ca and click on "Company Info."

REALITY FINANCIAL SNAPSHOTS

Organizations, whether for-profit or not-for-profit, are vigilant in the way that they manage their working capital. Managers of these organizations are aware that the management of working capital accounts is a constant and important responsibility. In 2008, Enbridge's statement of financial position showed a $3.7 billion amount in current assets for an increase of 13.6% over 2007. On the other hand, The Ottawa Hospital (TOH) showed an amount of $75.5 million in current assets for a 10.4% increase over the previous year. The next several paragraphs examine the various working capital accounts shown on Enbridge's and TOH's statement of financial position accounts under current assets and current liabilities.

ENBRIDGE[1]

As shown below, Enbridge's statements of financial position for the years 2008 and 2007 show a 13.6% increase in their current asset accounts and a 16.8% growth in their current liability accounts. The following gives the breakdown of the growth pattern for various current asset and current liability accounts, including current ratios, quick ratios, DWC, and CCE ratios for both years.

(in $ millions)	2008	2007	Change (%)
Current assets			
Cash and cash equivalents	541.7	166.7	225.0
Accounts receivable and other	2,322.5	2,388.7	–2.8
Inventory	844.7	709.4	19.1
Total current assets	3,708.9	3,264.8	13.6
Current liabilities			
Short-term borrowings	874.6	545.6	60.3
Account payable and other	2,411.5	2,213.8	8.9
Interest payable	101.9	89.1	14.4
Current maturities of long-term debt	533.8	605.2	11.8
Current maturities of non-recourse long-term debt	184.7	61.1	202.3
Total current liabilities	4,106.5	3,514.8	16.8
Net working capital	–397.6	–250.0	
Current ratio (times)	0.90	0.93	
Quick ratio (times)	0.70	0.73	
Days of working capital	17.1	27.1	
Cash conversion efficiency ratio (%)	12.3	10.9	

As shown above, net working capital for both years are in a negative position. In 2008, every dollar's worth of current liabilities was guaranteed by 90 cents of current assets and 93 cents in 2007. The quick ratio also showed a slight decrease from 73 to 70 cents.

DWC, which measures the number of DWC Enbridge holds in order to meet its average daily sales requirements, decreased from 27.1 days to 17.1 days. The CCE ratio, which measures the efficiency with which Enbridge converts revenue to cash flow within its operations, shows a slight improvement, from 10.9% to 12.3% between 2007 and 2008.

THE OTTAWA HOSPITAL[2]

The same calculations done for Enbridge regarding the management of working capital can also be done for TOH. However, because we are dealing with an NFP organization, the results of some of the numbers are meaningless and of no consequence. As shown on the following page, TOH's statement of financial position does

1. Enbridge Inc., *2008 Enbridge Annual Report*. Found at: http://www.enbridge.com/investor/financialInformation/reportsFilings/pdf/2008-annual-report-en.pdf.
2. *2008 Ottawa Hospital Annual Report*. Found at: http://www.ottawahospital.on.ca/about/reports/FS2008-e.pdf.

include current asset and current liability accounts. However, the nature of some of these accounts is somewhat different from those included in for-profit statements of financial position. For example, for-profit organization's accounts receivable may include hundreds, if not thousands of customers; in the case of TOH, only half of accounts receivable are payments to be made by patients.

Because NFP organizations are not in business to generate a profit, but instead to provide excellent patient care service, research, and so on, some of these ratios would be of little interest to financial analysts. Here is the breakdown of TOH's current asset and current liability accounts shown on their 2008 and 2007 statements of financial position.

(in $000s)	2008	2007	Change (%)
Current assets			
Cash held in trust	20,228	18,741	7.93
Accounts receivable	41,249	36,724	12.32
Inventories	9,674	9,205	5.10
Prepaid expenses	4,309	3,664	17.6
Total current assets	75,460	68,334	10.43
Current liabilities			
Bank indebtedness	51,294	19,355	165.2
Accounts payable and accrued liabilities	179,768	194,123	–7.4
Payable to TOH Residence Corporation	2,389	1,729	38.2
Deferred contributions related to trust funds	20,228	18,741	7.9
Total current liabilities	253,679	233,948	8.4
Net working capital	–178,219	–165,614	
Current ratio (times)	0.30	0.29	
Quick ratio (times)	0.26	0.25	
Days of working capital	–54.0	–67.2	
Cash conversion efficiency ratio (%)	0.8	0.7	

As shown above, net working capital shows a huge negative amount for both years and gives a 0.30 and 0.29 current ratio for the years 2008 and 2007, respectively. Because the net working capital is negative, the DWC shows a negative figure. The only meaningful ratio is the CCE ratio, which gives 0.8% in 2008 and 0.7% in 2007.

[DECISION-MAKING IN ACTION]

When Bill Webber, controller of Pickford Electronics Inc., attended the annual financial planning meeting with his management group, he made the observation that the company's profitability could be improved if certain working capital accounts moved faster. He continued his explanation by stating that if the turnover of Pickford's inventories and trade receivables moved faster, and trade and other payables slower, the company would improve its profitability, have more cash to work with, and be in a much better financial position.

Bill was not an operating manager and could not do anything to improve the company's cash performance. However, he made the point that all division and branch managers should take time and be more cautious in the way that the cash flow of the company is managed. As he pointed out, extra cash could be reinvested into the company and help Pickford grow at a faster pace. Janice Simmons, the general manager, thought that the point should be discussed further to determine how this cash flow idea could be implemented.

After several meetings between Janice and Bill, it was agreed that all managers should become sensitive to the importance of cash flow management and be given some training that would help them find solutions to improve the company's cash conversion cycle. During one of the management meetings, Janice pointed out that a portion of the future budgeting and financial planning meeting should be devoted to objectives that had to do with the function of cash management.

It was therefore decided that all managers at Pickford would be required to attend a two-day course on the topic of working capital management, given by an expert in the field. This course would be given to groups of 15 managers at a time over a two-month period.

After the training sessions, Janice convened all managers to a meeting and had Bill Webber explain the financial targets to be incorporated in Pickford's financial plan, namely the DWC and the CCE ratio. Bill pointed out that if all current asset and current liability accounts were improved, a responsibility shared by all managers, these two financial targets could be improved. He also indicated that once the operating budgets, the projected statement of income, and the projected statement of financial position were completed, he would present to them the improvements in the various working capital accounts and, particularly, the results related to the DWC and the CCE targets. He also added that if the cash flow objectives were not met, all operating budgets and plans would have to be redone until the targets were achieved.

A month later, Bill Webber presented a summary of the year-end 2009 and 2010 financial targets. Both he and Janice were pleased with the results as he pointed out that the cash flow from operations for the years 2009 and 2010 showed a $99,000 increase, that is, 50%. The makeup of the cash flow is as follows:

Cash Flow	2009	2010	Change
Profit for the year	$127,000	$179,000	$52,000
Depreciation/amortization	80,000	97,000	17,000
Adjustments in non-cash working capital accounts	−10,000	+20,000	30,000
Net operating cash flows	$197,000	$296,000	$99,000

As shown, the overall cash flow improvement was due to an increase in three operating activity accounts, profit for the year, depreciation/amortization, and a positive change in the adjustments in non-cash working capital accounts. The following paragraphs show how each cash flow item is calculated. The return on revenue improvement from 8.5% to 10.4% is due mainly to improvements in cost of sales.

Income Statement	2009	2010	Change (%)
Revenue	$1,500,000	$1,725,000	15.0%
Cost of sales			
Purchases	(735,000)	(784,000)	6.7
Manufacturing expenses	(315,000)	(337,250)	7.1
Subtotal	(1,050,000)	(1,121,250)	6.8
Gross profit	450,000	603,750	34.2
Other expenses and taxes	(323,000)	(424,750)	31.5
Profit for the year	$ 127,000	$ 179,000	40.9%
Return on revenue	8.5%	10.4%	

Here is the vertical analysis for the key expense items shown on the statement of income for the years 2009 and 2010.

Vertical Analysis	2009	2010
Revenue	100.0%	100.0%
Cost of sales	(70.0)	(65.0)
Gross profit	30.0	35.0
Other expenses including taxes	(21.5)	(24.6)
Profit for the year	8.5%	10.4%

The net change in non-cash working capital accounts in 2009 shows a net increase over 2008 in working capital (and a decrease in cash flow) in the amount of $10,000 and a decrease in 2010 in working capital (and an increase in cash flow) of $20,000. The favourable cash flow performance in 2010 is due in large measure to the acceleration in the cash conversion cycle, that is, a faster payment in trade receivables, an improved inventory turnover, and a slowdown in the payment of trade and other payables.

Working Capital Accounts	2008	2009	2010
Trade receivables	$150,000	$155,000	$150,000
Inventory	120,000	125,000	120,000
Sub-total	270,000	280,000	270,000
Trade and other payables	(110,000)	(110,000)	(120,000)
Net working capital	$160,000	$170,000	$150,000
Net change in working capital		+$10,000	−$20,000

As shown, Pickford invested an additional $10,000 in working capital in 2009 and plans to reduce it by $20,000 in 2010. Bill Webber indicated that the favourable cash flow performance would help the company significantly decrease its DWC from 41.4 days to 31.7 days and increase its CCE ratio from 13.1% to 17.2%.

By using a flip chart, Bill Webber explained how these working capital accounts would be improved and the impact on the company's cash flow position. He indicated that the adjustments in non-cash working capital accounts between 2009 and 2010 is expected to drop by $20,000 (from $170,000 to $150,000) despite the fact that the average daily revenue will show an increase of $616, or 15%. This change will improve the DWC by 10 days (from 41.4 days to 31.7 days). Bill Webber further explained this improvement with the following calculations:

Days of Working Capital

2009

$$\frac{\textbf{Net working capital}}{\textbf{Average daily revenue}} = \frac{\$170{,}000}{\$4{,}110} = \textbf{41.4 days}$$

Average daily revenue = $4,110 ($1,500,000 ÷ 365)

2010

$$\frac{\textbf{Net working capital}}{\textbf{Average daily revenue}} = \frac{\$150{,}000}{\$4{,}726} = \textbf{31.7 days}$$

Average daily revenue = $4,726 ($1,725,000 ÷ 365)

As Bill pointed out, the reasons net working capital dropped from $170,000 to $150,000 are improvements in inventory turnover, the average collection period of trade receivables, and the extension of the average daily payables. He gave the following explanation for each.

The *inventory turnover* improved from 8.4 times to 9.3 times despite the 6.8% increase in cost of sales. This inventory turnover's favourable performance is caused by a reduction in the inventory level in the amount of $5,000, or 4%. This is due to a better method in the way the raw materials will be purchased and the acceleration in the manufacturing process. The turnover is calculated as follows:

2009

$$\frac{\textbf{Cost of sales}}{\textbf{Inventories}} = \frac{\$1{,}050{,}000}{\$125{,}000} = \textbf{8.4 times}$$

2010

$$\frac{\textbf{Cost of sales}}{\textbf{Inventories}} = \frac{\$1{,}121{,}250}{\$120{,}000} = \textbf{9.3 times}$$

The *average collection period* improved from 37.7 days to 31.7 days because of a change in the policies and procedures regarding collection. Here is the calculation:

2009

$$\frac{\textbf{Trade receivables}}{\textbf{Average daily revenue}} = \frac{\$155{,}000}{\$4{,}110} = \textbf{37.7 days}$$

2010

$$\frac{\textbf{Trade receivables}}{\textbf{Average daily revenue}} = \frac{\$150{,}000}{\$4{,}726} = \textbf{31.7 days}$$

The *average payable period* increased slightly from 55 days to 56 days. Bill explained that this small improvement was due to the fact that the purchasing department was able to negotiate better prices and credit conditions with several of Pickford's key suppliers. Here is the calculation:

2009

$$\frac{\textbf{Trade and other payables}}{\textbf{Average daily purchases}} = \frac{\$110{,}000}{\$2{,}014} = \textbf{55 days}$$

Average daily purchases = \$2,014 (\$735,000 ÷ 365)

2010

$$\frac{\textbf{Trade and other payables}}{\textbf{Average daily purchases}} = \frac{\$120{,}000}{\$2{,}148} = \textbf{56 days}$$

Average daily purchases = \$2,148 (\$784,000 ÷ 365)

The CCE ratio also improved as a result of the 50.3% increase in operating cash flow (from \$197,000 to \$296,000) compared to the 15% increase in revenue.

Cash conversion efficiency ratio

2009

$$\frac{\textbf{Operating cash flow}}{\textbf{Revenue}} = \frac{\$197{,}000}{\$1{,}500{,}000} = \textbf{13.1 \%}$$

2010

$$\frac{\textbf{Operating cash flow}}{\textbf{Revenue}} = \frac{\$296{,}000}{\$1{,}725{,}000} = \textbf{17.2 \%}$$

Bill Webber concluded his presentation by saying that if a major effort had not been made in improving the working capital accounts, the company would probably have had to invest an additional 15% or \$25,000 instead of a \$20,000 reduction in these accounts. As a result, Pickford will be able to use this incremental \$45,000 cash flow amount for investment purposes, for their expansion program, and for buying capital assets.

FINANCIAL SPREADSHEETS—EXCEL

Several ratios calculated by the financial spreadsheets that accompany this manual are the DWC and the CCE ratio. The financial spreadsheets calculate the CCE ratio from two angles:

- Using the operating activities cash flow
- Using the profit for the year plus depreciation/amortization

The financial spreadsheets also include three decision-making tools dealing with the management of working capital. The first spreadsheet (cash discounts) determines whether a cash discount should be given to customers in order to improve cash receipts for different paying conditions (e.g., 60-day payment terms versus 90 days) and allowing different discounts (e.g., 1%/10, net 30 days, versus 2%/10, net 30 days).

The second spreadsheet (credit terms) helps to determine if existing credit terms should be extended to customers. It shows whether the incremental profit earned from increased revenue gives a larger (or lower) return on investment on the incremental investment in trade receivables than the cost of capital. The third spreadsheet (economic ordering quantity) calculates the number of units that a business should buy each time an order is made from a supplier.

Chapter Summary

1 Learning Objective

Define the meaning and importance of the cash conversion cycle.

Working capital management involves the management of all current asset and current liability accounts. Because these types of accounts vary on a day-to-day basis, managing this current portion of business activities is time-consuming. The objective of working capital management is to manage individual current accounts, and to ensure a proper balance between all asset accounts and all liability accounts. Also, there must exist a balanced relationship with other statement of financial position items such as non-current assets and long-term borrowings. Managing current assets includes inventories, trade receivables, marketable securities, and cash. The purpose of managing working capital accounts is to accelerate the cash conversion cycle and the operating cycle. There are two methods of measuring the efficiency and effectiveness of working capital management: (1) the DWC, that is the number of DWC a business holds to meet average daily sales requirements; and (2) the CCE that is how quickly a business converts revenue into cash flow from its operating activities.

2 Learning Objective

Explain different strategies related to managing inventories.

Managing inventories consists of replenishing stock in such a way that associated order and holding costs are kept at a minimum. Keeping inventories low helps to improve profitability. Three methods used to manage inventories are MRP, JIT, and economic order quantity (EOQ).

3 Learning Objective

Discuss various techniques related to trade receivables management.

Managing trade receivables involves six activities: setting credit terms; granting credit to customers; billing; monitoring payments made by customers; applying the necessary measures to maintain or reduce the average collection period; and obtaining proper credit insurance.

4 Learning Objective

Comment on managing cash and cash equivalents.

The essence of managing cash is to ensure an adequate reservoir of cash to enable a business to conduct its ordinary operating activities, handle emergencies, and take advantage of specific opportunities. The preparation of a cash budget helps management find what level of cash is needed and when. Managing marketable securities consists of investing surplus cash in profit-making investments, such as treasury bills, bank deposits, or bonds. Six different approaches can be used for managing marketable securities; it is a matter of selecting the one that best responds to the needs of a business.

5 Learning Objective

Show how current liability accounts can be managed to improve the cash flow cycle.

Management of current liabilities consists of using current debt, such as trade and other payables, accruals, and working capital loans, as effective sources of financing.

Key Terms

Aging of accounts receivable p. 270
Cash p. 272
Cash conversion cycle p. 252
Cash conversion efficiency p. 250
Credit insurance policy p. 272
Credit policy p. 268
Credit terms p. 264
Credit-scoring system p. 266
Days of working capital p. 250
Economic ordering quantity (EOQ) p. 260
Electronic funds transfer (EFT) p. 274
Float p. 274
Goal of working capital management p. 249
Holding costs p. 261
Indemnification policy p. 271
Inventories, types of p. 259
Inventory replenishment p. 263
Investment securities p. 276
Just-in-time inventory management p. 260
Material requirements planning (MRP) p. 260
Net working capital p. 248
Operating cycle p. 253
Ordering costs p. 261
Post office box p. 275
Regional banks p. 275
Working capital loans p. 282
Working capital management p. 248

Review Questions

1. What do we mean by net working capital?
2. What is the goal of working capital management?
3. What does the DWC measure? Why is it important?
4. What does the CCE ratio measure? Why is it important?
5. What do we mean by the cash conversion cycle? Show how it works.
6. With an example, differentiate between cash flow and profit.
7. Explain the various types of inventories that a company has to carry at all times.
8. What do we mean by "material requirements planning" within the management of inventories?

9. Explain how the economic ordering quantity method works.
10. Identify several ordering costs and several holding costs.
11. Comment on the different functions of the credit manager.
12. Differentiate between "average collection period" and "aging of trade receivables."
13. What types of insurance can a firm use to protect its trade receivables?
14. How can accelerating the flow of cash improve ROI?
15. What are the different approaches that can be used to improve the cash collection period?
16. Differentiate between the process related to the lockbox system and the traditional payment system.
17. Explain the various strategies related to managing marketable securities.
18. How can trade and other payables be a source of financing?
19. How can accruals be a source of financing?
20. What are working capital loans?
21. Why is it more difficult to manage working capital accounts than capital asset accounts?
22. Who is responsible for managing the working capital accounts? Discuss.

Learning Exercises

EXERCISE 1

With the following information:

a) Make a list of the working capital accounts.
b) Calculate the net working capital.

Buildings	$100,000
Cash	5,000
Trade receivables	25,000
Trade and other payables	40,000
Inventories	50,000
Cost of sales	150,000
Land	500,000
Wages payable	10,000
Prepaid expenses	12,000
Goodwill	50,000

EXERCISE 2

With the following information, calculate the company's DWC for the years 2009 and 2010.

	2009	2010
Profit for the year	$176,000	$225,000
Depreciation/amortization	55,000	70,000
Trade receivables	360,000	385,000
Inventories	450,000	490,000
Trade and other payables	400,000	440,000
Revenue	2,200,000	2,500,000

EXERCISE 3

With the information contained in Exercise 2, calculate the company's CCE ratio for the years 2009 and 2010. To do these calculations, assume that in 2008 the company's net working capital was $350,000.

EXERCISE 4

A company decides to market its products more aggressively. Current sales are 60,000 units per year and are expected to increase by 20%. Carrying costs are estimated at $0.50 per unit, and order costs are estimated at $10.00. The firm wants to minimize its inventory costs.

Question

Calculate the company's current economic ordering quantity.

EXERCISE 5

A company has decided to market its products more aggressively. Current sales are 30,000 units per year, and they are expected to increase by 50% next year. Carrying costs are estimated at $0.20 per unit, and order costs are estimated at $7.00.

The firm wants to minimize its inventory costs.

Questions

1. What is the economic ordering quantity?
2. What is the optimal number of orders per month once the new sales level is reached?

EXERCISE 6

A firm sells goods with an average retail sales price of $550.00. Customers usually pay 60 days after the date of purchase. Cost of producing the goods per unit is $125.00. If the cost of borrowing is 12%, would it be preferable for the company to offer 1/10, N/30?

Question

Should the company change its credit collection policy?

EXERCISE 7

A company is planning to change its credit policy. On the basis of the following information, would you recommend that the company change its policy?

The product details are as follows:

Current selling price	$5.00 per unit
Average cost	$4.50 per unit
Current annual sales	360,000 units
Current terms of sale	net 30 days

The company wishes to extend its credit period to terms of net 60 days. Allowing for the reaction of competitors, it is anticipated that such a move would produce the following results:

1. Sales are expected to increase to 420,000 units.
2. Bad debt losses are expected to increase by $6,000 per year.

The marginal cost per unit for the increased number of units to be produced would be $3.00. The company's after-tax rate is 40%, and its required minimum rate of return on such investments is 15% after tax.

Question

Would you recommend that the company change its credit policy?

EXERCISE 8

A company sells on terms of net 30 days and is considering a change to net 60 days. The firm wants to invest in projects that generate a ROA greater than 20%. The expected effect of the change in credit is summarized below.

	Net 30 Today (in $000s)	Proposed Net 60	Change
Revenue	$1,000	$1,200	$200
Profit for the year	100	120	20
Trade receivables	82	197	115
Total assets	500	630	130

Question

Would you make the change?

EXERCISE 9

A business can make 15% by investing its money in bonds. If the treasurer receives an amount of $20,000, 30 days sooner, how much would the company make?

EXERCISE 10

A company buys $2 million worth of goods each year. The treasurer of the company thinks that it would be possible to delay paying its bills up to 45 days without jeopardizing its relationship with suppliers. At the moment, the company's accounts payable are $165,000.

Question

If the company defers paying its bills to 45 days, how much financing would the company be able to obtain from that source?

EXERCISE 11

A company's trade and other payables amount to $500,000, and annual purchasing costs for materials from suppliers are $10,000,000. A new purchasing policy states that they should be paid in 30 days.

Question

How much cash would the company generate if it follows the 30-day policy? What if the firm negotiates a 40-day, or even a 60-day, payment term?

Case

CASE 1: KENT IMPORTS LTD.

Albert Cunningham began his career as a manufacturer's representative in the medical equipment business. Included in his lines were products imported from several European manufacturers. Albert's business gradually evolved into Kent Imports Ltd., a wholesaling business that purchased medical equipment from European manufacturers and sold to retailers through a sales organization. By purchasing shipments of medical equipment in large quantities from European manufacturers, Kent Imports was able to negotiate favourable prices and reduce shipping costs substantially. Furthermore, the company was able to assure delivery to customers because orders could be filled from a Toronto warehouse rather than from a European location. In 2007, Albert retired and turned over his business to his son David. At that time, revenue had reached $13 million a year and profit for the year was in excess of $400,000.

By late 2009, David could see that revenue for the year was going to be below $12 million and that profit would be in the $200,000 range. He decided to hire a marketing manager who would boost revenue more quickly.

David contacted an executive placement firm that recommended Ross Belman. Belman had a record of frequent job changes but had produced very rapid revenue increases in each position that he had occupied. He stayed with Kent Imports Ltd. for only 15 months (leaving in November 2010). In that short period of time, Belman was able to increase revenue from $12 million to over $18 million. Furthermore, profit for the year soared by 273% during that year. Even when Belman announced his resignation to take another position with a larger company, David felt the decision to hire him had been a good one.

David contacted the executive placement firm once again. This time the firm recommended Helen Tang, a young woman who was currently a district sales manager for another import manufacturer. Helen was very interested in the job because it would give her greater marketing responsibilities. Helen asked David what policy changes Ross Belman had implemented to increase revenue so dramatically. David explained Belman's belief that merchandise availability was the key to medical equipment import sales. Belman had insisted on increases in the amount of inventories carried by Kent Imports and had encouraged medical equipment retailers to carry more by extending more generous credit terms. Specifically, he established an unofficial policy of not pressing for collection as long as the merchandise was still in a store's inventories. The sales representatives—who were paid a commission at the time of sale—were given the responsibility of reporting what inventories the stores actually held. In addition, Belman implemented a change in credit standards so that the company could approve more new stores for credit. He felt that the old policy was biased against these new retail stores because they did not have a track record. Willingness to sell to this group had accounted for nearly half of the total revenue increase.

Helen asked if this policy had weakened the company's trade receivables, particularly the cash flow position. David responded by saying that he had been monitoring the average collection period very closely and there had been only a very slight change. Helen told David that although she was very interested in the position, she could not make a decision until she had looked at the company's financial statements. David was hesitant to show this information to an outsider, but he finally agreed to let her look at the records in the office. He allowed Helen to look at the statements of income and the statements of financial position. She did her own analysis of the company's financial statements in addition to determining to what extent the working capital policies actually helped improve Kent Imports' overall financial performance.

Questions

1. Do you agree with David Cunningham that the quality of the working capital accounts (inventories and trade receivables) showed only a slight change?
2. Comment on the company's overall financial performance for the years 2009 and 2010 particularly as it relates to the (1) liquidity ratios, (2) debt/leverage ratios, (3) asset-management ratios, and (4) profitability ratios.
3. Have the company's DWC and CCE ratio improved during the time Ross Belman was the marketing manager?
4. Did David do the right thing hiring Ross Belman?

Kent Imports Ltd.
Statements of Income
for the year ended December 31
(in $000s)

	2009	2010
Revenue	11,800	18,600
Cost of sales	(8,500)	(13,200)
Gross profit	3,300	5,400
Expenses		
Distribution costs	(1,100)	(1,620)
Administrative expenses	(1,500)	(2,100)
Depreciation/amortization	(200)	(300)
Finance costs	(200)	(320)
Total	(3,000)	(4,340)
Profit before taxes	300	1,060
Income tax expense	(110)	(350)
Profit for the year	190	710

Kent Imports Ltd.
Statements of Financial Position
as at December 31
(in $000s)

	2009	2010
Non-current assets (at cost)	2,900	3,700
Accumulated depreciation/amortization	(800)	(1,100)
Non-current assets (net)	2,100	2,600
Current assets		
Inventories	2,100	3,600
Trade receivables	1,600	2,100
Prepaid expenses	100	70
Cash and cash equivalents	160	240
Total current assets	3,960	6,010
Total assets	6,060	8,610
Equity		
Share capital	1,500	1,500
Retained earnings	2,100	2,810
Total equity	3,600	4,310
Long-term borrowings	1,300	1,800
Current liabilities		
Trade and other payables	850	1,400
Short-term borrowings	310	1,100
Total current liabilities	1,160	2,500
Total liabilities	2,460	4,300
Total equity and liabilities	$6,060	8,610

Note: In 2008, the company's net working capital was $2,700,000.

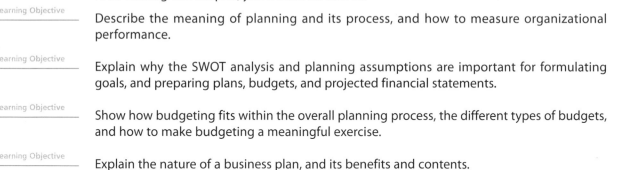

PHOTO/Kristian Sekulic/Shutterstock

CHAPTER 7

[PLANNING, BUDGETING, AND CONTROLLING]

Learning Objectives

After reading this chapter, you should be able to:

1 Learning Objective — Describe the meaning of planning and its process, and how to measure organizational performance.

2 Learning Objective — Explain why the SWOT analysis and planning assumptions are important for formulating goals, and preparing plans, budgets, and projected financial statements.

3 Learning Objective — Show how budgeting fits within the overall planning process, the different types of budgets, and how to make budgeting a meaningful exercise.

4 Learning Objective — Explain the nature of a business plan, and its benefits and contents.

5 Learning Objective — Describe projected financial statements and how to measure financial performance.

6 Learning Objective — Comment on the importance of controlling, the control system, and the different types of controls.

Chapter Outline

Planning
SWOT Analysis and Planning Assumptions
Budgeting
Business Plan
Financial Projections
Controlling

OPENING CASE

After spending several months going over the economics involved in opening a new retail store, the Millers were now preparing their business plan to be presented to several investors. In 2010, CompuTech was able to reduce its debt and purchase all assets from internally generated funds (see Self-Test Exercise No. 3.5 on page 130). The Millers were also pleased with their financial results in terms of managing their liquidity and debt structure. The financial statements also revealed that they had the ability to manage their assets (productivity) well and to generate a reasonable return on the company's assets (profitability). Financial statements and financial ratios that were calculated in the Self-Test Exercises in Chapter 4 would be presented to investors.

Based on the Millers' calculations (see Self-Test Exercise No. 7.5 on page 325), CompuTech's 2010 break-even point shows positive results only two years after the company started, that is, 80.3% ($337,374) of revenue ($420,000). Also, the Millers indicated that the new retail outlet that they want to open would be viable; in fact, it shows an excellent internal rate of return in the range of 25% (this topic will be covered in Chapter 11). Even the financing package that the Millers were considering appeared reasonable. The Opening Case on page 421 in Chapter 9 shows that of the $449,000 that they require for the new retail store ($350,000 in capital assets and $99,000 in working capital), 35% would be financed from internal operations, that is, $157,000, and about 15% or $70,000 from shareholders. The business and shareholders would therefore provide about 50% of the funds. The Millers would be seeking the remaining 50% of the funding requirements from lenders ($150,000 from long-term lenders and $72,000 from short-term lenders).

Everything looked positive. However, the Millers realized that they had to present to the lenders and to potential shareholders projected financial statements about their company for the next several years and a detailed cash budget for 2011. They also had to prove that they had an efficient accounting and financial reporting system in place to help them manage their monthly cash budget and to pay their bills as they came due. They also realized that the banks would probably not look at the company's detailed cost structure. However, the Millers planned to show them that they knew, through their planning process, how they made informed business decisions, and that they had in place an effective control system to reveal, in a precise and timely way, good or bad operating and financial results.

As part of their business plan, the Millers were to include the following:

- Mission statement
- Strategic goals and plans
- Past two years' financial statements
- Personal financial statements
- Projected statements of income (three years)
- Projected statements of financial position (three years)
- Projected statements of cash flows (three years)
- Projected working capital requirements (one year)
- Monthly cash budget (one year)
- Detailed inflows and outflows of cash (one year)
- Credit references
- Loan repayment schedule

In addition to the above information, the Millers were prepared to demonstrate that CompuTech would have the ability to manage its 90% increase in revenue in 2011, and that they were going to more than double their profit for the year, which would help finance their growth (sustainable growth). They also wanted to show that the company's overall financial health position (Z-score) is excellent.

The Millers wanted to prepare a business plan to satisfy not only investors' needs but also, more importantly, their own needs. They realized that planning and budgeting were a prerequisite to the success of any business and were prepared to take the time to go about their planning activity in an accomplished and professional way.

Chapter Overview

As shown in Figure 1.1, this is the third and last chapter dealing with operating decisions. Planning, budgeting, and controlling are ongoing operating activities that managers have to attend to in order to improve bottom-line results and financial position. This chapter covers six major themes: planning, strengths, weaknesses, opportunities, and threats (SWOT) analysis and planning assumptions, budgeting, the business plan, projected financial statements, and controlling. Because superior financial performance is a result of good planning, it is important to explain how various planning activities such as the formulation of goals and the preparation of plans and budgets can impact financial results. Every number contained in the statement of income and the statement of financial position is an outcome of what managers want to accomplish (goals) and how they intend to realize it (plans). As shown in Figure 7.1, each major theme that will be covered in this chapter includes a grouping of different activities (A to K). These activities will be explained in some detail throughout this chapter.

The first theme looks at planning in terms of its importance and how planning assumptions (A) can be used to formulate goals and prepare plans, budgets, and financial statements. The numbers shown on projected financial statements such as revenue, cost of sales, expenses, non-current assets, inventories, and trade receivables are meaningless unless they are supported by planning assumptions or premises considered "boundaries," which determine: (1) what a company plans to do, and (2) how the numbers shown on projected financial statements are put together. For instance, one would certainly want to know the reasons a company plans to increase its revenue by 15% while cost of sales only shows a 7% growth. Will the company introduce a new product? Market its products and services in new markets? Change suppliers or modernize its manufacturing facilities? This first theme also looks at performance indicators that can be used to gauge the organizational efficiencies (doing things right) and effectiveness (doing the right things) of a business. Planning consists of formulating goals and plans (strategic, tactical, and operational). As shown in Figure 7.1, all goals and plans (D and E) have an impact (positive or negative) on budgets and projected financial statements. A CEO who wants to introduce a new product line will most likely increase the company's revenue and expenses. If a plant is modernized, it will increase its capital assets and, because of efficiency improvements, most likely decrease its operating expenses.

Figure 7.1 **The Planning, Budgeting, and Controlling Process**

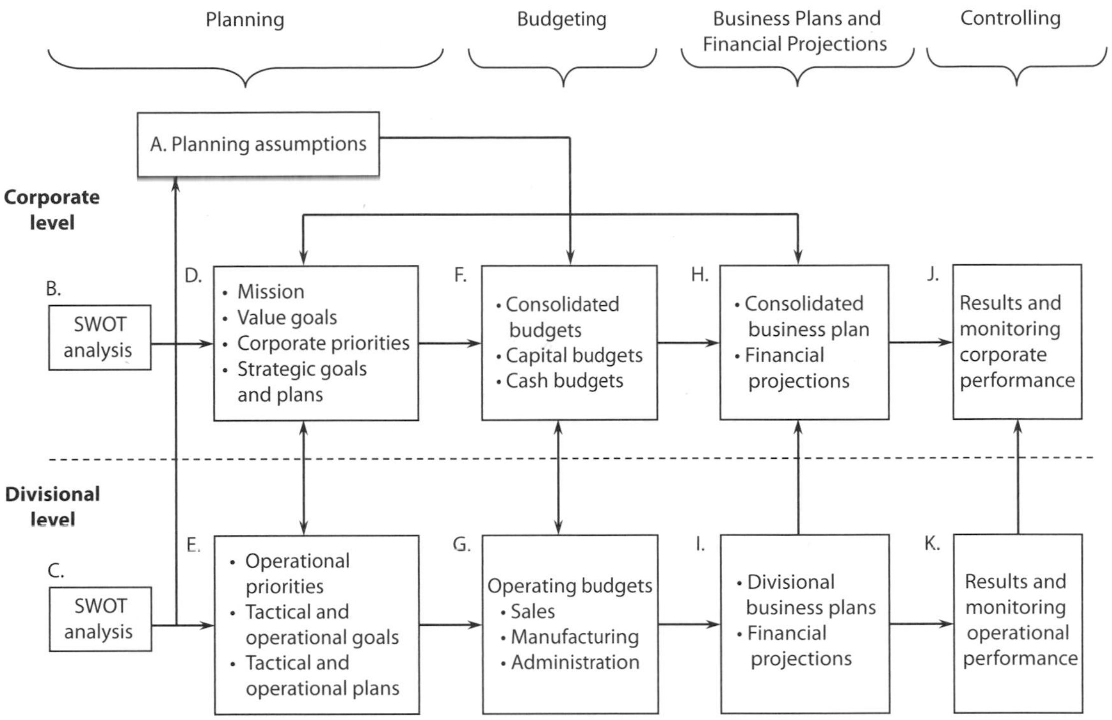

The second theme explains the importance of the SWOT analysis within the context of planning (B and C). SWOT is an acronym for identifying a company's strengths, weaknesses, opportunities, and threats. Both strengths and weaknesses deal with a company's internal operations (marketing, production, human resources); opportunities and threats focus on the company's external environment (general and industry). How can a company improve its financial performance if it wants to: (1) capitalize on its strengths and minimize its weaknesses, as well as (2) exploit opportunities that offer avenues for expansion and deal with threats that pose serious problems to its well-being? As shown in Figure 7.1, SWOT analysis helps not only to devise goals and plans but also to formulate planning assumptions.

The third theme explains the budgeting process, a crucial activity within the planning framework. Formulating strategic goals and plans, identifying corporate priorities, developing market/product strategies, and writing detailed operational plans and procedures are all essential steps in arriving at a perfectly orchestrated planning effort. Individually, these steps can accomplish very little; they become meaningful only as part of an integrated whole and eventually rolled up into consolidated projected financial statements. These planning efforts are translated into the common language of business—dollars—through the budgeting process. As shown in Figure 7.1, budgeting does not stand completely alone within the overall planning and controlling process (F and G). Budgeting flows out of the planning process. In essence, budgeting is the process of allocating resources, evaluating the financial outcome of managerial decisions, and establishing the financial and operational profile against which organizational performance will be measured. As shown in Figure 7.1, budgeting involves putting together operating budgets (sales, manufacturing, administration, R & D, etc.) and consolidated budgets, capital budgets, and cash budgets.

The fourth theme examines the preparation of the business plan, which is a document that summarizes goals, plans, and financial projections (H and I). A business plan can be prepared by owners of a small business interested in approaching lenders or by divisional managers of a large decentralized corporation showing what each **strategic business unit (SBU)** is expected to become in the future. An SBU is a divisional unit within a multi-business framework. This section explains in some detail the purpose of a business plan, and its benefits and contents.

Strategic business unit (SBU)
Divisional unit within a multi-business framework.

The fifth theme deals with projected financial statements (also part of H and I activities). Included in a business plan are projected financial statements that show the impact that the goals and plans are expected to have on a company's future financial performance. This theme also explains how to assess a company's financial performance by using financial ratios, the sustainable growth rate, and the financial health score.

The last theme looks at controlling (J and K). Basically, controlling is the feedback system designed to compare actual performance to predetermined standards, in order to identify deviations, measure their significance, and take any action required to assure that all corporate resources are being used effectively and efficiently. This section looks at the design of an effective control system, which includes the identification of performance indicators and standards, assessing performance, and analyzing variances that lead to corrective actions. It also explains the different types of controls, which include preventive controls, screening controls, and feedback controls.

Planning

1 Learning Objective

Describe the meaning of planning and its process, and how to measure organizational performance.

Planning
Process of formulating goals and outlining action plans to realize the goals.

Planning is the process of formulating goals and outlining action plans to realize the goals. It is a decision-making activity. There is no question that goals and plans have an impact on budgets and financial projections. Planning deals with two elements: *ends*, that is, where an organization wants to be in the future; and *means*, that is, the identification of the plans and resources needed to accomplish the results. As shown in Figure 7.2, the planning process includes five activities, each requiring decisions that impact a company's projected financial statements and performance. Because plans affect the amount of resources needed to achieve organizational goals, managers must deal with the following questions:

- Do we have enough resources to realize our goals?
- If not, what resources should we acquire?
- How much will the plans cost?
- Can we afford to buy capital assets?
- What impact do these goals and plans have on our bottom line?

Figure 7.2 The Planning Process

Activities	Decisions
SWOT	What have we achieved so far and what are our strengths, weaknesses, opportunities, and threats?
Goals	What do we want to accomplish and what impact will these goals have on the profile of our financial statements?
Planning	How and when are we going to implement our plans? Who is going to implement them? How much will these plans cost and what are the financial benefits?
Implementation	What should we do to ensure that we will be on course and that the goals and plans will materialize as planned?
Controlling	Did we reach our goals and implement our plans? Are the financial results in line with our financial projections?

IMPORTANCE OF PLANNING

There are many advantages to implementing an effective planning process. First, it encourages managers to evaluate alternative courses of action before making a decision. It forces them to be more *creative*, *innovative*, and *resourceful* in how resources should be deployed and how future activities should be carried out. Managers can evaluate the impact that various alternatives will have on their company's financial performance.

Second, planning helps to integrate short-term (operational) plans with long-term (strategic) plans. Planning leads to *goal congruence* as it links operational plans to tactical and strategic plans. Because each division prepares divisional business plans that contain short- and medium-term projected budgets and financial statements, these reports can be integrated into consolidated budgets and financial statements that are based on meaningful hypothesis.

Third, planning provides a *sense of purpose and direction*. Instead of continually reacting to circumstances, managers can, through planning, anticipate the future and determine the future courses of action required to help their company achieve superior financial performance. Goals tell what should be done; plans show step-by-step, where it should be done, how, and by whom.

Fourth, planning enables a business to *cope with change*. Businesses operate in a rapidly changing environment; planning makes managers aware of the state of the future environment and helps them develop reasonable and logical plans based on realistic assumptions about what to expect. Managers must therefore anticipate the environmental opportunities and threats before they happen if they hope to capitalize on what is going to happen in the future and prevent being bullied by existing and new firms.

Fifth, planning *simplifies managerial control*. Having identified the goals and the plans necessary to reach them, managers are in a much better position to monitor and evaluate their realization. Planning allows managers to identify what needs to be done, by whom, and when; controlling points out what was done and not done, and, if necessary, the steps needed to bring situations back in line. Both budgets and financial statements are excellent documents to make such comparisons.

HIERARCHY OF GOALS AND PLANS

Managers at all levels of an organization play different roles in the planning process. Consequently, as shown in Table 7.1, plans can be grouped under three categories: strategic, tactical, and operational.

A *strategic plan* involves the process of analyzing and deciding the mission and goals of an organization, examining the different alternatives for achieving the goals and allocating the resources needed to implement the plans in order to achieve superior long-range financial performance. Strategic planning helps managers harmonize their organizations with their environment. This is done by: (1) coping effectively with the elements of an organization's external environment (e.g., seizing opportunities and neutralizing threats); and (2) managing its internal environment (e.g., boosting strengths and eliminating weaknesses). Consolidated budgets and projected financial statements are documents that clearly demonstrate in quantitative terms the effectiveness of the strategic plans.

A *tactical plan* involves the process of preparing goals and plans to help divisional managers implement long-term strategies. A tactical plan is born out of a strategy. Managers responsible for divisional or functional units prepare their tactical plans, budgets, and medium-range financial statements to ensure successful implementation of the corporate strategies. Divisional budgets and financial statements also measure in clear terms the outcome of the plans.

An *operational plan* involves the process of developing in more detail shorter-range plans and operating budgets. These plans identify who is going to do what, when, and

Table 7.1 The Hierarchy of Plans

Types of Plans	Levels of Management	Responsibilities	Time Frame*
Strategic goals and plans (consolidated budgets and financial statements)	Top-level managers	Company-wide plans	5 years and more
Tactical goals and plans (divisional budgets and financial statements)	Middle-level managers	Divisions	1 to 5 years
Operational goals, plans, and budgets	First-level managers	Organizational units	1 year and less

* Time frame varies from industry to industry. In the petroleum industry, long-range plans can span as many as 20 years; in the clothing industry, the span may be one or two years.

where. First-level managers who are responsible and accountable for results prepare operating budgets. The controller uses these operating budgets to prepare the consolidated budgets and the projected financial statements.

There are many other plans that managers prepare. They include policies, procedures, methods, rules, regulations, programs, schedules, projects, and standards. All of these plans have an impact on budgets and financial statements.

PERFORMANCE INDICATORS

A key task of organizations (for-profit or not-for-profit) is to achieve a high level of performance, which is simply the attainment of organizational goals by using resources ingeniously and wisely. Performance indicators are used to evaluate organizations' performance. A **performance indicator** is a description of the type of measurement used to gauge organizational performance. For example, how should the trade receivables department be measured? In this case, the *average collection period* would be a good indicator.

Performance indicator
Description of the type of measurement used to gauge organizational performance.

Performance standard
Benchmarks against which performance is measured.

On the other hand, **performance standards** are benchmarks against which performance is measured. These involve numbers. For example, in the case of the trade receivables department, a *35-day average collection period* could be a performance standard. Performance standards can be grouped under four categories: time, output, costs, and quality. These will be explained in some detail in the section, "The Control System," beginning on page 339. The financial ratios presented in Table 4.6 on page 178 may very well be considered performance standards.

Economy
Process for determining the type of resources (human and materials) that should be acquired (least costly option) and how they should be processed.

Intelligent use of resources requires both economy and efficiency. **Economy** is the process for determining the type of resources (human and materials) that should be acquired (least costly option) and how they should be processed. This means assessing different alternatives available to reach a goal and selecting the one that is the most economical. Here, "costs" are linked to "benefits." Here are some typical cost–benefit examples:

- Would it be more economical to buy or lease a building?
- Would it be more economical to buy a machine to do our own printing, or have it done through contract work?
- Would it be more economical to automate the office and use only three workers, or use conventional equipment and six workers?

These are the types of decisions that are often made during the budgeting process, at a time when cost–benefit analyses are made to justify resources. There is no question that the options offering the best results will have positive effects on a company's financial performance.

Efficiency indicators
Refers to how well resources (inputs) are brought together to achieve results (outputs); it means doing things right.

Performance indicators can be grouped under two categories, efficiency and effectiveness. **Efficiency indicators** are used to gauge the amount of resources required to produce goods or services. These indicators relate goods and services produced (outputs) to the resources used to make them (inputs). Efficiency means *doing things right*.

There are three types of efficiency indicators. *Unit cost measures* relate the volume of work done to resources needed to produce the outputs. The cost per unit could therefore be considered an efficiency indicator and $0.75 per unit considered the standard. If 200,000 units are processed at a cost of $150,000, the efficiency standard for that particular organizational unit would be $0.75. *Productivity measures* relate products and services (outputs) and human resources (person-years). For example, a credit department that employs 100 workers to process 200,000 documents would show a productivity rate of 2,000 documents per person-year. *Work measurement* shows the output that a worker can produce within a given time period. Here are typical work measurements:

- 20 person-minutes per claim adjudicated (for an insurance company)
- 30 person-minutes per test (for performing X-rays in a hospital)
- 5 person-hours per case (for a social worker employed in a rehabilitation centre)
- 14 person-minutes per call (for sales agents making reservations for an airline company)

Effectiveness indicators
Measure the goal-related accomplishments of an organization; it means doing the right things.

Effectiveness indicators measure the goal-related accomplishments of an organization. They express how well an organization is accomplishing its goals. Effectiveness means *doing the right things*. These indicators are often expressed in terms of response time, percentage of mistakes, or number of complaints. Here are a few examples of effectiveness indicators and effectiveness standards:

Indicators	Standards
Telephone response time	15 seconds
Time delay between receipt and completion of an application	4 days
Percentage of mistakes	0.05%
Number of persons attending a seminar	25 persons
Percentage of defects	0.03%

There is no question that all organizations are trying to reach the highest level of effectiveness (goals) by using the least amount of resources (economy and efficiency). An organization that utilizes its resources well and on the right activities can be described as one that uses its resources in an *optimal way*. Figure 7.3 shows the relationship between organizational efficiency and effectiveness. As shown, an organization can reach its objectives (effective) yet waste much of its resources (inefficient). On the other hand, the organization can be extremely cautious in using resources (economy and efficiency) but not use them on the right things (ineffective). The ideal situation is this: Reach the intended objectives (be effective) and use the resources prudently (be economical) and ensure that the work is done rapidly (be efficient).

In the News 7.1 gives an overview of the importance of using quality indicators to measure client satisfaction and performance.

In The News [7.1]

Measuring Excellence in Quality Health Care Can Help a Hospital Become a Leader in North America

A goal or a measurement indicator can be considered a guiding force for anyone. A lack of clearly stated goals makes it difficult for an individual to focus on end results. As the Cheshire Cat told Alice in Lewis Carroll's 1865 *Alice's Adventures in Wonderland*, "If you don't know where you are going, any road will get you there."

Dr. Jack Kitts, president and CEO of The Ottawa Hospital, understands the basic principles related to objective setting and the use of quality measures as tools to help his hospital achieve positive end results. As he pointed out in his 2008–2009 Annual Report, "Quality indicators are the benchmarks we use to measure patient satisfaction and our performance. Our goal is to be in the top 10% of North America's teaching hospitals and we're working to make that happen by improving on such things as wait times, cancelled surgeries, infection rates, and other essential hospital services. It was a few years ago that our hospital began measuring quality by setting up a management information system capable of collecting and reporting important information. This valuable information is now helping us understand 'where we are,' 'where we are going,' and 'how far we are from certain goals'."

Source: Adapted from "The Ottawa Hospital's 2008–2009 Annual Report." Found at: http://www.ottawahospital.on.ca/about/reports/FS2008-e.pdf. For more information about The Ottawa Hospital's measurement indicators, go to http://www.ottawahospital.on.ca/about/reports/indicators/index-e.asp.

Let's go back to the trade receivables department and examine a managerial decision within a cost–benefit analysis framework. If the average collection period is 36.4 days, the manager could try to improve performance to 32 days by hiring one additional employee. If the additional employee costs $40,000, should the employee be

Figure 7.3 Organizational Efficiency and Effectiveness

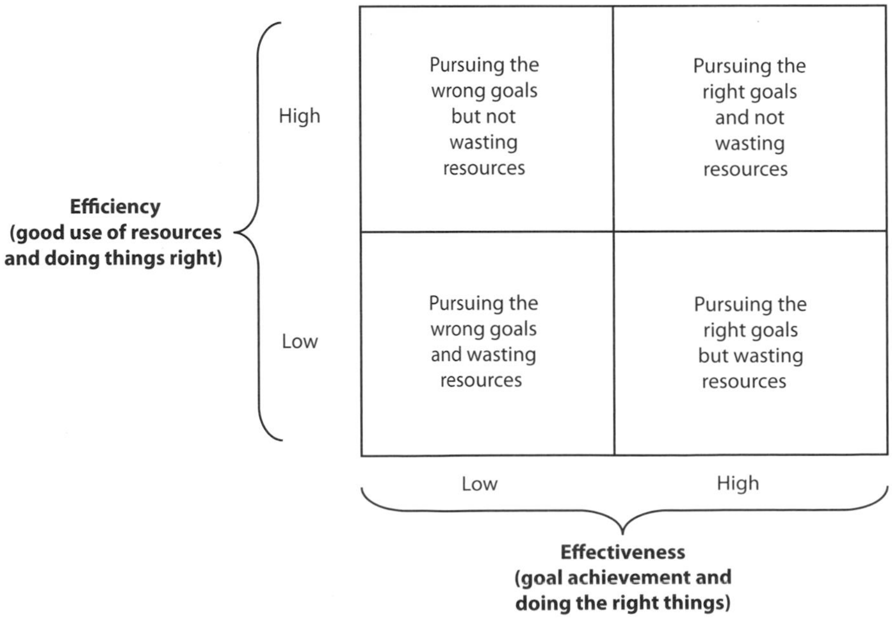

hired? Assuming revenue is in the $30 million range and trade receivables is $3,000,000, with an average daily sales of $82,192 ($30,000,000/365) and by reducing the trade receivables from 36.4 to 32 days, the company could generate an additional amount of $369,856 in cash. Here is the calculation:

Trade receivables	$3,000,000	
Improvement in trade receivables	2,630,144	($82,192 × 32)
Additional cash	$369,856	

By investing this additional cash in capital projects and earning, say, 12%, the company would generate $44,383 ($369,856 × 12%). Here we are comparing a cost in the amount of $40,000 to a benefit in the amount of $44,383. The company would just about break even with this decision. If the manager is able to reduce the average collection period, it would make the decision to hire the additional employee more economically attractive.

It is somewhat difficult to determine whether some of the financial ratios shown in Table 4.6 on page 178 are efficiency or effectiveness ratios in view of the fact that a combination of factors can impact on a particular ratio. For example, an increase of 5% in revenue could be determined as an effectiveness ratio because the decisions regarding pricing and advertising strategies have favourable effects on revenue. However, the company's revenue performance could very well be ineffective if the industry shows a 10% increase. This means that competing firms are making better decisions (doing the right things) to improve revenue. However, let's assume that return on revenue for the company is 9% compared to the industry average of 5%; this means that this organization is more efficient because the cost of doing business for each revenue dollar is less than that of the industry. On the other hand, if return on revenue drops from 9% to 7%, this means that the company has become less efficient; that is, the cost of doing business (cost of sales and expenses) is increasing faster than revenue. The vertical analysis of the statement of income shown in Table 4.2 on page 158 illustrates the level of efficiencies of Eastman Technologies Inc. at different profit levels (gross profit, profit before taxes, and profit for the year).

Self-Test Exercise No. 7.1

Performance Indicators

What could be efficiency and effectiveness indicators for each of the following organizational units or activities of CompuTech Inc.?

1. Retail store
2. Company
3. Sales associates
4. Security system
5. Promotional coupons

SWOT Analysis and Planning Assumptions

2 Learning Objective

Explain why the SWOT analysis and planning assumptions are important for formulating goals, and preparing plans, budgets, and projected financial statements.

Projected financial statements are not stand-alone documents or prepared in a vacuum. There are many reasons why the numbers presented on projected statements of income or statements of financial position increase or decrease over a period of time and the key factor that influences and explains these numbers are planning assumptions. As shown in Figures 7.1 and 7.4, planning assumptions are derivatives of the SWOT analysis. The SWOT analysis helps identify what is happening in a company's external environment (general and industry) and internal elements (e.g., marketing, production, etc.) that can help managers prepare a list of planning assumptions. These planning assumptions help managers formulate their goals, set up their plans, and prepare their budgets and projected financial statements.

SWOT ANALYSIS

As shown in Figure 7.1, the first step of the planning process is the analysis and diagnosis of a company's external environment and internal elements and the identification of planning assumptions. Because planning consists of making decisions, the first logical step is to assess the situation. Analyzing the external forces of the environment and the internal factors is done through the **SWOT analysis**, a process that identifies a company's strengths, weaknesses, opportunities, and threats.

SWOT analysis Acronym for identifying a company's strengths, weaknesses, opportunities, and threats.

The analysis and diagnosis of internal operations help managers to identify a company's strengths and weaknesses. A *strength* is something that a company is good at, or that gives an advantage or edge over competing firms. Examples of strengths are excellent financial resources, good relationships with suppliers, low cost of raw materials, and a superior sales force. A *weakness* is something that a company does poorly and that puts it at a competitive disadvantage. Examples of weaknesses are high inventory costs, weak after-sales service, high cost of wages, and high investment in working capital.

Figure 7.4 Relationship between Planning Assumptions and Projected Financial Statements

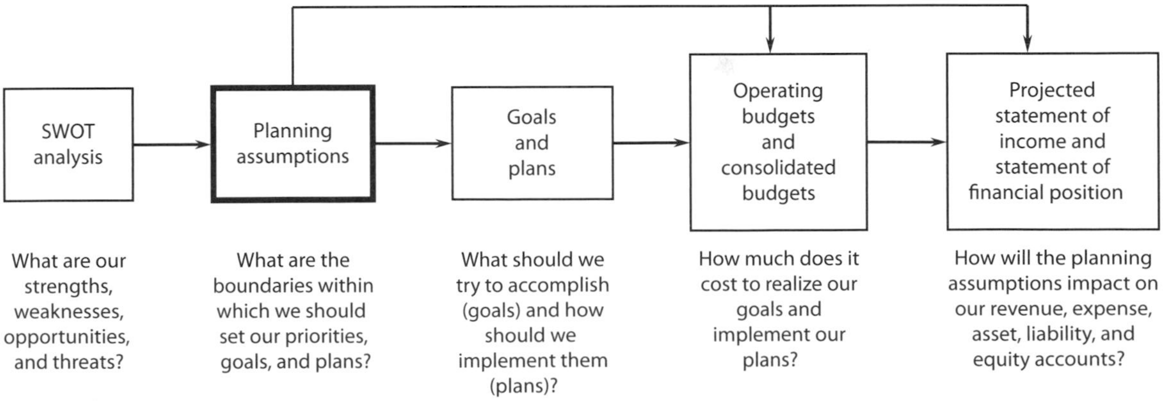

Opportunities are elements in the external environment that offer a company certain avenues for expansion. Examples of opportunities are the recovery of the economy, the rapid increase in market growth, and a reduction in the interest rate. *Threats* are those elements in the external environment that pose serious problems to the well-being of an organization. Threats can emerge from the entrance of a foreign competitor in the marketplace or the introduction of new products or services.

PLANNING ASSUMPTIONS

As shown in Figure 7.4, the SWOT analysis helps managers identify their planning assumptions (also known as planning premises).

Planning assumptions Boundaries upon which priorities, goals, plans, budgets, and financial projections are based.

Planning assumptions are important for two reasons. First, they establish boundaries upon which the company's plans and budgets are based. Without planning assumptions, company plans may very well be unrealistic. Planning assumptions related to the general and industry background and internal operations help managers to be more realistic in their projections. For example, if managers of a home electronics manufacturing company estimate a 4% increase per year in the electronics market over the next five years, the company will use this assumption to set its goals, plans, budgets, and financial projections.

Second, planning assumptions help all division, department, and organizational unit managers to be consistent in developing their goals, plans, budgets, and financial projections because all units use the same assumptions. For instance, if managers of a home electronics manufacturing company estimate a 1% population growth, and an increase of 4.5% a year in consumer disposable income, this information will be used by all unit managers of the company to formulate their respective goals, plans, budgets, and financial projections.

Some planning assumptions can be quantified while others are stated in general terms. *Quantitative assumptions* are hypotheses that can be expressed in specific terms. For example, external quantitative assumptions include statements such as:

- The Canadian dollar will remain at US$0.92 over the next two years.
- Market growth for Product A will be 3.7% a year over the next three years.
- Federal corporate tax rate will be 45%.
- GNP in real terms will increase by 2.2% over the next year.

Internal quantitative planning assumptions include the following:

- Labour costs will rise by 3.2%.
- Productivity will improve by 1.2%.
- Cost of raw materials for Product Y will be $2.15/unit.
- Employee absenteeism will be 1.5%.
- Overhead cost allocated to organizational units for computer services will be $90.00 an hour.

Qualitative assumptions refer to elements that are stated in broad terms. For instance, they may include potential changes in government regulations, company image, and employee morale.

Although some planning assumptions are generic in nature, such as the ones listed above, others are more specific and can be linked to specific accounts shown on financial statements. Let's now turn to how planning assumptions can help produce the projected statements of income and statements of financial position. Tables 7.9 and 7.11, which will be explained later in the chapter, show Eastman Technologies Inc.'s projected statement of income and statement of financial position for the year 2010. Each account is influenced by one or several planning assumptions.

Projected Statement of Income Planning Assumptions

Table 7.9 shows Eastman Technologies Inc.'s statements of income for two years. As shown, revenue is expected to show a 22% increase over 2009. After deducting all expenses from revenue, the company is expected to realize $264,000 in profit. To prepare a comprehensive business plan, Eastman will have to document financial targets for each line shown on the statement of income, and, more importantly, clearly pinpoint the assumptions used to realize the revenue and expense estimates.

This section gives a few examples of typical questions that can help formulate statement of income planning assumptions. Each line on Eastman's statement of income shows a financial goal, the increment over the previous year's (2009) operations, and a percentage related to the revenue line. For example, cost of sales is expected to reach $2,050,000 by 2010. This represents a 7.9% increase over the previous year ($2,050,000 ÷ $1,900,000). Also, total cost of sales is expected to be 67.2% of revenue ($2,050,000 ÷ $3,050,000) compared to 76% in 2009.

The statement of income shows the company's future revenue, costs, and profit performance. To examine the company's projected financial performance, managers can set financial goals similar to the ratios that were examined in Chapter 4 and also use vertical (see Tables 4.1 and 4.2) and horizontal analysis techniques (see Tables 4.3 and 4.4). Eastman's 2009 year-end forecast and 2010 budget year operating performance are summarized below.

As shown below, significant improvements were forecast in the cost of sales, which has a favourable effect on the gross profit and profit for the year. The horizontal analysis (increments between two consecutive statements of income) is also shown in the last column:

	As % of Sales		
	2010 Budget	2009 Year-End	Increase over 2009 (%)
Revenue	1.00	1.00	22.0
Cost of sales	(0.67)	(0.76)	7.9
Gross profit	0.33	0.24	66.7
Distribution costs	(0.06)	(0.06)	20.0
Administrative expenses	(0.09)	(0.09)	13.9
Profit for the year	0.09	0.04	170.8

Table 7.2 lists typical questions that can lead to formulating the statement of income planning assumptions as they relate to revenue and expense accounts.

Table 7.2 Planning Assumptions – Statement of Income

The following are typical questions related to the projected statements of income that can lead to the formulation of planning assumptions.

Revenue

- What will be our share of the market?
- How many units of different product lines will we sell?
- How many new customers will we serve? How many are we expected to lose?
- What will be the changes in the selling price for various products and services?
- What amount of inflation will be included in the selling price?
- Will we push our products/services in new geographic regions? How many will we sell in these new locations?
- Will our company's service/product mix change?

Cost of sales

- Are we going to keep the same suppliers? Will we change some? Have more?
- What type and quantity of supplies will we purchase from each?
- What terms or purchase agreements will we have with existing suppliers? With new suppliers?
- Will there be a change in the purchase of our product mix?
- Are we going to benefit from new discounts? Will they change (e.g., quantity, trade, etc.)?
- Will we be using the same distribution networks or different ones?
- Will there be a change in the freight prices? By how much?
- Does a change in the mix of suppliers affect our freight costs?
- Will there be a change in the number of workers in the plant?
- Will there be a new union agreement? If so, what are the new conditions?
- Will there be a new compensation package offered to our workers?
- What is the employee turnover rate? How much will it cost to train new workers?

Distribution costs

- Will there be a change in the number of employees working in the marketing organization?
- Will there be a new compensation package offered to our sales staff?
- Will the sales commission structure change next year?
- Will the policies regarding travel and entertainment programs change?
- How many conventions and meetings will we have next year?
- What products or services will we advertise? How many advertising programs will we have?
- What advertising media will we use (TV, Internet, magazines, newspapers, radio, billboards, etc.)? What are the rates for each?
- Will there be more (or less) promotional programs?
- How much will we spend on the purchase of capital assets?
- What will be the composition of the new capital assets?
- Will the depreciation rate be the same?
- Will the insurance premiums be changed?
- Will there be changes in costs (quantity and price) related to office supplies, telephone, utilities, postage, and management fees?

Administrative expenses

- Will there be more employees working in support or overhead units?
- Will there be a change in the compensation package for these employees?
- Will there be a change in the equipment that will be leased? What are the agreements?
- Will we buy new equipment such as computers, printers, fax machines, and office furniture?
- How will the purchase of the new equipment affect the depreciation expense?

Projected Statement of Financial Position Planning Assumptions

A similar analysis related to planning assumptions can be done for the statement of financial position accounts. Table 7.11 shows Eastman Technologies Inc.'s projected statement of financial position, including non-current assets, current assets, equity,

Table 7.3 Planning Assumptions – Statement of Financial Position

The following are typical questions related to the projected statement of financial position that can lead to the formulation of planning assumptions.

Assets

Non-current assets

- What assets will we buy next year (e.g., equipment, machinery, vehicles)?
- How much will these assets cost?
- Will we modernize our facilities? If so, how much will it cost?
- Will we invest in new plants? If so, how much will it cost?

Inventories

- How much will we invest in raw materials?
- How much will we invest in work-in-progress?
- How much will we invest in finished goods?
- Will there be a change in insurance premium rates for insuring our inventories?
- Will there be a change in the holding costs (warehouse and other storage facility expenses)?
- Will there be a change in the cost of ordering goods (e.g., paperwork, handling)?
- Will we change our inventory policies and procedures?

Trade receivables

- What is the aging of our trade receivables?
- What percentage of our revenue is made on credit?
- What percentage of our customers will take advantage of our trade discounts?
- What percentage of our customers will not pay their bills (bad debts)?

Prepaid expenses

- How many accounts make-up prepaid expenses?
- How much of our expenses (e.g., insurance, bonuses) will be applied to next year's statement of financial position?

Cash and cash equivalents

- How much cash do we need in order to meet our ongoing expenses over a 10-day period?
- What interest rate will we earn by investing cash in marketable securities?

Equity

- What amount will we need to raise from our shareholders?
- What are the conditions for raising funds from our shareholders?
- How much cash will be retained in the business in the form of retained earnings and how much will we pay in dividends?

Liabilities

Long-term borrowings

- What percentage of our non-capital assets will be financed by debt?
- What are the borrowing rates and agreements for the various long-term borrowings?

Current liabilities

- Are we going to negotiate new credit terms with our suppliers? If so, what are they?
- Will there be a change in purchase discounts?
- How much will we borrow from different short-term lenders?
- Will the short-term borrowing rates regarding our working capital loans and term loans be different? If so, what are the rates?
- How many accounts make up accrued liabilities and what is the amount of each?

non-current liabilities, and current liabilities. As shown in Table 7.11, Eastman Technologies Inc.'s total assets increased by $279,000—that is, from $1,800,000 to $2,079,000, or 15.5%, and the percentage of each account related to total assets changed between 2009 and 2010.

To determine where these increases took place, we have to examine the key elements of the assets such as non-current assets, inventories, and trade receivables as a percentage of total assets. The vertical analysis of the key components of Eastman's statement of financial position is as follows, and the horizontal analysis (increments between two consecutive statements of financial position) is shown in the last column below:

Percent of Total Assets

	2010 Budget	2009 Year-End	Increase over 2009 (%)
Non-current assets	0.68	0.67	17.7
Current assets	0.32	0.33	11.2
Total assets	1.00	1.00	15.5

Percent of Total Equity and Liabilities

	2010 Budget	2009 Year-End	Increase over 2009 (%)
Equity	0.37	0.31	38.6
Long-term borrowings	0.40	0.44	3.8
Current liabilities	0.23	0.25	7.8
Total liabilities	0.63	0.69	5.2
Total equity and liabilities	1.00	1.00	15.5

Self-Test Exercise No. 7.2

Planning Assumptions

With the following information, prepare an operating budget for one of CompuTech's departments for the year 2010. The operating results for the year 2009 for that particular department are as follows:

Revenue	$32,400
Cost of sales	(21,600)
Gross profit	10,800
Salaries	(8,000)
Profit	$2,800

In 2009, the department sold 5,400 units and the retail sales price per unit was $6.00. The purchase price per unit was $4.00. A portion of the salaries in the amount of $8,000 was allocated to that particular department. Both the controller and the sales manager formulated specific planning assumptions for the 2010 budget year. They projected a 6% increase in the number of units to be sold and that inflation was to increase by 2%. Salaries will show an 8% increase.

Budgeting

3 Learning Objective

Show how budgeting fits within the overall planning process, the different types of budgets, and how to make budgeting a meaningful exercise.

As shown in Figures 7.1 and 7.4, budgeting plays an important role in the overall planning process. The budgeting process fits right in the middle of activities related to formulating goals and plans and the preparation of the business plans and financial projections. Figure 7.5 shows that operating budgets are used to prepare the projected financial statements, such as the statement of income, the statement of financial position, and the statement of cash flows.

Budgeting
Process by which management allocates corporate resources, evaluates financial outcomes, and establishes systems to control operational and financial performance.

Budgeting is the process by which management allocates corporate resources, evaluates the financial outcome of its decisions, and establishes the financial and operational profile against which future results will be measured. If managers regard budgeting simply as a mechanical exercise, or a yearly ritual performed by planning groups or accountants, they will not really grasp how the company can improve its economic performance and operating efficiencies.

TYPES OF BUDGETS

Because different types of decisions are made in organizations, managers use different budgeting methodologies. Table 7.4 shows the different types of budgets prepared by organizations and the reasons they are prepared. These budgets can be grouped under four categories: (1) operating budgets, (2) complementary budgets, (3) comprehensive budgets, and (4) capital budgets. Let's examine the meaning of each.

Operating Budgets

Operating budgets
Budgets prepared by operating managers.

Operating budgets are prepared by managers. As shown in Table 7.5, three types of budgets are consolidated into a master budget that will be used to prepare the projected statement of income. The budgets used to prepare the projected statement of income are the sales budgets, the manufacturing budgets, and the staff or overhead budgets. At the start of a budget year, the master budget serves as a plan or standard. At the end, it is used as a control device to help managers gauge their performance against plans. Today, with the help of spreadsheets and customized software packages, budgeting can be used as an effective tool for evaluating "what-if" scenarios through sensitivity analysis and simulations. By incorporating different assumptions in the master budget, managers

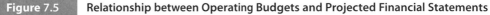

Figure 7.5 Relationship between Operating Budgets and Projected Financial Statements

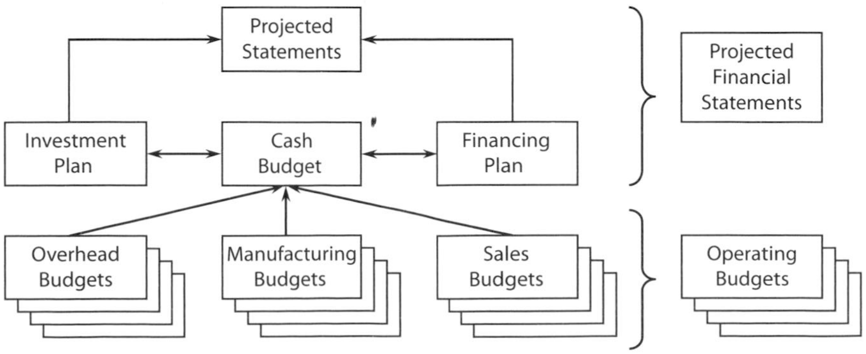

Table 7.4 Types of Budgets and Purpose

Types of Budget	Purpose
1. Manufacturing budget	Production requirement (materials, labour, energy, etc.)
2. Marketing budget	Sales and advertising plans
3. Branch, division, or regional budgets	Overhead units
4. Product budget	ROI on specific products
5. Executive staff budget	Specialized budgets (compensation and human resources)
6. Cash budget	To meet current cash obligations and obtain a line of credit
7. R & D budgets	Strategies upon which future sales and revenue depend
8. Capital expenditure budget	New plants, expansions, modernizations, R & D
9. Projected statement of income	Profit performance forecast
10. Projected statement of financial position	Financial structure forecast

can quickly find the best courses of action to follow to optimize their financial performance. Among the variety of budgets used in organizations, the marketing departments use the sales budget, manufacturing uses the flexible or variable budgets, and indirect or overhead organizational units use incremental or zero-based budgeting.

Table 7.5 Projected Statement of Income

	In $		
Revenue	1,000,000	}	Sales budgets
Less:			
Manufacturing expenses: variable and direct expenses such as labour, materials	(600,000)	}	Flexible budgets (manufacturing)
Contribution margin	400,000		
Fixed expenses such as depreciation, insurance, plant maintenance	(100,000)	}	Absorption costing
Profit margin on manufacturing operation	300,000		
Overhead expenses:			
Indirect and overhead expenses such as service organizations, support functions, projects and overhead units for:			
(1) operating units (tooling, quality control, scheduling)	(50,000)	}	Incremental budgeting or zero-based budgeting (staff or overhead units)
(2) corporate units (finance, human resources, engineering)	(100,000)		
Total overhead expenses	(150,000)		
Profit	150,000		

Sales budgets are prepared by the sales organization and are critical because they provide the basis for formulating other segments of the master budget. The sales budget includes the number of units expected to be sold and the selling price per unit, which translates into the revenue forecast. The sales budget is often broken down on a quarterly or even monthly basis.

Flexible or variable budgets are used by plant or production departments where costs of production (standard costs) are used as benchmarks for comparing actual results to identify price and quantity variances. The intent here is not only to verify if a production unit is within its budget but also, more importantly, whether it is within predetermined engineered standards.

Other costs, such as hydro, depreciation, or insurance, are fixed. They are, however, chargeable, or absorbed by individual products or divisions. Therefore, to determine operating margin on manufacturing for each product line, these fixed costs are included in appropriate units through a variable-costing mechanism. For example, under the absorption costing mechanism, if a plant produces six different products (or services) and incurs $50,000 in overhead expenses such as insurance, hydro, or general maintenance, this amount will be absorbed (or charged to) by each product, depending, of course, on the numbers of units produced or the amount of time it takes for each product to be manufactured.

Incremental budgeting or *traditional budgeting* works like this: Projected new expenses for the coming year are added to the previous year's total expenses and are expressed as percentages of the previous year's total. Such a budget might look like this:

		Increase (%)
Last year's expenses	$350,000	
Inflation	7,000	2.0
New activities	10,500	3.0
Increase due to volume	14,000	4.0
Next year's budget	$381,500	9.0

The incremental budgeting approach has the following flaws:

- It is difficult to relate the budget to specific objectives and plans.
- Past activities may be approved without being put to the test and really justified.
- Corporate priorities may get lost in the shuffle.
- The previous year's figures could have been inflated by one-time special expenses.

In the News 7.2 explains why a weekly budget, and analyzing percentages, can help a small business better manage its cash flows and be in a better position to enter the recovery.

Zero-based budgets (ZBB) (similar to activity-based budgets), popularized in the 1970s, are based on the premise that every budget dollar requires justification. Unlike

In The News [7.2]

Preparing a Weekly Budget, and Keeping Percentages in Line Can Help a Small Business Manage Its Cash Flow

Setting goals is one thing; knowing how to reach them is something else. The process that helps individuals reach their goals is the formulation of a plan, which is basically actions that someone intends to implement to reach them. Dreams are not necessarily backed-up by plans, but goals are!

One person who understands the importance of planning and budgeting is Tony Cappellano, owner of a chain of three restaurants in Toronto, Boom Breakfast & Co. He recognizes the fact that in the restaurant business, profit margins are extremely slim. So, in order to keep his business profitable, he manages his cash flow with a "fine-tooth comb." He credits his strong financial health and continued growth to the way that he manages his daily cash budget. As he points out, "I know what my fixed expenses are every day. I know what I need to bring in every day and I set a budget for the week and keep percentages in line." As one of his business advisors pointed out, the three-step process that is critical for managing the cash flow cycle includes the following:

- Analyze your financial statements.
- Create a three-year forecast that can be adapted to changing environments.
- Dictate how your business should be managed by adjusting the forecast with the cash situation.

Source: Adapted from Mary Teresa Bitti, "Living by the budget," *Financial Post*, June 15, 2009, p. FP8. You can learn more about Boom Breakfast & Co. by visiting their website at http://www.boombreakfast.com.

the traditional budgeting approach—whereby expenditures of the previous years are automatically incorporated into the new budget proposal, and only increments are scrutinized and subjected to debate—zero-based budgeting places all dollars, including last year's authorized expenditures and new requests, on an equal footing. It assumes that a manager has had no previous expenditures. It is much like the reengineering process, whereby managers ask the question, "If we were re-creating this organizational unit or company today, given what we know and given current technology, what would it look like?"

In the zero-based budgeting process, managers prepare budget proposals called "decision packages." These budget proposals are subsequently ranked against each other to compete for scarce corporate resources. Zero-based budgeting is a priority form of budgeting process whereby all budget proposals are ranked in order of importance. It is an effective tool used to analyze programs, proposals, or projects for the purpose of optimizing the use of a company's resources.

ZBB focuses on input–output relationships. It is a process that can be used by overhead organizational units such as purchasing, marketing, administration, engineering, human resources, legal services, and operations research.

The three steps involved in ZBB are the following:

1. The identification of the decision units (organizational units) in terms of their mission, activities, outputs, and performance indicators (efficiencies and effectiveness).

2. The preparation of the decision packages (budget proposals), which contain a description of the objectives, activities, programs, projects, outputs, efficiency and effectiveness standards, resource requirements (person-years, physical, budgets), risk, and time requirements.
3. The ranking of the decision packages based on corporate priorities and strategies.

Self-Test Exercise No. 7.3

Zero-Based Budgeting—Levels of Services

Identify the factors that you would take into consideration when determining the levels of services for CompuTech's retail store.

The Balanced Scorecard (BSC) is another management system that emerged some 10 years ago. It is a management process that can translate an organization's mission, vision, and strategies into a comprehensive set of quantifiable performance measures in addition to providing a framework for a strategic measurement and management system. It has made significant inroads in small, medium, and large businesses, as well as in not-for-profit (NFP) organizations. The BSC has been adopted by more than half of Fortune 500 companies and the growth momentum continues unabated. This management process has been hailed by the *Harvard Business Review* as one of the most effective management ideas of the 20th century for helping organizations yield swift benefits such as increasing financial return, promoting greater employee alignment with overall goals, improving communication, and being able to successfully implement strategies. The pioneers of the BSC management process, Robert Kaplan and David Norton,[1] were able to provide a meaningful integration of many issues helpful for decision makers when gauging their organization's performance.

The BSC scrutinizes a strategy through a "magnifying glass" from the following four perspectives:

- *Financial perspective*: How should our organization appear to our stakeholders?
- *Customer/client perspective*: How should our organization appear to our customers?
- *Internal process perspective*: What business processes should our organization excel at?
- *Employee learning and growth perspective*: How should our organization sustain its ability to change and improve?

1. Robert S. Kaplan and David P. Norton, *The Balanced Scorecard*, Boston: Harvard Business School Press, 1996.

Each scorecard perspective includes four elements: (1) an objective, (2) performance measures, (3) performance targets, and (4) initiatives. Initiatives are specific programs, activities, projects, or actions required to ensure that an organizational unit meets or exceeds its performance targets. For example, a student's scorecard would read as follows:

Objective:	Complete the introduction to finance course
Performance measure:	grade
Performance target:	80%
Initiatives:	• Complete case study No. 1 by November 30 • Present in class the findings of a research study on January 15

The BSC has the power to translate the mission statement, the value goals, the vision statement, and the strategies into measurable targets and action plans in addition to being capable of gauging to what extent overall targets are being realized. As shown in Figure 7.6, the "building blocks" components of the BSC process include the following: mission statement, value goals, vision statement, strategies, objectives,

Figure 7.6 **The Balanced Scorecard's Planning, Budgeting, and Controlling Management Process**

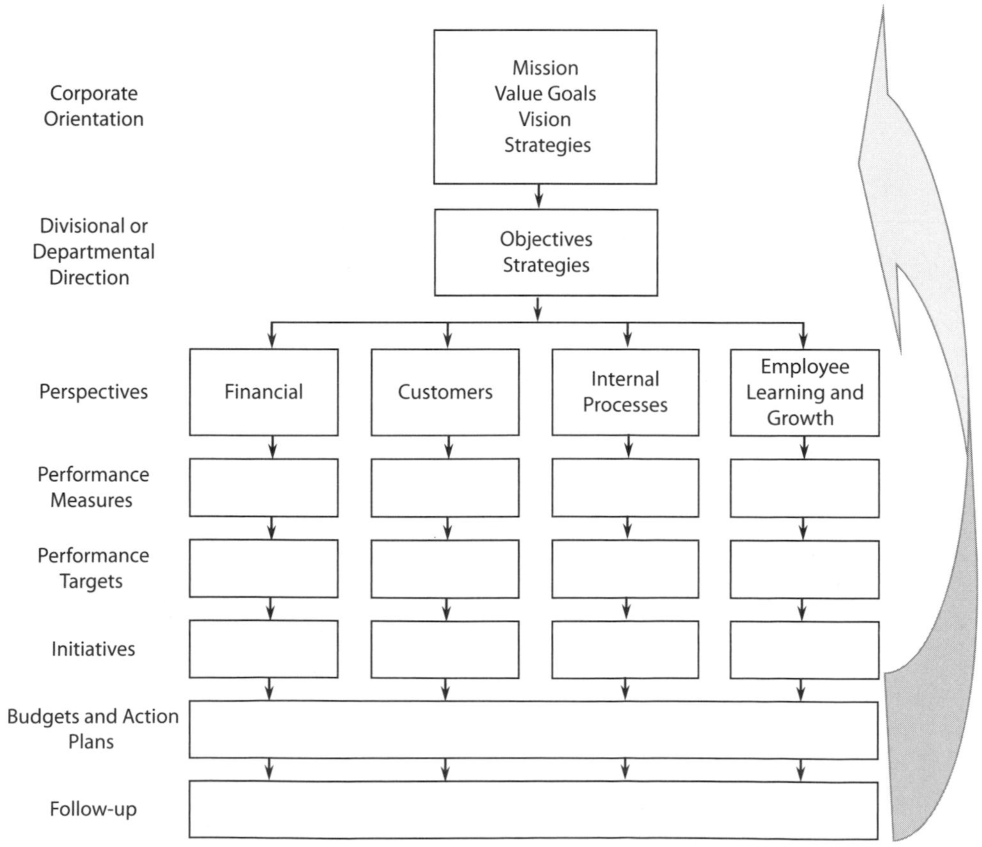

performance measures, performance targets, and initiatives, which all lead to the preparation of the organizational budgets, action plans, and follow-up.

The BSC's organizational performance system represents a balance among the following:

- External measures for shareholders and customers, and internal measures of internal processes, employee learning, and growth.
- Targets related to resources utilization (economy and efficiency) required to accomplish goal related accomplishments (effectiveness).
- Lagging indicators (results from past efforts) and leading indicators (measures that drive future performance).
- Easily quantifiable outcome measures and subjective performance drivers of the outcome measures.

Self-Test Exercise No. 7.4

Balanced Scorecard—Objectives, Measures, Targets, and Initiatives

For CompuTech's sales department, formulate examples of the following:

a) An objective
b) An efficiency measure and an effectiveness measure
c) An efficiency target and an effectiveness target
d) A lagging indicator and a leading indicator
e) Two initiatives

Complementary Budgets

Complementary budgets
Budgets that complement operating budgets whereby data are presented differently and in more detail.

Complementary budgets are the offspring of operating budgets and present operating budget data differently. They too can be classified into separate groups: product budgets, program budgets, item-of-expenditure budgets, and cash budgets.

Product budgets are used by marketing organizations to identify the profit performance of different products. For example, the budgets for three products may be prepared in the following way:

	Products		
	A	B	C
Revenue	$500,000	$770,000	$1,300,000
Cost of sales	(250,000)	(300,000)	(600,000)
Gross profit	250,000	470,000	700,000
Marketing budget			
Distribution costs	(50,000)	(75,000)	(100,000)
Advertising	(25,000)	(40,000)	(70,000)
Salaries and commissions	(100,000)	(150,000)	(250,000)
After-sales service	(50,000)	(40,000)	(100,000)
Total marketing budget	(225,000)	(305,000)	(520,000)
Net product margin	$25,000	$165,000	$180,000

From this budget, it is possible to find out how much money will be spent by each department (e.g., distribution, advertising, etc.) and on each product. This budget therefore gives an idea of the profitability level of each product. A business may also calculate the return on investment of each product by identifying, for each, the capital investments and the profit level (after allocating the company's overhead).

Program budgets are used mostly by NFP organizations, including federal, provincial, and municipal governments. Program budgeting has been called the *Planning-Programming-Budgeting System (PPBS)*. Five basic steps are involved in this budgeting process:

- The objectives of the major activities or programs are identified.
- The benefits (or results) to be generated by each activity or program are analyzed.
- The initial outlay and the future costs for each program are estimated.
- The alternatives are examined.
- The budget is prepared on the basis of the first four steps.

Item-of-expenditure budgets are the most popular format of budget preparation. Here, resources are classified in an entirely different way. For example, expenses might break down into salaries, supplies, equipment, travel, and utilities. A typical item-of-expenditure budget follows:

Items	Amounts
Salaries and wages	$200,000
Transportation and communication	25,000
Information	12,550
Professional services	35,500
Rentals	10,000
Purchases, repairs, and upkeep	5,000
Utilities, materials, and supplies	32,000
Other expenditures	20,000
Total	$340,050

Cash budgets are planning and controlling tools, and are used for negotiating a line of credit with commercial banks. These budgets trace, on a monthly basis, the funds that will be (1) available and (2) required. In short, cash budgets keep track of the adequate monthly cash balances that a business needs, avoiding unnecessary idle cash and possible cash shortages. As shown in Table 7.6, the cash budget is usually broken down into four sections:

1. Cash receipts section
2. Cash disbursements section
3. Cash surplus or deficit section
4. Financing section

Table 7.6 The Cash Budget

In $	January	February	March	April	May	June	July
1. Cash Receipts Section							
Revenue	225,000	285,000	290,000	300,000	400,000	500,000	600,000
Collections							
Within 30 days (10%)	22,500	28,500	29,000	30,000	40,000	50,000	60,000
In 30–60 days (40%)	80,000	90,000	114,000	116,000	120,000	160,000	200,000
In 60–90 days (50%)	142,500	100,000	112,500	142,500	145,000	150,000	200,000
Total receipts	245,000	218,500	255,500	288,500	305,000	360,000	460,000
2. Cash Disbursements Section							
Cost of sales (purchases)	(115,000)	(125,000)	(100,000)	(150,000)	(200,000)	(250,000)	(300,000)
Payments							
Cash (30%)	(34,500)	(37,500)	(30,000)	(45,000)	(60,000)	(75,000)	(90,000)
30 days (70%)	(70,000)	(80,500)	(87,500)	(70,000)	(105,000)	(140,000)	(175,000)
Total payments	(104,500)	(118,000)	(117,500)	(115,000)	(165,000)	(215,000)	(265,000)
Expenses							
Distribution costs	(52,300)	(50,300)	(50,060)	(50,500)	(38,000)	(56,000)	(55,000)
Administrative expenses	(108,000)	(82,000)	(111,500)	(85,860)	(88,000)	(84,000)	(71,000)
Total disbursements	(264,800)	(250,300)	(279,060)	(251,360)	(291,000)	(355,000)	(391,000)
3. Cash Surplus or Deficit Section							
Total receipts	245,000	218,500	255,500	288,500	305,000	360,000	460,000
Total disbursements	(264,800)	(250,300)	(279,060)	(251,360)	(291,000)	(355,000)	(391,000)
Gain (deficit)	(19,800)	(31,800)	(23,560)	37,140	14,000	5,000	69,000
4. Financing Section							
Beginning bank balance	27,200	7,400	(24,400)	(47,960)	(10,820)	3,180	8,180
Gain (deficit)	(19,800)	(31,800)	(23,560)	37,140	14,000	5,000	69,000
Closing bank balance (loan)	7,400	(24,400)	(47,960)	(10,820)	3,180	8,180	77,180

The cash budget is prepared in two steps. The first involves the calculations for each month of all receipts from cash sales and collections (section 1). Table 7.6 assumes that revenue for the months of November and December amounted to $285,000 and $200,000, respectively. Total receipts for the month of January shows an amount of $245,000. Here is the calculation:

	Revenue	Collection Period	Percent Received	January Receipts
January	$ 225,000	within 30 days	10%	$ 22,500
December	$ 200,000	30–60 days	40%	80,000
November	$ 285,000	60–90 days	50%	142,500
Total				$ 245,000

The same calculation is done for the months of February to July.

The second step requires that all cash disbursements for individual expense items be calculated (section 2). Cost of sales is done in two stages: 30% within 30 days and 70% within 60 days. It is assumed that purchases for cost of sales for the month of December is $100,000. Total payment for purchases amounts to $104,500. Here is the calculation:

	Purchases	Payment Period	Percent Paid	January Payments
January	$115,000	cash	30%	$34,500
December	$100,000	30 days	70%	70,000
Total				$104,500

The same calculation is done for the months of February to July.

Several departments must participate in the preparation of the cash budget, which requires a certain degree of judgment. For example, the sales department provides the revenue figures, while the credit manager provides a breakdown of the approximate percentage of revenue that will be made on a cash basis, on credit, or paid within 30, 60, or 90 days. Various departmental heads also provide information on operating expenses related to purchases, wages, salaries, lease payments, etc.

The difference between the receipts and the disbursements gives either a net cash surplus or a deficiency (section 3).

The financial officer then determines the amount of cash that should be (section 4):

- Kept in the bank at all times (cash at start of month);
- Invested in short-term securities (surplus cash); and
- Required from the bank in the form of a line of credit (outstanding loans).

The cash budget is a tool that allows for deliberate planning for the efficient acquisition of funds and for short-term investments.

NFP organizations also prepare cash budgets. Just like for-profit organizations, NFP organizations need to know how much cash they have to keep on hand. As shown below, a cash budget for an NFP organization displays cash that is expected to come in, cash expected to go out, and the difference between the two numbers plus an explanation of how any negative difference will be financed. The key lines for an NFP organization are at the bottom: the net cash flow for the month (positive or negative); beginning cash balance, which is last month's ending cash balance; and the ending cash balance, which shows the impact of that month's cash loss or gain.

Cash Budget for a Not-for-Profit Organization

In $	January	February	March	April
Cash Inflows				
Program services	280,000	300,000	295,000	315,000
Fundraising	50,000	60,000	40,000	50,000
Miscellaneous	10,000	15,000	15,000	20,000
Total cash inflows	340,000	375,000	350,000	385,000

Cash Outflows				
Salaries	(225,000)	(215,000)	(240,000)	(230,000)
Payroll taxes	(22,500)	(21,500)	(24,000)	(23,000)
Employee benefits	(22,500)	(21,500)	(24,000)	(23,000)
Legal/audit	(1,300)	(1,500)	(2,000)	(2,500)
Consultants	(3,000)	(2,300)	(3,000)	(4,000)
Contract services	(4,000)	(5,000)	(2,000)	(1,500)
Program supplies	(40,000)	(45,000)	(42,000)	(43,000)
Vehicle expenses	(2,000)	(1,500)	(2,000)	(1,400)
Leases	(3,000)	(3,000)	(3,000)	(3,000)
Rent	(25,000)	(25,000)	(25,000)	(25,000)
Utilities	(2,500)	(3,000)	(3,000)	(2,300)
Property insurance	(2,000)	(2,000)	(2,000)	(2,000)
Total cash outflows	(352,800)	(346,300)	(372,000)	(360,700)
Net inflow (outflow)	(12,800)	28,700	(22,000)	24,300
Beginning cash balance	10,000	(2,800)	25,900	3,900
Ending balance	(2,800)	25,900	3,900	28,200

Self-Test Exercise No. 7.5

Cash Budget

With the following information, prepare a cash budget for the months of January to April 2009.

The marketing department's sales forecast is:

December (2008)	60,000
January (2009)	60,000
February	70,000
March	75,000
April	80,000

The credit manager provides the following information:

80% of revenue is on a cash basis.

20% is collected after 30 days.

Cost of sales, which is 50% of revenue, is incurred in the month in which the sales are made.

These goods are paid for 30 days after the purchases are made.

Monthly selling and administrative expenses are as follows:

Salaries	$12,000
Finance costs	2,500
Leasing	800
Depreciation	3,000
Advertising	1,000

Other expenses are as follows:

Taxes: $10,000 in February, $10,000 in April, and $10,000 in September

Purchase of assets: $3,000 in January, $12,000 in February, $20,000 in March, and $3,000 in April

The cash balance on January 1, 2009, is $3,000.

Comprehensive Budgets

When the controller has received all revenue forecasts and budgets from the operating managers, the accountants consolidate and prepare the projected financial statements into a **comprehensive budget**. The various projected financial statements will be discussed later in this chapter, in the section, "Financial Projections," beginning on page 330.

Comprehensive budget
A set of projected financial statements such as the statement of income, the statement of financial position, and the statement of cash flows.

Capital Budgets

A **capital budget** reveals how much is required to invest in non-current assets (e.g., capital assets). This budget breaks down the capital assets by major category, how much funding is needed and when it is required, the location of the assets, and the reasons for spending. These budgets include investments such as cost-reduction programs or research and development projects, expansion of a manufacturing operation, replacement of obsolete equipment, installation of computer equipment, construction of a warehouse, or even the purchase of an ongoing business. Capital projects or capital assets generate benefits (returns, profits, savings) over an extended number of years. Projects that are included in capital budgets are critical because they usually require a significant amount of financial resources. The capital budgeting process and the evaluation methods will be discussed in Chapter 11.

Capital budget
Budget that shows how much will be spent for the purchase of capital assets.

RULES FOR SOUND BUDGETING

Table 7.7 summarizes the most important rules to follow when preparing budgets, especially operating budgets such as revenue, flexible, and overhead budgets. These rules are prerequisites for effective budgeting, and violation of any of them can easily jeopardize the budgeting process.

Business Plan

4 Learning Objective

Explain the nature of a business plan, and its benefits and contents.

A **business plan** gives a complete picture about an organization's goals, plans, operating activities, financial needs, and financing requirements. It is like a road map that demonstrates how an organization is to reach its goals. The business plan helps readers (lenders, investors, and other stakeholders) understand the intentions of the management team and what they want to accomplish. Business plans are produced by (1) heads of divisions, operating within large and decentralized corporations, and (2) entrepreneurs, managing small businesses. Because large corporations have divisions that operate more or less like independent businesses, each produces its own business plan and all are presented to corporate managers (CEO and vice-presidents) for review and approval. Ultimately, divisional business plans are consolidated into an overall corporate plan.

Business plan
Document that gives a complete picture about an organization's goals, plans, operating activities, financial needs, and financing requirements.

Owners of small businesses also prepare business plans for the purpose of communicating an investment opportunity to potential lenders and investors. For these entrepreneurs, a business plan is often considered a "ticket of admission" or a "calling card" that introduces their business and an opportunity to prospective investors. A business plan is also an important instrument for managers because it provides a blueprint regarding how their company will go about implementing its plans. The business plan gives a detailed description of a company's operational plans for each business function (marketing, production, distribution, finance, etc.) in terms of who is going to do what, when, how, where, and why.

Table 7.7	Ten Rules for Sound Budgeting

Rule 1: Pinpoint authority.
Make sure that reporting responsibilities are clear and that managerial authority is well defined.

Rule 2: Integrate all planning activities.
To be effective, budgeting must be linked in a systematic way to other planning activities, such as setting objectives, identifying corporate priorities and strategies, and establishing guidelines and management objectives.

Rule 3: Insist on sufficient and accurate information.
Information is essential to decision-making, the prime purpose of budgeting. All budget aspects, from cost–benefit analyses to the establishment of performance standards, depend upon the availability of current and accurate data.

Rule 4: Encourage participation.
Essentially, accountability is measuring achievement against objectives. Participation in goal setting encourages enthusiastic efforts. Few people like to be held accountable for hitting or missing someone else's targets.

Rule 5: Link budgeting to monitoring.
Budgeting is meaningless if it is not linked to monitoring. What is the point of spending endless hours formulating plans and budgets, if management does not follow up by comparing actual performance with standards?

Rule 6: Tailor budgeting to the organization's needs.
How information is presented, consolidated, and reviewed is a highly individualized matter. A system that works well for one organization will not necessarily produce the same results for another. Because management style, information needs, and corporate structures differ, each must create a budgeting system that meets its own special requirements.

Rule 7: Communicate budget guidelines and planning assumptions.
To ensure economy of time and effort, remove confusion in an organization and prevent the budgeting system from faltering, it is essential to establish and communicate premises, guidelines, and planning assumptions.

Rule 8: Relate costs to benefits.
It is essential to appraise every unit in terms of its contribution to the organization, the benefits expected from the services it provides, and the funds it needs to perform its tasks.

Rule 9: Establish standards for all units.
One reason for preparing budgets is to make sure resources are spent efficiently and effectively. To determine this, it is important to establish performance standards. Although it may be rather easy to establish performance standards at the production level, it is harder with overhead units (e.g., administration, research groups, or accounting operations). Nevertheless, every effort should be made to set performance goals.

Rule 10: Be flexible.
Managers should be able to respond easily to changing circumstances. On the manufacturing side, budget levels change with the level of production; managers responsible for production operations will clearly not be limited to their budget ceilings if sales levels are exceeded by 10% or 20%. They will respond to marketing needs. With overhead units, however, because of the absence of engineering standards, budgets often become permanently fixed. Yet it is only common sense that, during the operating year, managers responsible for overhead units should be allowed to increase or reduce their activities and, in turn, their budgets, to meet new requests or priorities.

BENEFITS OF THE BUSINESS PLAN

There are many reasons for carefully preparing a business plan. First, the company benefits because of the following:

- It shows specifically how management intends to go about implementing its plans and how it will be organized (who will do what and when).

- It forces managers to do a realistic assessment of different operating units of the business (strengths and weaknesses).
- It provides managers with a document that can be used to monitor their plans on a continual basis, and to take corrective action if necessary.
- It allows managers to see that all resources of the business are used efficiently and effectively.

To investors, a sound business plan offers many benefits for the following reasons:

- It provides a solid base on which they can judge a company and readily assess the past performance of the business, and find out whether it has adequate resources to successfully implement its plans.
- It assures them that management is aware of both the opportunities and threats related to the business.
- It indicates the company's ability to maintain and repay its debt within the short and medium term and shows the return generated by the projects contained in the business plan.
- It identifies all components of the company's operations, both internal, such as resources (financial, human, physical, technological, material), and external (industry environment, competition, trends).
- It identifies the timing and nature of future cash requirements.
- It enables investors to assess management's ability to plan and organize the use of the resources efficiently and effectively.
- It indicates how much funding is needed, who will provide it, and when it will be required.

STRUCTURE OF THE BUSINESS PLAN

The business plan includes an arrangement of information that is of interest to investors. The structure of a business plan can vary in style and detail; there is no perfect sequence of the contents of a business plan. Each investor may want to see sections in a different order or see different information emphasized. Also, the length of the business plan depends on the stage of development of a business (start-up versus ongoing) and the amount of funds being sought.

A typical outline of a business plan is as follows:

- Executive summary
- Company and ownership
- External environment
- Mission, statement of purpose, and strategy statements
- Products and services
- Management team
- Operations (marketing, production, etc.)
- Financial projections
- Appendices

Table 7.8 gives a brief description of the contents related to different sections of the business plan.

Table 7.8	Contents of a Business Plan
Cover sheet	**Name of business, address, and telephone number.**
Executive summary	Description of (1) the company's structure and major players; (2) company's purpose in the marketplace, as well as its products and services; (3) management team; (4) financial needs and financing requirements; and (5) key financial results.
Company and ownership	Includes (1) chronological history based on major milestones; (2) form of ownership (public or private company, date of incorporation); (3) names and addresses of founding shareholders and directors; (4) company's major successes or achievements; and (5) location of business.
External environment	Description of the company's operating environment and its ability to respond effectively to external forces in terms of opportunities and threats. The four key components are general environment (economic, political, etc.), industry characteristics, market dynamics, and competitive climate.
Mission, statement of purpose, and strategy statements	Statement of desired direction or achievement. With brief outlines of the overall picture and several "directional statements," lenders and investors should be in a good position to evaluate management's intentions in the context of the required financing and the company plans.
Products and services	Description of the products and services the company provides. It includes key product characteristics and distinctive features in terms of how they differentiate from competing firms.
Management team	Description of the (1) experience and skills of the key members of the management team; (2) key employees; (3) organizational chart; (4) number of employees and labour requirements of the business, including employee benefit package.
Operations	Description of the more important goals and strategies for each key function related to marketing, production, finance, and human resources. The following is a brief description of the type of information that can be included in each function: *Marketing/distribution plan*: market size, consumer profile, product strategy, pricing strategy, distribution strategy, marketing programs (advertising, promotions), composition of the sales force, sales revenue by product line, market share, product development. *Production/operations plan*: physical space, inventory and supplies, distribution system, patented processes, state of technology, type of equipment used, plant capacity, key suppliers and availability of raw materials, labour requirements, capital investment estimates, plant layout, government regulations. *Human resources plan*: personnel required by function, number and category of workers, training needs and costs, working conditions, compensation programs, turnover and morale, labour relations.
Financial projections	Audited financial statements, projected financial statements (statements of income, statements of financial position, statements of cash flows, cash budget), break-even analysis, and financial returns.
Appendices	Results of market research studies, corporate or product brochures, management resumes, summaries of key agreements, credit reports, copy of leases, copy of letters patent or corporate charter and by-laws, detailed plant layout and production process, articles, clippings, special reports, graphs and charts, glossary of terms, references from investors, lenders, trade creditors, and letters of intent from potential customers.

Financial Projections

5 Learning Objective

Describe projected financial statements and how to measure financial performance.

Projected financial statements
Results of some assumed events that are part of financial projections (e.g., statement of income, statement of financial position, and the statement of cash flows).

As shown in Figure 7.5, operating budgets are ultimately integrated into projected financial statements, also known as pro-forma financial statements. **Projected financial statements** show the results of some assumed events that are part of financial projections. The most important financial statements that managers, owners, lenders, and other interest groups examine to gauge the overall financial performance of a business are the statement of income, the statement of financial position, and the statement of cash flows.

STATEMENT OF INCOME

Table 7.9 presents Eastman Technologies Inc.'s projected statement of income for the year 2010. The statement shows the company's future revenue, costs, and profit performance. As shown in the table, significant improvements were forecast in the cost of sales, which has a favourable effect on the gross profit and profit for the year. To examine the company's expected financial performance, managers can calculate the

Table 7.9 **Projected Statements of Income**

Eastman Technologies Inc.
Statements of Income
for the year ended December 31
(in $)

	2010	2009	Increase or Percent of Revenue
Revenue	3,050,000	2,500,000	(22.0% increase)
Cost of sales	(2,050,000)	(1,900,000)	(67.2% of revenue for 76.0%)
Gross profit	1,000,000	600,000	(66.7% increase)
Other income	23,000	20,000	
Distribution of costs			
Sales salaries	(158,000)	(140,000)	(5.2% of revenue from 5.6%)
Advertising expenses	(34,000)	(20,000)	
Total distribution costs	(192,000)	(160,000)	
Administrative expenses			
Office salaries	(185,000)	(170,000)	(6.1% of revenue from 6.8%)
Lease	(29,000)	(20,000)	
Depreciation	(48,000)	(40,000)	
Total administrative expenses	(262,000)	(230,000)	
Finance costs	(41,000)	(35,000)	
Total other income and expenses	(472,000)	(405,000)	(16.5% increase, 15.5% of revenue from 16.2%)
Profit before taxes	**528,000**	**195,000**	
Income tax expense	(264,000)	(97,500)	
Net profit for the year	264,000	97,500	(8.7% of revenue from 3.9%)

ratios that were examined in Chapter 4 (see Table 4.6 on page 178) and also the vertical analysis of the statement of financial position and the statement of income (see Tables 4.1 and 4.2), and horizontal analysis of the statement of financial position and the statement of income (see Tables 4.3 and 4.4).

STATEMENT OF CHANGES IN EQUITY (RETAINED EARNINGS SECTION)

Table 7.10 shows Eastman's projected statement of changes in equity (retained earnings section) for the year 2010. The company will pay $50,000 in dividends, retain $214,000 in the business, and accumulate retained earnings in the amount of $469,000.

STATEMENT OF FINANCIAL POSITION

A similar analysis can be done for the statement of financial position. As shown in Table 7.11, Eastman Technologies Inc.'s projected statement of financial position presents the financial structure in terms of non-current assets, current assets, equity, non-current liabilities, and current liabilities, and how these elements are distributed during the years 2009 and 2010. As shown in the table, Eastman Technologies Inc.'s total assets increased by $279,000—that is, from $1,800,000 to $2,079,000.

The projected statement of financial position is formulated by starting with the statement of financial position for the year just ended and adjusting it, using all activities that are expected to take place during the budgeting period. The more important reasons for preparing a projected statement of financial position include the following:

- To disclose some unfavourable financial conditions that management might want to avoid.
- To serve as a final check on the mathematical accuracy of all the other schedules.
- To help managers perform a variety of financial ratios.
- To highlight future resources and obligations.

Table 7.10 **Projected Statement of Changes in Equity (Retained Earnings Section)**

Eastman Technologies Inc.
Retained Earnings Statement
for the year ended December 31, 2010
(in $)

Retained earnings (beginning of year)		255,000
Earnings	264,000	
Dividends	(50,000)	214,000
Retained earnings (end of year)		469,000

Table 7.11 Projected Statements of Financial Position

Eastman Technologies Inc.
Statements of Financial Position
for the year ended December 31
(in $)

	2010	2009	Increase or Percent of Revenue
Assets			
Non-current assets			
Property, plant, and equipment	1,600,000	1,340,000	(see capital budget for details)
Accumulated depreciation	(188,000)	(140,000)	
Total non-current assets	1,412,000	1,200,000	
Current assets			
Inventories	230,000	218,000	(0.2 time improvement)
Trade receivables	325,000	300,000	(5-day improvement)
Prepaid expenses	67,000	60,000	
Cash and cash equivalents	45,000	22,000	(Cash to revenue to 1.5% from 0.9%)
Total current assets	667,000	600,000	
Total assets	2,079,000	1,800,000	
Equity			
Share capital	300,000	300,000	(no change)
Contributed surplus	—	—	
Retained earnings	469,000	255,000	(see statement of income and statement of changes in equity for details)
Total other comprehensive income/(loss)	—	—	
Total equity	769,000	555,000	
Liabilities			
Non-current liabilities			
Long-term borrowings	830,000	800,000	
Current liabilities			
Trade and other payables	220,000	195,000	(slightly over 10% of cost of sales)
Short-term borrowings	140,000	150,000	
Accrued expenses	30,000	20,000	
Taxes payable	90,000	80,000	
Total current liabilities	480,000	445,000	
Total liabilities	1,310,000	1,245,000	
Total equity and liabilities	2,079,000	1,800,000	

To determine where these increments are recorded, we have to examine the key elements of the assets such as inventories, trade receivables, and non-current assets as a percentage of total assets.

STATEMENT OF CASH FLOWS

Table 7.12 presents Eastman's projected statement of cash flows for 2010. Essentially, it shows the amount of cash that will be used to finance the company's capital budget. As shown in the investing activities portion of the statement, $260,000 will be invested in non-current assets (capital assets). Operating activities will generate $280,000, which will be used exclusively to buy the assets and to pay the dividends to the shareholders.

Table 7.12 Projected Statement of Cash Flows

Eastman Technologies Inc.
Statement of Cash Flows
for the year ended 2010
(in $)

	Cash Inflows	Cash Outflows
Operating activities		
Profit for the year	264,000	—
Depreciation	48,000	—
Inventories	—	12,000
Trade receivables	—	25,000
Prepaid expenses	—	7,000
Cash and cash equivalents	—	23,000
Trade and other payables	25,000	—
Notes payable	—	10,000
Accrued expenses	10,000	—
Taxes payable	10,000	—
Total	357,000	77,000
Net cash from operating activities	**280,000**	—
Financing activities		
Payment of dividends	—	50,000
Long-term borrowings	30,000	—
Share capital	—	—
Total	30,000	50,000
Net cash from financing activities	—	**20,000**
Net cash from investing activities	—	**260,000**
Total	**280,000**	**280,000**

Note: The presentation format of this statement of cash flows is different from the one presented in annual reports, such as the one shown in Table 3.9 on page 129. This format is considered more a management tool, lists more details under operating activities, and the cash account is listed under operating activities and not as a separate item.

In the News 7.3 explains why cash flow is the lifeblood of small businesses and how growth potential should not be constrained by a cash flow crisis.

In The News [7.3]

Why Cash Flow Is the Lifeblood of a Business and Why Growth Potential Can Be Constrained by a Cash Flow Crisis

There is a reason why we sometimes here statements such as "Cash is king," or "Profits are an opinion, but cash is a fact." There is no question that cash flow management is essential to the success of every business. You can lose a customer without irreparable damage, but if you have a gap in your cash flow, which causes you to miss payroll or a payment to a supplier, it may be just the reason to tarnish your business's reputation.

David Wilton, director of small business at Scotiabank, makes the point that "to start a business, you need passion and prospective customers, but cash is the thing that makes that business flourish." In an article that appeared in the *Financial Post,* here are a few reasons why Wilton suggested that cash is important to a business and how it can be managed:

- Without cash, a business fails.
- You have to project future events to predict the effect that it will have on your cash flow.
- A business may be profitable on paper, but profits don't pay the bills, cash does.
- A growing business can strain the cash flow cycle.
- When sales go up, so do all other items shown on your financial statements (statement of income and statement of financial position).
- Choosing to make sales grow is a strategic decision.
- Be guided by your goals.
- Make cash flow a fundamental part of your success.

Source: Adapted from David Wilton, "Cash flow vital to business growth," *Financial Post,* June 15, 2009, p. FP8. For more information about managing a small business, visit http://scotiabank.com/ and click on the "Small Business" tab.

FINANCIAL INDICATORS

Now that management has produced different types of budgets and the projected financial statements, the next three key questions are:

- What is the company's financial performance?
- Is the company growing within its operating and financial capabilities?
- How healthy is the business? Will its financial health improve or deteriorate?

Financial Ratios

Lenders and investors will certainly want to assess the company's financial performance regarding its liquidity, debt/coverage, asset management, and profitability. The ratios presented in Table 4.6 on page 178 showing Eastman's performance relating to industry ratios can also be analyzed in terms of trends. As shown on the following page, Eastman's projected financial performance for 2010 compared to 2009 and 2008 continues to improve.

	Actual 2008	Year-end 2009	Budget Year 2010
Liquidity ratios			
Current ratio (times)	1.35	1.35	1.39
Quick ratio (times)	0.89	0.86	0.91
Debt/coverage ratios			
Debt-to-total-assets (%)	67.07	69.17	63.01
Time-interest-earned ratio (times)	7.52	6.57	13.88
Fixed-charges coverage ratio (times)	4.49	4.55	8.54
Asset-management ratios			
Average collection period (days)	45.42	43.80	38.89
Inventory turnover (times)	9.42	8.72	8.91
Capital assets turnover (times)	2.37	2.08	2.16
Total assets turnover (times)	1.51	1.39	1.47
Profitability ratios			
Gross profit to revenue (%)	22.53	24.00	32.79
Operating income to revenue (%)	6.89	8.40	17.90
Return on revenue (%)	3.33	3.90	8.66
Return on total assets (%)	5.04	5.42	12.70
Return on equity (%)	15.31	17.57	34.33

Sustainable Growth Rate

Most people equate growth with success, and managers often see growth as something to be maximized. Their view is simple: If the company grows, the firm's market share and profit for the year should also increase. However, growing too fast (if growth is not properly managed) may create problems. In some instances, growth outstrips a company's human, production, and financial resources. When that happens, the quality of decision-making tends to deteriorate under constant pressure, product quality suffers, and financial reserves often disappear. The bottom line is this: If growth is not managed, a business can literally grow broke.

There is no question that there are limits to how quickly a company should grow. Preoccupation with growth at any cost can overextend a company administratively and financially. Results can be lower profit, cash shortages, and, ironically, slower growth, as managers pause to regroup and repair the damage. Some signs of trouble associated with growing too quickly are substantial increases in inventories and trade receivables relative to revenue, declining cash flow from operations, and escalating interest-bearing debt.

Sustainable growth rate
Rate of increase in revenue a company can attain without depleting financing resources, borrowing excessively, or issuing new stock.

In order to understand growth management, we must first define a company's **sustainable growth rate**. It is defined as the maximum rate at which a company's revenue can increase without depleting financial resources. Managers must therefore look at different options when they target the company's sustainable growth rate. In many instances, management should limit growth in order to conserve financial strength.

If a company wants to grow, it has several options:

- Increase its profit for the year on revenue.
- Reduce the payout of dividends in order to retain earnings.
- Sell new equity.
- Increase leverage (more debt versus equity).
- Increase the productivity of its assets.

It is possible to develop a sustainable growth equation that shows a company's optimum growth rate. The formula that can help determine the optimum growth rate is the following:

$$\textbf{Growth} = \frac{(M)(R)(1 + D/E)}{(A) - (M)(R)(1 + D/E)}$$

where

M = Ratio of profit for the year to revenue
R = Ratio of reinvested profit to profit for the year before dividends
D/E = Ratio of total liabilities to equity
A = Ratio of assets to revenue

Eastman's 2009 and 2010 sustainable growth rates are 9.9% and 39.2%, respectively. The ratios used to arrive at these growth potentials are as follows:

	2009	2010
M = Ratio of profit for the year to revenue	0.04	0.09
R = Ratio of reinvested profit to profit for the year before dividends	0.51	0.81
D/E = Ratio of total liabilities to equity	2.24	1.70
A = Ratio of assets to revenue	0.72	0.68

Eastman can grow faster in 2010 than in 2009 because important favourable changes are expected. As shown, there is a significant change in the ratio of profit for the year to revenue. In 2009, the company had only $0.04 in profit for every dollar's worth of revenue to invest in growth such as investments in capital assets or research and development. This ratio jumped to $0.09 in 2010.

The ratio of reinvested profit to profit before dividends also increased. In 2009, the company's ratio was only 0.51 (with profit for the year of $97,500 and payment of $47,500 in dividends), compared to 0.81 for 2010 (with profit for the year of $264,000 and payment of only $50,000 in dividends). This means that the company will have more cash to reinvest in the business for growth purposes.

A similar improvement is taking place in the ratio of total liabilities to equity. In 2009, 69% of the company's total assets were financed by debt. This figure is expected to drop to 63% in 2010. As a result, the ratio of total liabilities to equity will improve from 2.24 to 1.70. This improved performance gives the company more flexibility to borrow in the future.

The fourth ratio used in the formula is the total value of assets needed to support every dollar's worth of revenue. As shown, in 2009, the company required $0.72 worth of assets to produce $1.00 in revenue; in 2010, the company required only $0.68. This is another improvement.

Because it has shown improvements in these four ratios, the company will be able to improve its sustainable growth to 39.2%, which compares favourably to the company's expected revenue growth in 2010 of 22.0%. This means that the company is well within its organizational and financial capabilities.

Financial Health Score

Let's turn now to measuring Eastman's financial health. In 1962, Edward Altman developed a mathematical model to help financial analysts predict the financial performance of businesses. Altman utilized a combination of traditional ratios and a sophisticated statistical technique known as *discriminant analysis* to construct a financial model for assessing the likelihood that a firm would go bankrupt. The model combined five financial measures utilizing both reported accounting and stock/variables to arrive at an objective overall measure of corporate health called the **financial health score**, or the Z-score. For example, if the five ratios give a Z-score of 3.0 or higher, the company is in a healthy financial position or in a safe zone. If the score falls between 1.8 and 3.0, the company is in the grey zone and could go either way. If the score is less than 1.8, the company is in danger of bankruptcy.

Financial health score (Z-score)
Linear analysis in which five measures are objectively weighted to give an overall score that becomes the basis for classifying the financial health of a business.

Table 7.13 shows Altman's Z-score formula and Eastman's five financial ratios for 2009 and 2010. As shown, Eastman scored 2.34 in 2009 (grey zone) and 3.11 in 2010 (safe zone). This indicates that the company was able to take positive financial steps to make the company more viable. Here is a brief explanation for each of these ratios.

- Ratio (a): There was no change in the ratio of net working capital to total assets between the two accounting periods.
- Ratio (b): The relationship between retained earnings and total assets increased substantially in 2010 over 2009 (from 0.14 to 0.23). This change is a result of an 84% increase in the retained earnings account shown on the statement of financial position. This reflects a strong profit performance ($0.09 profit for every dollar's worth of revenue in 2010 compared to $0.04 in 2009) with a small increase in dividend payments.
- Ratio (c): The ratio of earnings before interest and taxes to total assets also increased substantially. This reflects a strong profit performance in 2010 compared to 2009.
- Ratio (d): The equity-to-debt ratio also improved in 2010 (0.59 compared to 0.45).
- Ratio (e): The revenue-to-total assets ratio also improved in 2010 (1.39 to 1.47).

Table 7.13 Altman's Z-Score

Measuring the Financial Health Zone of Eastman Technologies Inc. for 2009 and 2010

Safe zone	3.0 and over
Grey zone	1.8 to 3.0
Bankrupt zone	0 to 1.8

$Z = 1.2\,(a) + 1.4\,(b) + 3.3\,(c) + 0.6\,(d) + 1.0\,(e)$

				2010	2009
a	=	$\frac{\text{Working capital}}{\text{Total assets}}$	=	0.09	0.09
b	=	$\frac{\text{Retained earnings}}{\text{Total assets}}$	=	0.23	0.14
c	=	$\frac{\text{Earnings before interest and taxes}}{\text{Total assets}}$	=	0.26	0.12
d	=	$\frac{\text{Equity}}{\text{Total liabilities}}$	=	0.59	0.45
e	=	$\frac{\text{Revenue}}{\text{Total assets}}$	=	1.47	1.39
		Z-score		**3.11**	**2.34**

Self-Test Exercise No. 7.6

Financial Indicators

By using CompuTech's financial statements for the year 2010 presented in Appendix A, calculate the following:

1. The company's sustainable growth rate
2. The company's Z-score

Controlling

6 Learning Objective

Comment on the importance of controlling, the control system, and the different types of controls.

Controlling is a function of the management process that closes the management loop. What is the point of planning and budgeting if managers are not informed of the results of their efforts? We sometimes hear people say "We have things under control"; that means that all activities involved in realizing a project are well coordinated. On the other hand, if someone says that an activity is "out of control," it means that it is at the mercy of events. Establishing strategic and operational control points is crucial to ensuring that objectives and plans are realized.

THE CONTROL SYSTEM

As shown in Figure 7.7, establishing an effective control system involves six steps:

Step 1: Design the subsystem.
Step 2: Establish performance indicators.
Step 3: Determine performance standards.
Step 4: Measure performance.
Step 5: Analyze variations.
Step 6: Take corrective action to resolve unfavourable situations that may arise.

Design the Subsystem

The first step in establishing a control system is to determine the type of subsystem within the overall management process that would be most effective. The control subsystem should fit the culture of the organization and be one that managers and employees at all echelons will benefit from. Managers in bureaucratic organizations may prefer a bureaucratic control system (extensive rules and procedures), while democratic organizations may opt for organic controls (employees monitor their own destiny). Managers should also ask questions such as: How do we want the system to help us? Should the control system be more future oriented (solve the problem before it appears) or reactive (give us information after an event takes place)? Or should we have both systems?

The system should be designed on the basis of what specific inputs (quantity and quality) are required by managers and when they need the information for analyzing their activities and making decisions. Managers will also prefer that the information output be presented in a certain way (e.g., online, reports, or presentations).

Figure 7.7 The Control Process

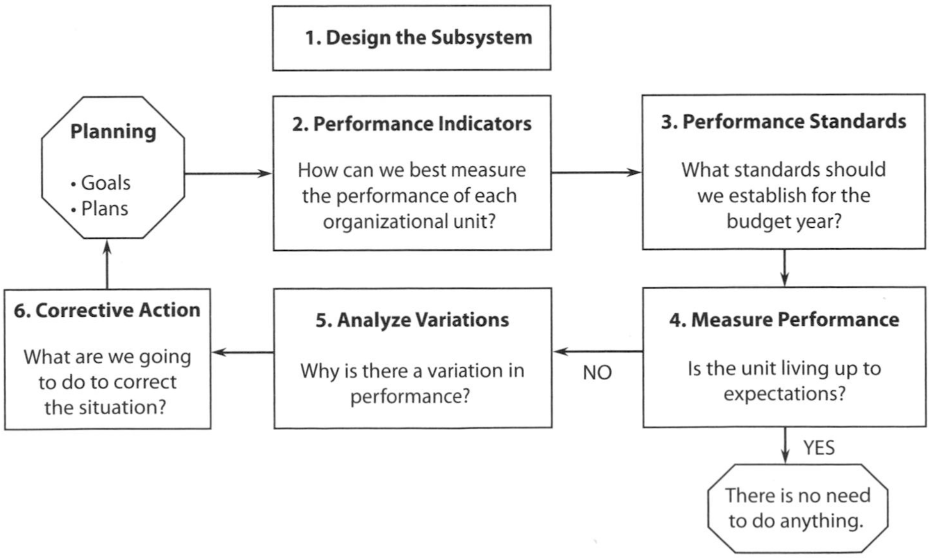

Establish Performance Indicators

As shown in Figure 7.7, the entire control process is closely linked to the planning activity. Establishing operational and financial goals during the planning phase allows managers to determine the type of performance indicators they should use for measuring accomplishments. The control process allows managers to determine how organizational units should be measured. First, determine the key elements or characteristics of the organizational units in terms of costs and benefits. Second, determine which of these elements need to be measured. We are referring here to the principle of selectivity (also known as Pareto's Principle[2]), which states that often only a small number of vital activities account for the largest number of outputs. If the appropriate indicators are not identified, it may be difficult for managers to measure the real organizational performance. For example, return on revenue is an appropriate indicator for assessing the global company performance, cost per unit is suitable for gauging manufacturing operations, and share of market is excellent for measuring marketing performance. Table 7.14 gives examples of performance indicators (operating and financial) suitable for gauging objectives for different organizational units.

Indicators can also be used to measure the performance of specific activities within a department such as marketing and production, or units such as sales and quality control. Indicators can also help measure employee performance.

Determine Performance Standards

Once performance indicators are selected, the next step is to pinpoint the standards applicable for a particular time period (day, week, month, or year). These standards are

Table 7.14 Standards for Assessing Performance

Organizational Units	Performance Indicators	Standards	Performance	Variations
Company-wide	Return on revenue (%)	7.5	7.7	0.2
Departments				
*Marketing	Share of market (%)	12.7	12.4	(0.3)
*Production	Cost per unit ($)	2.07	2.05	0.02
Organizational units				
*Sales	Number of units sold	200,000	210,000	10,000
*Quality control	Number of tests per day per technician	6	6	—
Employees				
*Marketing	Number of customers visited per day per sales representative	3	2.5	(0.5)
*Production	Number of units produced per hour	35	38	3

2. David Parmenter, *Pareto's 80/20 Rule for Corporate Accountants* (Hoboken, NJ: John Wiley & Sons, Inc., 2007).

established during the planning phase and serve as benchmarks for comparing results. There are four broad categories of performance standards: time, output, cost, and quality.

Time standards determine the length of time required to perform a specific task. For example, the length of time it takes to serve a customer at a bank or the length of time between a customer complaint and responding to it determines the quality of service offered and, thus, customer satisfaction.

Output standards measure the number of units that should be produced by individuals or groups. Managers of ticket agents for an airline company know the number of calls they can respond to on an hourly basis or the number of minutes it takes on average to provide information to their clients. For a telephone company, management knows the number of service calls technicians can respond to each day. At a university, student advisers know how many students they can meet daily.

Cost standards measure the resources required to produce goods or services. Holiday Inn or Westin Hotels know how much it costs to clean their rooms each day, Bic knows how much it costs to make a pen, and Gillette knows how much it costs to produce a can of shaving foam.

Quality standards pinpoint the level of quality needed to meet customer expectations. The total quality management concept focuses on quality standards that signal whether customers are receiving the expected quality products or services. For example, the services expected by guests at Holiday Inn or Comfort Inn will be different from those expected from the Westin Hotels or Four Seasons, and the customer expectations for a Rolex watch would be different than for a Timex. Although these organizations sell products of different qualities, the critical point is to gauge the quality standards anticipated by the customers and to carefully respond to their needs. Table 7.14 also gives examples of performance standards.

Measure Performance

Performance could be measured daily, weekly, monthly, or annually. To measure performance, managers need information that can be obtained from five sources: written reports, computer printouts, oral presentations, personal observations, and electronic media.

Written reports are used widely, particularly in large organizations. They are costly because of the time it takes to write the reports and for others to read them. To be effective tools, written reports should be brief (one page), in outline rather than narrative form, and structured to highlight the most critical information. *Computer printouts* can quickly provide all types of operating and financial data or information. Today, spreadsheets allow managers to enter data, which the computer calculates and presents numerically or graphically. From these printouts, managers can readily extract specific information. *Oral presentations* are effective as there is an immediate exchange of ideas during staff meetings between, say, subordinates and supervisors. Individuals communicating information at such meetings can use simple visual displays (e.g., simple line graphs or milestone charts), which are considered effective media for explaining performance and remedial action plans. To be effective, however, such meetings should be brief. Managers should establish before the meeting which reports should be presented and which should be distributed and read beforehand. Through *personal observations*, managers can see the status of an operation. *Management by walking about (MBWA)* is considered by many an effective management technique that can help managers make critical observations regarding the behaviour of individuals and groups, and operating activities. However, today information also can be provided to managers instantly through *electronic media*. A sales manager, for example, can open his computer before the day starts and look at sales performance for the previous days, weeks, or months for individual sales representatives, or area or regional managers.

To compare results to standards, managers must analyze information. Table 7.14 also shows how results are compared to standards. For example, the company established a target of 7.5% return on revenue and achieved 7.7%, a superior performance.

Analyze Variations

Variations between standards and results must be analyzed to determine the reasons for "off-performance" situations. Unfavourable variations do not necessarily mean mediocre performance. For example, is $10,000 over budget in manufacturing expenses unfavourable? A close analysis may reveal that the manufacturing department produced more units to meet marketing needs, and thus increased corporate profits. If the advertising department spent $100,000 less than was budgeted, does this represent a favourable situation? Perhaps at first glance it may. However, after scrutiny, the manager may find that corporate revenues are $800,000 less than expected and profit for the year $125,000 less than budgeted due to not having spent the $100,000 advertising budget. Overall, the company's profit for the year performance is down by $25,000.

Let's take another example to show the importance of properly analyzing variations. The credit department may have exceeded its salary budget by $14,000, but if credit officers worked overtime to recover the trade receivables more rapidly and succeeded in reducing the average collection period from 50 to 45 days, the benefits could have exceeded the $14,000 overtime cost.

It is not enough just to look at the column showing variations and judge quickly the performance of an organizational unit. Managers should investigate the reasons for the variations and determine whether they have favourable or unfavourable effects on the overall company performance.

Take Corrective Action

When variations have been identified and the exact causes are known, managers then take the necessary steps to solve the problems. Managers have three options. First, there is the status quo. If a manager is on target or the variation is only minimal, she may decide not to do anything. Second, a manager may wish to correct a situation. This is a likely option if the manager sees serious operating problems and wants to bring operations back in line. Third, the manager may want to change the standard. This may be appropriate if the original standard was set too high or if uncontrollable circumstances have changed the environment dramatically.

TYPES OF CONTROLS

Most control systems are one of three types: preventive controls, screening controls, or feedback controls (see Figure 7.8).

Figure 7.8 Types of Control Systems

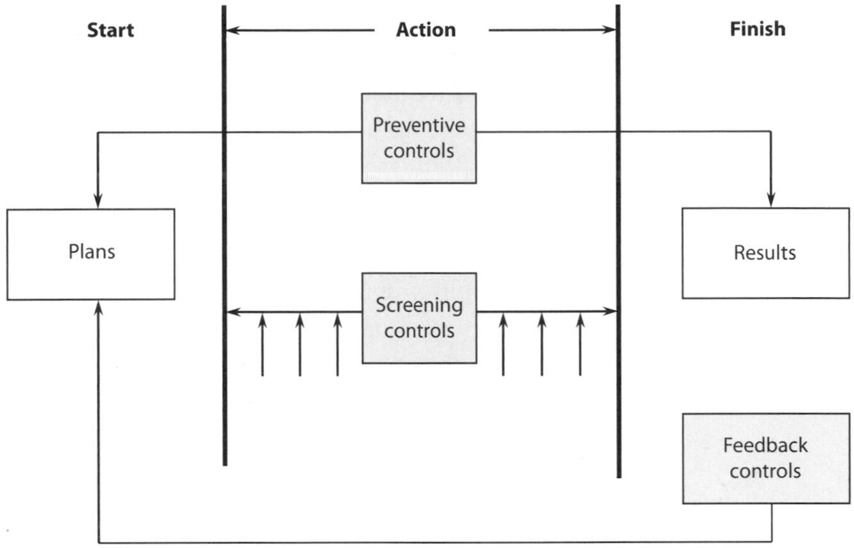

Preventive Controls

Preventive controls System that helps to guide actions toward intended results.

Preventive controls (also known as feedforward controls, preliminary controls, steering controls, or proactive controls) take place when one wants to guide actions toward intended results. A recipe for making a cake is a classic example. The recipe will guide the cook to help realize the intended results (the cake). This control system emphasizes the future; a manager knows what he wants, and puts in place the necessary mechanism to ensure that the intended results are achieved. Let's take two business situations to illustrate how preventive controls work. Before hiring bank tellers, the human resources department will identify the required qualifications to ensure that the manager hires efficient and effective tellers, and maintains the employee turnover at a low level. The job description prevents staffing officers from hiring unsuitable job applicants; that is why this system is called preventive control. Similarly, in a manufacturing operation that makes products such as soft drinks, coffee, chocolate bars, or hamburgers, management will specify the quality level and the ingredients before production actually begins.

Screening Controls

Screening controls System that helps to monitor performance while work is being performed.

Screening controls, also known as concurrent controls, take place during the implementation phase or as the process takes place. Some screening controls take the "yes-no" form. This means that the process can either be continued or stopped in order to take corrective actions. For example, when buying a house, a potential homeowner will say yes or no during each step of the purchase process (visit the house, negotiate the price or other terms, agree with the terms of the mortgage loan) before signing the final purchase agreement.

Screening controls can also be done by using what is called the "steering" mechanism. This means that as the process evolves, the degree of deviation is gradually brought back into line without actually stopping the process. In an automobile manufacturing plant, for example, control points are established at every critical step of the assembly line. As a car moves along the line, periodic control checks are executed to see that each job is performed according to standards before the car moves to subsequent assembly points. Steering controls reduce unnecessary manufacturing costs (e.g., having to remove the dashboard if the electrical wiring system is improperly installed).

Feedback Controls

Feedback controls System that helps to focus on variations of past performance.

Feedback controls, also known as corrective controls or post-performance controls, are like thermostats. They place emphasis on past performance and the manager takes corrective action only when comparisons are made and the variations detected. Managers are reacting to a given situation; for example, if your bank statement shows an overdraft, you will immediately take action by rushing to the bank to make a deposit. In organizations, daily, weekly, and monthly reports work the same way; they inform managers about performance so that they can take the necessary actions to correct unfavourable situations. Typical feedback controls are report cards, budget reports, and audit reports.

The objective of these three types of control systems is the same—to assist managers to gauge performance and take corrective action to reach stated objectives.

REALITY FINANCIAL SNAPSHOTS

All successful organizations, such as Enbridge and The Ottawa Hospital, formulate goals and plans (strategies) that show what they want to achieve and how they intend to reach the goals. When looking at Figures 7.1 (segment H and I) and 7.4, one can realize that financial statements (past and future) are only images or reflections of what organizations want to accomplish with their goals and plans. The following several paragraphs give some examples of the type of goals, strategies, and projects that both Enbridge and The Ottawa Hospital have presented to the members of their board of directors and stakeholders at large. A more complete description of these organization's goals and plans are available on their respective websites.

ENBRIDGE[3]

Enbridge's *vision* and key *objective* read as follows: "To be North America's leading energy delivery company and its key objective is to generate superior shareholder value." The company will deliver superior shareholder value through an investment proposition consisting of the following:

- Industry-leading earnings per share growth rate
- A low-risk commercial business model
- A balanced combination of near-term dividend income and capital appreciation

3. Enbridge Inc., *2008 Enbridge Annual Report*. Found at: http://www.enbridge.com/investor/financialInformation/reportsFilings/pdf/2008-annual-report-en.pdf.

Enbridge's 2008 Strategic Plan consisted of four key strategic priorities to generate superior shareholder value and position the company for the environment of the future.

1. Expand existing core businesses (pursue opportunities in both its liquids and natural gas delivery systems).
2. Focus on operations (consistently deliver safe, cost-effective, and high-quality service to customers and meet the broader expectations of communities it serves).
3. Mitigating and managing execution risk (key priorities include enhanced project management systems and processes, proactive human resource planning, and an increased focus on social investment, to both facilitate project development and meet the expectations of the company's stakeholders).
4. Developing new platforms for longer-term growth (new platforms currently being pursued include renewable energy, such as wind and solar; CO_2 transportation and sequestration; and investment in smaller start-up entities to enable the development of new technologies that complement the company's core operations).

The following gives examples of five key initiatives to be realized in different business units such as liquids pipelines, gas distribution and services, gas pipelines, sponsored investments, and international businesses in order to sustain growth and profitability.

- Alberta Clipper, Southern Lights Pipeline, and Line 4 Extension were approved by the National Energy Board (NEB) and construction began on the Canadian portion of Alberta Clipper Project, Line 4 Extension, and various segments of Southern Lights Pipeline.
- First phase of the U.S. Southern Access Expansion Project has been completed on schedule and construction commenced on phase 2 of the Southern Access Expansion Project.
- Waupisoo Pipeline, which was completed one month ahead of schedule and on budget.
- Spearhead Pipeline expansion commenced.
- Project financing of US$1.3 billion and $0.4 billion secured for Southern Lights Pipeline.

THE OTTAWA HOSPITAL[4]

The formulation of goals and preparation of plans are not done only by for-profit organizations. NFP organizations such as The Ottawa Hospital also prepare plans to make sure that they use their funds in the most efficient and effective way. Here are a few examples of institutional goals and plans that can be found in The Ottawa Hospital's planning documents that can be viewed on its website. Here are TOH's vision, mission statement, key success factors, and core values.

4. *2008 Ottawa Hospital Annual Report.* Found at: http://www.ottawahospital.on.ca/about/reports/FS2008-e.pdf.

TOH's Vision

The Ottawa Hospital will be nationally recognized as the academic health sciences centre of choice.

TOH's Mission

- TOH is a compassionate provider of patient-centred health services with an emphasis on tertiary-level and specialty care, primarily for residents of eastern Ontario.
- TOH provides a wide variety of educational opportunities across all health care disciplines in partnership with the University of Ottawa and other affiliated universities, community colleges, and training organizations.
- TOH develops, shares, and applies new knowledge and technology in the delivery of patient care through nationally and internationally recognized research programs in partnership with the Ottawa Health Research Institute.
- TOH plays an active role in promoting and improving health within our community. TOH collaborates with a wide range of partners to address the needs of the community and to build a strong, integrated system for regional health care delivery.
- TOH functions in English and French while striving to meet the needs of the culturally diverse community we serve.

TOH's Key Success Factors

- Set new standards in patient care, education, and research.
- Inspire innovation, learning, and growth.
- Build financial strength.
- Create enabling environments.
- Drive change through advocacy and partnerships.

TOH's Core Values

- Compassion
- A commitment to quality
- Working together
- Respect for the individual

The following gives examples of some of the initiatives, plans, or strategies that TOH will be implementing during the next few years in order to rise to the challenge for which its vision and mission statements strive.

- Maintain a deficit-free operation.
- Promote efficiencies through the optimization of health care services delivery.
- Give health care providers the right tools to do their job.
- Develop professional practices in 95 units across all three campuses.
- Reduce wait times for patients receiving hip and knee replacements, cancer surgeries, and MRI exams.
- Reduce the length of stay of patients in the department through the Emergency Departments.

- Launch the Privacy Program, which protects personal health information of patients and staff.
- Help train 2,000 nursing students, 570 residents, 533 medical students, 339 professionals, 117 clinical fellows, and 4 research fellows.
- Publish important studies in leading scientific and medical journals.
- Attract and retain highly skilled health care professionals by giving them the best possible tools.

[DECISION-MAKING IN ACTION]

In September of 2010, Dytex Ltd. began its annual planning process. At one of its monthly management meetings, John Lipton, CEO of the company, informed managers that, over the next several years, the economic and industry conditions appeared extremely positive. He made the point that he wanted Dytex to take advantage of this opportunity by significantly improving the company's financial performance. He stressed the importance that all managers in every division would have to take a serious look at their operating budgets and try to be creative in finding ways to improve their respective performance. He insisted that he wanted aggressive growth in the marketplace, and improvement in operating efficiencies in all divisions, departments, and organizational units.

He asked Arlene Gibson to make a brief presentation of the company's financial statements for the years 2009 (actual) and 2010 (year-end forecast). The statements of income are presented in Table 7.15 and statements of financial position in Table 7.16.

Table 7.15 **Dytex Ltd.'s Statements of Income**

Dytex Ltd.
Statements of Income
for the year ended December 31
(in $000s)

	2009 Actual	2010 Forecast	2011 Budget
Revenue	102,000	109,000	128,000
Cost of sales	(71,000)	(73,000)	(82,000)
Gross profit	31,000	36,000	46,000
Other income	100	150	200
Distribution costs	(11,000)	(12,000)	(13,000)
Administrative expenses	(10,000)	(10,700)	(11,300)
Finance costs	(2,000)	(2,300)	(2,500)
Total other income/expenses	(22,900)	(24,850)	(26,600)
Profit before taxes	8,100	11,150	19,400
Income tax expense	(3,300)	(4,500)	(5,820)
Profit for the year	4,800	6,650	13,580
Retained earnings (beginning of year)	13,000	17,800	24,450
Profit for the year	4,800	6,650	13,580
Retained earnings (end of year)	17,800	24,450	38,030

Table 7.16 **Dytex Ltd.'s Statements of Financial Position**

Dytex Ltd.
Statements of Financial Position
as at December 31
(in $000s)

	2009 Actual	2010 Forecast	2011 Budget
Assets			
Non-current assets			
Property, plant, and equipment	100,000	113,000	135,000
Accumulated depreciation	(30,000)	(33,000)	(38,000)
Net non-current assets	70,000	80,000	97,000
Current assets			
Inventories	6,000	8,000	8,500
Trade receivables	9,000	12,700	14,000
Prepaid expenses	300	200	300
Cash and cash equivalents	1,100	1,450	1,600
Total current assets	16,400	22,350	24,400
Total assets	86,400	102,350	121,400
Equity and liabilities			
Equity			
Share capital	25,000	30,000	31,000
Retained earnings	17,800	24,450	38,030
Total equity	42,800	54,450	69,030
Liabilities			
Non-current liabilities			
Long-term borrowings	34,400	38,000	41,000
Current liabilities			
Trade and other payables	4,000	4,100	4,700
Short-term borrowings	5,000	5,300	5,900
Accruals	200	500	770
Total current liabilities	9,200	9,900	11,370
Total liabilities	43,600	47,900	52,370
Total equity and liabilities	86,400	102,350	121,400

After the presentation, Mr. Lipton gave a rough idea of his key strategic goals based on the following planning assumptions:

> "First, we're going to be aiming for a 20% increase in revenue in 2011. This is based on the premise that three of the four sectors in which our divisions compete in will show growth close to 15%. With our new and improved product lines that we are going to introduce in the marketplace, coupled with some creative advertisements and innovative marketing strategies, we should not have problems in achieving that growth. Nevertheless, we will have to make sure that we have the physical, financial, and human resource means to achieve this growth rate.
>
> Second, the return on revenue over the past several years has been less than the ones experienced by our key competitors. In 2009, our return on revenue was 4.7% and based on our most recent forecast, we expect to show 6.1% by the end of this year. Our key competitors are showing performance in the area of 8 to 10%. In fact, we should use Gilmore Inc. as our benchmark; their return on revenue is 14%. I do know that there is room for improvement in efficiencies in both cost of production and marketing, and our managers should make every effort to cut costs, improve efficiencies, eliminate waste, and be more economical in the way that they operate.
>
> Third, our divisions expect to invest substantial sums of money in capital assets in 2011: modernizations, acquisition of new assets, investment in research and development, and the expansion of two plants. Following our discussions of the past several meetings and some preliminary reports that I have received from your divisional controllers, I estimate a $20 million investment in capital assets.
>
> Fourth, I would like to have these capital projects funded mostly by internally generated cash. This cash will come from increased operating efficiencies (profit for the year) and improvements in the way that we manage our inventories and trade receivables. This year, there appears to be deterioration in the way that inventories and receivables are managed. With the 20% projected increase in revenue, I surely don't expect inventories and receivables to increase in the same proportion. With improvements in these two working capital accounts, this will allow us to invest less cash in working capital accounts. Some members of the board of directors have expressed a willingness to invest more funds in Dytex. However, I would like to keep this at a minimum because we have several acquisitions that we have in sight over the next several years and I would like to keep our debt position as low as possible. We will need external funds for these acquisitions in later years.
>
> The bottom line is this: I want to make sure that Dytex's financial position is improved during the next several years. In 2009, the company's overall financial health score was 2.54. Based on our year-end forecast, we expect it to reach 2.66. I would like to see a continued improvement and reach a score of 3.00 by 2011. Also, our economic value added in 2009 was a meager $248,000 with a forecast of $707,000 by year-end. I would like to be able to show the members of the board of directors that EVA showed a sizeable gain for next year.

Now, we have three months of planning and budgeting. Arlene Gibson and her staff will be coordinating this process. They will consolidate the divisional and departmental budgets and present the projected financial statements at our late November meeting. If the financial results are in line with these broad goals, we will bring these numbers to the board members for review and approval. If not, we will have to ask our managers to redo their budgets in order to squeeze more cash from our operations."

During the November special budget sessions, Arlene Gibson presented the 2011 consolidated financial statements in addition to the projected statement of cash flows and key financial results (see Table 7.17). Also, she pointed out the following fixed payments during the planning period:

($000s)	2009	2010	2011
Lease payments	1,000	1,200	1,300

Mr. Lipton was pleased with the statements and indicated that he was prepared to present them to the next meeting of the board for review and approval.

Table 7.17 Dytex Ltd.'s Financial Performance

Dytex Ltd.
Statements of Cash Flows
for the period ending December 31
(in $000s)

	2010 Forecast	2011 Budget
Operating activities		
Profit for the year	6,650	13,580
Depreciation	3,000	5,000
Adjustments in non-cash working capital accounts	(4,900)	(430)
Cash flow from operating activities	4,750	18,150
Financing activities		
Share capital	5,000	1,000
Long-term borrowings	3,600	3,000
Cash flow from financing activities	8,600	4,000
Cash flow from investing activities	(13,000)	(22,000)
Increase in cash and cash equivalent accounts	(350)	(150)
Cash, beginning of year	1,100	1,450
Cash, end of year	1,450	1,600

Table 7.17 (Continued)

Financial Performance Measures

	2009 Actual	2010 Forecast	2011 Budget
Liquidity ratios			
Current ratio (times)	1.78	2.26	2.15
Quick ratio (times)	1.13	1.45	1.40
Debt/Coverage ratios			
Debt-to-total-assets ratio (%)	50.46	46.80	43.14
Times-interest-earned (times)	5.05	5.85	8.76
Fixed-charges coverage ratio (times)	3.70	4.19	6.11
Asset-management ratios			
Average collection period (days)	32.21	42.53	39.92
Inventory turnover (times)	11.83	9.13	9.65
Capital assets turnover (times)	1.46	1.36	1.32
Total assets turnover (times)	1.18	1.06	1.05
Profitability ratios			
Gross profit to revenue (%)	30.39	33.03	35.94
Operating income to revenue (%)	9.80	12.20	16.95
Return on revenue (%)	4.71	6.10	10.61
Return on total assets (%)	5.56	6.50	11.19
Return on equity (%)	11.21	12.21	19.67
Economic value added (in 000s)	248	707	4,631
Sustainable growth rate	12.63	13.91	24.49
Company's growth rate	N/A	6.86	17.43
Financial health score	2.54	2.66	3.00

FINANCIAL SPREADSHEETS—EXCEL

The financial spreadsheets that accompany this text are exceptional tools for looking at the financial performance of projected financial statements. Once the goals and plans have been formulated and financial results inputted onto the input documents (statements of income, statements of changes in equity, and statements of financial position), analysts and managers can immediately interpret results by looking at the output documents (vertical and horizontal financial statements, ratios, etc.). The most positive feature about the spreadsheets is that changes made on the financial statements as a result of altered goals and plans can quickly be measured in terms of the impact they have on financial performance (e.g., liquidity, profitability, asset-management, debt-coverage). The spreadsheets also calculate the more-complex ratios such as sustainable growth rate and financial health score. The spreadsheets also include decision-making tools that can help prepare monthly cash budgets, and sales and manufacturing budgets.

Chapter Summary

1 Learning Objective

Describe the meaning of planning and its process, and how to measure organizational performance.

Planning is the process of formulating goals and outlining action plans to realize the goals. Planning is important because it (1) helps managers to become more resourceful, (2) integrates their operational plans with strategic plans, (3) provides a sense of purpose and direction, (4) helps them to cope with change, and (5) simplifies managerial controls. Goals and plans can be grouped under three categories: strategic, tactical, and operational. One of the key priorities of managers is to achieve the highest level of performance with the least expenditure of resources, which means being efficient (doing things right) and being effective (doing the right things).

2 Learning Objective

Explain why the SWOT analysis and planning assumptions are important for formulating goals, and preparing plans, budgets, and projected financial statements.

The first step in the planning process is to go through the SWOT analysis that involves analyzing a company's internal environment to identify its strengths and weaknesses, and then its external environment to identify the opportunities and threats. The purpose of the SWOT analysis is to formulate planning assumptions that are benchmarks upon which priorities, goals, plans, budgets, and financial projections are based.

3 Learning Objective

Show how budgeting fits within the overall planning process, the different types of budgets, and how to make budgeting a meaningful exercise.

Budgeting is a vital element of the management planning and control process. It is the process that translates corporate intentions into specific tasks and identifies the resources needed by each manager to carry them out. Budgeting is only a part of the planning and controlling framework. An organization may have different types of budgets, which can be grouped under three categories: operating budgets (flexible and overhead budgets), complementary budgets (product budgets, program budgets, item-of-expenditure budgets, and cash budgets), and comprehensive budgets (projected financial statements and capital expenditure budgets). Flexible budgets are employed at the plant level, where costs of production are used as checkpoints to compare actual results and to ascertain price and quantity variances. A production budget will vary with the number of units produced. Zero-based budgeting is a management tool used by administrative or overhead units. Here, the manager of each unit reviews all activities—past, present, and projected—and evaluates them in terms of productivity versus costs. There is also the balanced scorecard management system, which is a process that translates an organization's mission, vision, and strategies into a comprehensive set of quantifiable performance measures in addition to providing a framework for a strategic measurement and management system. All managers should be responsible for preparing their own budgets. Because specific departments play important roles in improving various components of the statement of financial position and the statement of income, it is critical that they prepare their budgets in a responsible way.

4 Learning Objective

Explain the nature of a business plan, and its benefits and contents.

A business plan is a document that gives a complete picture about an organization's goals, plans, operating activities, financial needs, and financing requirements. Both managers and investors benefit from a carefully crafted business plan. The business plan includes an executive summary, an explanation about the company and its owners, the external environment, its mission and strategy statements, its products and services, its management team, its operations (marketing, production, human resources, etc.), its financial projections, and appendices.

5 Learning Objective

Describe projected financial statements and how to measure financial performance.

Financial planning is the activity that integrates all budgets into projected financial statements to determine whether the company is improving its financial performance. There are three projected financial statements: the projected statement of income; the projected statement of financial position, and the projected statement of cash flows. Management should also be able to manage the company's growth. This is important if the company is not to deplete its human and financial resources. The sustainable growth formula is a tool that identifies how fast a company should grow in order to conserve financial strength. The Z-score formula, which combines five ratios, is used to assess the financial health of a business.

6 Learning Objective

Comment on the importance of controlling, the control system, and the different types of controls.

Controlling is the management activity that helps managers determine whether they have realized their plans and objectives. Establishing a control system involves six steps: (1) design the subsystem, (2) establish performance indicators, (3) determine performance standards, (4) measure performance, (5) analyze variations, and (6) take corrective action to resolve unfavourable situations that may arise. Control systems can be grouped into three major categories: preventive controls, screening controls, and feedback controls.

Key Terms

Budgeting p. 315
Business plan p. 326
Capital budget p. 326
Complementary budgets p. 321
Comprehensive budget p. 326
Economy p. 305
Effectiveness indicators p. 306
Efficiency indicators p. 305
Feedback controls p. 344
Financial health score (Z-score) p. 337
Operating budgets p. 315
Performance indicator p. 305
Performance standard p. 305
Planning p. 302
Planning assumptions p. 310
Preventive controls p. 343

Review Questions

1. What is planning and why is it important?
2. What is the difference between a performance indicator and a performance standard?
3. What is the purpose of the SWOT analysis?
4. What is the usefulness of planning assumptions?
5. What is budgeting?
6. Why is budgeting so important?
7. Explain budgeting in terms of planning as a whole.
8. What are operating budgets?
9. Differentiate between incremental budgeting and zero-based budgeting.
10. Why is the balanced scorecard so effective as a management tool?
11. What do we mean by complementary budgets?
12. What is the purpose of a cash budget?
13. List the more important rules of sound budgeting.
14. What are the benefits of a business plan for a company?
15. What is financial planning?
16. What do we mean by the term "sustainable growth"?
17. Explain Altman's financial health formula.
18. What is controlling?
19. Explain the various steps involved in the control system.
20. Comment on the various types of performance standards.
21. Differentiate between preventive controls and screening controls.
22. Contrast control as a "policing activity" and control as a "steering activity."
23. Because managers cannot control everything, what factors should be considered when determining which activities should be controlled?

Learning Exercises

EXERCISE 1

Identify efficiency and effectiveness indicators for the following organizational units, individuals, or organizations:

1. Sales department
2. Telephone-answering service

3. Purchasing department
4. Politician
5. Rehabilitation centre
6. Student
7. General insurance company
8. Cleaning department
9. Security department
10. School

EXERCISE 2

Nick Strizzi owns and operates a pizza delivery and take-out restaurant. In 2010, he sold 100,000 pizzas at an average selling price of $15.00. The cost to make each pizza amounts to $3.00 for cheese, $2.50 for spices, and $3.75 for the crust and other ingredients. The annual cost of operating the business is as follows:

Rent	$55,000
Salaries	230,000
Insurance	15,000
Advertising	30,000
Car expenses	150,000

The income tax rate for the year 2010 was 18%. Nick is preparing a projected income statement for the year 2011. The planning assumptions are as follows:

Increase in number of pizzas sold	10%
Selling price per pizza	$16.00
Increase in cost of cheese	8%
Increase in cost of spices	5%
Increase in cost of crust and other ingredients	9%
Annual rent	$65,000
Increase in salaries	12%
Increase in insurance costs	10%
Advertising costs	$35,000
Increase in car expenses	15%
Income tax rate	17%

Questions

On the basis of the above information, do the following:

a) Prepare Nick Strizzi's statement of income for the year 2010.
b) Prepare Nick Strizzi's projected statement of income for the year 2011.
c) Calculate Nick Strizzi's return on revenue ratios for the years 2010 and 2011.

EXERCISE 3

Identify the factors that you would take into consideration when using zero-based budgeting to determine the level of services for the following organizational units:

- Sanitation department
- Training department
- Quality control department
- Police department
- Advertising department
- Telephone-answering service

EXERCISE 4

With the following information about Quantum Plastics Ltd., prepare a cash budget for the months of January to April 2011.

The marketing department's sales forecast follows:

November (2010)	$25,000
December	50,000
January (2011)	75,000
February	120,000
March	140,000
April	110,000

The credit manager provides the following information:

20% of sales are on a cash basis.
60% are collected after 30 days.
20% are collected after 60 days.

Cost of sales, which is 50% of sales, is incurred in the month in which the sales are made. These goods are paid for 30 days after the purchases are made.

Monthly selling and administrative expenses are as follows:

Salaries	$22,000
Telephone	1,000
Amortization	500
Rent	2,200
Hydro	1,100
Stationery	500

Other expenses are as follows:

Taxes: $3,000 in February and $3,000 in June.
Purchase of equipment in January for $24,000.
The cash balance on January 1, 2011 is $12,000.

EXERCISE 5

Using Eagle Electronics Inc.'s financial statements below, calculate the following:

1. The company's sustainable growth rate
2. The company's Z-score

Statement of Financial Position

(in $)

Non-current assets	2,000,000	Equity	
Current assets		Share capital	400,000
Inventories	600,000	Retained earnings	850,000
Trade receivables	300,000	Total equity	1,250,000
Cash and cash equivalents	100,000	Non-current liabilities	1,000,000
Total current assets	1,000,000	Current liabilities	
		Trade and other payables	350,000
		Notes payable	100,000
		Bank loan	300,000
		Total current liabilities	750,000
		Total liabilities	1,750,000
Total assets	3,000,000	Total equity and liabilities	3,000,000

Statement of Income and Statement of Retained Earnings

(in $)

Revenue	3,000,000
Cost of sales	(1,500,000)
Gross profit	1,500,000
Expenses*	(900,000)
Profit before taxes	600,000
Income tax expense	(300,000)
Profit for the year	300,000
Dividends	(100,000)
Retained earnings	200,000

* Includes $100,000 of finance costs.

Cases

CASE 1: SEABRIDGE DISTRIBUTORS INC.

Seabridge Distributors Inc. is a distributor of central air conditioners, purifiers, humidifiers, and dehumidifiers. It has the franchise for the distribution, installation, and servicing of products for a well-known national brand in eastern Canada.

In September 2010, Louise Lane, president of the company, asked Bill Vance, general sales manager, to prepare a monthly sales budget for 2011. Lane informed Vance of the importance of a sales budget, giving the following reasons:

1. It helps to set objectives for each sales representative and for individual product lines.

2. Manufacturers are informed at least six months ahead of time of Seabridge's short-term requirements for each product line; this ensures getting products in the right quantities at the right time.
3. The bank manager is informed of Seabridge's financial requirements for each month of the budget year; the bank provides Seabridge with short-term money to finance the company's inventories and is interested in its short-term repayment capability.
4. If Seabridge is to operate effectively, it should not be caught in a position of being short of products at times when demand is high. Similarly, it would be costly for the company to be left with excessive quantities of units in inventory at the end of a season.

Following this meeting, Bill Vance decided to have a meeting with his four area managers to get the ball rolling. In early October, Bill met with his managers, emphasizing the importance of sound sales budgeting and stressing that the foundation for the preparation of a sound sales budget is sales forecasting.

The four sales managers had sales territories with the following number of sales representatives.

Territory	Number of Sales Representatives
North	4
South	5
East	3
West	4
Total	16

At the meeting, Vance showed some Power point transparencies indicating the industry's demand projections for each product line, the company's 2010 share of market, and what he hoped to achieve in 2011. The figures are shown below.

		Share of Market	
	Total Market (in units)	Estimated	Objective
	2011	2010	2011
Air conditioners	15,000	14%	16%
Air purifiers	2,300	12%	15%
Air humidifiers	83,000	11%	13%
Air dehumidifiers	74,000	9%	11%

He also presented the following percentage breakdown of the number of units sold each month for different products based on the previous five years.

Percent of Sales by Month				
	Air Conditioners	Air Purifiers	Air Humidifiers	Air Dehumidifiers
January	—	3	1	—
February	—	2	1	—
March	2	2	—	—
April	4	4	—	—
May	10	8		5
June	28	22	—	33
July	44	33	—	56
August	12	8	6	6
September	—	6	12	—
October	—	6	38	—
November	—	4	28	—
December	—	2	14	—
Total	100	100	100	100

The average unit selling prices budgeted are as follows:

Air conditioners	$4,700
Air purifiers	650
Air humidifiers	515
Air dehumidifiers	450

At the end of the meeting, the concept of sales objectives was discussed at some length with the area managers. Although it had not been the company's practice to establish objectives for every sales representative, it was the consensus that in view of the company's ambition to increase its share of the market for 2011, objectives should be introduced.

Questions

1. On the basis of the information available, prepare a monthly sales budget for 2011 for individual and combined product lines.
2. Is there anything wrong with the way that the sales budget and sales objectives were introduced in this company? How would you have approached the situation?

CASE 2: ANDERSON EQUIPMENT LTD.

One day in March 2010, John Sutherland, industrial commissioner for the city of South Elk, received a telephone call from Nick Faranda, president of Anderson Equipment Ltd., who wanted to see him as soon as possible.

In early afternoon, when Sutherland arrived at Faranda's office, Faranda was sitting at his desk going over his current year's cash budget. Faranda informed Sutherland that as a result of the revised credit restrictions adopted by his bank, he was being asked to prepare an estimate of his financial requirements for the balance of the calendar year. All major customers of the bank were asked to provide this information.

Faranda also informed Sutherland that he was going to have a meeting with Joanne Armstrong, lending officer responsible for handling the company's account and that he wanted to be in a position to show her his financial requirements for the rest of the calendar year. Consequently, Sutherland was asked to help Faranda prepare a budget forecast. On the basis of the information available, Faranda felt that it would not be necessary to borrow funds before July 2010. The budget would therefore be prepared for the period July 1, 2010, to January 31, 2011.

The marketing department provided the following sales forecast:

July	$50,000
August	100,000
September	500,000
October	650,000
November	550,000
December	400,000
January	200,000

Ten percent of sales are for cash, 40% of sales are collected after 30 days, and the remaining 50% after 60 days. Purchases, which are 80% of sales, are incurred in the month in which the sales are made. These goods are paid 30% in cash and 70% within 30 days. Distribution and administrative expenses are $10,000 per month, plus 1% of monthly sales. Start-up costs in July are $30,000. Income taxes for the entire operating period are paid in April and are 40% of the profit. The monthly depreciation is $10,000. The company feels that it is necessary to maintain a minimum cash balance of $25,000 during the selling season.

The cash balance on July 1 is $75,000.

Question

Prepare a monthly cash budget from July 2010 to January 2011.

CASE 3: UNITED MANUFACTURERS LTD.

With the financial objectives and assumptions presented below, prepare the following for the company:

a) Projected statement of income for 2011
b) Projected statement of changes in equity for 2011
c) Projected statement of financial position for 2011
d) Projected statement of cash flows for 2011
e) Financial ratios for 2011, comparing them with the 2010 financial results

Also, calculate the following:

f) The company's 2011 sustainable growth
g) The company's 2011 Z-score

Financial objectives and assumptions:

1. Related to the statement of income:
   - Revenue will increase by 10.0%.
   - Cost of sales as a percentage of revenue will decline to 51.5%.
   - Distribution costs as a percentage of revenue will improve slightly to 10.5%.
   - General and administrative expenses will drop to 5.7% of revenue.
   - Research and development costs as a percent of revenue will increase to 2.0%.
   - Depreciation/amortization will be $120,000.
   - Other income will be $6,000.
   - Finance costs will be $35,000.
   - Income tax rate (as a percent of profit before taxes) will be maintained at the 2010 level.
2. Related to the statement of changes in equity:
   - An amount of $50,000 in dividends will be paid to shareholders.
3. Related to the statement of financial position
   a. Non-current asset accounts
      - Investment in new capital assets will be $660,000.
      - Other assets will be increased by $100,000.

   b. Current asset accounts
      - Inventories will improve to 4.9 times.
      - Trade receivables will improve to 44.9 days.
      - Cash and cash equivalents will be 2.0% of revenue.

   c. Equity
      - Shareholders will invest an additional $200,000 in the business.

   d. Non-current liabilities
      - Long-term borrowings will increase by $39,700.

   e. Current liabilities
      - Trade and other payables will increase to 11.31% of cost of sales.
      - Notes payable will increase to $268,685.

United Manufacturers Ltd.
Statements of Income
for the year ended December 31
(in $)

	2009	2010
Revenue	2,900,000	3,100,000
Cost of sales	(1,870,000)	(1,880,000)
Gross profit	1,030,000	1,220,000
Other income	4,000	5,000
Distribution, administration, and other expenses		

Distribution Costs	(325,000)	(330,000)
Administrative expenses	(220,000)	(210,000)
Research and development	(35,000)	(45,000)
Depreciation/amortization	(95,000)	(105,000)
Total distribution, administration, and other expenses	(675,000)	(690,000)
Finance costs	(27,000)	(30,000)
Total	698,000	715,000
Profit before taxes	332,000	505,000
Income tax expense	(166,000)	(252,500)
Profit for the year	166,000	252,500

United Manufacturers Ltd.
Statements of Financial Position
as at December 31
(in $)

	2009	2010
Assets		
Non-current assets		
Capital assets	2,719,000	2,919,000
Accumulated depreciation/amortization	(595,000)	(700,000)
Net capital assets	2,124,000	2,219,000
Other assets (intangible)	100,000	200,000
Total non-current assets	2,224,000	2,419,000
Current assets		
Inventories	256,000	268,000
Trade receivables	420,000	459,000
Cash and cash equivalents	48,000	54,000
Total current assets	724,000	781,000
Total assets	2,948,000	3,200,000
Equity and liabilities		
Equity		
Share capital	800,000	800,000
Retained earnings	652,000	904,500
Total equity	1,452,000	1,704,500
Non-current liabilities	950,000	1,000,000
Current liabilities		
Trade and other payables	140,000	131,600
Notes payable	256,000	263,900
Other current liabilities	150,000	100,000
Total current liabilities	546,000	495,500
Total liabilities	1,496,000	1,495,500
Total equity and liabilities	2,948,000	3,200,000

PHOTO/Sebastian Kaulitzki/Shutterstock

CHAPTER 8

[SOURCES AND FORMS OF FINANCING]

Learning Objectives

After reading this chapter, you should be able to:

1 Learning Objective — Differentiate between internal financing and external financing.

2 Learning Objective — Explain different types of risk-related financing options (ownership versus debt).

3 Learning Objective — Explain useful strategies when approaching lenders.

4 Learning Objective — Comment on the different categories of equity financing.

5 Learning Objective — Discuss the sources and forms of intermediate and long-term debt financing.

6 Learning Objective — Comment on the most important sources and forms of short-term financing.

7 Learning Objective — Identify the factors that can influence the choice between buying or leasing an asset.

Chapter Outline

Internal versus External Financing
Risk-Related Financing Options
Useful Strategies When Approaching Lenders
Equity Financing
Sources and Forms of Intermediate and Long-Term Debt Financing
Sources and Forms of Short-Term Financing
Lease Financing

OPENING CASE

Now that the Millers have identified their 2011 financial needs and financing requirements (shown below, representing the difference between the 2011 and 2010 statement of financial position accounts) and have completed their business plan, they are ready to approach investors (shareholders and long- and short-term lenders) for the purpose of raising funds.

In $	Financial Needs (cash outflows)	Financing Requirements (cash inflows)
Property, plant, and equipment	**350,000**	
Internal sources		
Profit for the year		77,000
Depreciation/amortization		80,000
Total internal sources		**157,000**
Working capital		
Inventories	45,000	
Trade receivables	45,000	
Prepaid expenses	5,000	
Cash and cash equivalents	4,000	
Total working capital	**99,000**	
Working capital financing		
Trade and other payables		27,000
Short-term borrowings		40,000
Current portion of long-term borrowings		5,000
Total working capital financing		**72,000**
External sources		
Share capital		70,000
Long-term borrowings		150,000
Total external sources		**220,000**
Total	**449,000**	**449,000**

As shown above, CompuTech needs $449,000 to finance its existing retail store and to open the new one. An amount of $350,000 will open the new store, and $99,000 will be needed to finance the working capital (inventories, trade receivables, prepaid expenses, and cash).

To help finance part of the $350,000 property, plant, and equipment, the Millers will be contacting various investors and will try to obtain $70,000 from shareholders (e.g., friends, family members, and private investors) and $150,000 from long-term lenders. Based on the Millers' financial projections for 2011, 35%, or $157,000, will be provided by internally generated funds (profit for the year and depreciation/amortization), and 16%, or $72,000, will be obtained from suppliers and short-term lenders. The Millers will approach a bank to obtain a $40,000 short-term loan, which is about 45% of the $90,000 required to finance inventories ($45,000) and trade receivables ($45,000).

Although the Millers have identified their financing requirements, they are unsure whether these various sources are the best mix to finance their $449,000 financial needs. They analyzed various sources of financing and raised questions such as, "From whom should we obtain more funds?"

- Lenders or shareholders?
- Friends or private investors (i.e., angels)?
- Banks or government institutions?
- Short-term lenders or suppliers?
- Leasing or owning?

They also questioned themselves about the best forms of financing. For example, "Which of the following should we consider?"

- Term loans or conditional sales contracts?
- A line of credit or a revolving loan?
- Secured loans or unsecured loans?
- Seasonal loans or factor our receivables?

This is what this chapter addresses.

Chapter Overview

Financing is one of senior management's most constant preoccupations. There are many ways a CFO can finance the purchase of assets, and cash can be obtained from a variety of sources and in different forms. Selecting the right source and form of financing can improve the long-term financial structure and profitability of a business.

As shown in Figure 1.1, sources and forms of financing is the first chapter dealing with financing decisions. Chapter 9 will focus on (1) how cost of capital is calculated and used as a management tool, (2) how leverage analysis can be used to maximize profitability and return, and (3) describing the profile of different financial markets, as well as various dividend strategies. This chapter examines the sources and forms of financing; that is, where, why, and how funds can be obtained and the different types of financing instruments available to businesses.

The more important considerations to take into account when choosing the right form and source of financing are the following:

- Firm's annual debt commitments or obligations
- Cost of financing
- Risk factors arising from a slowdown (or acceleration) in economic or market conditions
- Control factors (related to existing shareholders)
- Flexibility to respond to future financing decisions
- Pattern of the capital structure in the industry

- Stability of the company's earnings
- Common shareholders' expectations

Financial needs
The items for which a business needs money.

The first thing that a CFO has to do before approaching investors is to identify what is to be financed. Here, we are talking about **financial needs**. Financial decisions have to do with what needs to be financed and the amount needed. Here are a few examples:

1. Purchase of property, plant, and equipment
2. More investments in research and development
3. Launching of a new product requiring large expenditures in promotional and advertising activities
4. Acquisition of another business
5. Additional working capital (inventories and trade receivables)

Once the financial needs have been identified, the next step is to pinpoint where the financing will come from and the amounts required from different sources. Both the nature of the financial needs and the amount required will determine, to a large extent, the financing requirements in terms of sources and forms.

Figure 8.1 shows how the financial needs and financing requirements are related to one another. The left side of the figure shows that the company will require $1.0 million to finance the expansion of its business activities. This could be in the form of the purchase of capital assets that will appear on the statement of financial position (SFP) and operating expense items (e.g., advertising, promotion, salaries for research and development) that will appear on the statement of income. The composition of this $1.0 million financial need could be made up as follows:

Capital assets	$600,000
Marketing costs	100,000
Research and development	100,000
Working capital	200,000
Total	$1,000,000

Figure 8.1 **Financial Needs and Financing Requirements**

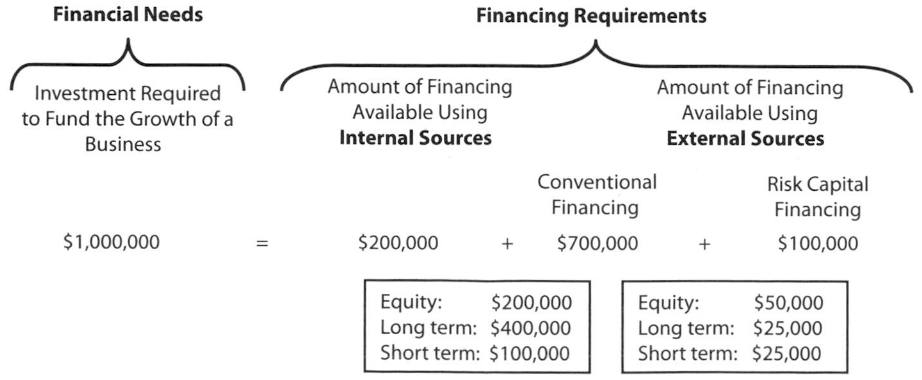

Before approaching lenders and shareholders, the CFO has to be very careful and precise when calculating the financial needs. Lenders want to be assured that the amounts that will be financed are supported by reasonable and consistent assumptions. Here are a few examples of questions the CFO should ask in examining planning assumptions:

- Are the revenue estimates reasonable relative to the expected market growth?
- Are the levels of inventories and trade receivables in line with the company's sales growth?
- Will the investment in non-current assets produce the estimated number of units and revenue?
- Will the company be able to service its debt with the projected sales growth?
- Are the company expenses incurred in cost of sales, distribution, and administration reasonable and in line with industry standards?

Financing requirements Who will provide the money (shareholders and lenders) to finance a business and in what form (e.g., mortgage, working capital loan).

The right side of Figure 8.1 (equity and debt) shows the **financing requirements**, that is, the amount of cash needed, and where it will come from to finance the $1.0 million expansion. This is the subject of the chapter. The $1.0 million financial needs identified in the figure will be financed in the following way:

a. Total internal sources			$200,000
b. External sources			
Equity			
Shareholders	200,000		
Risk capital	50,000	$250,000	
Long-term borrowings			
Conventional	400,000		
Risk capital	25,000	425,000	
Short-term borrowings			
Conventional	100,000		
Risk capital	25,000	125,000	
Total external sources			800,000
Total financing requirements			$1,000,000

As indicated above, a business can obtain money from a wide range of sources and in different forms. *Sources* are institutions that provide funds and include commercial banks, investment bankers, equipment vendors, government agencies, private venture capital investors, suppliers, trust companies, life insurance companies, mortgage companies, individuals (angels), institutional investors, and shareholders. *Forms* are the financing instruments used to buy assets or to finance the growth of a business. They include share capital (common and preferred), risk capital, mortgages, bonds, lease financing, short-term loans (secured or unsecured), term or installment loans, and revolving loans.

This chapter covers seven topics falling under two major themes. The first theme deals with the process of raising funds from investors. As shown in Figure 8.2, there are 10 fundamental steps to follow if a borrower is contemplating raising money from investors (shareholders or lenders). Of course, it is not always necessary to follow "all" these steps when approaching investors to raise a small amount of money to finance an increase in a working capital loan or to obtain a mortgage on a building. However, when a borrower prepares a business plan for the purpose of raising funds to finance a new venture or obtaining substantial sums of money to expand or modernize, a business should go through these steps in order to increase its chances of obtaining the funds. The second theme addresses forms and sources of financing. Table 8.1 shows different forms and sources of external financing broken down into four categories—equity, long-term, intermediate, and short-term financing—all of which will be covered in some detail in this chapter. It explores typical financing issues that businesses must often take into consideration.

The chapter's second theme explores seven topics. The first topic explains that financing requirements can be obtained from two broad sources: internal operations and external financing. The second topic looks at different types of risk-related financing options, namely business risk, financial risk, and instrument risk. The third topic explores various strategies that can be adopted before approaching lenders. It has to do with the matching principle, the criteria used by investors to evaluate borrowers, and how a company can become creditworthy. The fourth topic explains equity financing, in particular, shareholders, risk capital investors, and government institutions. The fifth topic lists the major sources and forms of intermediate and long-term financing such as long-term loans, conditional sales contracts, bonds, mortgages, and subordinated debt. The sixth topic analyzes the various forms and sources of short-term financing, namely, suppliers, chartered banks, confirming institutions, and factoring companies. The last topic analyzes the advantages of leasing versus owning, pinpoints the factors that influence lease-or-buy decisions, and explains how to calculate the economics of a lease-versus-buy option.

Figure 8.2 Approaching Investors—A 10-Step Process

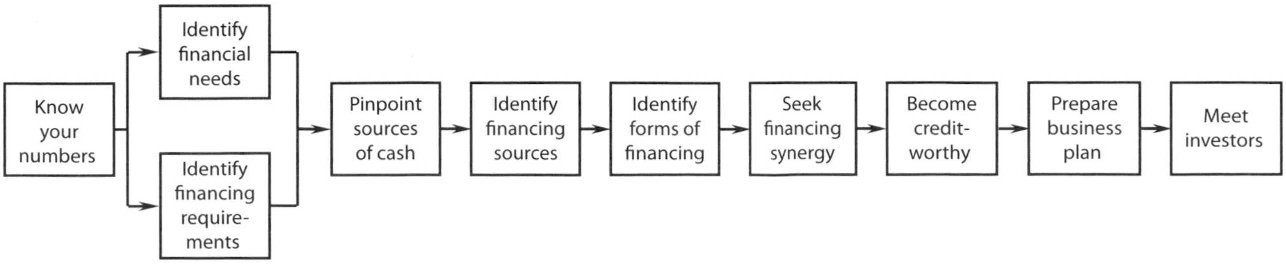

Table 8.1 Forms and Sources of Financing

Reasons for Financing	Forms	Sources
1.	**Equity financing**	
Intangible assets: R & D, promotional programs	Retained earnings	Reinvested earnings
	Share capital (common and preferred)	Ownership investment
	Grants and contributions	Institutional investors Government-backed corporations Private investors
2.	**Long-term debt financing**	
Capital assets: Property, plant, and equipment	Leases (services, financial, sale, and leaseback)	Leasing companies
	Bonds	Investment dealers
	Mortgages (secured and unsecured)	Pension, insurance and trust companies, chartered banks
	Subordinated debts	Government agencies Venture capitalists/private investors
3.	**Intermediate financing**	
Capital assets: Property, plant, and equipment	Term loans	Chartered banks
	Leases (as above)	Trust companies Finance companies Leasing companies
4.	**Short-term financing**	
Flexible current assets: Inventories	Inventory financing (general lien, floor planning, warehouse financing)	Confirming institutions
	Consignment	Suppliers
Trade receivables	Trade receivables financing	Factoring companies
Cash	Line of credit Seasonal loan Revolving credit Notes payable Single loan	Chartered banks
	Trade credit	Suppliers
Durable current assets: Inventories and trade receivables	Working capital loans	Chartered banks

Self-Test Exercise No. 8.1

Financial Needs and Financing Requirements

In one of their stores, Len and Joan are looking at investing some cash and are considering obtaining the financing from different sources. With the following information, make a list of Len and Joan's financial needs and financing requirements.

Short-term borrowings	$4,000	Inventories	$8,000
Trade receivables	4,000	Computers	4,000
Furniture	6,000	Depreciation	3,000
Suppliers	2,000	Chartered bank	4,000
Profit for the year	6,000	Len and Joan	3,000

Internal versus External Financing

1 Learning Objective

Differentiate between internal financing and external financing.

Internal sources
Funds generated by a business (e.g., profit for the year, depreciation/amortization).

External sources
Funds provided by investors (shareholders and lenders).

As explained in Chapter 3, businesses can obtain financing from two principal sources: internal and external. **Internal sources** are funds generated by the business itself. For example, Table 3.9 on page 129 shows the principal sources of internal financing under the heading "Operating activities," which includes profit for the year and depreciation/amortization. A decrease in working capital accounts is also a source of internal financing. **External sources** comprise funds obtained from investors. Under the heading "Financing activities" in Table 3.9, external activities show that the two principal sources of external financing are shareholders (equity) and lenders (loans). As indicated earlier in this chapter, equity financing can be obtained from conventional and risk capital investors. Similarly, debt financing can also be obtained from conventional lenders (e.g., banks, suppliers, insurance companies) and risk capital investors (e.g., factoring companies, confirming institutions). This chapter deals primarily with external financing. First, though, let's examine how a business can generate its own cash.

Profit for the year and depreciation/amortization are the main sources of internal cash flows. To calculate the amount of cash generated by a business, we can refer to the statement of income and the statement of changes in equity (retained earnings section). By examining Eastman Technologies Inc.'s statement of cash flows, shown in Table 3.9, we obtain the following:

Profit for the year	$97,500
Depreciation/amortization	40,000
Total cash generated by the business	137,500
Dividends paid to shareholders	(47,500)
Cash retained in the business	$90,000

In this case, after paying income taxes and dividends, an amount of $90,000 will be reinvested into the business. These funds can be used to purchase non-current assets, help finance working capital accounts, or reduce the principal on the debt.

Working capital is also an important source of financing. Working capital accounts, such as inventories and trade receivables, usually increase when a business grows. However, if a business is in financial difficulty, it can reduce the level of its net working capital and could generate extra funds. During the early 1980s, when interest rates reached unprecedented heights, many businesses had to cut back on their inventories and trade receivables.

Let's examine how a business can generate funds from its inventories and trade receivables accounts. To illustrate the calculation, let's refer to Eastman Technologies Inc.'s statement of income and SFP, shown in Tables 2.2 and 2.4 on pages 63 and 72, respectively.

In 2009, Eastman Technologies Inc. has $218,000 in inventories with an inventory turnover of 8.7 ($1,900,000 ÷ $218,000) times. If management sets an inventory target of 10 times, it can achieve this by introducing more efficient purchasing practices and better inventory management control systems. The 10-time ratio reduces inventories to $190,000 ($1,900,000 ÷ 10), thus generating an additional one-time cash inflow amount of $18,000.

Also, the SFP shows trade receivables in the amount of $300,000 with an average collection period of 44 days. If management wants to reduce this figure to 30 days, it will have to squeeze more funds from this account without placing sales performance in jeopardy; therefore, management may implement a more aggressive credit policy. With an average daily sales performance of $6,849 ($2,500,000 ÷ 365) and a collection period target of 30 days, trade receivables could be reduced to $205,470 ($6,849 × 30) from $300,000. This would produce an additional one-time inflow of cash in the amount of $94,530.

Self-Test Exercise No. 8.2

Raising Cash from Working Capital Accounts

How much additional cash could Len and Joan obtain from their working capital accounts by the end of 2010 if they are to improve the average collection period by 2 days and the inventory turnover by 0.5 times? In 2010, CompuTech's inventories account was $65,000; its trade receivables account was $45,000. The company's 2010 revenue is estimated at $420,000; its cost of sales is estimated at $209,000.

2 Learning Objective

Explain different types of risk-related financing options (ownership versus debt).

Risk-Related Financing Options

Once the company's financial needs have been identified, capital assets ($600,000), marketing costs ($100,000), research and development ($100,000), and working capital ($200,000), in addition to the financing requirements also identified earlier, the next step is to pinpoint the instruments (or forms) that could be used to finance the expansion program. To do so, the following questions will have to be considered:

1. What will be required to finance the capital assets, temporary working capital, and permanent working capital (financial needs)?
2. What are the financing options (or instruments) available to meet our needs? Financing instruments include conventional financing instruments and risk-capital financing instruments.

When selecting a specific financing source, it is important to understand that each source bears different costs. Risk is the key to determining how much it costs to finance a business, and there is a direct relationship between risk and return. Risk (the variability of returns, or the chance of losing on the investment) and return (what investors expect to earn) go hand in hand. As the risk of a project or business venture increases, the return (or cost of capital) that investors expect to earn on their investment to compensate for the risk will also increase.

Before examining the various forms and sources of financing, let's define the three different types of risks that businesses have to cope with. They are business risk, financial risk, and instrument risk.

Business risk
The uncertainty inherent in projecting the level of revenue and EBIT.

Business risk is intrinsic in a firm's operations. It has to do with the uncertainty inherent in projecting the future revenue and earnings before interest and taxes (EBIT). The industry and economic environment in which a firm operates impose business risk. A high-tech firm, for example, faces a great deal more business risk than a food processor business. Expected future demand and product life cycle for food are less difficult to predict than the future demand for most high-technology products. General economic cycles and changing industry conditions cause business variations. This is the single most important determinant that will influence a firm's capital structure (debt versus equity).

Financial risk
The way that a business is financed (debt versus share capital).

Financial risk has to do with financial leverage, that is, a firm's capital structure. In general, the more debt a firm employs, the greater the risk of insolvency and hence the riskier it is to finance the business. Essentially, financial risk is an additional burden of risk placed on common shareholders as a result of management's decision to use more debt. To be sure, highly leveraged firms may not have the financial strength to ride out a prolonged sales decline or an economic slowdown. The bottom line is this: Financial risk can magnify business risk because there is a greater reliance on fixed costs (finance costs) or the amount of cash required to pay for the loans.

Instrument risk
The quality of security available to satisfy investors.

Instrument risk is the quality of the security available to satisfy investors (e.g., secured versus unsecured loans). For example, a first mortgage loan is less risky (because of the guarantees) than a second mortgage. Also, a conditional sales contract is less risky than financing trade receivables through factoring.

It is also important for management to take into account the interplay between business risk and financial risk and to maintain an appropriate balance between the two. For instance, a firm facing a relatively low level of business risk can be much

Figure 8.3 **Risk-Related Financing Options (Risk versus Return)**

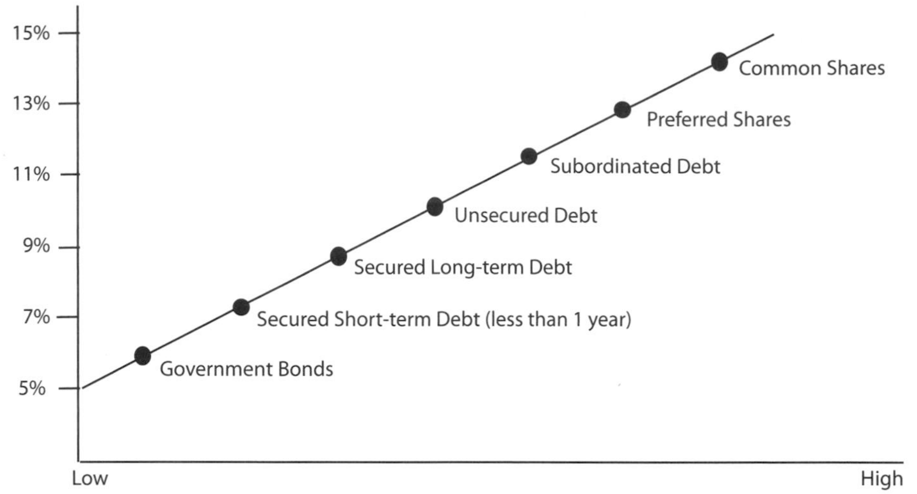

more aggressive in using debt financing than a business operating at a relatively high level of business risk.

Also, when risks are high, the financing instruments (common shares versus risk capital) must offer a corresponding high rate of return to attract investors. Figure 8.3 shows the risk curve, which is the relationship between risk and return for different financing instruments. As shown in Figure 8.3, financing instruments, based on their specific characteristics (security, claim on cash flow, liquidity/marketability, and pricing), can be placed at different points on the risk curve.

Although equity appears to command a high return, for a growing business, it is often the most stable and appropriate source of capital. Conventional financing, which is generally provided by commercial banks, credit unions, and trust companies, tends to accept a lower return as the risk related to the investment is low because of the collateral used to guarantee these loans. In contrast, high-risk investors tend to invest in projects with higher levels of risk and, for this reason, will demand a higher rate of return.

Useful Strategies When Approaching Lenders

3 Learning Objective

Explain useful strategies when approaching lenders.

Before looking at the various forms and sources of short-term financing, let's examine strategies that can be useful when approaching lenders. They are the matching principle, criteria used by investors to rate borrowers, and how a business can make itself creditworthy.

THE MATCHING PRINCIPLE

The basic idea of the matching principle is to match the maturity of the financial needs to the period of time the funds are required (financing requirements). For example, a company would use a line of credit to finance its working capital requirements and a mortgage to finance the purchase of capital assets. This principle takes into consideration two factors: cost and risk.

As shown in Figure 8.4, funds are needed to finance capital assets, durable (permanent or fixed) current assets, and flexible (or variable) current assets. The matching principle stipulates that capital assets and current assets should be financed by the appropriate sources of financing: capital assets by long-term borrowings, and current assets by short-term credit. As shown in Figure 8.4, the flexible component of the current assets fluctuates depending on the financial needs of a business. Durable

Figure 8.4 Strategies for Financing Working Capital

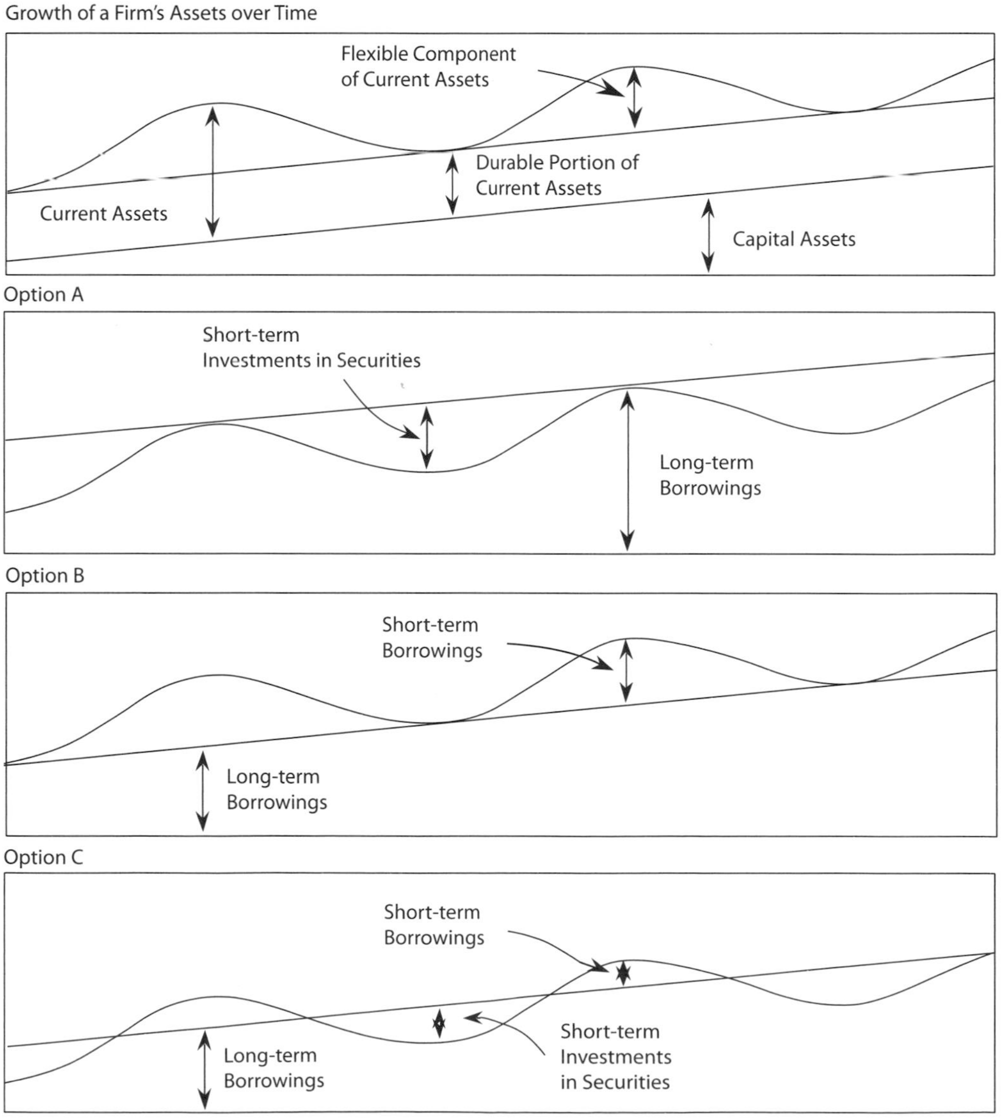

current assets are necessary in order to operate a business, and flexible current assets fluctuate with changing business conditions.

Three basic strategies can be used to finance current asset (or working capital) accounts. In the first strategy (option A), all current assets are financed by long-term borrowings; this is considered the most conservative strategy but the most costly. It is not risky because the business always has the required debt to meet its current needs. However, it is costly because if there is excess cash, it is invested in short-term securities. The return earned from the short-term investments (say, 3%) is far less than the cost of a loan (say, 6%).

In the second strategy (option B), all current assets are financed by short-term borrowings. This option is risky because interest rates may rise when it is time to renew a loan, and the lender may refuse to renew the loan if there is a tight money supply.

The third strategy (option C) is a compromise between the first option (conservative and more costly) and the second (risky and less expensive). In this option, the business uses a small amount of short-term credit to meet peak seasonal working capital requirements. However, during the off-season, excess cash or liquidity is stored in marketable securities. The crests above the line represent short-term borrowings; the troughs below the line represent holdings in short-term securities.

CRITERIA USED BY INVESTORS TO RATE BORROWERS

Investors require certain information before investing funds in a business. Some of the information will be provided by the business, and the investors will obtain the rest through their own files and networking. Investors look at potential borrowers using different criteria commonly referred to as the **C's of credit**: character, collateral, capacity, capital, circumstances (or conditions), and coverage.

C's of credit
Factors that investors look at to gauge the creditworthiness of a business: character, collateral, capacity, capital, circumstances, and coverage.

Character means two things to an investor (lender or shareholder). First, it means that the borrower should have the required skills and abilities to manage the business professionally and should be serious, dependable, and accountable. Second, investors look for persons who are true to their word, those who appear to feel morally obligated to pay their debt, dividends, or principal according to their promise. What investors are really looking for is reputation and honesty. Credit is derived from the Latin word *credere,* meaning "to believe" or "to trust," and it implies a promise to pay. There is no question that investors are concerned with borrowers' integrity and willingness to meet their financial commitments.

Collateral is the pledge offered by a business (particularly to lenders) in exchange for a loan. It is like a form of insurance on physical assets, which will be rightly owned by the lender if a business stops operating or is liquidated. This is vital to lenders because the absence of such security increases their risk. Businesses that have a high credit rating may obtain a loan on an unsecured basis, that is, on faith and trust; others, however, are obliged to back their borrowings with collateral.

Capacity means two things to investors. First, it means the ability of a business to generate enough cash to meet its obligations—repayment of the principal, finance costs, and dividends. A close examination of a business's cash flow forecast or cash budget can indicate a business's capacity to meet its financial commitments. Second, it means how capable the management team is in managing a new project or an expanded operation—essentially, managerial skills (planning, organizing, leadership, and controlling) and technical ability in the areas of production, marketing, manufacturing, distribution, finance, and competence in making a business expansion or a new operation a real success.

Capital refers to a business's financial structure—the mix between equity and the funds provided by lenders. The more money that shareholders have invested in their business, the more confidence the lenders will have about providing a loan.

Circumstances, or *conditions*, refer to the environment governing a business's performance, specifically the status of the industry in terms of trends in demand, prices, competition, profitability, and government regulations.

Coverage refers primarily to insurance coverage. Most businesses are subject to losses arising from different sources: death of a principal owner or an important partner; damage to the business property resulting from fire, explosion, or any violent cause; embezzlement, theft, or any dishonest acts committed by a shareholder, officer, or employee; and public liability suits. Investors feel less vulnerable when businesses to which they have lent money are adequately covered by insurance.

The information regarding the C's of credit is usually required by investors. If appropriate information is not provided, investors will seek it elsewhere, such as from business contacts, other investors, suppliers, or credit institutions. It is therefore a good strategy to know, before meeting investors, what they are looking for.

MAKING A COMPANY CREDITWORTHY

Making a company creditworthy is the first step for obtaining funds quickly and at a more attractive rate. The reasons for investors to turn down loans or share capital are numerous, ranging from objective to subjective.

Potential borrowers should analyze their business situation from an investor's perspective when considering the raising of funds. This is important as fundraisers should anticipate investors' questions and give careful consideration to the way they should be answered. Although specific and detailed questions vary according to a particular situation, here is a broad range of reasons investors tend to reject investment proposals or loan applications.

Factors related to creditworthiness:

- Poor earnings record
- Questionable management ability
- Collateral of insufficient quality or quantity
- Slow and past due in trade or loan payments
- Poor accounting system
- New firm with no established earnings record
- Poor moral risk (character)

Factors related to a bank's overall policies:

- Not enough equity
- Requested maturity of the loan too long
- Applicant has no established deposit relationship with the lender
- Type of loan not handled by the lender
- Line of business not handled by the lender
- Loan portfolio for the type of loan already full

The rest of this chapter deals with external forms and sources of financing. The features, including the advantages and disadvantages of each source of financing, will be examined for different types of forms and sources of equity, long-term, intermediate, and short-term financing.

Equity Financing

4 Learning Objective

Comment on the different categories of equity financing.

Equity is the interest an owner holds in a business. If a business is privately owned, the owners can also obtain funds from investors that specialize in small and medium-sized business loans and mortgages. In this case, owners of the privately owned business will prepare a business plan and will go directly to specific individuals and ask them to become shareholders of the business.

Prospectus
A document disclosing the details of a security and the underlying business to prospective investors.

For publicly owned businesses, the process is more complicated. The owners have to prepare a **prospectus**, which is a document disclosing the details of a security and the underlying business to prospective investors, and approach an investment dealer in order to raise funds from the general public through a public issue. A public issue exists when funds are raised from the general public. The investment dealer buys the securities from the firm and sells them to the general public.

Let's turn now to the role of the investment dealer and the cost of raising funds from the general public. As mentioned earlier, long-term financing can be obtained from two distinct sources: shareholders, when funds are raised by issuing shares, and lenders, when money is provided in the form of a loan, such as bonds or mortgages. Investment dealers (or investment bankers) facilitate the financing of businesses by buying (wholesale) securities issues of bonds or shares and reselling them (retail) to their clients. Investment dealers borrow the money they need to finance the issue. Usually, they get it from banks on a very short-term basis and repay their lenders when the issue sells out. This process may take a week or two, or it may all be completed in one day.

The cost of public issues of either bonds or shares is high because there are many legal details that must be taken care of. The process is lengthy, requiring approval by at least one provincial securities commission, and sometimes by several, depending on where the bonds or shares are issued. Thus, this source of funds can be used only at infrequent intervals and for large amounts of money. New firms are usually either too small to use investment dealers or find their services (which may cost as much as 10% to 25% of the funds raised) too expensive. Table 8.2 summarizes the steps involved in making a public issue.

Table 8.2	Steps Involved in Making a Public Issue
Step 1:	The firm decides to list (or not to list) its issue on an exchange (e.g., Toronto Stock Exchange).
Step 2:	The firm selects one or more investment dealers who will be responsible for buying and selling the issue, that is, the underwriter(s).
Step 3:	A preliminary conference takes place between the issuing company and the underwriter(s) to discuss the amount of capital to be raised, the type of security to be issued, and the general terms of the issue.
Step 4:	A preliminary prospectus is prepared. The preliminary prospectus discloses important aspects of the issue and forms the basis of the agreement among all parties.
Step 5:	A public accounting firm performs an audit of the company's financial situation, and management prepares the required financial statements to be included in the preliminary prospectus.
Step 6:	After it is signed, the preliminary prospectus is filed with the appropriate provincial securities commission. This is followed by a waiting period (usually around 15 business days), which gives the staff of the securities commission time to go over the prospectus to evaluate the accuracy of the data and content, and to ensure that there are no deficiencies or misrepresentations in the document.
Step 7:	After clearance is given by the securities commission, the final prospectus is prepared and final clearance is given. At this point, the underwriting agreement is signed between the issuing company and the underwriter. Here, an agreement is reached about the date of the issue, the actual price that the underwriter is prepared to pay, and his or her commission.

Let's now turn to the major sources of equity funds: shareholders, risk capital investors, and government institutions.

SHAREHOLDERS

Shareholders
The owners of a business (common and preferred shareholders).

Funds can be provided by **shareholders** in the form of common shares and preferred shares. The owners (shareholders) of a business provide common share financing. The collective and specific rights of the shareholders related to common shares are listed in Table 8.3.

To a company, the most attractive feature of issuing common shares is that they do not entail fixed charges. Unlike a mortgage payment, dividends are paid when earnings are generated. Common shares do not have fixed maturity dates and can be sold more easily than debt.

Preferred share financing has some characteristics of both common share and debt financing. The preferred share appears in the equity section of the SFP. Although this type of financing is considered equity, preferred shareholders do not have the same rights as common shareholders.

Table 8.4 lists the advantages and disadvantages of equity financing.

Table 8.3 Shareholders' Collective and Specific Rights

Collective Rights
- Amend articles of incorporation.
- Adopt and amend bylaws.
- Elect the directors of the corporation.
- Authorize the sale of capital assets.
- Authorize mergers and amalgamations.
- Change the amount of authorized common and preferred shares.
- Alter the rights and restrictions attached to the common shares.
- Create a right of exchange of other shares into common shares.

Specific Rights
- Vote in the manner prescribed by the corporate charter.
- Sell their share certificates to other interested parties.
- Inspect corporate books (practical limitations).
- Share in residual assets of the corporation (last among the claimants).

Table 8.4 Advantages and Disadvantages of Equity Financing

Advantages	Disadvantages
• Low risk.	• They extend voting rights or control to additional shareholders.
• Dividends are paid when profit is generated.	• Gives the right to more owners to share in profit; thus dilutes the equity interest.
• No restrictive covenants that could cause default.	• Takes time to access.
• Provides stability and permanency.	• Underwriting costs are expensive.
• Common shares do not have fixed maturity dates.	• Dividends are not tax deductible.
• Shares can be sold more easily and investors realize a return on their equity in the marketplace at no cost to the company.	

Risk capital investors Individuals or institutions that provide money to finance a business that entails relatively high risk; these investors seek a high potential return.

RISK CAPITAL INVESTORS

Risk capital investors provide equity financing to small or untried enterprises, thereby absorbing much of the risk that commercial lenders are unwilling to shoulder. Commercial lenders are rarely interested in inventions requiring further research, development, and engineering. They have certain preferences about the companies they want to back. These preferences are usually based on the type, history, and status of the company, and the amount of financing needed.

On the other hand, risk capital investors prefer dealing with companies whose products have potential to succeed in the marketplace or are already selling well, but that lack the capital to exploit their markets. Risk capital investors generally provide equity financing or both equity and long-term debt financing (e.g., subordinated debt).

Risk capital investments are unique in the following ways:

- They apply mostly to fast-growth businesses.
- Usually, several years are required before the risk capital investors can liquidate their investment or make an exit.
- During the early years there is usually no organized secondary market.
- The new firm faces a high risk of failure.
- Several infusions of capital are frequently necessary before the new enterprise becomes a "going concern."

Risk capital investments can be categorized as embryonic, start-up, development, expansion, turnaround, or buyout. *Embryonic investments* are made in firms intending to develop a new product or process up to the point where it is possible to make a prototype. *Start-up investments* are made in new firms just getting started with a new product or service in an established market. *Development investments* are made in small firms that are already in production and just about to realize profits but do not have sufficient cash flow to continue operations. *Expansion investments* are made in smaller firms in need of additional productive capacity, but without sufficient funds of their own. *Turnaround investments* are made in firms that are currently experiencing financial difficulties, but that have great potential for profitability with more capital and better management. *Buyout investments* are made in firms that are already established and have a proven and good track record, but whose owners are seeking to sell out and retire. Usually some or all of the current employees are the ones who want to buy the firm but do not have the funds to do so.

Here is a profile of the general types of risk capital investors.

Angel investors are professional investors, retired executives with business experience and money to invest, or high-net-worth individuals simply looking for investment opportunities. Angels will usually invest between $25,000 and $300,000 in a venture. Many angels are sophisticated investors and will go through the formal due diligence review.

Venture capital
Risk capital supplied to small companies by wealthy individuals (angels), partnerships, or corporations, usually in return for an equity position in the firm.

Private investors and **venture capital** firms are individuals or groups of professionals with a vast amount of experience, contacts, and business skills that can help a business become more profitable. The size of their investment can range from $25,000 to $5 million. Investors in this category have particular preferences, strategies, and investment criteria. While some private firms will be more interested in investing in the development stage, many will be interested in companies involved in the expansion, acquisition, and management/leveraged buyout stages. These investors include labour-sponsored venture funds such as Working Ventures Canadian Fund, Fonds de Solidarité, and Canadian Medical Discoveries Fund.

Institutional investors provide equity and subordinated risk capital investment to small- and medium-sized businesses. They include subsidiaries of commercial banks, investment banks, certain life insurance companies, and pension funds. These companies fund investments that are less than $1 million, as well as larger ones. Canada has a wide range of such organizations including Bank of Montreal Capital, Royal Bank Capital Corporation, CIBC Wood Gundy Capital, Penfund Partners, Investissement Desjardins, Roynat, Ontario Teachers' Pension Fund, and TD Capital.

In the News 8.1 shows how entrepreneurs should prepare themselves when meeting angel investors for the purpose of raising seed start-up capital funds.

In The News [8.1]

What Entrepreneurs Should Do When Meeting Angel Investors

Sometimes, securing funds from traditional investors is close to impossible, particularly if you are in a start-up situation and want to get your business off the ground quickly. So, the most logical thing to do is approach a venture capitalist, and more precisely, an angel investor, one who can offer expertise, experience, and contacts in addition to seed money.

There are an estimated 260,500 active angels in the United States. It is apparently the largest source of seed money available for ready-to-go entrepreneurs. The only problem is to know just how to approach them. If an entrepreneur gets all hyped-up about his product or service, an angel can easily lose interest during the first meeting. Also, if the entrepreneur is vague when replying to a question, that alone could be a turn-off. However, seed money received from angel investors helped American icons such as Starbucks, FedEx, Amazon, and Google. Several recent studies on obtaining financing from angels suggest that entrepreneurs, when approaching an angel, should make sure that (1) he has a product that is just about ready for market, (2) he has injected his own money into the business, (3) his business plan is crisp and clear, (4) he approaches angels that understand his business, and (5) he contacts every available angel, and if an angel turns him down, to ask for names of other angels that might say yes.

Source: Adapted from Brent Bowers, "In pitching to angel investors, preparation tops zeal," *The New York Times*, June 10, 2009. Found at http://www.nytimes.com/2009/06/11/business/smallbusiness/11hunt.html?_r=1#. For more information about angel investors and what information they expect from entrepreneurs, go to http://www.smallbusinessnotes.com/financing/angelinvestors.html.

Government-backed corporations make investments in smaller, regional communities where mainstream investors are less active. For example, the Atlantic Canada Opportunities Agency (ACOA) provides support to businesses located in the Atlantic provinces. The Business Development Bank of Canada (BDC) is unique in its status because it offers a one-stop shopping service. Its mission is to help create commercially viable business projects, together with counselling, training, and mentoring assistance. It provides the following:

- Venture loans (between $100,000 and $1 million) for expansion and market development projects.
- Working capital for growth funding (up to $100,000).

- Patient capital, directed at knowledge-based businesses in the early stages of development; offered on a long-term basis (up to $25,000).
- Micro-business programs for training and counselling to very small companies, along with up to $25,000 for new businesses and up to $50,000 for existing businesses.

Corporate strategic investors differ from traditional venture capital companies in that their motivation extends beyond financial reasons. Their business agreements are referred to as strategic alliances or corporate partnerships. A strategic investor may have a broad range of objectives that include enhancing innovation, gaining exposure to new markets and technologies, identifying and accessing acquisition candidates, ensuring sources of supply, assisting a client, initiating new ventures internally, and spinning off businesses when there are potentially profitable operations that are not appropriate for the original firm.

GOVERNMENT INSTITUTIONS

Government financing Funds obtained (directly or indirectly) from government institutions to finance a business.

Government financing is a direct or indirect form of financial assistance to businesses offered by a municipal, provincial, or federal agency to help businesses carry out capital expenditure projects or expansion of their activities that, without such assistance, would be delayed or even abandoned completely. Government financing (or programs) can be grouped into two broad categories: allowances for income tax purposes and direct and indirect grants. Federal financing aid can come from non-refundable grants, refundable grants, conditionally refundable grants, equity participation, direct loans, guarantee of loans, remission of tariff, export financing, cost sharing, fees for counselling purposes, training grants, and small business loans. Provincial financing aid can come from forgivable loans, direct loans (mortgage, small business loans), working capital loans, training grants, guarantee of loans, equity participation, inventory financing, leasebacks, and venture capital. Municipal financing aid can come through free land, deferred property taxes, and industrial sites (e.g., infrastructure assistance).

The more important governmental financial institutions include the Export Development Corporation (EDC), Farm Credit Canada (FCC), the Business Development Bank of Canada (BDC), and provincial venture capital organizations.

Export Development Corporation. The EDC is a Crown corporation that provides a wide variety of financial services, including export insurance, bonds, loans, and lines of credit to both Canadian exporters and foreign buyers. Canadian exporters can insure their export sales against non-payment by foreign buyers for up to 90% of the value of the shipments. This insurance can cover commercial and/or political risks of insolvency, default, repudiation by the buyer, cancellation of import licences, blockage of funds, and war. Virtually any export transaction can be insured by EDC, which provides export financing at either fixed or floating rates of interest to foreign buyers of Canadian goods. The money is paid in Canada directly to the exporting company, so the export sale is a cash sale for the Canadian firm. EDC can operate either on its own account or for the government, in case the Canadian government would like to assist exports in ways that may fall outside the normal purview of the more commercial transactions normally made by EDC.

Farm Credit Canada. FCC is a Crown corporation created in 1959 to provide domestic financial services to enable individual Canadian farmers to establish, develop, and/or maintain viable farm enterprises. The corporation also makes farm loans to groups or syndicates of farmers organized to share the use of farm machinery and specialized farm buildings and their equipment. Loans made by FCC are usually made at fixed rates of interest based on the combined overall cost of funds to FCC. These loans can be for terms of 5 to 15 years with amortization as long as 30 years.

An important innovation is the shared-risk mortgage, which was introduced in the spring of 1985. This type of loan has an interest rate that is adjusted each year. There is equal sharing between the FCC and the farmer in interest rate increases and decreases, up to the maximum allowable fluctuation of 2.5%. The normal term of the shared-risk mortgage is six years, and the loan limit is $350,000 for individuals or $600,000 for partnerships.

Another innovation is the Commodity-Based Loan Program, which began in 1986. Payments are calculated by linking the loan principal amount to a price index of one or two of the major commodities produced on the farm. If prices go up by 5%, for example, then both the principal of the loan and the periodic payments would also increase by 5%. Financial advisory services are also offered to new or existing borrowers on request.

The Business Development Bank of Canada. The BDC is a Crown corporation established in 1975 (under the name Federal Business Development Bank) to promote and assist the establishment and development of small and medium-sized Canadian businesses. It provides three types of services: financial (loans and loan guarantees), venture capital, and management (counselling, training, information, and financial planning). The BDC concentrates on helping new businesses that cannot obtain funds from other sources. It is, therefore, a supplemental or last resort lender. It has tended to concentrate most of its efforts on helping companies in manufacturing, wholesale and retail trade, and tourism.

The BDC provides loans, loan guarantees, equity financing, or any combination thereof in whatever way is best suited to the needs of the firm. The BDC provides funds for start-ups, modernization, expansion, change of ownership, or other business purposes to firms unable to obtain financing from other sources on reasonable terms and conditions. Term loans can be used to finance capital assets such as buildings, land, machinery, or equipment, with the assets used as collateral. In some cases term loans can also be made to finance working capital needs.

Provincial venture capital organizations. Most provinces have established legislation allowing private investors to set up small business development companies that act as suppliers of venture capital. In some provinces, such as Manitoba, the provincial government matches 35% of the capital raised by private investors. In Ontario, the provincial government provides a tax-free cash grant of 30% of the investor's contribution, thus reducing the risk for individual investors. Some provinces have direct financing programs for small businesses that meet certain qualifications. These programs change frequently.

The Small Business Loans Act. The *Small Business Loans Act (SBLA)* is a federal law intended to help new and existing small businesses obtain financing for capital asset needs from the chartered banks and other designated lenders (trust companies, credit unions, and caisses populaires) according to normal commercial procedures. The federal government guarantees the loans. The maximum amount is $100,000, and the maximum term is 10 years. The interest rate is usually prime plus and fluctuates as the prime rate changes. SBLA loans are restricted to firms whose gross revenues do not exceed $2 million annually.

Sources and Forms of Intermediate and Long-Term Debt Financing

5 Learning Objective

Discuss the sources and forms of intermediate and long-term debt financing.

At the risk of oversimplification, we will differentiate intermediate financing from long-term debt financing by the length of time funds are borrowed. Intermediate financing refers to a two- to five-year loan, while long-term financing refers to five years or longer. The next several sections deal with loans that are provided to businesses for a long term in order to finance the purchase of capital assets.

CONVENTIONAL INTERMEDIATE AND LONG-TERM FINANCING

Long-term loan
Loan to finance capital assets for a long period of time (over five years).

Term loan
Loan made to buy capital assets.

Intermediate and **long-term loans** usually finance capital (or non-current) assets. These may be straightforward term loans, usually secured by the physical asset itself. Banks, life insurance companies, pension funds, and federal and provincial government agencies provide longer-term financing on capital assets.

Term loans are a principal form of medium-term financing used for the purchase of capital assets (usually three to seven years). However, in certain circumstances, the maturity may be as long as 15 years. A term loan involves an agreement whereby the borrower agrees to make a series of interest and principal payments on specific amounts and dates to a lender. This differs from a bank line of credit, whereby repayment is at any time (demand) or at a specified time in one lump sum. The key characteristics of a term loan are the following:

- Terms of the loan are tailored to suit the needs of the borrower.
- Security is usually in the form of a chattel mortgage on equipment or machinery.
- In addition to collateral, the lender may place specific restrictions on the operations of the business (e.g., no additional borrowings and no increase in salaries to the officers of the company without prior approval of the lender).
- The loan is retired by systematic repayments over the life of the loan.

Let's take an example of a company that wants to borrow $200,000 at 8% over a 10-year period. In this case, the company would have to pay $29,806 each year in order to amortize the loan. Finding the annual loan repayment is relatively simple. All that is required is to divide $200,000 by the interest factor, 6.7101 found in Table D (Present Value Interest Factor of an Annuity) on page A-11 in Appendix B at the end of this book.[1] The factor is found under column 8% and year 10.

Self-Test Exercise No. 8.3

Annual Loan Payments

a) If the Millers borrow $100,000 for 5 years at 9%, what would be their annual loan payment?

b) If they borrowed $500,000 for 15 years at 14%, what would be their annual loan payment?

Conditional sales contract
Agreement made between a buyer and a seller regarding the purchase of an asset (e.g., truck).

A **conditional sales contract** is a written agreement between a buyer and a seller regarding the purchase of production equipment or other capital assets on a time-payment basis. Under this arrangement, the seller of the capital asset accepts a partial payment of the value of the asset as a down payment, which is usually a minimum of one-third; the rest is paid on a monthly installment basis. Legal ownership of the property is retained by the seller until the buyer has made all the required payments according to the term of the agreement, which usually runs from 12 to 36 months.

Table 8.5 lists the advantages and disadvantages of terms loans and conditional sales contracts.

Table 8.5 Advantages and Disadvantages of Term Loans and Conditional Sales Contracts

Advantages	Disadvantages
• Longer repayment terms.	• Ties up assets.
• Easy access.	• Increases financial risk given the cash payments of interest and principal.
• Flexibility.	• Commits the business because it is subject to penalties.
• Tax deductibility of finance costs.	• Often includes restrictive covenants.
• Suitable for long-term needs, e.g., permanent current assets and capital assets.	• Business may not have suitable security to offer because the business/financial risk may be too high.
• Low cost relative to other long-term sources of financing.	
• Commits the lender for a long term.	
• Does not dilute equity.	

1. Learning how to use interest tables will be covered in Chapter 10.

Bond
Long-term loan (10 to 30 years) that could be secured or unsecured.

Bonds are long-term contracts, typically for 10 to 30 years, under which a borrowing firm agrees to make payments of interest and principal, usually semi-annually, to the holder of the bond contract. The investor buys an annuity with regular payments until the maturity date, when the principal amount is repaid. An indenture is a legal document that spells out the rights of both the bondholders and the issuing firm. A trustee, usually a trust company, represents the bondholders and ensures that the firm lives up to its obligations. The firm pays the total interest payment to the trustee as scheduled, and the trustee then pays the bondholders, who are required to, when specified, clip coupons off the bond and cash them like cheques.

Bonds may be secured or unsecured. *Secured bonds* are essentially long-term promissory notes. Holders of secured bonds have prior claims over the assets and earnings (similar to first, second, and third mortgages). *Unsecured bonds* are called debentures. Only the earning power of the firm backs them up. Bonds may also be converted into shares of the issuing company, or redeemable before the stated maturity date, at the request of either the bondholder or the firm. Many variations on this theme are possible. The firm does not know who buys the bonds. Thus the issuance of bonds is a very impersonal and inflexible financing method, not suitable for all firms. These unsecured bondholders are similar to general creditors; they have a claim on the residual value of all assets that are left unencumbered.

Mortgage
Loan obtained against which specific real property is used as collateral (e.g., a building).

Mortgages are a pledge of a specific real estate property, such as land or buildings. Mortgages are long-term financing (e.g., 25 years). The amount of the mortgage is calculated based on the market value of the property. For example, 75% of the market value might be a common assessment, but a company can find companies that will finance up to 90% of the value of an asset. These investors frequently prefer long maturity periods. The repayment schedule is usually based on equal blended payments of interest and principal. The interest rate is fixed for a specific term and depends on the going market rate, the length of the term, and availability. Insurance companies, pension funds, chartered banks, and trust companies provide this type of financing.

Let's examine the concept of an amortized loan. Debt is amortized when the principal is paid off over the life of the loan. It is similar to home mortgages and car loans. Businesses borrow money from different lending institutions, and the loans are amortized over time. An amortized loan is normally structured so that there is a fixed payment, which is usually made on a monthly basis. The payment schedule includes interest and an amount (principal) that reduces the outstanding loan. Each successive payment contains larger proportions of principal repayment and smaller amounts of interest.

Let's examine the makeup of a loan amortization schedule for an amount of $300,000, bearing a 10% interest rate paid over a period of 10 years. The following shows the annual repayment schedule. As shown, over the 10-year period, the company paid a total of $488,230, which comprises $188,230 in interest and $300,000 in principal for the repayment of the original loan. The calculation is as follows. First, the yearly repayment amount of $48,823 is determined by dividing the $300,000 loan by the factor 6.1446 (column 2). This factor, which represents the 10% interest rate for a 10-year period, is found in Table D on page A-11 of Appendix B. The yearly interest payment is then calculated. During the first year, the $30,000 amount shown under column 3 represents the 10% interest multiplied by the $300,000 original loan (column 1). The next step consists of deducting the $30,000 interest payment from the $48,823 payment to determine the amount of principal that will be paid in that particular year. In year 1, the principal repayment is $18,823 (column 4). Finally, the ending balance (column 5) is calculated by deducting the principal repayment from the beginning balance. As shown, the ending balance is $281,177. This figure is used in column 1 for year 2. To calculate the interest and principal payments for the succeeding nine years, the same calculations are done for each year.

Period	Beginning Balance	Payment	Interest @ 10%	Principal Reduction	Ending Balance
	1	2	3	4	5
1	$300,000	$48,823	$30,000	$18,823	$281,177
2	281,177	48,823	28,117	20,706	260,471
3	260,471	48,823	26,047	22,776	237,695
4	237,695	48,823	23,769	25,054	212,641
5	212,641	48,823	21,264	27,559	185,082
6	185,082	48,823	18,508	30,315	154,767
7	154,767	48,823	15,476	33,347	121,420
8	121,420	48,823	12,142	36,681	84,739
9	84,739	48,823	8,474	40,349	44,390
10	44,390	48,823	4,433	44,390	—
Total		$488,230	$188,230	$300,000	

Table 8.6 lists the advantages and disadvantages of mortgage financing.

Table 8.6 Advantages and Disadvantages of Mortgage Financing

Advantages	Disadvantages
• Long-term commitment, without equity dilutions.	• Fairly rigid financing instrument.
• Maturity matches the long life of the assets.	• Increases financial risk due to fixed stream of interest and principal repayments.
• Interest is tax deductible.	• If company fails to make payment, it could be subject to penalties.
• Relatively inexpensive source of long-term financing.	
• Easy to access.	
• Considers the values of the asset more than the value of the business.	
• Standard documentation requirements. Restrictive covenants will be basic.	

Self-Test Exercise No. 8.4

A Repayment Schedule

Calculate the annual repayment, interest, and principal on the $100,000 loan presented in Self-Test Exercise 8.3a on page 386.

RISK CAPITAL LONG-TERM FINANCING

Risk capital investors invest funds in equity shares and equity-related debt in relatively small or untried enterprises, thereby absorbing much of the risk that commercial lenders are unwilling to shoulder. These investors prefer dealing with companies whose products are already selling and are proven successes, but that haven't yet exploited their markets.

Subordinated debt
Loan that is more risky, for which investors charge higher interest rates.

Subordinated debt is risk capital term debt whereby investors accept a higher level of risk compared to conventional sources. These instruments levy a rate of interest that typically ranges from 8% to 12%. However, the overall rate of return to the investor will be higher. Participation features could increase the rate of return and make the expected return range between 15% and 25% per year. This type of financing is good only if a business has exhausted secured financing (e.g., term loans based on capital assets, or short-term financing based on current assets, are not available). Subordinated debt is best suited to rapidly growing companies, expansion programs, management and leverage buyouts, and acquisitions.

Effectively, under such lending arrangements, investors structure the instrument to share in the expected success of the company. Here are a few examples:

- Royalties (percentage of net cash flow generated from operation)
- Participation fees
- Normal cost of common shares
- Warrants or options to purchase shares
- Rights to convert debt into common shares

Subordinated debt repayments can be tailored to the characteristics of individual businesses. Therefore, there is less risk of the borrower defaulting than with conventional long-term sources of financing. Sources of subordinated debt include private-sector venture capital firms, institutional investors, labour-sponsored funds, and government-sponsored corporations.

Table 8.7 lists the advantages and disadvantages of subordinated debt.

The payout of income, control, and risk factors related to common share financing, preferred share financing, and long-term debt are listed in Table 8.8.

In the News 8.2 shows the importance of obtaining debt financing in times when revenues are declining because of a recession.

Table 8.7 Advantages and Disadvantages of Subordinated Debt Financing

Advantages	Disadvantages
• Flexible and can be tailored.	• Takes time to access.
• Less expensive than equity.	• Expensive relative to other sources of short-term and long-term financing.
• Fills a financing gap, and high leverage is available.	• Some cash flow servicing requirements.
• Not as much dilution as straight equity.	• Investors will take a more active role in the company than other lenders.
• Available to a variety of industries.	• Set-up costs are high.
	• Restrictive covenants often apply.
	• Does not provide the stability of equity.

Table 8.8 Determining the Choice of Long-Term Financing

	Payout of Income	Control	Risk
Common shares	Paid after interest and preferred share dividends; by decision of the board of directors, all or a portion of the remaining funds may be retained by the business or distributed in the form of dividends.	Common shareholders have the legal right to make all major decisions and to elect the board of directors. They have the ultimate control of the corporation.	Because they have the last priority of claims in the event of liquidation, they bear the highest risk of any claimants.
Preferred shares	Dividends are paid before common dividends and may be cumulative if they are not paid during a specific year.	Preferred shareholders sometimes have a right to elect some of the directors on the board of directors (minority).	They have priority over the common shareholders regarding the assets (in the event of liquidation) and earnings for payment of dividends.
Long-term debt	There is a fixed payment of interest, which is made in the form of a sinking fund.	Usually, long-term creditors do not have the right to vote. However, if the bond goes into default, the bondholders may be able to take control of the company.	Bondholders have the first claim (secured) over the assets of a company (in the event of liquidation) and earnings.

In The News [8.2]

Debt Restructuring May Sometimes Be a Necessary Strategy during Economic Hardships

The tentacles of an economic slowdown have deep and far-reaching ripple effects on organizations' cash flow. When it hits them, organizations literally put a freeze on spending, up to a point where vulnerable organizations are caught in a "real pickle" have to be bailed out by investors.

This is what happened at CanWest Global Communications Corp. When businesses went through the 2008 economic recession, many of them simply stopped spending money on advertising. And CanWest, like many other media companies, experienced a severe drop in its advertising revenue. CanWest owns many news organizations, including *National Post*, the *Ottawa Citizen,* and the Global television network. With a decline in the advertising revenue, it put a strain on both the company's bottom line and its cash flow. The damage was so serious that CanWest had to go through a $3.8 million recapitalization plan. CanWest negotiated its restructuring plan with a group of lenders including CIT Business Credit Canada Inc.

Source: Adapted from "CanWest wins new extension," *Ottawa Citizen*, July 18, 2009, p. D1. For the latest corporate news releases on CanWest Global communication, see http://www.canwestglobal.com, and to learn more about how CIT gives financing support to small businesses, see http://www.cit.com/index.htm.

Sources and Forms of Short-Term Financing

6 Learning Objective

Comment on the most important sources and forms of short-term financing.

Short-term financing Sources of financing obtained for a period of less than one year (e.g., trade credit, line of credit).

Supplier credit Financing obtained from suppliers (trade payables).

Short-term financing can be obtained from suppliers (trade credit), chartered banks (trust companies), and specialized lenders that finance current assets such as inventories (confirming institutions) and trade receivables (factoring companies) on a secured basis for a period less than one year.

SUPPLIERS

Supplier credit is also known as trade financing. Almost all businesses use trade credit. When a firm (purchaser) buys goods or services from another firm (supplier), the former does not have to pay for the goods or services immediately. When this takes place, a debt becomes outstanding to the supplier. Invoices for materials, supplies, and services provided by suppliers are not received until some days after the materials are delivered or services performed. However, if a business can extend its trade payables, that can be considered an excellent source of financing. For example, if a company pays its bills within a 30-day period but then makes an arrangement with its suppliers to extend payments by an extra 15 days (to 45 days), this could generate more cash inflows. If the company has $195,000 in trade payables and the cost of purchases amounts to $2,372,500, it could generate an extra $97,500 in cash inflows.

Here is the calculation:

Existing trade payables	$195,000
Average daily purchases are $6,500 ($2,372,500 ÷ 365)	
New level of trade payables ($6,500 × 45)	292,500
Additional cash from trade credit	$97,500

Self-Test Exercise No. 8.5

Cash Inflows from Supplier Credit

How much additional cash could CompuTech obtain from its trade credit in 2010 if can extend its trade credit by an extra 10 days. The company has trade payables of $20,000 and buys $209,000 from various suppliers.

This type of debt is shown on the SFP as trade and other payables. This is a very attractive form of financing because, in most instances, buyers do not have to pay for the goods or services for a period of 30 days, or sometimes 60 days; furthermore, it is interest-free. As a business grows, supplier credit also grows. Trade credit is offered to buyers who usually have a good credit rating. Nevertheless, it may be dangerous for a business that does not know how to use this credit instrument. In some cases, businesses abuse their credit limit and have difficulty reimbursing their suppliers. This situation can easily damage a business's reputation.

Table 8.9 lists the advantages and disadvantages of supplier credit.

CHARTERED BANKS AND TRUST COMPANIES

Chartered bank An institution that provides short-term loans such as seasonal loans, operating loans, or working capital loans.

The second most important source of short-term financing is **chartered banks** and trust companies. Banks make short-term loans that usually appear on the borrowing firm's SFP as seasonal loans, operating loans, or working capital loans. These loans can fluctuate as often as daily to cover expected cash shortfalls. These credit instruments are designed to finance fluctuating current assets.

Short-term loans do not come spontaneously. Borrowers must specifically request them. Short-term loans are, of course, more flexible than trade credit because the money can be spent on a wider range of business needs. Bank loans can be either unsecured or secured by some form of collateral that the bank can foreclose on if

Table 8.9 Advantages and Disadvantages of Supplier Credit

Advantages	Disadvantages
• Inexpensive source.	• Usually not sufficient to bridge fully the timing difference between paying for supplies and receiving cash from sales.
• Limited documentation required.	• Very short term in nature.
• Easy access.	• If company does not pay on time, the supplier might cut off future supplies, which could have adverse effects on the business
• No costs.	
• No controls.	
• No security.	

the borrower cannot pay back the loan as agreed. Unsecured loans usually have a higher cost.

As a firm's financing needs increase, it usually asks its banker to increase its line of credit. If the bank refuses, the firm may be forced to forgo attractive growth opportunities. Most firms try to choose a bank that is willing to provide service, advice, and counsel; assume some risks; and show some loyalty to its customers. A business owner therefore expects to develop a long-term relationship with its banker. When an owner looks for financing, it is preferable to select a commercial bank (or branch) that will be an asset, not a liability, to the business. Here are some of the more important attributes to look for when selecting a commercial bank.

Financial counselling. It is a banker's job to stay abreast of financial developments, so one of the most valuable functions that a commercial loan officer can perform for a business is that of external financial expert. Management or owners should look for a bank where the commercial loan officers specialize in businesses of their size and type, and should develop a strong relationship with the person handling the loan.

Loyalty. The loyalty of a commercial bank to its customers is very important. Certain banks, when times get a little rough, may quickly shut the door on applications for increases in line of credit (especially for smaller businesses). Other banks will work with a business as much as possible to help ride out the storm.

Degree of loan specialization. It is important that lending arrangements be serviced by the department in the bank that specializes in the business's particular type of loan (e.g., working capital loan, revolving loan).

Understanding the nature of the industry. A banker who has adequate knowledge of the industry and particular financing requirements can be an invaluable resource. The banker will not have to get familiar with the business; taking the required time to find such a banker can help business owners receive the financial counselling they need to solve their problems.

Full range of services. Management should choose a bank that offers a full range of banking services.

Reputation. The reputation of the bank or branch in terms of counselling services and providing loans to businesses is also important. Bank loans exhibit much greater variability than other sources of business funds.

Types of bank loans. Most bank loans are short term and self-liquidating; that is, money is lent for a business purpose such as the purchase of inventories and repaid from the proceeds of the sale of the inventories. Because firms need to buy inventory before they can sell it, they need to borrow frequently to cover seasonal shortfalls in cash flow (e.g., the pre-Christmas sales season for retailers). Then, at the end of the sales season, they can pay off the loans.

Cost of short-term loans. A typical bank loan might have a maturity of only 90 days. When it is repaid, the bank can lend the money to some other firms that have different cash flow patterns. Most of the fixed maturity loans (e.g., 90 days) are made at what is called discount interest, which means that the interest is deducted in advance.

Calculating the cost of financing for the various sources of short-term financing is important. The equation used to calculate the annual percentage rate (APR) for short-term loans is as follows:

$$\textbf{APR} = \frac{\textbf{Finance costs}}{\textbf{Loan}} \times \frac{\textbf{365}}{\textbf{Maturity (days)}}$$

To illustrate the use of this equation, let's take the example of a business that borrows $20,000 for a period of 6 months (182 days) with a $600 finance cost. Assuming that the principal is paid only at maturity, the APR would be 6.02%. The calculation is as follows:

$$\textbf{APR} = (\$600 \div \$20{,}000) \times (365 \div 182) = 6.02\%$$

About half of the outstanding loans of the chartered banks are classified as operating loans, and they are used by businesses to finance inventories and trade receivables. These loans are frequently renewed year after year and basically amount to quasi-permanent working capital financing. Most of the operating loans are not made on a basis of fixed maturity but, instead, on a demand basis. This means that the bank can request payment at any time. Demand loans are risky because if the bank suddenly demands repayment, the company would have no choice but to negotiate another loan with another financial institution. Also, the interest rate of this type of loan is usually not fixed, but floating. The floating rate is usually specified as **prime rate**, which is the rate the banks charge their most creditworthy customers, plus some premium for risk. The cost of bank loans varies for different borrowers at any given time because of differences in the risk to the lender. The cost of bank loans also varies over time as economic conditions change and interest rates fluctuate.

Prime rate
The interest rate that banks charge to their most creditworthy customers.

Because the prime rate is the base interest rate established by the Bank of Canada, commercial banks may therefore charge a slightly higher rate to their customers. Other borrowers pay more, depending on the risk of the loan. A typical operating loan might have a cost stated as prime plus two, meaning that if the prime rate is 5%, the borrower would pay 7%. As the prime goes up or down, the loan rate also changes if it is floating. Usually interest is calculated each month and is deducted from the firm's bank account.

Banks offer different forms of credit to their clients. First, there is the **line of credit**, which is a formal or written agreement between a banker and a borrower regarding the maximum amount of loan that will be extended to a business during a given year. For instance, a business may estimate that it will require a $20,000 loan during a four-month period (say, October to January) to produce goods and to sell them on credit. Although the business may have a high credit rating and may be able to obtain as much as $50,000, the business owner will have to indicate to the loan officer the amount required and when it will be needed. The agreement (based on the cash budget)

Line of credit
A formal or written agreement between a bank and a borrower regarding a loan.

Table 8.10 Advantages and Disadvantages of a Bank Line of Credit

Advantages	Disadvantages
• Easy and fairly quick to access.	• Increases the financial risk because cash servicing is required.
• Relatively inexpensive.	• Amount available is limited by the ceiling.
• Flexible.	• If the company experiences problems, lender is in a position to demand/cancel the line, and go for the option of realizing on the security.
• Loan revolves up and down and maximizes the use of cash.	• Not suitable for long-term requirements where the company expects returns over a long term.
• Suitable for short-term temporary needs.	• The company may not have suitable security or financial risk may be too high.
• Reporting requests are usually minimal.	
• Interest/fees are tax deductible.	

confirms that the funds to be provided will be available in the form of a temporary loan. Table 8.10 lists the advantages and disadvantages of a bank line of credit.

In the News 8.3 illustrates that business confidence and economic recovery are the best cures for attracting financing from different sources and for undertaking capital investment projects.

In The News [8.3]

Economic Recovery Is the Best Cure for Attracting Financing and Undertaking Capital Investments

The best stimulus package for boosting profitability and cash flow is an economic recovery. A company can formulate strategies at different organizational levels or spend time and money on promotion and advertising to increase sales by just a fraction of 1%, but when there is an economic upswing, all components on the financial statements shift, and in the right direction.

Predictions for the mood of the Canadian economy, including those from economists at the Conference Board of Canada (CBoC), indicate prosperity. According to the CBoC, the business confidence index increased by more than 10 points to 81.9 during the second quarter of 2009. This was the index's highest level since the second quarter of 2008. Also, business executives mentioned that they were more optimistic about their financial statements. In fact, 40% of them expected better earnings during the next six months compared to 23% who predicted less optimism. Most executives stated that it was now a good time to invest in capital projects.

Source: Adapted from "Business confidence at highest level in year," Ottawa Citizen, July 29, 2009, p. D3. For the latest Conference Board of Canada economic outlook, visit http://www.conferenceboard.ca.

Self-Test Exercise No. 8.6

The Average Percentage Rate

During the next three months, Len and Joan are considering applying for a bank loan to finance primarily their inventories. They expect to increase their inventories by $30,000 and hope to obtain 60% financing from the bank. The bank manager indicated that it would cost them $400 in finance costs for the three-month period. Based on this information, what is CompuTech's APR for the three-month loan?

Cost of pledging trade receivables. A business may want to finance its trade receivables. Here is an example to illustrate how to calculate the APR for financing its trade receivables. Let's assume that a bank lends 60% of the trade receivables at 2% above the prime rate of 6%. The bank also charges a 1% service fee of the pledged trade receivables. Both the finance costs and the service fee are payable at the end of each borrowing period. The company's trade receivables totals $700,000 and its average collection period is 40 days. As shown below, the percentage rate for financing the trade receivables is 17.1%. Here is the calculation:

$$\begin{aligned}
\textbf{Loan} &= \textbf{0.60} \times \textbf{pledged trade receivables} \\
&= \textbf{0.60} \times \textbf{\$700,000} = \textbf{\$420,000} \\
\textbf{Finance costs} &= (\textbf{\$420,000} \times \textbf{0.08}) \times (\textbf{40} \div \textbf{365}) \\
&= \textbf{\$3,682} \\
\textbf{Service fees} &= \textbf{\$420,000} \times \textbf{0.01} = \textbf{\$4,200} \\
\textbf{APR} &= [(\textbf{\$3,682} + \textbf{\$4,200}) \div \textbf{\$420,000}] \times (\textbf{365} \div \textbf{40}) = \textbf{17.1\%}
\end{aligned}$$

Self-Test Exercise No. 8.7

Cost of Pledging Trade Receivables

During the next six months, Len and Joan will be entering a busy season. They expect their commercial trade receivables to reach $40,000 and will want to have the bank finance 70%. The bank charges 9% and an additional 1% service fee of the pledged trade receivables. The average collection period for CompuTech's commercial accounts is 50 days. What is the company's APR for the pledged trade receivables?

Self-liquidating loan Funds used to finance temporary or fluctuating variations in working capital accounts (e.g., inventories, trade receivables).

Second, seasonal or **self-liquidating loans** are used by businesses primarily to finance temporary or fluctuating variations in inventories and trade receivables, which are the working capital accounts that are flexible. For instance, a business that sells ski equipment may have a specific seasonal borrowing pattern. It may need some financing in July, as inventories begin to accumulate. Once inventories are shipped to retailers in September and October, buyers start to make their payments. Seasonal loans can be secured or unsecured, and interest rates can fluctuate over time. Like a demand loan, the bank can call such loans at any time. In most cases, these loans are repaid on an installment basis (amortized over the life of the loan), but they may also be repaid in a lump sum.

Revolving credit
Maximum amount of a loan a bank agrees to provide a business (borrower).

Third, there is **revolving credit**, which is similar to a line of credit. In this case, the bank signs an agreement with the borrower (business) to extend credit up to a maximum amount. This type of financing costs a little more because additional fees can be levied by the bank. For instance, if the bank offers a credit limit of $300,000, and the borrower uses only $200,000, the unused portion of the borrowing may be liable to a standby fee, say 0.5%, which is charged to compensate the bank for committing itself to the loan.

Interim financing
Loan made to a business to help finance a capital project, such as the construction of a new plant, until regular financing is obtained.

Finally, there is **interim financing**, also called bridge financing, which is a loan available to businesses to help them finance a capital project, such as the construction of a new plant or the expansion of an existing one, until regular financing, such as a first mortgage, is received. This financing is called interim because it is used to bridge the time gap between the date construction begins and the time that the long-term loan is received.

Secured loan
A loan that the borrower guarantees by pledging some assets.

Firms that are not able to obtain unsecured credit, such as a line of credit, a seasonal loan, or revolving credit, because of low credit standing (or because they want a lower interest rate) will have to pledge some of their assets as security in order to obtain a loan. In the case of a **secured loan**, the borrower puts up some assets such as marketable securities, equipment, machinery, buildings, land, inventories, or trade receivables, as collateral to be claimed by the lender if the borrower does not respect the loan agreement or if the business is liquidated. Because most of the capital assets are financed by long-term loans (mortgages), short-term lenders will use inventories and trade receivables as collateral to secure short-term loans.

An instrument frequently used by banks is *commercial paper* or *corporate paper*. For larger firms, commercial paper is an alternative to bank loans. The maturity of commercial paper is generally very short but may go as long as one year. When the maturity date arrives, the borrower must pay; extensions are usually out of the question. Failure to pay on time will cause irreparable damage to a firm's reputation, perhaps preventing it from borrowing in the future.

ASSET-BASED FINANCING

Asset-based lending is a form of short-term risk capital financing. Just like a bank line of credit, an asset-based loan is subject to a ceiling amount based on inventories and trade receivables margins. It also involves a security pledge on inventories and trade receivables. However, pure asset-based loans differ from bank loans because they rely on collateral coverage rather than being linked directly to financial forecasts. Therefore, business and financial risk are less of an issue with asset-based lenders compared to conventional short-term lenders. However, pricing is higher, and interest charges may range from the prime rate plus 2% to 5% per annum.

Short-term risk capital financing is offered by factoring companies and confirming institutions.

Factoring
Selling trade receivables to a financial institution.

Factoring companies. Under **factoring**, the business makes an outright sale of its trade receivables to finance a business. The customer is told that the invoice has been sold and is asked to make payments directly to the finance company (the factor). This arrangement clearly increases the lender's risk. To reduce the risk, the factor virtually takes over the work of the borrower's credit department. All orders received from customers are sent to the finance company, which does a credit check. Factoring is fairly costly for businesses. It involves a continuing agreement under which the factor purchases trade receivables as they take place. The factor assumes the risk of accounts becoming uncollectable and is responsible for collections. Although in the past factoring was practised primarily in the apparel, textile, and furniture industries, it was not practised in most other industries because any company using this method was considered to be in poor financial health. Today, factoring appears to be gaining acceptance in many industries.

There are two general types of factoring arrangements. First, there is *maturity factoring*. In this arrangement, the factor purchases all of the business's invoices, paying the face value less a discount or commission. The customer is then told to pay the amount due to the factor by an agreed due date, say 30 days. The factor may charge the customer interest on amounts outstanding after the due date.

Second, there is *old-line factoring*. Here, the factor performs a lending function. It will advance funds to the company based on 70% to 90% of the value of an invoice. The factor may charge interest at prime rate plus 2% to 5% per annum, as long as the invoice is outstanding. In this case, the company receives cash almost immediately after the sale is made.

The maximum advance a business can obtain from the factor is limited to the amount of factored trade receivables less the factoring commission, finance costs, and reserve that the factor withholds to cover any returns or allowances by customers.

The factor normally charges a service fee ranging between 1% and 3% of the factored trade receivables to cover the credit-checking costs, collection, and bad debts losses in addition to the 2 to 5 points over the prime rate on advances to the company. For a business seeking this type of financing, these higher costs are partly offset by administrative costs saved by the company. These costs include administrative and clerical costs of credit investigation and collection in addition to the losses on uncollected accounts.

Let's look at an example and assume that a company has $500,000 in trade receivables with a 60-day average collection period and decides to sell them to a factor. The factor may (1) require a 10% reserve for returns and allowances, (2) charge a 2% factoring commission, and (3) charge an annual interest rate of 3% over prime (assuming that in this case the prime is 4%). The 10% reserve for returns is not considered a cost of factoring because the factor will return the amount to the company if the customers make no returns or adjustments. Here is the calculation:

Funds advanced by the factor:	
Average level of trade receivables	$500,000
Less: Factoring commission (2%)	(10,000)
Less: Reserve for returns (10%)	(50,000)
Subtotal	440,000
Less: Interest on advance (0.07 × $440,000) × (60 ÷ 365)	(5,063)
Total funds advanced by factor	$434,937
Fees and finance costs calculation:	
Factoring commission	$10,000
Finance costs	5,063
Total	$15,063
Annual percentage rate:	

$$\textbf{APR } (\$15{,}063 \div \$434{,}937) \times (365 \div 60) = 21.1\%$$

Now, let's assume that the company manages its own trade receivables at a cost of $1,000 a month for administrative fees and clerical costs in addition to $2,000 a month in bad debt losses. This additional information allows the company to determine whether it is worth having a factor handling its trade receivables. Here is the calculation:

$$\textbf{APR } [(\$15{,}063 - \$6{,}000) \div \$434{,}937)] \times (365 \div 60) = 12.7\%$$

As shown, it costs the company more to use a factor than if it were to administer the trade receivables itself. This calculation is done for a 60-day period. This comparison would be used to make the decision. If the company enters into an agreement with the factor, this type of calculation would be done on a continuous basis.

Confirming institution Organization that finances inventories.

Confirming institutions. Inventory is an asset that can serve as excellent security for short-term loans by **confirming institutions**. The major factor that is taken into account by lenders before extending inventory financing is the marketability of the inventories. Work-in-process inventories, for example, are poor collateral. Raw materials may be more secure, because they can be sold to other manufacturers; finished goods, ready to be shipped to retailers, may not be as good collateral as raw materials. The level of financing obtained on inventories depends largely on the nature of the goods.

Inventories can be financed in a number of ways. First, it can be financed by having a *blanket coverage* or a general lien put on it, such as the one used for trade receivables. Then the lender can claim as collateral a percentage of the business's inventories. This type of arrangement is easy to set up, but the lender takes a risk in that it does not have absolute control over the quality and quantity of the goods held in stock.

Second, there is *floor planning*. This type of financing is used primarily in the durable goods industry to finance automobile, farm, and industrial equipment dealers. In this case, each product is identified by a serial number and, when the good is sold, a portion of the proceeds is forwarded to the lender for repayment of the loan. Each time

Table 8.11 Advantages and Disadvantages of Asset-Based Financing

Advantages	Disadvantages
• Ideal for growing highly leveraged and turnaround situations, because of the higher level of risk assumed by the lender.	• Not suitable for all industries; needs high levels of trade receivables and inventories.
• No complicated financial covenants, which require monitoring and compliance. This results in less chance of default under a loan agreement.	• Increases the financial risk, due to interest servicing.
• Given the heavy reliance on the value of the collateral, it increases the opportunity for leverage.	• More expensive than conventional short-term financing.
• Lowers the need to raise equity, avoiding equity dilution.	• Onerous inventories and trade receivables monitoring requirements, sometimes as often as daily.
• Interest is tax deductible.	

goods are replenished, the borrower must sign a new agreement that specifies the terms and conditions. Sometimes the lender will spot check to certify the quantity and quality of the physical assets.

Third, there is *warehouse financing*. This type of financing involves an independent third party that controls access to the goods as security for the lender. There are two basic types of warehousing arrangements. First, there is *field warehousing*. Here, the inventories are located in a specified area on the borrower's property, and the warehousing agent exercises very strict control. Second, there are *public warehousing* arrangements. Here, the merchandise is located away from the borrowers' premises, probably in a public warehouse under the control of the warehouse agent.

Fourth, there is *consignment*. This means that although a seller delivers goods to a buyer, the seller remains the owner until the goods are sold to the public. Because the buyer does not purchase the goods, the seller may need to obtain short-term loans to finance the product. In this case, the buyer takes no risk. The profit margin on consigned goods is normally smaller than that on similar non-consigned items.

Table 8.11 lists the advantages and disadvantages of asset-based financing.

7 Learning Objective

Identify the factors that can influence the choice between buying or leasing an asset.

Lease Financing

Almost any physical asset can be purchased or leased. We are all familiar with residential apartment leasing, whereby a lessee (the tenant) acquires the right from the lessor (owner) to inhabit the apartment in return for monthly rental payments.

Lessee
One who pays to use an asset without owning it.

Lessor
One who lends an asset to someone (lessee).

Operating lease
A lease that is cancellable by the lessee at any time upon due notice.

Financial lease
Mutually agreed commitment by a lessor and a lessee for a specified period of time.

Leasing is an alternative to more traditional financing for many assets, but especially for equipment that has a useful life of three to ten years. The **lessee** or user gets the full use of the assets without the bother of owning them, and frequently this can be accomplished with little or no down payment. The **lessor** is the one who lends the asset to the lessee. The three most popular forms of leases are operating leases, financial leases, and sale and leaseback.

Operating leases. **Operating leases** provide not only financing but also maintenance of the asset, so they are popular for office equipment and cars as well as highly technical types of equipment, such as computers. The operating lease is an agreement between a lessee and a lessor that can be cancelled by either party upon due notice. Usually, the lease price includes services and repairs. Operating leases are not always fully amortized during the original contract period; the lessor expects to recover the rest of its costs by either leasing the asset again or selling it. If the original lessee believes that the equipment has become obsolete, it is usually possible to cancel the contract at little or no penalty cost prior to the normal expiry date of the lease period.

Financial leases. A **financial lease** is a mutually agreed-upon commitment by the lessor and lessee under which the latter agrees to lease a specific asset over a specified period of time. The lease does not provide for maintenance, is usually fully amortized, and does not normally include a cancellation clause. Financial leases are commonly used for assets such as airplanes, office equipment, movable offshore oil drilling rigs, medical equipment, railroad cars, and construction equipment. Lessors generally borrow 80% of the cost of the asset from a third party (or parties) on a non-recourse basis. The loan is secured only by the lease payments and is not a general obligation of the lessor. Lease periods as long as 15 or 20 years are common. The lessor records on its SFP only the net investment (20%) but can deduct both finance costs on its debt financing and depreciation on the asset; therefore, income for tax purposes is usually negative in the early years of the lease. The lessee may get lower lease payments than would otherwise be the case, and its payments are usually tax deductible. Virtually all financial institutions are involved in leasing, either directly or through subsidiaries.

In a financial lease, three parties are involved: the lessee, the lessor, and a lender. Here is how a typical financial lease works. The company (lessee) decides on the equipment or machinery it wants to use. The company approaches a leasing company and specifies the asset it wants and the length of time for which it will be needed. The leasing company then (1) borrows money from a lender (if necessary), (2) buys the asset from a manufacturer, and (3) leases it to the company (lessee). Usually, the lease period lasts throughout the useful life of the asset so that the leasing company does not find itself in the position of having to lease it to another company. In this lease agreement, the leasing company does not even take physical possession of the asset.

Sale and leaseback Arrangement made by someone to sell an asset to a lessor and then lease it back.

Sale and leaseback. A **sale and leaseback** arrangement can be used only once, because it requires the firm to sell an asset and then lease it back. Thus, it still gets to use the asset while increasing the funds available within a particular time period. Lease payments in such arrangements are similar to mortgage payments or payments on a long-term loan. For example, a firm could sell its factory building and land to a financial institution and then lease it back. The selling firm in this case receives the full purchase price of the property, which it can use for any purpose. It is committed to making periodic payments to the financial institution, which is equivalent to paying rent.

LEASE-OR-BUY ANALYSIS

Medium- and long-term financing are generally used to acquire capital assets, such as buildings, machinery, and equipment. As long as the assets do the job, a business is not concerned about how assets are financed. Managers' prime interest is to see that the assets do the job at the lowest possible cost. To financial managers, however, the choice between owning versus leasing has significant financial implications. Their job is to ensure not only that assets are obtained at the lowest possible cost and on the most favourable terms but also that they produce the greatest financial benefits to the owners. Although leasing has far-reaching legal and accounting implications, we will deal here only with the cost factors in comparing the choice between leasing versus owning an asset. Table 8.12 presents a cost comparison between owning and leasing $1 million worth of assets. The assumptions underlying this comparative cost analysis are the following:

- Life of the assets is 10 years.
- Duration of the lease is 10 years with annual installments of $162,745 (before tax) and $81,372 (after tax) based on a 10% compounded interest charge.
- Debt agreement is 100% of assets; a 10-year repayment schedule with a 10% compounded interest charge. (Assets are rarely financed at 100% of value; however, this assumption is made only to illustrate the true economic comparison between the two options.)
- CCA is 15%.
- Income tax is 50%.
- Residual value of the asset is nil.

As shown in column 1, the annual cost of the lease is $81,372, or $162,745 × 50% (income tax rate). The second column shows the annual payment for the $1,000,000 loan. The $162,745 annual lease payment is obtained by dividing $1,000,000 by the factor 6.1446 (from Table D in Appendix B at the end of the book, column 10% and line 10 years). Columns 3 and 4 show how much will be paid each year for finance costs and principal, respectively. In the first year, with a $1,000,000 loan at a 10% interest rate, the finance costs will be $100,000 (column 3) and the principal

Table 8.12 Comparison of Cost of Owning versus Cost of Leasing

Computing Net Cost of Owning

	1	2	3	4	5	6	7	8	9
Year	**Lease Payment after Tax at 50%**	**Total Payment**	**Finance Costs**	**Principal**	**CCA**	**Income Tax Deductible Expenses**	**Tax Shield 50%**	**Net Cost of Owning**	**Net Advantage (Disadvantage) versus Lease**
		(col.3 + col.4)				(col.3 + col.5)	(col.6 ÷ col.7)	(col.2 – col.7)	(col.1 – col.8)
1	$81,372	$162,745	$100,000	$62,745	$75,000	$175,000	$87,500	$75,245	$6,127*
2	81,372	162,745	93,725	69,020	138,750	232,475	116,238	46,508	34,865*
3	81,372	162,745	86,823	75,922	117,938	204,761	102,380	60,365	21,008*
4	81,372	162,745	79,230	83,515	100,247	179,477	89,739	73,006	8,367*
5	81,372	162,745	70,880	91,865	85,210	156,090	78,045	84,701	(3,328)
6	81,372	162,745	61,693	101,052	72,428	134,121	67,061	95,685	(14,312)
7	81,372	162,745	51,587	111,158	61,564	113,151	56,576	106,169	(24,796)
8	81,372	162,745	40,472	122,273	52,329	92,801	46,401	116,344	(34,971)
9	81,372	162,745	28,245	134,500	44,480	72,725	36,363	126,383	(45,010)
10	81,372	162,745	14,795	147,950	37,808	52,603	26,302	136,444	(55,071)
	$813,720	$1,627,450	$627,450	$1,000,000	$785,754	$1,413,208	$706,604	$920,850	$(107,125)

* Favours owning
( ) Favours leasing

repayment will be $62,745. Column 5 shows the annual capital cost allowance for the $1,000,000 capital assets. Year 1 shows $75,000 [($1,000,000 × 15%) ÷ 2], and the remaining yearly figures are calculated on a declining basis. Column 6 shows the total tax-deductible amount made up of the finance costs (column 3) and capital cost allowance (column 5). Column 7 shows the yearly tax shield. Because the company is in a 50% income tax bracket, it will benefit from an $87,500 (column 6 ÷ 2) tax shield. Column 8 shows the net cost of owning the asset, which is the annual payment of the loan (column 2) less the annual tax shield. Column 9 (net advantage or disadvantage versus lease) shows the net difference between the after-tax lease payment and net cost of owning. As indicated, it is preferable to lease the asset. During the 10-year period, the total cost of owning is $920,850 versus $813,720 for leasing, for a net difference of $107,130.[2] In the early years, there is a distinct cash flow advantage to owning the asset; by the fifth year, however, cash flow favours leasing.

2. The difference in the totals is due to the rounding of the figures in individual columns. Adding the 10 numbers in column 9 gives $107,125 (difference between individual numbers shown in column 1 and column 8) and not $107,130, which is the result of the sum of the 10 numbers appearing in column 1 ($813,720) and the sum of the 10 numbers in column 8 ($920,850).

Self-Test Exercise No. 8.8

Lease or Buy a Truck

The Millers are not sure whether they should buy or lease a truck. A five-year lease could be arranged with annual lease payments of $5,000, payable at the beginning of each year. The tax shield from lease payments is available at year-end. CompuTech's tax rate is 35%. The truck would cost $25,000 and has a five-year expected life span, and no residual value is expected. If purchased, the asset would be financed through a term loan at 14%. The loan calls for equal payments to be made at the end of each year for five years. The truck would qualify for CCA allowances written off on a straight-line basis over five years.

Calculate the cash flows for each financing alternative. Which alternative is the most economically attractive?

FACTORS THAT INFLUENCE LEASE-OR-BUY DECISIONS

This example of comparative cost analysis does not consider all the cost factors affecting the economics of each option. Many other factors may also have to be considered. The most common include interest rate, residual value, obsolescence, risk factor, increase of financial leverage, adjunct costs, and capital cost allowance rate.

Interest rate. Although the example in Table 8.12 assumes the same interest rate for both leasing and owning, this may not always be the case. It is important to compare the lessor's interest rate with prevailing lending interest rates. Some leasing firms offer specialized services, and their costs will be included in the leasing charges, thus complicating the comparison.

Residual value. Most assets have a residual value at the end of a lease period. If a firm owns an asset and sells it at the end of a similar period, the resulting cash inflow would be a reason to favour owning.

Obsolescence. The type of equipment also influences owning versus leasing. If a piece of equipment will soon become obsolete, leasing may be the best option. Why purchase a piece of equipment with a 10-year lifespan when it will become obsolete to the company after four? Some will argue that the higher the obsolescence factor, the higher the cost of the lease. This is not always true, because lessors can often find other users for their equipment; not all users have the same obsolescence rate.

Risk factor. Leasing a piece of equipment with a high rate of obsolescence passes the element of risk to the lessors.

Increase of financial leverage. Leasing is often claimed to have a double effect on financial leverage. First, more money is usually available to finance assets through a lease than its alternate source, a loan. Assets can be leased at 100%, but chattel mortgage or conditional sales contracts can be obtained at only 50% or 75%. Second, financing part of a capital asset through leasing leaves room for future financing, if an expansion is contemplated right after start-up. However, while leasing may seem to hold out the promise of greater leverage, less risk of obsolescence, and lower cost, care should be used in considering this financing option. Lenders are wise to the financial obligations of "off-statement of financial position" financing and take them into account when assessing creditworthiness.

Adjunct costs. Certain costs, such as legal fees, are not as high for leasing as for debt financing; these should also be considered in the cost comparison.

Capital cost allowance rate. A change in the capital cost allowance rate may alter the decision. For example, if the CCA rate increases from 15% to 25%, this would favour the purchase option.

Self-Test Exercise No. 8.9

Lease or Buy Computers

The Millers are faced with the decision of purchasing or leasing several computers (including a cash register) for their new store. The computers can be leased for $8,000 a year or purchased for $30,000. The lease includes maintenance and service. The salvage value of the equipment five years hence is $6,000. The company uses the declining amortization method. The amortization rate is 35%. If the computers were purchased, service and maintenance charges (a deductible cost) would be $300 a year. CompuTech can borrow the entire amount at a rate of 14% if the purchase option is exercised. The tax rate is 35%, and the company's cost of capital is 11%. On the basis of the above, which method of financing would you choose?

Use the following capital cost allowance amounts to calculate the cost of the equipment.

Year	Amount
1	$10,050
2	6,825
3	4,436
4	2,884
5	1,875

REALITY FINANCIAL SNAPSHOTS

The following paragraphs give an overview of the sources and forms of financing obtained by Enbridge and The Ottawa Hospital (TOH).

ENBRIDGE[3]

In 2007, Enbridge had $19.9 billion in total assets and reached a total of $24.7 billion in 2008 for an increase of 24.1%. In 2008, current assets accounted for 15.0% of total assets. The following gives the split between the current asset and non-current asset accounts as shown in the company's SFP.

3. Enbridge Inc., *2008 Enbridge Annual Report.* Found at: http://www.enbridge.com/investor/financialInformation/reportsFilings/pdf/2008-annual-report-en.pdf.

Assets (in $ millions)	2008	Percent of Total	2007	% of Total
Current assets	3,708.9	15.0	3,264.8	16.4
Non-current assets	20,992.5	85.0	16,642.6	83.6
Total assets	24,701.4	100.0	19,907.4	100.0

Liabilities and Equity

In 2008, all of Enbridge's current assets ($3.7 billion) were financed by current debt ($4.1 billion). The following gives a breakdown of the broad categories of forms of current liability financing. As shown, more than half of the current liabilities were comprised of trade and other payables. In 2008, short-term borrowings accounted for 21.3% of total current liabilities.

Current Liabilities		Percent of Total		Percent of Total
Short-term borrowings	874.6	21.3	545.6	15.5
Trade and other payables	2,411.5	58.7	2,213.8	63.1
Interest payable	101.9	2.5	89.1	2.5
Current maturities of short-term debt	533.8	13.0	605.2	17.2
Current maturities of non-recourse long-term debt	184.7	4.5	61.1	1.7
Total Current Liabilities	4,106.5	100.0	3,514.8	100.0

Long-term borrowings

In 2008, 72.7% of Enbridge's long-term borrowings were made up of long-term debt such as debentures and medium-term notes, and 73.2% of the company's total assets were financed by debt, a slight decrease over 2007.

Long-term debt	10,154.9	72.7	7,729.0	69.5
Non-recourse long-term debt	1,474.0	10.5	1,508.4	13.6
Other long-term liabilities	259.0	1.9	253.9	2.2
Future income taxes	1,290.8	9.2	975.6	8.8
Non-controlling interests	797.4	5.7	650.5	5.9
Total long-term debt	13,976.1	100.0	11,117.4	100.0
Percent of long-term debt to non-current assets		66.6		66.8
Total liabilities		18,082.6	14,632.2	
Percent of liabilities to total assets		73.2		73.5

Shareholders' equity

In 2008, 26.8% of the company's total assets were financed by equity and the bulk of it was made up of common share (48.3%) and retained earnings (51.1%).

Share capital				
Preferred shares	125.0	1.9	125.0	2.4
Common shares	3,194.0	48.3	3,026.5	57.4
Contributed surplus	37.9	0.6	25.7	0.4
Retained earnings	3,383.4	51.1	2,537.3	48.1
Accumulated other comprehensive income/(loss)	32.8	0.5	(285.0)	(5.4)
Reciprocal shareholding	(154.3)	(2.4)	(154.3)	(2.9)
Total shareholders' equity	6,618.8	100.0	5,275.2	100.0
Percent of shareholders' equity to liabilities and equity		26.8		26.5
Commitments and contingencies	24,701.4		19,907.4	

THE OTTAWA HOSPITAL[4]

Sources and forms of financing for TOH are totally distinct from for-profit organizations. The composition of TOH's current and capital assets is as shown below. Current assets represent only a small portion of total assets (e.g., 13.3% in 2008).

(in $000s)	2008	Percent of Total	2007	Percent of Total
Current assets	75,460	13.3	68,334	12.9
Long-term assets	492,253	86.7	459,957	87.1
Total assets	567,713	100.0	528,291	100.0

While total current assets amount to $75.5 thousand, total current liabilities represent just over three times that amount ($253.7 thousand). This could very well mean that some of the bills included in trade and other payables ($179.8 thousand) were incurred for the purchase of long-term assets. This simply means that the matching principle (current assets and current liabilities) may not apply for NFP organizations. As shown, 44.7% of all assets are financed by current liabilities while deferred contributions related to capital assets finances 47.5% of total assets.

Current liabilities	253,679	44.7	233,948	44.3
Long-term liabilities				
Employee future benefits	15,959	2.8	13,945	2.6
Deferred contributions related to capital assets	269,826	47.5	259,450	49.1
Net assets	28,249	5.0	20,948	4.0
Total long-term liabilities and net assets	567,713	100.0	528,291	100.0

4. *2008 Ottawa Hospital Annual Report*. Found at: http://www.ottawahospital.on.ca/about/reports/FS2008-e.pdf.

[DECISION-MAKING IN ACTION]

Ted Bentley, the owner of Microplus Inc., is very encouraged about his company's expansion program and its capability to produce power modules (sounding amplifiers for audio components). He feels that the market is growing rapidly and that power modules would provide Microplus Inc. with higher margins that would help improve his company's financial performance. He points out that the key to Microplus' future growth and success is to market new highly profitable power modules.

Before meeting investors, the first thing that the company's controller did was to formulate financial projections based on the company's goals and plans. After several months of discussions with the key members of the management team, the controller was able to prepare three-year projections for the company's statements of income, statements of financial position, and statements of cash flows. The expansion program is expected to cost $1.1 million and is broken down as follows:

Financial needs

Capital assets		$600,000
Working capital requirements		
Inventories	$200,000	
Trade receivables	200,000	
Subtotal	400,000	
Trade and other payables	100,000	300,000
Marketing costs		200,000
Total		$1,100,000*

On the financing requirements side, Microplus's bank will lend a very small amount to the company on its increase in inventories (40%) and trade receivables (30%). Based on the estimated purchases, the controller calculated a $100,000 increase in credit outstanding with various suppliers. The bank is also prepared to finance part of the capital assets in the amount of $200,000 with annual payments bearing an annual 10% interest charge. The controller informed Ted that on the basis of the projected financial statements, particularly the statement of cash flows, an amount of $200,000 would be available to finance the expansion through internal sources. Shareholders are also prepared to invest an extra $100,000 into the business to finance the expansion.

Ted realizes that he will be short by $460,000 in financing to meet his $1.1 million investment need. After some discussion with several financial advisors, they suggest that he should approach non-conventional investors who would be prepared to provide risk capital financing. This suggestion is based on the nature of the business (high tech) and the fast growth that is expected to take place in the industry and particularly in Microplus. Ted decided to meet two risk capital investors.

The first was the Business Development Bank of Canada, which indicated that it would provide a subordinated debt in the amount of $200,000 with collateral on the capital assets. Ted also met an individual in risk capital lending who was also interested in investing $260,000 in equity funds in Microplus. Ted Bentley was aware that although the cost of equity would be high

* Note: This $1.1 million financial need is netted out after supplier financing (trade and other payables). Excluding supplier financing, Microplus would have to raise $1.2 million.

(typically in the 25% to 40% return), it would not have to be paid by Microplus on an annual basis. The high return expected by the risk capital investor would be earned at exit through a buyout situation probably in the fourth or fifth year after the expansion.

On the basis of the above information, the following presents how Microplus's financial needs will be financed. Table 8.13 summarizes both the company's financial needs and financing requirements.

Financial Needs (cash outflows)		Financing Requirements (cash inflows)	
Capital assets	$600,000	Bank	$200,000
Inventories	200,000	Bank (40% on inventories)	80,000
Trade receivables	200,000	Bank (30% on trade receivables)	60,000
		Suppliers	100,000
Marketing costs	200,000	Internal sources	200,000
		Shareholders	100,000
		BDC	200,000
		Risk capital firm	260,000
Total	$1,200,000	Total	$1,200,000

Financial requirements can be analyzed from different angles. First, on the basis of internal sources versus external sources, showing the percentages provided by short-term lenders and long-term investors. As shown below, 16.7% of the financing will come from internal sources, while total external funding represents 83.3% with long-term representing 63.3% and short-term 20.0% of the funding requirements.

		Amount		Percentage
Internal		$200,000		16.7%
External				
Long-term	$760,000		63.3%	
Short-term	240,000		20.0	
Subtotal		1,000,000		83.3
Total		$1,200,000		100.0%

Another way to analyze Microplus's financing requirements is to differentiate between the amount of funds generated from debt versus equity (capital structure or financial leverage) after internal sources have been provided. As shown below, lenders (debt) provide 53.3% of the total financing package.

	Amount	Percentage
Internal	$200,000	16.7%
External		
Equity	360,000	30.0
Debt	640,000	53.3
Subtotal	1,000,000	83.3
Total	$1,200,000	100.0%

Table 8.13 Microplus's Financing Requirements

	Internal Sources	External Sources				
	Cash Flow from Operations	Conventional	Risk	Conventional	Risk	Total
Internal						
From operations	$200,000					$200,000
External						
Equity financing						
1. Conventional shareholders				$100,000		100,000
2. Risk capital – institutional investors					$260,000	260,000
Intermediate and long-term debt financing						
1. Conventional financing – bank		$200,000				200,000
2. Risk financing – subordinated debt (BDC)			$200,000			200,000
Conventional financing – short term						
1. Suppliers		100,000				100,000
2. Inventories (40%) – bank		80,000				80,000
3. Trade receivables (30%) – bank		60,000				60,000
Total financing requirements	$200,000	$440,000	$200,000	$100,000	$260,000	$1,200,000

As shown below, risk capital financing accounts for 38.3% of the total financing package, and the remainder is split between internal sources (16.7%) and conventional sources (45%).

	Amount	Percentage
Internal	$200,000	16.7%
External		
Conventional	$540,000	45.0%
Risk	460,000	38.3
Subtotal	$1,000,000	83.3
Total	$1,200,000	100.0%

FINANCIAL SPREADSHEETS—EXCEL

Template 8 (Vertical Analysis of the Statement of Financial Position) of the financial statement analysis component of the financial spreadsheets accompanying this text can give a detailed view of the composition of the various liability and equity accounts over a three-year period. Template 8 (Lease/Buy Decision) of the decision-making tools spreadsheets is designed to calculate the cost of leasing an asset versus the cost of owning an asset.

Chapter Summary

1 Learning Objective

Differentiate between internal financing and external financing.

Financing can be obtained from two sources. First, *internally*, by using profit generated by operations including depreciation/amortization, and by managing the current assets more effectively; and second, *externally*, from shareholders (through purchase of common or preferred shares) and short-term and long-term lenders.

2 Learning Objective

Explain different types of risk-related financing options (ownership versus debt).

External financing can be obtained from different sources and in different forms. Each is used to finance a specific asset, different venture, or business undertaking. A business faces three types of risks. *Business risk* has to do with the uncertainty inherent in projecting future earnings of a business. *Financial risk* deals with a company's financial structure. *Instrument risk* focuses on the type of instrument that should be used to finance a business.

3 Learning Objective

Explain useful strategies when approaching lenders.

When considering financing, businesses should attempt to match, as closely as possible, the maturity of the source of funds to the period of time for which the funds are needed. To do this, both cost and risk should be taken into consideration. Investors use different criteria for assessing the worthiness of prospective clients. The C's of credit are character, collateral, capacity, capital, circumstances (or conditions), and coverage.

4 Learning Objective

Comment on the different categories of equity financing.

Equity financing can be secured from shareholders and risk capital firms. These types of funds can be obtained from private or public sources. If public offerings are made, investment dealers must be used to process the issue. Risk capital firms provide financing for smaller, high-risk firms. They generally provide equity financing or both equity and long-term debt financing. Risk capital investments can be categorized as embryonic, start-up, development, expansion, turnaround, or buyout. Risk capital investors include angel investors, private investors, institutional investors, and government-backed corporations. Government financing is a direct or indirect form of financial assistance to businesses offered by a municipal, provincial, or federal agency to help businesses carry out capital expenditure projects or expand their activities. The more important governmental financial institutions include the EDC, Farm Credit Canada, the Business Development Bank of Canada, and provincial venture capital organizations.

5 Learning Objective

Discuss the sources and forms of intermediate and long-term debt financing.

Sources of *intermediate and long-term financing* are commercial banks and trust companies. In addition, there are conventional long-term investors (e.g., banks, shareholders) and risk-capital investors including government institutions. Medium- and long-term financing are obtained from conventional institutions and include term loans, conditional sales contracts, bonds, and mortgages. Risk capital funds can also be obtained on a subordinated debt basis whereby investors accept a higher level of risk. When considering common share, preferred share, and long-term debt financing, different factors must be taken into account: the payout of income, control, risk, and the advantages and disadvantages of each.

6 Learning Objective

Comment on the most important sources and forms of short-term financing.

The most popular sources of short-term financing are suppliers, chartered banks and trust companies, and asset-based financing. The most popular forms of short-term financing are trade credit (suppliers) and lines of credit, seasonal or self-liquidating loans, revolving credit, and interim financing offered by chartered banks. Other financing institutions also offer secured loans on inventories and trade receivables. Lenders can offer asset-based loans. These include factoring on trade receivables and general lien, floor planning, warehousing agreements, and consignment to finance inventories.

7 Learning Objective

Identify the factors that can influence the choice between buying or leasing an asset.

Lease financing is another popular way of acquiring assets. The three major types of leases are service leases, financial leases, and sale and leaseback. Before deciding on buying or leasing assets, the cost of each option should be evaluated. The factors that will determine the choice are interest rate, residual value, obsolescence factor, risk factor, increase of financial leverage, adjunct costs, and capital cost allowance rate.

Key Terms

Bond p. 387
Business risk p. 373
Chartered bank p. 392
Conditional sales contract p. 386
Confirming institution p. 399
C's of credit p. 376
External sources p. 371
Factoring p. 398
Financial lease p. 401
Financial needs p. 367
Financial risk p. 373
Financing requirements p. 368
Government financing p. 383
Instrument risk p. 373
Interim financing p. 397
Internal sources p. 371
Lessee p. 401
Lessor p. 401

Line of credit p. 394
Long-term loan p. 385
Mortgage p. 387
Operating lease p. 401
Prime rate p. 394
Prospectus p. 378
Revolving credit p. 397
Risk capital investors p. 380
Sale and leaseback p. 402
Secured loan p. 397
Self-liquidating loan p. 396
Shareholders p. 379
Short-term financing p. 391
Subordinated debt p. 389
Supplier credit p. 391
Term loan p. 385
Venture capital p. 381

Review Questions

1. What is the difference between financial needs and financing requirements?
2. Differentiate between internal and external financing. Give several examples.
3. Discuss the concepts of business risk, financial risk, and instrument risk.
4. How can working capital become a source of internal financing?
5. Differentiate between flexible and durable current assets.
6. Explain the meaning of matching principle.
7. Identify the six C's of credit.
8. Explain the significance of the word capacity.
9. How can a company become more creditworthy?
10. What steps are involved when making a public issue?
11. Differentiate between shareholder collective rights and specific rights. Identify three of each type of right.
12. What is the purpose of a risk capital investor? Comment on some of them.
13. What types of capital investments do risk capitalist firms invest in?
14. How can government agencies help businesses?
15. Differentiate between a secured bond and an unsecured bond.
16. What is the purpose of a subordinated debt?
17. Why are suppliers considered an important source of financing?
18. What factors should a company consider before selecting a chartered bank as a lender?
19. Differentiate between a seasonal loan and revolving credit.
20. What is commercial or corporate paper?
21. What sort of financing do factoring companies and confirming institutions provide?

22. Differentiate between an operating lease and a financial lease.
23. Is it easier for a big firm to obtain a loan than a small business? Explain.
24. Why is it important for a business to understand the nature of its assets before approaching lenders?
25. If you were to provide a term loan to a small business entrepreneur, what provisions would you include in the contract in order to protect your interest?
26. Do you believe that leasing would be as popular if income taxes did not exist? Explain.

Learning Exercises

EXERCISE 1

A company needs $1.2 million to invest in different types of assets and operating expenses to launch a new line of products. With the following information, make a list of the company's financial needs and financing requirements.

Marketing costs	$55,000	Trade receivables	$175,000
Depreciation	50,000	Equipment	600,000
Shareholders	200,000	Suppliers	250,000
Inventories	350,000	Profit for the year	100,000
Working capital loan	100,000	Equipment vendors	200,000
Research and development	120,000	Commercial bank	300,000

EXERCISE 2

How much additional cash could a company obtain from their working capital accounts if it can improve its inventory turnover by 0.2 times, and average collection period by 5 days? The company's inventories are $500,000, and trade receivables are $250,000. The company's revenue is estimated at $1.8 million and cost of sales at $900,000.

EXERCISE 3

Calculate the amount of additional cash that a company could raise from suppliers if its trade credit is extended by 10 days. Assume that the company's trade payables are $300,000 and that it buys $2,300,000 from various suppliers yearly.

EXERCISE 4

During the next four months, a company is considering approaching banks to finance its increased level of working capital. The company expects to increase its working capital needs by $30,000 and hopes to obtain 55% financing from the bank. The bank manager indicated that it would cost them $700 in finance costs for the four-month period. Based on this information, calculate the company's APR for the four-month loan.

EXERCISE 5

During the next four months, a furniture manufacturer will be entering its holiday season. Management expects their commercial trade receivables to reach $900,000 and will be seeking a bank loan that will finance 60% of its receivables. The bank charges 8% and an additional 1% service fee of the pledged trade receivables. The average collection period is 45 days. Calculate the company's APR for the pledged trade receivables.

EXERCISE 6

A furniture company is considering using a factor to manage their trade receivables. The company has $1,600,000 in trade receivables with a 70-day average collection period. The factor charges a 10% reserve for returns and allowances, a 2% factoring commission, and an annual interest rate of 4% over prime (assuming that in this case prime is 5%). If the company manages its own receivables, it would cost $3,000 a month for administrative fees and clerical costs in addition to $4,000 a month in bad debt losses. Based on this information, what would be the company's APR?

EXERCISE 7

If a company borrows $300,000 for four years at 10%, what would be the annual loan payments?
If the company borrows $650,000 for 10 years at 12%, what would be the annual loan payments?

EXERCISE 8

Calculate the annual payment, finance costs, and principal repayments on a $300,000 loan bearing a 10% interest rate over a four-year period.

EXERCISE 9

Calculate the following lease-or-buy option.

A four-year lease could be arranged with annual lease payments of $90,000, payable at the beginning of each year. The tax shield from lease payments is available at year-end. The firm's tax rate is 40%. The machine costs $500,000 and has a four-year expected life, and no residual value is expected. If purchased, the asset would be financed through a term loan at 12%. The loan calls for equal payments to be made at the end of each year for four years. The machine would qualify for accelerated capital cost allowances written off on a straight-line basis over two years.

Calculate the cash flows for each financing alternative. Which alternative is the most economically attractive?

EXERCISE 10

Hull Manufacturing Co. is faced with the decision of purchasing or leasing a new piece of equipment. The equipment can be leased for $4,000 a year or purchased for

$15,000. The lease includes maintenance and service. The salvage value of the equipment five years hence is $5,000. The company uses the declining method to calculate depreciation. The rate of depreciation is 30%. If the equipment is owned, service and maintenance charges (a tax-deductible cost) would be $900 a year. The firm can borrow the entire amount at a rate of 15% if the purchase option is exercised. The tax rate is 50%. On the basis of the above, which method of financing would you choose?

Use the following capital cost allowance amounts to calculate the cost of the equipment.

Year	Amount
1	$4,500
2	3,150
3	2,205
4	1,543
5	1,081

Cases

CASE 1: GRIP CASE INC.

In April 2010, Miriam and Ben Friedman were thinking about starting their own business, Grip Case Inc. Their objective was to produce and market inexpensive attaché cases. It was not their intention to compete directly against expensive cases produced by companies such as Samsonite, Hartmann, Zero Halliburton, or Atlantic. Miriam and Ben felt that if their company produced an inexpensive case (retailing at about $50), they would sell at least 15,000 units during the first year of operation. Of course, the launching of the Grip Case Inc. would be conditional on obtaining the required financing that the company needs to borrow from various lending institutions.

Miriam and Ben intended to approach their venture in three phases. The first phase would consist of a detailed feasibility study, including legal work for patent registration and additional work on the product design. The second phase would involve the preparation of a detailed investment proposal required to seek the necessary financing for the purchase of the capital assets, the working capital requirements, and operating funds needed to market the products effectively. The third phase would be implementation through production and commercialization.

Attaché cases are marketed under private brands or manufacturers' brands. Private brands account for a smaller segment of the Canadian retail market. Most often, private brand cases are manufactured for retail outlets such as The Bay, Sears, Walmart, etc. Manufacturers' brand names include products such as Hartmann, Samsonite, Atlantic, SOLO, and Stebco.

After examining dozens of different types of cases, Miriam and Ben found that the four most important elements of the product, with regard to consumer choice, are construction, convenience, interior, and exterior. The quality of construction of a case depends on its frame, hinges, handle, feet, latches, and locks. Convenience is determined by what the case offers, such as files and pockets. Miriam and Ben found that cases are available with a wide variety of files and pockets. How the interior of a case is divided also interests buyers. Things that buyers look for are lining, stability, and file compartments. Some attaché cases have pockets for business cards, a calculator, airline tickets, and parking-lot receipts. The exterior comes in different qualities. This factor significantly affects the retail sales price. Cases are made of leather, vinyl, or moulded plastic. Good-quality leather cases are the most expensive, with a price range of between $250 and $800. Vinyl cases are priced between $75 and $250. The cheapest moulded-plastic case sells in the $70 range.

Although Miriam and Ben intended to market the three basic types of cases (attaché case, briefcase, and portfolio), they wanted to market only the attaché cases during the first year of operation in order to hold down their initial investment and production costs. The type of case that they wanted to market would retail between $40 and $60. The cost of production and the amount of markup sought by the middle parties would determine the exact price. They would focus primarily on the student markets (secondary, colleges, and universities). They believed that a practical, low-priced model could meet consumers' needs. Grip Case Inc. would sell its products directly to wholesalers and/or retailers. The exact distribution network had not yet been determined.

Grip Case Inc. is to manufacture cases for private brands and sell to retail stores such as Walmart, Zellers, discount stores, and drugstores. It would also sell cases bearing its own brand name, "Grip Case." By selling cases at about $25 to wholesalers/retailers, and with 15,000 units, the company would be able to cover its costs and begin to make a profit during the second year of operation. The following shows Grip Case Inc.'s financial needs.

FINANCIAL NEEDS		
Working capital		
Inventories	$60,000	
Trade receivables	40,000	$100,000
Capital assets		
Leasehold improvements	100,000	
Equipment	70,000	
Machinery/truck	80,000	250,000
Research and development		50,000
Marketing/promotion		50,000
Total financial needs		$450,000

Grip Case Inc.'s condensed projected statements of income for the first three years of operations are as follows:

	Year 1	Year 2	Year 3
No. of units	15,000	20,000	25,000
Unit selling price ($)	25	25	25

		(in $)	
Revenue	375,000	500,000	625,000
Cost of sales	(187,500)	(250,000)	(312,500)
Gross profit	187,500	250,000	312,500
Administrative expenses	(85,000)	(95,000)	(110,000)
Distribution costs	(90,000)	(70,000)	(80,000)
Depreciation	(30,000)	(30,000)	(30,000)
Finance costs	(25,000)	(25,000)	(25,000)
Total expenses	(230,000)	(220,000)	(245,000)
Profit before taxes	(42,500)	30,000	67,500
Income tax expense	—	—	(12,000)
Profit for the year	(42,500)	30,000	55,500

Miriam and Ben had accumulated an amount of $150,000 over the past 10 years and were planning to invest the entire amount in the business in the form of equity. They knew that they would have difficulty obtaining debt financing but had a $250,000 house of which 40% could be used as collateral. However, they were prepared to use this option only as a last resort.

Miriam and Ben were determined to adopt a conservative strategy, growing slowly and carefully in starting their business. Rather than investing huge sums of money in expensive equipment and buying a building, they intended to purchase some used equipment and rent a building belonging to Miriam's father. If, after the first three years, the attaché case product line reached the expected level of sales, they would then consider making the other cases, that is, the briefcase and the portfolio product lines. Depending on the company's financial position three years after start-up, Miriam and Ben might lease a larger building or even build their own.

Although Miriam and Ben were still at the research stage, they had done some costing to calculate how much profit they would make for each case. At 15,000 units, the cost of production would be in the $187,500 range, for a total unit production cost of approximately $12.50. The cost breakdown is as follows: direct materials, $6.30/unit; direct labour, $2.00 (for a total of $124,500 in variable costs); and the rest ($63,000) in fixed manufacturing costs.

Questions

1. What questions do you think lenders will want to ask Miriam and Ben regarding their venture?
2. How many units would the company have to sell in the first year of operation in order to break even? When will the company break even?

Is the break-even point in that year reasonable? Why or why not? (The break-even point concept was covered in Chapter 5.)

3. What type of investors or lenders should Miriam and Ben approach? Why?
4. What type of collateral would the lenders want to take into consideration?
5. How much do you believe they will be able to obtain from the different financing sources? Why?

CASE 2: BALDWIN EQUIPMENT INC.

Management of Baldwin Equipment is considering increasing the productivity of its plant. Management heard from suppliers that a certain piece of equipment could entail an after-tax cash flow savings of more than $35,000 a year if it was installed in Baldwin's plant. However, Jim Henderson, the controller of the company, is unsure whether the company should buy or lease the equipment. If the asset is leased for a 10-year period, it would cost the company $45,000 a year (before tax). The company's income tax rate is 50%. If the company buys the asset, it would cost $300,000 and be financed entirely through debt for a 10-year period at a cost of 10%. The asset's capital cost allowance is 25% (declining basis). On the basis of this information, Jim is now considering whether to purchase or lease the equipment. He is considering doing a sensitivity analysis regarding the two options by modifying some of the data in the base case, which is the information presented above.

Question

On the basis of the following, calculate the effect that each individual change in the base case would have on the decision. Changes to the base case are as follows:

- Capital cost allowance would be increased to 40%.
- The interest on the loan would be 8%.
- The company would be able to sell the asset for $50,000 in the tenth year.

PHOTO/Pixelbliss/Shutterstock

CHAPTER 9

[COST OF CAPITAL, CAPITAL STRUCTURE, AND FINANCIAL MARKETS]

Learning Objectives

After reading this chapter, you should be able to:

1 Learning Objective — Explain the financial and capital structure concepts in addition to the cost concepts.

2 Learning Objective — Clarify the meaning of cost of financing, why it is used, and how it is calculated.

3 Learning Objective — Explain that the economic value added concept is a financial technique used to measure managerial performance related to shareholder wealth maximization.

4 Learning Objective — Explain that the components of the average weighted cost of capital include common shares, retained earnings, preferred shares, and long-term borrowings.

5 Learning Objective — Explain the importance of leverage analysis and how the operating leverage, financial leverage, and combined leverage are calculated.

6 Learning Objective — Give a profile of the financial markets, the stock market, and various theories related to the dividend theories and payments.

Chapter Outline

OPENING CASE

By the end of 2010, the Millers were pleased with CompuTech Sales and Service's financial performance. In fact, they exceeded their financial expectations. During that year, they decided to incorporate their business. It is now called CompuTech Inc. The Millers were entering an important phase in their business development; they wanted to further expand their retail business. The one determining factor that limited the number of outlets they hoped to open was how much financing they would be able to obtain from investors. They were also considering asking a few friends to invest in their business.

Important elements that could encourage investors to invest in CompuTech are the quality of the collateral and the company's ability to service its debt. On the other hand, the factor that would entice potential shareholders to invest in the company is its ability to grow in terms of revenue and profit. The Millers would have to prove to potential investors that they have the ability to manage the company extraordinarily well and demonstrate that CompuTech Inc. would be able to generate substantial earnings.

The Millers began to prepare a business plan to be presented to different investors. They wanted to expand the working capital of their existing retail outlet and open another outlet in 2011. The amount of the required investment in non-current assets (property, plant, and equipment) was estimated at $350,000. The following shows how the Millers proposed to finance their expansion program.

	Cash Outflows	Cash Inflows
Property, plant, and equipment	$350,000	
Internal financing		$157,000
Share capital		70,000
Long-term borrowings		150,000
Working capital requirements	$99,000	
Short-term borrowings		72,000
Total	$449,000	$449,000

The Millers remembered their initial conversation with entrepreneur Bill Murray when he said, "You have to make sure that your business generates enough cash (or profit) to pay for financing its growth." Now that the Millers were facing growth and expansion, they began to realize the significance of Bill's statement. They had to make sure that sufficient cash would be available from the business to pay the finance costs and dividends. They also had to make sure that earnings from their business would be sufficient to reinvest into their business for the purchase of non-current assets (new store, equipment, etc.), and for working capital requirements.

A quick analysis of their projected financial statements for 2011 indicated that CompuTech would generate a 12.1% return on assets (ROA). The Millers had to ensure that the cost of borrowed funds from different financing sources would be less than the ROA. In order to encourage other shareholders to invest in CompuTech Inc., they had to demonstrate how much additional wealth the business would generate for them.

The Millers had more ambitious goals for the longer term. They wanted to go public by 2018. This meant that they had six to seven years to demonstrate that CompuTech Inc. had real growth potential with powerful earnings. They were thinking of approaching venture capitalists by 2013 to invest substantial sums of money in their business in the form of equity. They realized, however, that these types of investors were looking for 25% to 35% (if not more) return on their investment. If they wanted to entice these types of investors by 2013, the Millers had to show that CompuTech Inc. had substantial growth and earnings.

Chapter Overview

There is an important connection between three critical components of finance: capital structure, cost of capital, and capital budgeting. This chapter deals in large measure with capital structure and cost of capital while Chapter 11 covers the third component, capital budgeting.

Here is how these three key components of finance are connected to one another. As shown in Figure 9.1, one of the first steps in capital expenditure planning (or capital budgeting) is to determine how much funds (or cash) should be borrowed and from whom (capital structure). If the treasurer is asked to raise, say, $1 million, the cost of funds related to raising the money will have to be calculated (cost of capital). The

Figure 9.1 **Interplay Between the Major Components of Finance**

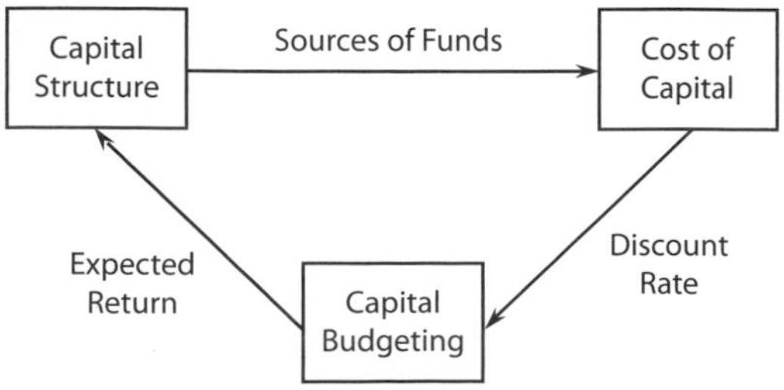

composition of the debt-to-equity makeup, which is made up of common equity, preferred equity, and long-term borrowings (bonds or mortgages), largely determines the cost of capital. As shown in the following example, because raising funds from equity costs more (12.0%) than from debt (5.0%), it would be less tempting to obtain funds from shareholders than from lenders.

As a result, different debt-to-equity structures may influence the relationship between the cost of funds and ROA. To illustrate, as shown in the following example, let's assume that a company has $1 million in assets, which gives a 9.0% ROA. The financial structure shown in option A gives a 9.9% weighted average cost of financing (WACF), while option B gives 7.1%. The **weighted average cost of financing** reflects the proportion of the component costs of each amount included in a company's financial structure. With a 9% ROA, the company is in a negative position with option A because the company is negative by 0.9% (9.0% ROA versus a 9.9% WACF). With option B, a different financial structure, the company's ROA would exceed the cost of funds by 1.9%.

Weighted average cost of financing Represents the proportion of the component costs of each amount included in a company's financial structure.

Option A

	Equity		Debt		Total
Amount	$700,000	+	$300,000	=	$1,000,000
Cost of funds	12.0%		5.0%		
Weight	× 0.70	+	× 0.30	=	1.00
WACF	8.40%	+	1.50%	=	9.90%

Option B

	Equity		Debt		Total
Amount	$300,000	+	$700,000	=	$1,000,000
Cost of funds	12.0%		5.0%		
Weight	× 0.30	+	× 0.70	=	1.00
WACF	3.60%	+	3.50%	=	7.10%

As shown in Figure 1.1 on page 7, Chapter 8, which covered the sources and forms of financing, was the first chapter dealing with financing decisions. This chapter, which also deals with financing decisions, examines six distinct but related topics. The first topic gives a broad definition of the words *cost* and *structure*. It explains the difference between cost of financing and cost of capital and also the difference between the financial structure and the capital structure. The second topic focuses on the importance of cost of financing and describes its purpose and how it is calculated. The third topic looks at the EVA, which is an index that measures managerial performance in terms of achieving the objective related to shareholder wealth maximization. This section also shows how EVA is calculated.

Cost of capital
The cost of borrowing money from one source (shareholders or lenders) to finance a business.

The fourth topic, a major theme in this chapter, explains the key characteristics of long-term capital financing sources and the cost of capital. **Cost of capital** has to do with the cost of borrowing funds from long-term investors (common shares, retained earnings, preferred shares, and long-term borrowings). For example, someone who obtains a mortgage from the bank at 7.0% to buy a house would have a 7.0% cost of capital. Similarly, if an entrepreneur wants to start a business that requires $500,000 in capital, the first thing that will be done is to determine how much it will cost to raise these capital funds from various investors. As illustrated in the following example, the cost to raise the $500,000 from investors to buy the assets is 6.1%. Also, assuming that the entrepreneur earns $50,000 in profit on a $500,000 investment in assets, the business would generate a 10.0% ROA. In this particular example, there is a positive 3.9% difference between the cost of capital at 6.1% and the amount that the entrepreneur expects to earn from the business. As we will see in Chapter 11, cost of capital is often used as the discount rate to determine whether to approve capital projects (see Figure 9.1).

The reason for comparing the ROA to the cost of capital is to ensure that the return generated from a particular investment in capital projects justifies the cost of borrowed capital. This is how banks operate: They borrow money at a cost, and lend it for a return; they refer to the difference between the two as the *spread*.

Statement of Financial Position	
Assets	Investors
Return on assets	Cost of capital
10.0%	6.1%

The following shows how the cost to raise capital dollars from different investors is calculated. For example, the $100,000 amount borrowed from Source A represents 20% (weight) of the $500,000 amount and accounts for 1.0% (5% × 0.20) of the weighted cost. This process leads us to calculating a 6.1% weighted average cost of capital. The weighted average cost of capital reflects a weighted average component cost where the weight of each long-term source reflects the amount used. In the future, the expression WACC will be used to differentiate the aggregate cost of capital from the cost of individual components.

Sources	Amount	Cost		Weight		Weighted Cost
Source A	$100,000	5%	×	0.20	=	1.0%
Source B	250,000	6%	×	0.50	=	3.0%
Source C	150,000	7%	×	0.30	=	2.1%
WACC	$500,000			1.00		6.1%

Leverage
Technique used to determine the most suitable operating and financial structure that will help amplify financial performance.

The fifth major theme of this chapter explains the meaning of **leverage**, a technique used to determine the most suitable operating and financial structure that can help amplify a firm's operating and financial performance. It focuses on the following questions: Should a business have more fixed costs than variable costs? What would be the right proportion? Should the business have more equity than debt? Again, what would be the best combination or proportion? This segment of the chapter explains the meaning of operating leverage, financial leverage, and combined leverage.

Revenue is a key element that helps decide the most suitable operating and financing mix (or structure). The more volume a business generates, the more management will be inclined to have a higher mix of fixed costs versus variable costs. For example, this was particularly critical when free trade agreements were signed with the United States and Mexico that gave wider access to markets for Canadian businesses. With expanded markets, many businesses restructured their operating and financial structures in order to maximize both profitability and the wealth to their shareholders.

Finding the most suitable operating structure can help amplify profitability. For example, if a business generates an increase in EBIT of 20% with a 10% increase in revenue, the business has a 2.0 (or 2 to 1) operating leverage; that is, each time revenue increases by 10%, EBIT is amplified by 20%. If management decides to change the composition of its operating cost structure and obtains a leverage of 3.0 (meaning that a 10% increase in revenue generates a 30% increase in EBIT), it simply means maximization of greater earnings. The importance of calculating operating leverage is this: If Company A operates with a 3.0 leverage and Company B with a 2.0 leverage factor, the former has a better competitive advantage. This section also explains how financial leverage and combined leverage can amplify a company's financial performance.

The sixth and final section of this chapter deals with financial markets, the stock market, and dividend theories and dividend payments. The segment related to financial markets examines the organizations and the procedures involved in the buying and selling of assets. As we will see, there are different types of markets such as money markets, capital markets, primary markets, secondary markets, spot and future markets, mortgage markets, consumer credit markets, and physical asset markets. The segment that deals with the stock market looks at the difference between a privately held company and a publicly traded company, including the meaning of an initial public offering and a listed company. The last segment of this section looks at various dividend theories, dividend policy, and dividend payments.

1 Learning Objective

Explain the financial and capital structure concepts in addition to the cost concepts.

Structure and Cost Concepts

Financial structure
The way a company's assets are financed by the entire right-hand side of the statement of financial position (long-term and short-term financing).

Let's examine the difference between financial structure and capital structure, and the contrast between cost of financing and cost of capital.

As shown in Figure 9.2, **financial structure** means the way a company's total assets are financed by the "entire right-hand side of the statement of financial

Figure 9.2 **Financial Structure and Capital Structure**

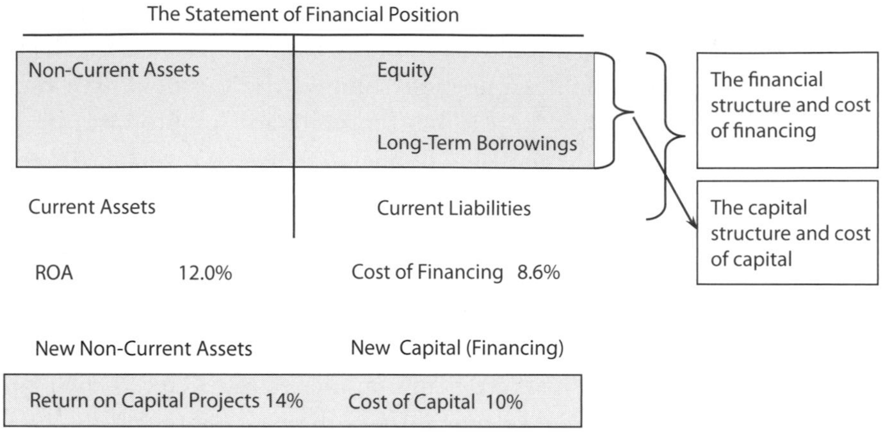

Capital structure
Components of the permanent or long-term financing sources used to buy non-current assets.

position" (equity, long-term borrowings, and current liabilities). On the other hand, **capital structure** represents the more permanent forms of financing such as equity (common shares, retained earnings, and preferred shares) and long-term borrowings (mortgages, bonds) that are normally used to finance non-current (or capital) assets. The shaded portion in the figure represents the portion related to the capital financial package. Capital structure therefore accounts for only a portion of a company's total financial structure. As shown, it excludes current liabilities.

Self-Test Exercise No. 9.1

Financial Structure and Capital Structure

From the following financing sources, identify CompuTech's financial structure and capital structure, and calculate the proportion or weight of each.

Sources	Amounts
Share capital	$100,000
Trade and other payables	20,000
Retained earnings	58,000
Long-term borrowings	50,000
Term loan	40,000
Working capital loan	—

Let's now look at the importance of calculating the cost of financing and the cost of capital. Cost of financing shows how much a business is charged to finance the assets that are shown on a company's statement of financial position (SFP). As shown in Figure 9.2, let's assume that a company borrows funds from different financial institutions, which cost 8.6%, and earns 12.0% ROA; in this case, the company's cost of financing is less than what it earns. This produces positive results and undoubtedly makes good business sense. However, if the cost of financing a business is more than its ROA, the shareholders would not be earning enough to justify the investments in total assets.

Cost of capital is a different concept, but it is calculated in a similar way. As indicated earlier, it deals with only the permanent forms of financing and has to do with the raising of new long-term capital to buy new non-current assets. As shown in Figure 9.2, the company raises new capital funds from different financing sources (equity and long-term borrowings) at a cost of 10.0% (cost of capital). These funds are invested in new non-current assets and produce a 14.0% return (capital budgeting). This means that the cost of the newly acquired capital or permanent financing is less than the return to be earned on newly acquired non-current assets. Again, this would make good business sense.

Cost of capital is associated with capital budgets as both have long-term implications. Bonds and mortgages, for example, are borrowed on a long-term basis (say, 15 years) and are used to finance capital projects that also have long life spans (say, 15 years). Referring to Figure 9.2, if the company's cost of capital is 10.0%, and it earns 14.0% ROA, this means that the business would have a 4.0% positive spread every year during the next 15 years. If the spread were negative, the shareholders would make less on their investments. If this were the case, management would surely not proceed with the investment decision.

In the News 9.1 illustrates one of the reasons why a business will raise debt financing as a strategy to battle difficult times.

In The News [9.1]

Raising Debt Financing Can Be Part of a Company's Strategy to Battle Financial Losses

Like most airlines, British Airways PLC, the flag-carrier airline of the United Kingdom and one of two airlines to operate the supersonic Aérospatiale-BAC Concorde aircraft back in 1976, was another wounded company caused by the recession-driven economy. They went through the most probable "cure-all" treatment taken by most organizations caught in this mess, debt financing.

During the middle of 2009, British Airways PLC was planning to raise $1.1 billion to help go through the recession and financial losses. The estimated three-month loss through June was $166 million. Despite the fact that the company had been trying to implement some cost-cutting activities by reducing staff and putting into operation innovative strategic plans (e.g., all-business service to New York on a 32-seat Airbus, and offering superior service like punctuality performance), it was able to (1) raise $500 million through a convertible debt issue, and (2) secure the return of $550 million worth of guarantees from pension fund trustees.

Source: Adapted from Associated Press, "British Airways announces plan to raise capital," *Globe and Mail*, July 18, 2009, p. B6. For updates on market conditions and strategic developments at British Airways, go to http://www.bashares.com.

Self-Test Exercise No. 9.2

Weighted Average Cost of Financing and Cost of Capital

With the information contained in Self-Test Exercise No. 9.1 and the following costs for individual financing sources, calculate CompuTech's weighted average after-tax cost of financing and cost of capital.

Sources	Cost (%)
Share capital	12
Trade and other payables	0
Retained earnings	11
Long-term borrowings	5
Term loan	7
Working capital loan	6

Cost of Financing

2 Learning Objective

Clarify the meaning of cost of financing, why it is used, and how it is calculated.

Let's now examine the importance of cost of financing and how it is calculated. Table 9.1 shows a company that raises $1,200,000 from seven different sources. Equity financing accounts for $450,000 (or 37.5%), long-term borrowings account for $500,000 (or 41.7%), and short-term borrowings or current liabilities account for $250,000 (or 20.8%) of the total financing package. The table also presents the cost of financing for each amount raised, on a before- and after-tax basis. For example, management raised $50,000 from Source A at a cost of 8.0% on a before-tax basis. Assuming that the company is in a 40% tax bracket, the after-tax cost of borrowing from Source A would be 4.8%. The same arithmetic is done for calculating all other long- and short-term loans. However, the cost of raising funds from equity is 12%, whether before or after tax, because dividends are paid to shareholders with after-tax profit. The last two columns of Table 9.1 present the WACF. As shown, based on that particular financing structure, it would cost the company 9.05% before tax to raise funds from different sources, and 7.12% after tax.

The WACF, however, is somewhat irrelevant unless it is compared to the return that the company earns on its assets. Table 9.2 gives us this comparison. As shown in the table on the left side of the SFP, the company earns a 14.20% ROA on a before-tax basis and 8.52% on an after-tax basis. The before-tax return is based on the assumption that the company generated $170,400 in profit before taxes ($1,200,000 × 14.20%) and $102,240 ($1,200,000 × 8.52%) after taxes on total assets of $1,200,000.

As indicated above, the after-tax return is based on the assumption that the company is in a 40% tax bracket. As shown in Table 9.2, the spread is positive using the before-tax calculation because the company's assets are generating more than the cost of borrowed funds (14.20% versus 9.05%). The spread is also positive on an after-tax basis (8.52% versus 7.12%). After-tax comparison is the common approach used for comparing cost of financing to ROA.

Table 9.1 Cost of Financing

	Amounts in $	Weight (%)		Cost of Financing Before Tax	Cost of Financing After Tax		Weighted Average Cost of Financing Before Tax	Weighted Average Cost of Financing After Tax
Equity								
Share capital	150,000	12.5	×	12.0%	12.0%	=	1.50%	1.50%
Retained earnings	300,000	25.0	×	11.0%	11.0%	=	2.75%	2.75%
Subtotal	450,000	37.5					4.25%	4.25%
Long-term borrowings								
Mortgage	200,000	16.7	×	7.0%	4.2%	=	1.17%	0.70%
Bond	300,000	25.0	×	7.5%	4.5%	=	1.88%	1.12%
Subtotal	500,000	41.7					3.05%	1.82%
Current liabilities								
Source A	50,000	4.2	×	8.0%	4.8%	=	0.34%	0.20%
Source B	100,000	8.3	×	8.4%	5.0%	=	0.70%	0.42%
Source C	100,000	8.3	×	8.6%	5.2%	=	0.71%	0.43%
Subtotal	250,000	20.8					1.75%	1.05%
Total debt	750,000	62.5					4.80%	2.87%
Total sources	1,200,000	100.0						
Weighted average cost of financing							9.05%	7.12%

Table 9.2 Comparing Cost of Financing to ROA

Statement of Financial Position

				Before tax	After tax
Assets		Equity	$450,000	@ 4.25%	4.25%
Non-current	$800,000	Liabilities			
Current	400,000	Non-current	500,000	@ 3.05%	1.82%
		Short-term	250,000	@ 1.75%	1.05%
Total	$1,200,000	Total	$1,200,000	9.05%	7.12%

	ROA	Cost
Before tax	14.20%	9.05%
After tax	8.52%	7.12%

Before tax

Debt $750,000	×	14.20% (ROA)	=	$106,500
Debt $750,000	×	7.67% (Cost)	=	(57,525)
Financial leverage				$ 48,975

After tax

Equity financing	15.04%	×	0.375	=	5.64%
Debt financing	4.60%	×	0.625	=	2.88%
Return on assets					8.52%

Let's push this analysis a little further and calculate how much the company is earning on borrowed funds. This is what the lower portion of Table 9.2 presents. The company borrowed $750,000 ($500,000 from long-term lenders and $250,000 from short-term lenders) and earned 14.20% (ROA) or $106,500. As shown below, the weighted average cost to borrow the funds from both long- and short-term sources is 7.67%. These amounts are drawn from different sources of financing that appear in Table 9.1.

Sources	Amounts	Weight (%)		Before-Tax Cost		Weighted Cost (%)
Mortgage	$200,000	26.67	×	7.0	=	1.87
Bond	300,000	40.00	×	7.5	=	3.00
Source A	50,000	6.67	×	8.0	=	0.53
Source B	100,000	13.33	×	8.4	=	1.12
Source C	100,000	13.33	×	8.6	=	1.15
Total	$750,000	100.00				7.67%

This means that there is a 6.53% spread (14.20% and 7.67%) on a before-tax basis between the cost of debt financing and the ROA. As shown in Table 9.2, the company's financial leverage—that is, the amount of money the owners earn by using other people's money—is $48,975.

The lower portion of Table 9.2 also shows how the shareholders' return can be amplified as a result of the company's earnings performance and financial structure. Because the cost of debt financing is 7.67% on a before-tax basis, the after-tax cost of financing (assuming the company is in a 40% tax bracket) would be 4.60%. Also, the proportion of the $1,200,000 raised from equity is $450,000, or 37.5%, and the balance, $750,000, or 62.5%, was obtained from debt. As shown, instead of earning an 11.30% return (12% for share equity and 11% for retained earnings), the shareholders are actually getting more, 15.04%.

Here is how this number is calculated. Debt financing is constant; that is, irrespective of what happens, the company has to pay the interest—here, 4.60%, which represents 2.88% of the total cost of financing. As shown in Table 9.2, the company earns an 8.52% after-tax ROA. By subtracting the 2.88% portion of the debt financing from the 8.52% ROA, we get 5.64% (15.04% × 0.375).

3 Learning Objective

Explain that the economic value added concept is a financial technique used to measure managerial performance related to shareholder wealth maximization.

Economic Value Added

A new term that has gained prominence in the business community to measure after-tax net operating profit relative to cost of capital is the **economic value added (EVA)**. EVA measures how profitable a company truly is in terms of creating shareholder wealth. Calculating the EVA begins with the company's revenue, and then subtracts the expenses incurred in running the business, which results in *net operating profit before taxes (NOPBT)*. Then it subtracts income tax expense to obtain *net*

Economic value added (EVA)
Tool that measures the wealth a company creates for its investors.

operating profit after taxes (NOPAT). By deducting the cost of all the capital employed from NOPAT, we get EVA. Capital assets include elements such as buildings, equipment, computers, and vehicles, as well as working capital.

EVA can be expressed by the following formula:

$$\textbf{EVA} = \textbf{(return on total assets – cost of capital)} \times \textbf{Capital}$$

In effect, EVA charges the company for the use of those assets at a rate that compensates the lenders and the shareholders for providing those funds. What is left is EVA, and it measures profits after all costs are covered, including the cost of using assets shown on the SFP.

EVA has become the financial tool of choice at leading companies such as Coca-Cola, AT&T, Walmart, Eli Lilly, and Quaker Oats. At Eli Lilly, for example, EVA was linked to the company's bonus-plan pay system.

The reasons for the increasing popularity of this performance measurement are the following:

- It more closely reflects the wealth created for shareholders.
- It promotes management accountability.
- It helps to make better decisions.

Table 9.3 shows an example of how EVA is calculated. As shown, the company's NOPBT is $1.0 million. On an after-tax basis, the NOPAT is $550,000. It is assumed here that the company is in a 45% income tax bracket. The company's cost of capital of 10.9% (after tax) to finance the $4,500,000 worth of capital funds (trade and other payables are excluded from this calculation because suppliers do not charge interest) produces $490,500 in finance costs. The difference between the NOPAT and the cost of capital gives a $59,500 positive EVA. EVA can also be calculated by using the formula:

$$\begin{aligned}\textbf{EVA} &= \textbf{(return on total assets – cost of capital)} \times \textbf{Capital}\\ &= \textbf{(12.22\% – 10.9\%)} \times \textbf{\$4,500,000} = \textbf{\$ 59,500 (rounded from \$59,400)}\end{aligned}$$

Table 9.3 The Economic Value Added

	Net Operating Profit	Minus	Cost of Capital	Equals	EVA
NOPBT	$1,000,000	Weighted cost	10.9%*		
Income tax expense	(450,000)	of capital	×		
		Total capital	$4,500,000		
NOPAT	$ 550,000	*MINUS*	$ (490,500)	*EQUALS*	$59,500

*10.9% equals to 60% of equity @ 14.5%, or 8.7%, plus and 40% of debt @ 5.5%, or 2.2% (8.7 + 2.2 = 10.9%).

These calculations show the importance of comparing the cost of capital to ROA. If the ROA is less than the cost of capital, management must either increase the return on its assets or restructure its financing package differently in order to improve the EVA or the wealth to its shareholders.

Self-Test Exercise No. 9.3

Economic Value Added

By using CompuTech's 2011 financial statements, calculate the company's EVA.

CompuTech Inc.
Statement of Income
for the period ended December 31, 2011
(in $)

Revenue	800,000
Cost of sales	(406,000)
Gross profit	394,000
Other income	5,000
Distribution costs	(140,000)
Administrative expenses	(110,000)
Finance costs	(30,000)
Total other income/expenses	(275,000)
Profit before taxes	119,000
Income tax expense	(42,000)
Profit for the year	77,000

The company's three major sources of financing will be from shareholders for $305,000, long-term borrowings for $200,000, and short-term borrowings for $85,000. The equity portion was split as follows: share capital in the amount of $170,000 and retained earnings for $135,000.

The cost of capital for these three sources of financing is as follows:

Common share equity	14.0%
Long-term borrowings	11.0%
Short-term borrowings	13.0%

4 Learning Objective

Explain that the components of the average weighted cost of capital include common shares, retained earnings, preferred shares, and long-term borrowings.

Cost of Capital

The cost of capital incurred by businesses is set out in contractual agreements made between a borrowing company and the different stakeholders. The key issues that will be focused on are (1) dividends and growth potential expected by the common shareholders (common shareholders and retained earnings), (2) the dividends it will pay to preferred shareholders, and (3) the amount of interest it will pay to lenders.

In this section, we will calculate the cost of capital for a hypothetical company called Wildwood Inc. Let's assume that Wildwood's management wants to raise $20 million to invest in different capital projects. We will calculate the cost of capital of four financing sources:

a. Common shares
b. Retained earnings
c. Preferred shares
d. Long-term borrowings

Afterward, we will define the meaning of marginal cost of capital. Let's first examine the characteristics of each of these major sources of financing.

CHARACTERISTICS OF LONG-TERM CAPITAL SOURCES

Common share, preferred share, and debt financing have one important common characteristic: They are all obtained from external sources. Retained earnings (that is, profit for the year generated by a business) is the only internal financing source. Table 9.4 summarizes the basic **characteristics of long-term financing sources** as seen from an issuing company's point of view.

Long-term financing sources (characteristics) Factors to consider when raising funds from long-term sources: payout, risk, voting rights, cost of capital, tax cost, and cost of issue.

These major long-term financing sources are examined in terms of payout, risk, voting rights or control, cost of capital, tax cost, and cost of a new issue.

Payout means the money that a business must pay its stakeholders in exchange for funds. Payout ranges from compulsory payment (debt) of principal and interest to non-obligatory payments, such as dividends on common shares.

Risk refers to the impact each source of financing has on a business if the business is unable to meet its contractual agreement. Debt financing is the riskiest choice, particularly when economic or business conditions are difficult to predict, because bondholders may demand that interest be paid as per agreement, and if it is not, force the business into receivership.

Voting rights refer to the control that different stakeholders have over a business. Those who have the ultimate control of a company are the common shareholders. The issue of a new bond or preferred shares does not take away the rights of existing shareholders, but the issue of new common shares dilutes common shareholders' voting control. Also, additional shareholders can force a company to spread earnings more widely and thinly (see the figures in Table 9.5 for the spread of profit to new and existing shareholders).

Cost of capital includes factors associated with the borrowing of money, such as payment of dividends for common or preferred shares, interest on debt, underwriting and distribution costs, and taxes. All these elements must be weighted to determine the costs associated with each source of financing. Costs related to preferred shares and debt are more easily determinable and relatively more certain than common share financing.

Tax cost plays an important part in deciding whether to go the route of share or debt financing. Common or preferred share dividends are not deductible as an expense for calculating a business's income tax; interest on bonds is. Taxes are a real cost that

Table 9.4 Characteristics of the Major Sources of Long-Term Financing

	Common Shares	Retained Earnings	Preferred Shares	Debt
Payout	Common share dividends are paid after debt and preferred dividends.	Reduced payment of dividends puts more funds into a business; may be unfavourable in the short term but favourable in the long term.	Same as debt, amount is specified by agreement.	Interest and principal must be paid as per contractual agreement.
	Company is not forced to make payment.		Dividends can be cumulated from year to year.	Bondholders do not participate in superior earnings.
Risk	Do not carry fixed maturity date.	Increases value and worth of a business.	Have maturity and is usually callable.	If lenders are not paid according to agreement, they can force a business into receivership.
			Have prior claim over common shareholders for receiving dividends and other assets if company is liquidated.	
Voting rights (control)	New issue creates change in ownership structure (extends voting rights). Legal right to make major decisions (elect board of directors).	When earnings are retained in a business, existing owners do not have ownership right.	Have limited voting privileges; if they do, it is for minority representation on board of directors.	Have no say in business unless bond goes into default.
Cost of capital	Rate is more difficult to ascertain because external factors and growth potential of a business form part of the cost.	Not easily determinable because of unpredictable growth trends.	Easy to calculate because it has a maturity date and a stated dividend rate and price of a share.	Easy to calculate and determinable because interest rate is stipulated.
Tax cost	Common dividends are not tax deductible.	Taxed before payments are made to shareholders.	Preferred dividends are not tax deductible.	Interest charges are tax deductible.
Cost of issue	Underwriting and distribution costs are usually higher than preferred share and debt financing.	Avoids cost of issue.	Flotation cost is expensive.	Underwriting cost is less expensive than other alternatives.

Table 9.5 **Impact of Debt and Share Financing on Profit**

	A Common Shares	B Preferred Shares	C Debt
Profit before taxes	$500,000	$ 500,000	$ 500,000
Financing costs	0	0	(50,000)
Taxable income	500,000	500,000	450,000
Income tax expense (at 45%)	(225,000)	(225,000)	(202,500)
Profit for the year	275,000	275,000	247,500
Preferred dividends	0	(60,000)	0
Profit to common shareholders	275,000	215,000	247,500
Profit to new shareholders	(123,750)	—	—
Profit to existing shareholders	$151,250	$ 215,000	$ 247,500

Financing assumptions:

A. ***Common share financing*** of $500,000 raised from new shareholders in exchange for 50% of the company's shares.
B. ***Preferred share financing*** of $500,000 raised from investors with a dividend rate of 12%.
C. ***Debt financing*** of $500,000 raised from lenders with interest rate of 10%.

must be examined carefully. Table 9.5 gives an example of the impact taxes have on debt and share financing, at a certain level of profit. As shown in the table, alternative C (debt financing) is the least attractive form of financing because the profit after taxes is $247,500 compared to $275,000 for alternatives A and B. However, alternative C is the most lucrative for the existing shareholders because they earn $96,250 ($247,500 – $151,250) more than common share financing offers, and $32,500 ($247,500 – $215,000) over preferred share financing.

Cost of issue includes charges associated with the underwriting and distribution of a new issue. Costs of issuing common shares are usually higher because the investigation is more detailed than preferred share and debt financing. A company that wants to raise funds will examine all the advantages and disadvantages of each source of financing and select the one that best meets its specific needs at the time of the issue.

The main factors that are taken into consideration when raising funds are as follows:

- The nature of a company's cash flows
- The company's annual burden of payments (existing debt)
- The cost of financing each type of capital
- The control factor
- The expectations of the existing common shareholders
- The flexibility of future financing decisions
- The pattern of the capital structure in the industry
- The stability of the company's earnings
- The desire to use financial leverage
- The market conditions that can easily dictate the use of one form of capital source over another

CALCULATING THE COST OF CAPITAL

Let's now calculate the cost of long-term capital sources, namely common shares, retained earnings, preferred shares, and debt.

Common shares. As we will see in future paragraphs, both preferred share and debt costs are easily calculated, quite determinable, and certain. They are contractual agreements signed by the company and the shareholders or bondholders.

Cost of common shares
Includes dividends paid to shareholders, flotation costs, and growth rate.

Calculating the **cost of common shares** is more complicated. The common shareholders know what they want, but it is difficult for the treasurer of a company to estimate the future expected values of the business in terms of growth, retained earnings, etc., all of which are incorporated in the calculation. There are two different approaches used for calculating the cost of common shares.

The first approach is based on past performance. By looking at trends related to common share prices and dividend payments, the treasurer can put a price tag on a new issue. For instance, if, during the past five years, the selling price of common shares has been \$25, and dividends paid were in the \$2.50 range, the average investor's rate of return is therefore 10% (\$2.50 ÷ \$25). If there are no significant changes in shareholders' expectations, interest rates, or investors' attitudes toward risk, the treasurer can assume that the future cost of common shares will be 10%.

The second approach is based on forecasts. Here, the treasurer takes into consideration three factors: (1) annual common dividends to be paid, (2) price of the common shares, and (3) expected growth in earnings and dividends. The formula to calculate the cost of common shares is as follows:

$$\textbf{Cost of common shares} = \frac{\textbf{Dividends on common shares}}{\textbf{Market price of the share} - \textbf{Issue costs}} + \textbf{Growth rate}$$

Let us refer to Wildwood Inc.'s financing package. The company intends to raise \$10 million from common shares. Also, the common share market price is \$100 and the company's current annual common dividend payout is 10%, or \$10 per share. Historically, the company's growth performance in earnings, dividends, and share price has been 4% a year, which is a growth that is assumed to continue during the next few years. Using the previous formula, Wildwood Inc.'s cost of common shares would be 14%.

$$\textbf{Cost of common shares} = \frac{\$10}{\$100} + 4\% = 14\%$$

The other factor taken into account is the flotation cost or the cost of selling a new issue. If Wildwood Inc.'s flotation costs are 10% on a \$100 common share issue, the company would net \$90. If we take this factor into consideration, the cost of the new shares would be 15.11%.

$$\textbf{Cost of common shares} = \frac{\$10}{\$100(1-0.10)} + 4\% = 15.11\%$$

The company is showing growth because a portion of the retained earnings is plowed back into investment opportunities. These investments would generate additional earnings and produce a favourable effect on the growth potential of the company. For example, if Wildwood Inc. earns 20% on its investments, and half of each dollar earned is paid in dividends and the other half retained in the business, this means that each new reinvested dollar produces 10 cents ($0.50 × 20%). Suppose, instead of reinvesting half of the earnings into the business, management decides to pay all its earnings in dividends; this may force a company to bring its growth to a halt. In this case, the market price of the share may remain at $100 as the investors would still receive a 14% return. (The topic related to the payment of dividends will be covered later in this chapter on page 451.) Here is how this rate is calculated:

$$\textbf{Cost of common shares} = \frac{\$14}{\$100} + 0 = 14\%$$

Retained earnings. An amount of $2 million is expected to be generated by Wildwood Inc. through its earnings. Some managers may think that retained earnings are "free money"; although it may be free to them, it is not to the shareholders. Shareholders also expect to make a return on their money (equity), because this is what they would expect to earn if they were to invest the $2 million in other investment securities. This is sometimes referred to as **opportunity cost**. In short, shareholders are making a sacrifice by not pursuing the next best investment alternative.

Opportunity cost
The income sacrificed by not pursuing the next best investment alternative.

Calculating the **cost of retained earnings** is similar to the common share calculation, except that issue costs are not incurred. If the company expects to earn $20 a share and pay $10 in dividends during the coming year, and the growth pattern is also 4%, the company's cost of retained earnings will be 14%.

Cost of retained earnings
Includes dividends and growth rate.

Preferred shares. Preferred shares are a hybrid of common shares and debt. Like debt, preferred shares carry a fixed contractual commitment for a company to pay—in this case, the dividends due to the preferred shareholders. In the event of liquidation, preferred shareholders take precedence over common shareholders. Also, dividends are paid to preferred shareholders before the common dividends are paid.

Calculating the **cost of preferred shares** is relatively easy because it carries a maturity date and a stated dividend rate with a current price. For example, if Wildwood Inc. issues preferred shares with a value of $1 million bearing 12%, the cost of this issue to the company would be $120,000 annually. If, one year from now, the preferred shares are sold in the market for 90% of their value, say $900,000, the interest rate to be earned

Cost of preferred shares
Includes fixed dividends paid to shareholders and the flotation costs.

by the new preferred shareholders would be 13.33% (12% ÷ 90%). The factors that may influence a decline in the market value of such shares are as follows:

- The general rise of the interest rate, which forces the price of the shares to drop
- A renewed fear of rampant inflation
- A decline in the general value of the business as an investment opportunity

Also, Wildwood Inc. would have to pay a commission to the investment dealers, and such flotation costs would be incorporated in the calculation.

Assuming that Wildwood Inc. sells 10,000 preferred shares at \$100 each, bearing a 12% dividend rate, and the investment dealers charge a selling and distribution commission of \$4 a share, Wildwood Inc. would net \$96 a share. The formula used for calculating the cost of preferred shares is as follows:

$$\textbf{Cost of preferred shares} = \frac{\textbf{Dividends on preferred shares}}{\textbf{Market value of the share} - \textbf{Flotation costs}}$$

Wildwood Inc.'s cost of the preferred share issue would be 12.5%, or \$125,000. The calculation is as follows:

$$\textbf{Cost of preferred shares} = \frac{\$12}{\$100 - \$4} = 12.5\%$$

So far, we have calculated the cost of raising \$13 million of the \$20 million that Wildwood Inc. wants to raise. The remaining \$7 million would have to come from debt financing.

Cost of debt
Finance costs less income tax expense.

Debt. **Cost of debt** financing is relatively easy to calculate. For example, if a company borrows \$100,000 for one year at 10%, the lenders would receive \$10,000 in finance costs. Ignoring income tax for the moment, the cost of capital for that particular source would be 10%.

Debt financing considers two fundamental questions. First, how should the cost be calculated when there are several different types of bonds? Second, because finance cost is a tax-deductible item, how does income tax affect the cost of debt?

First, if there are several bonds with different interest rates, we have to calculate the average rate of interest for that particular financing source. For example, let's assume that Wildwood Inc. decides to issue two bonds, a senior bond (like a first mortgage on a house) for \$5 million at 7%, and a \$2 million subordinated bond (like a second mortgage; it is paid only if the senior bonds are paid) at 9%. The average interest rate is calculated as follows:

$$\textbf{Average cost of bonds} = \frac{(\$5{,}000{,}000 \times 7\%) + (\$2{,}000{,}000 \times 9\%)}{\$7{,}000{,}000} = 7.57\%$$

Second, we must deal with the impact of income taxes on the cost of debt. Because finance costs are tax deductible, we must find the income tax rate in order to calculate the effective cost of debt. The higher the income tax rate, the lower the effective cost of debt will be. For example, if a company has a 40% income tax rate, the after tax cost of borrowing the aforementioned $7 million in bonds is 4.54% [7.57% × (1 – 0.40)], or $317,800. If the income tax rate is 25%, the after-tax cost of borrowing would be 5.68% [7.57% × (1.0 – 0.25)], or $397,600. If no taxes are paid, the cost of debt would be 7.57%, or $529,900, annually.

The formula used for calculating the after-tax cost of debt follows:

After-tax cost of debt = (before-tax cost) × (1.0 – tax rate)

By applying this formula to the $7 million bond issue, and assuming that Wildwood Inc.'s tax rate is 40%, the after-tax cost of the debt would be 4.54%, calculated as follows:

After-tax cost of debt = 7.57% × (1.0 – 0.40) = 4.54%

Weighted average cost of capital. We have now calculated the individual cost of capital for common shares, retained earnings, preferred shares, and debt. With this information, we can calculate Wildwood Inc.'s weighted average cost of capital; the arithmetic is simple. As illustrated by several examples before, we need to (1) compute the proportion of each source of capital relative to the total capital structure, and (2) multiply this number by the appropriate cost of that specific source of capital. As shown in Table 9.6, Wildwood Inc.'s weighted cost of capital is 11.169%. This rate would be the approximate value that would be used as the hurdle rate when reviewing potential capital investment projects.

Marginal cost of capital. Let's assume that, during the year, Wildwood Inc. wants to raise an extra $2 million in order to invest in more capital projects. It also wants to keep its capital structure in the same proportion. For the purpose of this exercise, let's assume that debt and preferred shares are raised at the same cost, while the cost for raising common

Table 9.6 Weighted Average Cost of Capital

Source of Capital	Amount of Capital	Percent of Total		After-Tax Cost of Capital		Proportion of Cost
Common shares	$10,000,000	0.50	×	15.11%	=	7.555%
Retained earnings	2,000,000	0.10	×	14.00%	=	1.400%
Preferred shares	1,000,000	0.05	×	12.50%	=	0.625%
Debt	7,000,000	0.35	×	4.54%	=	1.589%
	$20,000,000	1.00				11.169%

shares is higher. By using the common share dividend yield, say 12%, a 10% flotation charge, and a 4% growth rate, the new cost of common share issue would be 17.33%.

The calculation is as follows:

$$\textbf{Cost of common shares} = \frac{\mathbf{12.00\%}}{\mathbf{0.90}} + \mathbf{4\%} = \mathbf{17.33\%}$$

Marginal cost of capital (MCC) The increased level of average cost resulting from having borrowed new funds at higher rates than those previously borrowed.

As shown in Table 9.7, the calculation of Wildwood Inc.'s new cost of capital is 12.738%. The additional dollars raised above the $20 million figure mean that Wildwood Inc. would have a new average cost of capital of 12.738%; this is referred to as the **marginal cost of capital (MCC).** This means that Wildwood Inc.'s MCC, which was 11.169% to raise the $20 million, is now increased to 12.738% to raise $22 million (an extra $2 million).

Figure 9.3 shows graphically the relationship between the original $20 million capital structure and that of the new $22 million. The graph shows that the cost curve is flat up to the point where it reaches $22 million; at that point, it moves up

Table 9.7 New Weighted Average Cost of Capital

Source of Capital	Amount of Capital	Percent of Total		After-Tax Cost of Capital		Proportion of Cost
Common shares	$12,000,000	0.5455	×	17.33%	=	9.444%
Retained earnings	2,000,000	0.0909	×	14.00%	=	1.288%
Preferred shares	1,000,000	0.0454	×	12.50%	=	0.562%
Debt	7,000,000	0.3182	×	4.54%	=	1.444%
	$22,000,000	1.0000				12.738%

Figure 9.3 Marginal Cost of Capital

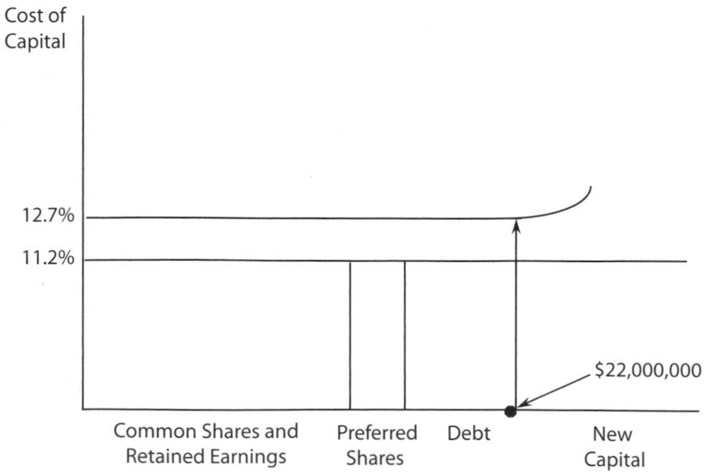

gradually and continues to rise. The reason for the rise is that Wildwood Inc. may find it difficult to raise new securities within a short time span. If it finds new sources of capital, they will be more expensive because of the higher risk to be borne by the stakeholders and the corresponding higher return they will demand from the company.

Self-Test Exercise No. 9.4

Weighted Average Cost of Capital

Len and Joan are considering buying a cottage valued at $175,000. They have a combined savings of $40,000, and the bank approved a $120,000 first mortgage. Len's father agreed to provide them with a $10,000 loan. Also, Joan was lucky enough to win $5,000 at a casino. If Len and Joan invested their money in short-term deposits, they would be able to earn 4.5%. The interest rate that was offered by the bank on the first mortgage was 10%. Len's father agreed to lend the money at only 5%. On the basis of this information, calculate Len and Joan's weighted average cost of capital.

Using the MCC in Capital Budgeting Decisions. The purpose of calculating the MCC is to ensure that the cost of borrowing does not exceed the return that will be earned from capital projects. For example, if it costs 15.0% to borrow capital dollars from different sources, the company will have to be assured that the aggregate return of all projects is at least equal to 15.0%; if it is less, the company would be in a negative return position. Let us examine how this works.

Once the MCC is calculated, the next step is to relate it to capital projects. Using the Wildwood Inc. example, if the company intends to invest $20 million in capital projects giving an 11.2% return, most projects would be accepted. However, if managers submit capital projects that exceed the $20 million level, management would then have to examine all investment opportunities and accept a mix of projects that will maximize the overall value of the business. The procedure is as follows.

The first step is to find the MCC, such as the one shown in Figure 9.4.

Second, projects are evaluated, and the rate of return of each project is determined. The capital budgeting technique used to assess the economic attractiveness of capital projects is called *internal rate of return (IRR)*. This technique will be explained in Chapter 11 on page 533. Using the IRR technique, the aggregate cash flow of all projects is discounted. The idea is to find the net present value of all projects that will give a zero figure. This happens when the total cash inflow of all projects equals the total cash outflow. In Wildwood Inc.'s case, management can approve a mix of projects that, when discounted by a rate of 11.2%, give $20 million. If the company's aggregate IRR does not equal the cost of capital, we have to proceed to the next step.

Figure 9.4 Marginal Cost of Capital and Internal Rate of Return

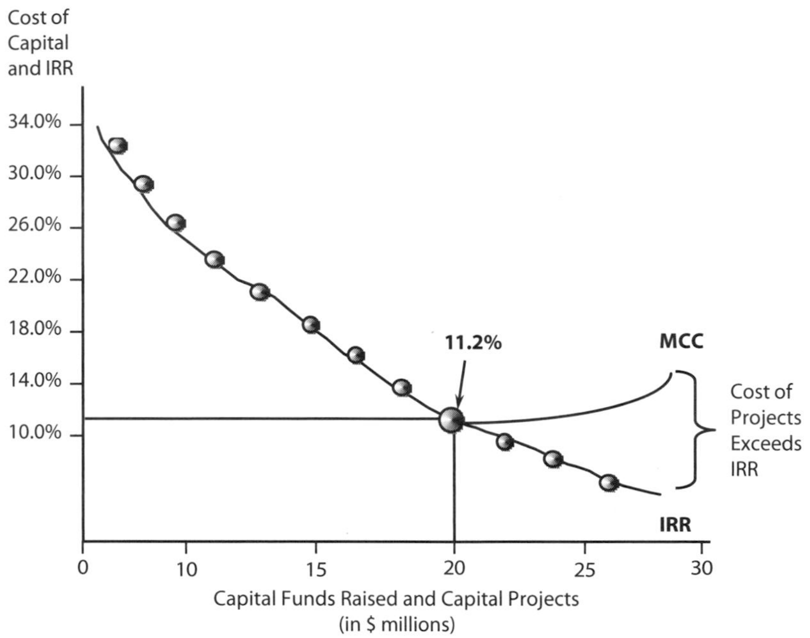

In this step, the discounted values of the cash flows of all projects are calculated at varying discount rates (say, 35% down to 5%) and the result is plotted on a graph (see Figure 9.4). If the company raises $20 million at a cost of 11.2%, it will approve $20 million worth of capital projects. If more projects are approved, the aggregate IRR will fall below the 11.2% point, and Wildwood Inc. would be in a negative return position.

Self-Test Exercise No. 9.5

Weighted Average Cost of Capital

Len and Joan are toying with the idea of investing $1.0 million to open up two other retail outlets in different cities. After reviewing the financial projections with their accountant, May Ogaki, the Millers determined that the two retail outlets showed a combined 8.5% return on investment. After several meetings with different financial institutions, the Millers would be able to obtain the following amounts:

Common shares	$250,000
Retained earnings	100,000
First mortgage	500,000
Second mortgage	150,000
Total	$1,000,000

The cost of capital for each source of financing is as follows:

Common shares	14.0%
Retained earnings	14.0%

Self-Test Exercise No. 9.5 (continued)

First mortgage	10.0%
Second mortgage	13.0%

The company's corporate income tax rate is 33%.

1. Calculate the company's weighted cost of capital.
2. Should the Millers go ahead with the project?

Leverage Analysis

5 Learning Objective

Explain the importance of leverage analysis and how the operating leverage, financial leverage, and combined leverage are calculated.

Leverage analysis is used to determine the financing package or cost structure that will optimize the worth of a business. The purpose of leverage analysis is to answer one fundamental question: What is the best financing mix or capital structure to use to finance our assets? An example will illustrate how leverage analysis works. Let us assume that a firm borrows $400,000 at 6% after tax to finance projects that cost $500,000 and earn 12% (after tax). Here, the owners earn $36,000 (after-tax profit of $60,000 less finance costs of $24,000) on their $100,000 investment, a return on equity of 36%. This compares favourably to the project's return of only 12%. Under these circumstances, where there is a wide spread between the rate of return and the rate of interest, management would use debt rather than equity funds. As mentioned before, debt is less expensive than equity financing.

Although this example is relatively simple, it is usually more intricate to figure out the leverage factor that produces the greatest financial benefits. To understand the mechanics of leverage, we have to examine the behaviour of revenue, fixed and variable costs, profit before taxes and finance costs, debt charges, and earnings per share (EPS). As shown in Figure 9.5, there are three types of leverage: operating leverage, financial leverage, and total or combined leverage.

Figure 9.5 The Leverage Concept

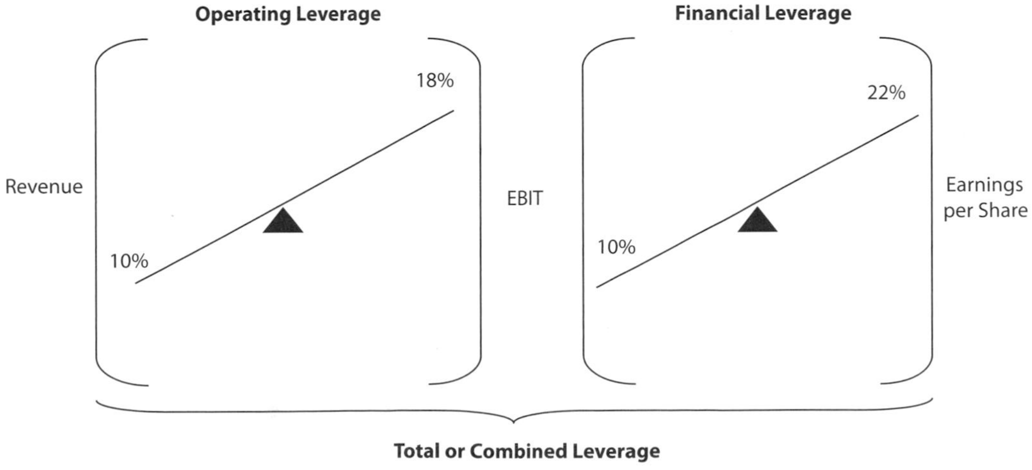

OPERATING LEVERAGE

Operating leverage Financial technique that determines to what extent fixed costs should be used relative to variable costs.

Operating leverage deals with the behaviour of costs at the operating level (e.g., company or plant); it does not take financing costs into consideration. This approach determines the most suitable costs (fixed versus variable costs) that will maximize earnings before the payment of finance costs or dividends and on total corporate charges, which, in turn, affect financial leverage.

Operating leverage is based on the break-even analysis concept, a decision-making tool that was examined in Chapter 5. It involves the analysis of relationships between three elements: revenue, fixed costs, and variable costs. The idea is to select the most appropriate cost mix that will maximize earnings under a set of economic or industry considerations. A favourable operating leverage is achieved when a change in revenue generates a larger change in EBIT. As shown in Figure 9.5, a 10% increase in revenue produces an 18% increase in EBIT. The element that amplifies the earnings is the relationship between fixed costs and total operating costs.

Here is an example of how operating leverage works. Let's assume that management contemplates modernizing a manufacturing plant that will require a $700,000 capital expenditure. To decide whether to modernize, management will have to identify the level of sales volume and revenue that will be achieved in the future and the impact that the new technology will have on the company's fixed and variable cost structure.

As shown in Table 9.8, the new technology will bring about changes to the company's operating cost structure. Under the present cost structure, the company's fixed costs amount to $200,000, and it also earns a $5.00 contribution (an amount that will be used to pay fixed costs). If the company decides to modernize, the cost structure would change, and the new fixed costs would be increased to $300,000 (an increment of $100,000 over existing operations). However, the unit variable costs will be reduced

Table 9.8 Impact of Plant Modernization on Operating Leverage

	Present Production Methods			Proposed Production Methods		
Fixed costs		$200,000			$300,000	
Selling price		15.00			15.00	
Variable costs		(10.00)			(8.00)	
Contribution		$ 5.00			$ 7.00	
	High	Expected	Low	High	Expected	Low
No. of units	100,000	70,000	40,000	100,000	70,000	40,000
(in $000s)						
Revenue	$1,500	$1,050	$600	$1,500	$1,050	$600
Variable costs	(1,000)	(700)	(400)	(800)	(560)	(320)
Fixed costs	(200)	(200)	(200)	(300)	(300)	(300)
Total costs	(1,200)	(900)	(900)	(1,100)	(860)	(620)
EBIT	$ 300	$ 150	$ 00	$ 400	$ 190	$(20)

to $8.00 (from $10.00) because of the decreased variable costs due to higher productivity. The new contribution margin would be increased to $7.00. In other words, the company would earn an extra $2.00 in contribution to pay for the $100,000 fixed cost increment. The question is this: Is the expansion worth the investment? To answer the question, the company would have to estimate the sales volume that it expects to achieve in the next year or two. Table 9.8 shows that if the level of sales is at 40,000 units, the company would break even with the existing facility, but if management modernizes its plant, the company would incur a $20,000 loss. However, if the company expects to sell 100,000 units, this new sales level would certainly justify the investment because it would generate $400,000 in EBIT instead of $300,000 for the present production methods.

Essentially, operating leverage measures how much the operating cost structure amplifies profit performance before interest and taxes. As shown in Table 9.9, a 10% increase in revenue (at the proposed production methods) generates a 17.5% increase in EBIT or a leverage of 1.75.

FINANCIAL LEVERAGE

Financial leverage Financial technique used to determine the most favourable capital structure (equity versus debt).

Financial leverage is used to choose the most favourable capital structure—the one that will generate the greatest financial benefits to the shareholders. It is reasonable to assume that shareholders will favour projects with return rates exceeding the cost of borrowed funds. Because debt is the least costly source of funds, shareholders will prefer to borrow the maximum amount possible from this particular source (provided that the projects can generate enough cash to pay off the debt).

Financial leverage can be gauged by looking at only one alternative and changing its capital structure mix to determine how much the leverage can enhance the EPS position for each option. By excluding the effect of operating leverage from this analysis (Table 9.9), Table 9.10 shows that a 10% increase in EBIT produces a 16% increase in profit before taxes. Here, the financial leverage is 1.6.

Table 9.9 Operating Leverage

	For the Proposed Production Methods (high)		
Revenue	$1,500,000	$1,650,000	10.00%
Variable costs	(800,000)	(880,000)	10.00%
Contribution margin	700,000	770,000	10.00%
Fixed costs	(300,000)	(300,000)	—
Profit (EBIT)	$400,000	$470,000	17.50%

$$\frac{\text{Contributing margin}}{\text{Contributing margin} - \text{Fixed costs}} = \frac{\$700{,}000}{\$400{,}000} = 1.75$$

Table 9.10 Financial Leverage

For the Proposed Production Methods (high)			
EBIT	$400,000	$ 440,000	10.0%
Interest	(150,000)	(150,000)	—
Profit before taxes	$ 250,000	$ 290,000	16.0%

$$\frac{\text{EBIT}}{\text{EBIT} - \text{Interest}} = \frac{\$400{,}000}{\$250{,}000} = 1.6$$

COMBINED LEVERAGE

Combined leverage Financial technique used to calculate both operating and financial leverage.

Combined leverage simply calculates both the operating and financial leverage. As shown in Table 9.11, when revenue increases by 10%, profit for the year (or profit before taxes) shows a 28% increase or a leverage of 2.8. It is assumed here that the income tax rate is at 40%.

Self-Test Exercise No. 9.6

Operating Leverage, Financial Leverage, and Combined Leverage

Using the following information, calculate CompuTech's operating leverage, financial leverage, and combined leverage.

Revenue	$420,000
Variable costs	$212,000
Fixed costs	$148,000
Finance costs	$14,000
Income tax rate	33%

Table 9.11 Combined Leverage

For the Proposed Production Methods (high)			
Revenue	$1,500,000	$1,650,000	10.0%
Variable costs	(800,000)	(880,000)	10.0%
Contribution margin	700,000	770,000	10.0%
Fixed costs	(300,000)	(300,000)	—
EBIT	400,000	470,000	17.5%
Finance costs	(150,000)	(150,000)	—
Profit before taxes	250,000	320,000	28.0%
Income tax expense	(100,000)	(128,000)	—
Profit for the year	$150,000	$192,000	28.0%

$$\frac{\text{Contributing margin}}{\text{EBIT} - \text{Interest}} = \frac{\$700{,}000}{\$250{,}000} = 2.8$$

or

$$1.75 \times 1.6 = 2.8$$

Self-Test Exercise No. 9.7

Effect of Changes in Costs on the Operating Leverage, Financial Leverage, and Combined Leverage

Using the data contained in Self-Test Exercise No. 9.6, assume that the Millers want to make the company more automated and are able to reduce the variable costs to $165,000, increase the fixed costs by $20,000 (i.e., to $168,000), and increase the interest charges (finance costs) from $14,000 to $18,000. Calculate the new operating leverage, financial leverage, and combined leverage.

Financial Markets

6 Learning Objective

Give a profile of the financial markets, the stock market, and various theories related to the dividend theories and payments.

Financial markets Organizations and procedures involved in the buying and selling of financial assets.

Financial markets deal with businesses, individuals, and government institutions including procedures involved in the buying and selling of financial assets. The objective of financial markets is to match buyers and sellers in an efficient and effective way. Organizations and individuals that want to raise money are brought together with those that have a surplus of funds in the financial markets. The financial market system serves as an important vehicle for the efficient and effective operation of the economy. Given that there is a transfer of funds between sellers (saving units or savers) to buyers (investing units), the latter must pay for the capital supplied by the savers, and the investment activity is highly influenced by the rate of return (cost of capital) that the firm must pay to entice funds from the savers.

Investment dealers (also known as investment bankers) facilitate the transfer of funds between sellers and buyers. As shown in Figure 9.6, when the transfer of these securities is done directly between a borrower (or business) and a lender (or saver), they are called *primary claims*.

Trading securities can also be done by financial intermediaries, which include banks, trust companies, credit unions, insurance companies, and caisses populaires. As shown in Figure 9.6, they differ somewhat from investment dealers in that they issue *secondary claims* (instead of primary claims) to the ultimate lenders. Financial intermediaries help the indirect transfer of funds between lenders and borrowers and are compensated for their services via an *interest rate spread.* For instance, a bank may loan money to an individual or a business at an average of 8% interest, pay depositors (savers) 5%, and earn 3%, which they will use to operate their financial institution (e.g., salaries and other expenses).

TYPES OF MARKETS

As mentioned earlier, businesses or individuals that want to borrow money are brought together with those having surplus funds in the financial markets. There are different categories of financial markets, each consisting of different types of institutions. It is important to note that each market deals with somewhat different types of securities, services different types of customers, or even operates in a different part of the country. Here are examples of the major categories of markets.

Figure 9.6 **Transfer of Funds Process**

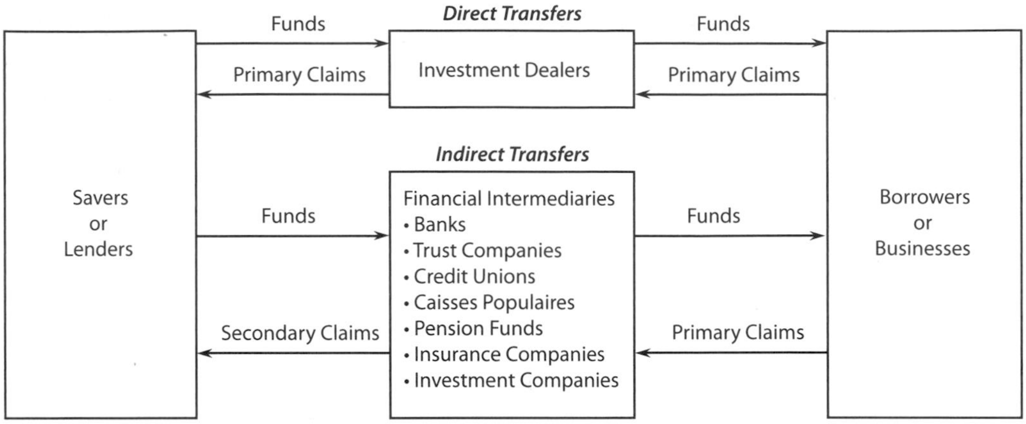

Money markets are defined as the markets for short-term (less than one year) debt securities. Most large corporations participate in the money markets, particularly when they have more cash than they need to run their business. For example, a business might have $100 million in cash and short-term investments. By investing the cash in money market securities, the business can earn interest rather than leaving it in a non-interest-bearing bank account.

Capital markets deal with long-term securities having maturities extending beyond one year. Businesses are interested in these markets when they want long-term funds, either equity or debt. This takes place when a business wants to raise funds externally in the capital markets. The Toronto Stock Exchange (TSX) and the New York Stock Exchange (NYSE) are examples of such markets.

Primary markets are those markets in which newly issued securities are bought and sold for the first time. For example, if RIM or Magna International were to sell a new issue of common shares to raise capital, this would be considered a primary market transaction. On a daily basis, in just about every business newspaper, announcements are made about the issuance of new equity or debt securities.

Secondary markets have to do with the reselling of existing securities. These markets are well established in North America, where shares are traded on the "floor" of a security exchange, such as the TSX as it deals in "used" as opposed to newly issued shares and bonds.

Spot markets and *future markets* are terms used to identify whether an asset is bought or sold for "on the spot" delivery within days or at a future date (e.g., three months).

Mortgage markets deal with loans on residential, commercial, and industrial real estate.

Consumer credit markets have to do with loans on large items such as automobiles and appliances, as well as loans to individuals interested in going to university or taking a vacation.

Physical asset markets (also called tangible or real asset markets) deal with real estate, machinery, etc. While financial markets deal with shares, bonds, and mortgages, physical asset markets deal with "real" assets.

STOCK MARKET

Stock market
A network of exchanges, brokers, and investors that trade securities.

The **stock market** is a network of exchanges, brokers, and investors that trade securities. It is a place where individuals go to buy and sell shares. The most active stock market in Canada is the TSX, and in the United States, the NYSE, where there are networks of exchanges and brokers.

A *stock exchange* is a physical marketplace where the transfer of securities take place. A brokerage firm is a company of stockbrokers generally having the right to trade on an exchange. It employs individuals (the brokers) who are licensed by the government to help individuals in selling and buying securities. While public companies pay fees to the exchange, investors pay fees to the brokers.

In Canada, the securities markets are regulated by provincial and territorial legislation. Depending on the province or territory, the securities regulations are established in the *Securities Acts* or consumer affairs legislation, and all jurisdictions require companies to disclose specific information to potential investors when they are about to issue new securities. *Disclosure* means that investors must be given complete and accurate information about the companies behind the shares that are offered for sale.

When someone starts a new business, funds are usually provided by the owner(s), family members, and sometimes friends. Normally, the entrepreneur is the owner of the unincorporated business. Due to the fact that the business is not incorporated, it is not a corporation, and has no shares to offer to the general public. However, if the business is successful and the entrepreneur wants to raise more money for growth purposes, he can incorporate and sell shares to others. If the entrepreneur incorporates, and wants to sell shares to a small group of individual and has no intention of becoming a public entity, the business would be considered a **privately held company**. These types of corporations can sell shares to a small group of individuals, but this type of transaction is rigorously restricted by provincial regulations.

Privately held company
A business that cannot sell shares to the general public.

After a while, if the business is successful and requires a considerable amount of additional funds to expand its operations and seize business opportunities, the entrepreneur can choose to go public and become a publicly traded company. The entrepreneur would then approach an investment dealer who would do the work related to whether a particular market would welcome the company's offerings and the price of the shares. If the response is positive, the registration procedure would begin with the preparation of a document known as a prospectus that discloses the details of a security and the profile in great detail of the business in question to prospective investors. The purpose of the prospectus is *disclosure*, which basically means that the document must give a true and accurate picture of the nature of the business and the risks involved.

Publicly traded company
A business that can sell securities broadly after a prospectus is approved by the appropriate securities commission.

Initial public offering IPO
Securities of a newly established public company offered to the general public for the first time.

Listed company
A company that is traded on an organized exchange and is listed on the exchange.

Publicly traded companies can offer securities to the general public but require the approval of the provincial securities commission. The process for obtaining approval and registration from the appropriate securities commission is know as *going public*. Going public requires the assistance of an investment dealer.

When a prospectus is approved by the appropriate securities commission, the investment securities may be offered to the general public. This initial offering is called an **initial public offering (IPO).**

If a business continues to grow and is successful among potential investors, it may want to list its name on the stock market. This would make it easier for investors to trade in the secondary market to buy or trade shares. If, in the future, the company decides to raise more funds from investors, the fact that it would be a **listed company** on the stock exchange would make it easier for the business to raise additional capital.

Share prices are reported on a daily basis in financial newspapers such as the *Globe and Mail* and the *Financial Post* and on financial websites. Table 9.12 shows typical and hypothetical financial information that is usually shown about companies trading on the stock market. The information includes the stock name, the ticker symbol, the share prices (opening, high, low, and closing prices during the trading day, including the change), the average volume during the trading day, the yield (dividends and percent), the EPS and price/earnings (P/E) ratio, the 52-week stock performance (high and low), and the number of shares outstanding and their value.

Table 9.12 Typical Stock Market Information

1. Stock	Abbreviated name of the company (e.g., Rogers for Rogers Communications Inc.)
2. Ticker	The company's tickertape or ticker symbol (e.g., RCI.B for Rogers)
3. Open	Price of the stock when the trading day opened (e.g., 30.00)
4. High	Highest price paid during the trading day (e.g., 33.50)
5. Low	Lowest price paid for the stock during the trading day (e.g., 29.90)
6. Close	Price of the stock at the end of the trading day (e.g., 32.80)
7. Net change	Net change (up or down) from the previous trading day (e.g., 2.80)
8. Average volume	Number of shares that changed hand during the trading (e.g., 2,100,000 shares)
9. Yield	
• Dividends	Dividends paid (e.g., 0.30)
• Percent	Dividend yield expressed as a percentage (e.g., 3.4%)
10. EPS	Earnings per share (e.g., 1.90)
11. P/E ratio	Price/earnings ratio (e.g., 14.9 times)
12. 52-week high	The highest price paid for the stock during the past year (e.g., 39.00)
13. 52-week low	The lowest price paid for the stock during the past year (e.g., 26.75)
14. Shares out	Number of shares outstanding (e.g., 506.900 million)
15. Quoted market value	Value of the shares on the market (e.g., 15.900 billion)

In the News 9.2 shows Rogers Communications Inc. financial stock market information as it appeared on the CNX Marketlink on July 24, 2009.

In The News [9.2]

Rogers' Communications Inc.'s Stock Market Information

Rogers Communications, with headquarters in Toronto, was founded in 1920. It is considered one of Canada's largest communications companies, particularly in the field of wireless communications and cable television. In 2008, the company employed 29,200 and realized annual revenues of $11.35 billion with net income of $1.26 billion.

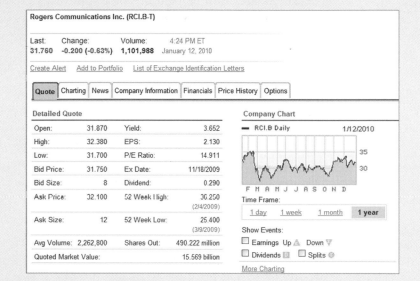

Rogers Communications Inc. (RCI.B-T)

Last:	Change:	Volume:	4:24 PM ET
31.760	**-0.200 (-0.63%)**	**1,101,988**	January 12, 2010

Create Alert | Add to Portfolio | List of Exchange Identification Letters

Quote | Charting | News | Company Information | Financials | Price History | Options

Detailed Quote

Open:	31.870	Yield:	3.652
High:	32.380	EPS:	2.130
Low:	31.700	P/E Ratio:	14.911
Bid Price:	31.750	Ex Date:	11/18/2009
Bid Size:	8	Dividend:	0.290
Ask Price:	32.100	52 Week High:	36.250 (2/4/2009)
Ask Size:	12	52 Week Low:	25.400 (3/9/2009)
Avg Volume:	2,262,800	Shares Out:	490.222 million
Quoted Market Value:			15.569 billion

Company Chart

— RCI.B Daily 1/12/2010

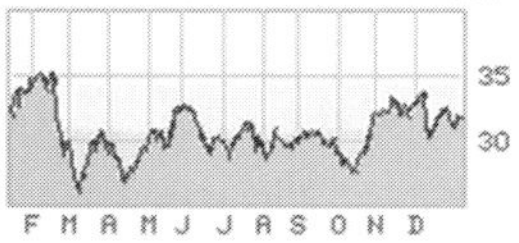

Time Frame: 1 day | 1 week | 1 month | **1 year**

Show Events:
☐ Earnings Up Down
☐ Dividends ☐ Splits

More Charting

Source: TMX. For more information about Rogers, visit their official website at http://www.rogers.com. To see the most current information about Rogers' stock market performance, go to http://cxa.marketwatch.com/tsx/en/market/quote.aspx?symbol=RCI.B&x=4&y=11.

DIVIDENDS

Most investors buy shares for the dividends that they expect to receive. As a result, the board of directors pays a considerable amount of attention to dividend payouts, as the decisions they make have an effect on shareholders' interest. Dividend payout also influences a company's cash flow and the level of retained earnings that remains available for reinvestment purposes.

Figure 1.5 on page 16 shows that there is a relationship between internal use of cash (retained earnings) and external use of cash (payment of dividends and debt reduction). Within the context of cash flow analysis, the amount of cash to be retained in a business for reinvestment purposes has to be balanced with the amount of cash to be paid out in the form of dividends. It is the role of the board of directors to determine the amount of cash that should be retained in the business for re-investment purposes (capital assets and working capital) versus the payment of dividends and debt reduction. Retained earnings are important for a business if it wants to stimulate growth in future earnings and, as a result, influence future share values. On the other hand, if dividends are paid now, it provides shareholders with immediate tangible returns.

Most provincial jurisdictions have laws that regulate the payment of dividends. For example, the Ontario Securities Commission (OSC) is the government agency that administers the *Securities Act* and the *Commodity Futures Act* for Ontario; the OSC also regulates securities and listed futures contract transactions in Ontario. In general, these laws about dividends state the following:

- A company's capital cannot be used to pay dividends.
- Dividends must be paid out of a company's present and past net earnings.
- Dividends cannot be paid when a company is insolvent.

Dividend Theories

The major issue about dividends has to do with the amount of dividends that a company should pay: Does the payment of larger or smaller amounts of dividends have a positive, negative, or neutral effect on a company's share price? Or do shareholders prefer current dividends or deferred dividends? There are three major theories regarding the preference of investors "for" or "against" dividend payments: the dividend irrelevance theory, the dividend preference theory, and the dividend aversion theory.

Dividend irrelevance theory
Theory suggesting that investors are indifferent to the payment of dividends because the value of lesser dividends now is offset by growth-created value in the future.

The **dividend irrelevance theory** advanced by Miller and Modigliani[1] states that dividends have little effect on share price because if earnings are retained in the business for growth purposes, the incremental re-invested cash may cause the business to become more profitable and/or grow faster in the future. That would, in turn, make the future selling price of the shares increase faster and also increase dividend payments in the future.

Dividend preference theory
Theory suggesting that investors prefer instant cash to uncertain future benefits.

The **dividend preference theory** advanced by Gordon and Lintner[2] maintains that, in general, investors prefer receiving dividends now compared to not receiving any. The argument is based on the uncertainty factor: What will happen in the future? They argue that investors prefer not to have management use their cash now on the assumption that they may not be able to make the company grow. It has to do with the question of "trust." The argument is often referred to as the "bird in the hand is worth two in the bush." (You may not be able to catch either of them in the bush!) The major flaw in this argument is this: If investors are concerned about re-investing their money into their company now, why have they invested their money in that particular company in the first place?

1. Merton Miller and Franco Modigliani, "Dividend Policy, Growth, and the Valuation of Shares," *Journal of Business 34*, October 1961, pp. 411–433.
2. Myron J. Gordon, "Optimal Investment and Financing Policy," *Journal of Finance*, May 1963, pp. 264–272; and John Lintner, "Dividends, Earnings, Leverage, Stock Prices, and the Supply of Capital to Corporations," *Review of Economics and Statistics*, August 1962, pp. 243–269.

Dividend aversion theory
Theory suggesting that investors may prefer future capital gains to current dividends because of lower tax rates on capital gains.

The **dividend aversion theory** is based on the premise that investors prefer not to receive dividends now in order to enhance share prices in the future. This argument is based on the assumption that dividends are often taxed at higher rates than capital gains. The decision related to "receiving" versus "not receiving" dividends has to do with trading immediate dividends for a higher selling price in a later period. The trade-off has to do with investment income (now) versus the appreciated price that represents a capital gain when the shares are sold. Therefore, the trade-off boils down to one question: Should I receive dividends today or possibly a benefit from a higher price at a later date?

Dividend Policy

Dividend payout ratio
Proportion of earnings that a business pays out in dividends.

Dividend policy has to do with the process in which a business determines what it will pay in dividends. This process deals with two things: the amount to be paid and the pattern under which dividends will be paid. Let's first examine the meaning of the term **dividend payout ratio**, which is the proportion of earnings that a business pays out in dividends. Many businesses usually have a payout ratio that they want to maintain over the long term. The dividend payout ratio is calculated as follows:

$$\textbf{Divided payout ratio} = \frac{\textbf{Divided}}{\textbf{Earnings}} = \frac{\textbf{Diviend per share}}{\textbf{EPS}}$$

For example, if a dividend payout ratio is 30%, it means that the business pays a cash dividend of 30 cents out of every dollar it earns. Sometimes a business may have difficulty in paying out its dividends in difficult times, or if it has other substantial priorities such as investing in capital assets or debt repayment.

The second thing has to do with the *dividend payment pattern*. Usually, businesses try to pay its dividends on a regular basis. A "stable" dividend refers to a constant amount of dividend paid from time to time and is normally increased on a regular basis. In the main, a decrease in the amount of dividends carries an unfavourable signal to investors. Consequently, the board of directors makes an effort to keep dividends per share from going down. The objective in the payment of dividends over the long term is to make it grow; sometimes the amount can flatten out, but not diminish.

Dividend Payment

At each quarterly meeting, the board of directors evaluates the company's performance and decides the amount of dividends that should be paid during the next period. As mentioned before, the board tries to keep the amount of dividends from

Figure 9.7 **The Dividend Payment Procedure**

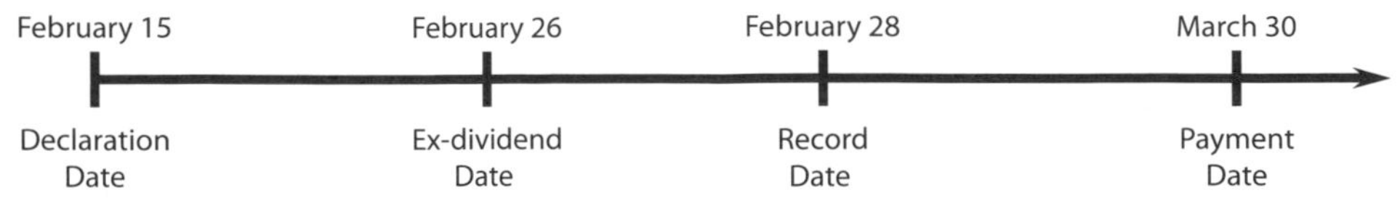

going down particularly if the company tries to follow a rigid dividend payment pattern strategy. Most businesses follow a dividend declaration and payment procedure such as the one shown in Figure 9.7. The procedure usually deals with a declaration date, an ex-dividend date, a record date, and a payment date.

The *declaration date* is the day that the board of directors meets to decide on the amount of quarterly dividend that should be authorized. As shown in the figure, February 15 happens to be the declaration date.

The major stock exchanges require two business days prior to the record date to have enough time to record ownership changes. This is referred to as the *ex-dividend date*, which is the date on which a share trades without a declared dividend that has yet to be paid. An investor that buys shares on or after this date is not entitled to receive the declared dividends. In this case, if investors buy shares on or after February 26, they are not entitled to receive the dividend.

The *record date* is the date on which a business makes a list from its stock transfer books of those shareholders who are eligible to receive the declared dividends. On February 28, the company makes a list from its stock transfer books.

The *payment date* is usually about four weeks or so after the record date. In the example in Figure 9.7, it happens to be on March 30. On this particular date, the company makes the dividend payments to the shareholders.

In the News 9.3 indicates that sometimes investors prefer cashing in immediate benefits (selling their shares for quick gains) instead of waiting for their shares to possibly grow in the future.

In The News [9.3]

Some Investors Prefer Trading Instant Benefits for Possible Growth in the Value of Their Shares

What else is new? During uncertain and risky times, investors may prefer cashing in their shares and making a profit *now* instead of waiting a few months or even years to collect more "hopeful" benefits. Risk has to do with uncertainty of outcome, which could either be good or bad!

In mid-August of 2009, the TSX dropped below the 11,000 mark. The reason: Profit-takers took advantage of a 230-point increase or a 2% surge right in the middle of the morning of Tuesday, August 4, 2009. While earnings and economic news were upbeat at the time, many investors and analysts feared that the stocks would begin to drift south after such a big boost. The investors made the right move because the S&P/TSX composite index fell by 30.42 points, down to 10,987.68 the following day.

Source: Adapted from The Canadian Press, Kristine Owram, "Toronto stock market slips back below 11,000 points as investors take profits," August 5, 2009, accessed at *Winnipeg Free Press* website, August 8, 2009.

REALITY FINANCIAL SNAPSHOTS

The following paragraphs give some examples of the type of financing and cost for Enbridge and The Ottawa Hospital (TOH).

ENBRIDGE[3]

In 2008, Enbridge's SFP showed an amount of $10,154.9 million in long-term borrowings. The following describes the composition of this debt in terms of its weighted average interest rates, maturity dates, and amounts.

($ millions)	Weighted Average Interest Rate	Maturity Date	Amount
Liquid Pipelines			
Debentures	8.20%	2024	200.0
Medium-term notes	5.88%	2009–2036	1,124.6
Southern Lights project financing (US$850.0 million; 2007 – nil)			1,358.9
Commercial paper and credit facility draws, net (2008 – nil; 2007 – US$365.0 million)			524.7
Other			15.3
Gas Distribution and Services			
Debentures	11.06%	2009–2024	485.0
Medium-term notes	5.77%	2014–2036	1,795.0
Commercial paper and credit facility draws, net			883.2
Corporate			
U.S. dollar term notes (US$1,372.0 million; 2007 – US$1,357.3 million)	5.50%	2014–2022	1,680.2
Medium-term notes	5.69%	2010–2035	1,568.0
Commercial paper and credit draws, net (US$690.0 million; 2007 – US$317.0 million)			2,034.1
Deferred debt issue costs and other			(105.7)
Total Debt			11,563.3
Current Maturities			(533.8)
Short-Term Borrowings	2.89%		(874.6)
Long-Term Debt			10,154.9

THE OTTAWA HOSPITAL[4]

TOH's SFP shows an amount of $51,294 thousand in bank indebtedness for the year 2008. All other liabilities consist of accounts payable, deferred contributions, and employee future benefits. The note included in the hospital's annual report related to the bank indebtedness reads as follows:

> The Hospital has an available line of credit of $24,000 thousand with its corporate bankers, of which $13,517 thousand was drawn against at March 31, 2008 (2007 – $Nil). This line of credit is unsecured and bears interest at prime minus 0.75%. The hospital also had an overdraft of $35,504 thousand (2007 – $19,355 thousand) that was covered by the capital cash account.

3. Enbridge Inc., *2008 Enbridge Annual Report.* Found at: http://www.enbridge.com/investor/financialInformation/reportsFilings/pdf/2008-annual-report-en.pdf.
4. *2008 Ottawa Hospital Annual Report.* Found at: http://www.ottawahospital.on.ca/about/reports/FS2008-e.pdf.

[DECISION-MAKING IN ACTION]

Management of National Electronics Ltd. is in the process of reviewing its upcoming operating plans and capital budgets. Prior to making important decisions, members of the management committee wanted some information to determine whether they should approve or reject some of the capital expenditure projects.

National Electronics Ltd.'s 2010 statement of income and SFP are shown below.

National Electronics Ltd.
Statement of Income
for the year ended December 31, 2010
(in $)

Revenue	5,000,000
Cost of sales	(2,900,000)
Gross profit	2,100,000
Finance costs	(100,000)
Operating expenses	(800,000)
Total expenses	(900,000)
Profit before taxes	1,200,000
Income tax expense (40%)	(480,000)
Profit for the year	720,000

National Electronics Ltd.
Statement of Financial Position
as at December 31, 2010
(in $)

Non-current assets	3,000,000	Equity	
		Share capital	1,000,000
		Retained earnings	1,000,000
		Total equity	2,000,000
		Long-term borrowings	
		Mortgage	1,500,000
		Bond	500,000
		Total long-term borrowings	2,000,000
Current assets		Current liabilities	
Inventories	1,000,000	Trade and other payables	500,000
Trade receivables	1,000,000	Working capital loan	500,000
Total current assets	2,000,000	Total current liabilities	1,000,000
Total assets	5,000,000	Total equity and debt	5,000,000

Treasurer Callan Hughes indicates to the committee that the shareholders were expecting to earn 12% on their equity. She also pointed out that the before-tax costs of financing the mortgage, bond, and working capital loan were 6%, 7%, and 9%, respectively.

The company's total capital budget was estimated at $2.0 million. Callan said that the financing of the total capital budget would come from equity in the amount of $800,000 and debt for $1.2 million. The cost of financing equity would be 14%; the cost for the debt would be 10%.

One important project that the committee was considering was the modernization of a small manufacturing plant. At the meeting, plant manager John Wyspianski indicated that the project would cost $200,000 and earn an 18% return. John indicated that the $200,000 modernization program would make significant changes in the operating cost structure. As he pointed out, the plant currently produces $450,000 in revenue with variable costs estimated at 80% of revenue and $100,000 in fixed costs. He stated that the modernization program would reduce the variable costs to 75% of revenue but increase the fixed costs to $115,000. The sales manager indicated that he expected revenue to reach $500,000 by the end of the current year and attain the $600,000 objective by the end of the following year.

Callan also indicated that the finance costs that were to be allocated to finance the plant's modernization program would be $8,000.

The CEO asked the following questions:

1. What is National Electronics Ltd.'s cost of financing?
2. What is National Electronics Ltd.'s cost of capital for modernizing the plant?
3. What is National Electronics Ltd.'s economic value added?
4. Should the modernization program be approved? Why? To answer this question, Callan has to produce a statement of income for the plant's three levels of revenue ($450,000, $500,000, and $600,000) for both current operations and the modernization program.
5. If the modernization program is approved, what is the plant's operating leverage using the $600,000 revenue objective?
6. What is the company's financial leverage, also using the $600,000 revenue objective, if the modernization program is approved?
7. What is the plant's combined leverage?

As evidenced by the discussion at the management committee, several managers (e.g., treasurer, plant manager, sales manager) are involved in the decision-making process.

Table 9.13 shows the calculations related to the questions raised by the CEO.

Question 1: What is National Electronics Ltd.'s cost of financing?

As shown in Table 9.13, Callan first has to determine the weighted cost before and after tax for each source of financing. The company is in a 40% tax bracket, which is evidenced by the amount of tax that the company pays ($420,000 in taxes deducted from the $1,200,000 profit before taxes). As shown in the table, the cost of financing for National Electronics Ltd. as an ongoing entity is 6.84%. The only account that does not bear a finance cost is trade and other payables, which is the financing provided by suppliers.

Question 2: What is National Electronics Ltd.'s cost of capital for modernizing the plant?

National Electronics's capital budget shows that $2,000,000 will be invested in a modernization program for a small manufacturing plant. By using the same financing proportion for the entire company (40% for equity and 60% for debt) as shown in the calculation for the first question, $800,000 will by financed by equity and $1,200,000 by debt. The cost for equity and debt is 14%

Table 9.13 Decision-Making In Action

Question 1: Cost of Financing

	Sources	Cost Before Tax (%)	Cost After Tax (%)	Weight	Weighted Cost of Financing (%)
Equity	$2,000,000	12.0	12.0	0.40	4.80
Mortgage	1,500,000	6.0	3.6	0.30	1.08
Bond	500,000	7.0	4.2	0.10	0.42
Trade and other payables	500,000	0.0	0.0	0.10	0.00
Working capital loan	500,000	9.0	5.4	0.10	0.54
Total	$5,000,000			1.00	6.84

Question 2: Cost of Capital for Financing the Modernization Program

	Sources	Cost Before Tax (%)	Cost After Tax (%)	Weight	Weighted Cost of Capital (%)
Equity	$ 800,000	14.0	14.0	0.40	5.60
Debt	1,200,000	10.0	6.0	0.60	3.60
Total	$2,000,000			1.00	9.20

Question 3: Economic Value Added

Net operating profit before taxes and finance costs	$1,300,000	Capital	$4,500,000
Income tax expense (40%)	(520,000)	Cost of financing	× 6.84%
Net operating profit after taxes	780,000	Cost of financing	$ 307,800
Finance costs	(307,800)		
Economic value added	$ 472,200		

Question 4: The Modernized Plant's Profit and Loss Statement at the Three Revenue Levels

	Before Modernization			After Modernization		
Revenue	$600,000	$500,000	$450,000	$600,000	$500,000	$450,000
Variable costs	(480,000)	(400,000)	(360,000)	(450,000)	(375,000)	(337,500)
Contribution margin	120,000	100,000	90,000	150,000	125,000	112,500
Fixed costs	(100,000)	(100,000)	(100,000)	(115,000)	(115,000)	(115,000)
Profit before taxes	$ 20,000	$ 000	$ (10,000)	$ 35,000	$ 10,000	$ (2,500)

Question 5: Operating Leverage Using the Modernization Option at $600,000 Revenue Level

			Increase
Revenue	$600,000	$660,000	10.0%
Variable costs	(450,000)	(495,000)	10.0%
Contribution margin	150,000	165,000	10.0%
Fixed costs	(115,000)	(115,000)	—
EBIT	$ 35,000	$ 50,000	42.9%

$$\frac{150{,}000}{35{,}000} = 4.29$$

Question 6: Financial Leverage

			Increase
EBIT	$35,000	$38,500	10.0%
Interest	(8,000)	(8,000)	—
EBT	$27,000	$30,500	13.0%

$$\frac{35{,}000}{27{,}000} = 1.30$$

Question 7: Combined Leverage

			Increase
Revenue	600,000	$660,000	10.0%
Variable costs	(450,000)	(495,000)	10.0%
Contribution margin	150,000	165,000	10.0%
Fixed costs	(115,000)	(115,000)	—
EBIT	35,000	50,000	42.9%
Interest	(8,000)	(8,000)	—
EBT	27,000	42,000	55.6%
Income tax expense	(10,800)	(16,800)	
Profit for the year	16,200	25,200	55.6%

$$4.29 \times 1.3 = 5.58$$

and 10% on a before-tax basis and 14% and 6% after tax. As shown in the table, the cost of capital for financing the project is 9.2%.

Question 3: What is National Electronics Ltd.'s economic value added?

As shown in the statement of income, National Electronics Ltd. produces an NOPBT in the amount of $1.3 million ($1,200,000 in profit before taxes + $100,000 in finance costs). On the investor's side of the SFP (equity and liabilities), the company raised $4.5 million from shareholders and lenders with a WACF of 6.84%. By deducting from the NOPBT the 40% income tax expense of $520,000 and the $307,800 finance costs, the company is left with an EVA in the amount of $472,200.

Question 4: Should the modernization program be approved? Why or why not?

A statement of income for the plant's three levels of revenue ($450,000, $500,000, and $600,000) for both current operations and the modernization program is shown in Table 9.13.

On the basis of the information provided by John and the sales manager, the management committee should approve the modernization program. This can be looked at from two angles. First, as shown in the table, the modernized plant would generate $35,000 in profit versus $20,000 at the $600,000 revenue level. The existing plant shows a ratio of 80% in variable costs, leaving a 20% contribution margin to pay for the $100,000 fixed costs. The modernization program would reduce the variable costs to 75% but increase fixed costs by only an extra $15,000, up to $115,000. The determining factor that will influence the management committee to approve (or not approve) the project is the sales estimates provided by the sales manager. Even at the $450,000 sales level, it would be economically attractive for the company to modernize. Nevertheless, the most probable estimate based on the sales manager's input is in the $600,000 range.

Second, John indicated that the modernization program would earn an 18% return. This compares favourably to the 9.2% cost of capital (an 8.8% positive difference). This is a good result in view of the fact that the modernization program would not be considered a high-risk investment.

Question 5: If the modernization is approved, what is the plant's operating leverage using the $600,000 revenue objective?

The operating leverage is very attractive at the $600,000 revenue level for the modernization option. As shown in Table 9.13, a 10% increase in revenue would generate a 42.9% increase in EBIT. The operating leverage is 4.29. Because National Electronics is in the 40% tax bracket, the leverage on an after-tax basis would be the same. The after-tax profit level for a 10% increase in revenue would also produce a 42.9% increase in earnings after interest and taxes ($21,000, which is 60% of $35,000, versus $30,000, which is 60% of $50,000).

Question 6: What is the company's financial leverage, also using the $600,000 revenue objective, if the modernization program is approved?

The financial leverage is not as attractive, but still good. A 10% increase in profit before taxes produces a 13.5% increase in profit after taxes. The financial leverage is 1.3. Here, it is estimated that $8,000 in finance costs will be paid to finance the modernization program.

Question 7: What is the plant's combined leverage?

The combined leverage is very positive. A 10% increase in revenue generates a 55.6% increment in profit before (or after) taxes, or a combined 5.58 (4.29 × 1.3).

FINANCIAL SPREADSHEETS—EXCEL

Template 13 (Economic Value Added) of the financial statement analysis component of the financial planning spreadsheets accompanying this text can calculate the EVA, which is essentially the incremental profit after taxes that a company earns after paying the cost of borrowed capital. There are three templates of the decision-making tools spreadsheets that are related specifically to this chapter. Template 3 calculates the operating leverage for three different volume levels. This template helps to determine whether a company, for example, should modernize a plant. Templates 4 and 5 calculate the cost of capital for privately owned businesses and for publicly owned companies.

Chapter Summary

1 Learning Objective

Explain the financial and capital structure concepts in addition to the cost concepts.

Financing decisions consider not only sources and forms of financing but also financial and capital structure, cost of financing, and cost of capital. *Financial structure* means the way a company's total assets are financed by the entire right-hand side of the SFP, long-term and short-term financing. *Capital structure* represents the permanent forms of financing, such as common shares, retained earnings, preferred shares, and long-term borrowings. *Cost of financing* represents how much it costs a business to finance all assets shown on a company's SFP. *Cost of capital* means the weighted rate of return a business must provide to its investors in exchange for the money they have placed in a business. Cost of capital is a critically important element in the financing decision process because it is the basis for determining the capital expenditure investment portfolio. To illustrate, if the average cost of capital is 10%, management of a company will approve a capital expenditure portfolio that will earn 10% or more.

2 Learning Objective

Clarify the meaning of cost of financing, why it is used, and how it is calculated.

To calculate the cost of financing, you have to go through four steps. First, you identify the amount obtained from each source. Second, you find the weight or proportion for each amount raised from their respective sources. Third, the cost of each source (before and after taxes) is identified. In the last step, you multiply the weight of each source by the after-tax cost of financing and obtain the weighted cost. By adding all individual weighted costs, you get the WACF.

3 Learning Objective

Explain that the economic value added concept is a financial technique used to measure managerial performance related to shareholder wealth maximization.

The EVA is a performance measure that attempts to measure how profitable a company truly is. It is calculated by deducting the cost of using the assets (finance costs) from the NOPAT.

4 Learning Objective

Explain that the components of the average weighted cost of capital include common shares, retained earnings, preferred shares, and long-term borrowings.

The most important factors to consider when determining a permanent financing scenario are payout, risk, voting rights, cost of capital, tax cost, and cost of issue.

The key elements to consider when calculating a company's cost of capital are: (a) the amount of funds obtained from each financing source (shareholders and lenders), (b) the proportion of each source, (c) the after-tax cost of each source, and (d) the weighted average cost of capital, which is arrived at by multiplying each amount calculated in (b) by each cost listed in (c). There is a connection between the cost of capital and investment decisions. Cost of capital tells management how much it cost to raise funds from long-term sources while techniques in capital budgeting such as the IRR tells management how much each project generates. If a project earns less than the cost of capital, it might be rejected.

5 Learning Objective

Explain the importance of leverage analysis and how the operating leverage, financial leverage, and combined leverage are calculated.

Leverage analysis is used to determine the financing package or cost structure that will maximize the worth of a business. There are two types of leverages: operating leverage and financial leverage. *Operating leverage* deals with the cost behaviour of an operating unit; it determines the most appropriate cost mix (fixed versus variable) that will maximize profitability under a given set of economic and industry conditions. *Financial leverage* is used to determine the most favourable capital structure—that is, the one that will generate the greatest financial benefits to the shareholders. *Combined leverage* is used to calculate both operating and financial leverage.

6 Learning Objective

Give a profile of the financial markets, the stock market, and various theories related to the dividend theories and payments.

The segment related to financial markets examined the organizations and procedures involved in the buying and selling of financial assets. There are different types of markets such as money markets, capital markets, primary markets, secondary markets, spot and future markets, mortgage markets, consumer credit markets, and physical asset markets. The segment that dealt with the stock market looked at the difference between a privately held company and a publicly traded company, including the meaning of an initial public offering and a listed company. The last segment of this section looked at various dividend theories, dividend policy, and dividend payment.

Key Terms

Capital structure p. 426
Combined leverage p. 446
Cost of capital p. 424
Cost of common shares p. 436
Cost of debt p. 438
Cost of preferred shares p. 437
Cost of retained earnings p. 437
Dividend aversion theory p. 453
Dividend irrelevance theory p. 452
Dividend payout ratio p. 453
Dividend preference theory p. 452
Economic value added (EVA) p. 431

Review Questions

1. What do we mean by financial structure?
2. What is the objective of using the leverage analysis technique?
3. What is the purpose of calculating the cost of capital?
4. What is the meaning of the EVA? What does it measure? Why is it important?
5. What are the major elements of the cost of capital?
6. What is the relationship between the cost of capital and the rate of return?
7. Define opportunity costs.
8. What major characteristics should be explored when considering the major sources of long-term financing?
9. Explain the meaning of leverage.
10. Comment on the major components of finance.
11. Differentiate between debt financing and common share financing.
12. What does the growth factor represent when calculating the cost of common shares?
13. What do we mean by marginal cost of capital?
14. What is the purpose of operating leverage analysis?
15. What is the purpose of financial leverage analysis?
16. What is the usefulness of the combined leverage?
17. How can leverage analysis be used to determine whether a plant should be modified or not?
18. What is the connection between the management of capital structure and the management of capital assets?
19. What are financial markets?
20. What is the difference between a primary financial market and a secondary financial market?
21. What is the purpose of a stock exchange?
22. What is a prospectus?
23. What does the dividend irrelevance theory suggest?

Learning Exercises

EXERCISE 1

From the following financing sources, identify the company's financial structure and capital structure and calculate the proportion or weight of each.

Sources	Amounts
Retained earnings	$450,000
Share capital	300,000
Trade and other payables	300,000
Long-term borrowings	900,000
Working capital loan	70,000
Short-term borrowings	200,000

EXERCISE 2

With the information contained in Exercise 1 and the following costs for individual financing sources, calculate the company's weighted average after-tax cost of financing and cost of capital.

Sources	Cost (%)
Share capital	14
Trade and other payables	0
Retained earnings	12
Long-term borrowings	6
Short-term borrowings	8
Working capital loan	6.5

EXERCISE 3

Daniel and Evelyn are considering buying a house valued at $250,000. They have combined savings of $20,000, and the bank approved a $200,000 first mortgage. Another financial institution agreed to provide them with a $20,000 second mortgage. Also, Daniel has just won $10,000 from a lottery. If Daniel and Evelyn invested their money in guaranteed certificates, they would be able to earn 4%. The interest rates offered by the bank are 6% for the first mortgage and 7% for the second.

Question

On the basis of this information, calculate Daniel and Evelyn's cost of capital.

EXERCISE 4

One of the capital expenditure projects included in a company's capital budget was a $10 million investment for the construction of a new manufacturing facility in South America. The preliminary information provided by the financial analysis department of the company indicated that the project would earn an 8% return on investment. The treasurer met several investors who showed an interest in the project and were prepared to provide the following:

Common shares	$3,500,000
Retained earnings	500,000
Preferred shares	1,000,000
Bonds	5,000,000
Total	$10,000,000

The cost of capital for each source of financing is as follows:

Common shares	12.0%
Retained earnings	11.0%
Bonds	7.5%
Preferred shares	10.0%

The company's corporate income tax rate is 45%.

The members of the management committee were reviewing all projects contained in the capital project. When they examined the $10 million manufacturing facility, several showed some concern about the project's viability and were not sure whether it should be approved.

Question

Ignoring flotation costs or brokers' fees, calculate the cost of capital for raising the $10 million. Should the management committee approve this project? Why?

EXERCISE 5

The CEO of an electronics business was contemplating going public. Let's assume that the prospectus shows an expansion plan that would cost $20 million, and the CEO wished to raise funds from the following sources:

a) $8 million from common shares. Each share would be sold for $15 and yield $2 in dividends. The flotation costs would be 10%.
b) $1 million through the company's retained earnings.
c) $1 million from preferred shares. The expected selling price would be $10, and the flotation costs would be $0.50 per share. An amount of $1 in annual dividends per share would be paid to the preferred shareholders.
d) $8 million from a mortgage at a cost of 5%.
e) $2 million from a second mortgage at a cost of 7%.

The corporate tax rate is 48%, and the prospectus showed the growth rate to be 5% per year.

Question

On the basis of the above information, calculate the company's cost of capital.

EXERCISE 6

Silverado Inc. is contemplating spending $25 million to expand its mining operation, a project that is considered to have a reasonable amount of risk. Based on some initial analysis, the project would expand the operation's production output by 18% and provide a 15% return on investment.

Prior to deciding whether to proceed with the venture, the CEO asks the treasurer to determine where the financing would come from and how much each source will cost. The following are the findings of the treasurer:

a) $11 million will be funded from common shares. Each share will be sold for $50, yielding $4 in dividends. The flotation costs will be 10%.
b) $3 million will be provided from internal sources (retained earnings).
c) $1 million will be generated from preferred shares. The expected selling price is $100, and the flotation costs will be $5 per share. An amount of $10 in annual dividends per share will be paid to the preferred shareholders.
d) $4 million will be funded by the selling of bond A and $6 million by the selling of Bond B. The cost of Bond A is estimated at 6% and the cost of Bond B at 8%.

The company's corporate tax rate is 47%. The treasurer expects the common shares to continue to grow at a rate of 5% per year.

Questions

1. Calculate the company's cost of capital.
2. Should the CEO approve the expansion program? Why?

EXERCISE 7

Oscar Lewitt, CEO of Ingram Corporation, had just read in a recent issue of *Fortune* magazine an article entitled "America's Wealth Creators" and noticed several names of corporations he was familiar with, such as Microsoft, General Electric, Intel, Walmart, Coca-Cola, Merck, and Pfizer. These top wealth creators were listed in terms of their market value added (MVA) and economic value added (EVA). Although he recognized that some of the MVA and EVA were in the billions of dollars, he noticed in the article two numbers, return on capital and cost of capital. He felt that if these corporations, despite their size, were able to figure out how much value they were adding to the wealth of their shareholders, it would be possible to calculate the EVA for Ingram Corporation.

At his next management committee meeting, Mr. Lewitt asked his controller to figure out the EVA for Ingram Corporation and to report the information to the management committee at their next meeting for discussion purposes.

After some research about this new financial technique, the controller knew that he had to refer to his financial statements to calculate the EVA. He had to draw several numbers from the statement of income and the SFP in order to figure out the cost of capital and ROA. The company's most recent statement of income and different sources of financing are shown below:

Ingram Corporation Statement of Income for the period ended December 31, 2010	
Revenue	$1,200,000
Cost of sales	(650,000)
Gross profit	550,000
Expenses	
Distribution costs	$(150,000)
Administrative expenses	(125,000)
Depreciation	(50,000)
Finance costs	(45,000)
Total expenses	(370,000)
Profit before taxes	180,000
Income tax expense	(67,500)
Profit for the year	$112,500

The company's three major sources of financing are from short-term lenders for $100,000, a mortgage for $325,000, and equity for $430,000. The equity portion was split as follows: capital shares in the amount of $130,000 and retained earnings for $300,000.

The cost of capital for these three sources of financing is as follows:

Short-term borrowings	12.0%
Equity	15.0%
Long-term borrowings	10.0%

Questions

Based on the above information, answer the following:

1. Calculate Ingram Corporation's EVA.
2. Comment on the EVA. How could EVA be improved?

EXERCISE 8

Using the following information, calculate the company's operating leverage, financial leverage, and combined leverage.

Sales volume	100,000 units
Price per unit	$11.30
Variable costs (per unit)	$8.30
Fixed costs	$100,000
Interest	$25,000
Corporate income tax rate	40%

EXERCISE 9

Using the data in Exercise 8, assume that the company wants to make its plant more automated and is able to reduce the variable costs to $7.30 per unit, increase the fixed costs by $100,000 (i.e., to $200,000), and increase the finance costs from $25,000 to $35,000.

Question

Calculate the new operating leverage, financial leverage, and combined leverage.

EXERCISE 10

In 2010, Pirex Ltd. earned $6 million in profit. The company had 2.3 million shares outstanding and had a 40% payout ratio. The company's market price for each share was $15.00.

Questions

With the above information, calculate the following:

a) The company's EPS
b) The company's dividends per share
c) The company's dividend yield
d) The company's P/E ratio

Case

CASE 1: SHARCO SYSTEMS INC.

Sharco Systems Inc., a manufacturer of auto parts, wants to make inroads in the European and Asian markets. Sharco's executives know that it will be a difficult task because of the strongly entrenched existing competitors in those markets. However, the company executives believe that if they formulate effective business goals and strategies and raise the resources required to implement their plans, they could become viable competitors in these markets.

The company's statement of income and SFP are presented below. As shown, in 2010, the company earned $176 million in profit for the year on assets worth $2.0 billion.

Sharco Systems Inc.
Statement of Income
for the year ended December 31, 2010
(in $ millions)

Revenue	2,500
Cost of sales	(1,610)
Gross profit	890
Expenses	
Distribution costs	(260)
Administrative expenses	(120)
Depreciation	(100)
Finance costs	(90)
Total expenses	(570)
Profit before taxes	320
Income tax expense	(144)
Profit for the year	176

The before-tax cost of financing the equity and debt as shown on the SFP is as follows:

Bank loans	8.0%
Current portion of long-term borrowings	7.0%
Mortgage	6.0%
Debentures	7.0%
Equity	12.0%

Sharco Systems Inc.
Statement of Financial Position
as at December 31, 2010
(in $ millions)

Assets		
Non-current assets		
Property, plant, and equipment (at cost)	1,800	
Less: accumulated depreciation	(500)	
Total non-current assets		1,300
Current assets		
Inventories	290	
Trade receivables	350	
Prepaid expenses	10	
Cash and cash equivalents	50	
Total current assets		700
Total assets		2,000
Equity		
Common shares	135	
Retained earnings	750	
Preferred shares	15	
Total equity		900
Liabilities		
Long-term borrowings		
Mortgage	500	
Debentures	300	
Total long-term borrowings		800
Current liabilities		
Trade and other payables	60	
Bank loans	100	
Income taxes payable	130	
Current portion of long-term borrowings	10	
Total current liabilities		300
Total liabilities		1,100
Total equity and liabilities		2,000

The company had to prepare a prospectus in order to raise $350 million from the following sources:

	In millions
Common shares	$100
Retained earnings*	70
Preferred shares	30
Long-term borrowings	150
Total	$350

* Although retained earnings are not funds raised from the general public, it is shown here for the purpose of calculating the cost of capital.

These funds would be used almost exclusively to expand their operations in Europe and Asia, which would generate a return of 22% on the company's investments. The company's vice-president of finance provided the following information:

- Common share dividend yield is estimated at 7% and growth rate during the past five years has been 6%. (This rate is expected to continue.)
- Internal funding from retained earnings is estimated at $70 million.
- Preferred shares would be sold at $75 and bear a 10% yield.
- Cost of new debt is expected to be 10%.

Questions

1. With the above financial statements, calculate the following:
   a. Sharco's before- and after-tax cost of financing for 2010
   b. Sharco's before- and after-tax ROA for 2010 and compare them with your answers to Question 1a
   c. Sharco's conomic value added for 2010
   d. The company's cost of capital to raise funds from the following:
      – Common shares only
      – Preferred shares only
      – Long-term borrowings only
      – All sources (WACC)
2. Should Sharco go ahead with the project?

PHOTO/Gemphotography/Shutterstock

CHAPTER 10

[TIME-VALUE-OF-MONEY CONCEPT]

Learning Objectives

After reading this chapter, you should be able to:

1 Learning Objective — Differentiate between time value of money versus inflation and risk.

2 Learning Objective — Explain financial tools that can be used to solve time-value-of-money problems.

3 Learning Objective — Differentiate between future values of single sums and future values of annuities.

4 Learning Objective — Make the distinction between present values of single sums and present values of annuities.

5 Learning Objective — Solve capital investment decisions using time-value-of-money decision-making tools.

Chapter Outline

Time Value of Money versus Inflation and Risk
Tools for Solving Time-Value-of-Money Problems
Future Values
Present Values
Solving Time-Value-of-Money Investment Problems

OPENING CASE

The Millers are currently examining several investment options. Even though they are interested in investing money in CompuTech Inc., they also want to make sure that they will invest enough in RRSPs and educational funds for their two children, Vincent and Takara. To evaluate their needs, the Millers knew that they had to become knowledgeable in the language of the banking and investment community and in terms of concepts dealing with compounding and discounting. They realized that if they were to invest money in RRSPs and educational funds today, the element of time would make their investment grow. They therefore had to learn how to use interest tables, financial calculators, and financial spreadsheets capable of performing *time-value-of-money* calculations.

The Millers also realized that if they were to communicate knowledgeably with bankers, insurance agents, and financial advisers, they had to understand financial concepts such as the notion that a "dollar earned today is worth more tomorrow." For example, if the Millers were to deposit $1,000 in the bank today for one year at 5%, "time" is the only factor that would make their investment grow to $1,050. Similarly, if Len Miller wanted a $100,000 life insurance policy, the insurance agent would determine the amount of premiums he would have to pay each year for a certain number of years (depending on average age expectancy). Similarly, financial advisers who want to recommend to clients how much they need to save each year in different investments, such as RRSPs or guaranteed investment certificates (GICs), have to have a good understanding of these time-value-of-money concepts.

Bankers, insurance agents, and financial advisers are also familiar with the concept that a "dollar earned tomorrow is worth less today." This is referred to as *discounting*. For example, if the Millers wanted to have $60,000 for both children by the time each child turns 20, they know that they would have to invest today an amount that would surely be less than $60,000.

The Millers also recognized that the time-value-of-money concept was important not only for personal financing but also for business decisions. The application, however, would focus almost exclusively on discounting. Because insurance companies pay death benefits in the future, the future values of the premium payments have to be compounded (future value) or brought into the future for comparison purposes (death benefit and all premium payments). Conversely, businesses make different calculations. Because business investments are made today (purchase of assets, opening of a new retail store, or the expansion of an existing one), all cash receipts that would be earned in the future are discounted in order to find their present value and compared to the initial investment to determine whether the investment is worth it.

The Millers understood that they had to make all types of personal and business decisions and, in order to make prudent and insightful decisions, they had to learn financial techniques related to the time value of money.

Chapter Overview

As shown in Figure 1.1 on page 7, this is the first chapter dealing with investing decisions. Chapter 11 deals with capital budgeting decisions such as the purchase of equipment or machinery; construction, modernization, or expansion of a plant; and research and development. These kinds of decisions involve outflows of cash (disbursements), which take place during the year a decision is made, and inflows of cash (receipts), which are generated years after the initial funds are disbursed. To make effective decisions in capital budgeting, it is important to understand why money has a time value; this is what this chapter is all about.

This chapter focuses on five major themes. The first theme explains that money has a time value because of the "existence of interest" and differentiates it from the concepts related to inflation and risk. For example, if you have a choice between receiving $100 today or $103 a year from now, which option would you prefer? If money is worth 3% (interest rate), it does not matter which option you select. You could invest the $100 in a term deposit, which would give you 3% interest and increase your initial $100 to $103 one year from now. "Time" is the only element that would have earned $3 or 3% for you. Conversely, we can say that the $103 you would receive one year from now equals today's $100. The fact that there is a *cost* (interest) associated with the borrowing of money, whether provided by shareholders or lenders, confirms the fact that money has a **time value**. The old saying that reminds us "not to count our cash before it is discounted" is still valid today.

Time value of money
Rate at which the value of money is traded off as a function of time.

However, if we were to introduce a 2% inflation rate into this equation, we would earn a net 1% after inflation. This illustration confirms that a dollar earned today is worth more tomorrow (compounded). Or, a dollar earned tomorrow is worth less today (discounted). In capital budgeting, if a company invests money in a long-term producing asset and wants to calculate the return on the investment of that asset, the company must take into account both time value of money and inflation. The reason is simple: The company invests cash today in exchange for cash that it will earn in future years. In order to respect the time-value-of-money notion, all monies, whether spent today or earned next year or five years from now (including inflation), must be placed on an equal footing. That is why it is important to understand the fundamentals of the mathematics of interest, compounding, and discounting.

Time value of money and risk are also connected to one another. The nature of the investment (risk) makes a difference. One would certainly expect to earn more on a high-risk investment (high-tech businesses) versus a low-risk investment (Canada Savings Bonds). If a company invests $100,000 in a low-risk capital asset that will generate a one-time inflow of cash of $10,000 next year (the original $100,000 plus a profit of $10,000, or 10%), we can ask a fundamental question: Should the asset be purchased? The business may borrow $100,000 for, say, 6% to purchase the $100,000 capital asset. Here, the decisions could be justified because the return would exceed the 6% cost of capital. The company would actually make a 4% return after the cost of borrowing the funds. However, the decision might change completely if the investment was made in a high-risk project because management would be looking for, say, 20% (instead of 10%). If that would be the case, the project could very well be rejected.

The second theme of this chapter looks at various useful tools that can be used to make time-value-of-money decisions. They are: (1) the algebraic notations that explain the makeup of the various financial equations used in calculating future and present value amounts; (2) interest tables shown in Appendix B at the end of this book; (3) financial calculators and spreadsheets used for making time-value-of-money calculations; and (4) the *timeline* concept, which shows graphically when cash is disbursed or received over a period of time (months or years).

The third and fourth themes show how to use interest tables, financial calculators, and financial spreadsheets to calculate the future value and present value of single sums and annuities. In particular, they explain how to calculate the following:

- The future value of a single sum
- The future value of an annuity
- The present value of a single sum
- The present value of an annuity

The last theme explains how interest tables can be used on a personal basis and in business. It gives different examples related to compounding, discounting, and annuity calculations. This section also serves as a brief introduction to the application of interest tables (time value of money) when making business decisions, which will be covered in detail in Chapter 11. Therefore, the objective of the fifth section of this chapter makes the link between the time-value-of-money concept and capital investment decision-making. Sometimes, businesses simply avoid the use of the more sophisticated capital budgeting techniques to calculate the return on capital projects. Their managers believe that the mathematics of interest, which is the foundation of time-value-of-money capital budgeting techniques, is complicated and cumbersome, and that they have to use complex mathematical compound and discount formulas. This is not so. All that is required is to understand the *concepts* related to time value of money. Once this is understood, it is easy to use the more effective capital budgeting techniques such as internal rate of return (IRR) and the net present value (NPV) method and assess the economic viability of capital projects in a more meaningful way. These capital investment decision yardsticks will be fully explained in the next chapter. Today, financial calculators and spreadsheets can help decision-makers perform complex financial calculations easily and quickly.

1 Learning Objective

Differentiate between time value of money versus inflation and risk.

Time Value of Money versus Inflation and Risk

People often believe that money has a time value because of inflation and risk. These are three concepts that are totally distinct. The following paragraphs explain the difference between time value of money and inflation and time value of money and risk.

TIME VALUE OF MONEY AND INFLATION

Inflation
Represents a price-rise characteristic of periods of prosperity.

Inflation, which is a general increase in price in periods of prosperity, is taken into consideration when capital decisions are considered. For example, if you invest $1,000 in a term deposit bearing a 4% interest rate at a time when inflation is running at 3%, next year's purchasing power of the $1,040 would be reduced to $1,010. Time value and inflation should not be confused, particularly in capital investment decisions, because the calculation of inflation is a separate exercise.

Let us examine a capital asset that generates a multi-year cash flow. The revenues and expenses generated by the investment during the entire economic life of the asset include two elements. First, there are the revenues that are calculated on the basis of the expected volume increments, and second, the anticipated increase in unit selling price, which should include the element of inflation. Expenses also take into consideration increments in wages and the costs of material, utilities, etc., due to inflation. The difference between the projected revenues and projected expenses gives a profit level for the year that incorporates the inflationary factor. Once the revenue and expense projections are calculated (which includes the built-in factor for inflation), the time-value-of-money calculation of the future cash flows (compounding or discounting) begins.

Self-Test Exercise No. 10.1

Cash Flow Forecast of a Photo Centre

Several months after opening up their retail store, Len and Joan were thinking about adding a new department—a photo centre. They felt that it was a very lucrative business with a markup in the 50% range. The cost of the equipment would be $150,000 and the first-year revenue was estimated at $125,000. The five-year revenue forecast consisted of a 20% annual increase (including 3% for inflation). Operating expenses had different growth patterns. The $25,000 amount for salaries increased by 8% (including 3% for inflation) and the $50,000 amount for materials showed a 15% increase (including 3% for inflation). The equipment was depreciated over a five-year period (straight line) and CompuTech's income tax rate was 35%. With this information, calculate the company's yearly profit and cash flow forecast for the five-year period.

TIME VALUE OF MONEY AND RISK

Risk
Represents the level of expectations (probabilities) that something will happen in the future.

People also confuse time value and risk. It is not because risks are inherent in capital projects that money has a time value. Nevertheless, it is important to consider the risk factor when contemplating capital investment decisions. A $1,000 investment in Canada Savings Bonds with a 3% interest rate bears little risk. **Risk** represents the level of expectations (probabilities) that something will happen in the future. The chances of recovering the $1,000 amount and the interest are virtually assured. However, if $1,000 is invested in an untried product, risk is paramount. Because of the relative inherent risk involved in these types of investment opportunities, the investor would be comfortable with the 3% interest rate for the Canada Savings

Bonds but would probably want to earn a 25% return on a high-tech product that is on the verge of being researched and not yet commercially tested.

Although risk and capital decisions are closely related, it is important to note that interest and risk are two distinct concepts. While interest implies time value, risk suggests the level of return one should expect to earn from a particular investment.

In the News 10.1 puts in plain words how a company is prepared to take a plunge in a project that management hopes will bring positive financial results, but in the process, it will have to race against an already entrenched powerful competitor.

In The News [10.1]

Investing in a Market Where Powerful Businesses Are Well Established Is Always a "Risky" Decision

Some individuals might say: Who in their right frame of mind would want to launch a business to compete against companies such as Facebook and Google? Facebook, a social networking website, has more than 300 million active users worldwide. In 2009, a Compete.com study ranked Facebook as the most used social network by worldwide users, followed by MySpace. And look at Google, a company with 19,786 full-time employees, running literally thousands of servers worldwide, processing millions of search requests each day, and running about 1 petabyte of user-generated data every hour. But it appears that there is a small niche in that market, and a Canadian company is willing to take the plunge and, with it, the risk.

The company is Canpages Inc., a privately owned Vancouver-based search engine firm. Their intention is to get into the social networking business by acquiring GigPark, a website that individuals spend time on to make recommendations on local businesses and services. Canpages, a profitable business that has a list of some 80,000 businesses along with maps and videos, earned more than $100 million in revenue in the past year. Their objective is to merge two systems: Gigpark.com into Canpages.ca. As Olivier Vincent, CEO of Canpages, said, "GigPark will add a whole new pillar to our strategy" for creating an all-inclusive hybrid search–social networking system in Canada. He hopes that the integration will bring "hundreds of thousands" of new users to the company. He also made the following point: "Forming a social networking system is not only a question of reinventing the wheel, that is, to create Facebook, but instead to leverage Facebook, MySpace, and Twitter." However, the race is not only with social networking organizations, but also with Google, by introducing a 360-degree image mapping of Toronto streets, and with Yellow Pages.

Source: Adapted from Eric Lam, "Canpages buys GigPark website," *Financial Post*, August 25, 2009, p. FP2. For more information about Canpages and GigPark, visit http://corporate.canpages.ca and http://www.gigpark.com.

Tools for Solving Time-Value-of-Money Problems

2 Learning Objective

Explain financial tools that can be used to solve time-value-of-money problems.

Several tools are available to solve time-value-of-money problems. Algebraic formulas, interest tables, financial calculators, and spreadsheets can quickly solve time-value-of-money problems. Because time value of money deals with different time periods, which are extended for many months or even years, we will explain the *timeline* concept. But first, let's examine three topics: algebraic notations, interest tables, and financial calculators and spreadsheets.

ALGEBRAIC NOTATIONS

Algebraic notations are introduced for three reasons: first, to show how the interest tables presented in Appendix B at the end of this book (page A-7) are calculated; second, to explain the makeup of the various financial equations used for calculating future and present value amounts; and third, to familiarize students interested in using financial calculators and spreadsheets with the keystrokes for solving time-value-of-money problems.

It is not necessary to understand the roots of the various algebraic formulas used to calculate future and present values. It is important, however, to grasp how interest tables are used to calculate the future value of a sum received today and the present value of a sum received in the future.

In general, algebraic equations use lowercase letters to symbolize percentage rates and length of time while capital letters normally stand for money or dollar amounts. For instance, the letter i stands for interest rates, n for number or periods (months or years), PV for present value amounts, FV for future value amounts, and PMT for constant stream of cash payments. The symbols and letters that should be remembered are as follows:

P	The principal, which is the amount available today. This is expressed in dollars.
PV	The present value of a sum. This is also expressed in dollars.
FV	The future value of a sum. This is also expressed in dollars.
i	The rate of interest. This can be expressed on an annual, semi-annual, quarterly, or monthly basis.
n	The number of periods over which funds are borrowed. This is expressed in months or years.
PMT	This is a constant stream of funds to be received or spent over a number of periods. This is commonly referred to as an annuity. This equal flow of funds is expressed in dollars.
A	The present value of a constant stream of funds to be received or spent over a number of periods. It is the present value of an annuity. This figure is expressed in dollars.
S	The future sum of a stream of funds to be received or spent over a number of periods. It is the future value of an annuity and is also expressed in dollars.
k	An interest rate required to obtain a targeted rate of return.
T	The tax rate.

These symbols will be used in algebraic formulas to calculate the following:

- Future value of a single sum (compounding)
- Future value of a stream of sums (compounding)
- Present value of a single sum (discounting)
- Present value of a stream of sums (discounting)

INTEREST TABLES

Let's now turn to interest tables and examine how they can be used as time-value-of-money decision-making instruments to calculate the following:

- Future (compounding) and present (discounting) values of a single sum of money received or paid out at a given point in time.
- Constant flow of sums of money (an annuity) received or paid out over a given time period.

Interest tables
Present calculated factors used for computing future or present values of single sums and annuities.

Why four interest tables? The four interest tables listed in Table 10.1 are presented in Appendix B at the end of this book. **Interest tables** present calculated factors used for computing future or present values of single sums and annuities. It is important to understand their function before using them. Compounding uses Tables A and C. If you want to find the future value of a single sum, use Table A. If you want to calculate the future value of an annuity, use Table C.

In capital budgeting, however, financial analysts use discount tables—that is, Tables B and D. If you want to calculate the present value of a single sum, use Table B. If you want to find the present value of an annuity, use Table D.

As shown in Appendix B, these tables are made up of columns and rows, which list numerous calculated factors. The *columns* represent the interest rates while the *rows* indicate the years.

How interest tables came about. The concepts of compounding and discounting have been known for hundreds of years. Interest tables, however, have been around for only the past eight decades. These tables were not conceived by bankers or accountants, but by actuaries working for insurance companies. Here is how they used these tables. As shown in the upper portion of Table 10.2, if someone wished to buy a $30,000 insurance policy, that person could have been asked to pay $1,000 a year during his or her expected lifespan, which in this case happened to be 20 years. The insurance companies would have invested these $1,000 receipts at, say, 6% and, over the 20-year period, these sums would have a future value of $36,786, which is arrived at by multiplying $1,000 by the factor 36.786. This factor is found in

Table 10.1 Using Interest Tables

These two tables are mostly used in capital budgeting. ↓

	To compound	To discount
Single sum	Table A	Table B
Annuity	Table C	Table D

Table 10.2 Insurance versus Industrial Businesses

Compounding

Insurance Business		
Year 1	→ to →	Year 20
Yearly premiums (cash inflows) $1,000		$+36,786
Money is worth 6% ($1,000 × 36.786)		
Death benefit (cash outflow)		$−30,000
Surplus or net future value (NFV)		$ +6,786

Discounting

Industrial Business

Company invests $200,000 (cash outflow) to increase plant output. As a result, the company's sales increase by $20,000 (cash inflows) each year.

$−200,000	cash outflow
$+229,398	present value of the savings if money is worth 6% ($20,000 × 11.4699)
$ +29,398	surplus or net present value (NPV)

Appendix B, Table C on page A-9 under column 6% (interest rate) and opposite row 20 (years). In 20 years, when the $30,000 amount was paid out (cash outflow), the insurance company would have made a surplus of $6,786, which is referred to as the *net future value (NFV)*.

In the 1950s, the industrial community decided to use the time-value-of-money idea as a capital budgeting decision-making instrument. Industrial managers said that if the time value of money was good for insurance companies, it would also be good for industrial companies, as both have cash outflows and cash inflows. However, there is one major difference: the timing of making the cash disbursements or outflows. In the case of insurance companies, the cash outflow (payment) is made later, that is, in 20 years. In the case of industrial companies, the cash outflow is made at the beginning, and it is for this reason that cash receipts have to be discounted (in order to compare them to the initial investment) instead of bringing them into the future.

As shown in the lower portion of Table 10.2, the $200,000 expansion project that earns $20,000 a year over the next 20 years gives a $229,398 present value, which is arrived at by multiplying the $20,000 amount by the factor 11.4699. The factor is drawn from Table D on page A-11 under column 6% (interest rate) opposite row 20 (years). As shown, using a 6% discount factor, the company generates a $29,398 surplus, which is referred to as the *net present value (NPV)*.

FINANCIAL CALCULATORS AND SPREADSHEETS

Fortunately, financial calculators and spreadsheets can remove the unpleasant chore of making endless calculations to find solutions to time-value-of-money problems.

Financial calculators. For compounding and discounting calculations, financial calculators operate in the same fashion as interest tables. For every problem, several variables are known and calculators have a key function for each variable. Of all the variables, one is not known. By inputting the appropriate key for each variable and pressing the key function "Compute," the calculator displays the answer. The more important function keys set up in financial calculators and their meaning are as follows:

n	Number of periods
i/y	Interest rate per year
PV	Present value
FV	Future value
PMT	Payment

For example, to calculate the future value of a five-year $1,000 annuity bearing a 5% interest rate, you calculate the following:

Enter 5 years (n)
Enter the $1,000 amount ($PMT$)
Enter the 5% interest rate (i/y)

The financial calculator displays a $5,525.63 amount made up of $5,000, that is, the $1,000 five-year annuity, and the $525.63 amount for interest.

Financial spreadsheets. Financial spreadsheets such as Excel can also be used to solve time-value-of-money problems. To use the Excel spreadsheet, go to the menu bar "Insert" and click on "Function." Then click on "Financial" in the function category.[1] This will give you many financial calculation options such as FV, IRR, NPER, PMT, and NPV. Click on the future value (FV) and enter the same information in the dialogue box (see Table 10.3) that we used for calculating the future value of the $1,000 five-year annuity bearing a 5% interest rate. Press OK and, as shown, the $5,525.63 amount is displayed.

TIMELINE ILLUSTRATIONS

Timeline
Graphic illustration of time-value-of-money problems.

At times, the time-value-of-money concept is conceptually difficult to grasp. One tool that can help students to comprehend more fully this concept is the **timeline**, which is a graphic illustration of time-value-of-money problems. Although Figure 10.1 shows various timelines used to solve different problems, they all have several common characteristics. As shown, they are divided into different time periods (in these cases years, although they could be months or quarters). These periods are portrayed on the horizontal lines.

1. Your version of Excel may require different actions to reach the financial functions available. For example, if you use a more recent version of Excel, such as Excel 2007, your actions are slightly different. Under the "Formula" tab, click on "Insert Function." Then click on "Financial" in the drop-down list box labelled "Or select a category."

Table 10.3 Excel Financial Spreadsheets

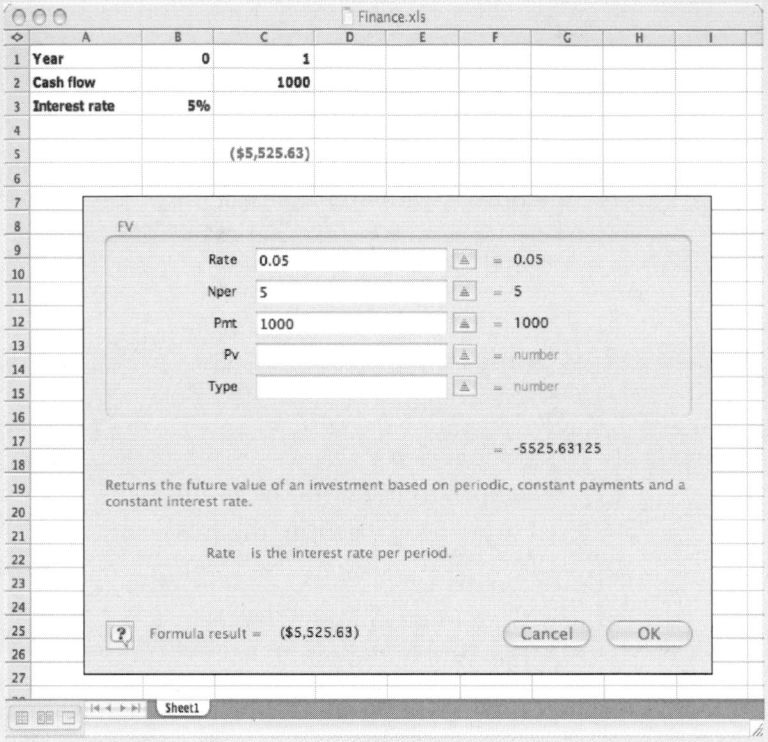

They all begin with time 0, which is the present, and add periods or years to the right. In these examples, time 1 is the beginning of the first period, time 2 the beginning of the second, and so on. The horizontal lines identify different components of the problems (e.g., amounts, targeted interest rates). Although, in most cases, there is no need to draw timelines, they become useful to comprehend the more complicated time-value-of-money problems. A timeline will be used in this chapter to explain certain time-value-of-money problems.

Figure 10.1 shows four timelines: two dealing with FV and two with PV. The first example, future value of a single sum (a), shows that a $1,000 amount received at the beginning of year 0 will increase to $1,050 ($1,000 × 1.050, factor drawn from Table A on page A-5) by the beginning of year 1. The second example (b) shows what the future value of $1,000 amounts received at the beginning of each year are worth at the beginning of year 5. These factors are also drawn from Table A. As shown, each year has a different factor indicating the number of years that the interest accumulates over time. The third

Figure 10.1 **Profile of Time-Value-of-Money Timelines**

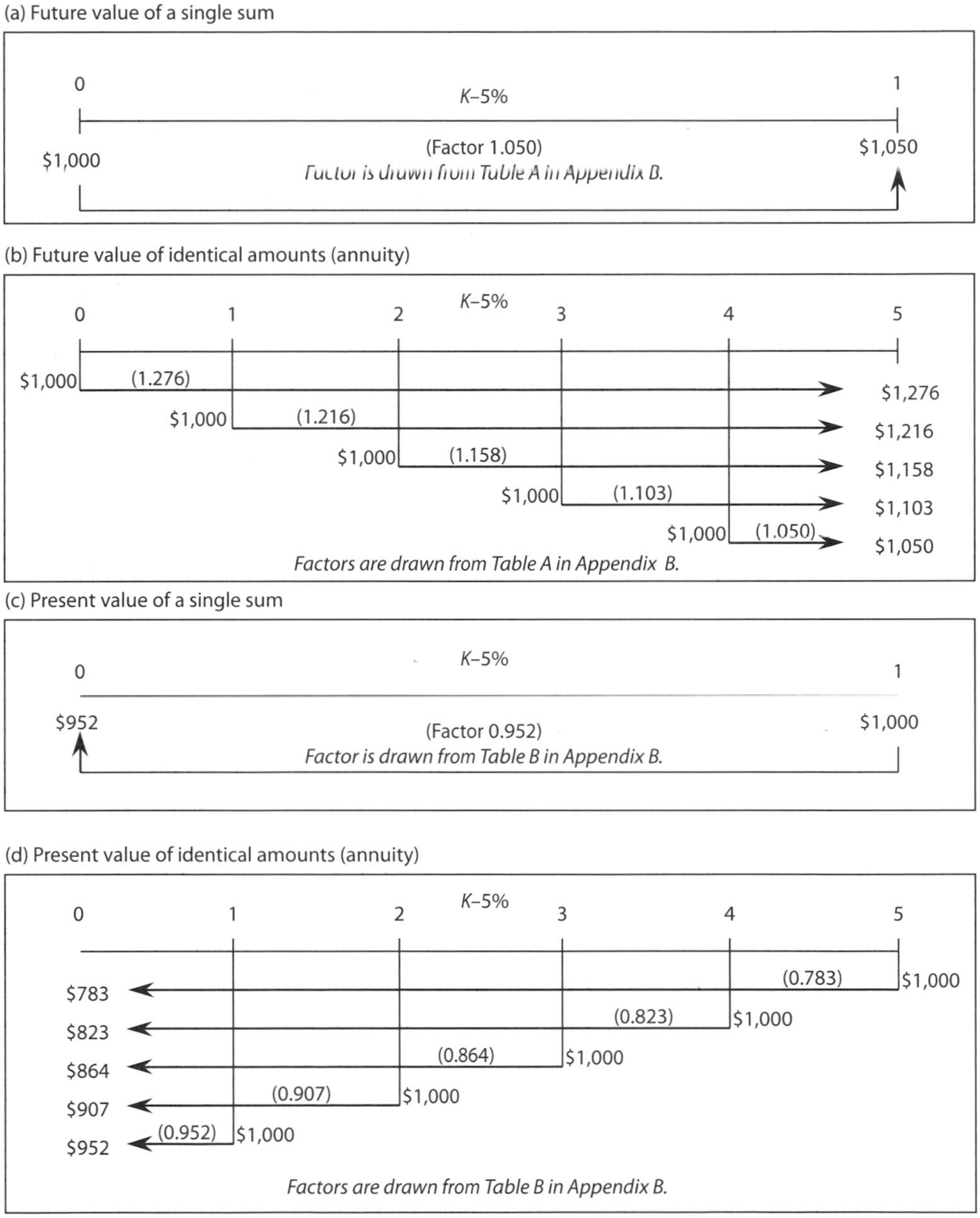

illustration (c) shows that the value of $1,000 received at the beginning of year 1 is worth $952 ($1,000 × 0.952, a factor drawn from Table B on page A-7) in year 0 or today. The last example (d) shows how much individual amounts received over a period of five years are worth today. These five factors are also drawn from Table B.

Future Values

3 Learning Objective

Differentiate between future values of single sums and future values of annuities.

The next two sections explain how to calculate, step by step, the following:

- Future value of a single sum
- Future value of an annuity
- Present value of a single sum
- Present value of an annuity

This section gives examples about how to calculate the future values of single sums and annuities and the next section shows present value calculations of single sums and annuities. First, let's look at the difference between simple and compound interest.

SIMPLE AND COMPOUND INTEREST

Simple interest Interest paid on the principal only.

Compound interest Interest rate that is applicable on the initial principal and the accumulated interest of prior periods.

Interest can be paid in two ways. First, it can be paid by means of simple interest, which is the simplest form. Here, the banker calculates **simple interest** only on the original $1,000 amount, or the principal. Interest paid is applied in the case of borrowed funds or earned in the case of invested money. If the original amount is kept in the bank for, say, three years, you would then earn $300 in interest using a rate of 10%.

Simple interest is not, however, the conventional way that interest is paid or earned. Usually, when money is deposited in a bank, the banker pays interest on both the original amount (the principal) and the accumulated balance, which increases each succeeding period as a result of the period interest that is added to the new balance. This form of interest is called **compound interest**.

Figure 10.2 illustrates the difference between simple interest and compound interest. As shown, the value of a $1,000 investment (principal) at 10% using simple

Figure 10.2 Simple and Compound Interest

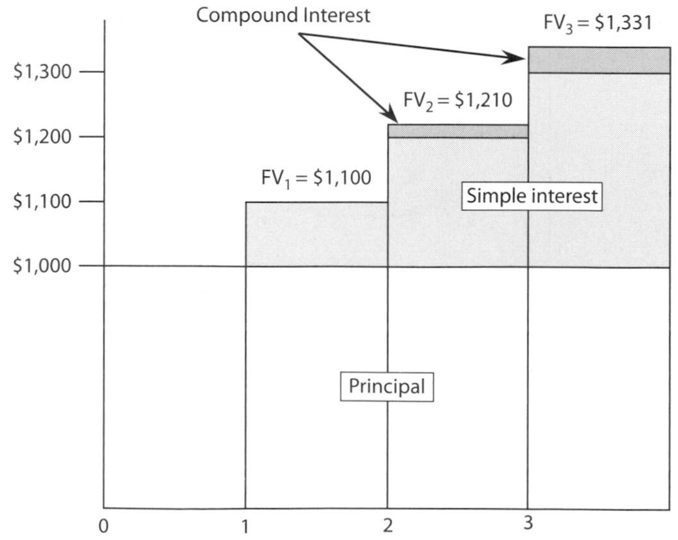

interest increases by $100 increments. If the investment is made at the beginning of year 1, the $1,000 amount would increase to $1,100 by the end of the first year. Simple interest would make the investment grow to $1,200 by the end of year 2 and $1,300 by the end of year 3. Using compound interest factors, the future value of the investment would grow to $1,100 by the end of the first years, $1,210 by the end of the second year, and $1,331 by the end of year 3. The compounding effect would add an extra $31 dollars by the end of the third year, which is due to the fact that during the second year, 10% (or $10) is earned on the $100 amount of interest earned during the first year and, in the third year, an additional 10% (or $21) is made on the interest earned during the first and second years (10% of $210).

FUTURE VALUE OF A SINGLE SUM

We said earlier in this chapter that money has a time value because of the existence of interest. This means that if you invest $1,000 today at 10%, you will collect $1,100 at the same date next year. If you keep your original amount invested for an indefinite period of time, interest will continue to accumulate, and your $1,000 will grow year after year. This future amount is referred to as the **future value (FV)** of a single sum.

Future value (FV)
The amount to which a payment or series of payments will grow by a given future date when compounded by a given interest rate.

Let's examine how the compound value of $1,000, invested today at 10%, would grow at the end of three years. Table 10.4 shows that at the end of the first year, the investor earns $100 and the ending amount is $1,100. During the second year, $110 in interest will be earned, which is made up of $100 on the original $1,000 and $10 on the interest earned during the first year. The balance at the end of the second year is $1,210. Figure 10.2 and Table 10.4 show the effect of compounding the future value of a single sum. The same arithmetic is done for calculating the interest earned during the third year; the value of the amount at the end of that period is $1,331.

An investor does not have to go through these calculations to determine the value of the initial investment for a specific period. This would be extremely cumbersome, particularly when one deals with a 10-, 20-, or 25-year time span. That is why interest tables come in handy. Here is how these tables are used. Table 10.5 shows interest factors for interest rates ranging from 9% to 20% covering 25 years. By looking at the 10% column, you can readily see that the future value of $1,000 at the end of the third year amounts to $1,331 ($1,000 × 1.331), the same amount that was calculated

Table 10.4 Calculating the Future Value of a Single Sum

Year	Beginning Amount	Interest Rate	Amount of Interest	Beginning Amount	Ending Amount
1	$1,000	0.10	$100	$1,000	$1,100
2	1,100	0.10	110	1,100	1,210
3	1,210	0.10	121	1,210	1,331

in Table 10.4. Table A in Appendix B at the end of this book contains factors for interest rates ranging from 1% to 36% for a 25-year period.

The algebraic equation used to calculate the future value of a single sum is as follows:

$$FV_n = P\ (1 + i)^n$$

$$FV_3 = \$1{,}000\ (1.10)^3$$

$$FV_3 = \$1{,}000 \quad 1.331$$

$$FV_3 = \$1{,}331$$

Rule of 72
Calculation that shows the approximate number of years it takes for an investment to double when compounded annually.

The Rule of 72. There is a quick and easy way to calculate the approximate number of years it takes for an investment to double when compounded annually at a particular rate of interest. It is called the **Rule of 72.** To find the answer, divide 72 by the interest rate related to the invested principal. Here is how it works. If you want to know how many years it takes for an investment to double at, say, 10% interest compounded annually, as shown below, you divide this figure into 72 and obtain 7.2 years.

$$\frac{72 \text{ (rule)}}{10 \text{ (\%)}} = 7.5 \text{ (approximate number of years)}$$

To verify this answer, look at Table 10.5. If we go down the 10% interest column, we see that the \$1.00 amount reaches \$2.00 between year 7 (1.949) and year 8 (2.144).

Self-Test Exercise No. 10.2

Future Value of a Single Sum

Joan Miller has just inherited $30,000 and has the option of investing this amount in different funds: GIC, safe mutual funds, or in stock options that are more risky. Based on her analysis, the historical performance for each fund is 5%, 9%, and 12%, respectively. If there are no withdrawals, how much will Joan have in these various funds at the end of 20 years?

FUTURE VALUE OF AN ANNUITY

Annuity
A series of payments (or receipts) of fixed amount for a specified number of years.

Up to this point, we have talked about the growth values of single sums. However, investors may want to invest money on a yearly basis and generate a flow of funds over many years. A series of periodic income payments of equal amounts is referred to as an **annuity**. A mortgage repayment, family allowances, RRSPs, whole-life insurance premiums, and even salaries and wages are considered typical annuities. In capital budgeting, if a company modernizes its plant at a cost of $100,000 and produces a "fixed yearly $25,000 savings" that would also be considered an annuity.

Because investors and capital budgeting decisions deal with multi-year funds flow situations, it is also important to understand how to calculate the future growth and the present value of annuities. Let's calculate the future growth of a five-year $1,000 yearly annuity bearing a 10% interest factor. There are two ways to do this calculation. First, we can go to the compound interest table in Table 10.5 and calculate the growth of each $1,000 individually. As shown in Table 10.6, the sum of all future receipts amounts to $6,105, made up of $5,000 in investment and $1,105 in interest. The calculation is done as follows. It is assumed that the annuity is paid at the end of each period—that is, on December 31—starting at the end of year 1. In five years, the $1,000 amount will grow to $1,464. Because the fifth payment is received on December 31 of the last year, this receipt does not produce any interest.

This is a very complicated and drawn-out way to calculate the future value of an annuity.

Table 10.5 Factors to Calculate the Future Value of a Single Sum

N	9%	10%	11%	12%	14%	16%	18%	20%
1	1.090	1.100	1.110	1.120	1.140	1.160	1.160	1.200
2	1.188	1.210	1.232	1.254	1.300	1.346	1.346	1.440
3	1.295	1.331	1.368	1.405	1.482	1.561	1.561	1.728
4	1.412	1.464	1.518	1.574	1.689	1.811	1.811	2.074
5	1.539	1.611	1.685	1.762	1.925	2.100	2.100	2.488
6	1.677	1.772	1.870	1.974	2.195	2.436	2.436	2.986
7	1.828	1.949	2.076	2.211	2.502	2.826	2.826	3.583
8	1.993	2.144	2.305	2.476	2.853	3.278	3.278	4.300
9	2.172	2.358	2.558	2.773	3.252	3.803	3.803	5.160
10	2.367	2.594	2.839	3.106	3.707	4.411	4.411	6.192
11	2.580	2.853	3.152	3.479	4.226	5.117	5.117	7.430
12	2.813	3.138	3.498	3.896	4.818	5.936	5.936	8.916
13	3.066	3.452	3.883	4.363	5.492	6.886	6.886	10.699
14	3.342	3.798	4.310	4.887	6.261	7.988	7.988	12.839
15	3.642	4.177	4.785	5.474	7.138	9.266	9.266	15.407
16	3.970	4.595	5.311	5.130	8.137	10.748	10.748	18.488
17	4.328	5.054	5.895	6.866	9.276	12.468	12.468	22.186
18	4.717	5.560	6.544	7.690	10.575	14.463	14.463	26.623
19	5.142	6.116	7.263	8.613	12.056	16.777	16.777	31.948
20	5.604	6.728	8.062	9.646	13.744	19.461	19.461	38.338
21	6.109	7.400	8.949	10.804	15.668	22.575	22.575	46.005
22	6.659	8.140	9.934	12.100	17.861	26.186	26.186	55.206
23	7.258	8.954	11.026	13.552	20.362	30.376	30.376	66.247
24	7.911	9.850	12.239	15.179	23.212	35.236	35.236	79.497
25	8.623	10.835	13.586	17.000	26.462	40.874	40.874	95.396

Table 10.6 Calculating the Future Value of an Annuity

Year	Amount Received	Interest Factor	Interest	Future Sum
1	$1,000	1.464	$464	$1,464
2	1,000	1.331	331	1,331
3	1,000	1.210	210	1,210
4	1,000	1.100	100	1,100
5	1,000	0.000	---	1,000
Total	$5,000		$1,105	$6,105

The second approach is to use annuity tables. Table 10.7 shows annuity factors for interest rates ranging from 9% to 20% for periods ranging from 1 to 25 years. By going down the 10% interest rate column to year 5, we find factor 6.105. If we multiply this factor by the $1,000 amount representing the fixed annuity receipts, we obtain $6,105. This is a much easier way to calculate future values. Table C in Appendix B at the end of this book gives annuity fatctors for interest rates ranging from 1% to 36%.

Table 10.7 Factors to Calculate the Future Value of an Annuity

N	9%	10%	11%	12%	14%	16%	18%	20%
1	1.000	1.000	1.000	1.000	1.000	1.000	1.000	1.000
2	2.090	2.100	2.110	2.120	2.140	2.160	2.180	2.200
3	3.278	3.310	3.342	3.374	3.440	3.506	3.572	3.640
4	4.573	4.641	4.710	4.779	4.921	5.066	5.215	5.368
5	5.985	6.105	6.228	6.353	6.610	6.877	7.154	7.442
6	7.523	7.716	7.913	8.115	8.536	8.977	9.442	9.930
7	9.200	9.487	9.783	10.089	10.731	11.414	12.142	12.916
8	11.029	11.436	11.859	12.300	13.233	14.240	15.327	16.499
9	13.021	13.580	14.164	14.776	16.085	17.519	19.086	20.799
10	15.193	15.937	16.722	17.549	19.337	21.322	23.521	25.959
11	17.560	18.531	19.561	20.655	23.045	25.733	28.755	32.150
12	20.141	21.384	22.713	24.133	27.271	30.850	34.931	39.581
13	22.953	24.523	26.212	28.029	32.089	36.786	42.219	48.497
14	26.019	27.975	30.095	32.393	37.581	43.672	50.818	59.196
15	29.361	31.773	34.405	37.280	43.842	51.660	60.965	72.035
16	33.003	35.950	39.190	42.753	50.980	60.925	72.939	87.442
17	36.974	40.545	44.501	48.884	59.118	71.673	87.068	105.931
18	41.301	45.599	50.396	55.750	68.394	84.141	103.740	128.117
19	46.019	51.159	56.940	63.440	78.969	98.603	123.413	154.740
20	51.160	57.275	64.203	72.052	91.025	115.380	146.628	186.688
21	56.765	64.003	72.265	81.699	104.768	134.840	174.021	225.026
22	62.873	71.403	81.214	92.503	120.436	157.415	206.345	271.031
23	69.532	79.543	91.148	104.603	138.297	183.601	244.487	326.237
24	76.790	88.497	102.174	118.155	158.659	213.977	289.494	392.404
25	84.701	98.347	114.413	133.334	181.871	249.214	342.603	471.981

The algebraic formula used to calculate the future value of an annuity is as follows:

$$S = PMT\left[\frac{(1+i)^n - 1}{i}\right]$$

$$= \$1{,}000 \quad 6.105$$

$$= \$6{,}105$$

Self-Test Exercise No. 10.3

Future Value of an Annuity

Joan Miller was given a choice on her $30,000 inheritance between receiving (1) the full payment today, or (2) a $3,000 annuity for the next 20 years and a lump-sum amount of $10,000 at the end of the 20th year. If Joan can earn 9%, which option is the most attractive?

Present Values

4 Learning Objective

Make the distinction between present values of single sums and present values of annuities.

The following several sections turn to the calculation of the present values of single sums and annuities in addition to showing how to calculate the future and present values of uneven series of amounts.

PRESENT VALUE OF A SINGLE SUM

Present value (PV) The value today of a future payment or stream of payments, discounted at an appropriate rate.

The opposite of compounding is discounting. Compounding means that when money is invested today, it appreciates in value because compound interest is added. The opposite takes place when money is to be received in the future; in this case, the future amount is worth less today. It is called the **present value (PV)**, which can be defined as the value today of a future payment or stream of payments, discounted at an appropriate rate. By referring to our previous example, because of the existence of the 10% interest rate, both amounts, $1,000 in year 1 and $1,331 ($1,000 × 1.331) in year 3, have equal values today. This, therefore, supports the argument that the $1,331 to be received three years from now has a $1,000 value today. Because discounting is the opposite of compounding, all we need to do is to reverse the compound algebraic equation as follows:

$$PV = F\left[\frac{1}{(1+i)^n}\right]$$

$$= \$1{,}000 \quad \frac{1}{(1 + 0.10)^3}$$

$$= \$1{,}000 \quad \frac{1}{1.331}$$

$$= \$1{,}000 \quad 0.75131$$

$$= \$751.31$$

This means that the $1,000 to be received three years from now at 10% is worth $751.31 today; or, to reverse the process, if you invest $751.31 today at a 10% interest rate, it would appreciate to $1,000 in three years' time ($751.31 × 1.331).

Like the compound interest calculation, calculating the present value of a promised future sum would be time consuming. To avoid this clerical chore, we can use present value tables. Table 10.8 shows present value factors for interest rates ranging from 9% to 16% between 1 and 25 years. Looking at the appropriate interest column (10%) and at year 3, we find factor 0.75131. This means that by multiplying the promised $1,000 future sum by 0.75131, we obtain a $751.31 present value. A more complete present value table appears in Table B in Appendix B at the end of this book.

In the News 10.2 makes clear that low interest rates can put a lid on borrowing costs, encouraging individuals to buy big-ticket items and businesses to invest in capital projects.

Table 10.8 **Factors to Calculate the Present Value of a Single Sum**

N	9%	10%	11%	12%	13%	14%	15%	16%
1	0.91743	0.90909	0.90090	0.89286	0.88496	0.87719	0.86957	0.86207
2	0.84168	0.82645	0.81162	0.79719	0.78315	0.76947	0.75614	0.74316
3	0.77218	0.75131	0.73119	0.71178	0.69305	0.67497	0.65752	0.64066
4	0.70843	0.68301	0.65873	0.63552	0.61332	0.59208	0.57175	0.55229
5	0.64993	0.62092	0.59345	0.56743	0.54276	0.51937	0.49718	0.47611
6	0.59627	0.56447	0.53464	0.50663	0.48032	0.45559	0.43233	0.41044
7	0.54703	0.51316	0.48166	0.45235	0.42506	0.39964	0.37594	0.35383
8	0.50187	0.46651	0.43393	0.40388	0.37616	0.35056	0.32690	0.30503
9	0.46043	0.42410	0.39092	0.36061	0.33288	0.30751	0.28426	0.26295
10	0.42241	0.38554	0.35218	0.32197	0.29459	0.26974	0.24718	0.22668
11	0.38753	0.35049	0.31728	0.28748	0.26070	0.23662	0.21494	0.19542
12	0.35553	0.31863	0.28584	0.25667	0.23071	0.20756	0.18691	0.16846
13	0.32618	0.28966	0.25751	0.22917	0.20416	0.18207	0.16253	0.14523
14	0.29925	0.26333	0.23199	0.20462	0.18068	0.15971	0.14133	0.12520
15	0.27454	0.23939	0.20900	0.18270	0.15989	0.14010	0.12289	0.10793
16	0.25187	0.21763	0.18829	0.16312	0.14150	0.12289	0.10686	0.09304
17	0.23107	0.19784	0.16963	0.14564	0.12522	0.10780	0.09293	0.08021
18	0.21199	0.17986	0.15202	0.13004	0.11081	0.09456	0.08080	0.06914
19	0.19449	0.16351	0.13768	0.11611	0.09806	0.08295	0.07026	0.05961
20	0.17843	0.14864	0.12403	0.10367	0.08678	0.07276	0.06110	0.05139
21	0.16370	0.13513	0.11174	0.09256	0.07680	0.06383	0.05313	0.04430
22	0.15018	0.12285	0.10067	0.08264	0.06796	0.05599	0.04620	0.03819
23	0.13778	0.11168	0.09069	0.07379	0.06014	0.04911	0.04017	0.03292
24	0.12640	0.10153	0.08170	0.06588	0.05322	0.04308	0.03493	0.02838
25	0.11597	0.09230	0.07361	0.05882	0.04710	0.03779	0.03038	0.02447

In The News [10.2]

Low Interest Rates Can Encourage Individuals and Businesses to Buy Capital Assets

There is one way to regulate the intensity of a fire: by feeding it with an adequate supply of gasoline, that is, the oxidizing agent. This is precisely one of the roles of the Bank of Canada. The Bank's monetary policy has to do with increasing or decreasing the interest rate to ensure a "well-functioning Canadian economy," which (1) allows Canadians to make spending and investment decisions with confidence, (2) encourages longer-term investments in the economy, and (3) sustains job creation and greater productivity. The bottom line is this: creating real improvements in Canada's standard of living.

This is what the governor of the Bank of Canada, Mark Carney, has been trying to do since the start of the recession: keep the economy moving in the right direction. He brought the interest rate to the lowest possible level, 0.25%, and promised to keep it there (conditions permitting) until 2010. As some economists indicated, this is a key factor for driving the Canadian economy back to growth. As a result of his effective monetary policy, Canada's home sale market soared by 18.2% in July 2009, making a cumulative 61% increase over the past six months. And in the commercial retail sector, the word recession does not seem to be part of the decision-making thinking process. In fact, retailers have added about 6.8 million square feet of space during the first six months of 2009, more than in 2008.

Source: Adaped from Paul Vieira, "Low interest rates come with high risk," *Financial Post*, August 27, 2009, p. FP1. For a peek at the Bank of Canada's latest news, visit http://www.bank-banque-canada.ca.

Self-Test Exercise No. 10.4

Present Value of a Single Sum

The Millers would like to have a $30,000 education fund for their son Vincent, who is now three years old, and the same amount for their daughter Takara, who has just turned one. The Millers expect that their children will start university by the time they reach 20 years of age. How much will the Millers have to invest today (in one lump sum) if the registered education savings plan guarantees a 7% annual interest rate free from any income tax?

PRESENT VALUE OF AN ANNUITY

Discounting
The process of finding the present value of a series of future cash flows.

Calculating the present value of an annuity is the reverse of compounding an annuity. Compounding gives the future growth of a series of fixed receipts or payments; **discounting** gives the present value of a series of receipts or payments. Let us figure out the present value of a $1,000 amount received every year during a five-year period that bears a 10% interest rate. This calculation can also be done two ways. First, we can multiply yearly receipts by their respective interest factors. We must therefore refer to Table 10.8 and calculate the present value of each amount. As shown in Table 10.9, the present value of the $1,000 five-year annuity totals $3,790.

Table 10.9 Calculating the Present Value of an Annuity

Year	Amount Received	Interest Factor	Present Value
1	$1,000	0.9091	$909
2	1,000	0.8264	826
3	1,000	0.7513	751
4	1,000	0.6830	683
5	1,000	0.6209	621
Total	$5,000		$3,790

However, there is no reason to go through this long process to calculate the present value of an annuity. By referring to Table 10.10, which contains a series of present value factors for annuities for varying interest rates, we can find the answer quickly and easily. Looking at the 10% interest column at the line for year 5, we find factor 3.7908. The more simplified approach is, therefore, to multiply this

Table 10.10 Factors to Calculate the Present Value of an Annuity

N	9%	10%	11%	12%	13%	14%	15%	16%
1	0.9174	0.9091	0.9009	0.8929	0.8850	0.8772	0.8696	0.8621
2	1.7591	1.7355	1.7125	1.6901	1.6681	1.6467	1.6257	1.6052
3	2.5313	2.4868	2.4437	2.4018	2.3612	2.3216	2.2832	2.2459
4	3.2397	3.1699	3.1024	3.0373	2.9745	2.9137	2.8550	2.7982
5	3.8896	3.7908	3.6959	3.6048	3.5172	3.4331	3.3522	3.2743
6	4.4859	4.3553	4.2305	4.1114	3.9976	3.8887	3.7845	3.6847
7	5.0329	4.8684	4.7122	4.5638	4.4226	4.2883	4.1604	4.0386
8	5.5348	5.3349	5.1461	4.9676	4.7988	4.6389	4.4873	4.3436
9	5.9852	5.7590	5.5370	5.3282	5.1317	4.9464	4.7716	4.6065
10	6.4176	6.1446	5.8892	5.6502	5.4262	5.2161	5.0188	4.8332
11	6.8052	6.4951	6.2065	5.9377	5.6869	5.4527	5.2337	5.0286
12	7.1607	6.8137	6.4924	6.1944	5.9176	5.6603	5.4206	5.1971
13	7.4869	7.1034	6.7499	6.4235	6.1218	5.8424	5.5831	5.3423
14	7.7861	7.3667	6.9819	6.6282	6.3025	6.0021	5.7245	5.4675
15	8.0607	7.6061	7.1909	6.8109	6.4624	6.1422	5.8474	5.5755
16	8.3125	7.8237	7.3792	6.9740	6.6039	6.2651	5.9542	5.6685
17	8.5436	8.0215	7.5488	7.1196	6.7291	6.3729	6.0472	5.7487
18	8.7556	8.2014	7.7016	7.2497	6.8399	6.4674	6.1280	5.8178
19	8.9501	8.3649	7.8393	7.3658	6.9380	6.5504	6.1982	5.8775
20	9.1285	8.5136	7.9633	7.4694	7.0248	6.6231	6.2593	5.9288
21	9.2922	8.6487	8.0751	7.5620	7.1016	6.6870	6.3125	5.9731
22	9.4424	8.7715	8.1757	7.6446	7.1695	6.7429	6.3587	6.0113
23	9.5802	8.8832	8.2664	7.7184	7.2297	6.7921	6.3988	6.0442
24	9.7066	8.9847	8.3481	7.7843	7.2829	6.8351	6.4338	6.0726
25	9.8226	9.0770	8.4217	7.8431	7.3300	6.8729	6.4641	6.0971

factor by $1,000; this gives us $3,790. Table D in Appendix B at the end of this book gives a more complete set of interest factors for annuities ranging from 1 to 25 years.

The algebraic formula used to calculate the present value of an annuity is as follows:

$$A = PMT\left[\frac{1-(1+i)^{-n}}{i}\right]$$

Using our example,

$$A = \$1{,}000 \times 3.7908$$
$$A = \$3{,}790$$

We now have two interest factors to keep track of: the compound interest factor and the present value factor. In the former case, factors are used to make a sum grow (compound), while in the latter case, factors are used to depreciate (discount) a sum expected to be received in the future.

Figure 10.3 shows graphically the impact that 10%, 20%, and 30% compound and discount factors have on a $1,000 amount over a 12-year period. For example, on the left side of the figure, a $1,000 investment at 10% grows to $3,138 in 12 years, while the same investment grows to $23,298 at 30%. The right side of the figure shows that $1,000 received 12 years from now is worth $319 today at 10%, and only $43 at 30%.

Figure 10.3 **Graphic Illustration of the Compounding and Discounting Process**

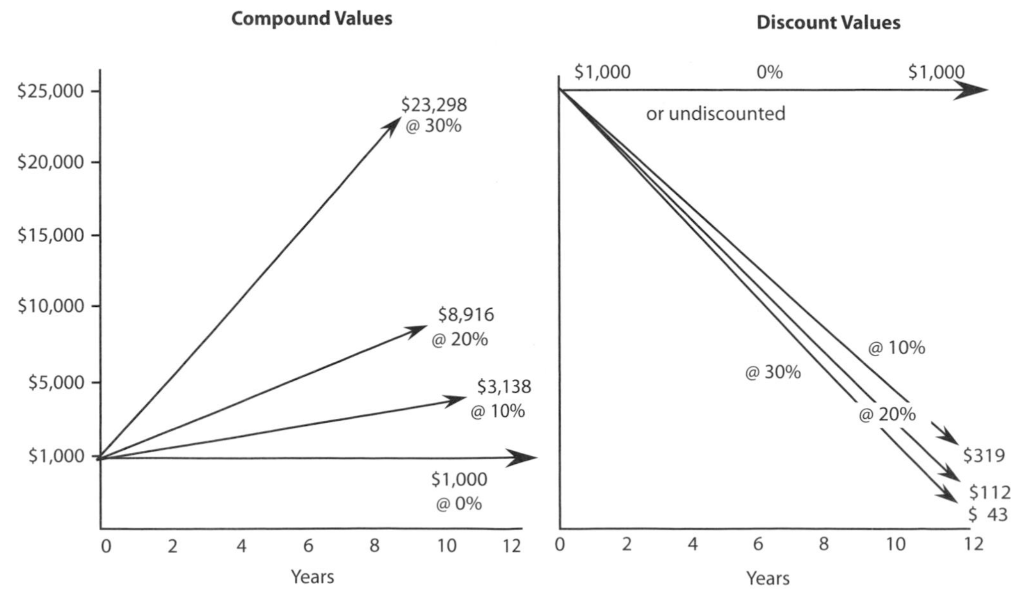

Self-Test Exercise No. 10.5

Present and Future Values of an Annuity

Len has just won $100,000 at a casino. If money is worth 10%, would it be better for Len to receive the full amount now or $15,000 each year for the next 10 years?

Questions

1. What is the value of each amount 10 years from now?
2. What is today's present value of each amount?
3. How much would Len have to receive each year to make the two amounts equal?
4. If Len received $15,000 each year instead of the $100,000 amount, what would be the effective interest rate or the IRR?

PRESENT VALUE OF AN UNEVEN SERIES OF AMOUNTS

Our definition of an annuity includes the term *fixed amount*. In other words, annuities are made up of constant and equal receipts or payments. But often, amounts received from investments are sporadic. If this is the case, in order to evaluate the economic desirability of an investment or a capital project (unless you have a financial calculator, spreadsheet, or software to calculate the present values of the future receipts), you must calculate each receipt or payment individually.

To illustrate the process of calculating uneven flows of receipts, let us assume that you contemplate investing $1,500, which would produce an inflow of funds of $200 in the first year, $500 in the second, $400 in the third, $600 in the fourth, and $200 in the fifth. If you want to make a 12% return on your investment, discounted-value calculations of the future receipts are shown in Table 10.11. In this case, the investment is not desirable because the discounted value of the future receipts, which amounts to $1,357, is less than the $1,500 initial outflow.

Table 10.11 Calculating the Present Value of Uneven Amounts

Year	Receipts	Discount Factor	Present Value
1	$200	0.8929	$179
2	500	0.7972	399
3	400	0.7118	285
4	600	0.6355	381
5	200	0.5674	113
Total	$1,900		$1,357

Using the same example except for changing the $200 receipt in the fifth year for a $200 annuity received over six years (from year 5 to year 10) would require a slightly different procedure to calculate the present value. As shown in Table 10.12, the present value of the receipts for years 1, 2, 3, and 4 are the same as those calculated in Table 10.11. However, because the last $200 receipt is an annuity, we can use a shortcut. In the first step, the $200 receipts from years 5 to 10 (for a total of six years) have to be discounted to year 4, which gives the amount of $822.28. In the second step, the $822.28 amount has to be discounted to year 0, which gives $522.56. The calculation process is shown in Table 10.12 and illustrated graphically in Figure 10.4. In total, the discounted value of the receipts amounts to $1,765.76, which is more than the original outflow. Therefore, in this case, the investment is desirable because it compares favourably to the initial $1,500 investment.

Table 10.12 Procedure for Calculating an Uneven Series of Amounts

A.	PV of $200 in year 1 (0.8929)	=	$178.58
	PV of $500 in year 2 (0.7972)	=	398.60
	PV of $400 in year 3 (0.7118)	=	284.72
	PV of $600 in year 4 (0.6355)	=	381.30
	PV of $200 in years 5 to 10		
B.	Step 1: $200 × 4.1114 = $822.28		
	Step 2: $822.28 × 0.6355	=	522.56
C.	PV of total receipts	=	$1,765.76

Figure 10.4 Graphic Illustration of the Present Value Calculations from Table 10.12

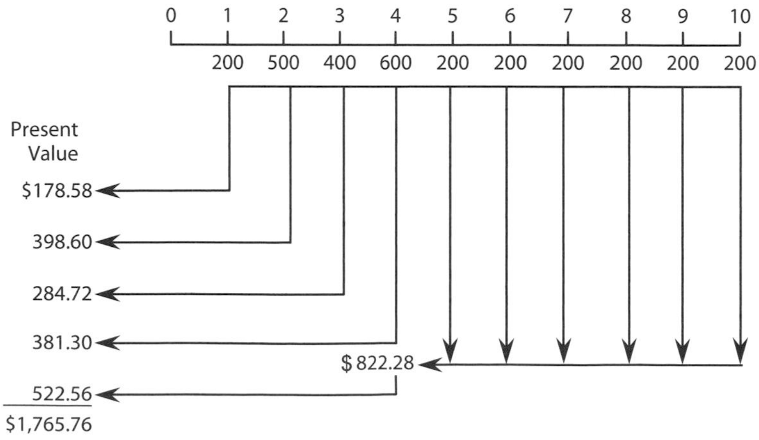

Self-Test Exercise No. 10.6

Present Value of Uneven Sums

Using the cash flow forecast that was prepared in Self-Test Exercise No. 10.1 on page 476, calculate Photo Centre's present value. Assume that the company's cost of capital is 10%.

Solving Time-Value-of-Money Investment Problems

5 Learning Objective

Solve capital investment decisions using time-value-of-money decision-making tools.

Let's now turn to the practical side of decision-making and examine how interest tables can help individuals and managers evaluate the economic desirability of different investment opportunities. The remaining segments of this chapter look at the meaning of time-value yardsticks within the context of the following investment and capital budgeting techniques:

- The future value (FV)
- The net future value (NFV)
- The present value (PV)
- The net present value (NPV)
- The internal rate of return (IRR)

To describe how these techniques are used, we will turn to a $100,000 lottery example and determine how much a winner should receive each year over a 10-year period in order to make the annuity equal to the lump sum. As shown in Figure 10.5, investment decisions deal with two key concepts: time and cash. Time is important because, as mentioned earlier, when managers invest money today, they expect to earn money from these investments over an extended number of years. For example, when a company invests $100,000 to modernize a plant that has a 10-year lifespan, that initial cash outflow must be compared to all the cash inflows that will be generated

Figure 10.5 Investment Decisions

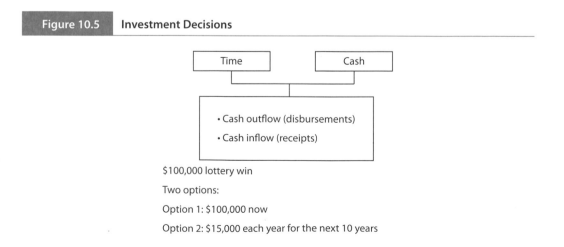

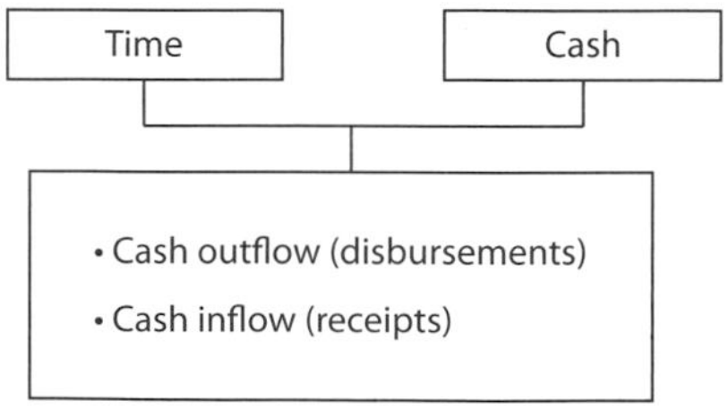

$100,000 lottery win

Two options:

Option 1: $100,000 now

Option 2: $15,000 each year for the next 10 years

through the savings in the future. There is no question that a $100,000 investment that generates $50,000 in savings during a three-year period (for a total of $150,000) would be more financially attractive than one that generates $15,000 a year during a 10-year period (also for a total of $150,000).

Cash outflow
Represents cash disbursements for the purchase of investments such as mutual funds or capital assets.

Cash inflow
Represents the receipt of money (interest or profit for the year plus depreciation) generated by an investment or a project.

The second critical element is cash. If someone invests money in mutual funds or a company invests money in equipment, machinery, or research and development, it invests "cash." Such an investment is commonly referred to as a **cash outflow** or cash disbursement. The investors or the managers will want to compare cash invested with cash generated by the investment. The cash that an investment generates is commonly referred to as **cash inflow** or cash receipts. The common denominator that ties a project together is cash. Therefore, in businesses, when preparing a project's projected statement of income, the profit for the year figure shown at the bottom of the statement of income must be converted into cash (e.g., by adding back depreciation) because time-value yardsticks use cash, not profit for the year, to calculate a project's viability. The bottom line is this: To make capital budgeting decisions meaningful, one has to compare apples (cash outflow) with apples (cash inflow).

In the News 10.3 points out that the two critical factors to consider when evaluating the economic benefits in a capital project are cash outflows and cash inflows.

In The News [10.3]

Cash Inflows and Cash Outflows Are Two Critical Factors Needed to Justify Investments in Capital Assets

Cash flow is one of the most important factors in the decision-making process that will determine whether to go ahead with a project. In fact, cash flow determines a project's rate of return value (IRR and NPV) and controls, to a large extent, a business's liquidity profile.

When Enbridge decided to proceed with the Alberta Clipper Pipeline project, cash (inflows and outflows) was certainly a preoccupation of the decision-makers. In August 2009, Enbridge Inc. received U.S. approval for going ahead with their project, which will carry oilsands crude to the U.S. Midwest. When the $3.7 billion pipeline (cash outflows) is completed in about a year, it will ship 450,000 barrels of bitumen a day to Superior, Wisconsin, with the potential to reach 800,000 barrels a day (cash inflows), which will be rerouted to refineries in Illinois and on to the main storage hub in Cushing, Oklahoma. The price tag for the Canadian portion is $2.5 billion, and for the U.S. portion, $1.2 billion.

Source: Adapted from "U.S. OKs Alberta clipper pipeline project," *Financial Post*, August 21, 2009, p. FP4. To learn more about Enbridge's Alberta Clipper Project, click on http://www.enbridge-expansion.com/expansion/main.aspx?id=1218.

The following illustrates the significance of time and cash in investment decisions. Assume that you have won a $100,000 lottery and are given the following options:

- Option 1: Receive the $100,000 lump-sum amount today.
- Option 2: Receive $10,000 each year during the next 10 years (also for a total of $100,000).

There is no question that you will go for the first option. In both options, we are dealing with cash and with time. It would be absurd to accept the $10,000 arrangement despite the fact that the total receipts equal $100,000. The fact that you could invest the $100,000 in mutual funds at, say, 10% would make option 1 more economically attractive. However, if you were offered $12,000 a year instead, would you go for it? How about $15,000 or $20,000? How about $25,000 during the next six years (for a total $150,000) instead of only $100,000? As you can see, different time factors and varying amounts call for an analysis to determine the most lucrative option.

The same applies in capital budgeting. If you were to invest $100,000 in a capital project that has a 10-year lifespan, how much should that project generate in cash in order to make it economically attractive? The following sections answer these questions.

FUTURE VALUE AND NET FUTURE VALUE

Question 1: Should the lottery winner accept the $100,000 lump-sum payment or $15,000 a year over the next 10 years?

Question 2: Should the manufacturing manager invest $100,000 in order to save $15,000 a year during the next 10 years?

Assuming that the lottery winner can invest money in mutual funds at say, 10%, here are the answers.

If the lottery winner is given the option of receiving a $100,000 lump sum now or $15,000 a year during the next 10 years, the future value of both amounts is calculated as follows:

$100,000	×	2.594	(Table A)	=	$259,400	(FV)
$ 15,000	×	15.937	(Table C)	=	$239,055	(FV)
Net future value					$ 20,345	(NFV)

Unquestionably, if the $100,000 were invested now in mutual funds at 10% over the next 10 years, this amount would grow (because of time) to more ($259,400) than if the $15,000 amount were put in the bank each year ($239,055). These amounts are referred to as future value (FV). As shown, by the 10th year, the lump-sum payment would give an extra $20,345, commonly referred to as the NFV. Individually, both amounts are referred to as the future value, and the difference between both future amounts is referred to as the NFV.

PRESENT VALUE AND NET PRESENT VALUE

On the other hand, if you want to justify which option to choose by comparing the discounted amounts, you would get a difference of $7,831 in favour of the lump-sum payment. Here is how the arithmetic works.

	–$100,000			
Present value	+$ 92,169	(PV)	=	or $15,000 × 6.1446 (Table D)
	– $7,831	(NPV)	=	Net present value

As indicated, whether you bring both sums into the future (10th year) or the present, the numbers are different, but the decision is the same—go for the $100,000 lump-sum payment.

If a business invests $100,000 (cash outflow) to modernize the plant in order to save $15,000 (cash inflow) a year, the economics would not justify the investment. As shown above, the discounted $15,000 (or $150,000 over the 10-year period) gives a present value (PV) of only $92,169. Using the 10% discount rate, the difference between the outflow and the inflow gives a negative $7,831 difference, which is referred to as the **net present value (NPV)**. Whenever there is a negative NPV, the return on the investment is less than the rate used to discount the future cash receipts, which in this case happens to be less than 10%. When the NPV is positive, it means that the return on the investment is more than the rate used to discount the future receipts.

Net present value (NPV) The present value of the future cash flow of an investment, less the initial cash outflow.

Self-Test Exercise No. 10.7

Net Present Value and Net Future Value

Using the cash flow forecast that was prepared in Self-Test Exercise No. 10.1, calculate Photo Centre's NPV and NFV. Assume that the company's cost of capital is 10%.

INTERNAL RATE OF RETURN

Now, if both amounts were to have the same value, the lottery winner would have to receive $16,275 each year for the next 10 years. This $16,275 amount is calculated by dividing the $100,000 amount by the factor found in Table D in Appendix B at the end of this book under column 10%, row year 10 (6.1446). As shown, both numbers are the same; that is, the lump-sum amount is equal to the present value of the $16,275 annual receipts—the NPV is 0.

Here is how the calculation is done.

	–$100,000		
Present value	+$100,000	=	or $16,275 × 6.1446 (Table D)
	$ 0	=	NPV

Now, if the management committee wants to make a 10% return on the $100,000, plant efficiencies would also have to generate $16,275 each year. If the savings is more than this, the plant would generate more than 10%; if it is less, the return would be less. The bottom line is this: When the interest rate makes the discounted future receipts ($100,000) equal the original investment ($100,000), it is referred to as the internal rate of return. The **internal rate of return (IRR)** can be defined as the interest rate that equates the cost of an investment (cash outflow) to the present value of the expected returns from the investment (cash inflow).

Internal rate of return (IRR) The interest rate that equates the cost of an investment (cash outflow) to the present value of the expected returns from the investment (cash inflow).

In this particular case, because 10% makes the future savings equal to $100,000 (the NPV equals 0), the IRR on this particular investment is 10%. If the savings are more than $16,275, the plant generated a higher return. For example, if the plant were to generate $18,429 savings per year during the next 10 years, the IRR would be 13%, because it is this rate that makes the NPV equal to 0.

	−$100,000		
Present value	+$100,000	=	or $18,429 × 5.4262 (Table D)
	$ 0	=	NPV

On the other hand, if the annual receipts were less than $16,275, then the IRR would be less. In the case of the manufacturing plant, the annual savings are $15,000. This means that the IRR would be less than 10% (8.1%). Here's the proof. This number is arrived at by looking at Table D in Appendix B at the end of this book, under the column 8% at row year 10, where we find factor 6.7101.

	−$100,000		
Present value	+$100,652	=	or $15,000 × 6.7101 (Table D)
	+$ 652	=	NPV

As shown, the 8% figure gives a positive $652 NPV, which means that the project generates 8% plus $652. If we were to convert this number on a percentage basis, the answer would be 0.144%. If Table D had a factor for 6.6667, then the PV would have been exactly $100,000, and the NPV would be 0.

Self-Test Exercise No. 10.8

Internal Rate of Return

Using the cash flow forecast that was prepared in Self-Test Exercise No 10.1, calculate Photo Centre's IRR.

Food for thought. As shown in Table 10.13, using traditional accounting methods to calculate the return on this project, one would divide the $15,000 amount by the $100,000 asset and obtain a 15% return (ROA). If a time-value-of-money yardstick were used, such as the IRR, the investment would give only 8.1%. In this case, the company would be losing 1.9% (after financing) each year during the next 10 years instead of making a net 5.0%.

This simple illustration proves that using accounting rates of return in capital budgeting decisions could be misleading. As we will discover in the next chapter, there are different ways of calculating the accounting rates of return, and they are not the most reliable capital budgeting yardsticks. As shown in Table 10.13, time-value yardsticks are more suitable for measuring the desirability of capital projects and can be compared more accurately to the cost of capital.

Table 10.13 Accounting Rate of Return versus the RR

Calculating the accounting rate of return using ROA

$$\frac{\textit{Receipts}}{\textit{Assets}} = \frac{\$15,000}{\$100,000} = 15\%$$

Statement of Financial Position

ROA	15.0%	Cost of capital	10.0%
IRR	8.1%		

USING INTEREST TABLES IN CAPITAL BUDGETING

To calculate the financial returns by using time-value-of-money yardsticks, you need four elements:

- Investment (cash outflow or disbursement)
- Annual cash inflow (receipts)
- Expected lifespan of the project
- Cost of money (or the return that management wants to make on the investment)

Let's use one more example to calculate the NPV and the IRR of a capital project by applying interest tables. As shown on the left side of Table 10.14(a), the company invests $25,000 in a new capital asset and obtains $1,000 in savings each year during the next 25 years. If management wants to make 10%, the present value of the $1,000 receipts gives $9,077. Here, the NPV is a negative $15,923. This means that the IRR is negative.

If management wants to earn 10%, how much should the project generate each year over the life of the asset? As shown on the right side of Table 10.14(a), the savings should be $2,754. As indicated, this annual savings discounted at 10% gives a present

Table 10.14(a) Investing in a Capital Project

1. A company invests $25,000 in a project. 2. It generates $1,000 in savings each year. 3. The expected life of the project is 25 years. 4. Cost of capital is 10%.		How much must the company save each year to make 10% on the project?	
1. Investment	– $25,000	– $25,000	Investment
2. Annual savings: $1,000			Savings per year: $2,754
3. Total savings: $25,000			Total savings: $68,850
4. Present value of savings (9.0770 × $1,000)	+ $ 9,077	+ $25,000	Present value of the savings (9.0770 × $2,754)
Net present value	– $15,923	0	Net present value

value of $25,000, or an NPV of 0. Here, the IRR would be 10% because it is the discount rate that makes the cash inflow equal to the cash outflow.

Now, if management wants to earn 16% (instead of 10%), the annual savings would have to be $4,100. As shown in Table 10.14(b), this annual savings gives a $25,000 present value. In this case, because 16% makes the outflow equal to the inflow, this rate would therefore be the IRR.

Now, let's put things in perspective. As shown in Table 10.14(c), assuming that the treasurer of a company raises $25,000 at a cost of 10% (cost of capital on the right side of the Statement of Financial Position) and repays $2,754 a year during the next 25 years, while managers invest this sum (left side of the Statement of Financial Position) in an asset that earns $4,100 or 16% percent per year, the company would make 6% after paying the financing charges, for a net $1,346 per year.

Table 10.14(b) Investing in a Capital Project

A company wants to make 16% on the $25,000 project.
How much must the project generate in savings or cash each year?

1. Investment	– $25,000
2. Annual savings: $4,100	
3. Total savings: $102,500	
4. Present value of savings (6.0971 × $4,100)	+ $25,000
Net present value	0

Table 10.14(c) Investing in a Capital Project

Statement of Financial Position

Asset $25,000	Loan of 10%
Saves $4,100	Repayment $2,754
Gives 16% per year	Cost of capital 10%

After financing, the company makes 6% or $1,346 per year

[DECISION-MAKING IN ACTION]

After spending several months researching how to go about planning their retirement and paying for their children's education, Steve and Lucy decided to meet Andrew Billingsley, a friend and personal financial adviser. Steve informed Andrew that he was very concerned about the future high cost of education and that he wanted some advice on how to plan ahead.

Steve became concerned when he read several articles about the spread between education inflation and cost-of-living inflation. Between now and 2030, a \$100 cost-of-living expense would rise to \$400, while a \$100 education expense would increase to \$500.

Steve and Lucy are both university graduates doing extremely well. Steve works as an accountant in a government agency while Lucy is employed as a librarian at a university. Both are making a contribution to a pension fund with their respective employers that would provide a combined pension of \$65,000 a year in addition to their Canada Pension Plan. They are both 30 years old and plan to retire at 55; that is, 25 years from now, or in 2035.

Steve explained that he and his wife would like to make a combined \$2,500 annual investment in an RRSP. Andrew examined several mortgage, bond, and equity fund performances for the last 10 years after looking at the facts and the couple's interests; Andrew suggested that if they invested in an equity fund they should expect to earn, on average, 10% over the 25-year lifespan.

The couple was also interested in saving money for the education of their three children, Sylvia (one year old), Phil (two years old), and Michael (six years old). They explained to Andrew that they would like to have enough money to pay for a university degree for their three children when each reached the age of 20. After reading several brochures published by Canadian banks, they learned that the cost of a university education (for four years) by the time their children reached their 20th birthday would be as follows:

- Sylvia: \$58,000
- Phil: \$55,000
- Michael: \$48,000

Steve and Lucy indicated that they were interested in making a contribution each year for their three children. The Canadian government would contribute 20% through the registered education savings plan (RESP) for a maximum of up to \$500 per child. Andrew indicated that the performance funds for this program are estimated to earn 8% a year tax-free over the life of the fund.

On the basis of the above information, calculate the following:

- How much will Steve and Lucy have in their registered retirement savings account the year they retire?
- How much will Steve and Lucy have to save each year (after the government contribution) in order to have enough money for their children's education by the time they each reach their 20th birthday?

The following calculations are made on yearly installments. These figures would be different if Steve and Lucy were to invest their money in these funds on a monthly or quarterly basis. Also, assume that all tax impacts are excluded from these calculations.

1. Steve and Lucy will have accumulated \$245,868 if they invest a combined \$2,500 a year in their RRSP.

   Calculation

   Yearly \$2,500 contribution for 25 years at a 10% annual compounded growth rate.

$$\$2,500 \times 98.347 \text{ (Table C)} = \$245,868.$$

2. An annual amount of $1,119.53 will have to be invested in Sylvia's RESP account.

Calculation

Steve and Lucy want $58,000 19 years from now bearing an 8% interest rate.

$58,000 ÷ 41.446 (Table C) = $1,399.41.

Total contribution:	$1,399.41
Government's contribution (20%)	279.88
Steve and Lucy's contribution	$1,119.53

3. An annual amount of $1,174.90 will have to be invested in Phil's RESP account.

Calculation

Steve and Lucy want $55,000 18 years from now bearing an 8% interest rate.

$55,000 ÷ 37.450 (Table C) = $1,468.62.

Total contribution:	$1,468.62
Government's contribution (20%)	293.72
Steve and Lucy's contribution	$1,174.90

4. An annual amount of $1,585.79 will have to be invested in Michael's RESP account.

Calculation

Steve and Lucy want $48,000 14 years from now bearing an 8% interest rate.

$48,000 ÷ 24.215 (Table C) = $1,982.24.

Total contribution:	$1,982.24
Government's contribution (20%)	396.45
Steve and Lucy's contribution	$1,585.79

Steve and Lucy would therefore have to invest a total of $6,380.22 each year in their RRSP and in their three children's RESP accounts.

Steve and Lucy's RRSPs	$2,500.00
Sylvia's RESP	1,119.53
Phil's RESP	1,174.90
Michael's RESP	1,585.79
Total	$6,380.22

FINANCIAL SPREADSHEETS—EXCEL

As indicated on page 481, Excel spreadsheets are excellent tools for solving time-value-of-money problems. The software can calculate different time-value-of-money calculations such as the FV, the IRR, and the NPV. Template 6 of the Decision-Making Tools spreadsheets is also an excellent tool to calculate the financial desirability of capital projects. This template will be explained in more detail in Chapter 11.

Chapter Summary

1 Learning Objective

Differentiate between time value of money versus inflation and risk.

Money has a time value because of the existence of interest. Because of interest, a dollar earned today would be worth more tomorrow (compounding). Conversely, a dollar earned tomorrow would be worth less today (discounting). In capital budgeting, *inflation* rates, like price or cost increases, are included in financial projections. Once the projected statements of income are completed, the time-value-of-money concept is used to discount all future cash inflows to the present. The element of *risk* has to do with uncertainties related to a project. The more uncertain the variables are that affect a capital project, such as the cost of the equipment, market condition, and competition, the more risky a project. If a project is highly risky, managers will use a high discount rate to calculate the net present value of a project and determine the IRR.

2 Learning Objective

Explain financial tools that can be used to solve time-value-of-money problems.

Tools used to calculate time-value of-money problems are financial equations, interest tables, financial calculators, and financial spreadsheets. The timeline concept shows graphically when cash is disbursed or received over a period of time (months or years).

3 Learning Objective

Differentiate between future values of single sums and future values of annuities.

Appendix B at the end of this book presents four different interest tables. Tables A and C deal with compounding. If you want to find the future value of a single sum, use Table A. If you want to calculate the future value of an annuity, use Table C.

4 Learning Objective

Make the distinction between present values of single sums and present values of annuities.

In capital budgeting, financial analysts use discounting tables, that is, Tables B and D in Appendix B at the end of this book. If you want to calculate the present value of a single sum, use Table B. If you want to find the present value of an annuity, use Table D. The four elements that must be taken into consideration in investment decisions are cash outflows (investments), cash inflows (receipts earned from the project), expected life of the project, and cost of capital raised that will be used to finance the project.

5 Learning Objective

Solve capital investment decisions using time-value-of-money decision-making tools.

A knowledge of compound and discount value concepts is essential for understanding many different topics in finance and for improving the quality of capital budgeting decisions. It is important to know how to use compound and discount tables. For example, for a business that invests $100,000 in a capital project and earns $40,000 over the following five years, the present value (if the cost of capital is 10%) of the $200,000 would be worth $151,632 ($40,000 × 3.7908). The NPV would be

+$51,632, or the difference between the $100,000 cash outflow and the $151,632 present value of the future cash inflows. The IRR would be 28.65%, which is the interest rate used to discount all future cash inflows so that the present value equals the cash outflow.

Key Terms

Annuity p. 486
Cash inflow p. 497
Cash outflow p. 497
Compound interest p. 484
Discounting p. 491
Future value (FV) p. 485
Inflation p. 476
Interest tables p. 479
Internal rate of return (IRR) p. 499
Net present value (NPV) p. 499
Present value (PV) p. 489
Risk p. 476
Rule of 72 p. 486
Simple interest p. 484
Timeline p. 481
Time value of money p. 474

Review Questions

1. Explain why money has a time value.
2. What is the difference between time value of money and inflation?
3. What differentiates time value of money and risk?
4. Why do you believe that cash and time are critical elements in investment decisions?
5. Within the capital budgeting framework, give a few examples to explain the difference between cash inflows and cash outflows.
6. Explain the Rule of 72.
7. What is the difference between simple interest and compound interest?
8. What is an annuity?
9. What is the meaning of net future value (NFV)?
10. What is the meaning of present value (PV)?
11. What is the meaning of net present value (NPV)?
12. What do we mean by internal rate of return (IRR)?
13. What is the difference between profit for the year and cash flows?
14. How did interest tables come about?
15. Give the full names of the four interest tables.
16. Why is time value more important in gauging capital decisions than the traditional accounting methods?
17. How can the internal rate of return help managers gauge the "economic value added" of investment decisions when compared to cost of capital?

Learning Exercises

EXERCISE 1

If you invest $10,000 at 8%, how much will your investment be worth at the end of the following time periods?

a) 5 years
b) 10 years
c) 15 years

EXERCISE 2

If you receive an inheritance and have two payment options, would you prefer receiving $85,000 now or payments made at the beginning of each year in the following way?

Year 1	$20,000
Year 2	$25,000
Year 3	$15,000
Year 4	$10,000
Year 5	$25,000

Calculate the future value of both options by the end of the fifth year if you can get 8% on your investment.

EXERCISE 3

Suppose you were offered the following options: a 10-year annuity of $10,000 at the end of each year or a $60,000 lump-sum payment today. If you want to make 10%, which option would you prefer? To answer this question, calculate the present value of both options and the future value of both options.

EXERCISE 4

If you were to sell a new car and the terms of the agreement are that you receive $5,000 as a down payment and three payments of $10,000 each year for next three years, what would be the real purchase price of the car if the interest rate is 5%?

EXERCISE 5

How much would you be willing to pay for an investment fund that is expected to generate $1,000 at the end of two years, $1,500 at the end of three years, and $2,000 at the end of four years if you wish to earn 16% annual interest on your investment?

EXERCISE 6

You have a choice between receiving (1) a $50,000 payment today, or (2) a $7,500 annuity for the next 10 years and a lump-sum amount of $20,000 at the end of the 10th year. If money is worth 10%, which option is the most attractive?

EXERCISE 7

If money is worth 12%, would you prefer receiving $200,000 now or $30,000 each year for the next 10 years?

Questions

1. What is the value of each amount 10 years from now?
2. What is today's present value of each amount?
3. How much would you have to receive each year to make the two amounts equal?
4. If you receive $30,000 each year instead of the $200,000 amount, what is the effective interest rate or the IRR (internal of return)?

EXERCISE 8

Hannah's parents want to put enough money aside for her education by the time she goes to university 10 years from now. If they invest the amounts listed below at the beginning of each year, how much will Hannah's education fund have grown by the end of the fifth year and tenth year? Assume that Hannah's parents earn 7% on their investment.

Year 1	$ 5,000
Year 2	$ 6,000
Year 3	$ 7,000
Year 4	$ 8,000
Year 5	$ 9,000

EXERCISE 9

Two young entrepreneurs want to invest $150,000 in a restaurant. Their business plan shows that the restaurant will generate $40,000 in cash from year 1 to year 5 and $50,000 from year 6 to year 10. They want to earn at least 20%. On the basis of this information, calculate (a) the present value, (b) the net present value, and (c) the internal rate of return.

EXERCISE 10

You plan to invest $150,000 in a retail business. The projected 10-year cash flows are as follows:

Year 1	$20,000
Year 2	$21,000
Year 3	$22,000
Year 4	$24,000
Year 5	$30,000
Year 6	$35,000
Year 7	$40,000

Year 8	$45,000
Year 9	$50,000
Year 10	$55,000

In the 10th year, the business will be sold for $100,000. The cost of capital is 12%. On the basis of this information, calculate the following for the project:

a) Present value
b) Net present value
c) Internal rate of return

Cases

CASE 1: THE FARM PURCHASE

Jan Schmidt is 45 years old and has the option of buying a farm for $500,000 or investing his money in an equity fund that has earned 14% over the past seven years. After a discussion with a few investment analysts, the conclusion was that the performance of this fund could continue over the next 20 years.

If Jan buys the farm, it would generate $75,000 each year over the next 20 years. In 20 years' time, based on real estate information, the farm would be worth approximately $2 million.

Questions

1. If Jan wishes to make the same return on his investment as on the equity fund, should he buy the farm? Why or why not?
2. What is the farm's net present value with and without the sale of the farm (using 10% as the discount rate)?
3. What is the farm's internal rate of return?

CASE 2: ED'S BOWLING ALLEY

In 2010, Ed intends to invest $1,500,000 in a bowling alley. After two years of operation, he plans to invest an extra $450,000 in the business by opening a restaurant. In 10 years, Ed anticipates selling the business for $3 million. Ed's cost of capital will be 11%. Ed would like to earn at least a 20% internal rate of return.

Ed can also lease a bowling alley that is located in a different city. The yearly cash flow from operations is estimated at $200,000 (net after the lease payment) for the next 10 years. Ed would also like to make 20% on this investment.

Questions

1. Is purchasing the bowling alley and restaurant a good investment? To answer this question, calculate the following:
   - The net present value by using the cost of capital
   - The internal rate of return

Ed predicts that the business will generate the following cash inflow:

Year	Amount	
0	−$1,500,000	
1	+200,000	
2	−450,000	(restaurant purchase)
2	+250,000	
3	+300,000	
4	+350,000	
5	+400,000	
6	+450,000	
7	+500,000	
8	+525,000	
9	+550,000	
10	+575,000	
10	+$3,000,000	(sale of business)

2. Is leasing the bowling alley a good decision?
3. If Ed can only do one or the other, should he go for the purchase or the lease? Why?

CASE 3: PALMTECH INC.

PalmTech Inc. is considering developing a software program that requires an initial investment of $450,000. The owners have put together a financial plan covering the company's additional investments in research and development. During the third year, the company expects to inject an additional $100,000 in research and development and another $50,000 in year 5.

During the first five years, the company expects to generate $100,000 per year in cash flow. However, they expect to increase its yearly cash inflows to $150,000 between years 6 and 10, $200,000 between years 11 and 15, and $250,000 between years 16 and 20. In the 20th year, if they were to sell the business, they expect to get $600,000.

The weighted average cost of capital is 8% but the company owners expect to earn 20%. On the basis of this information, calculate the project's net present value based on the company's weighted average cost of capital and the expected return on their investment. What is the project's internal rate of return? Should the owners proceed with the development of their software program? Why?

PHOTO/Dmitriy Shironosov/Shutterstock

CHAPTER 11

[CAPITAL BUDGETING]

Learning Objectives

After reading this chapter, you should be able to:

1 Learning Objective — Explain the capital budgeting process.

2 Learning Objective — Comment on the key elements used to gauge capital projects.

3 Learning Objective — Evaluate capital investment decisions by using time-value-of-money yardsticks.

4 Learning Objective — Assess capital investments using decision-making techniques that measure risk.

5 Learning Objective — Explain the reasons that can prevent a capital project from being approved.

Chapter Outline

The Capital Budgeting Process
The Capital Budgeting Elements
Evaluating Capital Expenditure Projects
Capital Budgeting Techniques That Cope with Risk
Capital Expenditure Constraints

OPENING CASE

By the end of 2010, the Millers were looking at several investment possibilities in order to expand their retail operations. The most viable and interesting option, one that was in line with their longer-term objective, was opening a new retail outlet. Now that they had several years of experience in the retail business and had accumulated enough cash, they were ready to move ahead with their plans.

The Millers estimated that it would cost around $350,000 to open their new retail store. Because they intended to lease a building for a 10-year period, the investment would be mainly in leasehold assets, the purchase of office equipment, and working capital. During the first year of operations, the Millers expected to invest $100,000 in working capital, mostly in inventories and trade receivables. During the second year, they expected to invest an additional $75,000 in working capital for a net investment amounting to $175,000.

The following summarizes the Millers' investment plan for their new retail store:

Year 0	Capital assets		$350,000
Year 1	Working capital	$100,000	
Year 2	Working capital	75,000	175,000
Total capital employed			$525,000

At the end of the 10-year lease, the Millers would have the option of either expanding the store to cope with the growth or moving to a larger building. If, instead of making these changes, they were to sell their business (inventories, leasehold assets, goodwill, etc.), they estimated that they would be able to get $900,000 in cash from a potential buyer.

CompuTech's weighted average cost of capital is 11.0%. This is based on funds that could be raised from lenders (short term and long term) and from shareholders.

The Millers hired a market research firm to determine the level of revenue that could be generated by the new store. On the basis of that information, they prepared the new store's projected financial statements to be included in the business plan and presented to potential investors. The cash inflows generated by the new store are estimated to be as follows:

Year	Cash Inflows
1	$75,000
2	80,000
3	100,000
4	125,000
5	140,000
6–10	150,000

As shown above, the new store's cash inflows during the first year are estimated at $75,000, with gradual increments between years 1 and 6. Starting in the sixth year, the Millers estimate that the cash inflow will remain constant until the tenth year. Based on these financial projections, the Millers would be pleased with the results because their investment would realize a positive $516,045 net present value using the 11% weighted average cost of capital and produce a 25.5% internal rate of return. (Self-Test Exercise No. 11.10 on page 539 shows how these numbers were calculated.)

Chapter Overview

Capital budgeting is the process of planning, evaluating, and choosing capital expenditure projects that generate benefits (returns, profits, savings) over an extended number of years. Capital budgeting decisions are critical to the financial destiny of a company because they are irreversible, usually require a significant amount of financial resources, and can alter the future success of a business for many years. Capital projects may call for the development of a new product, a major expansion of an existing product line, the launching of a new product line, the construction of a new facility, or a significant change in direction geared to take advantage of foreseeable opportunities.

Capital investment Project that requires extensive financial resources (cash outflows) made for the purpose of generating a return (cash inflows).

Expense investment A fully tax-deductible cost that should produce favourable effects on the profit performance.

A **capital investment** (expenditure or cash disbursement) may be defined as a project that requires extensive financial resources (cash outflows) in return for an expected flow of financial benefits (cash inflows) to be earned over a period of many years. A capital investment differs from an **expense investment** in that the latter generates benefits for a short period (less than one year). For example, a capital investment may represent the construction of a new plant costing $30 million (cash outflow) with an economic or physical lifespan of 20 years and generating a $3 million cash inflow each year. An expense investment may consist of a $20,000 advertising cost that produces favourable effects on profit during the current operating year. Table 11.1 compares capital investments and expense investments.

Capital investments are critical for a number of reasons. First, because new funds may need to be raised, the capital structure of a business can be altered significantly.

Table 11.1 Characteristics of Capital Investments and Expense Investments

	Capital Investments	Expense Investments
Size of cash outlay	Large	Small
Nature of commitment	Durable	Impermanent
Accounting treatment	Capitalized	Expensed
Cash turnover	Recurrent and spread over many years	One time and immediate
Financial impact of commitment	Significant	Minimal
Effect on financial structure	Minimal to sizeable	None

Second, long-term return on a company's assets and shareholders' yield can be highly influenced by the mix of projects undertaken. It takes only one ill-conceived capital decision to reduce a company's profit performance and return (often for many years) and with it, management's credibility. Third, the future cash position of a company can be affected significantly, a vital consideration for a firm that is committed to meeting fixed-debt obligations, paying dividends, and experiencing growth (which usually means undertaking more capital investments). Fourth, once committed, a project often cannot be revised, or can be revised only at a substantial cost.

Companies invest in capital projects for many reasons. A firm wishing to improve its financial performance could invest in cost-reduction programs or research and development, expand a manufacturing operation, replace obsolete equipment, install computer equipment, build a warehouse, or even buy an ongoing business. Each project varies significantly with respect to cash outlay, risk, profit levels, and time horizon. Capital projects can fall into several major categories:

- Necessary investments to reduce operating costs.
- Replacement investments to supplant worn-out equipment.
- Market investments to improve the distribution network.
- Expansion investments to increase sales volume, profit, and cash flows in existing product lines.
- Research and development investments to develop new products and new manufacturing or processing technologies.
- Product improvement investments to sustain the life cycle of a product.
- Strategic investments to alter a business's mainstream activity.

These types of capital projects can be grouped under two main categories: compulsory investments, which are essential to sustain the life of a business, and opportunity investments, which are discretionary and made only if management believes they will improve the firm's long-term prosperity. Table 11.2 compares these two types of capital investments.

Table 11.2 Comparing Compulsory and Opportunity Investments

	Compulsory Investments	Opportunity Investments
Effects	Maintain operating efficiencies	Increase momentum of the firm
Response	To a need	To an opportunity
Benefits	Immediate	Long-term
Risk	Negligible	High
Management involvement	Low-level	Top-level
Implications	Legislative, employee safety and satisfaction	Economic returns, share of market
Analytical techniques	Simple calculation	Mathematical models

Compulsory investments Investments made in capital assets to respond to a need, legislation, or employee demands that do not require in-depth analytical studies.

Generally, **compulsory investments** are made for three reasons: contingency, legislative, and cosmetic. Investments in this first category respond to a *need*. For example, a manufacturing department may have to increase its operating capacity to meet an expanded market need. Or a production manager may request that certain producing assets be replaced in order to eliminate substandard operations and maintain an acceptable level of operating efficiencies. In short, these types of investments prevent a company's rate of return from deteriorating. The second type of compulsory investment is dictated by *legislation*. For instance, the government may force businesses to invest in pollution-abatement machinery, in equipment that will meet regulatory quality control standards, or in assets affecting the safety of employees. The third type of investments are made for *cosmetic* reasons. These include expenditures for office furniture; for protecting existing company assets (e.g., fences, warehouses) from fire, pilferage, etc.; for improving the company image; and for making employees happier (e.g., cafeteria, sports facilities).

These types of capital expenditures do not require in-depth analytical studies. Because the investments have to be made for one reason or another, all that has to be done is to include the required capital amounts in the company's annual capital budget and to record them when the funds are disbursed. The major requirement in this process is to ensure that the firm obtains the best possible assets for the best possible price. The impact from such investments on profit position (minor expansion or modernization programs) can be measured with relative accuracy.

Opportunity investments Investments made in capital assets that are of a strategic nature and usually have far-reaching financial implications.

Opportunity investments, however, are far more complex and require sophisticated analysis, state-of-the art decision-making tools, and sound managerial judgment. Examples of these investments include launching a new product line, constructing a new plant, or substantially increasing manufacturing output to capture new markets. These capital projects are usually considerable and have far-reaching financial implications. The risk factor is enormous: If the venture is not successful, management's reputation suffers, and there will likely be a heavy cash drain from existing operations—or even worse, bankruptcy may result. These types of investments, however, can improve a company's competitive capability and profitability beyond current levels of performance.

Before the company commits to such investments, the first step is to appraise the investment's chances of success as accurately as possible. Because the investment's financial return is dependent on internal and external environmental forces, the investment appraisal demands an incisive analysis of all aspects of the capital venture. Figure 11.1 illustrates the impact that opportunity investments can have on a company's future. The vertical axis shows the return on investment; the horizontal axis represents the improvement profile of the return position against that of the industry over an extended number of years.

The main reason for injecting funds into capital assets is to improve a company's return on investment—either to close the "return gap" with that of industry or to improve further the company's financial position. For example, as shown in Figure 11.1,

Figure 11.1 **Growth Gap Analysis**

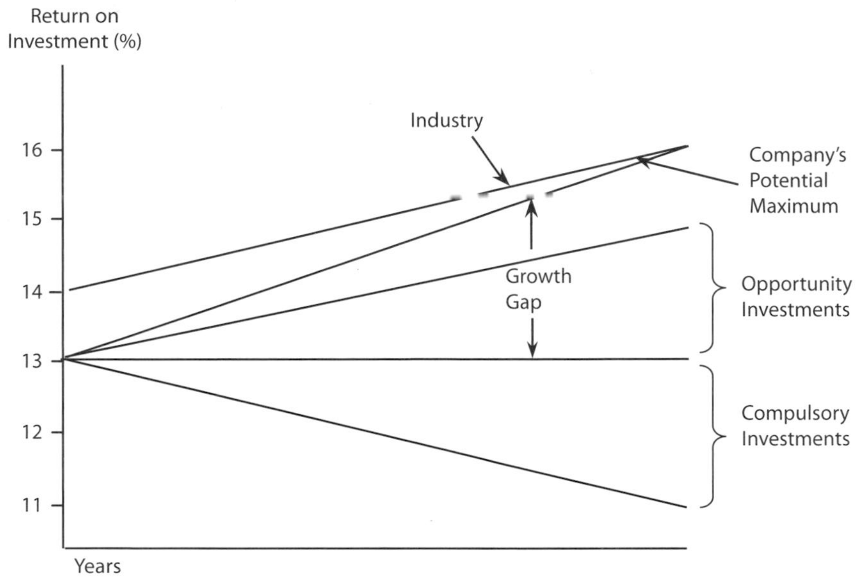

the company's return on investment may be at 13% compared to the industry's 14%. If nothing is done (e.g., improving the productivity of its existing capital assets, injecting funds into new equipment, or doing research and development on new product lines), over the long term, the company's return may drop to 11%, while the industry's climbs to 16%—the gap widens from 1% to 5%. If the company plows funds into compulsory investments, it can hold its position at 13%, and the gap with industry will be only 3%. With additional financial resources, the firm may make opportunity investments, thus reducing the gap further. But because of resource constraints, the firm may still not match the industry's growth. If, however, the firm is not financially bound, it could grow to a 16% level and reach both its full potential and the industry's growth.

As shown in Figure 1.1 on page 7 this is the second chapter dealing with investing decisions. It includes five sections. The first section looks at the steps involved in the capital budgeting process, which include establishing corporate priorities and strategies; formulating the plans and capital expenditure projects; ranking projects through capital budgeting methods (priorities, operations, and return/risk); calculating the weighted average cost of capital; determining the hurdle rate; and approving and implementing projects.

The second section explains the key capital budgeting elements, which include cash outflows, such as the initial cash outflow, net working capital, and normal capital additions; cash inflows, which include profit, depreciation, and the residual value of assets; the establishment of the economic life of the project; and sunk costs.

The third section examines different time-value-of-money yardsticks normally used by businesses to evaluate and rank capital expenditure projects. They include the accounting methods, the payback method, the net-present-value method, the internal rate of return, and the profitability index.

The fourth section looks at the more sophisticated time-value-of-money yardsticks that are commonly used to gauge the element of risk in capital projects. They are sensitivity analysis and risk analysis.

The last section explains the reasons that capital projects may not be approved. These include a lack of cash and the hurdle rate.

The Capital Budgeting Process

1 Learning Objective

Explain the capital budgeting process.

As shown in Figure 11.2, several steps are involved in capital budgeting. The first step is to establish the corporate priorities, and strategic and operational goals within the framework of the external general and industry environments (opportunities and threats) and internal environment (strengths and weaknesses). The future can never be predicted with certainty, but with the level of information available and modern risk-analysis techniques, it is possible to deal with the uncertainty factor in a relatively proficient manner. It is within this framework that the company's mission statement, strategic goals, and plans are formulated.

The second step is to prepare the business plan and the evaluation of the capital expenditure projects. Capital projects affect a business in different ways such as improving operating efficiencies and increasing market share. Management must therefore identify, select, and implement the most lucrative projects, that is, those that will best help the business achieve its strategic goals.

Figure 11.2 **Capital Budgeting Framework**

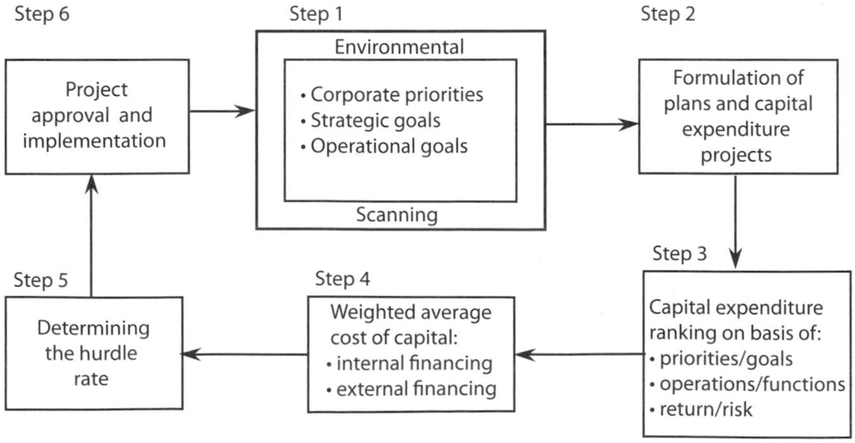

The third step is to rank the capital projects on the basis of the corporate priorities and goals, business needs (functional units), and returns:

- *Priorities and goals*. Most companies have priorities and a hierarchy of goals. Capital projects are therefore ranked according to how they will meet these overall priorities and strategic goals. (Are they to increase market share, improve manufacturing efficiencies, or diversify operations?)
- *Operations/functions*. Capital projects must also be ranked within their respective business units, operations, or functions (e.g., marketing, research, manufacturing, distribution).
- *Return/risk*. Because a healthy return is probably the ultimate objective of any business, the economic acceptability of a capital portfolio (opportunity investments) should be judged largely on this basis. However, there is a direct connection between risk and return. The higher the risk, particularly opportunity investments, the higher the expected return.

The fourth step is to explore fully the cost of alternate sources of capital. Funds are obtained from two sources: internally (e.g., through profit for the year and depreciation) and externally (e.g., from shareholders and lenders). If internal funds are to be used, management must decide what types of projects it intends to launch, several years before the funds are committed, so that the necessary cash can be set aside. External funds are generally obtained from long-term borrowings or share capital. As discussed in Chapter 9 (see Figure 9.1 on page 422), while equity and liability can be structured in a number of ways, it is critical to find the optimum financial structure, the one that combines the lowest cost with the least amount of risk.

The fifth step is to determine the hurdle rate, the level of return that each project should generate in order to be accepted (high risk, medium risk, and low risk). The hurdle reflects the cost of capital and an adjustment for the individual project's risk. For example, if a company's weighted average cost of capital is 10% and the business is dealing with a medium-risk project, management will probably require a 20% return, which will include 10% for the project's risk. Because the capital needed to finance an investment portfolio usually exceeds the funds available, a firm needs financial criteria for selecting those projects offering the most attractive returns. Hurdle rates that can be used for that purpose are determined in a number of ways, such as a company's weighted average cost of capital for financing new projects, long-term borrowing rates, ongoing internal rate of return, or even a figure chosen arbitrarily by top management. Hurdle rates are influenced by the following:

- Level of capital funds needed
- Reputation of the company or management
- Capital structure
- Type of issues to be offered
- Nature of projects (e.g., risk)
- Nature of industry

Once the hurdle rate has been agreed upon and projects have been ranked on the basis of objectives, operations, and return, all that remains is the last step, approving and implementing the projects.

The Capital Budgeting Elements

2 Learning Objective

Comment on the key elements used to gauge capital projects.

A few basic capital budgeting concepts should be understood before examining the time-value-of-money techniques used for gauging the economic desirability of capital projects. This section reviews the elements that serve as major input for capital project evaluation. They include cash outflows, cash inflows, economic or physical lifespan, and sunk costs.

CASH OUTFLOWS

When management decides to invest funds in a capital project, the decision entails outflows of cash in terms of the initial cash outflows (capital assets), working capital (inventories and trade receivables), and normal capital additions (future investments in capital assets).

Initial cash outflows. When a decision is made to proceed with a capital project, such as the purchase of equipment, initial cash outflows are recorded. Cash outflows could also take place over a period of several years. For instance, a new plant could be constructed over a three-year period with cash outflows taking place over that same time span. Irrespective of the accounting treatment, all initial cash disbursements must be considered cash outflows. For example, a firm may invest $10 million to modernize a plant; from an accounting perspective, part of that amount, say, $200,000, could be expensed the year the outflows take place, while the remaining $9.8 million is capitalized and depreciated over a 10-year period. However, for capital budgeting evaluation purposes, all outflows must be shown as disbursements in the year the money is spent.

Another point to consider about the initial cash outflows is that the financing of a project need not be taken into account. A company may receive 50% financing on the $10 million capital outlay. Irrespective of the amount of funds to be received from external sources, the project should be evaluated on the premise that the company uses its "own" cash or its equivalent for the entire project. Finance costs should not be considered an expense and thus should not be included in the projected statements of income. The intent of capital budgeting is (1) to gauge the economic returns of individual capital projects (stand-alone projects), (2) to compare each competing project with the others, and (3) to compare the return (i.e., IRR) to the weighted average cost of capital (see the lower portion of Figure 9.2 on page 426).

Working capital. Another cash outflow to consider is working capital. Some projects, such as modernization, replacement of obsolete equipment, or installation of antipollution equipment, may not require additional working capital. However, other projects such as the construction of a new plant or the expansion of an existing facility may cause revenue and working capital to increase. The working capital spending usually takes place at the time the project comes on-stream, usually the first and second year of operation. Incremental net working capital can take place several years after the launching of the new plant. These additions to working capital should therefore be included as cash outflows in the evaluation of the project.

Normal capital additions. Some capital projects may require additional capital expenditures for repairs and parts after the initial capital investment. If this is the case, these expenditures should be included as cash outflows when evaluating the capital project.

CASH INFLOWS

A capital project usually generates cash inflows during its entire physical life. These inflows of cash originate from several sources: profit for the year, non-cash expenses, and residual value.

Profit for the year. A new project will generate additional cash because of increased revenue (see Table 11.3) or produce savings resulting from more efficient operations.

Non-cash expenses. Because capital cost allowance, or CCA (equivalent to depreciation expense), is not a cash outflow but used solely for income tax relief purposes, the operating profit figure does not reflect the true cash inflow. The calculation of the profit for the year and cash inflow is shown in Table 11.3. As shown, because capital projects deal with cash flow and not profit, the amount incorporated in the project evaluation is $77,500 (cash), not $27,500 (profit for the year).

Residual value. Because money has a time value, it is important to anticipate not only the future cash inflows of a project generated by additional revenue or savings but also the sale of the assets at their **residual value** at the end of the life of the project. Estimating the residual value of an asset can be done in a number of ways:

Residual value
Represents the value from the sale of an asset or a business at the end of its physical life.

- Engineers can examine similar facilities and, based on historical experience, estimate the future residual value of the asset.

Table 11.3 Profit for the Year versus Cash Inflow

	Profit and Cash Inflow
Operating profit (other cash expenses)*	$100,000
Capital cost allowance	(50,000)
Profit before taxes	50,000
Income tax expense (45%)	(22,500)
Profit for the year	27,500
Add back capital cost allowance	50,000
Cash inflow	$77,500

* Could include incremental profit resulting from increased revenue, and excludes depreciation expense.

- Accountants can calculate the depreciated book value of the assets and determine the residual value of the newly acquired assets by using several assumptions.
- Suppliers of equipment and machinery can also provide valuable assistance in estimating residual values.

Residual values can have a significant impact on the return calculation. The impact of the present value of residual assets is examined in the next section.

In the News 11.1 gives an example about two critical capital budgeting elements—investments in capital assets (cash outflows) and the inflows of cash—that must be harmonized in order to maximize profitability over the long term.

In The News [11.1]

Cash Outflows and Cash Inflows Must Be Synchronized to Optimize Return

WestJet is a Calgary-based, non-unionized low-cost carrier. It is the second-largest Canadian air carrier behind Air Canada and is planning to be one of the world's top five most profitable international airlines. But they won't achieve that by "gut-feel" decisions. The company has a fleet of 81 Boeing aircraft and they want to add more. However, company executives want to make sure that the cost and timing associated with the acquisition of the new aircraft are in line with the harmonization of their cash flows.

WestJet was planning to expand its Boeing aircraft to total 86 by the end of 2009. However, the company renegotiated a reduced number with Boeing Co., down to three 737s (instead of five). The company also intends to extend its larger order to 2016, that is, three years further out than planned. The timing of the 737 purchase schedule will postpone the delivery of 16 aircrafts. The change in the delivery schedule is a direct result of the recession and the demand for air travel. WestJet's plans were to increase its fleet to 121 planes over the next four years, with about 20 new 737s for 2012 and 2013 delivery. But that has now changed. The timing of the outflows of cash (purchase of new aircraft) and the inflows of cash (demand for air travel) certainly played a key role in the rescheduling of the purchase decision.

Source: Adapted from Scott Deveau, "WestJet lowers flaps on 2010 expansion plan," *Financial Post*, August 25, 2009, p. F3. For more information about WestJet, visit http://www.westjet.com.

ECONOMIC OR PHYSICAL LIFE OF A PROJECT

Economic life
Number of years that a capital asset or investment opportunity will last.

A capital investment (cash outflow) is made in exchange for future profit (cash inflows). Because the **economic life** of a project plays a key role in determining the financial return of a project, this aspect of the analysis should be done with prudence. In one instance, engineers, suppliers, or accountants may determine that a piece of equipment (e.g., a vehicle) will last five years; in another instance (e.g., a plant), they may estimate 25 years. The longer the physical life of the project, the longer the cash inflows will be generated, and the more beneficial the financial return of the project will be. For example, if we refer to Table 10.10 on page 492, the present value of

Table 11.4 Present Values of $1,000 Residual Value

	Economic Life (Years)				
Discount Rates (%)	**5**	**10**	**15**	**20**	**25**
5	784	614	481	377	295
10	621	386	239	149	92
15	497	247	123	61	30
20	402	162	65	26	10
25	328	107	35	12	4
30	269	73	20	5	1

a five-year $10,000 annuity bearing a 10% interest rate amounts to $37,908 ($10,000 × 3.7908), while the present value of a 25-year $10,000 annuity bearing the same interest rate amounts to $90,770 ($10,000 × 9.0770).

Also, the physical lifespan of a project is important in order to calculate the present value of the residual value of the asset. The time span and the interest rate also have an impact on the financial return of a project. Table 11.4 shows the present values of an asset that has a residual value of $1,000 with varying discount rates and economic lives.

SUNK COSTS

Sunk costs
Investment cost incurred prior to making the decision to proceed with a capital project.

Sunk costs are funds that have already been spent on a project prior to making the decision to proceed with it. For instance, a firm may hire engineers to study the feasibility of investing huge sums of money in a project; the engineering costs may amount to $300,000. The recommendation may be to proceed or not to proceed with the capital project. The engineering fees are considered "sunk costs," meaning that these costs should not be taken into consideration when calculating the financial return of the project. The fact that management wants to make a decision on the project means that managers have discretion (go or no go); sunk costs, on the other hand, offer no discretion. Whether the decision is positive or negative, the $300,000 amount will still have been disbursed.

Evaluating Capital Expenditure Projects

3 Learning Objective

Evaluate capital investment decisions by using time-value-of-money yardsticks.

The main purpose of capital budgeting is to make decisions that will maximize a company's investments. Capital budgeting compels management to answer two basic questions: First, which of the many projects emanating from various departments should be approved? Second, how many projects, in total, should be approved?

In short, capital budgeting provides a methodology that helps management rank a multitude of investment proposals in order of priorities, strategic and economic importance, and return on investment.

Rate of return is probably the most widely used guide for helping managers make decisions related to the commitment of capital investments. The purchase of securities, acquisition of new assets, investment in product development, modernization, expansion, or construction of a new plant all have one common trait—they generate profit (or cash inflows) in return for cash disbursed. The rate of return can, therefore, be regarded as the relationship between cash committed and cash generated. This relationship is expressed in terms of a ratio or percentage. The arithmetic itself is relatively simple, but the fact that there is a choice in selecting the numerator and the denominator when calculating the return suggests that the results can vary substantially. The denominator, for example, can be expressed in terms of the original investment, depreciated capital assets, average investment, or capital employed. The numerator, where profit for the year is shown, also varies depending on the selected year of profit. The formula for calculating accounting returns also varies. The countless variables and formulas used for calculating return on investment have generated a good deal of bewilderment.

This section reviews different types of capital budgeting methods available and the arguments for and against each technique. Five capital budgeting methods used for gauging and ranking capital project proposals will be discussed. They are as follows:

- Accounting methods
- Payback method
- Net present value (NPV)
- Internal rate of return (IRR) or discounted cash flow (DCF)
- Profitability index (PI)

Each of these capital budgeting methods will be discussed in terms of (1) what it is, (2) what it does, (3) how it works, and (4) the arguments for and against it. After reviewing these capital budgeting techniques, sensitivity analysis and risk analysis will be discussed.

ACCOUNTING METHODS

Accounting methods Calculation of the book value rate of return by using data presented on financial statements.

What they are. The **accounting methods**, also referred to as the traditional yardsticks, the financial statement methods, the accountant's methods, and the book value rate of return, make use of data presented on financial statements to express the economic results of a capital investment.

What they do. The accounting methods give a rate of return of a capital project at a particular point in time (year) based on the profit for the year and a book investment.

How they work. The rate of return calculation based on these yardsticks is relatively simple: divide the profit for the year by an appropriate investment base. It can be calculated in one of the following ways: (1) return based on annual profit for the year divided by capital assets, (2) return based on annual profit for the year divided by capital employed, (3) return based on average profit divided by capital assets, (4) return based on average profit divided by capital employed, (5) return based on annual profit divided by average capital assets, (6) return based on annual profit divided by average capital employed, (7) return based on annual profit divided by depreciated assets, and (8) return based on annual profit divided by depreciated capital employed. Table 11.5 presents the formula used for each of these accounting methods.

By using the following assumptions, Table 11.5 shows how each accounting method can be used to calculate various rates of return for the first year of a capital project.

Original investment		$1,500,000	capital assets
		500,000	working capital
		$2,000,000	total capital employed
Salvage value		nil	
Life of the project		5 years	
Depreciation		20% per year (straight-line)	
Profit	Year 1	$50,000	
	Year 2	$90,000	
	Year 3	$150,000	
	Year 4	$200,000	
	Year 5	$250,000	

The following summarizes the different rates of return when using the accounting methods presented in Table 11.5. Although only eight accounting methods are presented in the table, there are numerous other accounting methods. As mentioned earlier, the table shows the calculations for the first year only. The returns for years 2 to 5 are presented on page 527.

Method 1 uses the annual profit divided by the initial investments in capital assets. By using this method, the return on the initial capital assets ranges from 3.3% to 16.7%.

Method 2 takes into consideration not only the investment made in capital assets but also the investments in working capital (inventories and trade receivables). This method shows the return ranging from 2.5% in year 1 to 12.5% by the end of year 5.

Some might argue that *method 3* is a more logical approach to calculate the return of a project. Instead of using the annual profit, the method considers instead the average profit. In this instance, the average profit for each year is $148,000 [($50,000 + $90,000 + $150,000 + $200,000 + $250,000) ÷ 5)]. By using this method, the calculation gives a 9.9% return throughout the five years.

Method 4 uses the same arithmetic with one exception: The same average profit for each year is divided by capital employed. This method gives a 7.4% return throughout the five-year period. Others might come out with a different argument and say that using *method 5*, the average investment in capital assets, gives a more accurate way for measuring a project's return. Because assets depreciate over a period of years,

Table 11.5 Accounting Methods

Method 1: Return based on annual profit divided by capital assets (first year only)

$$\frac{\text{Annual profit}}{\text{Initial capital assets}} \times 100 = \qquad \frac{\$50{,}000}{\$1{,}500{,}000} \times 100 = 3.3\%$$

Method 2: Return based on annual profit divided by capital employed (first year only)

$$\frac{\text{Annual profit}}{\text{Initial capital employed}} \times 100 = \qquad \frac{\$50{,}000}{\$2{,}000{,}000} \times 100 = 2.5\%$$

Method 3: Return based on average profit divided by capital assets (first year only)

$$\frac{\text{Average Annual profit}}{\text{Initial capital assets}} \times 100 = \qquad \frac{\$148{,}000}{\$1{,}500{,}000} \times 100 = 9.9\%$$

Method 4: Return based on average profit divided by capital employed (first year only)

$$\frac{\text{Average Annual profit}}{\text{Initial capital employed}} \times 100 = \qquad \frac{\$148{,}000}{\$2{,}000{,}000} \times 100 = 7.4\%$$

Method 5: Return based on annual profit divided by average capital assets (first year only)

$$\frac{\text{Annual profit}}{\text{Initial capital assets/2}} \times 100 = \qquad \frac{\$50{,}000}{\$750{,}000} \times 100 = 6.7\%$$

Method 6: Return based on annual profit divided by average capital employed (first year only)

$$\frac{\text{Annual profit}}{(\text{Initial capital assets/2}) + \text{Working capital}} \times 100 = \qquad \frac{\$50{,}000}{\$1{,}250{,}000} \times 100 = 4.0\%$$

Method 7: Return based on annual profit divided by depreciated assets (first year only)

$$\frac{\text{Annual profit}}{\text{Initial capital assets less depreciation}} \times 100 = \qquad \frac{\$50{,}000}{\$1{,}200{,}000} \times 100 = 4.2\%$$

Method 8: Return based on annual profit divided by amortized capital employed (first year only)

$$\frac{\text{Annual profit}}{\text{Initial capital assets less depreciation} + \text{Working capital}} \times 100 = \qquad \frac{\$50{,}000}{\$1{,}700{,}000} \times 100 = 2.9\%$$

supporters of this method argue that it does not make any sense to use the initial investment costs for calculating the return for the five-year period. Therefore, instead of using $1,500,000 throughout the five-year period, half, or $750,000, is used to calculate the return. In this case, the return ranges from 6.7% in the first year to 33.3% by the end of the fifth year.

The same logic is used for *method 6*. In this case, however, the $500,000 amount for working capital is added back to the average investment in capital assets ($1,250,000). If this method is used, the return ranges from 4.0% in year 1 to 20.0% in year 5.

Others claim that using the depreciated value of capital assets is a more accurate way to gauge a project's return. Because the assets are depreciated at 20% per year, the depreciated value of the assets is used in the calculation. In this case, *method 7* shows that the project's return ranges from 4.2% in year 1 to more than 100% in the last year. This is understandable because the assets are fully depreciated by the end of the fifth year.

By using *method 8*, the $500,000 amount in working capital is added back to the depreciated values of the capital assets. By using this method, the return goes from 2.9% in year 1 to 50% by the end of the fifth year.

The following shows the results of these various calculations.

Methods of calculation (%)	1	2	3	4	5	6	7	8
Year 1	3.3	2.5	9.9	7.4	6.7	4.0	4.2	2.9
Year 2	6.0	4.5	9.9	7.4	12.0	7.2	10.0	6.4
Year 3	10.0	7.5	9.9	7.4	20.0	12.0	25.0	13.6
Year 4	13.3	10.0	9.9	7.4	26.7	16.0	66.7	25.0
Year 5	16.7	12.5	9.9	7.4	33.3	20.0	100.0	+50.0

The bottom line is this: When someone says, "My project gives a 17.5% return," ask, "Exactly how did you go about calculating this return?"

If large corporations use the accounting rates of return method, during the capital budgeting process, the capital investment analysis department would usually issue written guidelines telling all departments or divisions how to go about making the calculations.

Arguments for accounting methods:

- They are simple to use and easy to calculate.
- The audit is simple because the information relates to accounting data.
- Emphasis is on profit for the year rather than cash flow.

Arguments against accounting methods:

- They do not take into account that money has a time value.
- They do not provide a "true" rate of return, which is essentially the exact earning rate of the dollars in use. The average book return method usually understates the rate of return, while the annual return method overstates it.

- The returns focus only on one specific year, while a project usually has a longer lifespan.
- It is meaningless to compare an accounting rate of return to other rates offered on bonds, loans, or any other figures quoted on the financial markets.
- They assume that a capital project will last for the depreciated life, when in fact this is generally not true.
- Because the time pattern of profit varies from project to project, it is difficult to make effective comparisons between them.

PAYBACK METHOD

What it is. This method measures the period of time it takes for the cash outflow of a project to be totally recovered by the anticipated cash inflows; in other words, it measures how soon the initial funds disbursed are recovered by the project. The **payback method** is also known as the *cash recovery period,* the *payoff method,* or the *payout method.*

Payback method
The number of years required for a capital investment to generate enough cash inflows to cover the initial cash outflow.

What it does. This technique measures *time risk* and not *risk conditions.* It is helpful in the project-selection process and also gives a valid measure of the expected project risk. The longer it takes for the initial investment to be recovered, the greater the risk. This is critical for a company engaged in an industry where product obsolescence is a factor, and where there are abrupt technological changes. A firm engaged in a relatively stable industry will be more likely to accept projects with longer payback periods. Payback can be considered an indicator of profitability. Projects that have a short payback period should have higher earnings in the short run. However, because this method favours immediate cash inflows, it may sacrifice future cash growth.

How it works. There are different ways of calculating the payback. It is true that the arithmetic process required to do the payback calculation is simple. For example, a business that invests \$1.5 million in a venture that generates an annual cash inflow of \$500,000 during its physical life will have a three-year payback period. The formula is as follows:

$$P = \frac{\mathbf{I}}{NCF}$$

where the original investment (I) is divided by the net cash inflow (NCF). It should be noted that this formula works only when cash inflow is equally distributed annually or when the irregular annual cash inflow is averaged out. The application of this formula to the above example is as follows:

$$\textbf{Payback} = \frac{\$1,500,000}{\$500,000} = \textbf{3.0 years}$$

The traditional payback method, the payback reciprocal, and the discounted payback are three methods used for calculating the economic desirability of a project.

Traditional payback method. When cash inflow is irregular, the calculation of the traditional payback period is done in the following way:

Years	Annual Net Cash Flows	Cumulative Cash Flows	
0	$(200,000)	$(200,000)	
1	25,000	(175,000)	
2	70,000	(105,000)	
3	80,000	(25,000)	← Payback
4	90,000	65,000	
5	$100,000	$165,000	
Total cash inflows	$365,000		

The illustration shows that the payback period takes place between years 3 and 4 as cash flow turns positive during the fourth year. In most cases, cumulative cash flow will not equal zero at specific given years, but instead, in fractions of a year or months. If this is the case, interpolation will have to be used by dividing the remaining cumulative negative net cash flow for the third year, amounting to $25,000, by the positive net cash flow for the fourth year of $90,000. This gives a fraction of a year of 0.278. The payback period therefore is 3.278 years.

Payback reciprocal
Capital budgeting technique that gives a rough estimate of the return on investment of a capital project.

Payback reciprocal. Another way of calculating the payback is by finding the **payback reciprocal**, which gives a very rough estimate of the return on investment. The calculation of the reciprocal is done in two steps. First, the average net cash inflows generated by the project must be calculated. In this case, the project generates an average net cash inflow of $73,000. The calculation is as follows:

$$\frac{\textbf{Total net cash inflows}}{\textbf{Number of years}} = \frac{\$365,000}{5} = \$73,000$$

Second, the average net cash inflows are divided by the initial cash outflow.

$$P = \frac{\$73,000}{\$200,000} = 36.5\%$$

Discounted payback period
The number of years required for a capital investment to generate enough discounted cash inflows to cover the initial cash outflow.

Discounted payback method. A company concerned about the element of time value will go beyond the traditional way of calculating the payback period. During the early 1980s, because of high interest rates (20% range), more businesses were taking into account the time value of money when calculating the payback period. Therefore, they calculated the **discounted payback period**. This was done by calculating the present value of future cash inflows to find the number of years it takes for the initial cash outflow to be totally recovered. Using a discount factor of, say, 15% to calculate the present value of the future stream of funds, the *discounted payback period* is 4.28 years. The calculation is as follows:

Year	Annual Net Cash Flows	Discount Factors	Present Values	Cumulative Present Values
0	$(200,000)	1.00000	$(200,000)	$(200,000)
1	25,000	0.86957	21,739	(178,261)
2	70,000	0.75614	52,930	(125,331)
3	80,000	0.65752	52,602	(72,729)
4	90,000	0.57175	51,458	(21,271) ←
5	100,000	0.49718	49,718	28,447

Arguments for the payback method:

- Because it is simple to use, it may be employed as a crude screening device. Before the company embarks on extensive, complicated, and costly feasibility studies, a quick calculation can easily distinguish between profitable projects and those that will produce marginal financial results. In short, the payback method can quickly separate the desirables from the undesirables.
- A firm that thrives on technological innovations would be inclined to use this method. In this type of business, management would want to be reasonably assured that the total cost of a venture could be recovered before better products or manufacturing processes are introduced. Here, management may have no alternative but to embark on capital projects that generate high initial cash inflows and recover their costs within a short time frame.
- A growth business that relies heavily on internal cash may find payback a useful method. Management of businesses in desperate need of cash may wish to trade off longer-term yield for short-term cash. A rapidly growing firm that opts for "dynamic projects" would find this method appropriate.
- Payback focuses on factors that are more visible. Even under dynamic environmental conditions, a firm equipped with good intelligence reports and forecasting techniques can, within reasonable limits, determine a project's potential initial cash outlays and cash inflows, at least up to the payback point. Time-value-of-money yardsticks, such as the internal rate of return (covered briefly in Chapter 10 and to be discussed in more detail later in this chapter), must incorporate into the calculation the more distant and unpredictable cash inflows (total physical life of the assets), which, in many circumstances, are merely "calculated guesses."

Arguments against the payback method:

- This technique fails to measure the *true economic worth* of a capital expenditure project because it focuses only on cash flow earned before the payback point, and it ignores the project's total physical lifespan. The payback methods place emphasis on liquidity and not return. The issue is this: Should a firm invest for the purpose of recovering its cash as quickly as possible, or should the decision be based on return? In other words, should management inject funds into a project that offers a short payback at the expense of lucrative cash inflows earned beyond the payback point?

- The opponents of this method say that it does not adequately compare the relative economic worth of projects, because it can encourage the deployment of capital funds toward less efficient projects rather than highly efficient ones. For example, a capital-intensive project with high initial cash outflows and start-up expenses and a 20-year physical life may show a long payback period. On the other hand, a labour-intensive project with minimal initial cash outlays but substantially higher labour and operating costs over its physical life may show a shorter payback and probably a shorter physical lifespan. Because of a shorter payback, the less efficient (or labour-intensive) project may be accepted instead of the capital-intensive project that could very well be more efficient.
- It does not take into consideration the timing of the flow of cash before the payback point. Although the payback method is geared to gauge liquidity, it fails to do this job properly. Consider the following hypothetical example. Two projects with initial cash outflows of $1.6 million may show a four-year payback period.

	Cash Flows in $000s		
Year	Project A	Project B	Difference
0	$(1,600)	$(1,600)	—
1	400	200	$200
2	400	200	200
3	400	600	(200)
4	400	600	(200)
Net cash flow	0	0	
Payback period	4 years	4 years	

Project A shows a superior cash flow profile because it produces $400,000 more by the end of the second year. These funds can be reinvested in lucrative endeavours. Also, if both projects cease to operate at the end of the second year, the firm would recoup 50% of the original outlays in project A and only 25% in project B. (This method is called the bailout payback period.)

Self-Test Exercise No. 11.1

Payback Period: Expansion

The Millers are considering a $200,000 expansion for their existing retail outlet. The expansion would generate $35,000 in cash each year over the next 10 years. On the basis of this information, calculate CompuTech's payback period.

Self-Test Exercise No. 11.2

Payback Period: Purchase of Existing Business

A retailer is interested in selling a retail business to the Millers for $1 million. This includes all physical assets, the working capital, and goodwill. The Millers estimate, based on the company's historical financial statements, that the annual cash inflows from the retail store would be in the $195,000 range. Calculate the company's payback period.

NET PRESENT VALUE METHOD (NPV)

What it is. The net present value technique measures the difference between the sum of all cash inflows and the cash outflows discounted at a predetermined interest rate, which sometimes reflects the company's weighted average cost of capital or the hurdle rate.

What it does. This method helps to establish whether a specific project will bring returns that exceed the cost of borrowing funds to undertake it. The rationale is relatively straightforward. If the net present value of a project, discounted at the company's weighted average cost of capital rate, is positive, the project may be classified as acceptable. If, on the other hand, the resulting net amount is negative, it would be economically unattractive and therefore rejected. This method is also useful for making realistic comparisons between projects. Because a common denominator (discount factor) is used in the calculation, it is easy to identify those projects that generate the most favourable results.

How it works. There are several steps in calculating the net present value of a project: (1) determine the projected cash flows, (2) determine the expected weighted average cost of capital, and then (3) compute the net present value itself. Referring to the example used in the payback calculation in "The Payback Method" section on page 528, the present value of the $200,000 investment with a 15% discount rate gives a total of $228,446 in discounted cash inflows for a net present value of $28,446.

Year	Net Cash Flows	Discount Factors	Net Present Value
0	$(200,000)	1.00000	$(200,000)
1	25,000	0.86957	21,739
2	70,000	0.75614	52,930
3	80,000	0.65752	52,602
4	90,000	0.57175	51,457
5	100,000	0.49718	49,718
Net present value (NPV)			$28,446

Arguments for net present value:

- This method is easy to use.
- It examines the total physical life of the assets. It facilitates the choice between different projects.

Arguments against net present value:

- The time-value-of-money concept is more difficult to grasp than other accounting methods such as return on assets.
- It is difficult to determine which cost of capital should be used to find the present value: Short-term or long-term? Current weighted average cost of capital or next year's? Current rate of return or the short- or medium-term rate? The hurdle rate?
- The net present value method does not measure the level of risk of a project. It is difficult to determine whether a project offers sufficient benefits in relation to its potential hazards. A statement like "This project gives a $28,446 net present value when discounted at 15%" is meaningless in the context of evaluating the risk of a capital project.

Self-Test Exercise No. 11.3

Net Present Value: Expansion

Using the information contained in Self-Test Exercise No. 11.1 on page 531, and assuming that CompuTech's weighted average cost of capital is 8%, calculate the project's net present value.

Self-Test Exercise No. 11.4

Net Present Value: Purchase of Existing Business

Using the information contained in Self-Test Exercise No. 11.2 on page 532, and assuming that the Millers want to make 20% on their investment and would like to sell the retail store for $4 million in the 20th year, calculate the company's net present value. Also, calculate the net present values for this project using the following discount rates: 18%, 19%, 20%, 21%, and 22%.

INTERNAL RATE OF RETURN (IRR)

What it is. The *internal rate of return,* also known as the *discounted cash flow (DCF) rate of return,* the *true yield,* or the *investors' method,* can be described as the specific discount rate used to discount all future cash inflows so that their present value equals the initial cash outflows. The financial community has used this discounting mechanism for many decades to calculate insurance premiums and bond yields. Later, the industrial community adopted it to evaluate capital projects.

What it does. It shows the economic merits of several projects and compares their returns to other financial indicators, such as the weighted average cost of capital and the company's aggregate rate of return.

How it works. The internal rate of return is found by trial and error (if a financial calculator or a spreadsheet is not available). Once the total annual cash flows are estimated, the net present value of the cash inflows and outflows is computed using an arbitrary interest rate. The totals are then compared. If the present value of the cash inflows is lower than the cash outflows, the procedure is repeated, this time using a lower interest rate. If, however, the present value of the cash inflows is higher than the cash outflows, a higher interest rate is used. The process continues until the total net cash flow equals zero. The required calculation for our earlier example is illustrated as follows:

Year	Undiscounted Cash Flows	At 18% Factor	At 18% PV	At 20% Factor	At 20% PV	At 22% Factor	At 22% PV
0	($200,000)	1.00000	($200,000)	1.00000	$(200,000)	1.00000	($200,000)
1	25,000	0.84746	21,186	0.83333	20,833	0.81967	20,492
2	70,000	0.71818	50,273	0.69444	48,611	0.67186	47,030
3	80,000	0.60863	48,690	0.57870	46,296	0.55071	44,057
4	90,000	0.51579	46,421	0.48225	43,402	0.45140	40,626
5	$100,000	0.43711	$43,711	0.40188	$40,188	0.37000	$37,000
NPV			$10,281		$(670)		$(10,795)

The calculation shows that it is the 20% interest rate that equalizes (near enough) the cash flows. (By using a financial calculator or a spreadsheet, we get exactly 19.87%.) The internal rate of return on this investment is therefore 20%. Trial-and-error calculations would have to be done if the net difference is more significant.

If the cash outflow takes place at year 0, and all cash inflows are constant each year of the project, it is quite easy to figure out the internal rate of return. For example, a $200,000 initial cash outflow and a $70,000 annual cash inflow give a 22% internal rate of return. First divide the $200,000 by the $70,000, which gives a factor of 2.8571. By referring to the present value of an annuity of $1 in Table D in Appendix B, we can obtain the internal rate of return by finding the 2.8571 present value factor in the row opposite year 5. The present value factor of 2.8571 lies between 22% (2.8636) and 23% (2.8035). In this case, the IRR is 21.11%.

Arguments for internal rate of return:

- It focuses attention on the entire economic life of an investment. It concerns cash flows and ignores book allocations.
- It considers the fact that money has a time value.
- It permits a company to compare the return of one project to the cost of capital (see Figure 9.2 on page 426).
- It facilitates comparisons between two or more projects.

Arguments against internal rate of return:

- This method covers activities that take place during the entire lifespan of a project. While this may be considered a strong point, it could also be a drawback. How can one predict internal and external environmental conditions 10, 15, and 20 years ahead?

- It ignores potential "cash throw-offs"—that is, should a company assess the financial desirability of a project in a vacuum, or should it include the added profit produced by the incremental cash that is generated by the project? For example, when a project generates, say, $25,000 during the first year of operation, should the interest earned on this money be taken into account when calculating the return of the project in question?
- The technique is relatively difficult to grasp. Operating managers understand ratios, such as the division of profit for the year by the project's investment; however, the internal rate of return calculation contains more than simple arithmetic. Concepts such as cash flows, time span, discounting, and present value—all essential components of the internal rate of return calculation—are introduced.
- This method poses some difficulty for determining the "true" financial benefits of a project. Because the investment return is expressed in terms of a percentage or a ratio, this method poses an element of delusion. For instance, a company's capital expenditure budget may contain several projects in the amount of $100,000, with internal rates of return in the 25% range. Other important projects in the $1 million range with a 20% internal rate of return may be weeded out, due to the comparative low factor yield. The absolute present-value sums are not evident. Put simply, you can invest $100 at 30% and $10,000 at 25% for a one-year period and, although the return on the first project is highly attractive, the absolute dollars earned are only $30. In the second case, the yield is lower; however, the dollars earned are $2,500. This cash throw-off can be reinvested in other projects generating additional profit or cash.
- It assumes that the cash flows can be reinvested at the calculated rate of return.

Self-Test Exercise No. 11.5

Internal Rate of Return: Expansion

Using the information contained in Self-Test Exercise No. 11.1 on page 531, calculate the project's internal rate of return.

Self-Test Exercise No. 11.6

Internal Rate of Return: Purchase of Existing Business

Using the information contained in Self-Test Exercises No. 11.2 and 11.4 on pages 532 and 533, calculate the project's internal rate of return.

In the News 11.2 illustrates that the purchase of a plant worth millions of dollars is the result not only of a handshake between a buyer and a seller but also of a detailed financial analysis that can justify its economic merits.

In The News [11.2]

The IRR, NPV, and Payback Period Calculations Were Surely Part of the Factory Acquisition's Decision-Making Process

Going to an auction to buy a plant was probably an excellent choice for Aquablue International, a manufacturer of quality concentrate, bottled water, and carbonated beverages. Aquablue bought Hershey's facility at Smith Falls, Ontario, via the auction sale mechanism. This was an effective way of softening the purchase cost of the capital assets, to ultimately improve profitability and return.

It was in June 2009 that the British Columbia bottled water company Aquablue International bought Hershey Chocolate's factory at Smith Falls. The company acquired some equipment at the auction, in addition to the facility itself. The auction paved the way for Aquablue to move into the facility to produce and bottle "enhanced water" and sugar-free drinks. The new facility, which would initially hire about 60 employees to help bottle its products, would employ an additional 70 by March 2010. Although the purchase price was not made public, the chief auctioneer indicated that buying the equipment "new" would have cost more than $70 million, an amount that the bidders at the auction would not see anywhere near that level. Aquablue and other bidders (as many as 200) were expected to participate at the bidding game.

Source: Adapted from Vito Pilieci, "Hershey plant auction draws a crowd," *Ottawa Citizen*, August 28, 2009, p. E1. For more information about Aquablue International, see http://www.aquablueinternational.com/index.htm.

PROFITABILITY INDEX

Profitability index (PI) Shows the ratio of the present value of cash inflows to the present value of the cash outflows, discounted at a predetermined rate of interest.

What it is. The **profitability index (PI)**, also known as the *present value index* or the *benefit-cost ratio,* shows the ratio of the present value of cash inflows to the present value of the cash outflows, discounted at a predetermined rate of interest.

What it does. This method helps to rank capital projects by the ratio of the net present value for each dollar to the cash outflow and to select the projects with the highest index until the budget is depleted.

How it works. Refer to the earlier example on page 532, where the initial cash outlay is $200,000, the cost of capital is 15%, the life of the project is five years, and the cash inflow is as follows:

Year	Cash Inflows	PV Using Discount Rate of 15%
1	$25,000	$21,739
2	70,000	52,930
3	80,000	52,602
4	90,000	51,457
5	$100,000	49,718
PV		$228,446

The present value of the future cash inflows is $228,446. The PI is calculated as follows:

$$\frac{\$228,446}{\$200,000} = 1.142$$

If the index is greater than 1.0, it means that the flow of cash discounted at a predetermined discount factor (e.g., weighted average cost of capital) is more than the cash disbursement. If it is less than 1.0, it means that the incoming cash flows of the project are less than the cash disbursed. For example, if 15% was used to calculate the PI of all projects shown in Table 11.6, it means that projects A to E generate more than 15%, and projects F to K, less.

This method helps to rank capital projects in a logical way because it looks at projects both in relation to budget constraints and in terms of which ones offer the highest total net present value. Table 11.6 illustrates this methodology. Let us say that a company has a maximum of $1.7 million to invest. As shown in the table, the company has 11 projects under review (A to K), each having specific cash outflows with corresponding net present values and profitability indexes. The company will give the green light to projects A to E for a total cash outlay of $1.7 million. This means that projects F to K would not be approved (unless they are compulsory projects such as antipollution abatement equipment or for employee safety). The aggregate PI for all approved projects is 1.36 ($2,310,000 ÷ $1,700,000).

Arguments for and against the profitability index:

The arguments for and against the profitability index are the same as those for and against the net present value method, with one exception: The NPV expresses results in absolute dollar terms, while the PI method expresses results in relative terms, that is, as an index.

Table 11.6 Capital Rationing and the Profitability Index

Projects		Cash Outflows	PV	PI	Aggregate PI
A		$300,000	$510,000	1.7	
B		200,000	320,000	1.6	
C	$1,700,000	600,000	840,000	1.4	1.36
D		400,000	440,000	1.1	
E		200,000	200,000	1.0	
F		200,000	160,000	0.8	
G		250,000	175,000	0.7	
H		150,000	60,000	0.4	
I		90,000	27,000	0.3	
J		300,000	60,000	0.2	
K		200,000	0	0	

Self-Test Exercise No. 11.7

Profitability Index: Expansion

Using the information contained in Self-Test Exercises No. 11.1 and 11.3, on pages 531 and 533, respectively, calculate the profitability index.

Self-Test Exercise No. 11.8

Profitability Index: Purchase of Existing Business

Using the information contained in Self-Test Exercises No. 11.2 and 11.4, on pages 532 and 533, respectively, calculate the profitability index.

Self-Test Exercise No. 11.9

Buy versus Lease Option

The Millers are considering two options: to buy or to lease another retail outlet.

Option 1: Purchase

Year		
0	Cost	$900,000
1	Additional cost	100,000
1	Cash flow from operations	150,000
2	Cash flow from operations	300,000
3	Cash flow from operations	400,000
4	Cash flow from operations	500,000
5	Cash flow from operations	600,000
5	Cash flow from sale of business	1,000,000

Option 2: Lease

With the lease option, the Millers would generate a net $70,000 annual cash inflow.

Question

If the Millers want to make 30%, should they buy or lease the retail store? To answer this question, calculate the following:

1. Net present value
2. Internal rate of return

Self-Test Exercise No. 11.10

Project Analysis

After looking at several options, including those described in Self-Test Exercise No. 11.9, the Millers were more interested in opening a new retail outlet. The investment in capital assets in the new outlet is estimated at $350,000, and an additional $175,000 in working capital (inventories and trade receivables) is to be spent over the first two years of operations. The economic life of the project is estimated at 10 years with a resale value of $900,000. The weighted average cost of capital is estimated at 11%, and the Millers would like to yield a 20% IRR. CompuTech's second retail store will generate the following cash flow during a 10-year period:

Year	Cash Inflows	Cash Outflows
0		$350,000
1	$75,000	100,000
2	80,000	75,000
3	100,000	
4	125,000	
5	140,000	
6–10	150,000	
10	900,000	

Questions

1. What is CompuTech's NPV using 11% and 20% WACC?
2. What is the retail store's payback period?
3. What is CompuTech's IRR?
4. What is the profitability index?
5. Should the Millers go ahead with the opening?

Capital Budgeting Techniques That Cope with Risk

4 Learning Objective

Assess capital investments using decision-making techniques that measure risk.

It was mentioned earlier that time-value-of-money yardstick results are based on a project's total physical lifespan. This implies the need to deal with the future, to use a series of underlying assumptions as benchmarks for computing the best possible estimates. The one overriding weakness in this approach is its vulnerability to the element of change. No one can predict, with any certainty, future environmental conditions, such as those related to economic, political, social, and technological factors, and, more specifically, elements affecting the industry, such as prices, competitors' aggressiveness, level of investment intentions by competitors, research and development, and labour costs. So the internal rate of return is based on the assumption that *all* estimates will materialize, that the price over the next five years will be x, that the cost of materials and wages will be y and z, etc. Thus, there are many chances for estimates to be off target. For example, a 15.6% internal rate of return can be increased or decreased by a change or several changes in the planning assumptions.

More sophisticated capital budgeting techniques have been developed to help decision-makers deal with probabilities or possibilities. These yardsticks can identify a range of results based on patterns of variations, rather than using one single set of factors to generate the best possible result (such as the one used to calculate the internal rate of return).

Two techniques used for dealing with range of results are sensitivity analysis and risk analysis.

SENSITIVITY ANALYSIS

Sensitivity analysis involves the identification of profitability variations as a result of one or more changes in the base case related to certain key elements of a project. These could include the purchase of land, buildings and equipment, sales volume, unit selling price, cost of material or labour, length of the physical life of the assets, and even the change in the tax rate. To illustrate, the internal rate of return of the project mentioned earlier in the section titled "Internal Rate of Return" was 20% based on one set of estimates. If selling prices vary by 10%, construction costs by 5%, and sales volume by 10%, the effect of these changes (individually) on the base case would be as follows:

Factors	% Variation in Factor	Internal Rate of Return
Base case	—	20.0%
Selling price	–10%	16.3%
Cost of construction	+5%	18.8%
Sales volume	–10%	17.5%

These factors may vary either individually or in combination. It is important to note that sensitivity checks do not contain the element of probability related to individual factors. This method simply illustrates the degree of change in the base internal rate of return as a result of one or more changes related to a project.

RISK ANALYSIS

Risk analysis
Process of attaching probabilities to individual estimates in a capital project's base case.

Risk analysis is the process of attaching probabilities to individual estimates in the base case. It was stated earlier that the process of appraising investment proposals has one weakness—the element of uncertainty. Those preparing the estimates to be included in the return calculation must know the degree of uncertainty related to their respective estimates.

Past experience alerts managers to the possible degree of error in their estimates. Therefore, management's knowledge should be used extensively to obtain the best-quality decision-making. The risk-analysis method will produce a full spectrum of return outcomes, from the most pessimistic to the most optimistic. Weighing the uncertainty factor, therefore, becomes an integral part of the project evaluation process. In this way, the sales manager, the production manager, the financial analyst, the plant engineer, the cost accountant, the purchasing agent, and others can all provide their calculated estimates regarding the likelihood of possible outcomes in the selling price, cost of labour, cost of machinery, cost of raw material, etc. Their input can be illustrated as follows:

Sales volume (in units)	100,000	200,000	300,000	400,000
probabilities	5%	15%	65%	15%
Selling price	$1.50	$1.70	$1.90	$2.10
probabilities	5%	15%	70%	10%
Cost of labour	$0.75	$0.80	$0.85	$0.90
probabilities	10%	15%	60%	15%
Project cost	$200,000	$250,000	$300,000	$350,000
probabilities	5%	10%	75%	10%
Life of project (in years)	10	11	12	13
probabilities	5%	10%	80%	5%

As mentioned earlier, the probabilities indicated under each variable (volume, price, etc.) are provided by managers based on their experience or calculated estimates.

The results of the risk analysis calculations could read as follows:

IRR Range (%)	Number of Occurrences	% of Total	% Cumulative
5–8	4	0.4	0.4
8–11	30	3.0	3.4
11–14	133	13.3	16.7
14–17	323	32.3	49.0
17–20	283	28.3	77.3
20–23	167	16.7	94.0
23–26	43	4.3	98.3
26–29	17	1.7	100.0
Total	1,000	100.0	

The above means that there are 4 chances out of 1,000 that the project's internal rate of return would fall between 5% and 8%, 30 chances out of 1,000 that it will fall between 8% and 11%, etc. The report could also indicate the following:

Minimum rate of return	5.3%
Maximum rate of return	29.3%
Mean	18.1%

Probability

68.3% that the return will fall between 15.6% and 22.0%.

95.5% that the return will fall between 9.0% and 23.9%.

99.7% that the return will fall between 5.9% and 29.0%.

This example indicates that of the 1,000 internal rate of return outcomes (an arbitrary number chosen by the financial analysts) under the most pessimistic circumstances, the financial return is 5.3%, while the most optimistic calculated estimates would predict a 29.3% return. Within these two extremes lies a full range of outcomes to help judge the risk factors inherent in a project.

In the News 11.3 gives an example of the type of risk analysis that a company may have to go through to determine the range of return outcomes by assigning a series of probabilities to various elements of a research project that may eventually result in a capital expenditure project.

In The News [11.3]

From Research to Reality, What Are the Probabilities of This Project to Succeed?

Cloaking is an advanced "stealth technology" that causes an object (just like the stealth bomber) to be partially or wholly invisible. The device has been used in many science fiction settings and games including *Doctor Who, Star Wars, Stargate,* and *StarCraft*. Now, the dream appears to be close to another reality. This is what Professor of Applied Mathematics Graeme Milton and his team at the University of Utah are working on. However, this is a dream that entails "real business risks." How much will it cost? How long will it take? What are the probabilities for the project to succeed? What are its chances to be commercially viable? And, how much of a return should private-sector partners, if any, ask for to compensate for the risk?

The research team at the University of Utah says that they have developed a device that could reduce the damage to buildings from tsunamis by sending out shockwaves of their own that would wear down the incoming tidal waves. The device could protect buildings from natural disasters. For instance, an operator of a building could fire electromagnetic waves at incoming shockwaves of an earthquake or tsunami and protect it against the destructive power. Because earthquakes and tsunamis are composed of waves in many different frequencies, the cloaking device could counter large vibrations generated by the main destructive waves and neutralize them by breaking down the waves into ever-smaller and less-destructive waves. The Utah scientists are now looking for partners in the private sector interested in commercializing the technology. The scientists say that the new device could become a reality within a decade.

Source: Adapted from Vito Pilieci, "Cloaking technology could protect buildings from disasters: study," *Ottawa Citizen*, August 21, 2009, p. E1. For more information about Graeme Milton's cloaking device, go to http://www.livescience.com/technology/080606-bts-milton-superlens.html.

Capital Expenditure Constraints

5 Learning Objective

Explain the reasons that can prevent a capital project from being approved.

Two reasons can prevent a business from proceeding with a large number of capital projects: cash insufficiency and hurdle rate (which determines in a large measure the extent to which projects are satisfactory or viable).

CASH INSUFFICIENCY

Before overloading a business with too much debt (a cheaper source than equity), management will calculate the appropriate debt-to-total-capitalization ratio. The risk factor largely determines this optimum capital mix. If a firm adds too much debt to its capital structure, future fixed charges will increase, affecting the firm's cash position. The question to answer is this: Will the capital projects generate sufficient cash to meet proposed fixed commitments or will there be a **cash insufficiency**?

Cash insufficiency
Not enough cash generated by a capital project to pay for fixed charges.

HURDLE RATE

The **hurdle rate** or the weighted average cost of capital can be used to rank the financial desirability of capital projects. Essentially, capital budgeting is the process of finding the break-even point between the yield of a capital project and the weighted average cost of capital. Obviously, the wider the spread between the aggregate yield or IRR of the projects and the weighted average cost of capital, the better it is for the shareholders.

Hurdle rate
Capital budgeting technique used to rank the financial desirability of capital projects according to their cost of capital.

To find this break-even point, the aggregate IRR must, of course, be known. It is also essential to pinpoint the sources and weighted average cost of the capital needed to finance all capital projects (e.g., internal financing, such as retained earnings, and external financing, such as bond or share issues).

The capital project selection system is often referred to as the capital rationing process, meaning that only the most viable projects—that is, those that exceed the hurdle rate (or the weighted average cost of capital, or WACC)—would be approved. Figure 11.3 presents this process. As shown in the figure, the company's total capital

Figure 11.3 Capital-Rationing Process

Projects	Project costs: Each project	Project costs: Cumulative costs	IRR: Each project	IRR: Cumulative
A	1.0	1.0	25.0	25.0
B	1.0	2.0	20.0	22.5
C-D-E	2.0	4.0	16.0	19.6
F	1.0	5.0	11.0	15.0
G-H	1.0	6.0	9.5	12.7
I	.5	6.5	2.5	12.0
J	.3	6.8	1.3	11.3
K	.2	7.0	—	10.0

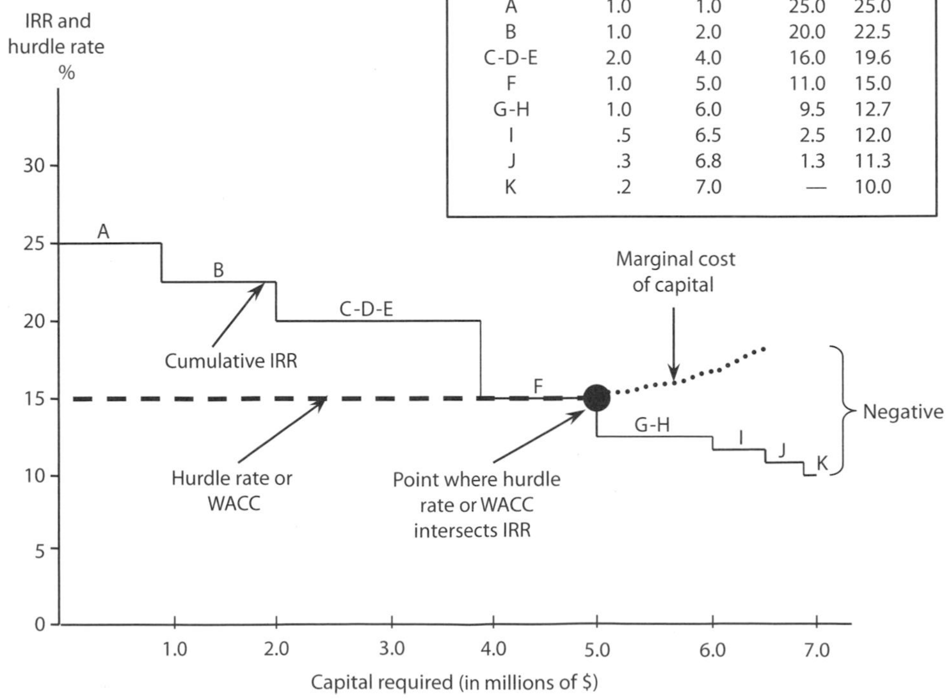

projects requested amount to $7 million, made up of 10 capital projects (A to J) and several other minor projects grouped under K (see the axis line at the bottom of the figure and the cumulative costs column in the enclosed box in the figure). Project A costs $1.0 million and generates a 25% IRR. Project B, which also costs $1.0 million, produces a 20% IRR. The cumulative IRR for these two projects is 22.5%. Projects C-D-E, which cost $2.0 million, return 16.0% for a cumulative 19.6% IRR. As shown, the cumulative IRR for all projects—that is, $7.0 million—is 10% (see under column cumulative IRR in the enclosed box and project K on the horizontal line). If management decides to set the project's hurdle rate or the WACC at 15% for the cut-off point (the broken line in the figure), projects G to K could very well be rejected. It is at that point that projects A to F give a cumulative 15% IRR and intersect the company's hurdle rate. If the company wants to raise more money (above the $5.0 million amount) to approve more projects, the company's hurdle rate would be raised in view of the fact the company's marginal cost of capital would also be raised (dotted line). However, under such circumstances, the cumulative IRR for additional projects would create a negative spread between the hurdle rate and the cumulative IRR.

REALITY FINANCIAL SNAPSHOTS

Each year, all types of organizations, big or small, manufacturing or service, for-profit and not-for-profit, invest large sums of money in capital projects. The following gives some examples of the amount of money and type of capital expenditure projects that Enbridge and The Ottawa Hospital invest in.

ENBRIDGE[1]

Based on Enbridge's statement of cash flows, in 2008, the company invested $3.6 billion in capital projects. The following is a partial list of capital expenditure projects, the size of the investment, and the year of completion contained in the company's annual report. One can only imagine the type of analysis and capital investment decision-making tools that were used to justify the economic desirability of these projects.

(in billions of Canadian dollars unless stated otherwise)

	Estimated Capital Cost	Expected In-Service Date
Liquids Pipelines		
Southern Access Mainline	$0.2 billion	2008
Expansion – Canadian Portion Line 4 Extension	$0.3 billion	Early 2009
Spearhead Pipeline Expansion	US$0.1 billion	First half of 2009
Hardisty Terminal	$0.6 billion	2009 (in stages)

1. Enbridge Inc., *2008 Enbridge Annual Report*. Found at: http://www.enbridge.com/investor/financialInformation/reportsFilings/pdf/2008-annual-report-en.pdf.

Southern Lights Pipeline	$0.5 billion+ US$1.7 billion	Light Sour Line – Early 2009; Diluent Line– Late 2010
Alberta Clipper – Canadian portion	$2.4 billion	Mid-2010
Fort Hills Pipeline System	≈$2.0 billion	No earlier than 2012
Sponsored Investments		
EEP – Southern Access Mainline Expansion – U.S. portion	US$2.1 billion	2008 – 2009 (in stages)
EEP – North Dakota System Expansion	US$0.1 billion	Q1 2010
EEP Alberta Clipper Pipeline U.S. Portion	US$1.2 billion	Mid-2010
EIF – Saskatchewan System	$0.1 billion	Q3 2010

Here are comments made in the annual report concerning the capital expenditure plans:

- Descriptions of each project are included in the strategy section of each business segment.
- These amounts are estimates only and subject to upward or downward adjustment based on various factors.
- Risk related to the development and completion of organic growth projects are described under Risk Management.

THE OTTAWA HOSPITAL[2]

Based on The Ottawa Hospital statement of cash flows, the organization invested $63.7 million toward the purchase of capital assets in 2008. Here is a partial list of capital expenditure projects that were committed for the upcoming years. Projects and programs reported in the hospital's annual report include the following:

- $5.9 million investment in the civic campus intensive care
- $15.8 million in a new cancer research floor
- State-of-the-art 30 Tesla MRI
- Educational training
- $47 million for renovating the general campus emergency department
- Research in various departments (cancer, chronic disease, genetic obesity, stroke, intensive care, rehabilitation, vision, etc.)
- Small and large amounts of funds invested in nursing, patient services, volunteer services, programs, and more

For these types of projects, however, the priority is not on obtaining the highest return on investment, but rather to provide the most cost-effective health care program.

2. *2008 Ottawa Hospital Annual Report.* Found at: http://www.ottawahospital.on.ca/about/reports/FS2008-e.pdf.

[DECISION-MAKING IN ACTION]

Let's now turn to analyzing capital expenditure projects to see how these various capital budgeting techniques are applied in different situations. Three projects will be analyzed:

- Modernization
- Launching a new product
- Constructing a new plant (New-Tech Inc.)

Modernization

Suppose a business contemplates investing $1.5 million to modernize a plant. On the basis of the following information, it is possible to determine whether a capital expenditure is worth the investment.

- The economic life of the project is estimated at 10 years.
- The savings (or cash inflows) are estimated at $300,000 per year.
- The cost of capital is 14%.

This information is sufficient for assessing whether the project has some economic merit. By referring to the discount tables, we can calculate the present value of the future savings by using the 14% discount factors. If the sum of the future savings, discounted to today's value, exceeds the $1.5 million initial capital outlay, it means that the project is economically attractive. If, however, the sum of the net inflow is negative, it means that the project should not go forward. As shown in Table 11.7, because the net present value between the initial cash outflow and the future cash inflows is positive by $64,830, the project could very well be approved.

Figure 11.4 graphically displays the results of the present value calculations for individual years. The shaded squares show the present values of each $300,000 receipt, while the white portion of each square shows the loss in value because of time.

Table 11.7 **Cash Flow Forecast of Modernizing a Project**

Year	Cash Outflow	Cash Inflows	Discount Factors	Present Value
0	$1,500,000	—	—	($1,500,000)
1	—	$300,000	0.87719	263,157
2	—	300,000	0.76947	230,841
3	—	300,000	0.67497	202,491
4	—	300,000	0.59208	177,624
5	—	300,000	0.51937	155,810
6	—	300,000	0.45559	136,676
7	—	300,000	0.39964	119,891
8	—	300,000	0.35056	105,167
9	—	300,000	0.30751	92,252
10	—	300,000	0.26974	80,921
Total Discounted Cash Inflows				1,564,830
Net Present Value				$64,830

Figure 11.4 **Graphic Illustration of the Yearly Cash Inflows and Initial Outflow**

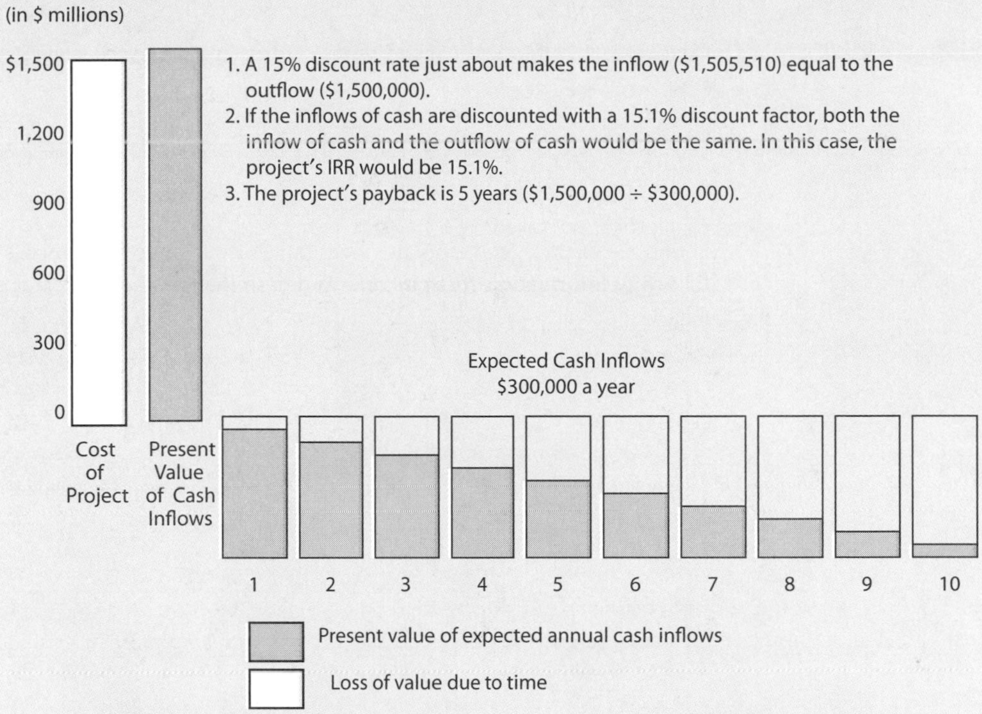
(in $ millions)
$1,500
1,200
900
600
300
0
Cost of Project
Present Value of Cash Inflows
1. A 15% discount rate just about makes the inflow ($1,505,510) equal to the outflow ($1,500,000).
2. If the inflows of cash are discounted with a 15.1% discount factor, both the inflow of cash and the outflow of cash would be the same. In this case, the project's IRR would be 15.1%.
3. The project's payback is 5 years ($1,500,000 ÷ $300,000).
Expected Cash Inflows
$300,000 a year
1
2
3
4
5
6
7
8
9
10
Present value of expected annual cash inflows
Loss of value due to time

Because we are dealing with an annuity situation, instead of using Table B in Appendix B (present value of a single sum), we can use Table D and look under column 14% (cost of capital) for year 10. By multiplying the $300,000 expected savings by the 5.2161 discount factor, we get the same number: $1,564,830 for a positive $64,830 NPV. If we used a 15% discount factor, the NPV would be $5,510. In this case, the IRR is 15.1%.

The following factors may reinforce or reverse our decision:

- A change in the economic life of the project
- A change in the corporate tax bracket
- A change in the initial cash outflows
- A change in the cash inflows
- A change in the cost of capital
- A change in the expected return on the capital assets
- The economic attractiveness of other projects considered by the company
- The shortage in the amount of funds available
- The nature of other projects, which may generate a lesser return but may be required by law—for example, antipollution equipment

Launching a New Product

Let's look now at the launching of a new product. Table 11.8 gives detailed information about the project and is divided into four parts:

- Part A shows the various components related to the $2.0 million cost or cash outflow of the project.

Table 11.8 Gauging a Capital Expenditure Project

A. The project

Assets	
R & D	$150,000
Equipment/machinery	850,000
Other assets	500,000
Net working capital	500,000
Total capital employed	$2,000,000

B. The projected statement of income

Year	Profit
1	$ 50,000
2	200,000
3	375,000
4	510,000
5	690,000

C. Projected statements of income and cash flows

Year	1	2	3	4	5
Revenue	$1,300	$1,700	$2,415	$3,000	$3,700
Cost of sales	(600)	(700)	(990)	(1,240)	(1,560)
Gross profit	700	1,000	1,425	1,760	2,140
Distribution costs and administrative expenses	(350)	(400)	(500)	(600)	(650)
Profit before CCA	350	600	925	1,160	1,490
CCA	(250)	(200)	(175)	(140)	(110)
Profit before taxes	100	400	750	1,020	1,380
Income tax expense (50%)	(50)	(200)	(375)	(510)	(690)
Profit for the year	50	200	375	510	690
Add back CCA	250	200	175	140	110
Cash flows	$300	$400	$550	$650	$800

D. Projected cash flow (000s)

Year	0	1	2	3	4	5
Assets	$(1,500)	—	—	—	—	—
Working capital	—	$(250)	$(250)	—	—	—
Pro-forma cash flow	—	300	400	$550	$650	$800
Sale of assets	—	—	—	—	—	300
Recovery of working capital	—	—	—	—	—	500
Total cash flow	$(1,500)	$50	$150	$550	$650	$1,600

- Part B gives the project's annual projected profit for five years.
- Part C shows the project's annual projected statements of income and cash flows.
- Part D gives the overview of the project's five-year cash flow forecast (the cash inflows and cash outflows for each year).

Here are the assumptions related to the project. As shown in Part A, management invests a total of $2.0 million in the project: $150,000 in research and development (R & D); $1,350,000 in equipment, machinery, and other assets; and $500,000 in working capital. The investment in net working capital consists of the following:

Trade receivables	$600,000	cash outflow
Inventories	300,000	cash outflow
Total	900,000	
Trade payables	400,000	cash inflow
Net working capital	$500,000	net cash outflow

Part B gives the five-year projected profits. If management wants to calculate the return outcomes of the project by using the accounting methods, it could compute the following yearly returns:

	Yearly Return on	
Year	**Capital Employed (%)**	**Capital Assets (%)**
1	2.5	3.3
2	10.0	13.3
3	18.7	25.0
4	25.5	34.0
5	34.5	46.0
Average return	18.2	24.3

	Return on Average Investment		**Return on Depreciated Assets**	
Year	**Capital Employed (%)**	**Capital Assets (%)**	**Capital Employed (%)**	**Capital Assets (%)**
1	4.0	6.7	2.9	4.2
2	16.0	26.7	14.3	22.2
3	30.0	50.0	34.0	66.6
4	41.0	68.0	63.7	170.0
5	55.2	92.0	138.0	+ 1000.0

Part C of Table 11.8 gives a more detailed forecast of management's projected statements of income and cash flows. The most difficult part of a project analysis is not calculating the payback or the internal rate of return but making the forecast related to the project itself. For example, the marketing department would have to estimate the company's revenue, which includes both the number of units sold (or service) and the selling price for each unit, adjusted for inflation.

The manufacturing department would have to forecast the cost of sales, which includes the cost of raw materials, freight-in, and the transformation of the raw materials into finished products. This forecast also includes anticipated inflation increments over the life of the project.

Similar cost forecasts would also have to be prepared by other organizational units that are expected to be part of the project. As indicated, this forecast takes into account the capital cost allowance (the tax-deductible item) rather than depreciation to calculate the income taxes to be paid each year over the life of the project. In order to determine the yearly cash flow generated by the project, because capital cost allowance is not a cash outflow (but a tax-deductible expense), it is added back to the profit for the year.

Part D of Table 11.8 gives the actual disbursements (cash outflows) and receipts (cash inflows) of the project. There are two distinct cash disbursements: the $1.5 million related to R&D, purchase of the machinery and equipment, and other assets made during year 0, and the $500,000 disbursements related to working capital, which in this case are spread equally over years 1 and 2. The third line is the projected cash inflows generated by the project. This line is drawn from Part C of the table. Other assumptions related to the project are that the assets have a five-year life span and that, at the end, the assets (equipment/machinery and other assets) will be sold for $300,000, and the $500,000 in working capital will be totally recovered.

Based on the above cash flows, the project's payback period, NPV, and IRR are as follows:

A. Payback period is 4.1 years.

Year	Annual Net Cash Flows (000s)	Cumulative Cash Flows (000s)	
0	($1,500.0)	($1,500.0)	
1	50.0	(1,450.0)	
2	150.0	(1,300.0)	
3	550.0	(750.0)	
4	650.0	(100.0)	← Payback
	$1,600.0	$1,500.0	

B. Net present value (NPV) is based on a 10% cost of capital.

Year	Annual Net Cash Flows (000s)	Discount Factors	Present Values (000s)
0	($1,500.0)	1.000	($1,500.0)
1	50.0	0.909	45.4
2	150.0	0.826	123.9
3	550.0	0.751	413.1
4	650.0	0.683	444.0
5	$1,600.0	0.621	993.6
Present value			2,020.0
Net present value (NPV)			$520.0

C. Internal rate of return (IRR) is 18.4%.

Year	Annual Net Cash Flows (000s)	Present Values (000s) 17%	18%	19%
0	($1,500.0)	($1,500.0)	($1,500.0)	($1,500.0)
1	50.0	42.7	42.4	42.0
2	150.0	109.6	107.7	105.9
3	550.0	343.4	334.7	326.4
4	650.0	346.8	335.3	324.1
5	$1,600.0	729.8	699.4	670.4
Net present value (NPV)		$72.3	$19.5	($31.2)

Someone who does not have a financial calculator or a spreadsheet has to find the internal rate of return on a trial-and-error basis, by using the 17%, 18%, and 19% discount rates until the NPV moves from a positive to a negative. As shown above, the calculation indicates that the internal rate of return is between 18% (NPV of +$19.5 thousand) and 19% (NPV of –$31.2 thousand).

Constructing a New Plant (New-Tech Inc.)

Let's look now at the third capital expenditure project. New-Tech Inc. is contemplating opening a new plant to manufacture pocket calculators. The cost of the project is as follows:

Land	$50,000	
Building	200,000	
Equipment/machinery	100,000	
Trucks	150,000	
Total capital assets		$500,000
Net working capital		150,000
Total capital employed		$650,000

The company expects to realize $2.0 million in revenue during the first year of operation, which would be maintained during the life of the plant. The company's projected statement of income is as follows:

Revenue		$2,000,000
Cost of sales		(1,700,000)
Gross profit		300,000
CCA	(25,000)	
Finance costs	(40,000)	
Other operating expenses	(145,000)	
Total expenses		(210,000)
Profit before taxes		90,000
Income tax expense		(40,000)
Profit for the year		$50,000

The company engineer indicates that the lifespan of the plant is 15 years. According to the company's real estate division manager, in 15 years, the market value of the land will have increased to $150,000, and the residual value of the buildings, equipment, and trucks will be in the order of $150,000. Working capital is expected to be totally recovered at the end of the project.

The company will borrow from different sources to finance the project, and the weighted average cost of capital, according to the company's treasurer, will be 11%. Management would like to obtain at least 25% on the project (hurdle rate). If you were a member of the management committee, would you go along with this proposal?

Table 11.9 gives the NPV, the payback period, and the IRR. As shown below, the first objective is to calculate the annual cash flow from operations. This is done by rearranging the statement of

Table 11.9 New-Tech Inc.

		25%		11%		15%	
Year	**Cash Flows**	**Factors**	**Cash Flows**	**Factors**	**Cash Flows**	**Factors**	**Cash Flows**
0	$(500,000)	1.0000	$(500,000)	1.0000	$ (500,000)	1.0000	$ (500,000)
1	$(150,000)	0.8000	$(120,000)	0.9009	$ (135,135)	0.8696	$ (130,440)
1	$ 97,280						
↕		3.8593	$ 375,432	7.1909	$ 699,530	5.8474	$ 568,835
15	$ 97,280						
15	$ 450,000	0.03518	$ 15,831	0.20900	$ 94,050	0.1229	$ 55,305
Net present value			$(228,737)		$ 158,445		$ (6,300)

Payback period: 6.7 years

Internal rate of return: 14.8%

income and converting the $50,000 profit for each year into cash flows; as shown, the calculation gives an amount of $97,280. Here are some of the assumptions and the arithmetic:

Gross profit		$300,000
CCA	($25,000)	
Other expenses	(145,000)	(170,000)
Profit before taxes		130,000
Income tax expense		(57,720)
Profit for the year		72,280
Add back CCA		25,000
Cash flow from operations		$97,280

It is assumed that the $300,000 gross profit is all cash inflows. The two other expense items deducted from the gross profit are CCA (for the purpose of keeping the example simple, CCA is treated on a straight-line basis), and other operating expenses. Because the company is in the 44.4% tax bracket (from the projected statement of income, $40,000 ÷ $90,000), the project itself will be taxed for $57,720 ($130,000 × 44.4%). Finance costs are excluded from the calculation because one of the objectives of finding the IRR is to compare it with the weighted average cost of the capital—that is, funds obtained from external sources. CCA is simply used as a tax shield; it is added back to the profit, which gives a net annual cash inflow from operations in the amount of $97,280. As shown in Table 11.9, using the cost of capital (11%) as the discount rate gives the project a positive NPV of $158,445. On the basis of this discount rate, company management would be tempted to approve the project. However, because of the risk factor, management has established a 25% hurdle rate. Using 25% as the discount factor gives the project $228,737 negative NPV, which is far less than expected. As shown in Table 11.9, using 15% as the discount factor gives the project a negative NPV of $6,300. With a financial calculator or a spreadsheet, we obtain exactly 14.81%. The bottom line is this: The project generates a 14.8% IRR, and after the weighted average cost of capital of 11% (or paying the external cost of financing the project), the company would be left with only 3.8%. This is much less than the 14.0% spread (25.0% – 11.0%) that management was hoping to realize to offset the risk associated with the project.

FINANCIAL SPREADSHEETS—EXCEL

Template 6 (capital project analysis) of the financial statement analysis component of the financial spreadsheets accompanying this text can calculate the net present value, the internal rate of return, the profitability index, and the payback period. Unlike financial calculators and other spreadsheets, this particular tool can calculate the annual capital cost allowance for different capital assets, which makes the project's cash flows more accurate and, ultimately, the time-value-of-money financial calculations more exact.

Chapter Summary

1 Learning Objective

Explain the capital budgeting process.

The capital budgeting process includes six key steps: (1) establishing corporate priorities and strategic goals; (2) formulating the plans and capital expenditure projects; (3) project ranking by using capital budgeting methods (priorities, operations, and return/risk); (4) calculating the weighted average cost of capital; (5) determining the hurdle rate; and (6) approving and implementing projects.

2 Learning Objective

Comment on the key elements used to gauge capital projects.

Capital-budgeting elements include cash outflows, such as the initial cash outlays, net working capital, and normal capital additions; cash inflows, which include profit, non-cash expenses, such as depreciation, and the residual value; the establishment of the economic life of a project; and sunk costs.

3 Learning Objective

Evaluate capital investment decisions by using time-value-of-money yardsticks.

Many different techniques are used for evaluating and ranking capital projects. There are the accounting methods, the payback method, the net-present-value method, the internal rate of return, and the profitability index. There are arguments for and against using each of these methods.

4 Learning Objective

Assess capital investments using decision-making techniques that measure risk.

More sophisticated methods are used to evaluate the element of risk; these methods are sensitivity analysis and risk analysis.

5 Learning Objective

Explain the reasons that can prevent a capital project from being approved.

Two reasons will cause a business to refrain from going forward with all capital budget submissions: lack of cash and the hurdle rate.

Key Terms

Accounting methods p. 524
Capital investment p. 514
Cash insufficiency p. 543
Compulsory investments p. 516
Discounted payback period p. 529
Economic life p. 522
Expense investment p. 514
Hurdle rate p. 543
Opportunity investments p. 516
Payback method p. 528
Payback reciprocal p. 529
Profitability index (PI) p. 536
Residual value p. 521
Risk analysis p. 540
Sunk costs p. 523

Review Questions

1. Why are capital projects so critical?
2. Differentiate between a capital investment and an expense investment.
3. What are compulsory investments? Give several examples.
4. What are opportunity investments? Give several examples.
5. What are the critical steps involved in the capital-budgeting process?
6. What items are usually included in the initial cash outflow?
7. Why is working capital part of cash disbursements in a capital investment, and what is its makeup?
8. Use an example to show how you would calculate the cash inflows by using the profit for the year.
9. What do we mean by residual value?
10. What do we mean by the economic life of a project?
11. Why are accounting methods not reliable yardsticks for measuring the economic desirability of capital projects?
12. Differentiate between time risk and risk conditions.
13. What are the arguments for and against the payback method?
14. What does the net present value measure?
15. What are the arguments for using the net present value method of calculating the economic viability of capital projects?
16. How is the IRR calculated?
17. How is the profitability index calculated?
18. What is sensitivity analysis?
19. What is risk analysis?
20. What factors prevent a business from proceeding with a large number of capital projects?
21. Why is capital cost allowance instead of depreciation expense used in capital budgeting?

22. Do you believe that "capital budgets are neither absolute limits on investment nor are they automatically affected by project ranking on purely quantitative grounds"? Explain.
23. Why is it that the weighted average cost of capital affects investment capability and risk tolerance?

Learning Exercises

EXERCISE 1

XYZ Inc. wants to invest $1 million in a capital project that would generate $300,000 in savings each year. The physical life of the project is 10 years, and the cost of capital is 10%. By using the above information, calculate the following:

1. Payback period
2. Net present value
3. Internal rate of return
4. Profitability index

EXERCISE 2

Today, you have some cash and the opportunity to buy a small retail store in a downtown location for the price of $700,000. This price includes all physical assets located in the retail store and the inventories. You also have the option of buying $700,000 of mutual funds paying 14% interest. The annual cash flow from the retail store operations is expected to be $115,000. In 20 years you plan to retire, and you feel that the store will be sold then for $2 million. If you wished to make the same return on your investment as you would with the investment securities, would you buy the retail store?

To answer this question, calculate the following:

1. Payback period
2. Net present value
3. Internal rate of return
4. Profitability index

EXERCISE 3

You have two options: to buy or to lease a video store.

Option 1: Purchase

Year		
0	Cost	$300,000
1	Additional cost	80,000
1	Cash flow from operations	45,000
2	Cash flow from operations	70,000
3	Cash flow from operations	90,000
4	Cash flow from operations	105,000

(Continued)

5	Cash flow from operations	140,000
6	Cash flow from operations	160,000
7	Cash flow from operations	165,000
8	Cash flow from operations	170,000
9	Cash flow from operations	175,000
10	Cash flow from operations	180,000
11	Cash flow from sale of business	400,000

If you want to make 25% on your money, should you buy the video store? To answer this question, calculate the following:

1. Net present value
2. Internal rate of return

Option 2: Leasing

You can lease a video store in another town. The net yearly cash flow from operations after deducting lease payments is estimated at $45,000 (net) from year 1 to year 10.

1. If you want to make 25% on your investment, should you lease the video store?
2. Which of the two options would you choose?

EXERCISE 4

Aaron Manufacturing Inc. intends to invest $70,000 in a modernization capital project that will generate the following cash inflows during eight years:

Year	
1	$12,000
2	17,000
3	18,000
4	23,000
5	15,000
6	11,000
7	9,000
8	8,000

Questions

1. Calculate the NPV at 12% and 18%.
2. Calculate the internal rate of return of the capital project.
3. If the annual cash flow were an even $15,000 per year for eight years, what would be the NPV at 12% and 18%?
4. What level of annual cash flow would be required to obtain a 20% IRR?
5. How would the results of (1) and (2) change if there was a capital recovery of $40,000 at the end of year 8?

EXERCISE 5

Luster Electronics Company is analyzing two capital projects, project A and project B. Each has an initial capital cost of $12,000, and the weighted average cost of capital for both projects is 12%. The projected annual cash flows are as follows:

Year	Project A	Project B
0	($12,000)	($12,000)
1	7,000	5,000
2	4,000	3,500
3	3,500	3,000
4	3,000	2,500
5	2,300	2,000
6	2,000	1,500

Questions

1. For each project, calculate the following:
   - Payback period
   - Net present value
   - Internal rate of return
   - Profitability index (using the 12% discount rate)
2. Which project or projects should be accepted if the two are independent?
3. Which project should be accepted if the two are mutually exclusive?

EXERCISE 6

Smith Manufacturing is subject to a 45% income tax rate and a 12% hurdle rate. Company management is considering purchasing a new finishing machine that is expected to cost $200,000 and reduce materials waste by $60,000 a year. The machine is expected to have a 10-year lifespan and will have a zero salvage value. For the purpose of this analysis, straight-line depreciation should be used instead of the CCA.

Questions

1. Calculate the cash flows.
2. Calculate the present value, the net present value, the internal rate of return, and the profitability index.

Cases

CASE 1: EXCEL PRODUCTS LTD.

One of Excel Products Ltd.'s strategies is to invest in new product lines. This involves periodic investments in research and development, plant, equipment, and working capital. This year, the company invested $4 million in a research and development project to develop a new product.

The managers are unsure whether they should invest an additional $9 million in capital assets for the launching of a new product line. The economic life of the project is expected to be 12 years, and straight-line depreciation will be taken over the project's lifespan. At the end of the life of the project, it is expected that the equipment and machinery will be sold for $2 million.

Working capital will also be invested over the first three years: $2 million during the first year, $1 million during the second, and $500,000 during the third; $2.9 million of that amount is expected to be recovered at the end of the 12-year period. The marketing department estimates that $1.2 million will be spent to promote the new product during the first year.

The company estimates that profit before depreciation, promotional expenses, and income taxes will be $3 million a year during the first five years, $4 million per year for the following five years, and $5 million during the last two years.

The company's income tax rate is 46%, and its cost of capital is 10%. For the purpose of this analysis, the depreciation expense will be used as the CCA tax deduction.

On the basis of the above information, calculate the following for the project:

1. Net present value
2. Internal rate of return
3. Profitability index

CASE 2: KOPLAYE INSTRUMENTS INC.

The board of directors of Koplaye Instruments Inc. is considering investing more than $5.8 million in the construction of a new plant to produce widgets for export. Although several members of the board have reservations about the project, many feel that the company has made a wise decision.

The treasurer of the company has been able to raise funds from different sources and indicates that the company's cost of capital would be 11.0%.

The board members feel that the project is not too risky and that a 15.0% hurdle rate would be acceptable.

The engineers of the company present the following information and estimate the life of the project to be 10 years.

	Costs (in 000s)	CCA
Land	$600	
Buildings	2,000	5%
Machinery/equipment	2,500	20%
Research and development	500	20%
Other assets	200	10%
Total assets	$5,800	

The marketing department indicates that there would be $300,000 invested in working capital in year 1, $250,000 in year 2, and $200,000 in year 3.

The controller provides the details of the project's projected revenue and cost data.

Year	Revenue (in $000s)	Cost of Sales (in $000s)	Other Expenses (in $000s)
1	$5,000	$2,000	$700
2	5,500	2,200	700
3	6,000	2,400	750
4	6,500	2,600	800
5	7,000	2,800	800
6	7,500	3,000	850
7	8,000	3,200	900
8	8,000	3,200	900
9	8,000	3,200	900
10	8,500	3,400	950

The company's controller estimates that $600,000 worth of the working capital will be recovered at the end of the project. The engineers estimate that the capital assets will be sold at the end of year 10 for $2 million. The company's income tax rate is 46%.

With the above information, calculate the following for the project:

1. Annual cash flow forecast during the 10-year period by using the actual CCA rates
2. Payback period
3. Net present value using the cost of capital and the hurdle rate
4. Internal rate of return
5. Profitability index

PHOTO/Yuri Arcurs/Shutterstock

CHAPTER 12

[BUSINESS VALUATION]

Learning Objectives

After reading this chapter, you should be able to:

1 Learning Objective — Differentiate between market value and book value.

2 Learning Objective — Discuss the various valuation models.

3 Learning Objective — Comment on the meaning of scanning the environment.

4 Learning Objective — Explain how to go about documenting planning assumptions.

5 Learning Objective — Show how to restate the statement of income and the statement of financial position.

6 Learning Objective — Present the various ways of price-tagging an ongoing business.

7 Learning Objective — Calculate the market value of publicly traded companies.

8 Learning Objective — Determine investment return on capital projects from an investor's (venture capitalist) perspective.

Chapter Outline

OPENING CASE

After three years of operations, CompuTech Inc. was doing extremely well in terms of meeting its financial goals. The Millers were now moving their business into another phase of its development, that of opening several retail stores. The retail concept that they had conceived had caught on very well with the general public, and the earnings generated by CompuTech were better than competing firms.

The Millers had two options in terms of growth. First, to grow slowly by opening a retail outlet (say, every two years) by using internally generated cash flows over the next 10 years and loans from conventional lenders. The second option was to approach a risk capital investor who would be interested in investing in their business. This option would help them grow more rapidly. It is a strategy that would enable the Millers to open five retail outlets in 2012, and more the year after. However, this strategy would require equity participation in CompuTech Inc. by a venture capitalist. If that were the case, the Millers would have to share business ownership.

They discussed this option with their advisors Bill Murray and May Ogaki, and both agreed that this course of action was a viable one. Bill made the following points:

> Risk capital investors are very demanding and require a substantial return on their investment. The investment proposal will have to be very complete and demonstrate clearly several key points. First, these investors want to see evidence that the investment opportunity generates a return commensurate with the risk—usually 25% to 40% compounded and adjusted for inflation. Second, they seek a good management team. Because most risk capital investors claim that management is the single most important aspect of a business opportunity, they regard reputation and quality of the team as key. Third, they will be looking for a viable exit strategy and options to realize their investment. Because these types of investors usually want to cash in their shares somewhere between three and seven years after making their investment, they want to be assured that you will have thought about how to comply with their wishes. This may require going public or selling their shares to another buyer. They might even want you to buy back the shares. Fourth, these investors will want to monitor and control their investment by having a voice on your board of directors, suggesting who should sit on your board and its composition, receiving monthly financial statements, having a say in hiring key managers, etc.

May Ogaki added the following points regarding the strategy for approaching private investors:

> You have to understand that these types of private investors often reject investment opportunities because entrepreneurs do not understand the needs, requirements, and specialization of a particular investor. If you approach the wrong investor, you run the risk of being rejected. The best approach to contacting private investors is to ensure that they will be able to provide the amount of capital that you require. Also, be certain that they are familiar with the industry that you are in and, most important, that they are located in your region. This is particularly important if they want to take an active part in your business. Another key criterion when selecting a private investor is to pick one who is a leader in the investment community and able to give you sound advice about your business. This type of deal should provide benefits to both sides: You offer a good investment opportunity in terms of a return, and the investor offers the capital you need to realize your dream.

The Millers realized that the investment proposal or business plan would have to be very convincing if they were to attract venture capital funds. The proposal would have to be very clear in providing information about financing needs, financial requirements, investment potential, and management capabilities.

Chapter Overview

Throughout this book, we have talked about book value: what a business owns and owes, or the value of a business's assets and liabilities. There was no mention of the market value of a business—how much it would be worth if it were sold as an "ongoing business." As an example, if we examine Oxford Inc.'s 2010 statement of financial position in Chapter 2 on page 101, we see that the company's total assets amount to \$3,180,000 and total liabilities to \$1,470,000 (\$900,000 in long-term borrowings and \$570,000 in current liabilities). In this case, Oxford's *book value,* being the difference between the asset and liability components of the statement of financial position, is \$1,710,000. If the owners were to sell Oxford Inc. at book price, they would sell the assets for what they are worth on the books (\$3,180,000), transfer to the new owners the liabilities (\$1,470,000), and ask for a \$1,710,000 cheque. However, if Oxford's owners were to sell the business, they would not sell it for book value but for what it is worth on the market. They would therefore assess the true market value of the business, as a going concern, and sell it for a price that would surely be different from what is shown on the books.

As shown in Figure 1.1 on page 7, this chapter deals with the third theme of investing decisions. It looks at investing decisions from the point of view of venture capitalists interested in investing in risk capital projects or buying ongoing businesses. As shown in Figure 12.1, there are six steps involved in the process of putting a price

Figure 12.1 Process for Price-Tagging an Ongoing Business

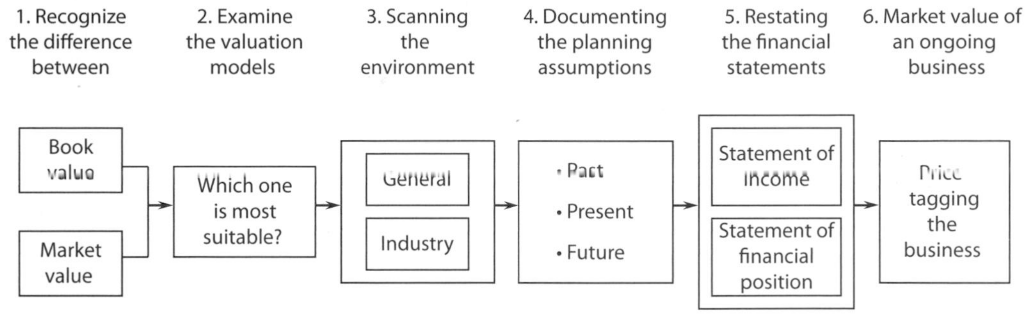

tag on an ongoing business. The first six themes of this chapter examine each of these steps while the last two themes show how to calculate the market value of publicly traded companies and the investment return on capital projects from a risk capital investor's perspective.

The first theme looks at the meaning of price-level accounting and current-value accounting, that is, the difference between book value and market value. The second theme turns to various valuation methods that organizations and investors use to determine the value of ongoing businesses. They are the liquidation value, the replacement value, the collateral value, the assessed value, and the economic value. The third theme describes what it means to scan the environment, that is, a method used during the planning process for pinning down planning assumptions or premises. The fourth theme looks at the process of formulating planning assumptions related to past performance, present capability, and future cash needs and profitability. The fifth theme shows how various components of the statement of income (revenue, cost of sales, etc.) and statement of financial position (non-current assets, inventories, trade receivables, etc.) can be restated, based on planning assumptions, to determine the real worth of a business. The sixth theme looks at how to determine the value of privately owned ongoing businesses. In particular, four methods will be explained: asset valuation, net present value, industry multipliers, and price-earnings multiple. The seventh theme looks at determining the value of publicly traded companies. The last theme of this chapter gives details about how investors, in particular venture capitalists, calculate their return on investment on both a before- and after-tax basis.

Market Value versus Book Value

1 Learning Objective

Differentiate between market value and book value.

To many individuals, it may not make much sense to report information on financial statements that does not really reflect the "true" or "real" market value of assets. For example, Table 12.1 presents a statement of financial position showing a house that was purchased in Toronto in 1970. The table indicates that after some 40 years, the $40,000 house, after allowing for depreciation, would have a $15,000 value on the books.

Table 12.1 Book Value versus Market Value

Statement of Financial Position (based on book value)

House			
Original cost	$40,000		
Depreciation	(25,000)		
Net book value	$15,000	New mortgage	$200,000

Statement of Financial Position (based on market value)

House			
Market value	$500,000	New mortgage	$200,000

As shown in the table, however, the "real value" of the house could be more in the range of $500,000. If the owner wants to borrow, say, $200,000, the owner's statement of financial position would look absurd (upper portion of the table) because the liability side of the statement of financial position would be $185,000 more than the book value of the house. As shown in this particular example, the **book value** would be considered as the accounting value of an asset (the original cost minus the accumulated depreciation). This is shown on the statement of financial position as net book value or net capital assets. However, as shown on the lower portion of the table, if the market value of the house were shown on the statement of financial position, the owner's financial structure would be more appropriate. In this case, the **market value** is considered as the price at which an item, business, or asset can be sold. Now, the owner could have done different things with the $200,000 mortgage money, such as the following:

Book value
The accounting value of an asset (the original cost minus total depreciation deductions made to date), shown on the financial statements as a firm's assets.

Market value
The price at which an item, business, or asset can be sold.

- Deposited in a bank account
- Used to make major alterations to the house
- Used to buy other assets such as a cottage, a car, or a trailer
- Used to take a year-long first-class trip around the world with family members

If the homeowner picked the fourth option, that mortgage money would have simply been spent and not shown on the asset side of the statement of financial position. If that had been the case, the statement of financial position would have shown $15,000 on the asset side and $200,000 on the liability side, similar to the amounts shown in Table 12.1.

Because of the difference between book values and market values, some individuals would challenge the validity of traditional accounting practices and ask the following question: Do financial statements prepared according to traditional accounting principles present fairly the financial position of a company in a period of inflation? Many would say no! For this reason, over the past decades, accountants have attempted to deal with this issue in order to present information on financial statements in a more sensible way. They have come up with two suggestions: price-level accounting and current-value accounting.

Price-level accounting Accounting method used to restate assets on financial statements in terms of current purchasing power (inflation).

Current-value accounting Accounting method used to restate assets on financial statements in terms of what they would be worth if purchased today.

Price-level accounting means that the numbers on financial statements are restated in terms of current purchasing power. Thus, if an asset such as a building were purchased five years ago for $1,000,000 at a time when yearly inflation was 4%, the value of the building would therefore be reported as $1,217,000.

Current-value accounting is based on what it would currently cost a business to acquire an asset with the same capability or capacity as the one it currently owns. In the above example, if the asset were to be purchased today at a cost of, say, $1,200,000 that would be the value that the existing asset would be reported on the statement of financial position.

Take the example of Eastman Technologies Inc.'s 2009 statement of financial position, shown in Table 2.4 on page 72. The statement of financial position shows the owners' equity to be $555,000. This is known as the book value and is based on the original or historical purchase price of all assets, adjusted for depreciation (total $1,800,000), less the amount of money owed to lenders, which amounts to $1,245,000.

If Eastman's owners were to sell their business for book value, they would sell the assets for what they are worth on the books, transfer the liabilities to the new owners, and ask for a $555,000 cheque. However, the company could be worth more than $555,000 for two reasons. First, Eastman's assets listed on the statement of financial position are historically based. This means that if the company purchased, in 2005, a piece of machinery for $100,000, the transaction provides an objective measure of the asset's value, which is what is shown on the company's statement of financial position. However, this 2005 value may not have much relevance today. In fact, the asset could be worth more (particularly if it was land).

Second, the assets of the company could generate excellent earnings. These earnings are not reflected in the statement of financial position. However, if the earnings produce a 20% or 25% annual return, anyone wanting to sell such a business would certainly take the level of earnings of these assets into consideration.

Some may argue that accountants should disregard the purchase price of capital assets and use a more meaningful current value in financial statements. The problem with this is that for many assets, objectively determinable current values do not exist. Therefore, accountants have opted for objective historical cost values over subjective estimates of current value.

Also, the government of Canada would have serious reservations about having company officials re-appraising capital assets higher than historical values. The reason is simple: The original $100,000 used to calculate the capital cost allowance would be increased and consequently reduce the amount of income taxes that the company would pay to the government. Furthermore, what government organization would be responsible for policing the activity of determining whether assets shown on statements of financial position reflect the true market value? Also, statements of financial position would have to be adjusted each year to reflect inflation or the changing prices of the capital assets. How would these changes be reflected on the liability and equity side of the statement of financial position?

To solve the valuation problem, the Canadian Institute of Chartered Accountants recommended that all Canadian enterprises whose securities are traded in the public market disclose in their annual reports, whenever appropriate, supplementary information about the effects of changing prices. In other words, if the value of a building is shown in the books at $600,000 (after depreciation) and the market value is $1,200,000, the annual report would comment on this difference through an appropriate footnote.

Self-Test Exercise No. 12.1

Book Value

With the information contained in CompuTech Inc.'s 2011 statement of financial position in Appendix A on page A-1, calculate the company's book value.

Valuation Models

2 Learning Objective

Discuss the various valuation models.

Different models can be used to value businesses. So far, we have talked about book value and market value. In Chapters 10 and 11, we examined the present value and the discounted cash flow methods to determine the value of an investment in capital assets (i.e., NPV and IRR). The time-value-of-money approach can also be used for business valuation purposes. Depending on the reason for valuing a business, organizations use different approaches.

In his book *Techniques of Financial Analysis*,[1] Erich Helfert identifies several valuation models. First is the *economic value*, which has to do with the ability or capacity of an asset to produce a stream of after-tax cash flows. For example, a person who invests $100,000 in Canada Savings Bonds does so in order to earn future cash receipts in the form of interest payments. However, the person may invest $100,000 in a capital asset for additional savings through productivity or for increased revenue. The investor would therefore compare the worth of the future receipts (cash inflows) to the original investment (cash outflows). The economic-value approach is a future-oriented concept based on the principles of trade-off and risk. For example, the investor might be prepared to accept a 3% return on the virtually risk-free Canada Savings Bonds investment or 25% in a revenue-generating business venture that is riskier. Risk is the price tag on the sought-after economic return. The economic value concept therefore looks at future cash flow expectations and the relative risk associated with the investment.

The second approach is based on *market value*, the worth of an asset traded on the market between a buyer and a seller without duress. The stock market is a

1. Erich A. Helfert, *Techniques of Financial Analysis*, 11th edition, Irwin/McGraw-Hill, 2002.

classic example of market value. At a particular point in time, some buyers would be prepared to buy (and others to sell) a share for what each party believes it is worth. By using this approach, the buyer and the seller are able to arrive at a mutually acceptable value for the commodity in question. A consensus is built between the two parties, where the value of a commodity is therefore subject to individual preferences and the psychological climate that exists at the time of the transaction.

Both the economic value method and the market-value approach deal with theoretical values, based exclusively on estimates. Unless the commodity is actually transferred between two parties, the market value is considered hypothetical. Consequently, one can establish a minimum and a maximum value of a commodity if a seller considers trading it on the market on a particular date.

We have already mentioned the third approach, the *book value* method. This method deals with the worth of an asset recorded on the statement of financial position, based on generally accepted accounting principles. Book value can be described as the historical value of an asset represented by its purchase price (original cost of the asset) less accumulated depreciation.

Liquidation value
Worth of an asset if sold under duress.

The **liquidation value** shows the worth of specific assets when sold separately. Liquidation means that a business must sell an asset under duress in order to obtain some cash. The liquidation value does not reflect the real worth of an asset or a business. In most cases, it is substantially below the economic value, the market value, and even the book value of an asset.

In the News 12.1 highlights several decisions made by a court judge when a business must sell its assets under duress during the liquidation process.

In The News [12.1]

Liquidating Assets of a Canadian Business Icon, Sold under Duress

After celebrating more than 100 years of growth and lucrative profits, it was in 1995 that Nortel decided, within the framework of a strategic move, to dominate the burgeoning global market for public and private networks. A company that employed more than 94,500 worldwide with market capitalization of $398 billion back in September 2000 filed for protection from creditors on January 14, 2009. A sad ending for a much-celebrated Canadian business icon!

It was in August 2009 that Nortel Networks Corp.'s remaining assets went on the selling block under the supervision of the accounting firm Ernst & Young Inc. This announcement was made after the resignation of chief executive officer Mike Zafirovski and most of the company's board members. Ontario Superior Court Judge Geoffrey Morawetz allowed Ernst & Young to administer the company's business operations and conduct the sale of Nortel's assets. The fact was that Nortel was "knee-deep in negotiations" and had no intention of replacing the outgoing CEO.

Sources: Adapted from "Nortel receiver takes over liquidation," *Ottawa Citizen*, August 15, 2009, p. D1. For more up-to-date news about Nortel's story, visit www.nortel.com.

Self-Test Exercise No. 12.2

Liquidation Value

With the information contained in CompuTech Inc.'s 2011 statement of financial position (see Appendix A at the end of this book) and the following assumptions, calculate the company's liquidation value. By liquidating the assets, the Millers would probably obtain the following:

- 30% for the non-current assets
- 50% for inventories
- 70% of trade receivables

Would the Millers have enough money to pay all their creditors? If the Millers' business cannot cover all its liabilities, what will they have to do?

Replacement value
Cost of acquiring a new asset to replace an existing asset with the same functional utility.

The **replacement value** or reproduction value is the cost of replacing an existing capital asset with an identical asset. This is a good approach for measuring the worth of an ongoing business because it is based on engineering estimates and judgments. However, this approach is flawed because it does not take into consideration the real worth of the management team, the reputation of the business, the strength of the organization, and the value of its products. Furthermore, it is difficult to equate the value of assets of an ongoing plant with so-called "equivalent assets." For example, what appears to be a "duplicate asset" may, in fact, have a higher or lower rate of productivity. With the passage of time, most physical assets are subject to some technological and physical wear and tear.

Collateral value
An assessment by lenders of the value of a particular asset taken as a guarantee for credit.

To secure their loans or other types of credit, lenders use the **collateral value** approach. This method is based on the premise that maximum credit will be allowed to a particular business against identifiable assets. Generally, in order to allow for a margin of safety, lenders will set a lower value than what the asset is worth on the market.

Assessed value
Method used by municipal governments for determining the level of property taxes.

Municipal governments use the **assessed value** approach for property taxation. The rules used to determine the assessed value vary widely between municipalities and do not necessarily reflect market values. The prime purpose of the assessed value is to levy tax revenues. Such values have little connection with other market values.

Economic value
Valuation method used to determine the ability or capacity of an asset to generate cash.

Economic value is the "price" that is placed on a business as an ongoing entity. For example, you will certainly pay more for a retail store that is operating (ongoing) than for the physical assets of a similar business that is on the brink of declaring bankruptcy. For the ongoing business, you would have to pay for the goodwill, which includes the customers, reputation, patents, employees, image, etc. This approach compares the cash outflows to future cash inflows. Future sections of this chapter will explore how to calculate values of ongoing businesses through time-value-of-money yardsticks such as the internal rate of return and the net present value approach.

Let's look at some preliminary steps involved in putting a price tag on an ongoing business. They include scanning the environment, documenting the planning assumptions, and restating the financial statements.

Scanning the Environment

3 Learning Objective

Comment on the meaning of scanning the environment.

Scanning the environment
Method used during the planning process for the purpose of pinning down planning assumptions or premises.

As shown in Figure 12.1, an important step involved in the valuation process is the nature of the industry in which a business operates and the competition it faces. This is commonly referred to as **scanning the environment** (step 3 in the figure). If the business operates in an extremely volatile and competitive environment, this affects its viability and profitability. Its risk is higher and the cash and earnings generated by the business may be more difficult to predict.

Scanning the environment means formulating planning assumptions on which the value of the business will be based. Here, we are talking about assessing the general and industry environments and formulating planning assumptions that could be expressed in quantitative and qualitative terms. *Quantitative factors* such as the GNP, labour rates, market demand, supply capability, imports, unemployment rate, and prevailing interest rates help to profile the conditions under which the business operates and to prepare the detailed operating plans related to marketing, manufacturing, research and development, engineering, and production.

Qualitative factors examine additional important perspectives such as government regulations and controls, labour activities, consumer preferences, and so on. The general environment includes economic, political, social/ethical, technological, and international conditions. Industry conditions include such factors as the profile of the consumers, number and power of suppliers, the competitive climate (rivalry among competing sellers), the threat of substitute products, potential entry of new competitors, and growth patterns. The main objective of scanning the environment is to pin down the *opportunities* and *threats* facing the business and the *strengths* and *weaknesses* within the various operating departments and divisions of a company.

The topic about planning assumptions was covered in some detail in Chapter 7 under the section "Planning Assumptions" beginning on page 310.

Documenting the Planning Assumptions

4 Learning Objective

Explain how to go about documenting planning assumptions.

As shown in Figure 12.1, the next step is to document the planning assumptions (or premises) that will help prepare the projected financial statements (step 4 in the figure). Investors will want to examine a company's past performance, determine whether the existing resources will be adequate to realize the new owners' strategic intentions, and also look at the company's projected financial statements (i.e., statement of income and statement of financial position); this will be discussed later in this chapter.

PAST PERFORMANCE

Looking at the track record of a business (for, say, the previous four or five years) is always important for investors. A history of healthy past performance supports the decision to purchase. A company's track record can be gauged in terms of overall performance, operating performance, and market performance.

Overall performance Ratios used to measure how well a business is deploying its resources.

Overall performance is a measure of how a company has used its resources in the past. Useful ratios to gauge overall performance may be grouped under two headings: those measuring financial conditions, such as current ratio, acid test ratio, and debt ratios; and those measuring profitability, such as return on revenue, return on assets, and return on equity.

Operating performance Method used for gauging the efficiency and effectiveness of management at the operating level (e.g., marketing, production).

Operating performance is a measure of managerial and technical competence. This is important in determining to what extent the existing management team is able to make the business profitable. Pertinent information on managerial performance relates to the major organizational functions. For example, under marketing is product acceptability, distribution efficiencies, sales performance; under manufacturing is operating expenses, cost of raw material, utilization of plant capacity, capital assets turnover, inventory turnover, and trade receivables turnover; and under human resources is labour turnover, quality of the workforce, and general working conditions.

Market performance Method used for gauging the efficiency and effectiveness of management within the industry in which it operates.

Market performance is a measure of a firm's position within its industry. Did it lose, maintain, or improve its market position? Was it able to manage its business under adverse environmental or industry conditions? How? Why? By how much? A number of firms compile industry data against which historical company performance can be compared. For example, *Dun & Bradstreet Canada, Standard & Poor's,* and several commercial banks disclose, through written reports or websites, pertinent industry ratios based on financial and taxation statistics. Dun & Bradstreet Canada provides with its *Canadian Industry Norms and Key Business Ratios* very comprehensive and essential financial data on company and industry key ratios related to solvency, efficiency, and profitability. Also, Standard & Poor's *Compustat Services* provides online information related to industry and company financial performance. Examples of this type of information are presented in Table 4.8 on page 183.

PRESENT CAPABILITY

If a business is purchased, the purpose of analyzing its present capability is to objectively review the company's strengths and weaknesses, and determine what needs to be done in order to carry out the new strategic and operational plans. It is also appropriate to specify how any deficiencies could be resolved. If, for instance, market share and profitability have been declining steadily, the new investors may strive to reverse this trend by introducing new products, modifying some existing products, and changing production processes to eliminate waste and inefficiencies.

The purchase of a business may call for different direction and orientation of the resources. Therefore, the analysis of present capability focuses on the following questions: Can the resources be extended? By how much? What new resources must be added in order to make the business more profitable? How will existing and new resources be integrated? Is there a need to redefine the company's mission, goals, and priorities? The new owners may have to plan in detail the new business's capabilities in the following areas:

- Human resources (technical and managerial)
- Financial resources
- Machinery, equipment, and facilities
- Sources of raw material (suppliers)
- Know-how (techniques, programs, systems)
- Internal relations (employees)
- External relations (union, image, financial community, community relations, government relations, associations)
- Organizational structure

FUTURE CASH NEEDS AND PROFITABILITY

This segment of the analysis is the most time consuming and demanding. It is difficult because, unlike analyzing past performance and diagnosing existing operating functions (e.g., marketing, production, research and development), looking into the future involves establishing a series of assumptions underlying the purchase decision. The point of the analysis is not only to justify the purchase but also to determine how much the business is really worth and what plans will be required to make the business achieve its strategic, operational, and financial goals.

Restating the Financial Statements

5 Learning Objective

Show how to restate the statement of income and the statement of financial position.

The key documents investors examine when buying a business are its financial statements, that is, the statement of income and the statement of financial position. On the statement of financial position, investors look at the book value of a company's assets and how much the business owes to creditors on these assets. By examining each item individually, investors can put a price tag on each asset to determine how much it is "actually worth," or its market value.

However, looking at the statement of financial position is not enough. The investor will also examine the statement of income to determine the company's existing and, most important, its potential earning power. The true value of a business is directly related to its ability to generate earnings, and the statement of income is the dominant element for arriving at this number. However, the earnings the existing owners are able to generate may be different from what the new owners will be able to realize. Therefore, as with the statement of financial position, there is a need to assess the individual components of the statement of income to determine, for example, if more revenue can be generated, and if there could be improvements in operating efficiencies in order to improve the bottom line. Each expense account on the statement of income is examined to determine whether cost savings could be realized through economy, downsizing, and increased productivity.

Financial ratios are used to analyze financial statements to assess a company's liquidity, debt/coverage, asset management, and profitability performance. Typical questions that investors ask include the following:

- Have these financial statements been audited?
- Is the business carrying too much debt?
- What is the real worth of the physical assets?
- Is the company profitable?
- Are the operating costs reasonable? Inflated? Out of line?
- Is the business carrying too much trade receivables compared to sales revenue? Too much inventories compared to the cost of sales? What is the real worth of these assets?
- How much is the reputation of the business worth?

After looking at a company's financial statements, the investors will formulate planning assumptions for each item included in the financial statements in order to help produce the projected statements of income and statements of financial position.

Let's now examine how each element shown on the statement of income and the statement of financial position can be restated to determine the real worth of a business.

RESTATING THE STATEMENT OF INCOME

Looking at only one year's statement of income does not give enough information to gauge the full meaning of a company's operating performance. The company's historical financial and operating performance must be analyzed in some detail. Several years are analyzed to determine how consistent a company is in generating revenue and earnings, and how each cost element has performed in the past. Specific things to look for are the following:

- Has revenue been on the increase?
- Have the operating expenses, such as cost of sales, distribution costs, and administrative expenses, been consistent from year to year?
- If we were to buy this company, would we be able to increase revenue? Reduce costs?
- If so, how would we be able to achieve such improvements?

Let's assume that an investor wants to purchase Eastman Technologies Inc. The potential investor would want to analyze the company's existing statement of income and, by exploring some of the questions mentioned earlier, could restate the numbers. In other words, every account on this statement would be examined in terms of how the business would operate under new ownership.

Eastman Technologies Inc.'s 2009 actual statement of income and 2010 restated statement are shown in Table 12.2. Comments related to the more important segments of the statement of income follow. Typical questions related to individual accounts appearing on the statement of income that can help formulate planning assumptions are listed in Table 7.2 on page 312.

Revenue

In 2009, the Eastman Technologies Inc. sold $2,500,000 worth of goods, and the new owners estimate $4,000,000 in 2010, a 60% increase. The new owner's marketing plan would determine how this growth will be realized. The so-called "marketing variables," which include selling, advertising, promotion, distribution, product, market finance, and market definition, have a direct influence on that all-important figure in the restated statements of income–revenue. Miscalculating the number of units to be sold and the selling price could severely affect profitability.

Predicting the mood of the consumer calls for a thorough investigation of wants or needs. The marketing plan usually includes the following:

- Marketing philosophy
- Description of the market (size, trends)
- Objectives (volume, price, share of market, and product mix)
- Consumer profile
- A list of the more important customers that will buy from the company (Who are they? Where are they located? Are they wholesalers? Retailers? Government organizations?)
- Marketing functions (strengths and weaknesses)
- Product description (features, patents, packaging, market test results, etc.)
- Marketing programs (sales promotion, sales organization, distribution, credit, warehousing facilities)
- Competitive advantage
- Distribution costs as a percentage of revenue
- Advertising and promotional budget
- Service arrangements
- Pricing strategies
- Warranties on products

Cost of Sales

Based on a marketing plan, each expense item included in the expense accounts shown on the statement of income is examined carefully. For example, even though the cost of sales shows one figure, the new buyers would want to examine the many different costs that are included in the $1,900,000 to determine whether efficiencies can be obtained through purchasing, freight, and manufacturing. Most expenses are incurred at the manufacturing level, through plant expenses, manufacturing costs, maintenance, raw material purchases, insurance, inventory costs, utilities, and wastage.

This plan focuses on efficiencies and shows production at competitive prices. Manufacturing's prime objective is to make a product that meets the needs of marketing (its selling agent) at the best possible price. The total manufacturing concept should incorporate the most modern techniques, equipment use, material handling, storage, inventory control, traffic, record keeping, and costing.

Calculating the break-even points for several future years of operation could highlight the relationship between revenue and costs (fixed and variable) and is considered a valid yardstick to determine level of risk. Several sensitivity checks can estimate the margin of safety regarding a price or volume drop, or an increase in operating expenses with no corresponding change in selling price.

Planning assumptions related to cost of sales looks at the following:

- Production operation (job-shop or mass production)
- Plant layout
- Production runs (capacity and forecast of utilization rate)
- Fixed and variable cost estimates (break-even point)
- List of equipment (auto equipment, trucks, vehicles)
- Raw material costs and reliability
- Maintenance costs
- Government regulations (health, security)
- Economics of a two- or three-shift schedule
- Quality control procedures

As shown in Table 12.2, vertical analysis helps to determine to what extent the new owners would be able to improve manufacturing efficiencies. Under the present owners, cost of sales as a percentage of revenue is 76% (or $0.76 for each $1.00 worth of revenue), and the new owners would show a $0.16 improvement, down to 60% (or $0.60 for each dollar's worth of revenue). Because of this exceptional improvement in cost of sales, the gross profit would jump from 24% to 40%.

Distribution Costs

The assumptions related to distribution costs can be covered in the marketing plan and reflect the planning assumptions related to sales and advertising. As shown in Table 12.2, despite the 60% increase in revenue, distribution costs will be increased by 106%, reflecting the emphasis that the new owners place on selling their products and services. As shown, distribution costs as a percentage of revenue increase from 7% to 8%.

Administrative Expenses

As shown in Table 12.2, administrative expenses include office salaries, rent, and depreciation. There is a 61% increase in these expenses, which is equivalent to the revenue increment. Because of this, total administrative expenses as a percentage of sales are maintained at 9%. Individually, office salaries increased by 12%, rental charges by 50%, and depreciation expense by 275%; the latter increase is due to the significant increase in capital assets.

Total other income and costs, which include other income, distribution costs, administrative expenses, and finance costs, increased by 113%; as a percentage of

Table 12.2 Restating the Statement of Income

	Actual – 2009		Buyer's Restated Estimates – 2010	
Revenue	$2,500,000	1.00	$4,000,000	1.00
Cost of sales	(1,900,000)	(0.76)	(2,400,000)	(0.60)
Gross profit	**600,000**	0.24	**1,600,000**	0.40
Other income	20,000	0.01	32,000	0.01
Distribution costs:				
Sales salaries	(140,000)	(0.06)	(245,000)	(0.06)
Advertising expenses	(20,000)	(0.01)	(85,000)	(0.02)
Total distribution costs	**(160,000)**	(0.07)	**(330,000)**	(0.08)
Administrative expenses:				
Office salaries	(170,000)	(0.07)	(190,000)	(0.05)
Rent	(20,000)	(0.01)	(30,000)	(0.01)
Depreciation	(40,000)	(0.01)	(150,000)	(0.03)
Total administrative expenses	**(230,000)**	(0.09)	**(370,000)**	(0.09)
Finance costs	(35,000)	(0.01)	(194,000)	(0.06)
Total other income and costs	(405,000)	(0.16)	(862,000)	(0.22)
Profit before taxes	195,000	0.08	738,000	0.18
Income tax expense	(97,500)	(0.04)	(369,000)	(0.09)
Profit for the year	$97,500	0.04	$369,000	0.09

revenue, they increased from 16% to 22%. Because of the significant improvement in revenue and costs of sales, profit before taxes increases by 278%; as a percentage of revenue, it improves from 8% to 18%.

Bottom Line

As a result of the changes in the revenue and expense accounts, profit for the year reaches $369,000, which represents a 278% increase. As a percentage of revenue, profit for the year increases from 4% to 9%. This means that in 2010, for every $1.00 of revenue, the company will make $0.09 in profit, compared to $0.04 in 2009.

The acquisition of the business by the new owners will therefore make the business more profitable. The new owners are expected to earn $369,000 in profit and $519,000 ($369,000 + $150,000) in cash flow (profit for the year plus depreciation).

Now that we know the potential earning power of the business, the next question is: Based on the statement of income projections, how much is the business worth? Restating the statement of financial position will give us this information.

RESTATING THE STATEMENT OF FINANCIAL POSITION

Table 12.3 shows Eastman Technologies Inc.'s statement of financial position of the present owners and the buyer's estimated value of individual asset and liability accounts. The buyer's estimated market value represents the new owner's projected statement of financial position. For this reason, items such as non-current assets, inventories, trade receivables, and retained earnings reflect what the investors would really buy from the present owners and how these assets would be financed. Let's look at the various components of the statement of financial position. Typical questions related to individual accounts appearing on the statement of financial position that can help formulate planning assumptions are listed in Table 7.3 on page 313.

Property, Plant, and Equipment

Property, plant, and equipment (also called capital assets or fixed assets), which include land, buildings, equipment, and machinery, are valued at $3,000,000 for an increase of 150% over the book value of the seller's assets ($1,200,000). Presumably, both the investor and the seller asked their respective real estate agents (to appraise the land value) and engineers (to evaluate the value of the machinery and equipment) to estimate the market value of the individual assets shown on the statement of financial position. Because we are dealing with the opening statement of financial position for the new company in 2010, there is no accumulated depreciation. At the end of the first fiscal year, however, this account would show a depreciation amount (drawn from the statement of income) for the use of the property, plant, and equipment assets.

Goodwill

Goodwill is a special asset that appears on a statement of financial position when a business is purchased. It represents the value of the reputation, faithful customers, and good name of the existing company. It is the excess paid for a business over the fair market value of the assets less the liabilities just prior to the purchase. In the case of Eastman, the new owners might pay $400,000 for the name and reputation. Like property, plant, and equipment, this $400,000 can be amortized over a period of years, and the amortization expense (just like depreciation used for capital assets) would be included in the buyer's statement of income.

Current Assets

Based on the market value, the worth of the current assets is estimated at $502,000. The value of both prepaid expenses ($60,000) and cash and cash equivalents ($22,000) shows their actual worth. Based on a detailed audit of the company's inventories and trade receivables accounts, they have been reduced to $170,000 and $250,000 respectively.

Share Capital

Share capital represents the amount of cash that the buyers would have to put up in order to buy the business. An amount of $1,457,000 would be invested in the business by the new owners, which represents 37% of the total equity and liabilities.

Table 12.3 Restating the Statement of Financial Position

	Actual – 2009		Buyer's Restated Estimates – 2010	
Assets				
Non-current assets				
Property, plant, and equipment	$1,340,000	0.75	$3,000,000	0.77
Accumulated depreciation	(140,000)	(0.08)	—	0.00
			3,000,000	0.77
Goodwill	—	—	400,000	0.10
Total non-current assets	1,200,000	0.67	3,400,000	0.87
Current assets				
Inventories	218,000	0.12	170,000	0.04
Trade receivables	300,000	0.17	250,000	0.06
Prepaid expenses	60,000	0.03	60,000	0.02
Cash and cash equivalents	22,000	0.01	22,000	0.01
Total current assets	600,000	0.33	502,000	0.13
Total assets	$1,800,000	1.00	$3,902,000	1.00
Equity and liabilities				
Equity				
Share capital	$300,000	0.17	$1,457,000	0.37
Contributed surplus			—	—
Retained earnings	255,000	0.14	—	—
Total other comprehensive income/(loss)	—	—	—	—
Total equity	555,000	0.31	1,457,000	0.37
Non-current liabilities				
Long-term borrowings	800,000	0.44	2,000,000	0.51
Current liabilities				
Trade and other payables	195,000	0.12	195,000	0.05
Short-term borrowings	150,000	0.08	150,000	0.04
Accrued expenses	20,000	0.01	20,000	0.01
Taxes payable	80,000	0.04	80,000	0.02
Total current liabilities	445,000	0.25	445,000	0.12
Total liabilities	1,245,000	0.69	2,445,000	0.63
Total equity and liabilities	$1,800,000	1.00	$3,902,000	1.00

*Note: **Shaded amounts*** denote items that are taken into consideration for the purchase of the business.

Long-Term Borrowings

As shown in Table 12.3, the buyers will borrow $2,000,000 to purchase some of the assets of the business.

Current Liabilities

All items reported under current liabilities are brought forward from the seller's statement of financial position to the new owner's opening statement of financial position. In Table 12.3, current liabilities amount to $445,000, or 12% of the company's total equity and liabilities.

Price-Tagging an Ongoing Business

6 Learning Objective

Present the various ways of price-tagging an ongoing business.

Now that we have created the projected statement of income and opening statement of financial position, we can determine how much the business is worth as a going concern. The going-concern value relates to the ability or capacity of an asset to produce a stream of after-tax cash flows. The investor would therefore compare the worth of the future receipts (cash inflows) to the original investment (cash outflows). The going-concern value approach is a future-oriented concept based on the principles of trade-off and risk.

Four techniques will be used to make that calculation: asset valuation, net present value, industry multipliers, and price-earnings multiple.

ASSET VALUATION

Asset valuation Methodology used to restate the numbers appearing on financial statements.

The **asset valuation** method looks at the buyer's restated statement of financial position (Table 12.3) and selects the items that the buyer is interested in purchasing. These items are shown in Table 12.4. The only assets that are of interest to the new owners are property, plant, and equipment; goodwill; inventories; and trade receivables. Property, plant, and equipment include assets such as land, buildings, equipment, machinery, and tools. These assets would be listed in detail at book price and market price. The value of these assets is $3 million. The other asset that the buyer will purchase is the goodwill. As shown, this is valued at $400,000.

The other item that the buyer will probably keep is trade and other payables ($195,000) because they are used to finance current assets such as inventories

Table 12.4 Cost of the Business

Property, plant, and equipment	$3,000,000
Goodwill	400,000
Total non-current assets	3,400,000
Inventories	170,000
Trade receivables	250,000
Total current assets	420,000
Less: trade and other payables	195,000
Net working capital	225,000
Purchase price	$3,625,000

($170,000) and trade receivables ($250,000). Based on the reappraised value, the buyer will purchase the seller's net working capital for an amount of $225,000 (that is, $170,000 + $250,000 – $195,000).

As shown in Table 12.4, the seller is asking $3,625,000 for the business. The question is this: Based on the projected statement of income, is the asking price worth it? The potential buyers could invest $3,625,000 in investment securities at 10% a year (before tax) and earn $362,500 a year. If they buy the business instead, they should expect superior earnings because of the risk factor.

NET PRESENT VALUE METHOD

The net present value method is based on the time-value-of-money concept and takes into account cash inflows and cash outflows. This topic was covered in Chapters 10 and 11. As shown in Table 12.5, the net present value is calculated by taking into account both the weighted average cost of capital and the hurdle rate. The seller's asking price is $3,625,000. This is the amount of cash that the buyer would have to pay and includes non-current assets, goodwill, and working capital (see Table 12.4).

The next step is to determine the amount of cash that would be generated over the life of the project. From the buyer's statement of income shown in Table 12.2, the cash inflow is estimated at $519,000. This is made up of the profit for the year in the amount of $369,000 plus depreciation amounting to $150,000. If we assume that the owner will want to keep the business for a period of 10 years, after which he or she will want to sell it for, say, $6,000,000, the net present value of the purchase,

Table 12.5 NPV Based on the Weighted Cost of Capital and the Hurdle Rate

In $	Cost of Capital 10%	Hurdle Rate 20%	Hurdle Rate 20%
Purchase price (outflows)	(3,625,000)	(3,625,000)	(3,144,968)
Cash inflows			
Cost of capital			
519,000 × 6.1446	3,189,047		
Hurdle rate			
519,000 × 4.1925		2,175,908	2,175,908
Sale of business			
Cost of capital			
6,000,000 × 0.38554	2,313,240		
Hurdle rate			
6,000,000 × 0.16151		969,060	969,060
Net present value	1,877,287	(480,032)	0

using a 10% discount rate, gives a positive $1,877,287. This means that the buyer would earn 10% on the investment plus $1,877,287 over the 10-year period.

In the News 12.2 shows how cash flow projections based on somewhat vague planning assumptions can even satisfy investors to fund research and development projects.

In The News [12.2]

No Money Is Spared in R&D When It Comes to Developing a Product Aimed to Change the Face of Optical Discs

WOW, what a sting on Sony's Blu-ray discs! Sony, the inventor of Blu-ray, had just won the battle of the high-definition DVD brands. It was only in July 2009 that Toshiba, its HD DVD rival, officially decided to surrender. And now, Sony is in for another big fight. This time, the challengers are the joint effort of two conglomerates: Mitsubishi Group and Hitachi Ltd., who are now putting on their venture capitalist hats. Both companies are in combat mode to wipe out Sony, the "emperor" of DVDs.

Hitachi Ltd., Mitsubishi Chemical Corp., and other organizations are in the process of developing the next-generation of optical discs. The new disc will have the capacity to store 25 times more data than a Blu-ray disc. This new technology is expected to be on the market by 2012. The new technology has the potential to (1) complement cloud computing, which allows more storage offline; (2) allow more efficient use of personal computers; and (3) increase the storage capacity of current PC hard drives. It is estimated that with a combination of hard drive and optical disc storage use based on the frequency data accessed, the power use per PC could be reduced by as much as 40%.

Source: Adapted from Yomiuri Shimbun, "Super disc promises to leave Blu-ray in shadows," *Ottawa Citizen*, August 11, 2009, p. D3. For more information about Hitachi and Mitsubishi, visit http://www.hitachi.com and http://www.m-kagaku.co.jp/english/corporate/index.html, respectively.

If the weighted average cost of capital were used as the rate for approving the purchase, the buyer would certainly buy the business. However, because of the risk involved, if the buyer's hurdle rate on the investment is 20%, the net present value would be negative, that is, a $480,032 negative amount. In this case, the buyer would earn less than the expected 20%. The buyer would probably not buy the business for the $3,625,000 asking price. However, if the buyer insists on making a 20% return, a counteroffer of $3,144,968 ($3,625,000 – $480,032) could be made—which, in this case, would make the cash outflow equal to the cash inflows. At that price, the IRR would be 20%. On the other hand, if the buyer still purchases the business for the $3,625,000 asking price, an internal rate of return of only 17.3% would be made.

INDUSTRY MULTIPLIERS

Industry multipliers A standard used to determine the value or worth of a business.

Another approach to putting a price tag on a business is the use of **industry multipliers**, which is a standard used to determine the value or worth of a business. Here, the buyer or seller would refer to a list of multipliers that applies to a particular industry. Although many individuals use multipliers, some (particularly buyers) refrain from using them because they focus too much on gross revenue, rather than the profit for the year. The argument is this: It's not the top line that counts but the bottom line.

Table 12.6 presents a list of typical industry multipliers. Although some of them are accurate in some industries, they should still be used with caution because they tend to simplify, to a large extent, the worth of a business. Nevertheless, these multipliers can be used as a complementary tool to obtain a rough estimate of an asking price. Using these multipliers with another technique such as NPV may result in roughly the same asking price. If that's the case, the valuation price would be an approximate estimate.

Because of a wide variation in gross revenue from year to year, it may be wise to calculate the asking price by using the company's last three or four years' statements of income. One may also want to average out the last three years' gross revenue to calculate the asking price.

PRICE-EARNINGS MULTIPLE

In the case of Eastman Technologies Inc., a price-earnings multiple can also be used to determine the value of the company. A price-earnings multiple is equal to the inverse of a capitalization rate. For example, if the investors want to use an 11% capitalization rate, the

Table 12.6 Industry Multipliers

Industry	Multiplier
Travel agencies	0.05 to 0.1 × annual gross sales
Advertising agencies	0.75 × annual gross sales
Collection agencies	0.15 to 0.2 × annual collections + equipment
Employment agencies	0.75 × annual gross sales
Insurance agencies	1 to 2 × annual renewal commissions
Real estate agencies	0.2 to 0.3 × annual gross commissions
Rental agencies	0.2 × annual net profit + inventory
Retail businesses	0.75 to 1.5 × annual net profit + inventory + equipment
Sales businesses	1 × annual net profit
Fast food (non-franchise)	0.5 to 0.7 × monthly gross sales + inventory
Restaurants	0.3 to 0.5 × annual gross sales, or 0.4 × monthly gross sales + inventory
Office supply distributors	0.5 × monthly gross sales + inventory
Newspapers	0.75 to 1.5 × annual gross sales
Printers	0.4 to 0.5 × annual net profit + inventory + equipment
Food distributors	1 to 1.5 × annual net profit + inventory + equipment
Building supply retailers	0.25 to 0.75 annual net profit + inventory + equipment
Job shops	0.5 × annual gross sales + inventory
Manufacturing	1.5 to 2.5 × annual net profit + inventory
	0.75 × annual net profit + equipment + inventory (including work in progress)
Farm/heavy equipment dealers	0.5 × annual net profit + inventory + equipment
Professional practices	1 to 5 × annual net profit
Boat/camper dealers	1 × annual net profit + inventory + equipment

Source: Richard W. Snowden, *Buying a Business* New York: AMACOM, 1994, pp. 150–151

price-earnings multiple would be 9.1 (100 ÷ 11%). If they want to use 13%, the price-earnings multiple would be 7.7 (100 ÷ 13%). To determine the company's market value by using the price-earnings multiple, the investor would therefore have to determine the appropriate capitalization rate and multiply this rate by maintainable after-tax cash flows, which in the case of Eastman is $519,000 ($369,000 + $150,000). If the investors want to use a 13% capitalization, the value of the business would be $3,996,300 ($519,000 × 7.7).

Market Value of Publicly Traded Companies

7 Learning Objective

Calculate the market value of publicly traded companies.

To calculate the value of publicly traded companies, analysts would have to use the number of common shares issued and the share market price. Here, in order to calculate the market value of the equity, one has to multiply the number of outstanding common shares by the share price on the last day that the shares were traded on the stock market.

Let's assume that Eastman Technologies Inc. is a publicly traded company and has 30,000 shares outstanding. With a $555,000 net worth, that means that the book value of each share outstanding would be $18.50 ($555,000 ÷ 30,000). However, if the shares were traded at, say, $25.00, the market value of the company, or the equity portion of the statement of financial position, would be $750,000 ($25.00 × 30,000). In this case, the ratio of the market value to the book value would be 1.35 times ($25.00 ÷ $18.50).

Self-Test Exercise No. 12.3

Common Share Valuation

The shareholders of CompuTech Inc., Len and Joan Miller, want to go public and are considering selling shares. CompuTech's statement of financial position for the year 2011 is as follows:

CompuTech Inc.
Statement of Financial Position
as at December 31, 2011

Non-current assets	$402,000	Share capital	$170,000
Current assets	235,000	Retained earnings	135,000
		Total equity	305,000
		Long-term borrowings	200,000
		Current liabilities	132,000
		Total liabilities	332,000
Total assets	$637,000	Total equity and liabilities	$637,000

Assume that CompuTech Inc. has 20,000 shares outstanding, which are currently trading at $35.50.

Questions

1. What is the book value of the shares?
2. What is the market value of the shares?
3. What is the ratio of the market value to the book value?

Return on Investment from an Investor's (Venture Capitalist) Perspective

8 Learning Objective

Determine investment return on capital projects from an investor's (venture capitalist) perspective.

Finding the value of an ongoing business for investors such as venture capitalists using the time-value-of-money approach can be done in a more detailed and sophisticated way. The method that will be described in the next few pages allows for the calculation of investments made in a business by several investors. For example, if several investors were interested in buying Eastman Technologies Inc., the return on investment for the portion of the investment made by each investor would be calculated. In this particular example, however, we are assuming that one investor (owner/manager) is interested in buying Eastman and will be referred to as the "investor."

Four steps are involved for calculating the return on investment based on this particular time-value-of-money yardstick. For example, using the four-step method, let's assume that a new owner or an investor wants to buy Eastman Technologies Inc. for $3.4 million in 2009. The amount comprises capital assets and goodwill. An additional $225,000 will be invested in working capital during the first year of operations, that is, 2010. The financial statements presented in Tables 12.2 and 12.3 will be used in the four-step calculation process as follows:

Step 1: The yearly after-tax cash flow
Step 2: The projected residual value
Step 3: The estimated market value
Step 4: The investor's before- and after-tax return (IRR)

Step 1: The Yearly After-Tax Cash Flow

The first step for calculating Eastman Technologies Inc.'s market value is to determine its after-tax cash flow forecast for the years 2010 to 2014. As shown in Table 12.7, Eastman's after-tax cash flow from operations increases from $519,000 (statement of income is drawn from Table 12.2) to $1,408,000 by 2014. As shown in Table 12.7, during the five-year period, Eastman will continue to invest in capital assets and in working capital. Investments in capital assets will be $100,000 a year while investment in working capital fluctuates on a yearly basis (e.g., $225,000 in 2010 and $410,000 in 2014). The lower portion of Table 12.7 shows how the increments in the working capital accounts were calculated and includes inventories, trade receivables, and trade and other payables.

After adding the investment in capital assets and working capital to the after-tax cash flow from operations, Eastman shows a negative cash flow in the amount of $3.4 million in 2009 (end of year investment) to a positive cash flow of $1,258,000 in 2014. This discretionary after-tax cash flow for each year in the forecast period is then discounted to its present value using an acceptable discount rate, in this case, 20% (which is the hurdle rate). (See the discount factors in Appendix B at the end of the book that were used to calculate the present value amount between 2010 and 2014.) The 20% discount factor reflects the risk associated with the nature of Eastman's operations. As shown, the projected cash flows lose more value (because of discounting) as

TABLE 12.7 Eastman Technologies Inc.'s After-Tax Cash Flows

In $000s	2009 Actual	2010 Forecast	2011 Forecast	2012 Forecast	2013 Forecast	2014 Forecast
Revenue		4,000	4,700	5,800	6,700	7,700
Cost of sales		(2,400)	(2,800)	(3,500)	(4,200)	(4,600)
Gross profit		1,600	1,900	2,300	2,500	3,100
Other income		32	30	28	30	30
Distribution costs		(330)	(360)	(380)	(400)	(420)
Administrative expenses		(370)	(400)	(410)	(420)	(440)
Finance costs		(194)	(270)	(288)	(300)	(300)
Total other income and costs		(862)	(1,000)	1,050	(1,090)	(1,130)
Profit before taxes		738	900	1,250	1,410	1,970
Income tax expense		(369)	(405)	(563)	(645)	(887)
Profit for the year		369	495	687	765	1,083
Add back: depreciation		150	200	250	300	325
Cash flow from operations		**519**	**695**	**937**	**1,065**	**1,408**
Capital assets	(3,400)	(100)	(100)	(100)	(100)	(100)
Incremental working capital	—	(225)	(45)	(60)	(30)	(50)
Total additional investment	(3,400)	(325)	(145)	(160)	(130)	(150)
Cash flow with additional investments		194	550	777	935	1,258
Discount factor (20%)	0.0000	0.8333	0.69444	0.57870	0.48225	0.40188
Annual discounted cash flows	**(3,400)**	**162**	**382**	**450**	**451**	**506**
Total present value for the five years	**(1,449)**					
Incremental working capital						
Inventories		(170)	(200)	(240)	(260)	(300)
Trade receivables		(250)	(300)	(350)	(400)	(450)
Total		(420)	(500)	(590)	(660)	(750)
Less: Trade and other payables		195	230	260	300	340
Net increase in working capital for the year		(225)	(270)	(330)	(360)	(410)
Previous year's working capital			225	270	330	360
Incremental working capital			(45)	(60)	(30)	(50)

we reach the end of the forecast period. For example, the cash flow generated during the second year of the forecast (2011) is discounted for two years only, while cash flow for the fifth year (2014) is discounted for five years. The cumulative net present value of the cash flows for the six years (2009–2014) is negative in the amount of $1,449,000 (−$3,400 + $1,951).

Self-Test Exercise No. 12.4

Cumulative Cash Flows and Net Present Value

By using 11% as CompuTech's weighted average cost of capital and the estimates shown below, calculate the following values for one of the company's retail stores:

1. The yearly present values
2. The cumulative net present values

In $000s	Year 1	Year 2	Year 3	Year 4	Year 5
Projected profit for the year	80	90	100	110	120
Projected capital cost allowance	6	8	9	10	11
Projected incremental investments in working capital	2	3	2	1	1

Step 2: The Projected Residual Value

At the end of the forecast period (in the case of Eastman, in 2014), Eastman will likely remain viable and continue to generate cash flows. The residual value represents the estimated present value of the after-tax cash flows expected to be earned throughout the company's lifespan. As shown below, the components of the residual value calculation include the calculation of the maintainable cash flow from operations beyond 2014 and the capitalization calculation.

Maintainable cash flow from operations. The cash flows before income tax expense for the last year of the forecast period (in the case of Eastman, 2014) are considered representative of the maintainable cash flows. As shown below, Eastman's cash flow from operations is $1,408,000. This figure is drawn from Table 12.7. Income tax expense and an estimate of annual ongoing capital spending (future average annual spending on equipment and other capital assets) are deducted to determine the maintainable after-tax cash flow. As shown, capital spending for each year after 2014 is estimated at $100,000. This amount will be spent each year to maintain the business at revenue levels equal to the last year of the forecast, that is, 2014. The illustration also shows that there will be a $50,000 yearly increase in working capital accounts. It is assumed here that Eastman will remain at the 2014 level of operations, generating a steady yearly cash flow from operations in the amount of $1,258,000.

	2014 Forecast
Cash flow from operations	$1,408,000
Sustainable spending in capital assets	(100,000)
Incremental working capital	(50,000)
Total additional investments	(150,000)
Net cash flow	$1,258,000

Capitalization calculation. The next step in calculating the residual value is determining the capitalization rate. Using capitalization is the same as discounting a maintainable cash flow in perpetuity (i.e., continually). The residual value is calculated by dividing the maintainable after-tax cash flow in the amount of $1,258,000 by an acceptable rate of return. In this case, the capitalization rate used for Eastman is reduced by 2% (from the 20% rate used in Table 12.7) to 18%. This difference between the discount rate used in the Table and the capitalization rate is adjusted for inflation, growth, and risk. Eastman's residual value amounts to $6,989,000.

Cash flow with incremental investments	$1,258,000
Divided by capitalization rate (20% less 2%)	18%
Residual value	$6,989,000

The last step in estimating Eastman's residual value is to calculate the present value of the $6,989,000 amount to be received in 2014 to the end of 2009 (the year of the investment by the new owner). By using the same 20% discount rate as the one used in Table 12.7, the present value of the residual value would be $2,809,000 and is calculated as follows:

Residual value	$6,989,000
Present value factor at 20%	0.40188
Present value of the residual value	$2,809,000

Self-Test Exercise No. 12.5

Capitalization Rate

Using the following information, calculate the after-tax cash flow from CompuTech Inc.'s operations.

Accounts	Amounts
Revenue	$800,000
Income tax expense	42,000
Distribution costs	135,000
Cost of sales	406,000
Administrative expenses	110,000
Finance costs	30,000

Depreciation amounts of $80,000 are included in both distribution costs and administrative expenses.

Questions

1. Calculate the value of the business as a going concern by using the following capitalization rates: 15% and 25%.
2. By using a 30% discount rate, calculate the present value of the business if it had a 15-year lifespan.
3. If an investor were to invest $300,000 in the business, how much cash should the business generate each year during a five-year period if the investor wants to earn 25%?

Step 3: The Estimated Market Value

This step in the process involves the calculation of Eastman's estimated fair market value. As shown below, the company's fair market value is estimated at $1,359,000, which reflects Eastman's five-year after-tax discounted cash flow in the amount of a negative $1,449,000 (drawn from Table 12.7) and its estimated positive residual value of $2,809,000 that was calculated in step 2.

Present value of cash flow from operations	($1,449,000)	(step 1)
Plus present value of the residual value	2,809,000	(step 2)
Estimated fair market value	$1,360,000	

Step 4: The Investor's Before- and After-Tax Return (IRR)

The last step involves the calculation of the investor's return on investment on a before- and after-tax basis. As shown below, the buyer invests $3,400,000 by the end of 2009 in Eastman (excluding the $225,000 amount in working capital, an amount that will be invested in 2010). As shown in Table 12.7, the business generates an after-tax cash flow from operations (with additional investments) in the amount of $1,258,000 by the year 2014. It is assumed that the investor would probably want to sell the business at a future date at a certain price. The total value at the time of the sale is determined by multiplying the maintainable after-tax cash flow of $1,258,000 by a multiple. The multiple is equal to the inverse of a capitalization rate. In this case, a 12.5% capitalization rate is used, which is equal to an eight times earnings multiple.

As shown below, by using the eight times multiple, the value at the time of selling the business is estimated at $10,064,000. The investor will have a 100% ownership in the business. By using a 24.2% discount rate, the present value of the $10,064,000 would be equivalent to the $3,400,000 investment. This discount rate would therefore be considered the investor's before-tax internal rate of return (IRR).

In $000s	2009	2010	2011	2012	2013	2014
Before-tax rate of return						
Initial investment	(3,400)					
Total value at exit						
After-tax cash flow						1,258
Multiple						8.0
Total value at time of selling						10,064
Initial investment	(3,400)					
Total cash flows	(3,400)					10,064
Before-tax return (IRR)	*24.2%*					

Similar calculations would have to be done to determine the investor's IRR on an after-tax basis. The after-tax calculation is shown below. The investor would receive $10,064,000 at the time of selling the business. The original $3,400,000 investment is then deducted from the cash proceeds, which would leave the investor with a capital gain on the investment of $6,664,000. If the investor's taxable portion is estimated at 75%, this means that the tax payable would be $2,499,000. If the investor is in the 50% tax bracket, an after-tax amount of $7,565,000 would be received. By using a 17.3% discount rate, the present value of the $7,565,000 would be equivalent to the $3,400,000 investment made by the investor. The discount rate would therefore be considered the investor's after-tax IRR. This discount rate is determined subjectively and represents the rate of return the buyer requires to assume the perceived risk associated with achieving the level of forecast cash flow.

In $000s	
After-tax rate of return	
Proceeds received on exit	10,064
Initial investment	(3,400)
Capital gains on investment	6,664
Taxable portion (say, 75%)	(4,998)
Investor's tax payable (50%)	2,499
Gross proceeds received on exit	10,064
Investor's tax payable	(2,499)
Net after-tax proceeds to investor	7,565

	2009	2010	2011	2012	2013	2014
After-tax rate of return						
Initial investment	($3,400)					
Total value at exit						
Total value at time of selling						$7,565
Initial investment	($3,400)					
Total cash flows	($3,400)					$7,565
After-tax return (IRR)	*17.3%*					

Self-Test Exercise No. 12.6

Business Valuation Using the Discounted Cash Flow (DCF) Method

The Millers are looking at the possibility of opening three new retail stores for CompuTech Inc. Len will be approaching a risk capital investor, Oscar Eden, hoping to obtain a $200,000 amount in equity participation. This amount represents 20% of the company's equity share.

When the Millers had their first meeting with Oscar, he presented the following financial projections:

Year	Cash Flow from Operations	Investments	Working Capital
0	—	$200,000	—
1	$200,000	200,000	$100,000
2	300,000	300,000	100,000
3	500,000	300,000	50,000
4	600,000	50,000	25,000
5	900,000	50,000	25,000

Self-Test Exercise No. 12.6 (continued)

During the conversation, Len and Oscar agreed that 15% should be used as a discount rate to calculate the present value of the company's cash flow and also as a capitalization rate. Oscar pointed out that he hoped that at the end of five years, when he would want to make his exit, the company would be worth at least five times its last year's cash flow.

Questions

1. What is CompuTech's net present value?
2. What is CompuTech's internal rate of return using only the five-year projections?
3. What is CompuTech's present value of the residual value?
4. What is CompuTech's fair market value?
5. What is Oscar Eden's internal rate of return on his investment?

In the News 12.3 shows why venture capitalists in Canada should be encouraged to invest more money in businesses engaged in research and development, and why the Canadian government should boost new-technology success stories via venture capitalist funds.

In The News [12.3]

Venture Capitalists Play a Key Role in the Development of the High-Tech Industry in Canada

Venture capital is not new. It has been around for more than 70 years, going back to 1938 when Laurance S. Rockefeller helped finance the creation of both Eastern Air Lines and Douglas Aircraft. But it was in 1946 that the American Research and Development Corporation, founded by Georges Doriot, the "father of venture capitalism" (former dean of Harvard Business School), that true private equity investments began to emerge. And now, it was just a few years ago that venture capitalists invested some $6.6 billion in 797 deals in the United States. A recent survey found that a majority (69%) of venture capitalists predict that venture investments in the U.S. will level between $20 and $29 billion in just a few years.

Well, with this type of introduction, no wonder why the Capital and Private Equity Association called on Industry Minister Tony Clement to establish a blue-chip panel to look at how to boost venture capital in Canada in an effort help Canadian new-technology success stories. The association noted that in 2008, funds invested by Canadian venture capital funds were only $1.3 billion into all technology sectors. That accounted for a 36% drop from the $2.1 billion invested in the previous year. This issue emerged as a result of the proposed US$1.13 billion sale of Nortel Networks Corp. assets to Ericsson of Sweden. The lobby group representing Canada's venture capitalists indicated that the government had to act promptly in order to ensure that maximum net benefit should accrue to Canada when intellectual property (in this case, Nortel) could eventually be transferred to other countries.

Source: Adapted from Paul Vieira, "Venture capitalists' group seeks tech strategy," *Ottawa Citizen*, July 31, 2009, p. F1. For more information about venture capital in Canada, visit the website http://www.cvca.ca.

[DECISION-MAKING IN ACTION]

Robin Pedwell, CEO of Amoco Sauna Inc., is considering launching a new product line in the Canadian market by the early part of 2011. The company is in the process of completing a prototype beauty care product—a compact, portable, and multifunctional facial sauna. If Amoco is successful in Canada, Pedwell would then market the product line in the U.S. and European markets.

The development of the multifunctional facial sauna began in 2007, when the company's marketing research department studied the market opportunities for health and beauty care products. The favourable market results encouraged Pedwell to design and develop a new line of products—a "family of products"—for health and beauty care. The leading product, called "Beauty Facial Sauna," was a portable, hand-held, steam-generating apparatus.

The only obstacle to Pedwell's dream was a shortage of the cash he needed to complete his research in 2010 on the facial sauna and to market the new product line in the early months of 2011. Because of the nature of the business venture, he was aware that conventional lenders would not be interested in financing his project. He realized that his only option was to obtain funds from high-risk capital investors. He was aware that obtaining funds from these types of investors would be a very difficult, time-consuming process, and also very expensive.

Therefore, Pedwell approached a long-time friend and financial adviser with excellent connections in the high-risk capital markets, Norm Woodstock. Woodstock would help Pedwell develop an investment proposal and a strategy on how to approach high-risk investors. The first thing that Woodstock suggested was to determine the value of the business as a going concern several years after the launching of the new product line. In other words, he was asking the question: What will Amoco's financial statements look like several years from now? Woodstock knew that high-risk investors are particularly interested in investing money in highly successful ventures, those that offer very high returns (somewhere in the 25% to 35% range). Also, these types of investors want to make sure that they have a clear option about how they would go about making their exit from the company by selling their shares four to five years after their initial investment. An exit strategy could take the form of a public offering or the possibility that Pedwell himself would buy back the investors' shares.

Before going through the detailed calculation and preparing the investment proposal, Woodstock analyzed Amoco's financial statements and indicated to Pedwell the different methods that could be used to determine the value of his company. He pointed out four methods: the book value, the liquidation value, the going-concern value, and the net present value method to calculate the investors' return on their investment.

Woodstock pointed out that the DCF method is the most suitable method to determine the real value of Amoco's potential return on the investor's investment. However, he decided to calculate the value of the business by using all methods just for the sake of getting some idea about Amoco's different economic values.

Book Value

As Woodstock pointed out to Pedwell, the book value of Amoco is the company's net worth or shareholders' equity, based on generally accepted accounting principles. Simply subtracting the liabilities from the book value of Amoco's assets gives the economic value called shareholders' equity or net worth. Illustration 1 shows Amoco's book value for year-end 2010. As shown in the illustration, the book value of the company is estimated at $700,000.

Liquidation Value

Woodstock explained that the liquidation value would be useful only if Amoco were sold in order to satisfy its creditors. By using this approach, tangible assets such as land usually have a liquidation value close to their market value. Inventories and trade receivables, on the other hand, are usually valued at less than what is shown in the books. Woodstock also added that in order to determine the liquidation value, all of Amoco's assets would be assigned a distressed value while all debts would be listed at book value. As he pointed out, most assets sold under duress are discounted from their book value. The difference between the distressed value of the assets and the actual or book value of the liabilities is considered the liquidation value. This value would not reflect Amoco's real worth.

In most instances, however, a liquidation value is substantially less than the market value and book value. This method would be used only if Amoco were in serious financial trouble and had to liquidate its assets to pay the creditors. As shown in Illustration 1, Amoco's liquidation value is estimated at $245,000. The book value of the company's assets is reduced by $455,000, or 28%, down to $1,145,000 while the liabilities (both current and long-term) remain the same at the $900,000 level.

Illustration 1
Estimated Statement of Financial Position
For year-end December 31, 2010
In $

	Book Value	Liquidation Value
Assets		
Non-current assets		
Property, plant, and equipment	900,000	700,000
Other non-current assets	50,000	20,000
Total non-current assets	950,000	720,000
Current assets		
Inventories	200,000	200,000
Trade receivables	300,000	125,000
Other current assets	150,000	100,000
Total current assets	650,000	425,000
Total assets	1,600,000	1,145,000
Equity and liabilities		
Total equity	700,000	245,000
Liabilities		
Long-term borrowings	300,000	300,000
Current liabilities	600,000	600,000
Total liabilities	900,000	900,000
Total liabilities and owners' equity	1,600,000	1,145,000
	Book value	Liquidation value

Going-Concern Value

Woodstock indicated that the going-concern value was a more relevant approach for determining a price tag for an ongoing business because it was related to the ability or capacity of Amoco to produce a stream of after-tax cash flows. This method would show the projected statements of income after the new sauna product line was introduced in Canada. As indicated to Pedwell, this forecast would require the help of many managers in the company involved in marketing, production, research and development, administration, finance, etc. Woodstock indicated that a high-risk investor would base his or her investment decision on revenue, distribution and manufacturing costs, profit for the year, and cash flow estimates. Most importantly, the investor would want to be confident about the reliability and accuracy of all revenue and cost estimates contained in the statement of income.

As Woodstock pointed out, typical non-risk investors are prepared to accept a 5% return if money is invested in relatively risk-free investments such as Canada Savings Bonds. However, high-risk investors, those prepared to invest in companies such as Amoco, expect to earn a return between 25% and 35% for such a revenue-generating business that presents some risk. Woodstock further explained that the level of risk is the price tag that helps determine a sought-after economic return. Therefore, the going-concern value incorporates future cash flow expectations and the relative risk associated with an ongoing business.

Illustration 2 presents Amoco's projected statement of income for 2011, that is, the year that Amoco expects to launch the new product line. As shown, Amoco anticipates earning $450,000 in profit and $550,000 in after-tax cash flow ($450,000 + $100,000). If a potential investor wants to earn, say, 20%, Amoco's going-concern value would be $2,750,000 million ($550,000 ÷ 20%). The $550,000 amount represents the maintainable, perpetual, or indefinite cash flows that

Illustration 2
Amoco Sauna Inc.
Projected Statement of Income
For the Year 2011
In $000s

Revenue		5,000	
Cost of sales		(2,960)	
Gross profit		2,040	
Other income	10		
Total distribution costs	(800)		
Total administrative expenses	(500)		
Finance costs	(100)		
Total income/costs		(1,390)	
Profit before taxes		650	
Income tax expense		(200)	
Profit for the year		450	
Add back depreciation		100	
After-tax cash flow from operations		550	550
Divided by capitalization rate		20%	30%
Going-concern value		2,750	1,833

Amoco expects to generate. A capitalization rate is a discount rate used to find the present value of a series of future receipts. In this particular instance, a 20% capitalization rate is the required rate of return expected by risk capital investors from Amoco. Woodstock indicated that this rate is based on a number of subjective factors and conditions at the time of valuation.

If the risk capital investors found Amoco's venture extremely risky and wanted to earn 30%, the cash flow receipts of $550,000 would give a $1,833,000 ($550,000 ÷ 30%) present value. Illustration 2 shows that the higher the capitalization rate (30% versus 20%), the lower the present value ($1,833,000 versus $2,750,000).

Net Present Value Method to Calculate the Investors' Return on Their Investment

The most appropriate approach for calculating the value of Amoco is the discounted cash flow (DCF) method. The primary benefit of the DCF method is that it allows for fluctuations in future cash flows over a period of time and shows the return on investment that potential investors would earn on their investments. The following lists the four steps involved in calculating Amoco's value by using the DCF method.

Step 1: Amoco's yearly after-tax cash flow. The first step for calculating Amoco's market value is to determine its after-tax cash flow forecast for the years 2011 to 2015. As mentioned earlier, these estimates are based on Amoco's management team and business-related experts in the field of sauna products.

Amoco hopes to have completed the research activities of the sauna's new product line by the end of 2009 and be ready for market full-scale distribution in Canada by early 2011. If the product line is well accepted in Canada (which is what Pedwell expects), Amoco would then be ready to launch the product line in the U.S. market. As shown in Illustration 3, the cash flow from operations generated by Amoco jumps from $550,000 (the detailed calculation for this figure is shown in Illustration 2) in 2011 to $1,450,000 in 2015. This represents a $900,000 growth over a four-year period, for a whopping 164% increase.

After adding the investments in capital assets and incremental working capital to the after-tax cash flow from operations, Amoco shows a negative $1,200,000 cash flow in 2010 (year of the investment) and positive cash flows between years 2011 and 2015 (from $350,000 to $950,000). As shown, a 20% discount rate to be considered by investors for this type of venture is used to determine the present value of the projected cash flows. This discount factor reflects the risk associated with Amoco's new product line. As shown, the projected present value cash flow loses more value proportionately to the undiscounted net cash flow (NCF) as it reaches the end of the

Illustration 3

In $000s	2010	2011	2012	2013	2014	2015
Cash flow from operations	—	550	800	900	1,200	1,450
Investments in capital assets	(1,200)	—	(400)	(400)	(300)	(300)
Incremental working capital	—	(200)	(200)	(200)	(200)	(200)
Subtotal	(1,200)	(200)	(600)	(600)	(500)	(500)
Net cash flows		350	200	300	700	950
Factor @ 20%		0.83333	0.69444	0.57870	0.48225	0.40188
Present values	(1,200)	292	139	174	338	382
NPV	**125**					
IRR	**23.7%**					

forecast period. This is due to smaller discount factors that are used in later years to reflect the loss of value as a result of time. The present value of the cash flow for each year is then added to determine the net present value (NPV). The net present value for the five-year forecast, using a 20% discount rate, is $125,000 ($1,325,000 – $1,200,000).

As pointed out by Woodstock, this is a lucrative venture if the projected cash flows are realized. The only obstacle and concern is to convince risk capital investors of the feasibility of realizing these cash flow estimates.

As shown above, by taking into account only the five-year cash flow forecast, the business venture would generate an internal rate of return of 23.7%. If the company's last year's $950,000 was maintained indefinitely and capitalized by using 18% (this will be discussed in step 2), this would give an additional inflow of cash in the amount of $5.3 million ($950,000 ÷ 18%). If the amount of $6,250,000 ($950,000 + $5,300,000) were incorporated in the return calculation for the year 2015, the company's internal rate of return would jump to 55.3% with a $2.3 million NPV using a 20% discount rate.

Step 2: Amoco's projected residual value. This step determines the residual value of a business. This is important to risk capital investors because they want to compare the amount of money that they will invest in the business to what the business today will be worth once it reaches maturity. In the case of Amoco, Pedwell is looking for $600,000 from private investors. He will have to demonstrate that the investment will multiply many-fold and earn a return that will offset the risk. This is explored in this second step.

At the end of the forecast period, that is, in 2015, Amoco will likely remain viable and continue to generate $950,000 in net cash flows for an indefinite period of time. Basically, the residual value is the present value of projected after-tax maintainable cash flows expected beyond 2015. As shown in Illustration 3, the maintainable cash flow from operations for 2015 is $1,450,000. Also, capital spending for each year after 2015 is estimated at $300,000 in addition to a $200,000 increase in working capital resulting from the anticipated introduction of the sauna product line in the U.S. market and possibly the European market. It is assumed here that Amoco will maintain its level of operations based on the 2015 performance (a realistic estimate, according to Pedwell).

When calculating the residual value, a capitalization rate has to be determined. Using capitalization is similar to discounting a maintainable cash flow in perpetuity. To calculate this figure, the maintainable after-tax cash flow amount of $950,000 is divided by an acceptable capitalization rate. In this case, the capitalization rate used for Amoco is 18% instead of the previous 20%. The difference between the discount rate and the capitalization rate is that the latter is adjusted for inflation, growth, and risk. By using this capitalization rate, the value of Amoco in 2015 would be $5.3 million ($950,000 ÷ 18%). Furthermore, the present value of this amount will be discounted to 2010, the year that the investor will advance the $600,000 to Amoco, by using a 20% discount rate. Amoco's present value of the residual value totals $2,121,033 ($5,277,778 × 0.40188). Here is how it is calculated:

	2015
Cash flows from operations	1,450,000
Investments	(500,000)
Net cash flows	950,000
Capitalization rate @ 18%	5,277,778
Present value factor @ 20%	0.40188
Prevent value of the residual value	2,121,033

Step 3: Amoco's estimated market value. This step in the valuation process involves the calculation of Amoco's estimated fair market value. As shown below, Amoco's fair market value is estimated at $2,446,033 and reflects Amoco's five-year after-tax discounted cash flow of $125,000 (step 1) and the estimated residual value of $2,121,030.

Present value of cash flow from operations	$125,000	(step 1)
Present value of the residual value	2,121,033	(step 2)
Estimated fair market value	$2,246,033	

Step 4: Calculate the investor's before- and after-tax return. This last step in the process involves the calculation of the investor's return on investment on a before- and after-tax basis. Pedwell will be seeking a $600,000 amount from a risk capital investor. This cash will be used to finalize the research and development on the sauna product line and help to fund a marketing program to launch it in Canada.

This investment will be required by the middle of 2010. Here, capitalization will also be used to determine Amoco's residual value. But first, the total value at exit must be determined by multiplying the maintainable after-tax cash flow by a multiple. Here, the multiple is equal to the inverse of a capitalization rate. In this case, a 12.5% capitalization rate is used and equals 8.0 (100 ÷ 12.5%) price-earnings multiple. As shown in Illustration 4, by using the 8 times multiple, the value at exit is estimated to be $7,600,000 ($950,000 × 8 times). Because it is assumed that the risk capital investor has a 40% equity participation in the company, this means that $3,040,000 in gross proceeds will be paid to him or her in 2015.

As shown in Illustration 4, by using a 38.3% discount rate, the present value of the $3,040,000 would be equivalent to the $600,000 investment made by the risk capital investors.

Illustration 4

In $000s	**2010**	**2011**	**2012**	**2013**	**2014**	**2015**
Before-tax return						
Initial investment	(600)	—	—	—	—	—
Total value at exit						
After-tax cash flow	—	—	—	—	—	950
Multiple	—	—	—	—	—	8.0
Total value at exit	—	—	—	—	—	7,600
Investor's share (40%)	—	—	—	—	—	3,040
Initial investment	(600)					
Total cash flows	600					3,040
Net present value	0					
Before tax IRR on investment	38.34%					

The discount rate would therefore be considered the investor's before-tax IRR on investment. As shown in Illustration 5, similar calculations would have to be done to calculate the investor's IRR on an after-tax basis.

Illustration 5

In $000s	
Gross proceeds received on exit	3,040
Initial investment	(600)
Capital gain on investment	2,440
Taxable portion (75%)	1,830
Investor's tax payable (50%)	915
Gross proceeds received on exit	3,040
Investor's tax payable	(915)
Net after-tax proceeds paid to investor	2,125

In $000s	**2010**	**2011**	**2012**	**2013**	**2014**	**2015**
After-tax return						
Initial investment	(600)	—	—	—	—	—
Total value at exit						
After-tax cash proceeds to investor	—	—	—	—	—	2,125
Initial investment	(600)					
Total cash flows	600					2,125
Net present value	0					
After-tax return on investment	28.78%					

Assuming that the after-tax cash flow is $2,125,000 at exit, the investor's after-tax IRR on investment would be 28.8%. Here, by using a 28.8% discount rate, the present value of the $2,125,000 received in 2015 would be equivalent to the $600,000 investment made by the risk capital investor today. This discount rate would therefore be considered the investor's after-tax internal rate of return (IRR).

The return on investment by the investor would be earned only when he or she sells shares at the planned exit in year 2015. The exit could be made in one of the following ways:

- Initial public offering
- Sale of all the shares of the company
- Sale of the investor's shares to a third party
- Buyback of the investor's shares by Pedwell

Chapter Summary

1 Learning Objective

Differentiate between market value and book value.

The *book value* of a business is what a business is worth on the books—that is, the difference between total assets and total liabilities. *Market value* is what a business is worth to a buyer as an ongoing entity. Because financial statements do not necessarily reflect the true market value of a business, accountants have attempted to resolve this issue through price-level accounting and current value accounting.

2 Learning Objective

Discuss the various valuation models.

Different valuation models exist. They include economic value, market value, book value, liquidation value, replacement value, collateral value, assessed value, and going-concern value.

3 Learning Objective

Comment on the meaning of scanning the environment.

When buying a business, it is important to scan the environment and to document the planning assumptions in order to construct a projected statement of income and projected statement of financial position.

4 Learning Objective

Explain how to go about documenting planning assumptions.

Documenting the planning assumptions means examining a company's past performance, determining whether the existing resources will be adequate to realize the new owner's strategic intentions, and looking at the restated company's projected financial statements, that is, the statement of income and the statement of financial position.

5 Learning Objective

Show how to restate the statement of income and the statement of financial position.

A new potential owners' financial statements should be restated (statement of income and statement of financial position) to reflect what the new owners see in terms of revenue, cost of sales, operating expenses, and statement of financial position accounts (assets, equity, and liabilities).

6 Learning Objective

Present the various ways of price-tagging an ongoing business.

Price-tagging a business can be done through the *asset valuation method*, which is the difference between the market value of the assets of an ongoing business and its liabilities; the *net present value method*, which takes into consideration cash outflows (purchase price of the business), cash inflows (profit for the year plus depreciation), and the potential resale value of the business at a later date; and *industry multipliers*, which reflect a percentage of the revenue.

7 Learning Objective

Calculate the market value of publicly traded companies.

To calculate the value of publicly traded companies, one has to multiply the number of common shares issued and the share market price.

8 Learning Objective

Determine investment return on capital projects from an investor's (venture capitalist) perspective.

Four steps are involved in calculating an investor's return on investment when buying an ongoing business. They are (1) determining the yearly after-tax cash flows, (2) projecting the project's residual value, (3) estimating the project's market value, and (4) calculating the investor's before- and after-tax return (IRR).

Key Terms

Assessed value p. 568
Asset valuation p. 578
Book value p. 564
Collateral value p. 568
Current-value accounting p. 565
Economic value p. 568
Industry multipliers p. 580
Liquidation value p. 567
Market performance p. 570
Market value p. 564
Operating performance p. 570
Overall performance p. 570
Price-level accounting p. 565
Replacement value p. 568
Scanning the environment p. 569

Review Questions

1. Differentiate between market value and book value.
2. What do we mean by price-level accounting?
3. What do we mean by current-value accounting?
4. Identify the most commonly used valuation models.
5. Explain the following valuation models:
   - Market value
   - Liquidation value
   - Collateral value
   - Assessed value
6. Why is it important for buyers of a business to scan the environment?
7. What are planning assumptions? Why are they important?
8. What do buyers look for when they assess the past performance of a business?
9. What financial ratios are useful for appraising a business?
10. How would you go about restating the statement of income of a business?
11. How would you go about restating the statement of financial position of a business?
12. What is goodwill?
13. What do we mean by asset valuation?
14. How can the net present value method help buyers to put a price tag on the worth of a business?
15. What are industry multipliers? What are their primary weaknesses?
16. What technique is used to put a price tag on the market value of publicly traded companies?
17. What do we mean by maintainable cash flows?
18. What is a residual value?
19. Discuss the meaning of *estimated fair market value.*
20. What do we mean by capitalization rate and price-earnings multiple?

21. Are the methods and techniques used for valuing a small business the same as those for a large business? Why?
22. Valuation techniques are essentially assessment tools that attempt to quantify the available objective data. Yet such quantification will always remain subjective in part. Explain.
23. Why is it that valuing a business for sale or purchase is one of the most complex tasks an analyst can undertake?

Learning Exercises

EXERCISE 1

John Hepworth, the sole proprietor of John's Variety, is having some difficulty with his retail store. He's concerned about the possibility of having to close it. He knows that the value of his business as an ongoing entity is not worth much because of the minimal level of profit that his store has shown over the past two years.

He's now thinking seriously about getting out of the business by liquidating his assets and paying his creditors in full. His bank manager informed him that if he liquidates his assets, he would probably obtain 60% for his non-current assets, no more than 40% for his inventories, and 65% of the trade receivables amount shown on his statement of financial position for the year ended December 31, 2010.

John was hoping to obtain at least $50,000 in goodwill. With the information listed below, prepare the following:

- John's statement of financial position for the year ended December 31, 2010.
- John's revised statement of financial position if he were to liquidate his business.

Accounts	Amounts
Revenue	$3,000,000
Inventories	200,000
Share capital	150,000
Accumulated depreciation	200,000
Distribution costs	130,000
Cash	10,000
Marketable securities	50,000
Retained earnings	385,000
Trade and other payables	150,000
Accrued expenses	50,000
Taxes payable	25,000
Other current assets	25,000
Long-term borrowings	350,000
Non-current assets (at cost)	900,000
Trade receivables	300,000
Short-term borrowings	175,000

Questions

1. What is John's book value?
2. What is John's liquidation value?
3. Will John have enough money to pay all his creditors?
4. If John's business cannot cover all his liabilities, what will he have to do?

EXERCISE 2

With the following information, calculate the after-tax cash flows from operations.

Accounts	Amounts
Revenue	$3,000,000
Finance costs	100,000
Income tax expense	175,000
Cost of sales	1,800,000
Distribution costs	400,000
Administrative expenses	300,000

Depreciation expense of $100,000 is included in distribution costs and depreciation expense of $200,000 is also included in cost of sales.

Questions

1. Calculate the value of the business as a going concern by using the following capitalization rates: 10%, 20%, 30%, and 40%.
2. By using a 20% discount rate, calculate the present value of the business if it had a five-year lifespan and a ten-year lifespan.
3. If an investor were to invest $400,000 in the business, how much cash should the business generate each year during a 10-year period if the investor wants to earn 30%?

EXERCISE 3

Trevor Johnson, CEO of Eastern Electronics Inc., is looking at the possibility of marketing a new product line. Trevor will be approaching a risk capital investor, Bill Miller, hoping to obtain $500,000 in equity participation. This amount represents 30% of the company's equity share.

When Trevor had his first meeting with Bill Miller, he presented the following financial projections:

Year	Cash Flows from Operations	Investments	Working Capital
0	—	$100,000	—
1	$300,000	800,000	$300,000
2	500,000	300,000	200,000
3	800,000	200,000	100,000
4	900,000	100,000	50,000
5	1,300,000	100,000	50,000

During the conversation between Trevor and Bill, both agreed that 20% should be used as a discount rate to calculate the present value of the company's cash flows and also as a capitalization rate. Bill pointed out that he hoped that at the end of five years, when he would want to make his exit, the company would be worth at least six times its last year's cash flows.

Questions

1. What is the company's net present value?
2. What is the company's internal rate of return using only the five-year projections?
3. What is the company's present value of the residual value?
4. What is the company's fair market value?
5. What is Bill Miller's internal rate of return on his investment?

EXERCISE 4

By using 10% as the company's weighted average cost of capital and the following estimates, calculate the following values for a manufacturing plant:

1. The yearly present values
2. The cumulative net present values

In millions	Year 1	Year 2	Year 3	Year 4	Year 5
Projected profit for the year	\$3.0	\$3.4	\$3.9	\$4.3	\$4.8
Projected capital cost allowance	\$1.1	\$1.2	\$1.3	\$1.4	\$1.5
Projected incremental investment in working capital	\$0.6	\$0.5	\$0.6	\$1.0	\$0.5

EXERCISE 5

The shareholders of Zimtex Electronics Inc. are considering selling their shares. The company's statement of financial position is as follows:

ZIMTEX CO.
Statement of Financial Position
(in \$)

Non-current assets	800,000	Share capital	200,000
Current assets	300,000	Retained earnings	350,000
		Total equity	550,000
		Long-term borrowings	400,000
		Current liabilities	150,000
		Total liabilities	550,000
Total assets	1,100,000	Total equity and liabilities	1,100,000

The company has 25,000 shares outstanding, which are currently trading at \$42.50.

Questions

1. What is the book value of the shares?
2. What is the market value of the shares?
3. What is the ratio of the market value to the book value?

Cases

CASE 1: LEWIN FOODS INC.

Helen Campbell and several business friends are considering buying Lewin Foods Inc., a privately owned company. Helen has just received the financial statements from the present owner and is trying to calculate the bid that should be made to the owners of the company.

Helen realized that the financial statements were not providing enough information to make a decision. So she hired several real estate agents, engineers, and accountants to help her determine the value of the land, machinery, equipment, and working capital.

Lewin Foods Inc.'s statement of income and statement of financial position are as follows:

Lewin Foods Inc.
Statement of Income
For the year ended December 31, 2010
(in $)

Revenue		5,600,000
Cost of sales		(3,400,000)
Gross profit		2,200,000
Distribution costs	(750,000)	
Administrative expenses	(440,000)	
Depreciation	(100,000)	
Finance costs	(35,000)	
Total expenses		(1,325,000)
Profit before taxes		875,000
Income tax expense (41.94 %)		(367,000)
Profit for the year		508,000

Although the company is generating $508,000 in profit and $608,000 in cash flow, Helen and her team estimated that they could increase revenue substantially and reduce costs. After much deliberation, the management team estimates that it could increase the profit for the year to $850,000 and cash flow to $975,000.

Lewin Foods Inc.
Statement of Financial Position
As at December 31, 2010
(in $)

Assets		
Non-current assets (at cost)	3,000,000	
Accumulated depreciation	(1,200,000)	
Non-current assets (net)		1,800,000
Current assets		
Inventories	1,200,000	
Trade receivables	765,000	
Prepaid expenses	60,000	
Cash	200,000	
Total current assets		2,225,000
Total assets		4,025,000
Equity and liabilities		
Equity		
Share capital	300,000	
Retained earnings	1,425,000	
Total equity		1,725,000
Liabilities		
Non-current liabilities		
Mortgage	500,000	
Long-term borrowings	600,000	
Total non-current liabilities		1,100,000
Current liabilities		
Trade and other payables	600,000	
Notes payable	400,000	
Taxes payable	200,000	
Total current liabilities		1,200,000
Total liabilities		2,300,000
Total equity and liabilities		4,025,000

The various consultants and auditors reported to Helen that the trade receivables are worth $650,000, or about 85% of what is currently shown on the company's statement of financial position. The value of the inventories, however, is not in as good shape. The auditors indicated that only $800,000 would be worth buying, which represents approximately 67% of what is shown on Lewin's statement of financial position. Helen is prepared to take over all of the trade and other payables.

The estimates regarding the property, plant, and equipment assets are as follows:

Land	$200,000
Buildings	800,000
Equipment	1,400,000
Machinery	600,000
Total	$3,000,000

During his conversation with Helen, Mr. Lewin, owner of Lewin Foods Inc., indicated that an amount of $700,000 in goodwill would have to be included in the selling price.

Because of the risk, Helen and her partners feel that they should earn at least a 25% internal rate of return on the business. The partners would be prepared to keep the business for 15 years and would hope to sell it for $8 million.

Funds raised to purchase the business would be obtained from various sources at a cost of 12%.

Questions

1. Would you buy the business?
2. If so, how much would you offer Mr. Lewin if you wanted to make a 25% internal rate of return?

CASE 2: NATIONAL PHOTOCELL INC.

In early 2010, Bill MacMillan, one of the shareholders of National Photocell Inc., was completing a proposal for the expansion of his research-oriented business into a commercial supplier of photochemical equipment.

MacMillan felt his proposal was sound. However, he was concerned that the business might have difficulty in raising funds, as the project would require a high level of financial support, particularly from high-risk capital investors.

Only a few firms, all with their own specialized production, characterized the photochemical equipment industry. There was little direct product competition, and many opportunities existed for new product innovations. Companies in the industry were typically small, with sales generally less than $3 million per year. MacMillan's revenue forecast is shown on the statements of income (see Illustration 1). As shown, revenue jumps from $1.0 million in 2011 to $8.0 million by 2016. The forecast period also shows that the net cash flows will show substantial increases from $70,000 in 2011 to $667,000 in 2016. However, National Photocell expects to show a negative net cash flow in 2012 of $536,000.

MacMillan felt that the company would require approximately $1.5 million in financing to set up production, marketing, and training of personnel and for equipment purchases. Investment in capital assets for production start-up would take place in 2011 and continue in 2012. Other funds would be used for working capital, with the heaviest investment in inventories and trade receivables, which would also be required in 2011.

MacMillan felt that traditional lenders would be willing to finance about $500,000 of the new financial needs. This would help finance the purchase of the capital assets and some working capital. The remaining $1.0 million would be raised from equity. About 60% of the new equity capital would be provided by existing shareholders and 40% by private investors. As shown on the statements of financial position (Illustration 2), the inflow of funds from the sale of the common shares would take place in 2011.

National Photocell Inc. would operate on a three-year cycle: high growth during the first two years, consolidation and planning for future growth during the third year. Marketing efforts will focus on North America for the first two years and then shift to a focus on Europe.

MacMillan was of the opinion that these financial needs and financing requirements were very accurate and realistic. Nevertheless, he felt that he would have to prepare a very effective and comprehensive investment proposal in order to attract one or two investors to finance the business. He fully understood that risk capital investors are interested in ventures that offer the following:

- A good business opportunity, one that generates a high return
- An excellent management team
- A feasible exit strategy
- The ability to monitor and control their investment

MacMillan was prepared to explain to potential investors how National Photocell could meet their needs. The most important factor would be the potential return that the investors expect to earn on this venture when they exit the business. MacMillan knew that the investors would want to reap their investment by 2016. He also knew that the business had to demonstrate a superior return performance. Also, the investors must earn a high return, something in the order of 30% to 40%.

ILLUSTRATION 1
National Photocell Inc.
Projected Statements of Income
For the period ended December 31

In $000s	2011	2012	2013	2014	2015	2016
Revenue	1,000	2,500	3,500	5,000	7,000	8,000
Cost of sales	(700)	(1,750)	(2,380)	(3,350)	(4,620)	(5,200)
Gross profit	300	750	1,120	1,650	2,380	2,800
Expenses						
Distribution costs	(100)	(250)	(420)	(650)	(910)	(1,040)
Administrative expenses	(56)	(140)	(214)	(301)	(462)	(520)
Finance costs	(30)	(125)	(110)	(105)	(105)	(95)
Total expenses	(186)	(515)	(744)	(1,056)	(1,477)	(1,655)
Profit before taxes	114	235	376	594	903	1,145
Income tax expense	(34)	(71)	(132)	(220)	(361)	(458)
Profit for the year	80	164	244	374	542	687
Add back depreciation	50	100	110	120	125	130
Cash flow from operations	130	264	354	494	667	817
Investments in capital assets	(40)	(600)	(200)	(200)	(200)	(100)
Incremental working capital	(20)	(200)	(100)	(100)	(100)	(50)
Subtotal	(60)	(800)	(300)	(300)	(300)	(150)
Net cash flows	70	(536)	54	194	367	667

ILLUSTRATION 2
National Photocell Inc.
Protected Statements of Financial Position
As at December 31

In $000s	2011	2012	2013	2014	2015	2016
Assets						
Non-current assets (cost)	2,800	3,400	3,600	3,800	4,000	4,100
Accumulated depreciation	(300)	(400)	(510)	(630)	(755)	(885)
Non-current assets (net)	2,500	3,000	3,090	3,170	3,245	3,215
Current assets						
Inventories	170	430	644	803	1,200	1,407
Trade receivables	150	380	500	750	965	1,250
Prepaid expenses	50	55	75	80	105	120
Cash	20	25	40	100	250	650
Total current assets	390	890	1,259	1,733	2,520	3,427
Total assets	2,890	3,890	4,349	4,903	5,765	6,642
Equity						
Share capital	1,400	1,400	1,400	1,400	1,400	1,400
Retained earnings	150	315	559	933	1,475	2,162
Total equity	1,550	1,715	1,959	2,333	2,875	3,562
Liabilities						
Current liabilities						
Trade and other payables	75	150	170	190	200	240
Short-term borrowings	100	400	400	350	450	500
Accrued expenses	30	80	70	80	90	90
Taxes payable	35	45	50	50	50	50
Total current liabilities	240	675	690	670	790	880
Long-term borrowings	1,100	1,500	1,700	1,900	2,100	2,200
Total liabilities	1,340	2,175	2,390	2,570	2,890	3,080
Total equity and liabilities	2,890	3,890	4,349	4,903	5,765	6,642

On the basis of the following assumptions, answer the questions below:

- The discount rate used to calculate the net present value is 20%.
- The capitalization rate to calculate the capitalized value of National Photocell is 18%.
- The times-multiple ratio to calculate the total value at exit in 2016 is 8.5.
- The taxable portion of the capital gain on investment is 75%.
- The company's income tax rate is 50%.

Questions

1. What will be the company's book value by 2016?
2. What is the company's net present value from 2012 to 2016?
3. What is the company's capitalized value?
4. What is the company's fair market value?
5. What is the company's internal rate of return during the five-year period (2012–2016)?

6. What is the company's internal rate of return using the estimated fair market value?
7. What is the risk capital investor's internal rate of return on the investment on a before-tax basis? On an after-tax basis?
8. Give your overall impression about the company's financial projections by using the liquidity ratios, the debt/coverage ratios, the asset-management ratios, and the profitability ratios.
9. Do you think that the risk capital investors will be interested in this venture? Why or why not?

[APPENDIX A]

CompuTech Inc. Financial Statements

STATEMENTS OF INCOME
STATEMENTS OF COMPREHENSIVE INCOME
STATEMENTS OF CHANGES IN EQUITY
STATEMENTS OF FINANCIAL POSITION
(FOR THE YEARS 2009 TO 2011)

CompuTech Inc.
Statements of Income
for the year ending December 31
(in thousands of $)

	2011	2010	2009
Revenue	800	420	350
Cost of sales	(406)	(209)	(177)
Gross profit	**394**	**211**	**173**
Other income	5	5	5
Distribution costs			
Salaries	(80)	(60)	(50)
Commissions	(5)	(3)	(2)
Travelling	(5)	(3)	(2)
Advertising	(10)	(5)	(3)
Depreciation/amortization	(40)	(20)	(20)
Total distribution costs	(140)	(91)	(77)
Administrative expenses			
Salaries	(60)	(38)	(30)
Leasing	(10)	(7)	(5)
Depreciation/amortization	(40)	(20)	(18)
Total administrative expenses	(110)	(65)	(53)
Finance costs	(30)	(14)	(10)
Total other income/expenses	**(275)**	**(165)**	**(135)**
Profit before taxes	119	46	38
Income tax expense	(42)	(13)	(13)
Profit for the year	77	33	25

CompuTech Inc.
Statements of Comprehensive Income
for the period ending December 31
(in thousands of $)

	2011	2010	2009
Profit for the year	77	33	25
Other comprehensive income/(loss)			
Exchange differences on translating foreign operations	—	—	—
Cash flow hedges	—	—	—
Gains on property revaluation	—	—	—
Other comprehensive income/(loss) for the year, net of tax	—	—	—
Total comprehensive income for the year	77	33	25

CompuTech Inc.
Statements of Changes in Equity
for the period ending December 31
(in thousands of $)

	2011	2010	2009
Common shares			
Balance at beginning of year	100	100	100
Common shares issued	70	—	—
Dividend reinvestment and share purchase plan	—	—	—
Shares issued on exercise of stock options	—	—	—
Balance at end of year	170	100	100
Retained earnings			
Balance at beginning of year	58	25	0
Profit for the year	77	33	25
	135	58	25
Dividends	—	—	—
Balance at end of year	**135**	**58**	**25**
Contributed surplus			
Balance at beginning of year	—	—	—
Stock-based compensation	—	—	—
Options exercised	—	—	—
Balance at end of year	—	—	—
Total shareholders' equity	305	158	125

CompuTech Inc.
Statements of Financial Position
as at December 31
(in thousands of $)

	2011	2010	2009
Assets			
Non-current assets			
Property, plant and, equipment	560	210	170
Goodwill	—	—	—
Other intangible assets	—	—	—
Accumulated depreciation/amortization	(158)	(78)	(38)
Total non-current assets	402	132	132
Current assets			
Inventories	110	65	50
Trade receivables	90	45	35
Prepaid expenses	10	5	5
Cash and cash equivalents	25	21	15
Total current assets	235	136	105
Total assets	637	268	237
Equity and liabilities			
Equity			
Share capital	170	100	100
Retained earnings	135	58	25
Contributed surplus	—	—	—
Total equity	305	158	125
Liabilities			
Non-current liabilities			
Long-term borrowings	200	50	60
Current liabilities			
Trade and other payables	47	20	17
Short-term borrowings	75	35	30
Current portion of long-term borrowings	10	5	5
Total current liabilities	132	60	52
Total liabilities	332	110	112
Total equity and liabilities	637	268	237

[APPENDIX B]

Interest Tables

TABLE A: FUTURE VALUE INTEREST FACTOR (FVIF)

(\$1 at *i*% per period for *n* periods)

FVIF = $(1 + i)^n$

Year	1%	2%	3%	4%	5%	6%	7%	8%
1	1.010	1.020	1.030	1.040	1.050	1.060	1.070	1.080
2	1.020	1.040	1.061	1.082	1.103	1.124	1.145	1.166
3	1.030	1.061	1.093	1.125	1.158	1.191	1.225	1.260
4	1.041	1.082	1.126	1.170	1.216	1.262	1.311	1.360
5	1.051	1.104	1.159	1.217	1.276	1.338	1.403	1.469
6	1.062	1.126	1.194	1.265	1.340	1.419	1.501	1.587
7	1.072	1.149	1.230	1.316	1.407	1.504	1.606	1.714
8	1.083	1.172	1.267	1.369	1.477	1.594	1.718	1.851
9	1.094	1.195	1.305	1.423	1.551	1.689	1.838	1.999
10	1.105	1.219	1.344	1.480	1.629	1.791	1.967	2.159
11	1.116	1.243	1.384	1.539	1.710	1.898	2.105	2.332
12	1.127	1.268	1.426	1.601	1.796	2.012	2.252	2.518
13	1.138	1.294	1.469	1.665	1.886	2.133	2.410	2.720
14	1.149	1.319	1.513	1.732	1.980	2.261	2.579	2.937
15	1.161	1.346	1.558	1.801	2.079	2.397	2.759	3.172
16	1.173	1.373	1.605	1.873	2.183	2.540	2.952	3.426
17	1.184	1.400	1.653	1.948	2.292	2.693	3.159	3.700
18	1.196	1.428	1.702	2.026	2.407	2.854	3.380	3.996
19	1.208	1.457	1.754	2.107	2.527	3.026	3.617	4.316
20	1.220	1.486	1.806	2.191	2.653	3.207	3.870	4.661
21	1.232	1.516	1.860	2.279	2.786	3.400	4.141	5.034
22	1.245	1.546	1.916	2.370	2.925	3.604	4.430	5.437
23	1.257	1.577	1.974	2.465	3.072	3.820	4.741	5.871
24	1.270	1.608	2.033	2.563	3.225	4.049	5.072	6.341
25	1.282	1.641	2.094	2.666	3.386	4.292	5.427	6.848

Year	9%	10%	11%	12%	14%	16%	18%	20%
1	1.090	1.100	1.110	1.120	1.140	1.160	1.180	1.200
2	1.188	1.210	1.232	1.254	1.300	1.346	1.392	1.440
3	1.295	1.331	1.368	1.405	1.482	1.561	1.643	1.728
4	1.412	1.464	1.518	1.574	1.689	1.811	1.939	2.074
5	1.539	1.611	1.685	1.762	1.925	2.100	2.288	2.488
6	1.677	1.772	1.870	1.974	2.195	2.436	2.700	2.986
7	1.828	1.949	2.076	2.211	2.502	2.826	3.185	3.583
8	1.993	2.144	2.305	2.476	2.853	3.278	3.759	4.300
9	2.172	2.358	2.558	2.773	3.252	3.803	4.435	5.160
10	2.367	2.594	2.839	3.106	3.707	4.411	5.234	6.192
11	2.580	2.853	3.152	3.479	4.226	5.117	6.176	7.430
12	2.813	3.138	3.498	3.896	4.818	5.936	7.288	8.916
13	3.066	3.452	3.883	4.363	5.492	6.886	8.599	10.699
14	3.342	3.798	4.310	4.887	6.261	7.988	10.147	12.839
15	3.642	4.177	4.785	5.474	7.138	9.266	11.974	15.407
16	3.970	4.595	5.311	6.130	8.137	10.748	14.129	18.488
17	4.328	5.054	5.895	6.866	9.276	12.468	16.672	22.186
18	4.717	5.560	6.544	7.690	10.575	14.463	19.673	26.623
19	5.142	6.116	7.263	8.613	12.056	16.777	23.214	31.948
20	5.604	6.728	8.062	9.646	13.744	19.461	27.393	38.338
21	6.109	7.400	8.949	10.804	15.668	22.575	32.324	46.005
22	6.659	8.140	9.934	12.100	17.861	26.186	38.142	55.206
23	7.258	8.954	11.026	13.552	20.362	30.376	45.008	66.247
24	7.911	9.850	12.239	15.179	23.212	35.236	53.109	79.497
25	8.623	10.835	13.586	17.000	26.462	40.874	62.669	95.396

Year	22%	24%	26%	28%	30%	32%	34%	36%
1	1.220	1.240	1.260	1.280	1.300	1.320	1.340	1.360
2	1.488	1.538	1.588	1.638	1.690	1.742	1.796	1.850
3	1.816	1.907	2.000	2.097	2.197	2.300	2.406	2.515
4	2.215	2.364	2.520	2.684	2.856	3.036	3.036	3.421
5	2.703	2.932	3.176	3.436	3.713	4.007	4.320	4.653
6	3.297	3.635	4.002	4.398	4.827	5.290	5.789	6.328
7	4.023	4.508	5.042	5.630	6.275	6.983	7.758	8.605
8	4.908	5.590	6.353	7.206	8.157	9.217	10.395	11.703
9	5.987	6.931	8.005	9.223	10.605	12.167	13.930	15.917
10	7.305	8.594	10.086	11.806	13.786	16.060	18.666	21.647
11	8.912	10.657	12.708	15.112	17.922	21.199	25.012	29.439
12	10.872	13.215	16.012	19.343	23.298	27.983	33.516	40.038
13	13.264	16.386	20.175	24.759	30.288	36.937	44.912	54.451
14	16.182	20.319	25.421	31.691	39.374	48.757	60.182	74.053
15	19.742	25.196	32.030	40.565	51.186	64.359	80.644	100.713
16	24.086	31.243	40.358	51.923	66.542	84.954	108.063	136.969
17	29.384	38.741	50.851	66.461	86.504	112.139	144.804	186.278
18	35.849	48.039	64.072	85.071	112.455	148.024	194.038	253.338
19	43.736	59.568	80.731	108.890	146.192	195.391	260.011	344.540
20	53.358	73.864	101.721	139.380	190.049	257.916	348.414	468.574
21	65.096	91.592	128.169	178.406	247.064	340.450	466.875	637.261
22	79.418	113.574	161.492	228.360	321.184	449.394	625.613	866.675
23	96.890	140.831	203.480	292.300	417.539	593.200	838.321	1178.680
24	118.205	174.631	256.385	374.144	542.800	783.024	1123.350	1603.000
25	144.210	216.542	323.045	478.905	705.640	1033.590	1505.290	2180.080

TABLE B: PRESENT VALUE INTEREST FACTOR (PVIF)

($1 at i% per period for n periods)

$$\mathbf{PVIF} = \frac{1}{(1 + i)^n}$$

N	7%	2%	3%	4%	5%	6%	7%	8%
1	0.99010	0.98039	0.97007	0.96154	0.95238	0.94340	0.93458	0.92593
2	0.98030	0.96117	0.94260	0.92456	0.90703	0.89000	0.87344	0.85734
3	0.97059	0.94232	0.91514	0.88900	0.86384	0.83962	0.81630	0.79383
4	0.96098	0.92385	0.88849	0.85480	0.82270	0.79209	0.76290	0.73503
5	0.95147	0.90573	0.86261	0.82193	0.78353	0.74726	0.71299	0.68058
6	0.94204	0.88797	0.83748	0.79031	0.74622	0.70496	0.66634	0.63017
7	0.93272	0.87056	0.81309	0.75992	0.71068	0.66506	0.62275	0.58349
8	0.92348	0.85349	0.78941	0.73069	0.67684	0.62741	0.58201	0.54027
9	0.91434	0.83675	0.76642	0.70259	0.64461	0.59190	0.54393	0.50025
10	0.90529	0.82035	0.74409	0.67556	0.61391	0.55839	0.50835	0.46319
11	0.89632	0.80426	0.72242	0.64958	0.58468	0.52679	0.47509	0.42888
12	0.88745	0.78849	0.70138	0.62460	0.55684	0.49697	0.44401	0.39711
13	0.87866	0.77303	0.68095	0.60057	0.53032	0.46884	0.41496	0.36770
14	0.86996	0.75787	0.66112	0.57747	0.50507	0.44230	0.38782	0.34046
15	0.86135	0.74301	0.64186	0.55526	0.48102	0.41726	0.36245	0.31524
16	0.85282	0.72845	0.62317	0.53391	0.45811	0.39365	0.33873	0.29189
17	0.84438	0.71416	0.60502	0.51337	0.43630	0.37136	0.31657	0.27027
18	0.83602	0.70016	0.58739	0.49363	0.41552	0.35034	0.29586	0.25025
19	0.82774	0.68643	0.57029	0.47464	0.39573	0.33051	0.27651	0.23171
20	0.81954	0.67297	0.55367	0.45639	0.37689	0.31180	0.25842	0.21455
21	0.81143	0.65978	0.53755	0.43883	0.35894	0.29415	0.24151	0.19866
22	0.80340	0.64684	0.52189	0.42195	0.34185	0.27750	0.22571	0.18394
23	0.79544	0.63416	0.50669	0.40573	0.32557	0.26180	0.21095	0.17031
24	0.78757	0.62172	0.49193	0.39012	0.31007	0.24698	0.19715	0.15770
25	0.77977	0.60953	0.47760	0.37512	0.29530	0.23300	0.18425	0.14602

N	9%	10%	11%	12%	13%	14%	15%	16%
1	0.91743	0.90909	0.90090	0.89286	0.88496	0.87719	0.86957	0.86207
2	0.84168	0.82645	0.81162	0.79719	0.78315	0.76947	0.75614	0.74316
3	0.77218	0.75131	0.73119	0.71178	0.69305	0.67497	0.65752	0.64066
4	0.70843	0.68301	0.65873	0.63552	0.61332	0.59208	0.57175	0.55229
5	0.64993	0.62092	0.59345	0.56743	0.54276	0.51937	0.49718	0.47611
6	0.59627	0.56447	0.53464	0.50663	0.48032	0.45559	0.43233	0.41044
7	0.54703	0.51316	0.48166	0.45235	0.42506	0.39964	0.37594	0.35383
8	0.50187	0.46651	0.43393	0.40388	0.37616	0.35056	0.32690	0.30503
9	0.46043	0.42410	0.39092	0.36061	0.33288	0.30751	0.28426	0.26295
10	0.42241	0.38554	0.35218	0.32197	0.29459	0.26974	0.24718	0.22668
11	0.38753	0.35049	0.31728	0.28748	0.26070	0.23662	0.21494	0.19542
12	0.35553	0.31863	0.28584	0.25667	0.23071	0.20756	0.18691	0.16846
13	0.32618	0.28966	0.25751	0.22917	0.20416	0.18207	0.16253	0.14523
14	0.29925	0.26333	0.23199	0.20462	0.18068	0.15971	0.14133	0.12520
15	0.27454	0.23939	0.20900	0.18270	0.15989	0.14010	0.12289	0.10793
16	0.25187	0.21763	0.18829	0.16312	0.14150	0.12289	0.10686	0.09304
17	0.23107	0.19784	0.16963	0.14564	0.12522	0.10780	0.09293	0.08021
18	0.21199	0.17986	0.15282	0.13004	0.11081	0.09456	0.08080	0.06914
19	0.19449	0.16351	0.13768	0.11611	0.09806	0.08295	0.07026	0.05961
20	0.17843	0.14864	0.12403	0.10367	0.08678	0.07276	0.06110	0.05139
21	0.16370	0.13513	0.11174	0.09256	0.07680	0.06383	0.05313	0.04430
22	0.15018	0.12285	0.10067	0.08264	0.06796	0.05599	0.04620	0.03819
23	0.13778	0.11168	0.09069	0.07379	0.06014	0.04911	0.04017	0.03292
24	0.12640	0.10153	0.08170	0.06588	0.05322	0.04308	0.03493	0.02838
25	0.11597	0.09230	0.07361	0.05882	0.04710	0.03779	0.03038	0.02447

N	17%	18%	19%	20%	21%	22%	23%	24%
1	0.85470	0.84746	0.84034	0.83333	0.82645	0.81967	0.81301	0.80645
2	0.73051	0.71818	0.70616	0.69444	0.68301	0.67186	0.66098	0.65036
3	0.62437	0.60863	0.59342	0.57870	0.56447	0.55071	0.53738	0.52449
4	0.53365	0.51579	0.49867	0.48225	0.46651	0.45140	0.43690	0.42297
5	0.45611	0.43711	0.41905	0.40188	0.38554	0.37000	0.35520	0.34111
6	0.38984	0.37043	0.35214	0.33490	0.31863	0.30328	0.28878	0.27509
7	0.33320	0.31392	0.29592	0.27908	0.26333	0.24859	0.23478	0.22184
8	0.28478	0.26604	0.24867	0.23257	0.21763	0.20376	0.19088	0.17891
9	0.24340	0.22546	0.20897	0.19381	0.17986	0.16702	0.15519	0.14428
10	0.20804	0.19106	0.17560	0.16151	0.14864	0.13690	0.12617	0.11635
11	0.17781	0.16192	0.14756	0.13459	0.12285	0.11221	0.10258	0.09383
12	0.15197	0.13722	0.12400	0.11216	0.10153	0.09198	0.08339	0.07567
13	0.12989	0.11629	0.10420	0.09346	0.08391	0.07539	0.06780	0.06103
14	0.11102	0.09855	0.08757	0.07789	0.06934	0.06180	0.05512	0.04921
15	0.09489	0.08352	0.07359	0.06491	0.05731	0.05065	0.04481	0.03969
16	0.08110	0.07078	0.06184	0.05409	0.04736	0.04152	0.03643	0.03201
17	0.06932	0.05998	0.05196	0.04507	0.03914	0.03403	0.02962	0.02581
18	0.05925	0.05083	0.04367	0.03756	0.03235	0.02789	0.02408	0.02082
19	0.05064	0.04308	0.03669	0.03130	0.02673	0.02286	0.01958	0.01679
20	0.04328	0.03651	0.03084	0.02608	0.02209	0.01874	0.01592	0.01354
21	0.03699	0.03094	0.02591	0.02174	0.01826	0.01536	0.01294	0.01092
22	0.03162	0.02622	0.02178	0.01811	0.01509	0.01259	0.01052	0.00880
23	0.02702	0.02222	0.01830	0.01509	0.01247	0.01032	0.00855	0.00710
24	0.02310	0.01883	0.01538	0.01258	0.01031	0.00846	0.00695	0.00573
25	0.01974	0.01596	0.01292	0.01048	0.00852	0.00693	0.00565	0.00462

N	25%	26%	27%	28%	29%	30%	31%	32%
1	0.80000	0.79365	0.78740	0.78125	0.77519	0.76923	0.76336	0.75758
2	0.64000	0.62988	0.62000	0.61035	0.60093	0.59172	0.58272	0.57392
3	0.51200	0.49991	0.48819	0.47684	0.46583	0.45517	0.44482	0.43479
4	0.40960	0.39675	0.38440	0.37253	0.36111	0.35013	0.33956	0.32939
5	0.32768	0.31488	0.30268	0.29104	0.27993	0.26933	0.25920	0.24953
6	0.26214	0.24991	0.23833	0.22737	0.21700	0.20718	0.19787	0.18904
7	0.20972	0.19834	0.18766	0.17764	0.16822	0.15937	0.15104	0.14321
8	0.16777	0.15741	0.14776	0.13878	0.13040	0.12259	0.11530	0.10849
9	0.13422	0.12493	0.11635	0.10842	0.10109	0.09430	0.08802	0.08219
10	0.10737	0.09915	0.09161	0.08470	0.07836	0.07254	0.06719	0.06227
11	0.08590	0.07869	0.07214	0.06617	0.06075	0.05580	0.05129	0.04717
12	0.06872	0.06245	0.05680	0.05170	0.04709	0.04292	0.03915	0.03574
13	0.05498	0.04957	0.04472	0.04039	0.03650	0.03302	0.02989	0.02707
14	0.04398	0.03934	0.03522	0.03155	0.02830	0.02540	0.02281	0.02051
15	0.03518	0.03122	0.02773	0.02465	0.02194	0.01954	0.01742	0.01554
16	0.02815	0.02478	0.02183	0.01926	0.01700	0.01503	0.01329	0.01177
17	0.02252	0.01967	0.01719	0.01505	0.01318	0.01156	0.01015	0.00892
18	0.01801	0.01561	0.01354	0.01175	0.01022	0.00889	0.00775	0.00676
19	0.01441	0.01239	0.01066	0.00918	0.00792	0.00684	0.00591	0.00512
20	0.01153	0.00983	0.00839	0.00717	0.00614	0.00526	0.00451	0.00388
21	0.00922	0.00780	0.00661	0.00561	0.00476	0.00405	0.00345	0.00294
22	0.00738	0.00619	0.00520	0.00438	0.00369	0.00311	0.00263	0.00223
23	0.00590	0.00491	0.00410	0.00342	0.00286	0.00239	0.00201	0.00169
24	0.00472	0.00390	0.00323	0.00267	0.00222	0.00184	0.00153	0.00128
25	0.00378	0.00310	0.00254	0.00209	0.00172	0.00142	0.00117	0.00097

TABLE C: FUTURE VALUE INTEREST FACTOR OF AN ANNUITY (FVIFA)

($1 per period at *i*% per period for *n* periods)

$$\text{FVIFA} = \frac{(1 + i)^n - 1}{i}$$

N	1%	2%	3%	4%	5%	6%	7%	8%
1	1.000	1.000	1.000	1.000	1.000	1.000	1.000	1.000
2	2.010	2.020	2.030	2.040	2.050	2.060	2.070	2.080
3	3.030	3.060	3.091	3.122	3.153	3.184	3.215	3.246
4	4.060	4.122	4.184	4.246	4.310	4.375	4.440	4.506
5	5.101	5.204	5.309	5.416	5.526	5.637	5.751	5.867
6	6.152	6.308	6.468	6.633	6.802	6.975	7.153	7.336
7	7.214	7.434	7.662	7.898	8.142	8.394	8.654	8.923
8	8.286	8.583	8.892	9.214	9.549	9.897	10.260	10.637
9	9.369	9.755	10.159	10.583	11.027	11.491	11.978	12.488
10	10.462	10.950	11.464	12.006	12.578	13.181	13.817	14.487
11	11.567	12.169	12.808	13.486	14.207	14.972	15.784	16.646
12	12.683	13.412	14.192	15.026	15.917	16.870	17.889	18.977
13	13.809	14.680	15.618	16.627	17.713	18.882	20.141	21.495
14	14.947	15.974	17.086	18.292	19.599	21.015	22.551	24.215
15	16.097	17.293	18.599	20.024	21.579	23.276	25.129	27.152
16	17.258	18.639	20.157	21.825	23.658	25.673	27.888	30.324
17	18.430	20.012	21.762	23.698	25.840	28.213	30.840	33.750
18	19.615	21.412	23.414	25.645	28.132	30.906	33.999	37.450
19	20.811	22.841	25.117	27.671	30.539	33.760	37.379	41.446
20	22.019	24.297	26.870	29.778	33.066	36.786	40.996	45.762
21	23.239	25.783	28.677	31.969	35.719	39.993	44.865	50.423
22	24.472	27.299	30.537	34.248	38.505	43.392	49.006	55.457
23	25.716	28.845	32.453	36.618	41.430	46.996	53.436	60.893
24	26.974	30.422	34.427	39.083	44.502	50.816	58.177	66.765
25	28.243	32.030	36.459	41.646	47.727	54.864	63.249	73.106

N	9%	10%	11%	12%	14%	16%	18%	20%
1	1.000	1.000	1.000	1.000	1.000	1.000	1.000	1.000
2	2.090	2.100	2.110	2.120	2.140	2.160	2.180	2.200
3	3.278	3.310	3.342	3.374	3.440	3.506	3.572	3.640
4	4.573	4.641	4.710	4.779	4.921	5.066	5.215	5.368
5	5.985	6.105	6.228	6.353	6.610	6.877	7.154	7.442
6	7.523	7.716	7.913	8.115	8.536	8.977	9.442	9.930
7	9.200	9.487	9.783	10.089	10.731	11.414	12.142	12.916
8	11.029	11.436	11.859	12.300	13.233	14.240	15.327	16.499
9	13.021	13.580	14.164	14.776	16.085	17.519	19.086	20.799
10	15.193	15.937	16.722	17.549	19.337	21.322	23.521	25.959
11	17.560	18.531	19.561	20.655	23.045	25.733	28.755	32.150
12	20.141	21.384	22.713	24.133	27.271	30.850	34.931	39.581
13	22.953	24.523	26.212	28.029	32.089	36.786	42.219	48.497
14	26.019	27.975	30.095	32.393	37.581	43.672	50.818	59.196
15	29.361	31.773	34.405	37.280	43.842	51.660	60.965	72.035
16	33.003	35.950	39.190	42.753	50.980	60.925	72.939	87.442
17	36.974	40.545	44.501	48.884	59.118	71.673	87.068	105.931
18	41.301	45.599	50.396	55.750	68.394	84.141	103.740	128.117
19	46.019	51.159	56.940	63.440	78.969	98.603	123.413	154.740
20	51.160	57.275	64.203	72.052	91.025	115.380	146.628	186.688
21	56.765	64.003	72.265	81.699	104.768	134.840	174.021	225.026
22	62.873	71.403	81.214	92.503	120.436	157.415	206.345	271.031
23	69.532	79.543	91.148	104.603	138.297	183.601	244.487	326.237
24	76.790	88.497	102.174	118.155	158.659	213.977	289.494	392.404
25	84.701	98.347	114.413	133.334	181.871	249.214	342.603	471.981

N	22%	24%	26%	28%	30%	32%	34%	36%
1	1.000	1.000	1.000	1.000	1.000	1.000	1.000	1.000
2	2.220	2.240	2.260	2.280	2.300	2.320	2.340	2.360
3	3.708	3.778	3.848	3.918	3.990	4.062	4.136	4.210
4	5.524	5.684	5.848	6.016	6.187	6.362	6.542	6.725
5	7.740	8.048	8.368	8.700	9.043	9.398	9.766	10.146
6	10.442	10.980	11.544	12.136	12.756	13.406	14.086	14.799
7	13.740	14.615	15.546	16.534	17.583	18.696	19.876	21.126
8	17.762	19.123	20.588	22.163	23.858	25.678	27.633	29.732
9	22.670	24.713	26.940	29.369	32.015	34.895	38.029	41.435
10	28.657	31.643	34.945	38.593	42.620	47.062	51.958	57.352
11	35.962	40.238	45.031	50.399	56.405	63.122	70.624	78.998
12	44.874	50.895	57.739	65.510	74.327	84.321	95.637	108.438
13	55.746	64.110	73.751	84.853	97.625	112.303	129.153	148.475
14	69.010	80.496	93.926	109.612	127.912	149.240	174.065	202.926
15	85.192	100.815	119.347	141.303	167.286	197.997	234.247	276.979
16	104.935	126.011	151.377	181.868	218.472	262.356	314.891	377.692
17	129.020	157.253	191.735	233.791	285.014	347.310	422.954	514.661
18	158.405	195.994	242.586	300.252	371.518	459.449	567.758	700.939
19	194.254	244.033	306.658	385.323	483.973	607.473	761.796	954.278
20	237.989	303.601	387.389	494.213	630.165	802.864	1021.810	1298.820
21	291.347	377.465	489.110	633.592	820.214	1060.780	1370.220	1767.390
22	356.444	469.057	617.278	811.998	1067.280	1401.230	1837.100	2404.650
23	435.861	582.630	778.771	1040.360	1388.460	1850.620	2462.710	3271.330
24	532.751	723.461	982.251	1332.660	1806.000	2443.820	3301.030	4450.010
25	650.956	898.092	1238.640	1706.800	2348.800	3226.850	4424.380	6053.010

TABLE D: PRESENT VALUE INTEREST FACTOR OF AN ANNUITY (PVIFA)

($1 per period at *i*% per period for *n* periods)

$$\textbf{PVIFA} = \frac{1 - \frac{1}{(1+i)^n}}{i}$$

Year	1%	2%	3%	4%	5%	6%	7%	8%
1	0.9901	0.9804	0.9709	0.9615	0.9524	0.9434	0.9346	0.9259
2	1.9704	1.9416	1.9135	1.8861	1.8594	1.8334	1.8080	1.7833
3	2.9410	2.8839	2.8286	2.7751	2..7232	2.6730	2.6243	2.5771
4	3.9020	3.8077	3.7171	3.6299	3.5459	3.4651	3.3872	3.3121
5	4.8535	4.7134	4.5797	4.4518	4.3295	4.2123	4.1002	3.9927
6	5.7955	5.6014	5.4172	5.2421	5.0757	4.9173	4.7665	4.6229
7	6.7282	6.4720	6.2302	6.0020	5.7863	5.5824	5.3893	5.2064
8	7.6517	7.3254	7.0196	6.7327	6.4632	6.2098	5.9713	5.7466
9	8.5661	8.1622	7.7861	7.4353	7.1078	6.8017	6.5152	6.2469
10	9.4714	8.9825	8.5302	8.1109	7.7217	7.3601	7.0236	6.7101
11	10.3677	9.7868	9.2526	8.7604	8.3064	7.8868	7.4987	7.1389
12	11.2552	10.5753	9.9539	9.3850	8.8632	8.3838	7.9427	7.5361
13	12.1338	11.3483	10.6349	9.9856	9.3935	8.8527	8.3576	7.9038
14	13.0038	12.1062	11.2960	10.5631	9.8986	9.2950	8.7454	8.2442
15	13.8651	12.8492	11.9379	11.1183	10.3796	9.7122	9.1079	8.5595
16	14.7180	13.5777	12.5610	11.6522	10.8377	10.1059	9.4466	8.8514
17	15.5624	14.2918	13.1660	12.1656	11.2740	10.4772	9.7632	9.1216
18	16.3984	14.9920	13.7534	12.6592	11.6895	10.8276	10.0591	9.3719
19	17.2261	15.6784	14.3237	13.1339	12.0853	11.1581	10.3356	9.6036
20	18.0457	16.3514	14.8774	13.5903	12.4622	11.4699	10.5940	9.8181
21	18.8571	17.0111	15.4149	14.0291	12.8211	11.7640	10.8355	10.0168
22	19.6605	17.6580	15.9368	14.4511	13.1630	12.0416	11.0612	10.2007
23	20.4559	18.2921	16.4435	14.8568	13.4885	12.3033	11.2722	10.3710
24	21.2435	18.9139	16.9355	15.2469	13.7986	12.5503	11.4693	10.5287
25	22.0233	19.5234	17.4131	15.6220	14.0939	12.7833	11.6536	10.6748

Year	9%	10%	11%	12%	13%	14%	15%	16%
1	0.9174	0.9091	0.9009	0.8929	0.8850	0.8772	0.8696	0.8621
2	1.7591	1.7355	1.7125	1.6901	1.6681	1.6467	1.6257	1.6052
3	2.5313	2.4868	2.4437	2.4018	2.3612	2.3216	2.2832	2.2459
4	3.2397	3.1699	3.1024	3.0373	2.9745	2.9137	2.8550	2.7982
5	3.8896	3.7908	3.6959	3.6048	3.5172	3.4331	3.3522	3.2743
6	4.4859	4.3553	4.2305	4.1114	3.9976	3.8887	3.7845	3.6847
7	5.0329	4.8684	4.7122	4.5638	4.4226	4.2883	4.1604	4.0386
8	5.5348	5.3349	5.1461	4.9676	4.7988	4.6389	4.4873	4.3436
9	5.9852	5.7590	5.5370	5.3282	5.1317	4.9464	4.7716	4.6065
10	6.4176	6.1446	5.8892	5.6502	5.4262	5.2161	5.0188	4.8332
11	6.8052	6.4951	6.2065	5.9377	5.6869	5.4527	5.2337	5.0286
12	7.1607	6.8137	6.4924	6.1944	5.9176	5.6603	5.4206	5.1971
13	7.4869	7.1034	6.7499	6.4235	6.1218	5.8424	5.5831	5.3423
14	7.7861	7.3667	6.9819	6.6282	6.3025	6.0021	5.7245	5.4675
15	8.0607	7.6061	7.1909	6.8109	6.4624	6.1422	5.8474	5.5755
16	8.3125	7.8237	7.3792	6.9740	6.6039	6.2651	5.9542	5.6685
17	8.5436	8.0215	7.5488	7.1196	6.7291	6.3729	6.0472	5.7487
18	8.7556	8.2014	7.7016	7.2497	6.8399	6.4674	6.1280	5.8178
19	8.9501	8.3649	7.8393	7.3658	6.9380	6.5504	6.1982	5.8775
20	9.1285	8.5136	7.9633	7.4694	7.0248	6.6231	6.2593	5.9288
21	9.2922	8.6487	8.0751	7.5620	7.1016	6.6870	6.3125	5.9731
22	9.4424	8.7715	8.1757	7.6446	7.1695	6.7429	6.3587	6.0113
23	9.5802	8.8832	8.2664	7.7184	7.2297	6.7921	6.3988	6.0442
24	9.7066	8.9847	8.3481	7.7843	7.2829	6.8351	6.4338	6.0726
25	9.8226	9.0770	8.4217	7.8431	7.3300	6.8729	6.4641	6.0971

Year	17%	18%	19%	20%	21%	22%	23%	24%
1	0.8547	0.8475	0.8403	0.8333	0.8264	0.8197	0.8130	0.8065
2	1.5852	1.5656	1.5465	1.5278	1.5095	1.4915	1.4740	1.4568
3	2.2096	2.1743	2.1399	2.1065	2.0739	2.0422	2.0114	1.9813
4	2.7432	2.6901	2.6386	2.5887	2.5404	2.4936	2.4483	2.4043
5	3.1993	3.1272	3.0576	2.9906	2.9260	2.8636	2.8035	2.7454
6	3.5892	3.4976	3.4098	3.3255	3.2446	3.1669	3.0923	3.0205
7	3.9224	3.8115	3.7057	3.6046	3.5079	3.4155	3.3270	3.2423
8	4.2072	4.0776	3.9544	3.8372	3.7256	3.6193	3.5179	3.4212
9	4.4506	4.3030	4.1633	4.0310	3.9054	3.7863	3.6731	3.5655
10	4.6586	4.4941	4.3389	4.1925	4.0541	3.9232	3.7993	3.6819
11	4.8364	4.6560	4.4865	4.3271	4.1769	4.0354	3.9018	3.7757
12	4.9884	4.7932	4.6105	4.4392	4.2785	4.1274	3.9852	3.8514
13	5.1183	4.9095	4.7147	4.5327	4.3624	4.2028	4.0530	3.9124
14	5.2293	5.0081	4.8023	4.6106	4.4317	4.2646	4.1082	3.9616
15	5.3242	5.0916	4.8759	4.6755	4.4890	4.3152	4.1530	4.0013
16	5.4053	5.1624	4.9377	4.7296	4.5364	4.3567	4.1894	4.0333
17	5.4746	5.2223	4.9897	4.7746	4.5755	4.3908	4.2190	4.0591
18	5.5339	5.2732	5.0333	4.8122	4.6079	4.4187	4.2431	4.0799
19	5.5845	5.3162	5.0700	4.8435	4.6346	4.4415	4.2627	4.0967
20	5.6278	5.3527	5.1009	4.8696	4.6567	4.4603	4.2786	4.1103
21	5.6648	5.3837	5.1268	4.8913	4.6750	4.4756	4.2916	4.1212
22	5.6964	5.4099	5.1486	4.9094	4.6900	4.4882	4.3021	4.1300
23	5.7234	5.4321	5.1668	4.9245	4.7025	4.4985	4.3106	4.1371
24	5.7465	5.4509	5.1822	4.9371	4.7128	4.5070	4.3176	4.1428
25	5.7662	5.4669	5.1951	4.9476	4.7213	4.5139	4.3232	4.1474

Year	25%	26%	27%	28%	29%	30%	31%	32%
1	0.8000	0.7937	0.7874	0.7813	0.7752	0.7692	0.7634	0.7576
2	1.4400	1.4235	1.4074	1.3916	1.3761	1.3609	1.3461	1.3315
3	1.9520	1.9234	1.8956	1.8684	1.8420	1.8161	1.7909	1.7663
4	2.3616	2.3202	2.2800	2.2410	2.2031	2.1662	2.1305	2.0957
5	2.6893	2.6351	2.5827	2.5320	2.4830	2.4356	2.3897	2.3452
6	2.9514	2.8850	2.8210	2.7594	2.7000	2.6427	2.5875	2.5342
7	3.1611	3.0833	3.0087	2.9370	2.8682	2.8021	2.7386	2.6775
8	3.3289	3.2407	3.1564	3.0758	2.9986	2.9247	2.8539	2.7860
9	3.4631	3.3657	3.2728	3.1842	3.0997	3.0190	2.9419	2.8681
10	3.5705	3.4648	3.3644	3.2689	3.1781	3.0915	3.0091	2.9304
11	3.6564	3.5435	3.4365	3.3351	3.2388	3.1473	3.0604	2.9776
12	3.7251	3.6060	3.4933	3.3868	3.2859	3.1903	3.0995	3.0133
13	3.7801	3.6555	3.6381	3.4272	3.3224	3.2233	3.1294	3.0404
14	3.8241	3.6949	3.5733	3.4587	3.3507	3.2487	3.1522	3.0609
15	3.8593	3.7261	3.6010	3.4834	3.3726	3.2682	3.1696	3.0764
16	3.8874	3.7509	3.6228	3.5026	3.3896	3.2832	3.1829	3.0882
17	3.9099	3.7705	3.6400	3.5177	3.4028	3.2948	3.1931	3.0971
18	3.9279	3.7861	3.6536	3.5294	3.4130	3.3037	3.2008	3.1039
19	3.9424	3.7985	3.6642	3.5386	3.4210	3.3105	3.2067	3.1090
20	3.9539	3.8083	3.6726	3.5458	3.4271	3.3158	3.2112	3.1129
21	3.9631	3.8161	3.6792	3.5514	3.4319	3.3198	3.2147	3.1158
22	3.9705	3.8223	3.6844	3.5558	3.4356	3.3230	3.2173	3.1180
23	3.9764	3.8273	3.6885	3.5592	3.4384	3.3254	3.2193	3.1197
24	3.9811	3.8312	3.6918	3.5619	3.4406	3.3272	3.2209	3.1210
25	3.9849	3.8342	3.6943	3.5640	3.4423	3.3286	3.2220	3.1220

[GLOSSARY]

A

Accounting: Process of recording and summarizing business transactions on a company's financial statements. p. 58

Accounting equation: Assets = Equity + Liabilities or Assets – Liabilities = Equity. p. 54

Accounting methods: Calculation of the book value rate of return by using data presented on financial statements. p. 524

Accrual method: Accounting method that considers sales when made and costs when incurred, regardless of when the transaction takes place. p. 62

Accrued liability: Represents what a company owes for services it has received and not yet paid or an expense that has been incurred but not recorded. p. 79

Adjustments in non-cash working capital accounts: The cash flow provided (or used) by working capital accounts such as trade receivables, inventories, and trade and other payables. p. 127

Administrative expenses: Expenses that are not directly related to producing and selling goods or services. p. 65

Aging of accounts receivable: A report showing how long trade receivables have been outstanding; it gives the percentage of receivables past due for one month, two months, or other periods. p. 270

Annual report: Report issued annually by corporations to their shareholders that contains their financial statements as well as management's opinion of the company's past year's operations and prospects for the future. p. 80

Annuity: A series of payments (or receipts) of fixed amount for a specified number of years. p. 486

Assessed value: Method used by municipal governments for determining the level of property taxes. p. 568

Asset-management ratios: Evaluate how efficiently managers use the assets of a business. p. 170

Assets: Resources that a business owns to produce goods and services (e.g., buildings, equipment, trade receivables, inventories). p. 71

Asset valuation: Methodology used to restate the numbers appearing on financial statements. p. 578

Auditor's report: Report prepared by an independent accounting firm that is presented to a company's shareholders. p. 82

Average collection period (ACP): Measures how many days it takes for customers to pay their bills. p. 171

B

Balanced scorecard (BSC): A process that can translate an organization's mission, vision, and strategies into a comprehensive set of quantifiable performance measures in addition to providing a framework for a strategic measurement and management system. p. 27

Benchmarking: Process of searching for the best practices by comparing oneself to a competitor's excellent performance. p. 179

Benchmarks: Excellent industry norms to which one's own financial ratios can be compared. p. 153

Bond: Long-term loan (10 to 30 years) that could be secured or unsecured. p. 387

Bookkeeping: Activity that involves collecting, classifying, and reporting accounting transactions. p. 53

Bookkeeping and accounting cycle: Steps involved in processing financial transactions for preparing financial statements. p. 54

Book value: The accounting value of an asset (the original cost minus total depreciation deductions made to date), shown on the financial statements as a firm's assets. p. 564

Break-even chart: Graphic that shows the effect of change in both revenue and costs on profitability. p. 220

Break-even point: Level of production where revenues equal total costs. p. 216

Break-even wedge: Method that helps managers to determine the most appropriate way of structuring operating costs (fixed versus variable). p. 231

Budgeting: Process by which management allocates corporate resources, evaluates financial outcomes, and establishes systems to control operational and financial performance. p. 315

Business plan: Document that gives a complete picture about an organization's goals, plans, operating activities, financial needs, and financing requirements. p. 326

Business risk: The uncertainty inherent in projecting the level of revenue and earnings before interest and taxes (EBIT). p. 373

C

Capital assets: *See* non-current assets.

Capital assets turnover ratio: Measures how intensively a firm's capital assets are used to generate revenue. p. 173

Capital budget: Budget that shows how much will be spent for the purchase of capital assets. p. 326

Capital cost allowance (CCA): A tax deduction that Canadian tax laws allow a business to claim for the loss in value of non-current assets due to wear and tear and/or obsolescence. p. 73

Capital investment: Project that requires extensive financial resources (cash outflows) made for the purpose of generating a return (cash inflows). p. 514

Capital structure: Components of the permanent or long-term financing sources used to buy non-current assets. p. 426

Cash: Cash holdings and short-term deposits. p. 272

Cash break-even point: Number of units or revenue that must be reached in order to cover total cash fixed costs (total fixed costs less depreciation/amortization). p. 224

Cash budget: A treasury function that determines the cash flow of business at the micro level to determine the level of liquidity. p. 124

Cash conversion cycle: Periodic transformation of cash through working capital accounts such as inventories, trade receivables, and trade and other payables. p. 252

Cash conversion efficiency: Measures how quickly a business converts revenue to cash flow from its operations or operating activities. p. 250

Cash flows: Has to do with the procurement (cash provided by) or allocation (cash used in) of cash. p. 114

Cash inflow: Represents the receipt of money (interest or profit for the year plus depreciation) generated by an investment or a project. p. 119

Cash inflow guidelines: A cash inflow takes place when there is a decrease in an asset account or an increase in an equity or liability account. p. 122

Cash inflows: These include profit for the year, proceeds from sale of non-current assets, proceeds from sale of investment securities, and obtaining loans or new equity. p. 497

Cash insufficiency: Not enough cash generated by a capital project to pay for fixed charges. p. 543

Cash method: Accounting method of recording business transactions when cash is received or disbursed. p. 62

Cash outflow: Represents cash disbursements for the purchase of investments such as mutual funds or capital assets. p. 119

Cash outflow guidelines: A cash outflow takes place when there is an increase in an asset account or a decrease in an equity or liability account. p. 122

Cash outflows: These include a loss from operation, the purchase of non-current assets, and the purchase of investment securities. p. 497

Chartered bank: An institution that provides short-term loans such as seasonal loans, operating loans, or working capital loans. p. 392

Chart of accounts: A set of categories by which accounting transactions are recorded. p. 53

Chief executive officer (CEO): Person who plays a major role in the complete management process and is responsible for the strategic plans and seeing that they are effectively implemented. p. 12

Chief financial officer (CFO): Person in charge of the finance function and responsible for all accounting functions and external activities. p. 12

Collateral value: An assessment by lenders of the value of a particular asset taken as a guarantee for credit. p. 568

Combined leverage: Financial technique used to calculate both operating and financial leverage. p. 446

Committed fixed costs: Costs that must be incurred in order to operate a business. p. 233

Complementary budgets: Budgets that complement operating budgets whereby data are presented differently and in more detail. p. 321

Compound interest: Interest rate that is applicable on the initial principal and the accumulated interest of prior periods. p. 484

Comprehensive budget: A set of projected financial statements such as the statement of income, the statement of financial position, and the statement of cash flows. p. 326

Compulsory investments: Investments made in capital assets to respond to a need, legislation, or employee demands that do not require in-depth analytical studies. p. 516

Conditional sales contract: Agreement made between a buyer and a seller regarding the purchase of an asset (e.g., truck). p. 386

Confirming institution: Organization that finances inventories. p. 399

Consecutive statements of financial position: Consecutive statements of financial position help to determine whether a change in each account is a cash inflow or a cash outflow. p. 120

Contribution margin: The difference between revenues and variable costs. p. 216

Controllable costs: Costs that operating managers are accountable for. p. 234

Controller: Person responsible for establishing the accounting and financial reporting policies and procedures. p. 12

Corporate culture: Shared system of values and beliefs within an organization. p. 33

Cost of capital: The cost of borrowing money from one source (shareholders or lenders) to finance a business p. 424

Cost of common shares: Includes dividends paid to shareholders, flotation costs, and growth rate. p. 436

Cost of debt: Finance costs less income tax expense. p. 438

Cost of financing: Effective after-tax cost of raising funds from different sources (lenders and shareholders). p. 22

Cost of preferred shares: Includes fixed dividends paid to shareholders and the flotation costs. p. 437

Cost of retained earnings: Includes dividends and growth rate. p. 437

Cost of sales: Cost incurred in making or producing goods that are sold. p. 65

Cost-volume-profit analysis: Tool used for analyzing how volume, price, product mix, and product costs relate to one another. p. 210

Credit: Accounting entries recorded on the right side of an account. p. 55

Credit insurance policy: Insurance to cover losses suffered from a firm's trade receivables that become uncollectible. p. 272

Credit policy: Decision about the extent of credit that should be extended to customers. p. 268

Credit-scoring system: System used to analyze the creditworthiness of potential customers. p. 266

Credit terms: Conditions under which credit is extended, especially how quickly the customer is expected to pay the account. p. 264

C's of credit: Factors that investors look at to gauge the creditworthiness of a business: character, collateral, capacity, capital, circumstances, and coverage. p. 376

Current assets: Assets such as inventories and trade receivables expected to be turned into cash, usually in one year or less). p. 74

Current liabilities: Debts that a business must pay within one year (i.e., trade and other payables). p. 78

Current ratio: Gauges general business liquidity. p. 165

Current-value accounting: Accounting method used to restate assets on financial statements in terms of what they would be worth if purchased today. p. 565

D

Days of working capital: The number of days of working capital a business holds to meet average daily sales requirements. p. 250

Debit: Accounting entries recorded on the left side of an account. p. 55

Debt/coverage ratio: Measures the capital structure of a business and its debt-paying ability. p. 167

Debt-to-equity ratio: Measures the proportion of debt used compared to equity to finance all assets. p. 167

Debt-to-total-assets ratio: Measures how much debt a business uses to finance all assets. p. 167

Demassing: Recession-driven technique to remove management layers from organizational charts to cut costs. p. 25

Depreciation: An accounting entry allocating the cost of a non-current asset against revenue over an asset's life and an estimated decrease in the value of non-current assets due to wear and tear and/or obsolescence. p. 65

Direct costs: Materials and labour expenses that are directly incurred when making a product. p. 234

Discounted payback period: The number of years required for a capital investment to generate enough discounted cash inflows to cover the initial cash outflow. p. 529

Discounting: The process of finding the present value of a series of future cash flows. p. 491

Discretionary fixed costs: Costs that can be controlled by managers. p. 233

Distribution costs: Costs incurred by a marketing organization to promote, sell, and distribute its goods and services. p. 65

Dividend aversion theory: Theory suggesting that investors may prefer future capital gains to current dividends because of lower tax rates on capital gains. p. 453

Dividend irrelevance theory: Theory suggesting that investors are indifferent to the payment of dividends because the value of lesser dividends now is offset by growth-created value in the future. p. 452

Dividend payout ratio: Proportion of earnings that a business pays out in dividends. p. 453

Dividend preference theory: Theory suggesting that investors prefer instant cash to uncertain future benefits. p. 452

Double-entry bookkeeping: System for posting financial transactions so that the accounting equation remains in balance. p. 54

DuPont System: Presentation of financial ratios in a logical way to measure return on assets (ROA). p. 187

E

Earnings before interest and taxes (EBIT): Profit before taxes and finance costs. p. 28

Earnings per share: Measures how much profit is available to each outstanding share. p. 177

Economic life: Number of years that a capital asset or investment opportunity will last. p. 522

Economic ordering quantity (EOQ): Method that determines the optimum quantity of goods that should be ordered at any single time. p. 260

Economic value: Valuation method used to determine the ability or capacity of an asset to generate cash. p. 568

Economic value added (EVA): Tool that measures the wealth a company creates for its investors. p. 431

Economy: Process for determining the type of resources (human and materials) that should be acquired (least costly option) and how they should be processed. p. 305

Effectiveness indicators: Measure the goal-related accomplishments of an organization; it means doing the right things. p. 306

Efficiency: The relationship between profit (outputs) generated and assets employed (inputs). p. 15

Efficiency indicators: Refers to how well resources (inputs) are brought together to achieve results (outputs); it means doing things right. p. 305

Electronic funds transfer: Means for transferring funds between customer and supplier by using the Internet or any other electronic medium. p. 274

Equity: Funds provided in a business by its shareholders, i.e., share capital, contributed surplus, retained earnings, and total other comprehensive income/(loss). p. 76

Expense investment: A fully tax-deductible cost that should produce favourable effects on the profit performance. p. 514

External financing: Cash obtained from investors (long-term lenders and shareholders). p. 19

External sources: Funds provided by investors (shareholders and lenders). p. 371

F

Factoring: Selling trade receivables to a financial institution. p. 398

Feedback controls: System that helps to focus on variations of past performance. p. 344

Financial benchmarks: Financial performance ratios that can be calculated by using dollar figures shown on financial statements (statement of income and statement of financial position) for the purpose of pinpointing excellent financial performance. p. 180

Financial health score (Z-score): Linear analysis in which five measures are objectively weighted to give an overall score that becomes the basis for classifying the financial health of a business. p. 337

Financial lease: Mutually agreed commitment by a lessor and a lessee for a specified period of time. p. 401

Financial leverage: Financial technique used to determine the most favourable capital structure (equity versus debt). p. 445

Financial management: Activity involved in raising money and buying assets in order to obtain the highest possible return. p. 9

Financial markets: Organizations and procedures involved in the buying and selling of financial assets. p. 447

Financial needs: The items for which a business needs money. p. 367

Financial ratio: Comparison or relationship between numbers shown on financial statements. p. 150

Financial risk: The way that a business is financed (debt versus share capital). p. 373

Financial statements: Financial reports, which include the two-statement report called the statement of income and the statement of comprehensive income, the statement of changes in equity, the statement of financial condition, and the statement of cash flows. p. 50

Financial structure: The way a company's assets are financed by the entire right-hand side of the statement of financial position (long-term and short-term financing). p. 425

Financing activities: Portion of the statement of cash flows that shows how much cash was provided (or used) from external sources (e.g., proceeds from the issue of shares or borrowings, repaying long-term debt, or payment of dividends). p. 127

Financing decisions: Decisions related to borrowing from long-term lenders and shareholders. p. 22

Financing mix: Proportion of funds raised from lenders and shareholders. p. 23

Financing requirements: Who will provide the money (shareholders and lenders) to finance a business and in what form (e.g., mortgage, working capital loan). p. 368

Fixed-charges coverage ratio: Measures to what extent a business can service all its fixed charges (e.g., interest charges, leases). p. 170

Fixed costs: Costs that remain constant at varying levels of production. p. 210

Float: The amount of funds tied up in cheques that have been written but are still in process and have not yet been collected. p. 274

Forms of financing: Financing instruments used to buy assets (e.g., term loans). p. 22

Future income taxes payable: Future tax liability resulting from the difference between depreciation and capital cost allowance. p. 77

Future value (FV): The amount to which a payment or series of payments will grow by a given future date when compounded by a given interest rate. p. 485

G

Goal of working capital management: To accelerate the cash flow cycle in a business after sales have been made. p. 249

Governance: Process of decision-making and the process by which decisions are implemented (or not implemented). p. 31

Government financing: Funds obtained (directly or indirectly) from government institutions to finance a business. p. 383

Gross profit: Difference between revenue and cost of sales (also referred to as gross margin). p. 28

H

Hard financial benchmarks: Financial targets that can be applied to any business or industry to gauge financial performance. p. 182

Holding costs: Category of costs associated with the storing of goods in inventories (e.g., insurance, rent). p. 261

Horizontal analysis: Shows percentage change of accounts shown on two consecutive financial statements. p. 160

Hurdle rate: Capital budgeting technique used to rank the financial desirability of capital projects according to their cost of capital. p. 543

I

Income tax: A percentage of taxable income paid to the provincial or federal governments based on taxable income less certain tax deductions. p. 68

Income tax expense: The total amount of taxes due to federal and provincial governments on the taxable income earned by the business during the current fiscal accounting period. p. 68

Indemnification policy: Insurance that a business takes against a catastrophic loss in cash. p. 271

Indirect costs: Costs that are necessary in the production cycle but that cannot be clearly allocated to specific products or services. p. 235

Industry multipliers: A standard used to determine the value or worth of a business. p. 580

Inflation: Represents a price-rise characteristic of periods of prosperity. p. 476

Initial public offering: Securities of a newly established public company offered to the general public for the first time. p. 450

Instrument risk: The quality of security available to satisfy investors. p. 373

Intangible assets: Assets that cannot be seen, touched, or physically measured and are included in the non-current asset section of the statement of financial position). p. 73

Interest tables: Present calculated factors used for computing future or present values of single sums and annuities. p. 479

Interim financing: Loan made to a business to help finance a capital project, such as the construction of a new plant, until regular financing is obtained. p. 397

Internal financing: Cash provided from retained earnings, depreciation/amortization, and a reduction in working capital accounts. p. 18

Internal rate of return (IRR): The interest rate that equates the cost of an investment (cash outflow) to the present value of the expected returns from the investment (cash inflow). p. 499

Internal sources: Funds generated by a business (e.g., profit for the year, depreciation/amortization). p. 371

International Accounting Standards Board (IASB): Organization that develops, in the public interest, a single set of high-quality, understandable, and enforceable global standards that require transparent and comparable information in general-purpose financial statements. p. 8

International Financial Reporting Standards (IFRS): Accounting standards issued by the IASB. p. 8

Inventories: Monetary value a company places on the material it has purchased or goods it has manufactured. p. 75

Inventories, types of: Raw materials, work-in-process, and finished goods. p. 259

Inventory replenishment: Decision related to when to order goods from supplier. p. 263

Inventory turnover: Measures the number of times a year a company turns over its inventories. p. 172

Investing activities: That portion of the statement of cash flows that shows how much cash was provided (or used) to buy or sell non-current assets (e.g., purchase or proceeds from the sale of a building). p. 129

Investing decisions: Decisions related to the acquisition of non-current assets. p. 20

Investment securities: Funds invested in short-term deposits such as treasury bills, bank deposits, etc. p. 276

J

Journalizing: Process of recording, electronically or manually, transactions in a journal (e.g., sales journal, salaries journal). p. 56

Journals: Also referred to as books of original entry, used to record accounting transactions in chronological order. p. 56

Just-in-time inventory management: An inventory management technique that obtains supplier materials just when they are needed. p. 260

L

Ledgers: Also referred to as books of final entry, show all amounts debited and credited in individual accounts (e.g., trade receivables, revenue, inventories and salaries) including a running balance). p. 56

Lessee: One who pays to use an asset without owning it. p. 401

Lessor: One who lends an asset to someone (lessee). p. 401

Leverage: Technique used to determine the most suitable operating and financial structure that will help amplify financial performance. p. 425

Liabilities: The debts of a business. p. 76

Line of credit: A formal or written agreement between a bank and a borrower regarding a loan. p. 394

Liquidation value: Worth of an asset if sold under duress. p. 567

Liquidity: Ability of a firm to meet its short-term financial commitments. p. 16

Liquidity ratios: Measure the ability of a firm to meet its cash obligations. p. 165

Listed company: A company that is traded on an organized exchange and is listed on the exchange. p. 450

Long-term financing sources (characteristics): Factors to consider when raising funds from long-term sources: payout, risk, voting rights, cost of capital, tax cost, and cost of issue. p. 433

Long-term loan: Loan to finance capital assets for a long period of time (over five years). p. 385

M

Marginal cost of capital (MCC): The increased level of average cost resulting from having borrowed new funds at higher rates than those previously borrowed. p. 440

Market performance: Method used for gauging the efficiency and effectiveness of management within the industry in which it operates. p. 570

Market value: The price at which an item, business, or asset can be sold. p. 564

Market-value ratios: Measurement tools to gauge the way investors react to a company's market performance. p. 177

Matching principle: Process of selecting the most appropriate financing source when buying an asset.p. 22

Material requirements planning (MRP): Method for developing a schedule to help coordinate and utilize resources in production. p. 260

Miscellaneous assets: Assets such as bonds and shares purchased from other businesses. p. 74

Mortgage: Loan obtained against which specific real property is used as collateral (e.g., a building). p. 387

N

Net present value (NPV): The present value of the future cash flow of an investment, less the initial cash outflow. p. 499

Net working capital: The difference between current assets and current liabilities. p. 248

Non-controllable costs: Costs that are not under the direct control of operating managers. p. 234

Non-current assets: Statement of financial position accounts such as land, buildings, equipment, and machinery; also called *capital* or *fixed assets.* p. 20

Non-current liabilities: Debts that are not due for a least one year. p. 77

Not-for-profit organizations: Organizations that operate exclusively for social, educational, professional, religious, health, charitable, or any other not-for-profit purpose. p. 89

O

Operating activities: The portion of the statement of cash flows that shows how much cash was provided by the business itself (e.g., profit for the year, depreciation/amortization, and adjustments in non-cash working capital accounts). p. 125

Operating budgets: Budgets prepared by operating managers. p. 315

Operating cycle: The number of days inventories and trade receivables take (in days) to be converted into cash. p. 253

Operating decisions: Decisions related to accounts appearing on the statement of financial position (current assets and current liabilities) and the statement of income (e.g., revenue, cost of sales, distribution costs). p. 24

Operating lease: A lease that is cancellable by the lessee at any time upon due notice. p. 401

Operating leverage: Financial technique that determines to what extent fixed costs should be used relative to variable costs. p. 444

Operating managers: Person in charge of organizational unit such as marketing, manufacturing, and human resources, and responsible for making operating and investing decisions. p. 13

Operating performance: Method used for gauging the efficiency and effectiveness of management at the operating level (e.g., marketing, production). p. 570

Operating section: Section of the statement of income that shows a company's gross profit and profit before taxes. p. 64

Opportunity cost: The income sacrificed by not pursuing the next best investment alternative. p. 437

Opportunity investments: Investments made in capital assets that are of a strategic nature and usually have far-reaching financial implications. p. 516

Ordering costs: Category of costs associated with the acquisition of goods (e.g., receiving, inspecting, accounting). p. 261

Other income: Revenue that is not directly related to the central operations of a business. p. 65

Overall performance: Ratios used to measure how well a business is deploying its resources. p. 570

Owners' section: Section of the statement of income that shows the amount of money left to the shareholders (i.e., profit for the year). p. 67

P

Payback method: The number of years required for a capital investment to generate enough cash inflows to cover the initial cash outflow. p. 528

Payback reciprocal: Capital budgeting technique that gives a rough estimate of the return on investment of a capital project. p. 529

Performance indicator: Description of the type of measurement used to gauge organizational performance. p. 305

Performance standard: Benchmarks against which performance is measured. p. 305

Planned downsizing: Systematic way of cutting costs. p. 25

Planning: Process of formulating goals and outlining action plans to realize the goals. p. 302

Planning assumptions: Boundaries upon which priorities, goals, plans, budgets, and financial projections are based. p. 310

Posting: Process of transferring recorded transactions from the journals to the appropriate ledger accounts (e.g., revenue, trade receivables). p. 56

Post office box: Location where customers pay their accounts (local post office box), which are subsequently transferred to the seller's bank account. p. 275

Prepaid expenses: Payments made for services that have not yet been received. p. 75

Present value (PV): The value today of a future payment or stream of payments, discounted at an appropriate rate. p. 489

Preventive controls: System that helps to guide actions toward intended results. p. 343

Price/earnings ratio (P/E): Indicates how much investors are willing to pay per dollar of reported profits. p. 177

Price-level accounting: Accounting method used to restate assets on financial statements in terms of current purchasing power (inflation). p. 565

Prime rate: The interest rate that banks charge to their most creditworthy customers. p. 394

Privately held company: A business that cannot sell shares to the general public. p. 449

Productivity: A measure of performance that gauges how resources are used. p. 154

Productivity measures: Ways of measuring organizational performance (i.e., return on assets). p. 26

Profitability index (PI): Shows the ratio of the present value of cash inflows to the present value of the cash outflows, discounted at a predetermined rate of interest. p. 536

Profitability ratios: Measure the overall efficiency and effectiveness of a business. p. 175

Profit before taxes: Difference between gross profit and expenses (distribution costs and administrative expenses), the addition of other income, and the subtraction of finance costs. p. 67

Profit break-even point: Number of units or revenue that must be reached in order to cover total costs plus a profit objective. p. 224

Profit for the year: Difference between profit before taxes and income tax expense. p. 29

Profit margin: Represents the profit before tax, after adjusting for non-operating accounts such as other income and finance costs. p. 175

Profit margin on revenue: Measures the operating efficiency of a business. p. 175

Profit-volume (PV) ratio: The contribution margin expressed on a per-unit basis. p. 217

Projected financial statements: Results of some assumed events that are part of financial projections (e.g., statement of income, statement of financial position, and the statement of cash flows). p. 330

Property, plant, and equipment: Types of assets that are considered permanent and are to be used over an extended period of time, i.e., many years (previously called *capital assets* or *fixed assets*). p. 71

Prospectus: A document disclosing the details of a security and the underlying business's legal, operational, and financial position. p. 378

Prosperity: The ability of a firm to grow (i.e., revenue, profit, equity). p. 17

Publicly traded company: A business that can sell securities broadly after a prospectus is approved by the appropriate securities commission. p. 450

Q

Quick ratio: Shows the relationship between the more liquid current assets and all current liabilities. p. 166

R

Ratio analysis: Helps readers of financial statements to assess the financial structure and performance of a business. p. 151

Regional banks: Locations where customers pay their accounts (local bank), which are subsequently transferred to the seller's bank account. p. 275

Relevant costs: Cost alternatives that managers can choose from to operate a business. p. 218

Relevant range: Costs (fixed and variable) that apply to a certain level of production. p. 218

Replacement value: Cost of acquiring a new asset to replace an existing asset with the same functional utility. p. 568

Residual value: Represents the value from the sale of an asset or a business at the end of its physical life. p. 521

Retained earnings: The profit generated by the business for which the owners have not claimed the amount in the form of dividends. p. 76

Return: Adequate cash and profit to finance a company's growth. p. 155

Return on equity: Measures the yield shareholders earn on their investment. p. 176

Return on revenue: Measures a company's overall ability to generate profit from each revenue dollar. p. 175

Return on total assets: Gauges the performance of assets employed in a business. p. 176

Revenue: What a business earns for the sale of its products and services. p. 64

Revenue break-even point: Revenue that must be reached in order to cover total costs. p. 223

Revolving credit: Maximum amount of a loan a bank agrees to provide a business (borrower). p. 397

Risk: Represents the level of expectations (probabilities) that something will happen in the future. p. 476

Risk analysis: Process of attaching probabilities to individual estimates in a capital project's base case. p. 540

Risk capital investors: Individuals or institutions that provide money to finance a business that entails relatively high risk; these investors seek a high potential return. p. 380

Rule of 72: Calculation that shows the approximate number of years it takes for an investment to double when compounded annually. p. 486

S

Sale and leaseback: Arrangement made by someone to sell an asset to a lessor and then lease it back. p. 402

Scanning the environment: Method used during the planning process for the purpose of pinning down planning assumptions or premises. p. 569

Screening controls: System that helps to monitor performance while work is being performed. p. 343

Secured loan: A loan that the borrower guarantees by pledging some assets. p. 397

Self-liquidating loan: Funds used to finance temporary or fluctuating variations in working capital accounts (e.g., inventories, trade receivables). p. 396

Self-regulated financial benchmarks: Financial targets that are determined by a business's own policies and practices and other financial measures. p. 182

Semi-variable costs: Costs that change disproportionately with changes in output levels. p. 212

Sensitivity analysis: Technique that shows to what extent a change in one variable (e.g., selling price, fixed costs) impacts the break-even point. p. 225

Share capital: Amount of money that is put into the business by the shareholders. p. 76

Shareholders: The owners of a business (common and preferred shareholders). p. 379

Short-term financing: Sources of financing obtained for a period of less than one year (e.g., trade credit, line of credit). p. 391

Simple interest: Interest paid on the principal only. p. 484

Soft financial benchmarks: Most financial benchmarks fall in this category and should be used with some degree of interpretation. p. 182

Solvency: Ability to service or pay all debts (short- and long-term). p. 154

Sources of financing: Institutions that provide funds (e.g., commercial banks). p. 22

Stability: Relationship between debt and equity. p. 17

Statement of cash flows: Financial statement that shows where funds come from (cash inflows) and where they went (cash outflows). p. 60

Statement of changes in equity: Represents the interest of the shareholders of a business, showing the cumulative net results in equity with respect to share capital, contributed surplus, retained earnings, and accumulated other comprehensive income/(loss) for the year. p. 60

Statement of comprehensive income: Financial statement that shows items of income and expense that are not recognized in the statement of income. p. 59

Statement of financial position: Financial statement that shows a "snapshot" of a company's financial condition (assets, equity, and liabilities). p. 60

Statement of income: Financial statement that shows a summary of revenue and costs for a specified period of time. p. 58

Stock market: A network of exchanges, brokers, and investors that trade securities. p. 449

Strategic business unit (SBU): Divisional unit within a multi-business framework. p. 302

Subordinated debt: Loan that is more risky, for which investors charge higher interest rates. p. 389

Sunk cost: Investment cost incurred prior to making the decision to proceed with a capital project. p. 523

Supplier credit: Financing obtained from suppliers (trade payables). p. 391

Sustainable growth rate: Rate of increase in revenue a company can attain without depleting financing resources, borrowing excessively, or issuing new stock. p. 335

SWOT analysis: Acronym for identifying a company's strengths, weaknesses, opportunities, and threats. p. 309

T

Term loan: Loan made to buy capital assets. p. 385

Timeline: Graphic illustration of time-value-of-money problems. p. 481

Times-interest-earned ratio (TIE): Measures to what extent a business can service its interest charges on debt. p. 168

Time value of money: Rate at which the value of money is traded off as a function of time. p. 474

Total assets turnover ratio: Measures how intensively a firm's total assets are used to generate revenue. p. 173

Total comprehensive income/(loss) for the year: Transactions and other events (e.g., asset revaluation) that will have an impact in the equity account. p. 59

Trade and other payables: Money owed to suppliers of goods or services that were purchased on credit. p. 78

Trade receivables: Money owed to the company by its regular business customers for the purchase of goods or services. p. 75

Transparency: Extent to which business processes and related information resources, assets, and outcomes are visible and open to inspection by stakeholders. p. 29

Treasurer: Person responsible for raising funds and regulating the flow of funds. p. 12

Trend analysis: Analyzing a company's performance over a number of years. p. 185

Trial balance: Statement that ensures that the general ledger is in balance (debit transactions equal credit transactions). p. 56

U

Unit break-even point: Number of units that must be sold in order to cover total costs. p. 223

V

Variable costs: Costs that fluctuate directly with changes in volume of production. p. 211

Venture capital: Risk capital supplied to small companies by wealthy individuals (angels), partnerships, or corporations, usually in return for an equity position in the firm. p. 381

Vertical analysis: Method of listing (1) all numbers on the statement of financial position to a percentage of total assets, and (2) all numbers on the statement of income to a percentage of revenue. p. 159

W

Weighted average cost of capital: Composite weighted after-tax cost of raising funds from long-term investors (bonds, mortgages, common shares, preferred shares). p. 22

Weighted average cost of financing: Represents the proportion of the component costs of each amount included in a company's financial structure. p. 423

Working capital accounts: Statement of financial position accounts such as inventories, trade receivables, and cash (current assets), and trade and other payables and short-term borrowings (current liabilities). p. 24

Working capital loans: Short-term loans made for the purpose of financing working capital accounts (e.g., inventories, trade receivables). p. 282

Working capital management: Managing individual current asset and current liability accounts to ensure proper interrelationships among them. p. 248

[INDEX]

D

G

H

I

Q

R

X

Y

Z